Who Will Lead Us?

The publisher gratefully acknowledges the generous support of the Jewish Studies Endowment Fund of the University of California Press Foundation.

Who Will Lead Us?

The Story of Five Hasidic
Dynasties in America

Samuel C. Heilman

UNIVERSITY OF CALIFORNIA PRESS

University of California Press, one of the most distinguished university presses in the United States, enriches lives around the world by advancing scholarship in the humanities, social sciences, and natural sciences. Its activities are supported by the UC Press Foundation and by philanthropic contributions from individuals and institutions. For more information, visit www.ucpress.edu.

University of California Press
Oakland, California

Library of Congress Cataloging-in-Publication Data

Names: Heilman, Samuel C., author.
Title: Who will lead us? : the story of five Hasidic
   dynasties in America / Samuel Heilman.
Description: Oakland, California : University of
   California Press, [2017] | Includes bibliographical
   references and index.
Identifiers: LCCN 2016046899 (print) | LCCN 2016048638
   (ebook) | ISBN 9780520277236 (cloth : alk. paper) |
   ISBN 9780520966482 (eBook)
Subjects: LCSH: Hasidism. | Leadership—Religious
   aspects—Judaism.
Classification: LCC BM198.2.H43 2017 (print) |
   LCC BM198.2.H43 2017 (ebook) | DDC 296.8/332—
   dc23
LC record available at https://lccn.loc.gov/2016046899

Manufactured in the United States of America

25 24 23 22 21 20 19 18 17
10 9 8 7 6 5 4 3 2 1

For Menachem M. Friedman,
my dear friend, who has taught me much and
given me courage to write this alone

May the LORD our God be with us, as He was with our
fathers; may He not leave us or forsake us.

—1 Kings 8:57

Contents

Illustrations

Prologue

During much of the twentieth century, when European Jews moved rapidly out of the ghettoes where they had lived for generations and toward incorporation into the larger host culture, those who chose to stay behind and remain attached to Jewish parochialism and tradition, who resisted acculturation and sought to reverse the losses of ghetto life, were a dwindling minority. Generally identified as "Orthodox" and considered a "residual category" of Jews, they held fast to parochial Jewish loyalties and time-honored practices.[1] Although their pietistic, charismatic folk religious movement, which emerged in eighteenth-century eastern Europe and flourished during the nineteenth century, had once been among the most radical challengers to tradition, Hasidim were by the twentieth century among the most distinctive of Orthodox Jews and were identified with the traditionalism of the ghetto. By midcentury, after mass migration, two world wars, a communist revolution, pogroms, and the Holocaust had shaken and decimated their world, one might have been tempted to write their epitaph.

Yet while Hasidism was seemingly on the wane as both Zionism and assimilation into melting-pot cultures attracted Jews, Europe became largely emptied of Jewish life, and the Soviet Union repressed it, it did not die. The last century turned out to be a tale of near death and resurrection. The very places Hasidim once believed would be most hostile to them—the Zionist state and the democratic countries of the West, primarily North America—became havens that gave them stability, relatively little persecution, and conditions where they could flourish and gain confidence and numbers they could never have dreamed of during the early 1900s.

A movement many believed had passed its golden age would revive and reinvent itself. These post-Holocaust Hasidim created ghettos where inhabitants sought to reverse the losses they had suffered and to create their own world. When their expanding numbers could not fit into those spaces, they built new settlements all their own. For anyone today walking the neighborhoods of Brooklyn's Borough Park or Williamsburg, New York's Kiryas Joel or New Square, London's Stamford Hill, Montreal's Outremont, Melbourne's Caulfield, or in Israel B'nai B'rak or Jerusalem's Kiryat Belz or Geula, to name but a few of their redoubts, the distinctive sight of Hasidim filling the streets is remarkable because the once unimaginable is today routine. Hasidism is alive and growing.

All this is not to say that this rebuilding has been easy. At the heart of Hasidism is a charismatic leader, a rebbe. Without him, there can be no Hasidim. An intermediary between his followers, the Hasidim, and the heavenly powers, he is capable of both bestowing blessings and transmitting the will of God. Like a father, he guides his followers in the most personal decisions of their lives, such as whom to marry, where to live, what to do, when to see a doctor, how to respond to adversity, even whether to have hope. He qualifies for this position only if he can bear this heavy burden and spiritual responsibility and if his followers believe he has charisma, a superordinary quality of charm and power.

Every Hasid believes his rebbe is extraordinary and has the ability to provide such leadership. Yet in spite of this belief and profound trust in him, rebbes are flesh and blood, subject to all infirmities that come by nature or accident, to physical and mental decline in old age, to the moral defects that show up in other people, to death. When that happens, the Hasidim need a successor. While Hasidism has managed transitions from one rebbe to the next, they have not always been easy. In contemporary times, and after many generations, succession is still not simple or automatic. It is filled with drama and complexity. The story of succession in contemporary Hasidism is what this book is about.

I will consider five successions. In two situations, there were too few successors; in two, there were too many; and in one, the Hasidim denied a need for a successor at all, claiming that their rebbe had never really died. Each of these stories offers a narrative of continuity and transformation in a group at once mysterious and yet transparent that seeks permanence in a modern world seemingly inimical to it. These are stories of the making and unmaking of men, of a search for charisma and struggles for power, of families united and divided, of death and resurrection as well as hopes raised and dashed. They answer the eternal question of Hasidism: Who will lead us?

I have benefited greatly from work that preceded mine and from what others have taught me. A review of this book's notes will reveal many of the writers whose insights and discoveries inform my own. I will not repeat their names here, but without them and their work I could not have written much at all. Although many people graciously offered help, I want to single out a few who were especially important to me. I thank Gabi Abramac, Henry Abramovitch, Zalman Alpert, David Assaf, David Biale, Yoram Bilu, Yigal Brayer, Benjamin Brown, Levi Cooper, Pinny Dunner, Eli Epstein, Shifra Epstein, Immanuel Etkes, Steven Frankel, Menachem Friedman, Uriel Gellman, Arthur Green, Israel Guttman, Susannah Heschel, Menachem Keren-Kratz, the late Chaim Elazar Rabinovich and other members of his family, Gadi Sagiv, and Duvid Singer. A special word of appreciation to my son Adam Heilman, who, though very busy at work and with his family, took the time to read every word of an earlier draft and gave me invaluable advice about what he thought worked and what did not. Children are commonly a lesson in humility, but this one helped far beyond that. Of course, no one but myself is responsible for the final form this book has taken.

I also was immeasurably aided by many Hasidim from each of the groups I have discussed and was helped immensely by several rebbes who graciously consented to be interviewed and who for long hours and over many months and years opened their lives to me. Many of these people from within the Hasidic world who helped me prefer to remain anonymous, and I thank them publicly, knowing that while they may not be willing to have me acknowledge who they are they have given me knowledge and the confidence without which I could not have proceeded.

Readers may wonder why so many of those Hasidic insiders who helped me would choose to remain anonymous. To understand this one needs to know something about the Hasidic world's view of biography and history, two of the domains from which this book draws. The late rabbi Shimon Schwab, an articulate spokesman for the right wing of Orthodoxy, once wrote:

> Now, if a historian would report truthfully what he witnessed, it would make a lot of people rightfully angry. He would violate the [Jewish] prohibition of Loshon Horah [evil tongue,] which does not only apply to the living but also to those who sleep in the dust and cannot defend themselves any

more. What ethical purpose is served by preserving a realistic historic picture? Nothing but the satisfaction of curiosity. We should tell ourselves and our children the good memories of the good people, their unshakable faith. . . . That means we have to do without a real history book. We can do without. We do not need realism, we need inspiration from our forefathers in order to pass it on to posterity.[2]

Books and accounts (like this one) that aim at a "realistic historic picture" and a sociological analysis of what actually happened or was said, that offer an unsentimental look at the facts of life rather than exclusively singing praises or adjusting a narrative to comport with how people want to be seen, run the risk of undermining the faith of believers in the rebbes, of making the holy seem mundane. This strikes at the core concerns of Hasidim, for whom their leaders must be presented as ideal if not sublime.

That is why books that deal with the sorts of events and personalities I have described here commonly come from the very world they describe, reflect the attitude that Schwab articulates, and, as Marc Shapiro puts it in his book on how Orthodox Judaism rewrites its history, are "designed to instill the proper education and 'outlook' in the reader." Thus they are often hagiographies in which "not only censorship but even outright distortion is permissible, all in the name of a higher truth."[3] I was not prepared to write such a book.

Many of those Hasidim and rebbes who helped me continue to live in a world where normative behavior and hagiography rate "much higher than the needs of the historical record."[4] While willing to help me, they were not willing to be publicly associated with my approach.

While no one can claim to be without bias, the academic and scholarly ideal to which I aspire in writing about the past and about people is to try to retain ethical neutrality, to put my own prejudices on the shelf, and to present the facts as I understand them without censoring what I have discovered. My composition of the narratives and my selection of the facts are guided exclusively by my desire to make sense out of them, rather than a wish to paint only a flattering portrait of all those described and to avoid embarrassing anyone.

Embarrassment is of course in the eye of those embarrassed. Is it humiliating to say that someone did not want to become a rebbe, even though he later did? Is it mortifying to describe a break between a father and his son if it was an essential step in what led to succession? Is it upsetting to describe the unflattering views that some hold toward their competitors in a struggle over succession? Is it embarrassing to describe the misgivings a rebbe has about his role and his desire to occasionally escape its constraints? Perhaps. But in a book that seeks to reveal and explain what actually goes on as Hasidim try to find successors for the position of rebbe, it is unavoidable.

By focusing on the generally unseemly disputes over succession my work will no doubt be understood as profaning the contenders. These accounts are therefore not likely to be endorsed. At best, members of the communities I have detailed will reply that one who does not share in a Hasidic life cannot be expected fully to appreciate the events, achievements, and motives that characterize individual Hasidic leaders. The paths that they followed, the nature of their experiences, and the nuances of their specific lives and history will be lost on someone like that. That is why so many of the insiders who helped me reach the conclusions I did have chosen to remain anonymous. An outsider who will not continue to live among the people he is describing can risk telling the story as I have; insiders have to be far more circumspect. If I have caused embarrassment, I regret it. I do have profound respect for the world I describe.

Finally, I should add a word about what this book is *not*. Although I reference them, this book is not a consideration of the writings, ideological arguments, and teachings of Hasidic rebbes or the spirituality that animates followers' attachment to them. To those who will object that I did not explain the depth of the attachments that drive Hasidism and its adherents, my response is that tracing the patterns and processes of contemporary Hasidic succession was more than enough for me.

Succession in Contemporary Hasidism

Who Will Lead Us?

When the modern Hasidic movement first emerged in the late eighteenth century, it was led mostly by charismatic men, commonly called *zaddikim* (loosely translated as the saintly or pious), who were themselves the successors of *ba'aley shem* (wonder masters of the name of God or healers) and their counterparts, the *maggidim* (itinerant preachers).[1] While the *ba'aley shem* were said to possess the mystical knowledge of Kabbalah that enabled them to invoke and in shaman-like fashion manipulate powerful, esoteric names of God in order to heal people, do battle with their demons, or liberate the human soul to unify itself with God, powers they used on behalf of those who believed in them, and while the *maggidim* were powerful preachers and magnetic orators who told tales and offered parables or sermons that inspired their listeners, *zaddikim* had a combination of these qualities and more. With *ba'aley shem* they shared a knowledge of how to apply Kabbalah to the practical needs of their followers and to perform "miracles," using their mystical powers ultimately to help their Hasidim (as these followers became known), and from the *maggidim* they took the power to inspire and attract with stories and teaching while inserting into these what their devotees took to be personal messages tailored just to them. With both, they shared the authority of charisma.

Charisma, Max Weber explained, should be "applied to a certain quality of an individual personality by virtue of which he is set apart from ordinary men and treated as endowed with supernatural, superhuman, or at least specifically exceptional powers or qualities."[2] Whether the supernatural was an essential aspect of early Hasidism has been debated, but what is almost universally accepted is the idea that the men who became its leaders were viewed by their followers as extraordinary and exceptional. Those who believed in them were convinced that they had qualities "not accessible to the ordinary person" and in the context of Hasidic Judaism regarded these leaders as being "of divine origin" or at the very least "exemplary" and worthy of emulation.[3]

Zaddikim were endowed with what their Hasidim considered remarkable personalities and righteous character that they could and would use for the good of others. While perceived as having a powerful connection to and association with the Almighty God as *mysterium tremendum*, the *zaddik* (or "rebbe," as he often came to be called) was a category of leader that challenged the Weberian notion of what a mystic was supposed to be. To Max Weber, a mystic was one who withdrew from the world and became a passive vessel of the divine, one for whom "the extrusion of all everyday mundane interests is always required."[4] Some *zaddikim* did indeed seek withdrawal—cases in point are Abraham (the so-called Angel) (1740–76), the short-lived son of Dov Ber; the Maggid of Mezherich, who led the life of an otherworldly ascetic Kabbalist; and Menachem Mendel, the Rebbe of Kotsk (1787–1859), who for the last twenty years of his life locked himself away and was seen only very rarely by a few family members and disciples.[5] Other Hasidic leaders isolated themselves at least during prayer or spiritual exercises, a process called *hitbodedut* (self-seclusion).[6] Yet most of the *zaddikim,* in contrast to the classic mystics, were seen as using their Kabbalistic powers and essential religiosity to serve *this-worldly* ends by helping their followers to smooth the naturally rough path of life in the real world. In short, these men (they were always men) were charismatic mystics or Kabbalists who were "active in the world" and worked not only on behalf of individuals but for the sake of the entire community of their followers, if not for the entire Jewish world, seeking to intensify spiritual life in the process.[7]

In contrast to the more staid and predictable scholars and rabbis, the *zaddikim* emerged as important figures on the eastern European Jewish scene and gained followers. Replacing the *maggidim* and the *ba'aley shem,* they challenged the monopoly on religious leadership that scholar rabbis held.[8] Although exceptional intermediaries between God and their Hasidim, rebbes inserted themselves, spiritually and practically, into the this-worldly, mundane lives and demands of their followers. They did all this not with asceticism (although some would invoke that) but with charisma and practices that opened up the esoteric elements of the mystical to all Jews who were devoted to them. They used public prayer, song, dance, the communal breaking of bread, and a host of other methods to connect the human with the divine, turning even profane activity into a means of spiritual ascent. Some Hasidim understood these practices more deeply than others, but all were expected to be transformed by the encounter with the rebbe, and therefore attached themselves to him, voluntarily submitting to their rebbe's authority and even giving it ascendancy over the rule-based dominance of traditional Judaism.

Ultimately, Hasidim viewed their leaders as model individuals to be emulated and embraced with devotion (*dvekut*). In return, the rebbes would (sometimes miraculously) provide for their followers the blessings of children (*bonei*), health (*chayei*), and livelihood (*mzonei*). Hasidism held that the material and spiritual well-being of the entire community was part of the rebbe's responsibility.

So attached did Hasidim become to their rebbes that they sought to spend as much time as possible with them, basking in their presence. Celebrating around the table (*tish*) with the rebbe, toasting him with "*L'chaim!*" (To life), singing or dancing with him, even eating his leftovers (*shirayim*), enhanced the relationship as much as praying or studying with him. At the heart of the *tish* were the rebbe's words, a *maymer,* or discourse by which those listening to and learning from him believed they came closer to God.

In some cases, even the rebbe's smallest gestures were judged as having cosmic significance, and his Hasidim dwelt endlessly on the meaning of them.[9] They might watch the rebbe to see, for example, "how he brought his spoon to his mouth, whether he bent his mouth close to the food or whether he brought the food up to his lips, whether he tasted only an olive's bulk [the ritual minimum] . . . and left the remainder for *shirayim*" for them to eat. "How much did he eat and how much did he drink? How did he sit—erect or bent over?" And of course, what tunes did he choose to sing?[10] Every detail mattered in this drama, in which both the observers and the observed were certain heaven was involved because the *zaddik* was after all able to ascend spiritually to the highest regions and powers.

Attachment to a rebbe became so pervasive that Hasidim were expected to travel, repeatedly if necessary, to be near him in order to request his advice and counsel or seek blessings and spiritual support.

No matter was too small or too complex for his help and guidance.[11] The longing to be near him even competed with the Hasid's attachments to his own family, and often attachment to the rebbe and the other Hasidim trumped family obligations, so that men left home, wife, and children to spend extended time near their master. To be sure, the attachment to a particular rebbe and court did not happen overnight. Hasidim might feel attachments to a number of *zaddikim* who shared a common forebear.

The Hasidim who were attached—really, who belonged—to the rebbe saw him as a projection of their attachments to one another and to God. He became a "collective representation," a collective symbol.[12] Hasidim often measured their rebbe by the intensity and power he could demonstrate. The more Hasidim he could sustain, the more supported him, in a synergy that led to rebbes being like royalty and Hasidim competing against other groups of Hasidim over whose king was greater.

The Hasid's ultimate goal was a *personal* relationship with his rebbe. It might be confirmed by the rebbe's gaze into his eyes at a *tish* or his shaking the Hasid's hand (either in reality or in a gestural way). A blessing, in a personal letter from the rebbe or a message sent by a *shaliach*, an emissary, might also suffice. But it was expressed most powerfully through a direct one-on-one, face-to-face private meeting with him called *yechidus, praven-zich,* or *gezegenen-zich.* Hasidim treated this moment as akin to an encounter with the numinous, if not the otherworldly. They might prepare for it with ritual immersion in a *mikveh* to purify themselves or other spiritual exercises.

Paradoxically, newcomers might be offered this sort of direct encounter, which also served as a kind of recruitment strategy. In many accounts Hasidim report how transformative their first meeting with the rebbe was for them and how it led to their personal attachment and life-changing experiences that were religiously meaningful in the extreme. Perhaps the best-documented such encounter is found in the autobiography of Solomon Maimon.[13] At least initially this encounter aroused not only "admiration" for the *zaddik* but "a desire to belong to the group of Hasidim connected to him."[14] Reports such as these, passed by word of mouth or letters, as well as propaganda by Hasidim, whose enthusiasm for their master was often infectious, served to encourage more young men to join. For those who were already Hasidim, seeing newcomers become attracted to their rebbe reaffirmed their own attachments.

Often direct meetings with the rebbe were accompanied by a *kvittel*, a note of supplication the Hasid brought along with hopes that the rebbe would accept it and intercede on high on his behalf. The note, accompanied by a *pidyon nefesh* (sometimes called acronymically a *PaN*), a monetary "ransom" of one's soul (essentially atonement for sins, almost like a papal indulgence), cleared the way for the rebbe's blessing or prayers to work.[15] In addition, among confirmed Hasidim there emerged the custom of giving *ma'amad,* a standing donation to the rebbe, equivalent to about 5 or even 10 percent of the Hasid's income. The more Hasidim a rebbe had, the more *pidyon* and *ma'amad* he received. As *pidyon* and *ma'amad* become a routinized aspect of the rebbe/Hasid relationship, they not only symbolized moral purification but came to play a growing economic role in the *rebistve* (a rebbe's reign or career).[16]

In time, beyond spiritual guidance and blessing, a whole array of services that the rebbe provided for his Hasidim developed, institutionalizing the economic relationship that bound them together. These might include the certification and therefore the provision of kosher meat—an important source of income for the certifier—or the provision of matzah for Passover, another staple that was paid for by users. These became an income source for some rebbes, especially if these leaders were also appointed official rabbis of a town or community, as was often the case in Poland and Galicia—a reason why many Hasidic rebbes sought such a position.[17] At the outset only the official rabbi could control these sorts of certifications and services, but by the time Hasidism had relocated to America and Israel particular rebbes acquired this entitlement as well, and with it important economic and hence political power. Later, after Hasidic yeshivas and other institutions (*mosdos*) became established features of the community, they became a critical conduit for funds and a cadre of new Hasidim.

As a Hasid and his family would go to their rebbe's schools, eat the meat and foods he certified as permissible, or look to him for approval over whom to marry and how to live, this strengthened his authority and power. His control over their personal lives became extraordinary and intimate. As they shared their troubles and hoped for his blessings, they elevated him over almost everyone in their lives. Rebbes, Hasidism, and Hasidim became a formidable economic, commercial, social, and political force wherever they established communities.

THE HASIDIC COURTS

All this became institutionalized in the formation of Hasidic courts, with their own set of practices, customs, and organizations, along with administrative personnel. "The court of the Maggid of Mezirech, which was active from the mid-1760s until the Maggid's death in 1772, was, as far as we know, the first Hasidic court." [18]

The term *court* refers to the physical enclosure in which the Hasidic leader lived, prayed, and received followers and visitors. Life at the court regulated contact between the leader and the Hasidim. [19] Some who lived near the rebbe populated his court regularly. Others who lived at a distance might make regular pilgrimages to it, often on special days, commonly holy days and the month leading up to and including the High Holy Days of Rosh Hashanah and Yom Kippur or days of significance in the life of the rebbe.

Though viewed as steeped in spiritual vitality and religious meaning, goings-on there also became routinized and ritualized. The tension between the routine and the numinous was always present, so certain moments were made to seem extraordinary. The entrance of the rebbe at the *tish* or moments of *yechidus,* as well as any rite of passage in his family, stood out. Of course, those on pilgrimage were less affected by the routine than family members, those who spent more time at court, or the administrative staff, *gabbaim* (aides) or house *bochurim,* young Hasidim serving as butlers or footmen. The latter lived not only *for* the sake of the *rebistve* but also *off* it, financially depending on it. Of course, the rebbe also lived *for* his calling as well as *off* it. [20]

THE POWER OF REBBES

Unlike the biblical prophets who in Jewish tradition felt called by God to speak to the people, one might say rebbes were those whom the people called on their own, believing them to have abilities far beyond those of mere mortals to arouse the human spirit in the service of heaven and to move heaven to reciprocate. Yet, as with the prophets, when a rebbe engaged in extraordinary behavior many of his followers believed that it was as if "the holy spirit descended upon him." [21] Indeed, there were those who asserted that a *zaddik* was only apparently selected by his followers but in truth was chosen by God. [22]

Certainly in the early years of Hasidism's emergence, this belief in rebbes' extraordinary thaumaturgic powers was encouraged by some of the leaders themselves. No less a leader than the Maggid of Mezherich (d. 1772), the man some have called the first true *zaddik,* a direct disciple of the reputed progenitor of modern Hasidism, Israel ben Eliezer (d. 1760), the so-called Ba'al Shem Tov (Besht), asserted that his followers had to believe that "a *zaddik* can modify [the higher and lower regions] at any time he desires," and his great-grandson, Yisrael Friedman of Ruzhin (1796–1850), was said to have claimed, "Had I wanted to, I could make all barren women fecund, even those whose menses have ceased."[23] Meir Horowitz of Dzikov (1819–77) insisted on the power of the *zaddik* "to resurrect the dead and to create heaven and earth."[24] While these and similar claims may seem extreme, the conviction widely held was that these leaders were endowed with *ruach ha'kodesh,* the Holy Spirit. Some went so far as to assert that "the spirit of Moses, the master of all prophets, the redeemer of Israel, beat in the souls of the *zaddikim.*"[25] The rebbe could help followers "acquire spiritual and religious perfection."[26]

With supreme confidence and power projected on them by their Hasidim, rebbes acted as agents of God, dispensing blessings, effecting miracles, even looking into the hearts of human beings. While Hasidim may have affirmed the rebbe on their own by virtue of his charisma and powers, spiritually and metaphysically his appointment, no less than that of the prophets, was increasingly seen as coming from on high.[27] The closer the Hasid was to his rebbe, the more he shared in the rebbe's reflected grace. That was why the personal encounter was so vital.

THE PROBLEM OF SUCCESSION

It was in the nature of such powerful beliefs in and attachment to these charismatics that few if any Hasidim imagined that their rebbe would die. And if the *zaddik* himself did think about it, he was unlikely to stress that prospect, for to do so would undermine the confidence of his followers in him as an instrument of God. But, like all mortals, rebbes did die, although in the language of Hasidism they were sometimes said simply to have "departed" in what was known as *histalkus* (leavetaking). They were described as having simply thrown off the human limitations of the earthly realm and mystically returned to God, with whom they had such a special relationship.[28]

In line with the Talmudic dictum (Berachot 18b) that "zaddikim b'motam nikraim chaim" (the righteous in their death are called living), some Hasidim tried to maintain their relationship with the departed *zaddik* as if he were still guiding them and acting on their behalf from the world beyond, a continuation of an old tradition of praying at the graves of the righteous and hoping for their intercession on high. In some cases this made a Hasidic leader's tomb a place of pilgrimage.[29]

But graves could not do what a living master could. To maintain attachments, those left behind had to find a *memaleh makom* (stand-in) to act as a channel between the departed leader and the Hasidim, sometimes operating on the basis of instructions left behind. It was not unusual for a body of texts (recorded talks) associated with a particular rebbe to become increasingly important after his passing.[30]

During Hasidism's earliest period, the view that that there would be some designated or logical successor of a departed rebbe "had not yet gained currency."[31] The aftermath of the first generation of leaders was rather characterized by a "loose affiliation of distinct communities connected ... by a common legacy" of teachings and attachments but no clear notion of succession.[32] In fact, the Maggid of Mezherich, in the generation of leaders following the Besht, "actively worked to promulgate Hasidism as a decentralized movement, with no thought of bequeathing a unified body of followers to his own biological heir."[33] Accordingly, most of those emergent courts that survived the death of the Maggid in 1772 were led by disciples, students, or those who had been close to him and shared his approach to Judaism and some charismatic qualities rather than blood descendants. Forcing Hasidim to follow all sorts of others after a leader died was seen as a mechanism that could spread Hasidism's influence into a wider domain than would be possible with a succession to a court led by a son in one place.[34]

A close reading of events suggests that early Hasidim did not think in terms of succession.[35] If we speak of the Maggid as the successor of the Besht, it is not because there was some formal process by which he inhabited the position or office of his preeminent predecessor. Rather, it is that through his personal charisma he was able in a few short years to fill a vacuum and emerge as a leader in his own right who became renowned and ultimately was considered a preeminent leader of Hasidism. Having come to his preeminence this way, the Maggid likewise encouraged his disciples to contend for followers in various Jewish communities. In the emerging Hasidic scene, the field was open. People were drawn toward a rebbe by his charisma and not his pedigree.

There were even some who solved the problem of a rebbe's death by ignoring it. The followers of Nachman of Breslov, known as the "dead Hasidim," continue even today to consider him their only and current rebbe. At the time of Nachman's death in 1810, the norm—if there was one—was for the group who had come together around a particular rebbe to simply scatter upon his demise and look for another to whom to attach themselves. What made the followers of Nachman stand out was their decision to try to remain together *even after his death*. One of them, Nathan Sternhartz of Nemirov, collected and disseminated

Nachman's writings, teachings, and stories to help the Hasidim stay unified.

Some *zaddikim* who died around the same time—perhaps most notably the well-known Levi Yitzchak of Berditchev (d. 1809)— did not have successors, and their followers did not remain together. Thus there were no Berditchever Hasidim who after Levi Yitzchak's death remained united and continued gathering followers, even though two of his sons tried unsuccessfully to succeed him.[36] While his life and tales about him continued to influence Hasidism, and his writings are studied still, as is the narrative of his life, the issue of succession was not essential to his leadership.

THE EVOLUTION OF SUCCESSION

Ultimately, however, succession became critical to Hasidism. While this book will look at succession in the present, to do so requires an understanding of its evolution. As long as there was no mechanism to keep Hasidim of a particular rebbe together, the open competition among would-be rebbes for followers continued apace. In line with a "tradition of non-centralist communal organization," characteristic of European Jewry, whose communities had been self-governing for centuries, Hasidism at first likewise maintained a "pluralist pattern of communal organization."[37] It was not unusual for a Hasid to travel to more than one rebbe, sharing loyalties rather than being attached exclusively to one man.

However, as rebbes established courts with their special customs, rituals, administrative personnel, and institutions and as they developed clearly marked territories of influence, the formerly pluralistic competition for Hasidim was challenged by the notion of loyalty to a *particular* rebbe. Gradually, the "norm which required of every hasid that he should be 'connected' to his own *rebbe* and no other" became dominant.[38] For Hasidim, their rebbe became essential to their identity. They were not simply "Jews"; they were *Hasidic* Jews. Moreover, they were not just Hasidim; they were Hasidim *of* a particular rebbe. In a changing world—and as the eighteenth century gave way to the nineteenth and twentieth, change became endemic—that particular Hasidic identity became a singular constant in their lives. Hasidim became what Richard Werbner has called "a charismatic fellowship."[39]

Long after some Jews left the precincts of Jewish traditional practice, those whose parents or grandparents had been Hasidim might still identify themselves by saying they came from a Hasidic background, often specifying the court of a particular rebbe. What that meant might vary, but it usually signified attachment to certain customs and practices associated with those Hasidim and a feeling about the power and authority of the rebbe. At the very least, it signified a kind of nostalgic set of spiritual attachments.

After their rebbe's death, the charismatic fellowship wanted to remain together. Leaving was less attractive, particularly when they had begun to identify themselves through their Hasidic allegiances and fellowship. They shared a soulful bond, *dvekut,* not only with the rebbe but also with one another.[40] This worked against the breakup of the Hasidic group and its dispersion after the *zaddik*'s death. For "orphaned" Hasidim to depart as individuals in order to find someone new became considered undesirable—even a kind of betrayal. Moreover, if one was particularly attached to one's rebbe, had grown up with him, was close with the family, and had risen in the court to a position of some seniority, one might be reluctant upon the rebbe's death to go in search of another court, where, as a new Hasid, one would suddenly find oneself a neophyte or newcomer, low in the hierarchy, and with a new identity.

If, on the other hand, all the Hasidim remained in the same court with an agreed-upon successor, the charismatic fellowship would remain intact and the senior Hasidim, who linked past and future, might even retain the higher status of those who had been close to the departed leader. A clear line of succession might mitigate the inherent instability of charismatic authority. A living stand-in could provide minimal instability, as long as he was agreed upon by all. As for the remaining family and staff, they could share in the charisma of the rebbe, deriving from him not only their social position and identity but also some of his gift of grace. They eagerly embraced the practice.

As Hasidism became a mass movement that swept across eastern European Jewry, the thought of being without a rebbe became unimaginable to Hasidim. Committed Hasidim were unprepared to simply melt back into the non-Hasidic world or to lose the connection to the others who shared their attachments to the rebbe. Succession became essential. The question now became: Who constituted a worthy successor?

WHO IS A SUITABLE SUCCESSOR?

Would the successor be any charismatic who made a claim? Was the "market" open to all comers, as it had been at the dawn of Hasidism? What would a successor need in order to hold on to the Hasidim and lead the court? Would he need to be a disciple who was particularly close to the rebbe and had shared some of his special knowledge, one who might even have aided the rebbe in the past and could teach what he had learned to those left behind, as seemed so often to have been the case as Hasidism first began its spread throughout eastern Europe? Or would the successor need to be a relative of the *zaddik*, either a son, a brother, or a son-in-law? Could that person even be the widow of the leader? These were questions that began to emerge as the eighteenth century drew to a close and questions of succession emerged.

Could it be only someone designated by the rebbe as his heir—either while he was still alive or in a moral will (a will that functions not to legally distribute assets but to offer counsel to those left behind, in a kind of teaching)? Did such a designation have to be explicit, or could it be implied? If implied, who would be the ones to infer the truth and act upon it, and with what authority?

If the choices the Maggid of Mezherich made were to be the standard, then the preferred choices for a successor would be disciples, not descendants. They were the best informed about what the rebbe taught and because of their intense involvement with him were best suited to continue what he had begun. Yet some argued that the succession from the Maggid to his disciples—like the Maggid's assumption of office following the Besht—was the consequence of offspring who were particularly unsuited charismatically.

Those who in contrast argued in favor of succession by blood descendants, most prominently sons, did so out of a presumption that the rebbe was a holy man and his spirit so sublime that "at the time of conception" of his offspring this act "would bring down an exceptional soul from heaven and that a child conceived and brought up in holiness would himself be holy."[41] The "term 'holy seed'—*zera kodesh*—occurs frequently" in rebbes' characterizations of their offspring.[42] The Besht reputedly told his son, "I know that I gave you a holy soul, for when I joined in union with my wife the heavens shook."[43] This concept also empowered sons-in-law, for their seed, impregnating the holy offspring of a rebbe, could join and even strengthen the rebbe's bloodline and perceived holiness and could produce a grandchild who was also *zera kodesh*. To make sure that no pollutants entered into the holy seed, rebbes' daughters would commonly be matched with sons of other rebbes, not infrequently with their cousins, thereby keeping the holiness in the family.

Like all royalty, Hasidism evolved "a theology of genealogical sanctity."[44] One succeeded not only to the position of rebbe but also to family leadership, and often inherited family property and control over precious objects like manuscripts or Judaica freighted with the iconic power of leadership.[45]

This did not happen all at once. In the early years of Hasidism, competition between those who favored distinguished disciples and those who favored family as successors was complicated by the existence of many distinguished disciples, no less than the presence of a number of sons or brothers or even sons-in-law who were potential successors. Indeed, as Uriel Gellman has shown, between 1772 and 1815 only 22 rebbes out of the approximately 120 active *zaddikim* at the time were sons or sons-in-law of their predecessors.[46] As succession became normative following the rebbe's demise, the identity of the "natural" successor was at first not obvious and the potential for conflict and tension was great, regardless of whether the choice was a disciple or a blood relative.

At first, the absence of set procedures offered some flexibility. To be sure, precedents of succession based on traditional Jewish norms of primogeniture and rules of inheritance were powerful influences. Yet the fact that there were many locations where younger sons could go to establish a following helped defuse tensions over who would succeed. A loser in one place could still try to become a rebbe elsewhere, developing a court that might be very much like the one from which he came, yet not really competing with it because of the geographic distance or the fact that his new followers were not yet connected to a particular Hasidic tradition and practices. Given the geography of Hasidism and the difficulties of travel, a relatively small distance might suffice to set up a new court. Moreover, a younger son or a disciple could capitalize on his ties to the older rebbe. Thus a single rebbe could have a number of successors, part of a single core dynasty, who coexisted in time but not in place. This allowed for the emergence of masters who led by dint of their own charismatic gifts even as it reinforced the idea of a dynasty. Perhaps the most famous Hasidic dynasty of this type was the Chernobyl one founded by Menachem Nachum Twersky (1730–97), student of the Besht and disciple of the Maggid of Mezherich, whose son, Mordechai (1770–1837), was succeeded by all of his eight sons, each of whom became a rebbe in a different city.[47]

Ultimately, successors would have to possess personal magnetism and offer evidence of charisma. As the teachings and practices of Hasidism reached the point of saturation among Jewry in the nineteenth century and became increasingly similar if not standardized, so that the variations among many courts became matters more of nuance than of obvious distinctions, the advantage of family ties to a *zaddik* increased, leading to kinship as the preferred basis of succession. Occasionally a rebbe's surviving brothers might become the chosen heirs (as happened in the Gerrer dynasty), impervious to the generation-advantaged sons.

So important did blood ties become that in some cases even a minor child, called a *yenuka,* might be made the rebbe, just to keep the *rebistve* in the family. Perhaps the first such was Abraham (1787–1813), the fifteen-year-old son of Shalom Shakhna (1769–1802), the grandson of the Maggid of Mezherich, who had become rebbe in Prohobitch, Ukraine. Almost immediately after the burial of his father, Abraham sat down in his father's place and assumed the position of leadership.[48] In so doing (perhaps at the urging and encouragement of his mother, Chava, who came from the Chernobyl dynasty and well understood the advantages of keeping the crown within the family), he kept his father's Hasidim from dispersing and the succession from going to another.[49] Later, when Abraham died, his younger brother, who would become Yisrael Friedman of Ruzhin, repeated the same seizure of position. The child-rebbe thus became a leader not primarily because he demonstrated a wisdom beyond his years or was greater than any of his father's disciples but because he was "holy seed." Choosing a son—even a young child—kept family members (especially the dowager *rebbetzin,* his mother) and some of his father's staff or relatives (who often acted as regents) in the ranks of the elite and powerful—something that would not happen if leadership went out of the family to a disciple.

Succession by a disciple would replace the family with the disciple's family, leaving the rebbe's widow and children as well his staff dislocated from a life in which they were not only treated as special but also supported financially. But having a son take over affirmed their gift of grace and allowed them to continue to partake in its benefits. Absent such succession, the dowager *rebbetzin* would become just another widow, her children mere fatherless children—all with "uncertain prospects." [50] Women therefore had a vested interest in seeing to it not only that their husbands held on to their Hasidim but that their sons inherited them as well. Sons-in-law or brothers of the late rebbe were not quite as good, for their own mothers or wives often outranked and displaced the dowager.

THE CHABAD CASE

No case better illustrates many of these issues than what happened following the death in 1812 of Schneur Zalman of Lyadi (1740–1812).

When Menachem Mendel of Vitebsk (1730–88) decided to move, with approximately three hundred of his followers, from Europe to the Holy Land, he appointed his disciple Schneur Zalman as a day-to-day guide for those of his Hasidim who remained behind. But Menachem Mendel's plan for maintaining his active leadership this way failed. The distance to the Holy Land was simply too great, while Schneur Zalman's powers and charisma were too impressive. Consequently, the latter evolved into a rebbe, founder of ChaBaD Hasidism. (For an explanation of the acronym ChaBaD, see chapter 6, note 2.)

Father to three sons and four daughters, he became very popular, with his own prime disciple, Aaron HaLevy Hurvitz, who often served as an intermediary between the rebbe and his Hasidim. Aaron even tutored the rebbe's son, DovBer. When Schneur Zalman died, his followers were not ready to break up. The question was who would continue to lead them. The choice devolved to either Aaron or DovBer, with each man having his supporters. Part of the conflict resulted from the fact that although he surely realized he would not live forever, the Alter Rebbe (Yiddish for the "old rebbe"), as Schneur Zalman came to be known, left no clear will as to who, if anyone, should succeed him. Some Hasidim might have been forgiven for assuming it would be Aaron because of all the tasks of leadership he had carried out during the Alter Rebbe's lifetime.[51] As preeminent disciple, Aaron, in his words and actions, blurred "the boundary between one who acts on behalf or on the authority of his *rebbe* and one who acts on his own authority."[52] Hence some Hasidim imagined that the rebbe had been grooming Aaron as his successor, especially because he would not have asked Aaron to instruct his son DovBer in the ways of Hasidism if he had not trusted that the former, eight years older than the boy, knew what needed to be known. Moreover, it was no secret at court that Aaron urged the boy forward whenever he struggled over some difficult idea, leading to the younger man's dependence on his teacher, who in writing referred to him as "my dear brother."[53] Hasidim might therefore legitimately believe that Aaron would be the one to lead not only the rebbe's children but all the Hasidim who had been orphaned by their master's death.

But there was no definitive proof. Given that DovBer ultimately became successor, ChaBaD sources—in retrospect—claimed that "following the death of his father, our grand rabbi, may he rest in peace, most of our fellows [the Hasidim] set their eyes on [his son] to succeed his father . . . for that was the opinion of our grand rabbi."[54]

There was an alternate argument, reportedly found in Schneur Zalman's opinion of who should succeed the Besht. A well-known tradition (probably untrue) claims that during an 1808 visit between Baruch of Medzibezh (1782–1811), the latter's grandson, and Schneur Zalman, the two argued over "how the authority of the leader was to be transmitted, whether from father to son or from teacher to disciples." In that argument, Baruch was purported to have argued for heredity ("I am the grandson" and therefore "I should be shown respect"), while Schneur Zalman argued for discipleship ("I, too, am the grandson of the Ba'al Shem Tov, his spiritual grandson, for the great Maggid [of Mezherich] was an outstanding disciple of the Ba'al Shem Tov, and I am the disciple of the Maggid").[55]

But in the wake of Schneur Zalman's passing, heredity succeeded. Championing DovBer were first and foremost the members of the family. Shterna, the widow, heavily involved in the affairs of the court, pressed to have Aaron forced into exile.[56] Others in the family uniformly argued for DovBer. In return, he reportedly swore at his father's grave that he would continue to support the family, a promise that undoubtedly helped hold their loyalty.[57] Yehuda Lev, Schneur Zalman's brother, aware of this undertaking, took the most public lead in trying to persuade the Hasidim that the Alter Rebbe had always meant to have his son lead the court next, arguing that "there is none among his brothers [including Aaron, who may have called him 'brother'] who is greater than him."[58] In the end, DovBer held on to the office, and Aaron left town with a small group of followers, but his once-prominent leadership within ChaBaD ultimately declined. In spite of his assertion that DovBer "was mistaken and fostered mistakes in all that was connected to serving God in accord with Schneur Zalman's instructions," DovBer and the family won the day.[59]

The contest may have seemed ideological or personal, but in fact it was structural and economic. Schneur Zalman had "eighty-thousand hasidim," many of whom were teachers of other Hasidim, and "each one had a charity box for him."[60] Those were resources the family was unwilling to give up to a stranger, even one as prominent as Aaron, who would be unlikely to share with them. So in fact succession was driven as much by a desire of the family to hold on to the Hasidim and the economic and political power of the court as any matter of ideology or spiritual development.

When the contest was over, ChaBaD accounts stressed the charisma and holiness of the winner as being decisive; they even suggested that he had won not because he was simply a son but because he—not Aaron—was really his father's top disciple. From then onwards, ChaBaD power and leadership (as we shall see later in these pages) remained within the family, and succession went from fathers to sons and sons-in-law who, by virtue of cross-cousin arranged marriages, were also members of the family by blood—albeit always with the proviso that the successor was also spiritually superior to all other possible claimants.[61]

The line of succession might go via a daughter if there were no male lines available, but the successor would always be male, even if he was informally governed by a woman—commonly a dowager *rebbetzin* (his mother or mother-in-law). "The situations surrounding the succession of a Rebbe have been as varied and as complex as family life itself, and decisions have turned on struggles within rabbinic families and between court factions, and on emotions as generous as love and willingness to sacrifice, or as onerous as jealousy and avarice."[62]

The Hasidim and their loyalties were ultimately decisive. Additionally, "The value of lineage and ancestral merit was one of east European Jewry's most ancient Ashkenazic legacies," and however revolutionary Hasidism might have been at the outset, it would in time fit back into traditional forms of that Jewry.[63]

One of the hallmarks of Schneur Zalman's Hasidism was his willingness to share widely Kabbalistic knowledge, what is called *toras ha'nistar,* or secret mystical teachings. He had done so in his seminal work, the *Tanya,* and in many of his addresses. This had been criticized by some other Hasidic leaders. DovBer announced that he would continue this tradition and "would not limit those loyal to him" from learning a thing that his father shared with him, including the hidden (*nistar*).[64] That decision, combined with his family tie to the *zaddik,* ensured his succession to the leadership. And when DovBer's knowledge of the ways of his father was published in pamphlets and volumes distributed to his Hasidim, he essentially used these publications to buttress his position—a practice all the succeeding rebbes of ChaBaD would embrace. In the interests of continuity, they were simply willing to reveal the unrevealed to the widest possible audience, often claiming that this was what the Messiah had always meant in his famous apocryphal conversation with the Besht in heaven when, in response to the question of when he would come, the Redeemer replied: "Through this you will know—when your teachings are publicized and revealed in the world and your wellsprings will be spread to the outside—that which I have taught you, and which you have grasped [will be understood by those you have taught,] and they too will be able to make 'unifications' and ascents like you."[65] While perhaps the Besht understood in the Messiah's reply "a striking demand for the communication of esoteric power to the people" and a need to delineate the mysteries of Kabbalah so that "every man should be able to make spiritual ascents just like his," ChaBaD Hasidim took this as a mandate to pass their message to the Jewish people and to carry out his mission to prepare the ground for the imminent arrival of the Messiah and Jewish redemption.[66]

The successful aspirations of Schneur Zalman's son to succession essentially served to centralize leadership. The more that efforts like DovBer's succeeded, the more they served as a model for others. For those Hasidim far from the rebbe, his emissaries grew in importance, as did the idea of regular pilgrimage to the court. Tensions were created, however, when rebbes established courts in the territory of another *zaddik*.[67] Indeed, the aforementioned argument between Baruch of Medzibezh and Schneur Zalman over who would succeed the Besht was actually a territorial dispute, with the former wary if not angry about the latter's visit, which he considered an effort to create a presence and levy a tax (*ma'amad*) on Hasidim in an area that Baruch considered his.[68] The visit ultimately resulted in the eviction of Schneur Zalman and his followers from Podolia.

The complications and conflicts over succession also reflect the classic pattern of what happens when new religious experiences and movements enter the stage of routinization and become part of established religion. As Richard Werbner points out, "After the peak of religious enthusiasm, fragmentation follows."[69] However, when life in a court is routinized, the idea of succession by a son is aided. On the other hand, particularly charismatic and innovative larger-than-life rebbes who have long worn the crown, especially those who embraced an *après moi le deluge* attitude, make it much harder for would-be successors to lay claim to their position. It takes time to become larger than life, and some never manage to do it: the offspring of great fathers who take over at a young age have an especially hard act to follow.

Rebbes with a more forward-looking view and organizational understanding sometimes made matters easier by announcing their wishes regarding a successor in the form of a moral will, describing what qualities a true successor should have (but leaving out names to avoid unleashing the "evil eye" on the chosen one or to allow some flexibility by not necessarily specifying exactly who they had in mind). Sometimes of course a father was unable or reluctant to choose among his possible successors, or he loved all of his sons and wanted them all to follow in his footsteps. The rebbe Yisrael Perlow of Karlin left such a will, which on his death in 1922 was opened. He left the following directions for choosing his heir: "And this will be the sign verifying who among my sons [should be my heir], the one who has all the following qualities: He will not be a bootlicker, nor double-faced, he will keep himself away from lies and not mingle with good-for-nothings. . . . Rather, he will join the company of God's faithful. He won't send his children to [public] school, even if it is a Jewish one. He will make no efforts to gain the leadership. He is the one who should be your head and leader." [70]

As it turned out, among the rebbe's sons, six considered themselves qualified to reign by their father's criteria, and a royal battle broke out among them, until the Karlin Hasidic elders sided with Avraham Elimelech, the fifth son, while the fourth son, Moshe, set up a court in Stolin. The third son, Yaakov Hayim, emigrated in the early 1920s to the United States, becoming one of the first Hasidic rebbes there, initially in Williamsburg, New York, and then in Detroit. The youngest son, Yochanan, was too immature to ascend to a leadership position upon the father's death but, once he married he set out to the Vohlin district in Europe and established his own court in Lutczek, far away from both Karlin and Stolin. Homogeneity gave way to diversity, aided by geography, which allowed each contender to find his place. As for his material inheritance, that was decided by a Polish court. [71]

TERRITORY AND SUCCESSION

Territoriality, as already hinted, became part of Hasidism. To signal their attachment to the rebbe, his Hasidim would identify themselves with the name of the locale of his court, which would become their brand. Hence the *zaddik* was often identified by a place-name: Dov Ber the Maggid of Mezherich, Baruch of Medzibezh, Schneur Zalman of Lyadi, Levi of Berditchev, Elimelech of Lyzhansk, Yisrael of Ruzhin, and so on. Sometimes the only way to solve the problem of succession when there were several potential candidates was to find a new locale for each potential successor. Names at first were easy to come by, for it was the rebbe who was the center of attachments, and wherever he came to establish himself and his court, that place-name would in time come to denote him and his followers. The rebbe gave the place its importance. A would-be leader who sought to obtain followers or to establish a court but found it impossible to do so in one locale (either because of competition, hostility, or inaccessibility to large numbers of followers) might find another location where such obstacles did not exist and might establish (or reestablish) himself there (either via a formal rabbinic appointment or by making himself prominent in other ways) and thereby attract the needed followers. If he succeeded, he and his followers eventually became known by the new place-name, or more precisely by a Yiddish variant of it. As mobility throughout Jewish Europe became easier during the late nineteenth and early twentieth centuries, the spread of Hasidim reached its apex. The number of rebbes multiplied with the popularity of Hasidism; new names grew in number.

This geographic dispersion and the names associated with it provided positions for a number of leaders from the same dynasty simultaneously. Geographic dispersion and the availability of new names as brands could mitigate conflict and competition over succession when there were several claimants to a throne, all the while also spreading Hasidism to new corners of Jewish life. While hard feelings and some elements of rivalry might have remained, the fact that a *zaddik* could establish himself in another place and be known by that name allowed all members of the family to retain some element of a *rebistve*, even if some of those who moved away from where their father the rebbe lived lost the advantages of the home court.

A rebbe's geographic location and accessibility to his followers mattered. Of course, a *zaddik* with extraordinary power and charisma could make a little town grow by attracting Hasidim, but one located near many Jews often fared far better than one in a distant village. Yet a significant rebbe would want to be located in a significant place. Surely the importance of Yitzchak Meir Alter was related to the fact that he established his court in the town of Ger (Gura-Kalvarya), just twenty-five kilometers southeast of Warsaw, where many Jews were concentrated.[72] Ultimately, a synergy between a dynasty and a place arose, so that importance flowed in both directions: from *zaddik* to place and from place to those who succeeded to the *rebistve* there. Only later would the place-name become more, a brand name, over which successors fought.

With new locations and names to match, a particular dynasty might enlarge its influence, with sons (or sons-in-law or even stellar disciples) establishing a new court related to the original, like a branch to the root. Such dispersed succession also allowed for divergence and differentiation in ways that did not necessarily lead to conflict and tension. Thus, for example, the Ruzhin Hasidic dynasty founded by Yisrael Friedman dealt with the fact that several of his offspring chose to pursue the "family business" and become rebbes in their own right by evolving offshoots, including Bohush (led by Friedman's grandson Yitzchak), Sadigura (led by a son, Avraham Yaakov), Boyan (led by another grandson, Yitzchak, son of the Sadigura Rebbe), Chortkov (led by a son, Dovid Moshe) and Husiatyń (led by a son, Mordecai Shraga).[73] While each of these could and did compete for prominence and prestige with the others, their dispersed locations diminished intrafamilial tension over matters of leadership, economics, and prominence. Moreover, the fact that none of these place-names had yet established a brand distinction of its own allowed for the competition to be gradual. Finally, because geographic distances mattered more at a time when travel was more complicated, the competition among rebbes in different locales for followers and influence was minimized, since the choice to attach oneself to someone elsewhere required an often difficult and expensive journey.

SUCCESSION, THE CHARISMA OF OFFICE, BRANDING, AND INHERITED IDENTITY

In time, however, certain place-names became brands with cachet and standing of their own, endowing the one attached to them with authority and esteem beyond what he brought personally to his position as rebbe. In part, such names offered inherited prominence, or what Max Weber called "the charisma of office." As Weber explained, the holder of "genuine charisma . . . would be ennobled by virtue of his own actions," which generated a personal following. But to someone who had charisma of office, legitimacy and prominence came by virtue of inheriting the position or title that had become the institutionalized expression of the charisma possessed by its previous incumbent.[74] When a successor became the Rebbe of Ger or of Bobov or any such illustrious title, he was enhanced by bearing that title.

With the institutionalization of succession, charisma of office became an inalienable part of leadership. Simultaneously, place-names associated with renowned Hasidic groups took on iconic power and deeper meaning. The leader *and* the place-name became a single entity of symbolic import, a focus of cohesion and a source of identification. So important did these names become that geography became secondary. Thus, even after the court moved to Rostov, Leningrad, Riga, Otwock, or Crown Heights, the famous Lubavitcher Rebbe (whose dynasty was once headquartered in the Byelorussian town of Lubavitch [Lubovici]) and his Hasidim never chose to call themselves anything other than Lubavitchers—so important had the name become. The same was true for many other Hasidic groups. Once the place-name had become iconic it was an identity and not a denotation of where the court was.

If originally Hasidim might attach themselves to a particular rebbe because they believed the "doctrine of the affinity of souls," a Kabbalistic notion that they had a mystical spiritual bond with him, after the institutionalization of succession their attachment was a matter of a family history of association with a particular dynasty and brand.[75] If a father was attached to a particular rebbe, his offspring would in time become attached to his successor, and their identities were expressed by the brand or place-name. As this inherited identity took root, the idea of poaching Hasidim or switching loyalty, once considered unacceptable only spiritually, became unthinkable institutionally.[76]

THE NEW WORLD AND RISING CONSERVATISM

By the time Jews were becoming modern, and certainly by the mid-twentieth century, when large numbers of Hasidim had reached America and Israel, Hasidism, "having emerged as an upstart movement seeking to upend established norms of Jewish behavior in the name of spiritual revival," had become "the guardian of traditional Jewish observance."[77] Hasidim saw the Holocaust and forced migration as proof of the hopelessness of assimilation and endorsed instead cultural ghettoization. They saw modernity as a counterfeit prize and as a threat that would dilute Judaism and Jewry, considered Zionism as religiously heretical and as a false promise, and demonized all non-Orthodox Jews as antireligious and dangerous to Jewish continuity. While ChaBaD and Breslov engaged in outreach to retrieve modern Jewry and Zionists, even they saw themselves as committed to revitalizing and strengthening traditional Jewish culture in its Hasidic form and like all other Hasidim turned their backs on the "various degrees of cultural accommodation and social integration with gentile society" that were so much the norm for most Jews.[78] Additionally, mid-twentieth-century Hasidism adopted a post-Holocaust ideology of rebuilding. As refugees and immigrants, they hoped to rebuild their lives while nostalgically projecting their European past as a sacred, golden age. Such collective sacred nostalgia, inflated by survivor guilt of the refugees, powerfully motivated many Hasidim to protect their young from the acculturative tendencies of the postwar world. Hasidism thus located itself among the more conservative and counteracculturative elements of Orthodoxy. This also affected succession. Any pretenders to the throne had to demonstrate that they shared these attitudes.

Succession continued to be by inherited charisma; dynasty rather than discipleship was determinative. In effect, once the belief was established that "charisma is bound to a blood relationship," even after the exodus from Europe "only the deeds of his forefathers could legitimate" a man as a rebbe.[79] The possibility of a disciple breaking away and starting his own court remained as rare in these years as it had become in Europe, although in the very early twentieth-century transitional years in America there were some disciples who, far from Europe, tried to establish themselves as rebbes in this new world while others at the time invented family connections with famous *zaddikim* back in Europe so as to establish a following.

After the Holocaust, leadership largely fell to those who were Holocaust survivors or those who escaped beforehand to Palestine or America and avoided the threats of communism, Nazism, secularism, and assimilation. These rebbes became ennobled not only by their charisma of office but by the sacred nostalgia for a lost world that marked the post-Holocaust world of Hasidism. This extra measure of charm would have a profound impact on succession because their offspring had to live up to predecessors who had been made holier by their having gone through the fire.

After its transplantation in the post-Holocaust era, Hasidim and their rebbes were no longer as dispersed as they had been in Europe, separated by sometimes shifting national borders and the vagaries of different political contexts and jurisdictional settings that affected movement. Instead, at first they found themselves often living in metropolitan New York and even in the same neighborhoods, or, in the case of Israel, in a small country under Jewish jurisdiction. In such a crowded environment, followers and leaders rubbed shoulders in sometimes uncomfortable ways. Even those far away were reachable by new, faster and easier options of travel and communication. Likewise, finding virgin territory where multiple sons of a rebbe might set themselves up was nearly impossible. Competition became inevitable and more intense. If one was not impressed with a successor, going to a competing court across the street or in a nearby neighborhood was easy. Even the opportunity to take on a new name lessened, for the old names now were enhanced and made more valuable by sacred nostalgia. They became holy trademarks.

Given that establishing a new court in another geographic location was no longer easy, yeshivas connected with the courts of specific rebbes became important for those who harbored ambitions for the *rebistve,* serving rebbes both as a recruitment tool and as a source of stable income. Headship of the yeshiva typically fell to the rebbe's sons or sons-in-law, who in the process were building a cadre of followers who would easily shift their allegiance to them when a new generation of leadership came to power. Large Hasidic groups established multiple schools: for primary grades (*yeshiva ketana*), for secondary level (*mesifta*), for married young men (*kollel*), and even for young girls (seminary). Often these were in other neighborhoods (or, in Israel, other settlements). The competition for students was fierce.[80] Many of these young people would in time be the first in their family to become Hasidic.

With so many institutions (*mosdos*), the role of rebbe became more complex—often beyond what any single man could handle. This led to roles for other family members to help run them. But that could also lead to succession battles. Such struggles became more frequent in the late twentieth and early twenty-first centuries. In some cases, they emerged because there were too many pretenders to a throne who had no other profession to pursue and who wanted to move up. In other cases, they occurred because a single rebbe could not maintain a sufficiently close and intimate relationship with *all* his followers, so that the group split, with different subgroups gravitating to different potential successors who nevertheless claimed the same title, often in the same neighborhood. In still other cases, succession issues developed because too many family members of a rebbe chose to exit from the Hasidic world and take advantage of opportunities that beckoned in the modern open society.

What had become a routinized pattern of succession, a family inheritance meant to provide stability and maintain authority, gradually became a source of increasing tension and competition. Brothers and brothers-in-law, as well as their supporters, might quarrel over who would be successor. If no sons or sons-in-law were available, the quest for some blood relative who could take over might lead Hasidim to create a rebbe out of someone who, although unprepared, was a blood relative. Failure to do so could lead to the disappearance of some dynasties, even those illumined by sacred nostalgia. The candidate would have to be made conservative and ultra-Orthodox.

WHO WILL LEAD US?

With a birthrate higher than any other in the Jewish world and a retention rate that remains near 80 percent, the number of Hasidim has grown to around 350,000 in North America and about 445,000 in Israel, with perhaps another 100,000 elsewhere in the world. Their population increase continues to be rapid, along with the proliferation of their institutions and the expansion of their economies—trends reflected in the power of the rebbes and whoever succeeds them.

Despite or perhaps because of this growth, transition and succession remain of great concern to Hasidim, who understand that their own collective continuity is at stake in them. Hasidim are always aware of this threat to their stability and future. They follow succession vicissitudes with extraordinary interest and worry, for they know that if there is no successor their anchor is missing; if there are too many successors, the community risks fragmentation; and if a successor is weak or uncharismatic or if he is not to be found, the community may lose adherents. This makes smooth transitions moments of celebration and collective effervescence that are socially magnified and exaggerated in importance, particularly in the insular and limited world of the Hasidim. In the eyes of the Hasidim, they take on a fateful character, as if determined by God.

But there is also turmoil, because increasingly successions have become fraught in the crowded and competitive world of charismatic leadership. Much as Hasidim might like to believe heaven is involved in the selection of their rebbes, followers believe that the majority should decide who will lead them. That means that besides God, power politics and popularity have entered into the mix, and candidates have to campaign for the position, even though they do so with subtlety and proxies. These campaigns may divide families, strain communal resources, and lead to epic battles that can spin out of control. Even rabbinic courts or civil courts are enlisted to resolve successions. Or in the absence of a successor, the Hasidim must try to create one, sometimes out of thin air, often testing the limits of charisma. As Hasidim seek a way out of this turmoil, ironically they may lose precisely the order and stability that they have sought to preserve.

The rest of this book will illustrate how all this plays out in the six different cases. The first three—Munkács, Kopyczynitz, and Boyan—represent cases where the Hasidim ran out of successors and had to find new ones. The next two—Bobov and Satmar—among the largest courts—illustrate two cases where competing successors have emerged. Finally, the last—ChaBad/Lubavitch—is a case where the Hasidim tried to avoid the problem of succession by denying the death of their rebbe and hence any need for succession.

What follows are the stories of each of these Hasidic successions and what led up to them. Each provides a unique and riveting narrative of continuity. Sometimes there is intrigue or and rivalry; sometimes near death and rebirth. These are accounts of personal and collective transformation, inspired by messianic hopes and shadowed by the Holocaust's genocidal destruction, as well as of migration and a search for continuity in new worlds that many once believed would be inimical to Hasidism but that turned out to be quite the opposite. These are chronicles of the making and unmaking of men, a search for charisma, leadership, and struggles for power. They tell of families united and divided, of death and resurrection, and of hopes raised and dashed. They give substance to the eternal question of Hasidism: Who will lead us?

2

Munkács

An Oedipal Challenge

The story of Munkács is a remarkable tale of what happens after a scion who is the only successor of a prominent rebbe has abdicated. It is a narrative deeply shaken by the historical events of the Holocaust, Zionism, and the relocation of European Jews to North America, the new state of Israel, and elsewhere in the Diaspora. It is also an account of a father born into Hasidism who after inheriting a crown gradually felt it no longer suited him and who after removing it could not make his peace with a son who took it for himself. Within this narrative are complicated relationships between fathers, sons, mothers, daughters, and the chorus of Hasidim who stand behind them all.

MUNKÁCS AND THE SHAPIRAS

The story begins in Munkács or Mukačevo, today a city along the banks of the Latorica River in the district of Subcarpathian Rus', in southwestern Ukraine. When they lived there, Jews called the town by its Hungarian name—Munkács—often written as "Munkatch" and sometimes pronounced in Yiddish as "Minkatch." In the interwar period, Munkács belonged to Czechoslovakia. By November 1938, it was absorbed into the Bereg district of Hungary. In 1941 it had 13,488 Jewish residents, some 42.7 percent of the total population of the town.[1]

Munkács Hasidism traces itself to Zvi Elimelech Shapira (sometimes "Spira"; 1783–1841). When in 1825 he moved from Munkács to

---

The Munkács Dynasty

ZVI ELIMELECH SHAPIRA (1783–1841): Known as the Bnai Yisosschor; Rebbe of Munkács, Hungary, and later of Dynów, Poland

ELAZAR SHAPIRA (1808–65): Known as the Yodai Bina; Rebbe of Łańcut, Poland; second son of Zvi Elimelech

DAVID SHAPIRA (1804–74): Rebbe of Dynów; youngest son of Zvi Elimelech

SHLOMO SHAPIRA (1832–93): Known as the Shem Shlomo; Rebbe of Munkács; grandson of Zvi Elimelech

ZVI HIRSCH SHAPIRA (1850–1913): Known as the Darchei Tshuvah; Rebbe of Munkács; son of Shlomo

CHAIM ELAZAR SHAPIRA (1871–1937): Known as the Minchas Elazar; Rebbe of Munkács; only son of Zvi Hirsch

BORUCH YEHOSHUA YERACHMIEL RABINOVICH (1914–97): Known as Boruchel; Rebbe of Munkács; son-in-law of Chaim Elazar

MOSHE YEHUDA LEIB RABINOVICH (1940–PRESENT): Rebbe of Munkács, in New York; third son of Baruch Yehoshua Yerachmiel

---

Dynów in the Lvóv district of Poland and established a court there, Shapira became known as the Dynover Rebbe. Since place-names did not yet carry the cachet of a brand and were not yet freighted with history or imbued with the sacred nostalgia we associate with them today, Shapira was better known as Bnai Yisosschor, after the name of his magnum opus of discourses on the Torah. A powerful opponent of Jews who had abandoned the traditional paths of Judaism, he called these modernizers and reformers "the descendants of the 'mixed multitude,'" those Egyptians who attached themselves to the Israelites during the exodus from Egypt.[2] With this attitude, Munkács Hasidism became associated with the culture war against modernizing tendencies in Judaism.

After his oldest son predeceased him, Zvi Elimelech's two surviving sons continued as Hasidic rebbes, but neither of them was associated with the name of Munkács. His second son Elazar (died 1865), went to the Polish town of Łańcut, where he became a rebbe, known by his book of adages and commentary, *Yodai Bina*. His third son Shmuel chose not to take up a *rebistve,* and his youngest son David (died 1874) remained in Dynów and was known as the Dynover Rebbe.

Zvi Elimelech's grandson, Shlomo (1832–93), son of Elazar and a disciple of Hayim Halberstam, the Rebbe of Sanz, a major Hasidic leader, held numerous rabbinical posts in Galicia before returning to Munkács. Leaving Strzyżów, Galicia, where he was head of the rabbinical court, Shlomo acceded to the request of some Hasidim in Munkács and reestablished his grandfather's court there in 1882. With only about four thousand Jews residing there at the time, Shlomo drew young Hasidim who had known him in Galicia to Munkács. Like his grandfather, he was a rigid opponent of the Haskalah or Jewish enlightenment and Neolog (Hungarian Jewish Reform) movements and embraced a highly conservative brand of Judaism. His court began to grow during his last decade.[3]

Shlomo's son, Zvi Hirsch (d. 1913)—also known as the Darchei Tshuvah—continued that tendency and became a leading advocate of Hungarian separatist Orthodoxy, a militant movement strongly opposing any association with the reformist general Jewish community as well as Jewish innovations, even forbidding his Hasidim to send their children to schools that offered instruction in the Hungarian language, which he considered a vehicle of assimilation. His failure to speak Hungarian led to his dismissal from his official position as town rabbi by the authorities, something that may have affected his economic situation but did not undermine his authority over Hasidic and much of traditional Orthodox Jewry in Munkács.[4]

CHAIM ELAZAR SHAPIRA, THE MINCHAS ELAZAR

Zvi Hirsch's only son, Chaim Elazar Shapira (1871–1937), born in Strzyżów, Poland, and later known as the Minchas Elazar, after his five-volume book of commentary, is really the start of this story.[5] "Lacking a formal secular education, he acquired a high school certificate from the town of Nitra in Slovakia so that he could fulfill the Austro-Hungarian authorities' requirement for a general education in order to serve as rabbi."[6] A man whose hegemony over Jewish life in Munkács would ultimately become nearly absolute, especially after 1903, when he was appointed chief of the rabbinical court, Chaim Elazar became a renowned Hasidic personality. A year after his father's death in 1913, at the age of forty-six, he formally succeeded him as rebbe.

Chaim Elazar "extended and deepened his father's tradition of rabbinical scholarship combined with extreme religious, social, and political conservatism."[7] His early years of leadership were marked by the "Great War" that he and many other rabbinical leaders saw as Armageddon and as a possible harbinger of imminent messianic redemption—the proverbial darkness before the light. Throughout his *rebistve,* he was known for dramatically invoking the need to hasten the coming of the Redeemer.[8]

He became ever more confrontational and ideological, denouncing and demonizing Jews whose behavior and thinking he considered led their followers away from "true" redemption: secularists, assimilationists, reformers, and Zionists.[9] Zionism especially bothered him. When in 1917 the British foreign minister Lord Balfour announced that "His Majesty's government view with favour the establishment in Palestine of a national home for the Jewish people," Shapira called this statement, over which thousands of Zionists cheered, a "tragedy" of idol worship.[10] Exile, he believed, was God's plan, and only the Messiah could end it. Shapira considered Zionism to be a movement aimed at circumventing the role of the Messiah in the redemption of the Jewish people. He seems to have believed that the true redemption was imminent but that the Zionists endangered its coming and therefore viewed his battle with them as apocalyptic in character.

Part of Shapira's growing influence came from a belief among many of his Hasidim in his ability to give blessings and to miraculously see what others could not. When, for example, in 1915 the Russian army was nearing Munkács, many rabbis declared that Jews should flee the town to save themselves from the cruelty of the czar, and some did. But Shapira confidently assured his Hasidim that all would be well and that they need neither flee nor fear the arrival of Russians. When the Russian army failed to enter Munkács after all, his reputation as a *zaddik* became even more enhanced.[11] Among a growing number of Hasidim in the demographically developing community, he was seen as oracular, in many ways eclipsing his father and grandfather.

The rebbe became renowned for a virulently uncompromising opposition to even minute changes in what he viewed as Jewish tradition, setting the bar even higher than his predecessors.[12] He denounced Jews who had emigrated to America or Palestine for their failure to uphold the traditions and practices of Orthodox Judaism as he defined it. He issued a famous warning (serendipitously caught on film in 1933) to the Jews of America to observe the Sabbath, telling them that if they increased their observance of the Sabbath all would be well with them but that if they did not they would suffer grim consequences.[13]

THE NEED FOR AN HEIR

Like other Hasidim, those in Munkács were concerned with their court's continuity. They had good reason. Engaged since both were about eight years old, in what was a not uncommon custom at the time, Chaim Elazar and Chaya Chasya, the daughter of his grandmother's sister, wed when they were fifteen. After nearly twenty years of an apparently loving marriage, the couple, however, still had no children. This troubled his Hasidim, for they were anxious to assure the future of their group. While Shapira emphasized his belief in the imminence of the Messiah, which would make the question of succession and the couple's infertility moot, the Hasidim nevertheless wanted Munkács to be led by its holy seed. Shapira, then still only the crown prince, was urged to find someone who could give him a child, preferably a son.

Bowing to the pressure and embracing the belief that he had a destiny to fulfill, Chaim Elazar divorced Chaya Chasya at the end of 1905. According to a number of sources, the couple wept bitterly at the divorce proceedings, sorry to end their happy but tragically unfruitful wedlock.[14] Even after their parting, Chaim Elazar maintained his caring feelings toward his former wife and, after Chaya passed away (still childless) in April of 1924 he continued to mark the anniversary of her death with a great deal of sadness, according to members of his family.[15]

In October of 1906, the thirty-five-year-old Chaim Elazar remarried.[16] His new bride, Rachel Perl, daughter of the Komarno (Ukraine) Rebbe, was half his age. Again there were no children. At last, after more than eight years of marriage, when Chaim Elazar was almost forty-four years old, and two years after he had assumed his father's *rebistve,* he and his wife had a daughter, Chaya Frima Rivka.[17] Although like all rebbes he had thirsted for a son and successor, the Shapiras would have no other children. The rebbe doted on and deeply loved his daughter. At his Passover seder, which of course he celebrated with his Hasidim, Frima (as she was known) would come in year after year from the adjacent room where the women sat and stood at the rebbe's table, surrounded by men and boys, to ask the famous four questions. Some of the Hasidim were troubled by what they considered to be this breach of protocol—for in line with the rigorous separation of the sexes that had become gradually de rigeur in Munkács, women were generally banished from the rebbe's *tish,* the communal table. They argued that with so many young Hasidic boys present at his seder table it was inappropriate—indeed, immodest—for a young girl to stand in their midst. "It could be," Chaim Elazar replied, "that you are right that a young woman like my daughter should not be at the table with us. But then the Hasidim will have a problem," he added, "because their rebbe will also not be here, for I cannot be here without my daughter." [18]

AN IMPORTED SUCCESSOR

With eighteen years of marriage to two women and the birth of only one daughter, the rebbe and his Hasidim were of course focused on whom she would marry. The groom would have to be someone both worthy and capable of carrying on the Munkács tradition. He would also be following a larger-than-life figure, never an easy task. A match was found: the son of Nosson David Rabinovich, the late rebbe of Parczew, a small town in eastern Poland, who in turn was eldest son of the Yitzchak Ya'akov of the Biala Hasidic dynasty. The young man's mother was the daughter of Reb Moshe Leib Shapira of Strzyżów (1850–1916) of the Munkács dynasty and also the cousin of his intended bride. The boy was also a cousin of his future father-in-law's first wife. The match seemed perfect.

In 1926, twelve-year-old Boruch Yehoshua Yerachmiel Rabinovich (1914–97) and eleven-year-old Frima were formally betrothed. Seven years later, in March of 1933, almost twenty years after Chaim Elazar had been anointed the Rebbe of Munkács, they were married at a wedding, attended by tens of thousands, that became one of the most famous such events in the 1930s and was captured on film (figure 1).[19] The groom was by then someone whom the Hasidim knew. The long betrothal, along with the panoply of the wedding itself, in which the new groom rode through town in an open carriage seated to the left of the Grand Rabbi, surrounded by throngs of people and guarded by the local gendarmerie in a scene reminiscent of a wedding of royalty, left no room for doubt that Boruch was the heir apparent.[20]

In effect, from the day he was engaged onward, Boruch (commonly called by the diminutive "Boruchel") was treated by his future father-in-law almost like the male heir he never had. Before the *kiddushin* (betrothal), the rebbe had reportedly examined his young future-son-in-law's prodigious Talmudic knowledge and concluded, in the words of the psalmist, "Thou art my son; this day I have begotten you." [21] The future leadership of Munkács Hasidism seemed assured at last.

For Boruchel's mother, Yutta, who lost her son from Poland where he had grown up and saw him taken away to Munkács, these events

1. The bride, Frima Shapira, and her mother-in-law the dowager *rebbetzin* of Parczew at her wedding to Boruchel Rabinovich, 1933. By permission of Ichud Archives, Brooklyn, New York.

were a mixed blessing. As a dowager *rebbetzin* she saw herself not just as a rebbe's widow and daughter but as something of an expert on matters related to the court and its customs; she spoke many languages and had begun inculcating her son with some of the court's values and the broader worldview that she believed would be missing in the community to which he was moving. Thus she feared he would become narrower in his outlook as he was groomed for the Hungarian Hasidism of Munkács. Also, like many a dowager *rebbetzin* whose son was a rebbe, she naturally sought to share in the power and prestige of his accomplishments. But he would be far away where she could not benefit from the power and influence that a rebbe's mother who lived near him naturally had; all that would go to the Shapira family, and to Frima's mother when Boruchel would ascend to the chair of rebbe.[22]

There were signs the Shapiras were seeking to absorb her son. In 1930, three months after Boruchel's father died, Chaim Elazar took his future son-in-law on a pilgrimage to the Holy Land. Some have suggested that the trip was driven by Kabbalistic calculations and hopes as well as by Chaim Elazar's communication with Shlomo Eliezer Alfandari, and that it had as its goal the possible revelation and crowning of Alfandari as the Messiah; the rebbe wanted the boy with him for this extraordinary occasion, but of course no such coronation occurred.[23] Whatever its true purpose, one senses that this was not just a trip abroad but an effort by the older man to become the young man's mentor, if not to act *in loco parentis*.[24] That view was certainly shared by the

Hasidim who watched how the older man took the boy under his wing and remained close to him.

Accordingly, when in 1936 Chaim Elazar died of melanoma, the succession of the twenty-three-year-old Boruchel to the throne of Munkács was expected and accepted. Indeed, in one version of events, at the cemetery Yitzchak Eisik Weiss (1875–1944), the Spinka Rebbe, had ostentatiously passed the young man a *kvittel,* a note of supplication that *zaddikim* are given by their followers as a sign that they accept his succession to the crown, announcing aloud, "The house of the righteous [*zaddikim*] will stand," (Prov. 12:7).[25] It was a sign that the young man was accepted into the Hasidic pantheon. Another report recounts the enthusiasm with which the young successor's discourse on the first Sabbath was received, when the principal of the yeshiva jumped up on a table and dramatically recited the blessing one is to make upon encountering a Jewish scholar, "*Boruch* [Blessed] art thou, o Lord our God, King of the Universe, who has given wisdom to those who are in awe of him." The play on the new rebbe's first name in this benediction was not lost on those in the room.[26]

Boruchel not only viewed his position as rebbe as beyond question, despite his youth, but also assumed his authority in Munkács would be as absolute as that of his illustrious predecessor.[27] If the twenty-three-year-old newcomer from Poland was naive in this assumption, he did not show it. Perhaps he supposed that since he had no competition as successor he would be able to grow in stature quickly and with the many years ahead of him his reputation and authority would grow beyond his own court. Moreover, as head of the yeshiva and as *av beit din* (chief justice of the law court) too, he might be forgiven for thinking his authority would be near absolute.[28]

Although the transition in 1937 seemed seamless, the years leading up to it had not been without incident. Boruchel sometimes found it difficult to get along with his mother-in-law and as a result had gone for a time to live in Warsaw, leaving his wife in Munkács with her parents and coming back to his mother. But his father-in-law knew this situation was untenable and sent his daughter to Poland to reunite with her husband. Later Boruchel had gone to Budapest, ostensibly to gather new followers for Munkács, but also no doubt because he too wanted to rise above the provincialism of the court, go to a place where people lacked the memory of his mother-in-law's being the *rebbetzin,* and like Chaim Elazar become a leader who transcended his *rebistve.* When he compared Munkács to his home village of Siedliszcze (about an hour's journey south from the slightly larger Parçzew in the Chelm district of Poland), he may have felt as if he had moved to the big city. But when he went to the cosmopolitan Budapest, Boruchel began to imagine himself as a leader on a far greater stage, a *rav*, or leader not only of Hasidim but of all Jews who accept the authority of Jewish law: "He wanted to be a *rav* in Budapest rather than a rebbe in Munkács," as his son years later articulated it. Later in life, Boruchel would tell his son many times that had the Holocaust never happened and transformed his life irrevocably, "Even if the world would go back to what it was, I would never have gone back to Munkács but would have moved the yeshiva" and the court to Budapest.[29]

To be sure, many Hasidic rebbes were removing their courts from remote villages to the big cities as even the most religious of Jews became urbanized. With such moves, they began to see themselves as operating on a bigger stage. Not unlike his mother, Boruchel saw himself not only a Hasid but also as a bit of an intellectual; he thought he could transform a Hasidic *rebistve* into a new sort of rabbinate that would allow him to be not just a rebbe for his Hasidim but also a public religious leader for all Jewry. Other Hasidic leaders had imagined themselves in such a role, perhaps most famously Yosef Yitzchak Schneersohn, the Sixth Lubavitcher Rebbe, who as we shall see in 1914 began to become more than a local rebbe and was later described by his representatives to the US State Department as a "sort of Pope of the Jews."[30]

DEATH AND NEW LIFE

Within a few months of Boruchel's trip to Budapest, however, his father-in-law was diagnosed with cancer; learning his poor prognosis, he persuaded the couple to return to Munkács. Shortly thereafter, on February 14, 1934, the eve of the Hebrew month of Adar, their first child, a son, was born. Of course, the birth was a great event for the court. This first male heir, a boy for whom the old man had been waiting a lifetime and the one who, if all went as expected, would someday succeed to the crown of Munkács, was for his maternal grandfather and the Hasidim the embodiment of hope, the holy seed. As described in the Munkács history, *Toldos Rabeinu* (The generations of our rabbi), the child's arrival was described with words from Isaiah 9:6 normally understood as announcing the birth of the Anointed One: "Unto us a child is born, unto us a son is given."[31]

But from the very beginning, this holy seed grew in troubled soil. Arguments arose over the boy's naming. In Chaim Elazar's mind, the boy had to be named Zvi Hirsch, after his maternal grandfather, the Darchei Tshuvah. Boruchel, however, wanted to name his first son for *his* late father, Nosson Dovid. The symbolism of the name would be important, for it would signal whether the ascension of Boruchel would move the future in the direction of his Polish family's Hasidic roots or continue the traditions of Munkács. All this of course had to be worked out in the eight days before the *bris*—the ritual of circumcision at which the child would be named and inducted into the Jewish people and family. The dying rebbe turned to his son-in-law and said, "You're going to have children, *brisn,* and you're going to have names. As for me, who knows if I will ever live to see another child?" [32]

Everyone concerned understood that the choice of name for this first son was not of the same order of meaning as any other child's name. Boruchel also looked upon the name as a chance for him to establish his own authority. He took a stand, arguing that by Jewish law he had to honor his late father by calling his son after him. The dying rebbe of Munkács was no less adamant. Finally, they compromised—something Chaim Elazar had commonly disallowed, saying it was not a good thing to mix names of two people together. They named the boy Zvi Hirsch Nosson Dovid. Yet in practice it was not really a compromise, for the boy's father would always call him "Duchu," a Yiddish diminutive for Dovid, the name of his paternal grandfather, while his maternal grandparents and all of Munkács called him "Hirschele," a Yiddish translation of Zvi, after the Darchei Tshuvah. [33] Every time someone called the boy by his name, it recalled the tension that the naming had occasioned and that existed between Boruchel and his adopted court. As for the boy, according to his brothers, because so many people called him by alternate names, he never really knew who he was.

The boy's grandfather nevertheless doted on him. In a famous story, repeated in Munkács, he acceded to the boy's entreaty when he was sick to blow shofar for him on the day before Rosh Hashanah, when by custom the ram's horn should *not* be blown, and later turned the transgression into a theme of a sermon he offered before sounding the shofar the next day. [34] But soon the grandfather was dead, and his son-in-law and successor took over.

In the early days of Boruchel's leadership of the court, while his young wife, increasingly sick with tuberculosis, was having three children before 1940, his newly widowed mother-in-law (the dowager *rebbetzin*), with whom he had a fraught relationship, largely managed the affairs of his household. [35] She knew more about the customs of Munkács than her Polish son-in-law. Clearly Boruchel's assumption that he had no competition in the *rebistve* did not take into consideration the desires of the dowager *rebbetzin* to remain a power in the court. With her daughter's physical limitations, the dowager's position as the effective *rebbetzin* grew. She guarded her position jealously.

In later years, as Boruchel reflected on those days, he confided to one of his Hasidim, Binyomin Wulliger, his difficulties as the heir in Munkács: "When my father-in-law took over the *rebistve* from his father he was forty-six years old. When my turn came, I could speak well, write well, lead the prayers well, but I had a major problem—I was only *a son-in-law* of the great Minchas Elazar, who could do all that as well and who had died at sixty-eight, and I had to take over when I was only *twenty-three*" and run the court with the constant presence of his mother-in-law.[36]

Although he had generally revered his late father-in-law, the new rebbe's domineering mother-in-law, on whom he continued to depend, remained troubled. Every time she insisted on calling his son Hirschele instead of Duchu, it was a symbolic challenge to her son-in-law's authority, exacerbating the enmity simmering between them. She continued to try to change what she and some of the Hasidim considered his more open attitude toward the world and his intellectual curiosity about mainstream culture into the more insular Hungarian Hasidic way.[37] She stressed that in his will her late husband had written that he was making his son-in-law his successor, "on the condition that he will follow the ways of Munkács." If she felt he was not, then, as much as any woman could, she would dominate him, almost to the point of trying effectively to replace him.

Thus, in spite of the absence of other heirs, Boruchel felt less than completely secure in his position. As in all cases of dynastic succession, senior disciples who remember and revere the previous leader, especially those whose shared charisma comes from their connection to him, necessarily perceive imperfections in the successor, who is often younger and less experienced than they are and whose charisma comes primarily from his new office. Often the most conservative forces dominate the early transitional period. Moreover, if the new rebbe, as was the case here, comes from outside, he may seem to them wanting, lacking an insider's interiority, *pnimius*. In twentieth-century Hasidism, where tradition became a cardinal value and organizing principle, and change was considered troubling, the young new outsider was always a problem for those who were anchored more powerfully to the past. This was exacerbated if the previous leader died while still actively engaged in leadership and was deemed a giant of his time, as was the case with

Chaim Elazar, whose funeral filled the streets of Munkács with thousands of mourners and onlookers.

Only with time, as the older Hasidim pass from the scene and as the younger ones who grow up with the new rebbe and have few memories of his predecessor come into their own, does the new rebbe's charisma of office morph into personal charisma. In the early years of his reign, this had not yet occurred for Boruchel. Add to that the counterclaims of a vital dowager *rebbetzin,* and even in a prepared succession where the new rebbe has no real competition and has been schooled by his predecessor, personal, cultural, and religious tensions may emerge.

Boruchel soon discovered that the court he inherited was not what it had once been. As he confided to his wife, he had taken over a court that had many financial debts and a series of adversaries, many of whom had been alienated by his late father-in-law's sometimes overly aggressive territorial and authority claims and who were now ready to cut Munkács down to size, albeit posthumously. To rebuild the court, the young new rebbe traveled often to Budapest, trying not only to attract new followers there but also to somehow move the court there so he might start fresh, preach to a far more cosmopolitan Jewry, and come out from the shadow of his predecessor, the influence of old Hasidim, and the dowager.

In spite of all this, during the brief time he had before the Nazis would come for him, Boruchel tried to put his stamp on the institutions and the Jewish community in Munkács, occupying all three posts of his office: *rav* and *av beit din* (the formally appointed chief rabbi of the town), *rosh yeshiva* (head of the yeshiva), and rebbe.[38] As *av beit din,* he once even overexercised his authority when he decreed unkosher the meat of a Munkács butcher who in his opinion had not cleaned his shop's shelves sufficiently, leaving the butcher with a huge financial loss, since this rabbinical declaration made his stock forbidden (meat was expensive, and it was unwise to anger kosher butchers, who were often among the richer and influential laity).[39]

As *rosh yeshiva* Boruchel rebuilt and reorganized the Darchei Tshuvah Yeshiva in Munkács with new classes and created vacation camps for the boys by moving the entire yeshiva to the countryside during the summer months. He hoped to transform the institution into the Hungarian version of the grand modern yeshiva, something modeled on the great yeshiva of Chachmei Lublin.[40]

During his first year as rebbe, on the two days of Shavuot, the festival celebrating the Jewish people's receipt and acceptance of the Torah, and on the following Sabbath, Boruchel offered three days of rabbinic discourses viewed by both the community and the Hasidim as an inspirational tour de force. His apparent knowledge of all the customs and practices of Hungarian Hasidism was impressive. When he had finished, one of the Hasidim with great drama stood up and recited the blessing of *shehechiyanu,* praising the Almighty for having allowed them all to live and see that day that their new rebbe graced them with his Torah and *hasidus* (discourses on Hasidism). For the young "outsider" from Poland to so impress them all was understood by the cognoscenti as auspicious. The charisma of his office was becoming his personal possession.

THE NAZI ERA

All these matters, which loomed large at the outset of his reign, proved minor compared to the events of history that would ultimately upend it and abort the natural progression during which a new rebbe and his Hasidim develop and deepen ties.

The first of these was the outbreak of the Second World War in 1939. By July of 1941 this resulted in the young rebbe's deportation from Munkács as a Polish citizen and his repatriation in Poland.[41] Although Borochel was from Siedliszcze, when he was expelled from Munkács with his son Duchu they were marked for deportation to Kamenets-Podolski in the Poland/ Ukraine (Galicia) border area. (The other children, all boys, had been spared deportation by the dowager *rebbetzin,* who hid them in a blanket.) During their journey, while at a stop in Jagelnica, Boruchel and Duchu managed to separate from the crowd and, after several weeks of hiding in the village, escaped on foot to Kolomyja in eastern Galicia.[42] There Boruchel learned that those Jews who had been brought to Kamenets-Podolski had been forced to dig a pit and then had been summarily shot and buried in that pit. Two months of hiding in Galicia, often with the help of local Jews, changed the young rebbe's assessment of what the future held for Hungarian Jewry and left his eldest son and heir so traumatized that he would never again be considered as a possible Rebbe of Munkács.[43]

After word reached Boruchel's mother-in-law concerning his whereabouts, she managed to get the still relatively free Jews of Budapest to intercede with the Hungarian government on his behalf. This intervention "and of course large sums of money" yielded a note from the head of the Division of Foreigners that permitted the return of the rebbe and Duchu to Hungary.[44] After their brushes with death, the two returned in September 1941, days before the Jewish new year. They went first to Munkács. During these same days, Poland's Jews were already being imprisoned in ghettos and sent off to concentration and slave labor camps, many to their deaths—among them Borochel's brother Yitzchak. His mother, Yutta, would die in the Warsaw ghetto of typhus.[45] In time, Boruchel's sisters, another brother, and his nieces, nephews, uncles, and aunts all perished.

Fearing a repeat of his deportation, Boruchel moved into hiding in the capital, where he believed he would be less likely to be identified. He stayed in an old age home managed by the Jewish community of Budapest. At last, he received notice from the authorities that he could appear in public but not "register officially as a citizen."[46] Looking to establish himself and bring his family to Budapest, which in 1941 was still a relatively safe haven for Jews, he thought again about moving his court to the big city with its nearly a quarter of million Jews. Budapest's Jews, feeling protected, continued to believe that they would not suffer the fate of Jews under Nazi occupation. At first believing this too, Boruchel tried to help other Jews come into Hungary. He managed to help hundreds in the brief time he would have.[47] By his own testimony, he tried, particularly in the summer of 1942 as the killings and deportations of Polish Jewry took place, to save as many as he could. In the spring of 1943, with the assistance of the Hungarian aristocrat Erzsébet Szapáry, a patron of Polish refugees, Boruchel arranged for Jewish Poles to be included in a temporary quota for non-Jewish Polish immigrants, as long as they hid their Jewish identity. His desperate efforts moved him to cooperate with all sorts of people to find financial support, including the so-called Neolog (Reform) as well as Zionist Jews (who helped him get certificates that would enable Jews to immigrate to Palestine) and a variety of Hungarian nobles.[48] Ultimately the project foundered as the situation worsened. In the opinion of his son, Moshe Leib, Boruchel, despite all his efforts, "never climbed out of the Holocaust."[49]

For three years he also desperately tried without success to enlarge his following in Budapest. His efforts to save Jewish refugees and his ability to speak with all kinds of people, from Hungarian aristocrats to non-Orthodox Jews, persuaded him that he could, as he wanted to be, become an actor on a larger stage, trying to organize and lead all of Hungarian Jewry against the extraordinary menace of Nazism. Feeling that he had received what he would later tell his son was "a call from heaven," he ran to officials of the government, speaking to lawyers, even donning a necktie—something rebbes did not do—all the while hoping to organize the Jews to resist the coming Nazis.[50] He encouraged a plan for the active self-defense of Hungarian Jewry, including a strategy (supported by some in the Hungarian government) to arm Jews who would be able to violently resist the Nazis, but, as he put it, the plan "fell on deaf ears."[51] One who recalled him in those days said, "To me the Rebbe looked like a king exiled from his palace, and his fate touched my heart."[52]

As the situation for Jews worsened, Boruchel concluded that only escape and emigration from Hungary offered hope of survival. His despair grew immeasurably greater when even members of his own family and Hasidim resisted his warnings that the future of European Jewry was coming to an end. These resistant family members were "certain that no evil would befall the remaining ones because my father-in-law, of blessed memory, had said that the enemy would not find a way to come to our country," a prediction that had proved true in World War I and for those who remembered it was a sign that they were blessedly protected forever from all such wartime catastrophes.[53] By 1944, after working assiduously to help save as many Polish and Slovakian Jews as he could from the Nazis and trying unsuccessfully to arouse the Jews of Hungary to their imminent danger, Boruchel concluded that the time had come for his own escape. His destination was the Zionist settlement in the Land of Israel.

In February of 1944 he wrote a letter to his Hasidim telling them of his plan to travel to "the Holy Land" and how "difficult is my departure from you, even though while our bodies will be distant our hearts will remain close." He closed the missive with the wish that "every one of you receive blessing, peace and rest and that you merit to be among the first to ascend to Zion in gladness with the help of the Messiah of David and Elijah." He signed it with the words, "I have beseeched [heaven] that you be saved from the birth pangs of the Messiah [by which he meant the pain and suffering that Jewish tradition believes will precede his arrival] and merit redemption."[54] The failure of his earlier efforts to get papers to America led the scion of an anti-Zionist Hasidism to look for his salvation in the Zionist homeland. It was a move that saved him and his family but would prove catastrophic for his *rebistve*.

In March, on the eve of his exit from Hungary and a month before the forced ghettoization of Munkács, Boruchel addressed a crowd that packed the Great Synagogue of Budapest.[55] He shared with them his pessimism over the Jewish future in Europe and one last time implored them to leave, to follow him via Turkey and come to the Land of Israel, where they could yet rebuild all that was about to crumble. Had his advice been taken, many in his audience would have been saved. "There were those who had reservations, and those who burst out crying," he would recall.[56] Few could have imagined a rebbe of Munkács, with its powerful anti-Zionism, making such a call.

Even the dowager *rebbetzin,* who had managed to get visas for her daughter, son-law, and grandchildren, refused to accompany her weak and pregnant daughter and grandchildren. Though, as she escorted them to the train, she surely realized that her sickly daughter and her trauma-tized grandson Duchu as well as his brothers Chaim Elazar (born March 1939 on the holiday of Purim), Moshe Leib (born December 1940, the first day of Chanukah), and Yitzchak Yaakov (born April 1942, the first night of Passover) needed her, she turned away as they got on, saying that whatever happened she wanted to be buried in Munkács.*

On May 11, nine transports began to deport the nearly 29,000 Jews of Munkács to what for most of them would be certain death. "A day before the evacuation of the Munkács ghetto, the Germans gathered all the Jews with beards and earlocks and ordered them to destroy what was left of the famous Yeshiva of Rabbi Shapira, singing while they labored. The Jews carried out their task under a hail of lashes."[57] On May 23, 1944, the final deportation train left Munkács, carrying 3,080 people. These were the last Jews of the Munkács community on their way to Auschwitz-Birkenau.[58] The dowager *rebbetzin* was among those who perished in its crematoria.

THE TRANSFORMATION OF A REBBE

As he prepared to flee Europe with his family, Boruchel no longer thought of himself simply as the successor to the crown of Munkács Hasidism. He imagined a future on another stage. The reality was otherwise. A month after his sermon in Budapest, and finding himself in Palestine with five children (including a baby daughter Yutta, known as Zuta, born en route in Istanbul on the day after Purim, 1944) and a wife who was sick with what would turn out to be an ultimately fatal flare-up of her tuberculosis and who upon landing had to be sent almost immediately to a sanitarium, Boruchel tried to reestablish himself in Jerusalem. But Jerusalem in 1944 was not Munkács in 1937. Gone now were the crowds who had listened to him in Budapest, as were the three hundred yeshiva students he had in Munkács. Although there was a Munkács *kollel* (yeshiva for married

---

* According to *Going Forward,* a memoir written by Boruchel's sister Peska Fried-man, she received a postcard from the dowager *rebbetzin,* written when the Nazis were coming near to Budapest, admitting, "I should have left when I had the chance."

men) in Jerusalem that supported a few students and their families, his efforts to use it and some of its resources as a base of operations were rebuffed. Indeed, not even all of those in the *kollel* saw themselves as his Hasidim. The great bulk of Munkács Hasidim had remained in Europe, if they were still among the living. Their rebbe was cut off from them, powerless, a war refugee with young children to care for and a wife in the hospital. Living in Palestine in the middle of a world war, he had in a short time gone from being a rebbe of repute with near-absolute authority in Hungary to having almost nothing.

By the war's end, Boruchel's widowed mother was dead, as were his siblings, in-laws, uncles, and aunts—and even many of those who had helped save him when he was on the run. Separated from the court and its trappings of power, lacking the presence of the dowager *rebbetzin* as an icon of his connection to the Munkács past, and absent the many Hasidim, he could not count on the charisma of his office to sustain him in his new circumstances. The institutions and local traditions he might once have depended upon and been nurtured by were missing. In America, a small group of Munkács Hasidim subsisted on Manhattan's Lower East Side, but by 1947 when he visited he discovered that he could not organize them as he wanted, that they resented his having chosen to live among the Zionists, and that America was not a place for him. Whatever his hopes of becoming more than a rebbe, the realities he now faced forced him to rethink his life's trajectory.

An intellectual with a broad vision, a scholar who knew Maimonides's *Guide for the Perplexed* by heart, he nevertheless lacked the savvy, funds, personal magnetism, and followers he needed to rebuild his life under new circumstances.[59] Few of the Hasidim he found thought he could provide them with *chayei, bonei,* and *mzonei* (the blessings of life, progeny, and livelihood), despite his pedigree. Although still a believer and convinced that the Almighty had rescued him for some grand purpose, he had questions. In a memoir written and published many years later, he exhorted God to "remember what wonderful Jews You had when Your people fell into the hands of the enemy; so many Jews who endangered their lives to help their brothers when they were subject to a vicious enemy," and asked, "Why did You send them to slaughter?"[60] Was this question an echo of abiding theological difficulties spawned by the horrors of the Holocaust or something more complicated and deeply rooted in the trajectory of his life? While Boruchel remained a devout Jew, the events of the Holocaust and its aftermath in his life clearly took a spiritual toll.

2. Boruchel Rabinovich speaking with Ben Gurion, first prime minister of Israel and former head of the Zionist Jewish Agency. By permission of Ichud Archives, Brooklyn, New York.

He still yearned to be a public figure, harboring the dream that he had had in Budapest and that he had shared with his predecessor to be a kind of Grand Rabbinic public figure and to build a yeshiva that would propel him beyond the limited orbit of Munkács. On one occasion, he stood on a stage with David Ben Gurion and Golda Meir, adding his voice to a mass protest in Habimah Square in Tel Aviv against the British White Paper that limited Jewish immigration into Palestine (figure 2). The powerfully anti-Zionist Munkács Hasidim surely found the sight of him standing side by side with these "heretic" leaders of modern socialist Zionism, whom their previous rebbe and his followers had so vilified, difficult to bear. But Boruchel considered it critical to get Jews out of harm's way immediately, and he stood with anyone sharing that goal.

Personally, life grew harder for Boruchel. Feeding his family was a struggle, and no help came from Munkács or its refugees. Worse, some even cheated him out of his quota of white flour in the ration-dominated Palestine where he now made his life.[61] A year to the day after his arrival in Palestine, Boruchel's wife succumbed to tuberculosis. On rare occasions the children had seen her, but because of the communicable nature of her illness, they were prevented from coming near. Her presence in their lives receded, so by the time she died she had already said her farewells. For all of them this was a loss, but certainly for eleven-year-old

Duchu, whose memories of his mother were more vivid, this was one more trauma in a string of events that had upended his life.

Boruchel's tribulations were known to the Hasidim, for he wrote to some, including those few who had escaped to New York.[62] But while they realized his dire straits, they were not inclined or able to help support him, especially after his Zionist activities. He felt abandoned and grew increasingly alienated from Munkács.

Feeling quite overwhelmed, the thirty-one-year-old widowed father desperately sought a way to support himself and his children, but what skills did a former rebbe have, and what sorts of jobs could he pursue in a place like Palestine? At the urging of his older sister Devora Perel Landau, who had been in the country since 1934 and had arranged the certificates that enabled his immigration, he prepared his candidacy in 1946 for the position of chief rabbi of Tel Aviv.[63] Through this office he believed he might restore his rabbinic authority—with Tel Aviv replacing Munkács—but on a different stage and in a new age. Although the common understanding was that Munkács remained anti-Zionist, Boruchel claimed he had never embraced that view, so powerful among Hungarian Hasidim, even if at times he had been forced by the Munkács tradition to express it. Having watched the stubborn refusal of Hungarian Hasidism to embrace the promise of Zionism lead to its entrapment in Nazi Europe and its decimation, he could at last come out as a Zionist. During his 1930 trip to the Holy Land with his anti-Zionist predecessor, young Boruchel had sneaked out at night to meet secretly with Rabbi Yaakov Moshe Charlap, the head of the Zionist Mercaz HaRav Yeshiva.[64] He hoped he would now get the tentative backing of some among the local Hasidim who might wish to influence the office of the rabbinate by putting forward a Hasidic rebbe as a chief rabbi in the emerging Zionist settlement.

These hopes were dashed when his candidacy failed even before becoming formal. Some among the local Belzer Hasidim who had an old score to settle with Munkács Hasidim characterized him as the embodiment of his late father-in-law and unsuited to the position. In addition, the largest and most powerful Hasidic group in Palestine, the Gerrers, whose support might have offset Belzer objections, were still smarting over the attacks by his predecessor against their now eighty-year-old rebbe, Avraham Mordechai Alter (1866–1948), for what he claimed was the latter's tolerance of Zionist "heresies."[65] When they saw that his successor from Munkács now proposed to enter *their* territory and take a share of rabbinic power, they would have none of it.

As for the Zionists, they recalled the strident opposition to them in Munkács and dismissed out of hand the proposition that a successor to that crown would hold an official position in a Zionist rabbinate. Even though Boruchel began saying publicly in 1946 that Jewish immigration to Israel "brings comfort to the mourning land and renews her youth with prosperity and vigor," Palestinian Zionists would not accept a change of heart from the Rebbe of Munkács.[66] Back in Hungary, Zvi Bederim, among the leaders of the socialist, antireligious Zionist Shomer Hazair movement, complained about "Zionist-hating rabbis," among whom he included Boruchel. He resented that they, "whose entire accomplishments amount to anti-Zionist propaganda," had obtained certificates to get to Palestine, where they were "jeopardizing our enterprise." [67]

In an indignant letter to the editor published in *Davar,* the Hebrew newspaper of Socialist Labor Zionism, and headlined "Hayitachen" (Is it conceivable?), which was later turned into a extensively circulated broadsheet, Chaim Kugel, head of the Holon Municipal Council, had written of Boruchel,

> Is it conceivable that this man, who did not spare an opportunity to launch calumnies and slurs against Hebrew educational institutions that were founded with prodigious effort and expense by our colleagues in Sub-Carpathian Ruthenia . . . , who hounded Zionism and Zionists . . . , who loyally continued the line of the Munkács court, which cursed and banned any Jew who pronounced the word *Zion* on his lips and which proscribed the stores and workshops of Jews who . . . sent their children to these Hebrew schools . . . is it conceivable that this man will appear as a representative and moral leader in the first Hebrew city, and be a guide to its residents and Zionists?[68]

What Kugel did not add was that Boruchel's father as well had been powerfully anti-Zionist, instructing in his will that his children share that ideology.[69] Boruchel withdrew from consideration.

If the Zionists saw Boruchel as too redolent of anti-Zionism for the Tel Aviv rabbinate, and if the local Hasidim saw him as too closely identified with grudges they held against his predecessor and with territorial threats, the Hasidim of Munkács saw his candidacy, though aborted, as too Zionist. If the successor to the Minchas Elazar aimed to become a leader in the new Zionist entity, then he could no longer be their rebbe.

With no position or court, he was now simply a widowed immigrant with five young children who was not particularly adept at parenting. His relationship with his children was fraught. His sons could not remember a single time he had hugged or kissed them but recalled many occasions of *chapen a patch,* getting beaten. Next to his relationship with his oldest son, Boruchel's relationship with his daughter Zuta was perhaps the most difficult, and since she had been an infant when her mother died, this left her particularly vulnerable. In later years she would hold him responsible for their mother's early death. At his wits' end, Boruchel persuaded his unmarried sister, Peska, to move in and help him care for his children. But Peska had fallen in love with a man in Europe, Wolf "Volvie" Friedman, whom she'd met during the war, and when after the war she heard he had been widowed and was in Paris looking for her she left immediately to reunite with him in hopes that they could marry, as they later did.

Her sudden departure left Boruchel with a desperate need to find help with his five children. Before she left, Peska put an ad in the paper looking for a nanny. Yehudit Wallhaus, a teenage German-Jewish immigrant, arrived for an interview. Peska didn't approve of the "immodest" way the girl dressed, realized Yehudit knew no Yiddish—the language of the household—and summarily dismissed her as inappropriate. But when Peska left, Boruchel was frantic for help. He turned to his married older sister Devora, and she advised him to try out the young nanny.

The nineteen-year-old really had no experience for such a position and found it overwhelming to care for five children, having particular difficulty with the oldest son who at twelve years old—just a few years younger than her—was already showing signs of continuing mental and emotional decline, post-traumatic stress disorder, and bipolarity. For all Yehudit's disadvantages, Boruchel realized he could not take care of the children alone. Having a nanny was a temporary solution, and by strict Orthodox custom it was religiously and socially inappropriate that he remain with an unmarried young woman in his home.

In tears, he called his Hasid Binyomin Wulliger in New York, with whom he was still close, sharing his frustration over his situation.[70] Marriage seemed to him the only solution to his life situation, but he could not find anyone. Boruchel decided that his children's nanny, although fifteen years his junior and a woman who had neither Hasidic background nor understanding of what it meant to be a rebbe, would become his new wife.

This marriage, however, would not begin with a great public wedding like what he had had in Munkács. Vows were exchanged quickly and without fanfare in a small hall in Ra'anana, north of Tel Aviv. Although Boruchel wore the *shtreimel* (fur hat) of a Hasid to the ceremony, it was not a Hasidic wedding. No one from Munkács was formally invited, and most of the few guests there were from Ra'anana and the bride's side. Even Boruchel's children did not attend the wedding.[71] Afterward, some Munkács Hasidim mocked the marriage, singing ditties outside his window referring to his having married a "servant girl."[72]

After the wedding their father matter-of-factly informed his children that they were to call the erstwhile nanny *Ema* (Mommy).[73] For the younger children who had very little in the way of memories of their mother the change was surprising but not as jarring as it was for Duchu; the new reality seemed to push him over the edge. He began to lose himself in his past. On the day after his father's wedding he banged on the window of his bedroom.[74]

While the children bore some feelings of abandonment by their father at the time, feelings that would grow when the new couple had children of their own, Yehudit's parents, living on an agricultural settlement in Ra'anana, made them feel cared for and at home. In Hebrew, the children called them *Saba* and *Savta* (Grandpa and Grandma), not *Bobeh* and *Zayde* in the preferred Yiddish of Hasidism.

As Moshe Leib, Boruchel's third son, would recall years later, "We went through a total change of what life had been like in Munkács and Budapest." They were not living like Hasidim anymore. Although the boys discreetly wore short sidelocks behind their ears, they dressed and increasingly acted like the children around them. In fact, while there was a school nearby run by Belzer Hasidim, this school was considered "too *hasidish* [Hasidic]" for the boys.[75] Instead, they went to a more generic religious school where there were a few children with earlocks like theirs.

ONE MORE TRY

Having failed to become chief rabbi of Tel Aviv and still looking to reconstruct his life, Boruchel tried one last time to rebuild his Hasidic life and court in America. Leaving four of his children behind with his second wife's parents in Israel, he went in June of 1947 to America for about five months to see if he could succeed there, taking along thirteen-year-old Duchu, whom he deposited in a yeshiva in New York. But it was a halfhearted trip, since by then he had "decided that his mission after the war would not be constrained to the community of Munkács but rather to the Jews in the world at large," a goal that he held for most of the rest of his life.[76]

In America, Boruchel appeared at a welcome reception in the Manhattan Plaza on the Lower East Side, ostensibly to report on the situation in the Land of Israel and on the refugees there. Binyomin Wulliger and his family set up as many gatherings as they could, financing whatever was needed. But nothing succeeded in raising Boruchel's profile as a rabbinic leader or a Hasidic rebbe, nor did he raise significant funds. By mid-October and the Holy Day of Sukkot, he was in Chicago giving speeches in some of the synagogues there in a campaign to find support for his plan to found religious schools in the Tel Aviv area.[77] Again he failed to marshal sufficient funds, and his visit was eclipsed by an appearance of Yoelish Teitelbaum, the Satmar Rebbe, in the same city at around the same time.[78] Back in Israel, his children on the Ra'anana farm spent what according to Moshe Leib were among the happiest times since their arrival in Palestine, unaware of what their father was going through and of his frustrating and unfulfilled search for a new role.[79]

Twenty-year-old Yehudit (or Irene, as she called herself on her travel documents) was not enthusiastic about the prospect of being a Hasidic *rebbetzin*. Her new husband tried to assure her that she would be able to adjust and find happiness if he managed to rebuild the court. But try as he might, he could not do it. He had little patience for those Hasidim still reeling from the Holocaust, whom he now met and who looked to him for sympathy, a blessing, something to restore them spiritually. He urged them to depend on their own inner resources, return to the Talmud, to the Torah, and make their own blessings rather than depend on him. Yet because so many had spent the years when they might have become Jewishly knowledgeable running from or suffering under the Nazis, the generation who now looked to him lacked the abilities to draw on such resources. They just wanted a rebbe on whom to lean, who would bless them, sing with them the heartwarming tunes of Munkács around a *tish,* and tell them what they could believe in. Boruchel was not the sort of rebbe who could or would do that. Something inside him had broken. He could no longer promise them *chayei, bonei,* and *mzonei,* in part because they no longer supported him with their *pidyonos,* the gifts and money.

OFF TO BRAZIL

Leaving Duchu in New York at the Torah Voda'as Yeshiva, where the boy became increasingly despondent, disoriented, and suicidally depressed, as he would for much of the rest of his life, often heavily dependent on medication, Boruchel and Yehudit returned to Palestine.[80]

3. Boruchel Rabinovich, while still the Rebbe of Munkács, with his children, after being widowed. His successor is frowning. (Inset) The children in Brazil. By permission of Ichud Archives, Brooklyn, New York.

Although Boruchel continued some work for Holocaust refugees, this was not a full-time position for him.[81] Finally, despairing of making a new life in the new state of Israel, he made a drastic move and in 1951 took his family to São Paulo, Brazil, to assume a rabbinic post, essentially abdicating his position as Munkács Rebbe (figure 3).[82] He even got a dog, which his new wife wanted, something unthinkable for a rebbe, for whom such impure and unkosher animals are viewed as unfitting. At the Sabbath table the dog would rush to Boruchel, and the erstwhile rebbe would share food with him, an honor once reserved for his Hasidim and the chosen few.[83]

There were still a few people who recalled his past, and they were not ready to let him leave them. In 1952, a last effort from some of the Hasidim urged him to resurrect his Munkács *rebistve*.[84] At a gathering on the Upper West Side of Manhattan, organized by a supporter from the Bronx, there were speeches and discussions about the glory days of Munkács before the war and about the influence of the Shapira line of rebbes and how the refugees and survivors of that Hasidism had an obligation to reestablish it and its traditions in the New World. In spite of all, they now looked to Boruchel, citing not only his family heritage but his efforts to save Jews from the Holocaust. They recalled the crowds in Budapest. Even now, they argued, although he was in Brazil, they were sure that he was free of the Zionist state, and they could lure him back to the "blessed land" of America to renew the glory of Munkács. A committee was established to bring this all to fruition. Nothing came of it.

As he wrote to the committee, "*I* am the one who is not suited to America and its ways, and therefore have not found my place there. . . . From whom could I have learned the ways of America? Not in my father's house and not in my father-in-law's—and you cannot teach an old man what you can teach a youngster." [85] In the winter of 1954, he tried for the last time to see if he could resurrect Munkács in the United States but finally returned to and remained in Brazil, settling in what the Hasidim called "the exile in the Exile."

To some it might seem that Reb Boruchel's abdication came from a series of material and concrete exigencies. Others might say that the competition from Satmar, a Hasidic dynasty no longer in another part of Hungary but in Brooklyn where of the remnants of Munkács lived, was overwhelming. Yet while Boruchel's failures and Satmar's successes undoubtedly raised questions about his ability to count on the Hasidim to bring him back or his ability to adjust to the new situation of Munkács in America, where the territory and the character of the population were different, the cataclysmic events through which his life had passed had raised many existential and religious questions that must also have played a part. As he put it in a 1952 letter, "My heart is afflicted over the situation in the aftermath of the spilt blood and the destruction of the House of Israel." [86] These afflictions included doubts about some of the hallmarks of Munkács Hasidism, such as its virulent antagonism toward Zionism and modernity and its powerfully conservative view of Judaism, doubts as to whether the world from which he came had been on the right side of history, questions about why he had been able to persuade so few of his family and followers to escape to Palestine, questions about why he felt so abandoned when he was in Jerusalem—questions hinted at in his memoir, *Binat Nevonim* (The understanding of the wise). In the end, he had accepted a version of Rabbi Abraham I. Kook's notion that in Zionism and the miraculous events of history that led from the darkness of Jewish exile to the redemptive light of the return to Zion one had to see the hand of God.[87] He no longer wanted to be dependent on Munkács Hasidim or to be limited by their outlook and world.

In Brazil, Boruchel confirmed his new direction and lived a modern life, driving (and even learning to fix) his own car, walking the dog, helping his wife with the dishes, acting as what was called "chief rabbi" (really the only Orthodox rabbi) in São Paulo, and serving also as a *mohel* (ritual circumciser), a task that became a mainstay of his income. He read voraciously, from Aristotle and the classics to modern literature and art, earned a university degree in philosophy and psychology, and later taught a course in philosophy at the University of São Paulo.[88] Even though the letterhead of his printed stationery identified him as "Rabbi B.S.R. Rabinovich da Munkatch," he was now quite cut off from the real life of Munkács Hasidism. When he needed ideas or materials to inspire Brazilian Jewry, he wrote not to the Hasidim but to Rabbi Leo Jung, the German Jewish spiritual leader of the Jewish Center in New York, a flagship modern Orthodox synagogue, asking for material that he could have translated into Portuguese.

The people in Brazil with whom the Rabinovich family was friends were Jewish, but their level of Jewish engagement and commitment was considerably lower than what the norm had been in the Hasidic community of prewar Munkács. While Boruchel retained the serious and somewhat standoffish demeanor of his office as rabbi in São Paulo, his wife was comfortable with these new friends, and there are photos of her with many of them. Often she would attend a movie, either with friends or accompanied by Boruchel's second son Chaim Elazar—who was tall and looked older than his years—while her husband remained involved with his own concerns.

Hasidim occasionally would arrive at Boruchel's office or home to talk to him, even in São Paulo, affording him a chance to function as something like what he once had been. When a Hasid once saw on his shelf not only holy books and Hasidic tomes but also the *Encyclopedia Britannica,* he questioned how the rebbe could have such heresy on his holy shelves; Boruchel found the questioning offensive.

As he gradually fell out of a relationship with the Hasidim, Boruchel began to harbor hopes for a different future for his children, who attended Brazilian public schools, where there were crucifixes on the classroom walls. In the afternoons, for three hours daily, the boys were tutored by a local Jewish *melamed* (teacher)—Boruchel chose not to teach them himself. He hoped that they would someday get a university degree, something that only his son Chaim Elazar and daughter Zuta would achieve.

RETRIEVING THE SONS

When Eliezer Sorotzkin, then collecting funds for the famous Lithuanian Telshe Yeshiva that had been newly reestablished in 1941 in a suburb of Cleveland, Ohio, arrived in Brazil, he approached the chief rabbi, hoping for help in gathering money from Brazilian Jewry. Staying in the Rabinovich house, Sorotzkin was stunned by what he found there—not only the secular books on the shelf but also and to him more importantly the fact that the Rabinovich sons had an abysmally low level of Talmudic and Jewish knowledge. How could a rebbe's sons and the grandsons of the Minchas Elazar be in such a state? he wondered aloud. He worried they were losing their rich and storied Jewish heritage.

Sorotzkin guessed correctly that Boruchel would not want to send his boys to a Hasidic yeshiva—certainly not to the anti-Zionist Satmar schools that had been absorbing so many from a Hungarian Hasidic background, and Munkács Hasidism had nothing yet that would be suitable for the boys. Nor, given his oldest son's unhappiness at Torah Voda'as, would he likely be prepared to send his boys there. Telshe, calling itself a rabbinical "college" in its 1941 Ohio reincarnation, had a rich tradition in Torah education, dormitories, and a campus where students could live and learn Torah; it also had a department of secular studies granting a high school diploma. In short order, Sorotzkin managed to persuade his host to send his sons, Chaim Elazar and Moshe Leib, to Telshe, where they could increase their Jewish knowledge, get secular learning, and be in an Orthodox Jewish environment. The fourth son, Yitzchak Yaakov, went a year later.

Although as a Lithuanian-style yeshiva, Telshe was not a place for Hasidic training, Sorotzkin believed that the Rabinovich boys needed above all else to become Torah scholars. The old enmities between Hasidism and the Lithuanian-style yeshiva world had waned in these early years after the Holocaust, when both groups sensed they were engaged in a salvage operation for Jews committed to maintaining fervently the age-old traditions of the Orthodoxy of eastern Europe. Just as in the 1940s, before the Hasidic courts had reestablished their own schools, Torah Voda'as, a Lithuanian-style yeshiva in New York, had become a Judaic training ground for children of Hasidic heritage in America, so too Telshe was for others.

While Chaim Elazar and Moshe Leib, at ages sixteen and fourteen, understood why they were being sent to a school thousands of miles away in another country and distant from their family, a part of them felt as if they were being banished, much as their eldest brother had been. Moshe Leib in particular worried about his sister, Zuta, whom he believed he alone could protect from their father's increasingly dark moods.

On the way to the yeshiva Chaim Elazar and Moshe Leib stopped in New York at their aunt Peska's. There the boys spent two weeks preparing for their new course of learning. Although his father had warned them not to depend on the Munkács community, the teens spent some time among the Hasidim in New York, seeing more people from Munkács and feeling welcome. The Hasidim showered more attention on the older brother, asking him for blessings for a livelihood, as if he were already a rebbe.

At Telshe, Chaim Mordechai (Mottel) Katz, son-in-law of the previous head, was head of the yeshiva. He took the boys aside as they prepared to enter its *mechina* (preparatory school).[89]

"We [in this yeshiva] come from Telshe, a small place in Lithuania—I'm even ashamed to say how small a place it was. When I travel now in America on behalf of the yeshiva I hear about all sorts of *hassidishe* [Hasidic] rebbes, most of whom I never heard of before the war. But I have to tell you, of Munkács we heard. And what do you think we heard of Munkács?" The two boys, scions of Munkács, sat quietly and listened intently. "Do you think it was the *niggunim?*" the songs for which so many Hasidic courts were known, "No." He continued: "Do you think it was for the *sherayim,*" the distribution of morsels from rebbe's meal to the Hasidim? "No. What we heard about Munkács was that they know how to learn [Torah]. We heard of the *Darchei Tshuvah* and after him the *Minchas Elazar,* whom no rabbi in Lithuania would dare ignore in any legal judgments he made. And who are these people? They are the rebbes who were your great-grandfather and grandfather." Then he added, "I understand there's a possibility that the Hasidim might want you to become their rebbe one day. If you don't sing the songs or hand out the *sherayim,* they might let it pass. But if you can't learn Torah like a scholar, then you can never be their rebbe." [**Interview by author with family member, October 16, 2012**]

Both boys threw themselves into their studies, realizing that although their forebears were Jewish scholars they themselves knew next to nothing about the great corpus of Jewish law and lore. Away from their father's rages, they found a new happiness in the school. Moshe Leib began studying with Mordechai Gifter, who would one day be the head of the school but who now became his *chavruse* (study partner) and mentor, taking the first steps that would ultimately lead him to succeeding his father.

Around the same time, Munkács Hasidim looked toward their future. They had carried on without a rebbe, but it did not work. Without a rebbe, they were losing young people. Those relative few who remained attached to Munkács turned to the *gabbaim,* most prominently Chaim Dov-Ber Greenfeld—known simply as "Chaim Ber." He had been not only *gabbai* to the Minchas Elazar but also houseboy for the Darchei Tshuvah, whose father had been the *sandak* (godfather) at Chaim Ber's circumcision.

In 1954, a delegation led by Chaim Ber and Binyamin Wulliger arrived at Telshe to inquire about the Rabinovich boys, just as Mottel Katz had predicted. Satisfied with what they heard, they began to think about how to create a path that would enable a succession to a new rebbe, even though the previous one was still living and nominally still rebbe. Although such a move was unprecedented, if they could bypass Boruchel they might mold his son into the rebbe they needed and maybe resurrect their court. The time had come, Wulliger believed, to bring the rest of the sons into the court and groom one of them as the next leader. Chaim Ber resisted—he was used to his position as senior Hasid and acting leader.

Chaim Ber protested that the boys' beards were just starting to sprout, a sign to him that they were not yet ready to lead. They were still too far from the Hasidic life—why, they were even regularly exposed to the television that was often on at their aunt and uncle's house in Crown Heights, Brooklyn (where everyone in the family was a fan of the *Perry Mason* detective series).[90] But Wulliger and a few others kept trying to persuade him that these were small matters that could be fixed and that if there was to be a future for Munkács Hasidim one of these holy seeds was it.

With Duchu out of consideration, the search committee turned to the next in line, Chaim Elazar.[91] A number of Hasidim tried to convince him take on the role. "They wanted another rebbe named Chaim Elazar," as the boy later explained.[92] Hasidic names were freighted with symbolic meaning, and to a group looking to recapture its lost glory the idea of a leader who was holy seed *and* bore the same name as the Minchas Elazar was most attractive and mystically meaningful.

But Chaim Elazar refused immediately. He had watched how his father's life had been repeatedly judged by those who came from the world he was being asked to lead. He had seen how he had been for-saken by these Hasidim who were supposed to be his followers and how he chafed under the heavy burden of his Hasidic crown. He recalled the expressed contempt from the Hasidim when his father decided to pur-sue a university degree, how they were troubled by the fact that he wore a gold watch and a diamond stickpin in his necktie, in a style that seemed far more cosmopolitan than they approved. He had seen not only how his father had to deal with his own life's problems but how, even after he no longer actively served as a rebbe, he was expected to solve personal problems that the Hasidim brought to him, and how delicate his father always needed to be in dealing with those.

He recalled especially an incident when a Hasid complained about his father's *Encyclopedia Britannica*. "I saw my father forced to justify himself before others who challenged him. I didn't really know at the time what the *Encyclopedia Britannica* was, but I knew it was some-thing intellectual, and I knew that he was being challenged by people who knew nothing about why he owned it and displayed it on his shelf." None of that appealed to him.[93]

Even the great Satmar Rebbe, Chaim recalled, whose towering, almost legendary, authority appeared beyond challenge, was confronted by one of his Hasidim who had somehow invaded the rebbe's bedroom and discovered there were mirrors in there; how, the Hasid wanted to know, could the great rebbe be so vain as to have a looking glass in his private chamber? Chaim Elazar decided that if that kind of life was what it meant to be a rebbe he wanted none of it. Years later, in his seventies, he could still recall his reaction: "I valued my privacy, and when I saw how a rebbe's life is not his own, I knew that I did not want that life." He added, "Whenever I saw charisma or people who were impressed by it, I ran the other way."[94] Chaim returned to Israel and enrolled in the highly Zionist Mercaz HaRav Yeshiva founded by Rabbi Abraham I. Kook.

MOSHE LEIB IS CHOSEN

Turned down by Chaim Elazar, the men from Munkács became even more desperate to fill the vacuum of leadership. They turned to Moshe Leib, the third son, who at the time was sixteen and a half and still studying at the Telshe Yeshiva. So far down in the birth order of Munkács royalty, he had never thought of himself as a successor. Although now more attached to Torah learning than he had been in

Brazil, he, like Chaim, was quite comfortable in the non-Hasidic Orthodox religious environment of his aunt and uncle's home in Crown
Heights during breaks from school.[95]

For the Hasidim, he was the new object of their hopes. On the third
of the Hebrew month of Shvat, 5719 (January 12, 1959), Wulliger
finally convinced a reluctant Chaim Ber to return to Telshe and offer the
crown to Moshe Leib. Taking the sleeper train, they were met early the
next morning at the station by the boy and his younger brother Yitzchak
Yaakov, along with the yeshiva's cook, Joseph Margulies, a Holocaust
survivor from Munkács. Chaim Ber was not wholly convinced about
the plan, but Wulliger begged him to keep an open mind. "Let me do
the talking," he said as they stepped off the train, to which the former
shot back, "What am I, a monkey?"[96] He would not be led.

After a series of conversations during which they reviewed the illustrious history of the Munkács Hasidic dynasty and whether it still had
a future, they turned to Moshe Leib: "The holy community of Munkács
looks to you." Nothing was said about his father or his brothers. Everyone understood why he was their new hope.

"I cannot say no," the teenager replied.

He would have to have a noticeable beard and be tutored in what it
meant to be a rebbe. He would not be the kind of rebbe his father had
been, but he was holy seed and therefore had it in him to succeed.

By the holiday of Purim, just a little over a month later, when he
arrived in the Brooklyn neighborhood where most of Munkács Hasidim
were to be found, Moshe Leib's face was framed by a small beard—all
he could raise on his teenage cheeks and chin. Chaim Ber was satisfied.
On Passover, the next month, the two brothers, Moshe Leib and
Yitzchak Yaakov, spent the seder with their aunt and uncle in Crown
Heights, but for the last days of the festival they were with Chaim Ber;
the process of preparing the next rebbe was now actively under way.

"I felt that great wrong had been done in abandoning the *rebistve*,"
Moshe Leib explained years later. "If I said no, my younger brother
would automatically also say no," and then there would be no one to
continue a great family tradition. That, he believed, "would be a crime
forever." And if he let that happen, "we would never be forgiven." He
felt that the burden of history had fallen on his shoulders and "someone
from the family has to say 'yes.'"

Still, he harbored lingering reservations about whether he indeed was
the one. Like so many of the figures he had read about in the Bible and
Hasidic tales he had heard, and also thinking like the teenager he was, he

sought a "sign" that he was meant to take up the leadership of this dynasty. But what would it be?

As he and a few boys walked the Telshe campus to his dorm, most of them wearing brightly colored polo shirts and looking like the American teens they were, an older man whom they passed asked them: "*Bochurim* [boys], you were just learning *Toyreh* [Torah] and now you're wearing polo shirts?"

"What's wrong with polo shirts?" one of the boys shot back.

"Where I come from," the old man replied, "we always wore only white shirts. I had a rebbe who learned *Toyreh* with a white shirt, suit and a hat." This, he explained, was the proper uniform of a yeshiva.

"Who was your rebbe, where are you from?" another boy asked.

"I'm from Munkács, and my rebbe was the Minchas Elazar." Moshe Leib felt a chill on his neck. This, he decided, was a sign from his late grandfather, speaking through this old man, confirming the choice he was preparing to make.

Only one step remained; he would have to ask his father for permission to go to New York and take up his crown. Moshe Leib understood that if he acted like a successor he would effectively end any claims that his father might have to the Munkács *rebistve*.

But while his father was no longer ready to carry on the *rebistve*, he had deep misgivings about his son's plans, afraid, he said, that he too would suffer disappointments and doubting that he would be given support, both financial and social, or even the authority he would need from the Hasidim. He warned him that "*hasidus* [Hasidism] in America," in the post-Holocaust world in general, was not what it had been in the past.

"They won't be able to teach you; they don't understand," his father said, referring to the Old World elders who would guide him. More than that, the inner life of a rebbe was not something anyone, even a *gabbai*, could explain. To do the job, he would have needed to grow up in a court, as Boruchel had done with his father and father-in-law. "Now," his father told him, it was all technical and soulless. "A rebbe in America has to know 'PR.'" The two spoke in Yiddish, as they always did, but these last words Boruchel spoke in English.

Moshe's father had other hopes for him; he wanted him to go to college—to study "anything that you want." This was an immigrant's postwar dream for his son, not the vision of a rebbe for his successor.

"Every person who will come in to see you," he continued, "will see you have a diploma and that you can do anything that you want." For Boruchel a university education for his children was not just an expression of so many refugee Jewish parents' hopes but also a conviction based on his own life experience that it would free his son from a risky dependence on the Hasidim. Boruchel worried that his son would take the *rebistve* and then be at the mercy of his Hasidim, in danger of their "dropping you," as he felt he had been dropped. With a college degree, however, he would be able to make a living in ways other than through his *rebistve,* and Boruchel felt "that the Hasidim should know that." Perhaps nothing so reflected his own distance from the *rebistve* as this wish. It was also a repudiation of what had been a principle for his predecessor, who had vehemently opposed any secular education for Jews.

Moshe Leib, however, understood what his father did not appreciate: in the emerging world of postwar ultra-Orthodoxy, a university education, with its exposure to foreign ideas and a culture that late twentieth-century Hasidism had decided was corrosive and religiously threatening, would disqualify and stigmatize him in the eyes of the Hasidim and among other rebbes, who would see him as damaged goods. "Today," he told his father, "if someone puts a college diploma on his wall, his *rebistve* is finished." Even Menachem Mendel Schneerson, soon to become the Seventh Lubavitcher Rebbe, who claimed to have attended the Sorbonne and other European universities and held an engineering degree from France, would after taking his crown discourage his Hasidim from university attendance.[97]

To avoid even the temptation of college attendance, as he came close to the end of high school at Telshe, Moshe Leib skipped the examinations that would make college admission possible. His choices were no longer his own, and his life would have to follow a trajectory diverging from the college dreams his father had for him. "No rebbe can do the things that a rebbe is not supposed to do," he recalled years later.

Assured that his father was unwilling to hold the reins of Munkács, but without the paternal blessing he had sought, Moshe Leib sent Chaim Ber the message that he was ready. His decision would ultimately estrange him from Boruchel, who by virtue of his son's most unusual succession during his father's lifetime would be known in the collective history of Munkács Hasidism as a failed and overthrown rebbe. Although Boruchel no longer wanted to be rebbe, the idea that he had "lost" his crown and his son to Munkács, which was now writing him out of their chronicle, troubled him, as would become dramatically obvious in the days ahead.

That the Hasidim would act on the decision of a teenager who had only a vague understanding of what was involved in being a rebbe, who had never really seen a Hasidic court from the inside, who had been educated in Israeli public schools and later in Brazilian ones, whose Torah knowledge came from a non-Hasidic yeshiva in Ohio and some brief mentoring in Brooklyn, and whose father had once held the position but was urging him to forego the crown and go to college instead was remarkable—a huge gamble by the Hasidim. At a time when everything in the Orthodox Jewish world was changing, the challenge of resurrecting and running an Hasidic court with an untrained neophyte was not going to be simple. Could he attract new followers while holding on to the old-timers when the big draws in the neighborhood were the charismatic old-time rebbes who survived the Holocaust? Could he establish institutions and build schools, gain a reputation as an organizer and a mover, and negotiate with the open society of America while keeping its seductions at bay? It was almost like running a corporation, and not simply being a charismatic leader.[98] Could an untested young man whose father, the former rebbe, was still very much alive provide his Hasidim with *chayei, bonei,* and *mzonei?*

Understanding what awaited him, Moshe Leib tried to stave off his actual crowning, claiming he had much to learn first. They also had to find him a wife, for no bachelor could be a full-fledged rebbe. In 1962, a match was found by the son-in-law of the Satmar Rebbe. As everyone understood, the marriage would be the first step in a process that would culminate in his succession to the Munkács *rebistve.* The twenty-two-year-old was to wed Nechama Perl Bernstein of Jerusalem, whose family traced its roots to the Besht. A distant relative, she was the daughter of the head of the Chaye Olam Yeshiva, who was also a *dayan* (rabbinic judge) on the Agudat Yisrael rabbinical court.

Moshe Leib would be wed shortly before Passover in New York, where he would set up his court, in the presence of his future Hasidim. Ironically, his older brother, Chaim Elazar, who had rejected the *rebistve,* would be getting married the next week in Jerusalem, and therefore missed the wedding.

THE WEDDING

In normal circumstances, the wedding of a likely successor of a rebbe is an event freighted with communal, social, religious, and even mystical significance. It is an opportunity for the Hasidim publicly to celebrate continuity, a cultural performance during which the group animates and displays sentiments essential to who and what they are. As the rebbe blesses the marriage, dances with the groom and later the bride in the presence of all the Hasidim, speaks about the cosmic and religious meaning of the event, and breaks bread with all the assembled, there is a sense among the Hasidim that this celebration is occurring in their lives and in heaven itself. So it was when the Minchas Elazar married off his daughter to Boruchel and all of Munkács rejoiced.

Moshe Leib's wedding would not be like that. Munkács was much diminished in numbers and influence from its heyday. The groom's father, the erstwhile rebbe, was marking not the continuity of his court but rather an unprecedented change to it, and his own eclipse. His arrival from Brazil would also mark the onset of his official repudiation of the rebbe role. His son was not just crown prince but a usurper of his father's throne who was becoming rebbe without his father's blessing. Still harboring hopes that Moshe Leib would attend college, Boruchel was unenthusiastic about his marrying before he had a "profession." This displeasure and concern constituted an implicit denial that becoming the Rebbe of Munkács *would* be his profession.

Although Moshe Leib's aunt Peska and uncle Volvie Friedman helped get him a *shtreimel* and a *bekeshe* (frock coat), the de rigeur garb for a Hasidic groom, the wedding itself was overseen by Chaim Ber and the Hasidim as well as their supporters. Boruchel, uninvolved in the planning, was preparing to leave as soon as possible to spend the upcoming Passover in Israel, where he would attend the wedding of his older son, Chaim Elazar. Moshe Leib's New York wedding was on April 7 and his older brother's on April 15, just three days before the first seder.

As the wedding day approached, Yoelish Teitelbaum, the Satmar Rebbe, who was now mentoring Moshe Leib and encouraging him to take up the crown, agreed to officiate at the marriage. Since he had met Moshe at sixteen, Yoelish had tried to wean him from the ways of Telshe, which represented the opponents of Hasidism. He wanted the new Munkács as a satellite of Satmar, which was fast becoming the premier court of reconstituted Hungarian Hasidism in the post-Holocaust world.

There was a history behind this interest, built against a background of acrimony between him and the Minchas Elazar. Many years before, Yoelish had publicly mentioned the paucity of Shapira heirs compared to his own, a declaration that deeply grieved the great Munkács Rebbe and that the Satmar later was known to regret, especially after all his own offspring died during his lifetime, leaving him with no grandchildren or heirs, while Shapira had many.[99] By the time he met one of those heirs on the path to be the Munkács successor, he saw it as his penance and destiny to take the boy under his wing and shape him into the rebbe he would become, especially as the boy's Zionist father would not.[100] Throughout his *rebistve,* Moshe Leib would look to Yoelish—perhaps even more than to his father—as the image of what a contemporary rebbe should be. That he rather than Boruchel would officiate was a powerful symbol of these feelings.

Although the wedding would be grand, with over a thousand attending, Boruchel was curiously passive about it. For a time no one was certain he would even attend. But at last he decided to come. When asked about the suggestion that the chuppah (the ceremony under the canopy) take place on a Saturday night—a most unorthodox choice and not considered a propitious time for marriage, but one that would result in the Satmar Rebbe's wearing his *shtreimel,* which he put on for Sabbaths and would still have on Saturday night, something considered a mark of honor—Boruchel replied: "I don't care; just make sure I can make it in time to Israel for Chaim Elazar's wedding and *Pesach.*"[101]

Boruchel's indifference may have come from ambivalent feelings about all that the wedding portended, about the prominent role that the Satmar Rebbe (it still bothered Boruchel that it was to the Satmar court that many Hasidim from Boruchel's Munkács had defected) would have in the ceremony and the groom's life, and about how his son would eclipse his own *rebistve.* Part of it might have arisen from the fact that he had neither the financial nor social resources to give his son a big wedding. Instead, Chaim Ber, a *gabbai,* found financing for and controlled the nuptials; *he* and not Boruchel chose and *insisted* on the Saturday night April 7 date.

The ceremony began after midnight, since the Satmar Rebbe, as was his wont, arrived late. Now Boruchel's diminution in public began in earnest. According to family custom, if a father was not with the mother of the groom, he would not escort his son to the chuppah. Instead, Boruchel's half brother Chaim Shlomo Horowitz, the Strzyżówer Rebbe of New York, led Moshe Leib to the bridal canopy, where the Satmar Rebbe in his *shtreimel* waited.[102] Boruchel's relatively minor honor was to recite the Aramaic text of the *ketubah* aloud. The bride's father offered the highly significant last of the seven blessings that would seal the marriage, and the *gabbai* Chaim Ber was awarded the recitation of another of the seven blessings. Such a prominent honor for a *gabbai* was unusual—like giving an old butler a formal role in a royal family wedding. Boruchel swallowed this breach of Hasidic etiquette. Chaim Ber had been kingmaker and rainmaker at what was happening tonight. Everyone watching knew the backstory and could imagine the feelings of all those who stood under the canopy.

As the ceremony ended and the wedding party moved to the festive meal, the Satmar Rebbe made his exit, while bride and groom went off for *yichud,* the first time they would be alone together in a room as wife and husband. Well past 1:00 a.m., the new couple made their entrance to the Grand Paradise Hall in Brooklyn, and the dancing commenced.

At a Hasidic royal wedding, where men and women are strictly segregated, the dancing that matters most takes place among the men. During the initial dancing among the men, a huge circle is created by the mass of Hasidim, and into it moves the rebbe, who dances, first by himself, then with the groom. Then they all dance together, and different people take turns dancing with the groom inside the large circle while the crowd sings and claps. Of course, in this wedding these customs were disturbed by the fact that the groom was on the verge of becoming the rebbe, while his father, nominally still the rebbe, was on the verge of disappearing from the community's life. So the first dance by the rebbe was impossible.

"Reb Boruchel," as the Hasidim were starting to refer to the father, and his son, Moshe Leib, soon to be called "the *neier* [new] rebbe," took the first dance. Clasping both hands, they galloped around the circle together, as the sea of Hasidim clapped and sang. It was a singular sight, making it appear that the tensions were gone and that the father rejoiced with the son and was even presenting him as his successor. But it would soon turn out that this was not true.

When father and son finished dancing, a few of the other Hasidic rebbes who had come to the wedding took their turns with the bridegroom. Following protocol, all of them made sure to dance with the groom (and rebbe-to-be) only briefly, always for a shorter time than Boruchel had, so as not to outshine him. Finally Chaim Ber claimed his turn. And then, as the son would much later put it, *"things went very wrong."*

Recalling the event fifty years later, one who had been there explained what had happened next: "Chaim Ber forgot he was a *gabbai* and not a rebbe." Dancing not with the self-effacement of a *gabbai* but with an ostentatious display of enthusiasm that might be expected of a host, he twirled around inside the circle with Moshe Leib, while Boruchel stood on the margins. As they danced longer than any of the preceding, Chaim Ber seemed as if *he* were leading the young man around, as if he was first among equals—the "master of the Munkács." This was perceived by some of those present, by the groom and certainly by his father, as a self-aggrandizing breach of protocol and a show of stature that was beyond what a *gabbai*—even one with such a long history in Munkács and with the distinction of having hand-picked the new rebbe—deserved. The dance seemed to celebrate replacement rather than succession.

In a drama overladen with Oedipal overtones, Boruchel exploded over what he viewed as a public affront. The choreography that turned the dance into a dramatic tableau in which his son was symbolically taken away from him by the Hasidim in the person of the *gabbai* and from which he himself was marginalized and ultimately excluded was too much for Boruchel to bear. Exasperated, Boruchel lunged at Chaim Ber, tearing hair from his beard, then grabbing the microphone from the band and stopping the dancing. The abrupt violence and sudden silence was frightening. Now Boruchel began a stunning tirade, letting out all his feelings. Overwhelmed by what he saw as a public slight and embarrassment, he talked about why he had left Munkács and had not settled in America. He justified his disappointments with his Hasidim.

He could not give his approval to the transition taking place before his eyes. In the tug-of-war within him that played itself out before everyone, he seemed to express his desire to celebrate his son's wedding even as he mourned what it portended. He was unready and *un*willing to be parted from his son and his *rebistve* in so humiliating a way.

Then, remembering that Chaim Ber had financed the wedding, Boruchel lamented that in America, unlike the Munkács he knew, everything was about money. If you have it you get honor, but if not you are forced to wait outside. Everyone understood how he felt that this reality had made it possible for the *gabbai* to be on the inside of the circle with his son, while he, the true rebbe, was now forced to watch from the outside.[103]

Boruchel had made a scene, but the crowd was not sympathetic to him; they were with Chaim Ber and the *new* rebbe. Some began to boo him, urging the band to start up again and resume the dancing. Binyomin Wulliger gently drew Boruchel off the stage. Zuta ran out of the room, and others were in tears or shock. That a day so filled with hope would be broken in this way was tragic. Boruchel soon departed; he did not stay to take that last dance with the bride, and he did not stay for the *sheva brachot,* the seven days of feasting and blessings following the wedding.

BECOMING A REBBE

On the first Sabbath after the wedding, the last day of *sheva brachot,* Chaim Ber stood up in the synagogue following the chanting of the Torah portion and announced, "Mazel tov, we have a new rebbe."

For two more years, the new rebbe stayed in a small yeshiva in Crown Heights, Kollel Gurari, with only about twenty students, all married and devoted to Torah study as a calling, staving off the full weight of the crown, often suffering "nightmares" when he thought about the responsibilities that awaited him and about his fraught relations with his father. He thought about instruction he had learned from the writings of the *Divrei Chaim,* which he read from cover to cover, memorizing its contents: the word *rebbe* could be understood as an acronym, with its three Hebrew letters, רבי, standing either for *Rosh B'nai Yisrael,* the head of the Jewish people, or *Rasha b'ainai Hashem,* an evildoer in the eyes of God. Being an intermediary between his Hasidim and the Almighty, he would be seen as a leader when all went well for his followers. But if he failed, they would conclude that God looked upon him as an evildoer. After all, they had already rejected one rebbe.

No matter how much Moshe Leib tried to delay the day, the Hasidim demanded that he become fully engaged. People started asking him for blessings, advice, and counsel. Although Moshe Leib tried to remain the same person he was, people treated him differently. He uncurled his sidelocks from behind his ears and wore them loose so that they were more prominent. After the anniversary of the death of the Minchas Elazar that year, the new rebbe began accepting *kvittlach* from his Hasidim.

He would do a lot of on-the-job learning, and there were always some of the older Hasidim or *gabbaim* (especially Chaim Ber) who would help. To make sure that every Hasid came along, Chaim Ber would upbraid laggards, telling them that "the rebbe has not seen you for too long a time." And if the new rebbe did something his *gabbai* thought was wrong, he would be sure to tell him, adding that he had done the same with his father when the young Polish rebbe had needed guidance about Munkács customs. Once they told Moshe Leib, "People are upset. You walk around in black socks. A rebbe should wear white stockings; we are your Hasidim and we want our rebbe to wear white stockings, as did the Minchas Elazar and as do all rebbes these days." From then on, he wore white stockings. He was learning the limits of privacy and leadership, and the sweep of what his Hasidim could demand of him.

After 1969, when he fully embraced his role, he moved his court from Williamsburg to Borough Park and, as his father had at the outset, tried to bolster the educational arm of the court. He founded a primary school. Moshe Leib also sought to be a fixer for Jews in trouble, an intermediary with the powers-that-be. He became, as one New York newspaper described him, "the ultra-Orthodox community's most influential rabbi in governmental affairs in New York."[104] Working behind the scenes for some of the most prominent Hasidic Jews and their supporters who ran afoul of the law, he pled in their defense and mitigated their punishments. He was understanding and fair, and perhaps most importantly discreet and frequently successful in his efforts.

As for being a wonder rabbi, he was not happy to play that role. But when Hasidim came to him for blessings, he responded. "Any Jew can give a blessing," he explained. Did God not tell the patriarch Abraham, that first Jew, to "be a blessing"? One need only give a blessing "with a full heart." "That is what I do. I give it with a full heart, and," he smiled, "I've had good results."

In spite of his illustrious Hasidic roots, in post-Holocaust Brooklyn a whole new generation was growing up that did not remember the grandeur of Munkács—a generation that could easily sample a number of rebbes in an afternoon and linger in their courts in order to see who suited them best and who put on a better display of charisma. Moshe Leib was not always their first choice. Still he hewed to what his grandfather had written in *Chayim v'Shalom* as his recipe for leadership: not to agitate, propagandize, or send out emissaries to gather large audiences for one's words, not to poach Hasidim, and to remain religiously repulsed by the honor of being a rabbi.[105] These recommendations suited his grandfather's situation, where he dominated the territory, but they were not prescriptions suited to growth or organization in a place like Brooklyn, where everyone rubbed shoulders with all sorts of Hasidim and the territory was up for grabs.

Those who were his Hasidim looked to his past for signs that he had always been destined for his crown. Someone recalled that at his *bris* on the last day of Chanukah, Shalom Elazar Halberstam, the old Ratzferter Rebbe and youngest son of the great founder of the Sanz dynasty, had been *sandak* (godfather). After the infant Moshe Leib was named, the Ratzferter Rebbe blessed him and in doing so took the unexpected step of standing up and reciting the words, "May he go higher and higher."[106] At the time, no one would have expected this third son to ascend to the throne of Munkács, but now, as the Hasidim reflected backward on their new and unexpected rebbe, they saw these words as a prophetic sign of his election. There were no coincidences; all had been ordained in heaven, and the scion of Sanz had seen it in Munkács years before.

Things did not always go smoothly. When Yitzchak Yaakov, the youngest son of Frima and Boruchel, married, he too sought to establish himself as rebbe. For a while in the 1980s, he tried to also share the name Munkács from his base on Ditmas Avenue in Kensington, Brooklyn, calling himself "Munkács/Flatbush." Although he had no real Hasidim there, this appellation was a challenge to his older brother, for it seemed to assert that the latter was not the only Rebbe of Munkács, just one of two. Moreover, whenever he publicly was identified by this title, Yitzchak Yaakov was in effect challenging the status of his older brother, if not the entire project of a unified, renewed Munkács dynasty that the Hasidim and Moshe Leib had been working so hard to reestablish. Some of the members of Yitzchak Yaakov's family wanted his older brother to be called the "Munkácser Rebbe of Boro Park" in an explicit challenge to the new order. The relations with his brothers deteriorated.

In a move that ultimately defused this challenge, others in the community persuaded the Flatbush brother to yield, assuring him that it would be to his financial and personal benefit. This was helped with his move in 2008 from Flatbush to Williamsburg. There he found himself deep in a territory dominated by Satmar Hasidim, whose dynasty was being aggressively contested by two brothers, Aaron and Zalman (see below).[107] Even before his relocation, Yitzchak Yaakov had begun to call himself "the Dynover Rebbe" (an option possible because, as noted earlier, the founder of the dynasty and his ancestor, Zvi Elimelech Shapira, had been a leader in both Munkács and Dynów). Even though there had been no other Dynover Rebbe since then, the younger Rabinovich was able to resurrect this title and make it his own, leading to a reconciliation with his brother Moshe Leib and eventually drawing a new Hasidic following, including from among those Satmar Hasidim who found the feud between the two Satmar Rebbes sufficiently disturbing that they turned to Dynów for a neutral place to worship. Indeed, the resolution of this Munkács conflict ultimately enhanced the prestige and esteem of both brothers, whose dignity was no longer profaned by an unseemly competition and conflict.

CODA

What about Boruch? In 1962, a week after attending the wedding of his son Moshe Leib in New York and while he was visiting Israel for the wedding of his son Chaim Elazar (greeted, according to newspaper reports, by hundreds of Munkács Hasidim, some of whom wanted him to remain), he tried unsuccessfully to get a position in the Israeli state rabbinate as chief rabbi of Hadera.[108] Despairing of transforming Jewry in Brazil, in 1963 he returned to Israel and found a position in the

4. Moshe Leib Rabinovich, the current Rebbe of Munkács, dancing before his Hasidim. Photo by Shmuel Lenchevsky. By permission of Ichud Archives, Brooklyn, New York.

Israeli state rabbinate in Holon, later moving to Petach Tikva. Yet he never really found himself in a situation that he believed suited him or fulfilled his ambitions. With his financial situation continuing to be precarious, while his son settled into his role as the Munkács Rebbe, seeking to resurrect the influence and grandeur of its years in Europe, the father tried to build a new position: a kind of chief rebbe of all Hasidim. The quest would set him against his sons in ways that neither sons nor father wanted.

On the surface the conflict was about a library. As with so many other Hasidic rebbes, books—*seforim,* as they are called—and other manuscripts, letters, and certain ritual objects are often inextricably linked to a Hasidic dynasty's identity and legacy. Not only are they of spiritual importance; they also are often financially valuable. Manuscripts and first editions, along with other artifacts, were part of the heritage of the Rebbes of Munkács, the treasury of the court. Boruchel wanted to sell some items to finance his plans.

The family became riven by the question of who controlled and owned the treasury. But this was a proxy dispute about who controlled the House of Munkács. The quarrel was no less bitter than the one that had broken out at the wedding. In December 1980, Boruchel wrote a letter on stationery with a letterhead identifying him as "chief rabbi of Munkatch, São Paulo and Holon." In it he stipulated that neither his son Chaim Elazar nor his son Moshe Leib nor their sister nor their spouses, sons, daughters, or grandchildren were to attend his funeral or say Kaddish for him, or visit his grave. The prohibitions, he explained, came because "each one of them sinned against me," and he did not want those sins recalled by their visits to his grave. Still, he prayed that "the Holy One, blessed be He, have mercy upon them." [109]

When Boruchel lay dying and his son, Moshe Leib, sought to have his father bless his own son before the young man's impending wedding and offer what both surely understood would be their final farewells, Yehudit, his second wife, offered only to let the grandson come but not his son. In the end, neither of the two entered the room.

On December 26, 1997, the day after the birthday of his son and successor, Boruchel Rabinovich passed away in Petach Tikva, Israel. It is customary that each year on the *yarzheit,* the anniversary of the death of a previous rebbe, the Hasidim and the current rebbe mark the occasion, considered in mystical tradition to be a time when the soul of the departed rises to a higher level in paradise, with a festive gathering and recollections of their departed leader. In Munkács today, however, no such celebrations for Boruchel occur.

As for Chaim Ber, he remained an *eminence grise* in the Munkács court for many years, and when on the Sabbath, November 3, 1984, he died at the ripe age of ninety-six, he would be eulogized as one who took the "young leftover fruit of the great tree, the grandchildren of the Rebbe of Munkács, to raise them in holiness." [110]

Today in the Munkács court in Borough Park Brooklyn, the crown rests firmly on seventy-four-year-old Moshe Leib (figure 4). His position in the Hasidic league of leaders is securely established. His open and warm character, and his willingness to serve his Hasidim and many others, fill his days with activity. Both of his sons, Chaim Elazar and Yerucham Fishel, as well as the rest of his family and even his grandchildren are involved with the court, though how succession will unfold is not clear. There is in the meantime, no hurry to move toward a transition.

3

Boyan and Kopyczynitz

Running Out of Rebbes

THE ORIGINS OF THE DYNASTIES

The Hasidic dynasties of both Boyan and Kopyczynitz trace their origins to the Ruzhin dynasty founded by Yisrael Friedman of Ruzhin (1796–1850), great-grandson of Dov Ber, the Maggid of Mezherich, who was among the founding fathers of Hasidism. Both ultimately confronted the problem of running out of successors, and each arrived at a different resolution.

Boyan begins with Yitzchak Friedman (1850–1917), known as the Pachad Yitzchak after his major work. Son of Avraham Yaakov Friedman, the Sadigura (Sadhora in Bukovina Austria) Rebbe, Yitzchak and his younger brother Israel drew lots in 1883 to see who would stay in Sadigura and succeed their father. Israel won, while Yitzchak, along with his wife, Malka (née Twersky), moved three years later to neighboring Bojany and established his court there, becoming known as the Boyaner Rebbe.[1]

After the First World War, during the Russian (later Soviet) occupation of the town, the Jewish quarter was destroyed and the rebbe's court burned to the ground, while he and his family escaped to Vienna.[2] Capital of the Austro-Hungarian Empire, which this war would dismantle, Vienna was a city of high culture.[3] Before 1914 Hasidism was effectively absent there, but with about one hundred thousand Jewish refugees, many from Galicia and Bukovina, finding their way to the city, a great number of rebbes and even more Hasidim established themselves

The Boyan Dynasty

YITZCHAK FRIEDMAN (1850–1917): Known as the Pachad Yitzchak; First Boyaner Rebbe

MENACHEM NACHUM FRIEDMAN (1869–1936): Rebbe of Boyan in Czernovitz; eldest son of Yitzchak

YISRAEL FRIEDMAN (1878–1951): Rebbe of Boyan in Leipzig; second son of Yitzchak

AVROHOM YAAKOV FRIEDMAN (1884–1941): Rebbe of Boyan in Lvóv (Lemberg); third son of Yitzchak

MORDECHAI SHLOMO FRIEDMAN (1891–1971): Rebbe of Boyan in New York; youngest son of Yitzchak

NACHUM DOV BRAYER (1959–PRESENT): Rebbe of Boyan in Jerusalem; grandson of Mordechai Shlomo

The Kopyczynitz Dynasty

YITZCHAK MEIR HESCHEL (1862–1934): First Rebbe of Kopyczynce; great-grandson of Yisrael Friedman, Rebbe of Ruzhin

AVRAHAM YEHOSHUA HESCHEL (1887–1967): Rebbe of Kopyczynce; eldest son of Yitzchak Meir

MOSHE MORDECHAI HESCHEL (1928–75): Rebbe of Kopyczynce in New York; second son of Avraham Yehoshua

there. According to a contemporary register, twenty Hasidic courts, including sixteen descended from the Sadigura dynasty, operated in Vienna during the interwar years.[4] The most influential leaders of this dynasty, those from Chortkov, Boyan, Husiatyń, and Sadigura, remained in Vienna after the end of the war, and although they made sporadic visits to their followers in the more important towns in Galicia, their influence in the Hasidic world weakened considerably and their successors had rather small followings. It may also be that a willingness to adopt elements of European culture, already evident among the Rebbes of Sadigura, led to or reflected their more acculturative tendencies. Many Hasidim became increasingly charmed by and attracted to the big city life and culture. Yet there were also some Viennese Jews who became attracted to Hasidism.

There had always been *zaddikim* who settled in large cities, but until the end of the nineteenth century these had been isolated cases. After the dislocations of the First World War, this development became far more common. Before his death in 1917, Yitzchak had remarked to his Hasidim that they were fortunate not to have to worry about the future of the Boyan dynasty: "For we have, thank God, those to whom we can leave [our legacy]: our [four] holy and pure sons."[5] He therefore left a will in which he offered his outline for the future of his dynasty and the role his sons would have in it.[6]

After the November 11 Armistice, all the sons realized that Vienna, with its growing anti-Semitism, was not for them and that going back to Boyan was not an option. Each one, seeking to continue his father's dynasty, moved to a different place, hoping to set up a court and establish a reputation on his own. The eldest, Menachem Nachum (1869–1936), became a rebbe in Czernovitz, Bukovina.[7] The second son, Yisrael (1878–1951), established himself in Leipzig, Germany, though he would end his days in Tel Aviv. The third, Avrohom Yaakov (1884–1941), became rebbe in Lvóv (Lemberg). Finally, the youngest, Mordechai Shlomo Friedman (1891–1971), remained temporarily in Vienna, caring for his widowed mother until her death in December 1920. After that, he considered a move to Drohobych, in an area that shifted politically between Ukraine and Poland. New York, at the time far beyond the pale for many Hasidim, since so few observant Jews were to be found there, was also considered.

Mordechai Shlomo's mentor and uncle, Yisrael Friedman of Chortkov, as a matter of principle supported the idea of establishing religious institutions as cultural and religious bulwarks against secularity. He therefore urged Mordechai and his cousin, thirty-nine-year-old Yitzchak Friedman, the Rebbe of Sadiger-Rimanov, to go to the United States and build Hasidism there.[8] The Chortkover Rebbe's plan had been for these two cousins to sustain each other spiritually and thus gain the fortitude to tame and colonize the Jewish and Hasidic wilderness that was America in those years.[9] Although coming with a pedigree more distinguished than that of many other Hasidim moving to America in those early days, both cousins had doubts. But as the youngest of his brothers, whose "social and economic prospects" were comparatively poor, Mordechai Shlomo had limited choices; in Vienna he had not really stood out, nor had he attracted "greater numbers by outshining his older, better-known bothers and cousins."[10] His cousin Yitzchak Friedman was in much the same situation.

As they pondered their choices, both knew that few Hasidic leaders believed America held promise for Hasidism in the future. A quick scan of those few Hasidic leaders coming in the early part of the twentieth century revealed men either unable to establish themselves in the Jewish heartland of Europe or Jews on the run for their lives. As for the rest of the immigrants, most appeared ready to reinvent themselves in the New World and abandon Jewish observance along the way. How could a true *zaddik* build a following there? Those who did found their followers to be far from truly Hasidic. Nevertheless, the Friedman cousins chose a trial visit.

Yitzchak of Sadiger-Rimanov came first in 1924 but soon decided that America was *not* the solution for him.[11] Overwhelmed by the fact that so many American Jews—including those who came to consult with him—publicly desecrated the Sabbath, he decided that whatever the problems in Vienna, he would return. But before he could, he was overtaken by tragedy. In line with Hasidic custom, he went for a ritual immersion in a *mikveh* on a cold December morning in 1924. This dip into the cold waters of the bath led to pneumonia, to which he succumbed just after midnight on 11 Kislev (December 8).[12] There were rumors of foul play, as none of the money he had reputedly collected from his consultations was found in his possession after his demise. Nothing was ever proven. At his funeral, a eulogizer declared: "The sufferings of the Jews of Europe, in which he was himself a full participant, brought him to New York; and there, the sorry religious and spiritual state of American Jewry, added to his other burdens, broke him completely."[13] This was an inauspicious beginning for the Chortkover Rebbe's grand plan.[14]

When Mordechai Shlomo of Boyan and his wife, Chava Sarah, daughter of the Mezhbizher Rebbe, arrived, soon after his cousin's sudden death, he was in despair about succeeding and quickly left after his trial stay. Back in Vienna, he reconsidered his options. They were not improved since his sojourn abroad. Heeding the advice of his oldest brother to choose New York over Drohobych, he returned permanently in November of 1927 to try to make a go of it.[15] Establishing a *shtibbel* or small synagogue at 247 East Broadway on the Lower East Side in Manhattan, where there were dozens of other such small quasi-Hasidic congregations and a few men who called themselves Boyaner Hasidim, he built a small following. But his situation remained difficult and daunting. When his older brother in Chernovitz heard of his difficulties that had come in spite of his advice, he reportedly explained, "America is a source of falsehood and my brother is a source of truth, and oh such a contradiction in terms."[16] Calling himself the Boyaner Rebbe of New York, Mordechai Shlomo acquired a modest congregation largely of nominally Orthodox Jews.

During the early years, many of his congregants and supporters were not necessarily Hasidic or even very observant. Like some Jewish immigrants at the time, they felt an attachment to him because he embodied their nostalgia for the Old Country. Inside his synagogue, they could share feelings of hope and anxiety, anticipation and wistful homesickness, all of which often were projected onto this relic of a lost world. They had less an attachment to his charisma than an affection for his person and warmth, an appreciation of his obvious concern for them that expressed itself in a connection to him.

Reflecting back on those days, many Hasidim today see rebbes like the Boyaner as driven by the desire to bring Jewishly unschooled and illiterate immigrants closer to Judaism, as pioneers of the "Return to Judaism" movement often associated with the last quarter of the twentieth century and often most commonly identified with the Lubavitcher outreach campaigns.[17] That is probably a stretch, if not an anachronism. In fact, those first rebbes in America like the Boyaner were simply trying to carve out a small space for themselves on a new Jewish frontier where they had to adapt.

ADAPTING TO AMERICA

The Boyaner Rebbe's need to adjust to American Jewish life recalibrated his view of Hasidic life. His Viennese background helped his understanding of what it meant to be a rebbe in a big and cosmopolitan city like New York. As he worked to help reconstruct the lives of immigrants and later refugees arriving just before or during the Holocaust (he served on the Va'ad Hatzola of Agudath Israel, trying to save as many as possible from the Nazis and their allies), he learned to be open and accepting, even as he tried to anchor them in his kind of Hasidic Judaism.[18]

Not unlike many of those who worshipped with him, the Boyaner became known for the modesty of his life—in sharp contrast to the so-called "regal way" that many rebbes of the Ruzhin dynasty had been known to embrace.[19] Unlike many rebbes who would arrive after the Holocaust, he was not bent on fighting a culture war with America.

Mordechai Shlomo read the *New York Times* daily and bought into parts of the American dream; his two sons and a daughter went to college.[20] The former did not grow beards and did not stand out as Hasidim while at school. One became a social worker, and the other, after getting a degree in architecture and marrying a college graduate, went into real estate. The rebbe's daughter, with an advanced degree in chemistry,

5. Mordechai Shlomo Friedman, the old Boyaner Rebbe (seated, with folded hands).
By permission of Yigal Brayer.

married a man who, although quite learned in Jewish matters, became a
Yeshiva University professor and psychologist.[21] The rebbe was proud of
their accomplishments, which exemplified the modern Orthodox ideal
(so popular in the immediate post-Holocaust period) of remaining committed to uncompromising Jewish religious observance while not separating from the larger culture and surrounding society.[22] Asked once
how he maintained his "purity in America," the rebbe reportedly replied:
"I sit here, in my corner, and I think about Boyan," even if his children
no longer did (figure 5).[23] What this would mean for succession one
could only guess.

KOPYCZYNITZ

Like the Boyaner Rebbe, another of his cousins, the Kopyczynitzer
(Kopyczynce) Rebbe, Avraham Yehoshua Heschel (1888–1967), was
an early arrival in America. Heschel, who on his father's side traced his
ancestry to the Apter Rebbe (Opatów, Poland) (1748–1825), his

namesake and great-grandfather, was the second to take this crown. The first was his father, Yitzchak Meir Heschel (1862–1934), who on his mother's side was a great-grandson of Yisrael Friedman, the Rebbe of Ruzhin. Establishing himself in the small whistle-stop town on the then Austrian-Russian border from which he took his court's name, Yitzchak Meir died in Vienna, where, like many of the Ruzhiner dynasty, he had fled during World War I.[24] After his death, his son, at age forty-eight, succeeded him. But 1934 was not good time to be a Jew, much less a rebbe, in Vienna. After the 1938 *Anschluss,* the political union with Nazi Germany, life for him became unbearable. He and his older son were beaten by "the SS and by the local Nazi hoodlums" and were subjected to repeated public humiliations.[25] Fleeing in 1939, he and his family arrived in New York.[26]

He too settled on Manhattan's Lower East Side, near the Boyaner. By the time Heschel, known as "Ruv Avrumenyu," arrived at Henry Street, Friedman had been on East Broadway for twelve years.[27] Heschel and Friedman not only were related through marriage over the generations and a mutual history in cosmopolitan Vienna but also now shared spheres of influence and territory.

In 1965, with the ethnic changes going on in Manhattan's Lower East Side and the migration of many Orthodox Jews to Brooklyn, Heschel moved his small court to Borough Park in Brooklyn. By then he was one of the honorary presidents of Agudath Israel.[28] Yet while his profile grew, he, like his cousin the Boyaner, watched his family adapt to America. He too had family members, including some of his children and their spouses, who had left the orbit of Hasidism. Perhaps most prominent was his brother-in-law and cousin Abraham Joshua Heschel, professor at the Conservative Rabbinical Jewish Theological Seminary, prominent author and public figure in the American civil rights struggle. While the Kopyczynitz court was not large, the rebbe was able to maintain a following until his death at seventy-nine in 1967.[29]

THE KOPYCZYNITZ SUCCESSION

The Kopyczynitzer and his wife, Sara (who was also his cousin), had three sons and seven daughters. The sons were first in the line of succession: Yisrael (Sruel), Moshe Mordechai, and Meshulam Zyshe. The daughters included Leah, married to Ephraim Fishel Horowitz, a rabbi in Tisminitz (Tysmienica), Galicia; Chava, married to Schneur Zalman Gurary, a Lubavitcher Hasid closely associated with the Sixth Lubavitcher Rebbe and a cousin of the latter's son-in-law Shmaryahu Gurary; Batsheva, married to Aaron Flintenstein; Mirel, married to Aaron Gartenhaus; Miriam (Manja), married to Yosef (Mottel) Fink; Malka, married to Aaron Lemberger; and Chaya Perel, married to Yaakov Yosef Twersky, who, although clean-shaven, served as the Chotiner Rebbe in the Bronx.[30] With so many offspring, one might assume succession would not be a problem. But it was.

Upon the death of their rebbe, Kopyczynitzer Hasidim naturally turned to his children, the holy seeds. But the question of succession and continuity was not easily answered. The oldest son, unmarried at the time (a status incompatible with succession), refused repeated entreaties to be rebbe, preferring to keep his job as an accountant and marrying much later.

After a period of mourning, the Hasidim turned next to the second son, who was seventeen years younger. He too refused, claiming he was neither a Hasidic scholar nor particularly charismatic. But the Hasidim persisted, and thus on the first anniversary of his father's passing in July of 1968 Moshe Mordechai Heschel acceded to their requests.[31] As his younger brother explained: "He gave up a lot to become the Rebbe. He accepted the position because he felt he had a responsibility to the Hasidim of my father. He didn't do it on account of guilt, although a lot of people used that on him."[32]

Having grown up in America, where he studied in the non-Hasidic Mesifta Tifferet Jerusalem, a yeshiva headed by the non-Hasidic Moshe Feinstein from whom he later received rabbinic ordination, Moshe Mordechai was comfortable in English. In the early 1950s, he directed a program whose goal was to release public school students for an hour of Jewish studies. Moderately successful in the diamond trade (then dominated by Hasidim), he worked on Manhattan's famous Forty-Seventh Street diamond district. As a rebbe, he developed a talent for marital and other interpersonal counseling, a skill that seemed well suited to the changing situation of modern Hasidim. This attracted a new flow of Hasidim to him, who "admired how he immersed themselves in their problems."[33] Many of his new followers came from non-Hasidic backgrounds, attracted by this modern-inflected rebbe with an open, gregarious, and warm personality who spoke their language and was a gifted counselor. While the Kopyczynitz synagogue never attracted more than about two hundred Hasidim, Moshe Mordechai's reputation as a counselor in the larger Brooklyn Hasidic world made him more popular than these numbers suggest.

Unlike more regal rebbes who waited for their Hasidim to approach them, Moshe Mordechai reached out to them personally, calling his Hasidim and supporters on the telephone, asking about their welfare. He was ready often to "put himself on the line for others by cosigning and guaranteeing loans," clearly seeing this as part of the mandate of a rebbe under the expectation of *mzonei,* providing for their economic welfare.[34]

As his reputation grew, a hagiography about him emerged that retroactively transformed his biography so that his ascent to the position of rebbe was seen not as an accident of history but as a matter of divine intention. For example, one story recounted how in the late 1920s his father had "made the long arduous journey from Vienna" to visit the Holy Land and "on the 15th of Sivan [had] . . . traveled to Me'aras Eliyahu, a cave high on Mount Carmel, where it is believed Eliyahu Hanavi [Elijah, the Prophet] had hidden." There the then rebbe prayed "for another son," and "One year later to the day his wife gave birth to a baby boy," Moshe Mordechai. There were stories of how Moshe Mordechai helped Jews in need or drew them closer to Judaism even while he was still in the business world, as if that period were the necessary precursor to his ascent.[35]

But the new rebbe had suffered from health problems ever since contracting rheumatic fever as a youngster. His eighteen- to twenty-hour days as rebbe took their toll. In March 1975 on Passover Eve, seven years after succeeding his father, he suffered a cerebral hemorrhage and died three days later at the age of forty-eight. Although his widow sought to place their son as his successor, she failed. Once again, the Kopyczynitzer Hasidim were in search of a leader.

They turned to Meshullam Zyshe, the old rebbe's youngest son and Moshe's brother. Ordained as rabbi at New York's Torah Voda'as Yeshiva, he had worked for Agudath Israel as head counselor in their popular summer camp. Many of the young boys who had once been campers there and might have seen him as a mentor were now leaders in the Orthodox world. But Zyshe, as he was called, never imagined himself as his father's successor. As he recalled, "Was I my father's Hasid? No. There were too many things that got in the way. He wanted me to be somebody else than I really was, and he made too many demands of me that I couldn't live up to. And so things got in the way."[36] Instead, Zyshe, who wished to go to college, did so for a time, until dropping out and going into office work.

Now, suddenly, the continuity of Kopyczynitz depended on his becoming successor. After his brother's funeral, Zyshe listened as Yerachmiel

Yehuda Myer Kalish, the Amshinover Rebbe, tried to persuade him to accept and "grow into the role," adding, "You say you're not a Rebbe? None of us are [*sic*] Rebbes today. None of us are like the *rebbeim* [rebbes] of old times. I'm not like my father and I imagine you're not like your father. But the role of a rebbe has changed today. A rebbe is just somebody who binds his people together. He has to strive to keep them together and give them spiritual strength. . . . And that's what I do, and that is what you can do."[37]

Zyshe said simply: "Much to my regret and sorrow, that wasn't me." Comparing himself to his father and brother, he concluded, "I wasn't up to such standards."[38] Nothing convinced him to change his mind, even though he understood the needs of the Hasidim. Informally, he helped facilitate the activities of the court, all the while fleeing the authority and imputed charisma of office a rebbe would have. He became a computer programmer, and later in 1998 began to work at the Union of Orthodox Jewish Congregations of America, serving as its "Webbe Rebbe," a kind of virtual rebbe, responding to the many kashruth questions e-mailed to its kosher certification division.[39] For the small court, things might have continued this way, but in 2003 Zyshe suddenly died as a result of a freak accident.[40] Once again the question of Kopyczynitz succession arose.

There were the sons-in-law, who in theory might have been suitable candidates for successor. But by 2003 they were mostly gone from the scene. Ephraim Horowitz, the oldest of them, had perished in the Holocaust. Schneur Zalman Gurary, the second one, who actively lived the Hasidic life, preferred to retain his deep Lubavitcher affiliations.[41] The Sixth Lubavitcher Rebbe had urged him to move out of his father-in-law's house, and Gurary had done so, becoming a key figure in running Lubavitcher yeshivas.[42]

The third son-in-law, Aaron David Flintenstein, had been dead fifteen years, and the fourth, Aaron Gartenhaus, had been dead for more than twice that.[43] So too had all the others.[44] With Zyshe's tragic death, Kopyczynitz had reached a dead end.

Perhaps as a reflection of the revitalization of Hasidism in the late twentieth and early twenty-first centuries, Yitzchok Meir Flintenstein, the only son of Aaron David and Batsheva, years later anointed himself as a rebbe in Israel, calling himself the Rebbe of "Kopyczynitz-Jerusalem." By invoking this hyphenated title, however, he meant to indicate that, as his aunt, Moshe Mordechai's dowager *rebbetzin*, had insisted, he would not succeed either his uncle or his grandfather.[45] Kopyczynitz remained a court in search of a rebbe.

In 1999, together with the assistance of his mother and older brothers, Moshe's youngest son, Avraham Heschel, founded Chasdei Moshe-Kopyczynitz, an outreach organization dedicated in memory of his father.[46] In 2015, Mordechai Twersky, American-born son of Perel and Yaakov Yosef, who had been a journalist living in Israel, declared his intention to activate his paternal and maternal Hasidic heritage and decided to call himself the Azarnitz-Chotiner-Kopyczynitz Rebbe.[47] But he too made no claims to be the successor to his maternal grandfather, and as of 2015 he had few if any Hasidim who looked upon him as their leader.

THE BOYAN SUCCESSION

Boyan seemed also to be heading toward a dead end. For years Friedman led his Hasidim from his headquarters on the Lower East Side, although in his last years he also maintained a small synagogue in an elegant building on Manhattan's Upper West Side, far from the Hasidic heartland. Throughout, he remained open to the modern world, and people who might not have worshipped in a Hasidic synagogue found their way to his. He traveled America, trying to build followers, even at a time that the trends in America were away from Orthodoxy.[48] While spending hours alone in his private room next to the main study hall "hunched over the Talmud" and hallowed by his followers, he stayed in touch with the outside world. That was probably why some of those he attracted were modern Orthodox who saw in this rebbe someone who could understand and maybe even sympathize with their religious and contemporary life choices. Such rebbes were increasingly difficult to find.

As Hasidism flourished in America and in Israel, the Boyaner, who became vice president of Agudath Israel in America and a member of its council of Torah sages, experienced the pressures that had gradually become part of the Hasidic and ultra-Orthodox world to separate from or even demonize modern America culture and secular Israel.[49] These pressures were particularly powerful in Israel and perhaps nowhere more than in Jerusalem, where he helped establish the large Ruzhin Yeshiva, which would one day be the headquarters of his successor. According to his grandson, from his first visit in 1949 to his fourth and last in 1960, whenever the rebbe would call on the Hasidim there, his wife would be given a list of restrictions, including, for example, not to wear lipstick.[50] Yet Mordechai Shlomo was able throughout his days to navigate the narrowing path between the growing insularity of late twentieth-century Hasidism and the more open approach that he had settled on in America.

In 1967, the year the Kopyczynitzer Rebbe died, Mordechai Shlomo suffered a massive stroke and ceased to function fully as rebbe. For a while his wife mediated between him and his Hasidim, but then she too suffered the same fate. In March 1971, the rebbe suffered a second fatal stroke.

The rebbe had known for many years that the question of who would succeed him was complicated. He watched as his older brother Menachem Nachum, Rebbe of Chernovitz, had died in 1936 of kidney disease and as the older of his sons, Aaron, refused for more than a year to succeed him, only to be taken by the Nazis two years later and killed with his younger brother and their families.[51] He saw that his second brother, Israel (1878–1951), had two daughters whose husbands did not become his successors. His third brother, Avraham Ya'akov (1881–1941), was killed in Lemberg and had no successors. By 1971, all that was left of the Boyan *rebistve* was Mordechai Shlomo's. But he had not made a choice for a successor, understanding that even within his family the possibilities were limited. Boyan was at risk of going the way of Kopyczynitz.

For the Hasidim, there was no obvious solution. By now most of the active and engaged Boyaner Hasidim were in Israel, while a smaller number were dispersed throughout Manhattan and Brooklyn. Any new rebbe would probably have to relocate to Israel, adding a complication to the succession.

Mordechai Shlomo's eldest son, Israel, held a high position in the New York City Welfare Department. His wife Nathalie, the widowed daughter of Rabbi Joseph Lookstein, one of the preeminent modern Orthodox leaders of New York, held a PhD in sociology from Columbia University and was a professor at Barnard College; her engagement with modernity was a matter of principle and family pride. She did not cover her hair as most Hasidic women did and was known to be freethinking, so she would never be a suitable *rebbetzin*.[52] Although she had children from her first marriage, Israel and Nathalie had no children of their own who might theoretically be candidates for succession. The Hasidim's obvious reluctance to try to persuade Israel to succeed as rebbe—dramatized when, upon his return from his father's funeral attended by more than twenty-five thousand people in Israel, none of the local Boyaner Hasidim came to meet him at the New York airport, as would be expected for a man who would be their leader—spoke volumes.[53]

In spite of their mutual misgivings and all these issues, the Hasidim and Israel Friedman talked briefly about his taking over his father's *rebistve*. But with Hasidism in Israel—and in America too—sliding toward the religious right, a modern Orthodox executive with a sociologist wife was not a good fit for them.[54]

"I could not," he explained in an interview, "give up all my worldly interests to become somebody who was at the beck and call of a very strict Orthodox community, especially the one in Israel." Nor, as he added, did he "see anything wrong" with having children "going to college," a prospect that the Hasidic world increasingly considered beyond the pale.[55] If the Boyan court led by his father had once accepted that possibility, it now no longer would.[56] Any successor to his father had to feel comfortable going where his Hasidim could follow, and they had to believe his entire being was shaped to their spiritual, social, and concrete needs. Although he ran the small Boyaner synagogue on Manhattan's West Side, Israel never took the next step.[57]

The Hasidim whose center of gravity had shifted from New York to Israel put their collective energy into enlarging their institutions there, knowing that while their yeshiva drew students they had a pipeline for bringing young people to Boyan. The older Hasidim, however, realized that without a successor rebbe they would have a hard time holding onto those young people and would risk ultimately losing them to one of the many competing courts and their charismatic rebbes. Indeed, some did move to the Sadigura Rebbe.

The Hasidim could have turned next to Israel's brother Yitzchok, but they understood that as an architect, engaged in real estate construction, he was even less likely than his brother to abandon his way of life to be their rebbe. They went next, therefore, to the late rebbe's daughter, Malka. A graduate of Brooklyn College with an MA degree in chemistry, she was married to Menachem Mendel Brayer, who, although having Hasidic roots and ordained as a rabbi, held doctorates in biblical studies and clinical psychology, while serving as a practicing psychotherapist as well as a professor of education in Yeshiva University. With his full beard and distinguished bearing (and the fact that on Sabbaths he sometimes wore a caftan), Brayer retained an image that some felt could morph him into a rebbe.

The Brayers lived in Washington Heights close to Yeshiva University (later moving to the Bronx) and summered at Sackett Lake in the Catskill Mountains, where Menachem Mendel played a kind of *shtikel* (partial) rebbe role in the small bungalow colony. Perhaps with a little encouragement he could be nudged away from his more worldly pursuits to trade his doctoral accomplishments, his academic career, and all his other lives for the Boyan crown. True, a life in the university was usually an unforgivable sin for a rebbe—as Moshe Leib of Munkács had argued to his father—but the Hasidim were desperate to find a candidate from within the family, and they trusted that Brayer was past the point of being damaged by his encounter with university life. They could explain his involvement in it as dictated by the needs of a livelihood and say that now those needs no longer existed.

Indeed, Brayer once told an interviewer, "When I am with Hasidim wearing Hasidic garb, I am a Hasid, period, totally divorced from the outside world." [58] He sometimes spoke at a Boyaner *tish* and felt that he was helping "keep the Hasidim together." [59] The famous Rabbi Yitzchak Hutner, the head of the Chaim Berlin Yeshiva, reportedly tried to persuade Brayer to take on the role, promising him that if "you become Rebbe, I'll give you the first *kvittel*," meaning he would publicly acknowledge Brayer's power to bestow blessings. [60] Brayer replied, "I never considered myself as being a Rebbe—far from it." [61]

His two sons nevertheless believed his distance was not so absolute. Indeed, perhaps because of who did ultimately become the successor, Brayer's obituaries in the ultra-Orthodox press when he died in 2007 focused exclusively on his Jewish accomplishments, referring to him as "the Hasidic scholar, the renowned pleasant and wise man, their crowning glory. A great leader in [the people of] Israel. Sharp and knowledgeable in all the inner workings of the Torah, a great scholar, who disseminated Torah among the flocks." [62] During the week of the shivah in Jerusalem where he had closed out his life, and after a new Boyaner Rebbe had long been appointed, hardly a word was mentioned about his academic achievements.

FASHIONING A REBBE FROM SCRATCH

With the idea of Professor Brayer as the successor fading away, the Hasidim turned now to their late rebbe's grandsons, the Brayer children. These young boys were holy seed—more legitimate claimants than their father, who was only a son-in-law. The heads of the yeshiva in Israel had observed them from afar. But now they focused upon them with far greater interest—particularly on the older of the two boys: Yisrael Avraham, known as "Yigal."

The Brayers were not going to force this sort of responsibility on their sons, but they were willing to set in motion events that might lead one of them to consider the possibility. Yigal was sent to Israel, after high school, for three years studying in the Ruzhin Yeshiva in Jerusalem. As first son he was the natural first choice. He was made painfully aware that for ten years since his grandfather's death the Hasidim had been without a rebbe and that they needed a successor. In the yeshiva, he was given special classes, private tutors, and special attention. Unlike his uncles and his father, he had as yet not committed himself to another life and could be fashioned into someone able and ready to continue the line. The old Hasidim, remembering the old ways, would aid in his makeover. As he would recall years later, he felt "like a rebbe in training." [63] He received rabbinic ordination and for a while thought that perhaps he could do the job. He felt a sense of responsibility to the Boyan tradition and understood that as the oldest grandson he was a crown prince.

But living inside the Hasidic world now, he saw close up the people he would have to lead and the life he would have to have among them: he would need to leave behind forever the far more modern American environment to which he remained attached. He surely realized that as a rebbe, within the far more restricted cultural and social—and even political—world of Israeli Hasidism as it had evolved, he would not lead even the sort of mildly open life his grandfather had had. He would have to marry someone the Hasidim considered suitable, and his private life would be far more limited than he could imagine. Pondering all this, he found overwhelming the weight of the crown the Hasidim wanted to place on him.

Years later, when speaking about those obituaries of his father in the ultra-Orthodox press that had entirely ignored his academic accomplishments, Yigal expressed exasperation at how that side of him, which the son respected and had been proud of, was so meaningless to the Hasidim. He could not lead people who would hide it. During those years of the late 1970s, he came to believe the role was not for him.

"I avoided making a decision for three years," he recalled. In the end, he returned to America, going on to get a degree in engineering at the City College of New York and ultimately becoming a rocket scientist. Yigal, in chronicling the family's Hasidic history, said half jokingly and half seriously that maybe he had refused the position of rebbe back then partly because he had suspected, from seeing his father act a bit like a rebbe, that his father, in some corner of his mind, "wanted it for himself."

Even when he worked as an engineer in California, Yigal—reflecting some of the same ambivalence that his father had felt—set up a kind of one-room chapel where "I played the role." But he did so avocationally, not as a calling, nor did he ever see himself as an object of veneration. Some of his congregants were former devotees of Shlomo Carlebach's House of Love and Prayer in San Francisco, while others were Los Angeles exiles, Californian seekers. In the end he gave up even that limited role, worshipping in a ChaBaD congregation in Long Beach, California, where he often was the Torah reader. His career remained in aerospace.

With the oldest grandson out of the running, the Brayers' younger son, Nachum Dov, five years Yigal's junior, became the Hasidim's person of interest. A letter written to Professor Brayer requested that the boy be sent to the yeshiva in Israel on the occasion of his grandfather's *yarzheit* (the anniversary of his passing). Four years after Yigal's trip, Nachum Dov followed.

In the accounts that emerged after Nachum Dov became successor, all the candidates who preceded him disappear from the record. For example, a recent version of the story of Nachum Dov's ascension to the throne tells the following tale:

> It is Adar 5731/1971 on a side street in Haifa, and two young Gerrer chassidim are pressing Rabbi [not Professor or Dr.] Menachem Mendel Brayer to meet with their rebbe, the Beis Yisrael [Yisrael Alter (1895–1977), the fourth Gerrer Rebbe]. The timing seems strange. Just days before, Rabbi Brayer's esteemed father-in-law, Rav Mordechai Shlomo Friedman of Boyan had left This World [*sic*]. The Boyaner Rebbe's two sons will carry on his activities, but neither will assume the position of rebbe. Rabbi Brayer, the Rebbe's son-in-law, is a scholar and author whom the Rebbe admired and loved—but has also refused the rabbinic mantle.

The complexities of succession are barely hinted at; what is fit for inclusion is only the summons to the leader of Israel's largest Hasidic group, a man who is revered as a member of the generation of Holocaust survivors and as a link between European Hasidism and the postwar generation, someone who by 1971 has become a towering figure in the political and social firmament of Israeli if not world Hasidism. The Gerrer Rebbe is concerned about Boyan continuity. As the story goes on,

> Just a few hours later, Rabbi Brayer is in the Gerrer Rebe's Yerushalayim [Jerusalem] home. "I hear that you have a son close to bar mitzvah age," the Beis Yisrael said. "You must provide him with the proper education, because when the time is right, he will become the Rebbe of Boyan." [64]

NACHUM DOV

When his grandfather died, Nachum Dov was about twelve. His memories of the rebbe were shaped by family occasions—especially the Jewish holidays—that he had spent with him. More than forty years later he still recalled them, as well as his first realization that his grandfather was not like everyone else's. At the Hasidic *tish* over which his grandfather presided, the boy played under the table. As he grew older, he was struck by those who came for the old man's blessings and counsel, how they danced with joy when they were in his grandfather's presence, and how he sensed that "something very special" was happening.[65] The visitors from Israel were not like those whom the young boy encountered in his life in New York. "Someone from *Eretz Yisrael* [the Land of Israel] was like a *chefetz shel mitzvah* [a special article used for a religiously significant act]."

He was drawn to these Boyaner Hasidim from Israel. Years later, when he joined them as a young boy in the yeshiva, he felt the same special attraction. Together with them, his memories of his grandfather sharpened. He remembered asking his sister, "Is *Zaide* [Grandpa] a *zaddik?*"

"Of course," she replied.

Overhearing this little conversation, his grandfather turned to the boy's father and said in his modest way, "*Nu,* if the kids make that mistake that I'm a *zaddik,* it's not a problem; but let's hope the older people don't make this same mistake of thinking I'm a *zaddik.*" For the boy, who would succeed to the same throne, the memory captured his grandfather's special humility and served as a lesson for him to never be carried away by his sense of grandeur—even if those around him thought him extraordinary.

Perhaps because he was younger and more impressionable, or perhaps because there was something in his character that resonated with the Hasidic and mystical aspect of his heritage, Nachum Dov—though by no means eager to take up the task of being a rebbe at age fifteen—did not have the same misgivings about leaving his American life that his older brother had had. Or perhaps he did not quite realize how radical the change would be if he did become a rebbe.

Before his preparation for succession, Nachum Dov had studied in yeshivas that were quite traditional. In elementary school he had attended Yeshiva Zichron Moshe, which featured instruction in Yiddish and was headed by Rabbi Yerucham Gorelick (1911–83), who came from Slutsk, Belarus, and had studied in the famous non-Hasidic yeshiva there. The school aroused in Nachum Dov a veneration for European traditions. When his father took the family on a sabbatical to Jerusalem, his son attended the Ruzhin Yeshiva, even though they lived in the distinctly non-Hasidic neighborhood of Rechavia. Returning to America, his parents sent him to high school at the Chasam Sofer Yeshiva in Brooklyn, and for a few months a year he was instructed by a Boyaner Hasid, Eliezer Rabinowitz, who taught him about the customs of Boyan. Perhaps all that made him more open to the idea of becoming his grandfather's successor.

"It's his own choice," his father had said when the Hasidim came to ask that the younger son become their leader, adding, "Maybe he wants to be a doctor."

"A rebbe is also a doctor," one of them replied, "a doctor of the *neshama* [soul]."

While Nachum Dov loved the experience of learning in the yeshiva, like Moshe Leib of Munkács he did not feel ready to embrace fully the idea of being a rebbe and deferred his answer to the calls that, once the leaders and *gabbaim* among the Hasidim decided he could be their leader, steadily increased. "I put it out of my mind."

The later hagiographic accounts describe those days altogether differently. "The distinguished chassidim who'd been charged with the sensitive task of preparing the future Rebbe for his position were surprised to discover his knowledge of the secrets of Ruzhiner leadership. . . . In their conversations with him, these early mentors ascertained that the future leader of Boyan already possessed a noble character and rare spiritual stature." [66]

Nachum Dov was increasingly invited to "sit at the dais at every gathering of the Hasidim," a visual signal of his impending coronation. [67] The fact that elders among the Hasidim appeared to defer to him in public underscored his privileged position.

A SPECIAL MARRIAGE

As long as he remained unmarried, Nachum Dov could not be a rebbe, so a match had to be found. The solution would revitalize another branch of the family even as it completed the steps for the continuity of this one. Like royalty of all sorts, Hasidism had over the years evolved a pattern of marriage that encouraged endogamy, so that the high status and charisma of select families could be preserved rather than becoming diluted. In Kabbalistic terms, they also saw this as a way of creating offspring who were more intensely holy. Such matches forged alle-giances and alliances between courts, while creating a separate class of people who were like royalty and considered exceptional. When mem-bers of this class wed outside the family, the marriages were with people who were self-made, by either the superior Torah scholarship of a young man or the financial prowess of the parents, or who had the high social standing of an elite family, with accomplishments perceived as reflecting divine favor.

For Nachum Dov, the rebbe-in-waiting, a rendezvous with the daughter of Zyshe Heschel of Kopyczynitz was arranged. She too had come from America and was studying in a girls' seminary in Jerusalem. After several meetings, including one at the Brayers' summer house at Sackett Lake, the nineteen-year-old Shoshana, granddaughter of the Kopyczynitzer Rebbe, and the now twenty-year-old grandson of the Boyaner Rebbe agreed to marry in Jerusalem in June 1980. Their wed-ding, officiated by Moshe Yehoshua Hager, the great rebbe of Vizhnitz in B'nai B'rak, and attended by all the rebbes descended from the Ruzhin dynasty, would breathe new life into the two related courts.[68]

Married, and in the minds of the Hasidim ready to take up the reins of leadership, Nachum Dov still tried to put off his succession. As he later recalled, he "didn't want to think about it too much," hoping "something else would happen," though he could not imagine what that something else would be. Perhaps, he mused, "Moshiach [the Messiah] would come," changing the course of all events and ending the pressure on him. References to the Messiah always emerge when succession is problematic. But the Messiah did not come and the succession moved forward.

After the wedding, Nahum Dov's uncles, father, and even his older brother felt relieved that he was now emerging as the anointed one to take on the responsibility they could and would not. A quarter of a century after his succession, Nachum Dov admitted privately that he still did not want the role, any more than he had at the beginning. He simply could no longer refuse it. With a sense of his destiny, he quoted the Psalmist: "The steps of a man are established by God, who desires his ways."[69]

JOINING THE FRATERNITY

Along with his father, many of "the most important rabbis and Hasidim" in the Ruzhin dynasty shared their knowledge and guided the young

American as he joined the fraternity of *zaddikim*. His great-uncle, the Sadigura Rebbe, Mordechai (Motl) Shalom Yosef Friedman (1897–1979), who had taken over the leadership of the court in Tel Aviv, took a special interest in him. Nachum Dov spent many Sabbaths, the day in the week when a rebbe's public activities were most dramatic, at the Sadigura court watching how the older man led a *tish*, offered words of Torah, greeted his Hasidim, and carried himself. Nachum Dov also visited the Mezhbizher Rebbe in Haifa, the Bohusher, and others of the Ruzhin dynasty to observe them in action. He took trips to visit other rebbes, ostensibly for their blessing before he formally took the position as leader but also to spread the word that he was joining their ranks and giving them a chance to express their assent to his ascent. As the neophyte, he needed to show this deference—and it was appreciated by the more senior rebbes, as reflected in their ultimate ratification and welcoming of him into their pantheon. He renewed the training he had begun years earlier with Eliezer Rabinowitz. In his imagination, the rebbe-in-training began to inhabit his family history, and gradually it filled the spaces of his personal past.

As the rebbes of leading courts in Israel accepted him into their rarified circle, he detached himself bit by bit from the American modern Orthodox life in which he had once been at home. The rebbes were all happy to take him in, not only because he was an eager and humble learner with a good pedigree, but also because in the intensifying contest for who would define the character of observant Orthodoxy they were convinced that their way was the right one and modern Orthodoxy was a historical and cultural aberration with no future. Nachum Dov's turn to the full-time Hasidic life was an important victory that confirmed their beliefs.

He visited the Gerrer Rebbes, Yisrael Alter and later his brother, Simcha Bunim Alter (1898–1992); the Klausenberger Rebbe, Yekusiel Yehudah Halberstam (1905–94), who had been close both to the Boyaner and Kopyczynitzer Rebbes; and even the Lubavitcher Rebbe, Menachem Mendel Schneerson in Brooklyn. They welcomed and encouraged him to follow the "special path" of Boyan, assuring him that they were certain his forebears wanted him to lead others on that path. To leave this path with no leader, to embrace the more modern options as other possible contenders for the role had done, was to reject the Hasidic renaissance they all espoused and incarnated. The "old boys' network" welcomed a new generation that guaranteed continuity.

When he shared his anxieties about taking on the responsibility of a rebbe's life, they confided that they too had had these feelings and doubts when they began. If he believed that he was different from them, he was wrong. He was one of them, and he needed to learn that "when the Almighty gives someone a job, he also gives him the strength and shows him the ways to do it."[70] Delaying the inevitable became more and more difficult.

TAKING ON THE CROWN

On the holiday of Sukkot in 1983, one of the elder Boyaner Hasidim turned to Nachum Dov with a simple argument that he believed would end his hesitations. In so many other Hasidic courts, he explained, there were several contenders for the crown—sons or sons-in-law, even brothers, who believed themselves suited to lead or whom various factions in the court championed. But in Boyan, *everyone* agreed that Nachum Dov was the one. He had not a scintilla of opposition, so why hesitate? The rebbe-select knew he was right. At last, a few months later, on Chanukah, nearly fourteen years after the death of his grandfather and almost four years after his wedding, Nachum Dov Brayer became the Boyaner Rebbe. He led his first *tish* on Friday night, December 2, 1983, and his second five days later on the last night of the holiday—often referred to as *zot Chanukah*. He donned a *kolpik,* the tall brown-furred hat worn by his predecessors, and he accepted the petitions of his Hasidim (figures 6 and 7).

Many Boyan Hasidim of his generation had never had a direct encounter with a rebbe of their own or had been preschoolers when the previous rebbe died. Most would not even be able to compare their new rebbe with memories of his predecessor. Indeed, many had never lived in either Vienna or New York. They were Israelis, and Jerusalem was their home. The new rebbe would have to stay here with them, in the more aggressively Orthodox fundamentalist culture of Israeli Hasidism.

For the few old-timer Hasidim who had been waiting for this day, Nachum Dov's physical resemblance to his grandfather and his similar gestures fired their enthusiasm and brought tears to their eyes. Their excitement inspired the younger generation. With the unpretentiousness that would mark him, Nachum Dov, recalling that reaction, said, "It was all because of the *kolpik.*"

But it was not just the hat on his head that convinced the Hasidim they had a new rebbe. His acceptance of *kvittlach* was the signal event, making him the focus and locus of devotion, a magnet for the Hasidim. No longer would they submit these requests (as they had for years in the

6. Nachum Dov Brayer, the current Boyaner Rebbe, wearing a *kolpik* peaked hat, dancing with his father, Professor Menachem Brayer. By permission of Yigal Brayer.

7. Nachum Dov Brayer walking with his father. By permission of Yigal Brayer.

absence of their own rebbe) to Yitzchak Friedman, Rebbe of Bohush and dean of the Ruzhin dynasty, who was nearly seventy years older than their new rebbe.

In the years before his ascension to the throne, they had been on their own, going to other rebbes and gathering for prayers in a variety of places and times; now they all began to pray together with their own rebbe and broke bread at his *tish*.

Emile Durkheim has argued that religion is created and sustained out of moments of "collective effervescence," moments when a group of otherwise separate individuals comes together to perform a ritual that holds cultural, social, and spiritual importance for them.[71] The process of coming together, in which everyone communicates, experiences, and participates in the same actions, thoughts, and feelings—particularly when they also recite or sing the same words in unison—not only unifies individuals in ways that are special but also creates a certain extra energy or collective effervescence that they feel. These group prayers and gatherings with the rebbe were such moments, and they projected all those feelings onto him.

Their new rebbe made the Hasidim feel as if they were animated by an outside force that made them stronger and lifted them to a higher spiritual level than they had been for years. They felt transported to new spiritual heights, elevated outside themselves and their individual lives. These feelings were of course reflections of their own collective energy, voices, and devotions that as one they focused upon him.[72] But they remained persuaded that he, their holy man and leader, was responsible for the "unbelievable change" in their community, as the rebbe's *gabbai*, Mordecai Dovid Schneid, put it.[73]

LIFE AS A HOLY MAN

The young rebbe did not always find it easy to be their holy man. He found giving blessings quite daunting, especially when people came near him for a magic touch, bared their souls to him, and asked him to intercede for them with God. Even after other rebbes had given him "the secrets of the trade," as he put it, this was difficult. When people handed him a *pidyon* of significant monetary value, which they barely could afford, in the hopes that he would help, he admitted he could respond only by imagining himself as the petitioner turning to a trusted "brother."[74] It was also difficult to remain humble, especially when everyone surrounding him thought him so endowed with the gift of grace.

"Sometimes," Nachum Dov explained, "the rebbe feels at first that he is simply unable to help, that he has no advice to give. But the hasid, through his faith, can generate the help he needs, can elicit the right advice. In hasidic thought, faith is not only belief; it is a force through which a person can bring about the thing he needs." [75] This psychological insight reflected a modern man's sensitivity—if not that of a devoted son of a psychologist—to the power of suggestion and its capacity to transform not only the petitioners but also the petitioned. With it, the rebbe freed himself of the assertion that he was the power behind the fulfillment of his followers' prayers; they were the agents themselves.

About seven years into his *rebistve,* he told an interviewer that among rebbes there was a belief "that the first answer that comes to one's mind is the right answer." He sometimes felt this to be true for himself. "I find this ability developing with time. But it's not in my *zechus* [merit]. I don't attribute it to myself." Then he added, "If a person believes that God can help him, if he believes in the *zechus* of the *zaddik,* then it happens. Even if the *zaddik* feels that it is not through his *zechus.*" [76]

The late Bostoner Rebbe Levi Yitzchak Horowitz expressed this idea in a pithy story. "A Hasid comes to the rebbe and says: 'Rebbe, I dreamed that I became a rebbe,' to which the rebbe replies: 'Yes, but did any Hasidim dream it too?'" [77] As the Boyaner Rebbe described it, his Hasidim were dreaming that with him as their leader their brand and group would have greater power, esteem, and influence in the Hasidic world.

The reputation of the new rebbe grew with the enthusiasms of his Hasidim. That in turn increased the crowds, which of course, mobilized and magnified the charismatic nature of those collective gatherings with the rebbe. Even the new rebbe could feel himself transformed in the process, although he always described this transformation with a kind of bemused humility. He learned the craft. The new rebbe understood that his role, the pillar of history on which he stood, made his petitioners see him in a different way. "When a hasid comes to consult his rebbe," Nachum Dov explained, "that is a special occasion. The hasid prepares himself. The rebbe has prepared himself too." It was a special spiritual encounter. But as for himself, "I don't feel that I talk any differently. I try to think and act the same with people as when I'm by myself. I don't see any difference in myself." [78] If a Hasid saw or felt a special power in him, thought of him "in magical or mystical terms— that's his side of the story," as the rebbe put it. [79]

Money flowed in to enlarge the yeshiva in Jerusalem and to build a new one in Brooklyn. Nachum Dov's success in building Boyan neighborhoods in the new settlement of Beitar Illit, a town in the northern

8. Nachum Dov Brayer lighting the pyre in Meron on Lag B'Omer, with his father, Professor Brayer, at his side. By permission of Yigal Brayer.

Judean Hills not far from Jerusalem that was becoming a *haredi* redoubt, as well as some in Modi'in Illit in the West Bank territory and Kiryat Gat in the area near Beersheba, the popular growth of Boyan schools that were attended by many young *haredi* youngsters, boded well for the future.[80] In today's Hasidic precincts success is measured not only by the charisma of the rebbe but by the ability to grow in numbers and create *mosdos,* institutions. Nachum Dov did both well.

As Boyaner Rebbe he had a high-profile role in the emerging Hasidic traditions of Israel; he was the one who lit the great bonfire on Lag B'Omer on the roof above the grave in Meron of the famous Rabbi Shimon Bar Yochai, a ritual that had become tremendously important to many of the Hasidim (figure 8). This privilege was purchased by Yisrael Friedman, the Rebbe of Ruzhin, who bequeathed it to his son Avrohom Yaakov Friedman, the first Sadigura Rebbe, from the guardians of Meron and Safed; the Sadigura Rebbe bequeathed this honor to his eldest son, Rabbi Yitzchok, the first Boyaner Rebbe, and his progeny.[81] For many years, the lighting was carried on by an emissary of the Boyaner Rebbe, Chief Rabbi Kaplan of Safed. Already as a teenager, Nachum Dov accompanied Kaplan, and when the older man died, as the rebbe he at last kindled on his own the great blaze that would burn for more than twenty-five hours.

9. Nachum Dov Brayer (center) praying incognito at a synagogue outside his court. Copyright Samuel Heilman.

Nachum Dov's days were long—often ending at 2:00 a.m.—and filled with activity. On a regular day, he would come downstairs around 6:00 a.m. from his apartment in Jerusalem's Makor Baruch neighborhood, immerse himself in a *mikveh* nearby, and then return to the chapel in his house. At 6:45 Boyaner boys on the cusp of their bar mitzvah might come by to don their *tefillin* for the first time and be taught by the rebbe how to properly do so. At 7:15 he would pray in the adjoining chamber to the chapel, and during the 2012–13 year he would enter the chapel to recite the Kaddish for his mother, whose death he was still mourning. After the nearly two-hour prayers he would have a regular session of Talmud learning with his study partner, Nochum Mordechai Tirhaus, a Hasid especially selected for his scholarship. He then sat at a large table covered with books, meeting with various people who sought his counsel, sometimes setting aside time for calls from around the world for his guidance. Mostly he met with men, but he would also sometimes meet with couples. Frequently, he would travel to satellite Boyan communities in Israel and abroad. Called upon to rally with other Hasidic rebbes on issues of political concern, he became a public figure. His endorsements of social protests and the like increasingly mattered. And of course he was the man of the hour on Lag B'Omer. Nachum Dov today leads a Boyan court that in numbers is the largest of all the Ruzhin dynasties.[82]

In later years, he would occasionally run away to a synagogue in Rechavia, where as a child he had prayed with his late father when the latter was on sabbatical, to "clear his head," as he put it. He needed a place where no one treated him as a rabbinic master, where he could pretend he was a simple Jew. There he sat quietly in the pews and prayed like everyone else, remembering perhaps the days before he was the Grand Rebbe of Boyan, when he was still the younger son of Professor Brayer (figure 9).

As his *gabbai,* the former American Mordecai Dovid Schneid, saw it, his rebbe's "old life was 'gone with the wind.'" Yet he had not changed the way he "sits on his chair, the color of his tie, nothing." In this world that tried so hard to hold on to the past, or at least its imagined image of the past, the absence of variation was viewed not as weakness but as strength and power. Schneid, who probably spends more time in the day with and around the rebbe than anyone, added, "In all the years I've been with him I never saw a single sign of regret, but I never saw a sign that he's happy with it either." And when the rebbe, now a grandfather and nearly thirty years on the job, was asked if he would recommend the job to his sons, he paused for a long time. "They themselves know that it's not easy." [83]

4

Bobov

A Clash of Families

Perhaps the fastest-growing Hasidic group in Brooklyn's Borough Park, the heartland of New York Orthodoxy, the Bobovers are embroiled in a bitter feud over who is the current rebbe.[1] The battling claimants to the title of Fifth Rebbe in the dynasty are Benzion Aryeh Leib Halberstam (figure 10), half brother of the Fourth Rebbe and son of the Third, and Mordechai Dovid Unger (figure 11), the younger son-in-law of the Fourth Rebbe. Both men lead courts just blocks apart. Each man and his Hasidim point to a line of succession leading inexorably to his being the legitimate holder of the crown. The battle in contemporary Bobov no longer represents just a spiritual and religious contest; it is about the power and appeal of an illustrious brand name and control over *mosdos,* the institutions of a complex organization and an international empire the founders of Hasidism could never have imagined.

WHO IS BOBOV?

Established in and named after the village of Bobov (Bobowa), Poland, the dynasty is an offshoot of the followers of Chaim Halberstam (1797–1876), the Rebbe of Sanz (Nowy Sącz) in southern Poland, who was also known as the Divrei Chaim. His grandson, Shlomo Halberstam (1847–1905), orphaned at eight years of age, became the First Bobover Rebbe, also known as the Ateret Shlomo. Like many of his cousins, he established his own following only after leaving Sanz, where others were

---

The Bobov Dynasty

SHLOMO HALBERSTAM (1847–1905): Known as the Ateret Shlomo;
First Bobover Rebbe

BENZION HALBERSTAM (1874–1941): Known as the Kedushas Zion;
Second Bobover Rebbe; son of Shlomo

SHLOMO HALBERSTAM (1907–2000): Known as the Kerem Shlomo;
Third Bobover Rebbe; son of Benzion

NAFTALI HALBERSTAM (1931–2005): Fourth Bobover Rebbe, in New
York; older son of Shlomo

BENZION ARYEH LEIB HALBERSTAM (1955–PRESENT): Fifth Bobover
Rebbe; younger son of Shlomo and half-brother of Naftali

MORDECHAI DOVID UNGER (1954–PRESENT): Rebbe of Bobov45;
son-in-law of Naftali Halberstam, the Fourth Rebbe

---

ahead of him in line to take leadership of that great dynasty. At the age
of seventeen, he moved first to the village of Bikofsk (Bukowsko), then
fifteen years later to Oświęcim (Auschwitz), and a year later about fifty
kilometers north of Sanz to Vishnitsa (Nowy Wiśnicz), Poland, where,
opening a yeshiva in 1881, he tried to establish a court. While his original supporters were Hasidim of his grandfather who turned to him
because he was a "holy seed" and local, over time his following grew on
his own merits. The yeshiva was critical for this; its students developed a
special closeness to him as its head. Later, when—ostensibly for health
reasons—he repaired to Bobov, about 60 kilometers to the southeast
and only 30 kilometers from Sanz and about 115 from the bigger city of
Kraków, the Ateret Shlomo took his yeshiva with him. In Bobov he and
later his son and successor attracted more followers. While his origins in
nearby Sanz remained important to his Hasidic pedigree, the Bobov
name gradually took on a reputation of its own. Many Kraków Jews and
others from Galicia also became Bobover Hasidim.

Born in Bikofsk, the Ateret Shlomo's only son, Benzion (son of Zion)
(1874–1941), a name reputedly given him by his grandfather, who believed
that in the child's lifetime the Almighty would rebuild Jerusalem and send
the Messiah to return the Jews to Zion, became known as the Kedushas
(holiness of) Zion after his book of the same name. Starting as a teacher
in the Bobover yeshiva, he took on more duties beginning in 1893, as
his father's health deteriorated.[2] Following his father's passing on July

10. Benzion Aryeh Leib Halberstam, the current (Fifth) Bobover Rebbe, with his aides and Hasidim. By permission of Duvid Singer.

11. Mordechai Dovid Unger, son-in-law of the Fourth Bobover Rebbe and now head of Bobov45, addressing his Hasidim at a *tish*. By permission of and copyright Stanley Weiss.

4, 1905, the thirty-one-year-old son succeeded him, becoming the Second Bobover Rebbe. Coming after his acting as a stand-in for his father during his physical decline, Benzion's transition had an air of inevitability. Lacking brothers to challenge his claim, he easily inherited the crown.

Benzion enlarged Bobover numbers, in part by establishing other branches of the yeshiva throughout Galicia. Not only was the Second Bobover Rebbe a Hasidic and spiritual leader, he was also known for the way he used his yeshivas and summer camps to "civilize" the young boys who studied in them. Many of these youngsters from small villages were sons of simple folk, with little knowledge of the world. "He would take these 'Mountain Jews' who didn't own a pair of shoes and would make *mentshen* [civilized people] out of them," not only "teaching them Torah" and Hasidism, but also "teach[ing] them how to speak properly, teach[ing] them how to eat using cutlery—fork and knife—and how to take care of themselves." [3] Many of the alumni became important leaders in other yeshivas throughout Poland and Ukraine, thereby spreading the reputation and authority of their rebbe and of Bobover Hasidism. The fact that the cities of Kraków and Tarnów, with their thousands of Jews, many of whom embraced Hasidism, were not that far away also helped increase the influence and reputation of the Bobover Rebbe in the region.[4] Bobovers were known for their ability to maintain ties with more urbane Jews even as they were intensely Hasidic. Several of the rebbe's daughters married into genteel families.

The increasing mobility during the period allowed more Hasidim to come on pilgrimage to Benzion, further spreading Bobover influence. His creation of Bobover *mosdos* in various locales allowed a Hasid to move from one place to another while still praying or studying in Bobover institutions and thus to maintain his allegiance to the rebbe.

During the First World War, the Bobover Rebbe found refuge in sophisticated Vienna, establishing ties and raising his profile with a number of other Hasidic leaders who also moved there at the time. Following the Armistice, after some time in a spa at Marienbad, he returned to Bobov, though with a higher profile.[5] Finding the yeshiva building in ruins, he rebuilt and reestablished it at great personal expense by 1922, now calling it Etz Chaim, a tree of life, where in time it enrolled three hundred students.[6] As branches of the school and Bobover Hasidism continued to spread to other towns and villages, the rebbe became a larger-than-life figure in Poland (figure 12). By 1931, at least thirty yeshivas in the region had affiliated with Bobover Hasidism, and by the time

12. Photos of the Second, Third, and Fourth Bobover Rebbes adorning the wall of the old synagogue in Bobov, Poland. Copyright Samuel Heilman.

of the outbreak of the Second World War there would be forty yeshivas with about 1,500 students.[7] Alumni and their parents were everywhere.

The rebbe attracted followers not only because of his organizational abilities but also by virtue of his musical talents. The many tunes he composed became part of the repertoire of Hasidic music entering the synagogues. When the rebbe led prayers, he would stand near the open window, and crowds who could not get into the hall would stand outside to listen to his chanting and singing, all adding to his charisma and reputation as a spiritual giant.[8] Even university students and others who had abandoned ties to traditional Judaism or Hasidism were known to be attracted.

Benzion translated his fame to Jewish politics as leader of the Rabbinical Organization (Agudat HaRabonim) of Western Galicia (where increasingly rabbis in the villages and towns were Bobovers). Under his leadership, Bobover Hasidism developed a reputation for zealotry in its opposition to modernity, Zionism, acculturation, and those Jews who supported it.

With the rise of the Nazis, the rebbe and his Hasidim found themselves pursued, persecuted, and targeted for destruction. The story of their efforts to escape and what happened to the rebbe, his son Shlomo, his grandson Naftali, and the rest of the family became a foundation narrative for the Bobovers when they rebuilt themselves, their court, and the *rebistve* in the post-Holocaust world. It also complicated the line of succession. This story of death and miraculous rebirth is one that Bobovers, even those born after the war, have assimilated as if it were part of their personal biographies. Indeed, to understand the roots of the current conflict over succession, we need to briefly review that period that was so painful but also spiritually essential for them.

SURVIVAL AND SUCCESSION DURING THE HOLOCAUST

In 1939, like most of Polish Jewry, the Bobovers realized, perhaps too late, that what was happening in neighboring Germany would affect them profoundly. Three days before the September 1 German invasion into Poland, some Bobover Hasidim, sensing the precariousness of their situation, organized an escape for the rebbe, his sons, and his sons-in-law eastward toward the Soviet border and what they believed would be safety. The rumor was that only Jewish men were endangered. Protecting the rebbe and his holy seed was of paramount concern.

Wherever they went, they made contact with local Bobover Hasidim, who were also in fear about their own future and took their rebbe's arrival as a fortuitous sign from heaven. They believed that his holiness would shield them from calamity. In every Bobover outpost the locals were spiritually fortified by their sixty-five-year-old leader, whose royal bearing had always awed them but never more than now. His willingness to suffer the travails of the journey and to face the clear dangers of the road without panic or loss of dignity inspired them with confidence, even in the midst of their dread. All this took place during the Days of Awe in 1939, and the beginning of the High Holy Days of the Hebrew year 5700, a time when normally Hasidim made pilgrimage to him. At each stop, they converged around him. Yet he and his retinue kept on running for their lives.[9] Nevertheless, the Hasidim always believed that as long as "the holy Rebbe is still alive . . . we get our strength from him."[10]

With bombs exploding around them and obstacles everywhere, the escape was sapping Benzion's physical strength. The hope that he and his retinue would find safety near the Soviet border was fast fading. Still they pressed eastward. The Soviets, Benzion explained to the Kashivka Rebbe, whom he met en route, "are evil and there is a future danger to be under their power, but nevertheless, they do not murder [Jews] immediately [upon contact] as do the Germans, and in the interim perhaps the Almighty will help us."[11]

Finding themselves under Soviet control, the rebbe and those with him adapted to the new rules of communism, one of which was that all able-bodied males had to be employed. If they sustained themselves in any other way, they were labeled "speculators" and subject to sanction or arrest. What this meant for the rebbe or his retinue was unclear; religion—which was their vocation—was officially banned by the Soviets. Looking to escape Soviet control, they sought papers that would enable them to get to America.[12] For a while it looked as if they might be able to travel on Costa Rican passports. But the Soviets had other plans. Those who did not manage to escape were deported, mostly to the east.

Among those caught in the Soviet net were the rebbe's younger son Chaim Yehoshua and his family, who were exiled to Siberia. In hopes of retrieving them, Benzion reputedly refused the efforts to procure an exit visa to the United States. He soon changed his mind as the Nazi-Soviet pact fell apart and he prepared to reach Lvóv. But it was too late.

Late on the afternoon of July 25, 1941, the first day of the Hebrew month of Av—a month fraught with the sorrows of Jewish history—Nazis broke into the house where the rebbe was staying and captured him and those with him. Maintaining his dignity, he had donned his Hasidic finery: a *shtreimel* on his head and a fine brocade *kapote* or kaftan. Together with about a hundred other Jews collected from throughout the city, they were stood at a street-corner. The rebbe was beaten and his *shtreimel* knocked off; he bent down to pick it up. Several times this scene repeated itself. At last, on the orders of the Nazis, they began to walk. "Benzion was weak, and could not keep up with the fast pace of the march. When he fell to the back of the column, the policemen whipped him and shouted at him to move faster. The march continued until the prisoners arrived at the Gestapo headquarters. Rabbi Benzion's family tried everything to win their release, but after three days, he was executed at the Yanover forest together with his son Moshe, three sons-in-law, and the other prisoners."[13] Thus ended the second rebbe's reign over Bobover Hasidim. News of his tragic fate soon reached the Hasidim and his family.

SUCCESSION OF THE THIRD REBBE, SHLOMO HALBERSTAM

The ascent of the man who would become the Third Rebbe, Shlomo Halberstam, who would lead the Bobovers to resurrection and growth in America and the world, took place without any formal coronation. In those dark days no one knew if any future remained for Bobover

Hasidism. Shlomo was alive, but he had not been spared suffering, having been with his father during that fateful last journey. Indeed, he was himself on the run still.

This was not what anyone had imagined when he was born in Bobov on November 7, 1907. As the oldest son, he was heir apparent of this new and thriving dynasty. Raised and educated in the yeshiva in Bobov, a holy seedling raised and instructed by his father, he represented continuity and hope. In 1924, nearly eighteen, he married his cousin, Bluma Rachel Teitelbaum, whose mother was his father's sister and whose father was the *av beit din* (chief judge in the Jewish court—essentially chief rabbi) in Limanov.

While Shlomo effectively became the Third Bobover Rebbe in the midst of the Holocaust following his father's brutal murder, his succession had actually been prepared years earlier. The year was 1932 and Shlomo's father had reached the age of fifty-eight, the same age his own father had been when he passed away. Imagining that he too might be nearing the end of his days, Benzion resolved, much to the consternation of his Hasidim, to "exile himself" and his immediate family from his court in Bobov and move three hundred kilometers eastward to the town of Tschebin (Trzebinia). Before departing on his self-imposed separation, however, the rebbe was persuaded by his Hasidim to appoint his son, Shlomo, as head of the large Hasidic court in Bobov (*av beit din*), an honorific that effectively anointed him as the *rav-tza'ir* (*yinger ruv* [Yiddish], young rabbi), or crown prince.[14] Whether this appointment was really at the Hasidim's urging, as contemporary lore has it, or part of the father's strategy at a time when he thought he might be close to death to prepare for the ultimate transition to his heir, we cannot really be certain. But no doubt these events, puzzling as they might have seemed at the time, helped smooth the path to succession. The appointment provided the son ample opportunities to display his leadership abilities during his father's lifetime.

Benzion's removal to his "exile" did not really cut him off from his Hasidim. "Rabbi Benzion resided in Trzebinia from 1932–1937, and thousands of his disciples streamed to his court, mostly on the Sabbath and festival days. Many of the town's residents, including those who lived there during those years, made their livelihood through their proximity to the court of the Rebbe."[15] In the meantime, Shlomo, who ran the larger home court in the village of Bobov, grew in social stature through his leadership of the yeshiva, where he also offered a regular discourse. His organizational abilities helped him establish more branches of the yeshiva. His reputation as an up-and-coming leader grew, especially among the younger Hasidim in the yeshivas. Indeed, when his father sent Shlomo's younger brother Moshe back from Tschebin to study with and be mentored by him, this further raised the rebbe-in-waiting's reputation in the eyes of the Hasidim. Even when at last his father returned to Bobov from his sojourn in Tschebin, Shlomo continued to run the day-to-day activities at the court and serve as *av beit din*. While the Rebbe Benzion's word was always paramount, the Hasidim's assurance that his son, Shlomo, knew precisely what his father's will was and had the elder man's full confidence and even shared in the instruction and guidance of his younger brothers allowed him to become a powerful intermediary between them and his father. For the yeshiva students, he was the most immediate representative of Bobov, and as they grew to maturity so did he and his authority over them.

Traveling throughout Poland and to all the branches of the yeshiva, Shlomo became the face of Bobov. When disputes among Jews arose that made it into the state or regional courts, it was not unheard of for judges to turn to the Bobover court and its *av beit din* for some guidance on how to resolve matters. The fact, as well, that Moshe Stempel, who had married Moshe's sister in a wedding that "was widely reported in all the Yiddish newspapers," was the son of a member of the Polish Parliament and a wealthy man whose family owned a chain of well-known hotels, a founder of the Agudat Yisrael Party as well as a communal leader in Kraków, only enhanced the sense that the Bobovers and their rebbe and his heir were more than simply a parochial group of Galician Hasidim.

When in 1936, in what was a continuing controversy in Poland, if not a barely camouflaged attack on Jews, the government prohibited kosher slaughter of meat, on the pretext of its cruelty to animals (though many saw it as an effort to remove the lucrative business of butchering from Hasidic and Jewish control), Bobovers led the resistance to this. A sixteen-day meat boycott supported by them demonstrated to authorities that Jews could learn to live without meat and hurt the government tax coffers. In short, by the mid-1930s, the Bobovers and their rebbe were a force to be reckoned with and one that seemed to have its house in order.

BOBOV ON THE RUN

All this influence and activity, and the expected transition from Benzion to Shlomo, were thrown into chaos, as we have seen, by the outbreak of the war. By the time Shlomo and his father found themselves on the run and living under Soviet rule, they were no longer a force to be reckoned with but Jews trying survive. Yet it was their connection to the large network of Bobover Hasidim and supporters that would in the end be the key link to their survival.

Life under the Soviets was bitter, and it made the Bobovers understand that however bad things were for Jews under the Nazis, life under the communists was only marginally better. Jews were often terrorized by the locals. Like everyone else, they needed to find official registered work. Before his murder, Benzion had urged his sons and sons-in-law to find some formal occupations. Now, most of the holy seeds found jobs as factory workers, often completing their jobs at home.[16]

With some help from connections and from bribes, Shlomo found a job as a factory night watchman. But this was no simple position. As the communists took over and confiscated private property, former owners might be expected to steal from their factories and former property in order to salvage what they could sell on the black market and thereby support themselves and their families. This made the job of a watchman more than a sinecure. Watchmen needed to be snitches. Alternatively, they might be accomplices to the thefts, or assumed to be by the authorities. Shlomo was in constant danger as he walked through the various parts of the factory seven nights a week in the dark, and he barely eked out a living to support himself and those dependent upon him. Still the job was viewed as a godsend, since it did not require major desecration of the Sabbath. But when after a few months as part of the position he was required to frisk and empty the pockets of all workers leaving the factory, he quit and found work in a rope mill, remaining until the Nazi-Soviet pact collapsed in June of 1941 and the war brought the Germans into Lvóv.

There was one silver lining in this dark event. Now that the Nazis had advanced to where he was, Shlomo was no longer separated by a border from those who remained in Bobov. The family could be reunited. The death of Benzion and the others, however, changed everything.

For a brief time, Shlomo found work in the local *Judenrat* (Jewish council) and tried in this capacity to save Torah scrolls in advance of the destruction and confiscation of synagogues. The fact that he had this official position saved him for a time from the deaths and deportations that many other Jews suffered. Indeed, when his father, brothers, and brothers-in-law were rounded up and taken off to their deaths, that was how he and his son Naftali (who actually saw them loaded on a truck) managed to avoid being included.[17]

In July of 1941 in Lvóv (renamed Lemberg by the Germans), after he was effectively the new rebbe, still in mourning for his murdered father, one of Shlomo's first acts was to "cut off his beard and *payos* [earlocks]," for he realized that "his 'Jewish' appearance could only be a liability." [18] A rebbe on the run needed to look as Gentile as possible if he were to survive. Few other rebbes had ever experienced a succession like this one.

Broken in spirit by the events that had made him the leader of the Hasidim and his family, Shlomo realized that there was no reason left to remain in Lemberg. [19] His surviving brother, Yecheskel Dovid, who had become the rebbe in Pokshinvitz (Koprzywnica, Poland), a village some 140 kilometers northeast of Bobov where Jews were about a third of population in the 1920s or about eight hundred people, had returned to Bobov. [20] He and his sister Gitcha worked to get money to bribe the Gestapo for a travel permit and to send a car to pick up Shlomo and his family to get them back to Bobov.

No sooner did Shlomo and his son Naftali, now the new crown prince, return to Bobov than they learned that their presence there had been reported and that it was likely that the Gestapo would soon come to get them. Even though he had shaved his beard and shorn his earlocks in an effort to evade capture, he was certain he would be recognized here as the leader of Bobover Hasidism. [21] Two days after his arrival in Bobov in November of 1941, therefore, he and Naftali fled to Kraków, leaving behind his wife, mother, brother, and other children. [22]

From Kraków, the two great hopes for Bobov were hustled to Bochnia in southern Poland, where they hoped to "disappear" in the ghetto there. In January 1942, Shlomo's wife, younger children, and mother-in-law joined more than eight thousand Jews who flooded into what would become a large labor camp in Bochnia. Shlomo's mother, the dowager *rebbetzin* Chaya Freidel, remained in Bobov with her son Yecheskel Dovid and her six daughters and grandchildren. [23]

Through the skills of one or two of his Hasidim with a talent for forging documents, Shlomo acquired false papers as a Hungarian. Identified thus as one Germans called an *auslander* (foreigner), he was able to escape the restrictive boundaries of the Bochnia ghetto, as well as to help others flee by providing them with forged papers or with food. [24] "A Rebbe who is not willing to descend into hell in order to rescue his followers," Kalonymus Kalman Shapira, the Piaseczner Rebbe who, turning down opportunities to escape, perished in a labor camp in 1943, was reputed to have said, "is not a rebbe." [25] By this standard, Shlomo was still very much the Bobover Rebbe. Although he had not had a coronation and no longer looked like a Hasid, Shlomo's actions and experiences in these terrible days endowed him with a charisma of his own.

Among Shlomo's concerns was new work he got supervising delousing, running the bathhouse and showers, all part of a job he had been given by the *Judenrat*. He arranged for a clandestine *mikveh* or ritual bath, where some Jews immersed themselves in religious preparation for their death, to which they hoped to go in a state of religious purity. For Hasidim, immersion in a *mikveh* was a signature practice, and the fact that a rebbe was able to assist them in this was of high spiritual significance. This further raised Shlomo's profile among the devout, albeit in an underground and clandestine way.

The moral choices Jews had to make were overwhelming: whether to hide or not, whether to take their young children and babies into bunkers (where their cries might inadvertently alert the Gestapo and lead to the capture or death of all who hid along with them), whether to go on the transports with their loved ones or separate from them and try to hide or escape, and whether to arrange for children to be hidden among Gentiles. And what if the parents never came back alive to retrieve them and they were raised outside their Jewish faith? Was leaving them in the hands of Gentiles where they might convert to Christianity permissible, or was that a cardinal sin and, for the children, a fate worse than death? Accustomed to taking important questions in their lives (and even some simple ones) to their rebbes, many Bobovers came to Shlomo even in these days, and even though he was hiding his true identity, to ask for his guidance in these extraordinary matters.

The moral weight of such inquiries crushed the thirty-four-year-old. If in these days he began to think about abandoning the role of rebbe or questioning his position as a Hasidic master, feelings that would only grow as the situation grew ever more desperate, who could blame him? Again and again, he shaved his beard and cut any shred of earlocks so that he would not look like a Hasid, or even a Jew.[26] Yet Hasidim continued to look to him to help them through the moral and existential chaos in which they found themselves or for blessings before they met their fate. When he answered them, "You must do all in your power to save your children in any way that you can, and may the Almighty have mercy upon all of us speedily and in our days," they could only assume he had the strength he needed. But Shlomo was slowly losing what he had.[27]

In early September 1941, as he and his son Naftali reviewed the biblical portion of the week, including Deuteronomy 28—the curses the

Almighty vowed to inflict on the Jews in days to come—he confessed that only now did he fully understand the meaning of those verses.[28] As the gradual liquidation of the Jewish ghetto began, the two hid in a bunker with about fifty others. Those who had remained outside the ghetto walls, depending on their forged papers, were caught and killed on the spot; those boarding the transports went to their fate, mostly death and destruction. The few with Shlomo and Naftali in hiding managed to survive that day unscathed, but who can say with what degree of survivor guilt.

Coming out of hiding after the transports had departed, Shlomo sensed that the long-term prospects for his continued survival were poor. Indeed, on the Sabbath eve of February 27, 1942, the Gestapo arrested him. Imprisoned, he prepared himself spiritually and emotionally, thinking of himself as joining a long history of Jewish religious leaders whose murder over the generations by the enemies of the Jews had been understood as an expression of *Kiddush Hashem,* the sanctification of God's name—the ultimate Jewish sacrifice. He began reciting chapters of the Psalms, which he knew by heart, in spiritual preparation for his inevitable death at the hands of his persecutors. He also began to write a moral will in which he shared his religious and ethical thinking for his children and all those who might survive, proclaiming, "We must always believe [in the famous biblical oath] that 'we shall do and we shall listen' to the will of the Holy One, may He be our blessing, even when a sharp sword rests upon our neck." [29] But he did not finish the document, and when later in the night the door opened and his jailers came to get him, he whispered the words of the *Shema Yisrael* and the credo of *Ani Ma'amin,* expressing the confidence that the Messiah would soon arrive. The Gestapo led him into the dark streets, where he saw the Jewish policeman whose job was to carry the dead to the cemetery and called out to him to tell his wife to raise their children to fear God and observe his commandments. But the policeman assured him he was not about to be killed, and indeed after some further interrogations Shlomo was released, likely as a result of bribes that had been paid on his behalf by his supporters and Hasidim.

Back outside the ghetto with his forged papers, Shlomo would slip into the ghetto to spend some time with the remaining Bobover Hasidim. In secret gatherings at Sabbath's end, after curfew, when the Hasidim would gather together, hold hands, and form a silent circle, as if dancing and singing, he would offer hushed words of Torah, Hasidic teaching, and spiritual encouragement. At times he stole Naftali, who was eleven years old at the time, in with him, taking the risk that if he were caught on the streets after curfew they would both be punished, if not shot. He wanted the boy to see how a rebbe had to act. Shlomo talked a great deal about the idea of religious self-sacrifice and how to prepare for it, something he had learned about in these last months as never before. He argued that the best method to prepare for the imminent coming of the Messiah (whose arrival would surely end Jewish suffering, a belief that roared through the hearts of many of those whose belief in God's redemption rose in the face of horror) was to pave his way by saving Jewish children from death or abandonment at the hands of non-Jews.[30]

As the situation deteriorated in 1943 and another large transport of Jews from the Bochnia ghetto left for the concentration camps, a plan took shape to smuggle Shlomo and his family to Czechoslovakia via Neumark (Všeruby) on the German-Czech border and then on to Hungary, where Jews still were relatively safe. The family was divided into separate groups so as not to arouse suspicion, but at the train station in Podgórze near Kraków and a stone's throw from the infamous Płaszów concentration camp, Shlomo and Naftali, who were traveling together, were detained by the police after the son was identified by some local boys as "a little Jew."[31] Flashing his false papers, Shlomo successfully bribed their way onto the train and continued toward the border. By Friday, June 18, 1943, they reached Neumark, where the Gestapo, particularly interested in penetrating the network that had smuggled him thus far, were quick to arrest them. When Shlomo refused to reveal names, he and Naftali were thrown into a cell, after the youngster begged not to be separated from his father.

Covering their bare heads with their coats, they began the Sabbath prayers. Transported by their own chanting, Shlomo recalled that they had been on the verge of death before. But maybe this time they would not be saved. As he hovered between hope and despair, he wondered if this suffering was the famous birth pangs of the Messiah, moments before redemption. Perhaps his death would be prologue to Judgment Day. He turned to prepare his son for this moment of supreme sacrifice that he believed was now upon them.

"Naftali, my delight," he began, "know that a Jew's body is dust of the earth, and it is subject to death, but his soul remains eternal and no murderer or evildoer in the world can shoot at it. Today, Naftali, I am your father and you my son, and you can still perform the commandment of honoring thy father, one of the most solemn commandments in our Torah. Tomorrow, it seems, we shall be two souls together in the holiness of heaven. Do you know what an extraordinary merit it is for a Jewish soul to perform the commandment of sanctifying God, *Kiddush Hashem?* Tomorrow, if that be the will of the Holy One, Blessed be He, we two shall merit the fulfillment of that great commandment. In this final moment of our lives, I make of you, my son, one request." [32]

Naftali swore to abide by any and all requests his father made of him. The moment bound son and father together in ways that few could ever imagine, let alone experience.

"Do you recall," Shlomo continued to his son, according to an internal account, "[the holiday of] Simchas Torah in Bobov, when with complete happiness we danced with the Torah scrolls in our arms or the deep joy we shared baking *matzah* on the eve of Passover? In a few hours, the only *mitzvah* remaining for us to perform together will be that of *Kiddush Hashem,* which we must carry out with the same profound gladness. The murderers will torture me because they want to learn who are those who have been smuggling Jews out and who have been forging the stamps and documents for them. But I will call out only the *Shema* until my soul leaves my body. When you see my suffering, my son, pay it no heed. Recite the *Shema* too, and fear nothing else in this world. Be strong and do not weep, for your tears will only bewilder me in that awesome and holy moment. Naftali, this is my last request of you, will you obey?"

"Father," he replied, "I will ask the murderers to kill me first, for I shall surely not be able to watch your torture."

Whether or not this conversation, so freighted with martyrdom, took place exactly as recounted, it has become a part of Bobover collective memory, enshrining the attachment of the two men who would be the Third and Fourth Rebbes and their powerful bond to each other, as well as their courage in facing their imminent destruction. It became part of their shared charisma and sanctity. Throughout the rest of that night, the two could not sleep, waiting for the morning and what they believed to be inevitable. Both were horrified by the thought of watching the other suffer and die. In the morning, however, when Shlomo was called into the office of the Gestapo, he was told that since he was obviously a Hungarian citizen he would be made to pay a fine for breaking the law and then would be returned to Bochnia. Shlomo could barely contain himself at this good fortune that he was certain was a sign of God's deliverance. The Nazi took a fine of six hundred zlotys and drove them to the railway station, sending father and son back with a note for his counterpart in Bochnia.

In fact, all this was the result of the fortuitous presence of a Bobover Hasid in the Gestapo office in Bochnia when the call from Neumark inquiring about the Halberstams came in. The Hasid was able to persuade the official who answered the phone to call back and in the name of the SS in Bochnia to request their return.[33] Once again, the network of Bobovers had saved the young rebbe and his son.

Shlomo's mother, wife, other son, and mother-in-law had not been as lucky and remained in Gestapo custody. This wore heavily on Shlomo; he initiated desperate efforts to liberate them. Through the people still making their way to him for his blessings, he learned of various routes and strategies for escape. Thus he had discovered a car belonging to a German official that could be hired for a price and used to ferry people to the Slovakian border. He hoped to use it to ferry family there, the first of whom he hoped would be his son and successor, Naftali.

Those with the car demurred, explaining that the procedure they had developed was based on forged work permits and that an eleven-year-old boy—even a future rebbe—could not be given such papers. Putting him in the car would endanger the entire effort. Shlomo used the power of the *rebistve:* he told them that God's blessings and protection would ensure their success because they were transporting the holy seed of the Bobover Rebbes.[34] Such was the belief in a rebbe's powers and the conviction that preserving the holy line of succession mattered that they agreed.

Notwithstanding, the car was stopped and its passengers were brought to the police authorities in Kraków. Keen to discover who was behind the effort, they put pressure on the young Naftali. But despite the blows they rained upon him, he said nothing, claiming ignorance. Through further bribes and influence, Naftali was freed, but the others remained in Gestapo custody. Shlomo and his brother Yecheskel Dovid continued to scheme in order to find passage for the family. Finally reaching the banks of the Biały Dunajec River along the Polish-Slovakian border, they planned to ford the river and then run twelve kilometers to a house at the foot of the Pieniny Środkowe mountain range of the Tatra Mountains. All this would take place in August 1943, weeks before the final liquidation of the Bochnia ghetto on September 12.[35]

After a harrowing run and more bribes, they reached Prešov in Slovakia, regrouping to get to Hungary. At Košice (called "Kashau" by the Hasidim) on the Hungarian border, in late 1943, with the help of Bobover locals, bribes, and a good deal of luck, Shlomo, Naftali, and some of the Bobovers made it to the Hungarian capital, where they would be united with Shlomo's sister, Nechama (Chumtche) Golda, the widow of Moshe

Stempel, her son Shmuel, her daughter Shoshana, and more Bobover supporters. Willing to come out in public here, Shlomo spoke before the
congregation at the Chevra Shas. Quoting the prophet Jeremiah's famous
warning that "from the North shall the evil break forth" (1:14), he
reported on the events in Poland, on what he had experienced and witnessed, and on the evil that he was sure would move southward toward
Hungarian Jewry. Just as the sacred Temple sacrifices were slaughtered
on the northern parts of the Temple Mount, he told them so too were the
holy Jewish people first being sacrificed and slaughtered to their north,
for every slain Jew was made holy by having been murdered. His desire
to arouse the community to action, to recognize the danger on their doorstep—not unlike the same warning that we have already seen Boruchel
Rabinovich of Munkács offer in the same Budapest—moved him deeply.
The situation was far from secure in Hungary. Already Polish Jews discovered living in Pest were being expelled to concentration camps.

In time, dressed again in clothes that disguised both their Hasidic and
their Jewish identity, the rebbe and Naftali fled toward Oradea (Gross-
wardein, as the Germans called it) three hundred kilometers from neighboring Romania, where the situation for Jews was marginally better.
His wife, younger son, and daughter as well as his mother-in-law had
made it there too and had gone into hiding. With his forged papers and
in Tyrolean disguise, Shlomo moved cautiously but freely throughout
the city, even as Nazis constructed a series of ghettos there from which
Jews would be taken to death camps.

As the situation grew worse, he and Naftali also went into hiding,
even as the *rebbetzin,* his younger son, his daughter, and his mother-in-
law were captured in their hideout. Shlomo tried to buy their release
through an intermediary, but this time he failed. On June 29, 1944, the
thirty-eight-year-old *rebbetzin,* Bluma Rachel, as well as her mother, his
son Mordechai Dovid (b. 1934), and his daughter Henchi (b. 1938),
were deported to Auschwitz and their deaths.[36]

Reaching Bucharest, Romania, Naftali and Shlomo, who continued
to be clean-shaven and bareheaded or wearing a Tyrolean-style hat,
stayed free. No Bobover Rebbe had ever looked like this. With half his
family gone or dead, on the run, trying to preserve the life of his son and
heir, and staying a step ahead of disaster, he hung between hopelessness
and terror, despair and anticipation, both rebbe and refugee. Romania's
Jews were increasingly subject to deportations and arrests. After three
weeks of living there, Shlomo focused his energies on saving Naftali,
and with him the future of Bobov and his own family.

SAVING THE SUCCESSOR AND BOBOVER CONTINUITY

Desperate to get the future Bobover Rebbe out of Romania, Shlomo knew doing so would cost a major ransom. After receiving a substantial payment, the Bucharest head of the Gestapo permitted three ships to sail for Turkey, allowing for the exodus of about a thousand people— including Jews. This flotilla of the *Morina, Mefkura,* and *Bulbul* had been arranged through bribes and efforts by the Zionists and local Jews.[37] Shlomo exerted all his influence and cajoled enough money from supporters to place Naftali on board. Once his heir was safe, Shlomo hoped to find ways to save himself and those in his family who were still alive. Arrival in Turkey, as we have seen in the case of the Rabinoviches of Munkács, eased entry into Palestine, Naftali's ultimate destination.

In the summer of 1944, Naftali boarded the *Bulbul.* As father and son parted, after their intense five years together on the run, Shlomo adjured his son:

> I ask of you that you remember always who you are, who your father is and who your grandfather. Remember always the source of great holiness from which you come. If the Lord, may He be blessed, saves me, then I will be able to reunite with you and see that you are provided with a worthy match. But if heaven forbid not, and you are the only one who has escaped from my family, then know that a great and holy responsibility rests upon you, and therefore beware of bad friends and be diligent in your studies so that you remain the pleasant plant in the garden of Bobov and the glory of your father and grandfather.[38]

There could be no mistaking that saving Naftali was not simply the desire of a father to save a beloved first son but, at least as the story of those days has come down to us from Hasidic and Bobover sources, nothing short of a rebbe's assuring succession in Bobov. Moreover, given the extremity of the circumstances and the drama of all that had led up to it, no one could ever question that, whatever happened, Naftali was to be the next Bobover Rebbe, even though he was only a boy just past his bar mitzvah.

The three ships that left Constanta, Romania, in August of 1944 for Turkey did not all make it. The *Morina* and the *Bulbul* arrived safely, but the second ship, the *Mefkura,* was shelled in Bulgarian waters, and only 5 or 6 of the 374 people on board survived the shelling and fire that broke out.[39] The sight of the burning *Mefkura* rattled the captain of the *Bulbul,* and he tried to jump ship. But before he could escape, he was captured by some of the passengers, who told him, "Our destiny will be yours." With the first mate taking over, the ship diverged from the route taken by the ill-fated *Mefkura*. After a severe storm and a mistaken effort to land in a part of Turkey where there was no port, the passengers disembarked via small boats that took them to the Turkish mainland, from which they continued on to Istanbul. They were met there by agents of the Zionist Jewish Agency, who arranged their passage via a train that passed through Aleppo and Beirut to the safety of Palestine.[40] These were the very Zionists that previous Bobover Rebbes had railed against in Poland before the outbreak of the war. Now the Bobover future was being protected by them.

Shlomo's mother and his brother Yecheskel Dovid were not so fortunate. Caught near Oradea, they were taken to Pest and imprisoned. Without sufficient funds to use as bribes to release them, Shlomo, still in Bucharest, frantically searched for resources that he could use to ransom his family. He turned to Chaim Yisroel Eiss, an Agudat Yisrael founder and activist who from his sanctuary in Zurich was working to save as many Jews as he could. This was the same Agudat Yisrael that the old Bobover Rebbe had opposed in Poland, and now his son was turning to it for help to save his family. Eiss sent money.

In January 1945, the Soviets were already entering Pest and leaving a path of destruction. In the chaos, Shlomo's brother, Yecheskel Dovid, fled and arrived at Shlomo's doorstep. Exhausted and dispirited, he reported on the Bobover women who had been with him and what a horror life had been during the previous ten months and the destruction in Budapest. Interviewed by the Jewish Telegraphic Agency, he reported that thirty to forty thousand Jews were all that remained of the quarter million who had once lived in Budapest.[41]

In the meantime, Shlomo, seeking to reach those left behind, went to Arad, on the Hungarian border, and bribed a Russian officer to drive him into Budapest and to arrange documents that would ease his passage to collect his mother and sister and bring them to relative safety. Although the siege around the city was nearing an end, the battles were still ongoing when he arrived. After reuniting with his mother, he traveled throughout the city searching for people he knew, hoping he could take them back to Arad or Bucharest and save them as well from the difficult straits in which they found themselves. Quite a few of the rabbis he came upon and offered to help did not recognize the clean-shaven man in the Tyrolean hat as the Bobover Rebbe.

Shlomo's sister, Rebecca Baila, hiding with two of her children in a village outside Budapest, found herself caught in the battle. Hoping to convince his driver to remain a few extra days so that he might retrieve her, Shlomo discovered that the man's fear of getting caught behind German lines was too great. Meanwhile his sister and her children found their own way to Budapest. In the Bobover recounting of these events, all these escapes and the apparent assurance of continuity they portended were viewed as no less than the hand of God saving Bobov from destruction.

With the war ending, Shlomo, writing in German to his family in Palestine on May 30, 1945, expressed concern about Naftali and regret that he had "sent the child away" because "he needs his father and mother to raise him." At that point, he reported that the dowager *rebbetzin* was "in good health"; she would die in 1974 in New York. He still harbored hopes that his wife and the children who had been taken to Auschwitz would be among those few who survived, and he fretted as well about the fate of his brother Chaim in Siberian exile.[42] Both those hopes would be dashed. Chaim died in a Soviet prison in 1944, and as we know the rebbe's wife and other children were exterminated by the Nazis. Of the Kedushas Zion's twelve children, two sons and seven daughters survived the war.[43] But only Shlomo was the "*heilige* [holy] rebbe" and only Naftali his chosen successor.

STARTING OVER AFTER THE HOLOCAUST

By July 1945 and war's end, Shlomo, claiming he was Italian, which he documented through yet another set of his nearly endless supply of forged papers, sought repatriation to Italy and out of Soviet jurisdiction.[44] He traveled via the Balkans and Belgrade to the coastal city of Bari, Italy, part of a flood of "new refugees," mainly from eastern Europe. Over time, Jews became predominant in Italy's displaced persons community. Many took off from Italian ports to Palestine, even though British authorities occupying Italy strongly opposed this. But the refugees kept coming, and postwar Italy adopted a humanitarian practice of turning a "blind eye" at the border so that immigration—and, ultimately, illegal migration to Palestine—continued.[45]

But Shlomo was not headed for Palestine. Trying to avoid the displaced persons camps, Shlomo sought housing in Bari, Italy, as the summer gave way to the period of Rosh Hashanah and the Jewish High Holy Days. Through some influence with the British army, he found a large house that had been confiscated by the Allies.[46] Refugee youths, particularly from Hasidic families, found their way to him, looking for some sort of emotional anchor in his presence and some continuity with their past that they tried to retrieve in this chaotic time. They looked to heal the breach in their lives; now more than ever, cleaving to a rebbe, whose survival was for them the embodiment of hope, was for many even more compelling than finding their family. There was no question in their minds that he was the legitimate successor of his murdered father, and they wanted to spend the Days of Awe from Rosh Hashanah through Yom Kippur close to him, inspired by his prayers, as if transported to a time before the murder and destruction that had so decimated their lives.

After the holy days, Shlomo traveled via London to New York to begin a new life. Settling first on Manhattan's West Side, he felt relieved to be safe but, according to reports of those who knew him at the time, also depressed and broken. Although he had begun to regrow his beard in Bari, in some ways he still felt clean-shaven and not ready to take up the full weight of a crown. Widowed and still bereaved, he was troubled about how his wife and some children had been left behind to die while he and his son Naftali, who was still in the Holy Land studying at the Slonim Yeshiva, had survived. For all of his activity on behalf of others during the war, Shlomo, now facing the daunting task of rebuilding Bobov in an American cultural and social environment that many believed was hostile to Hasidism, was not certain he had the strength or even the desire to go on as a rebbe.[47] He was emotionally spent and unsure what his natural vocation was. Around him were many other Jewish refugees and other displaced persons who were on the cusp of reinventing themselves in the New World. Many of them too had doubts about a God who had seemed to be silent while the Holocaust had taken place. If he shared their doubts, who would have blamed him?

Shlomo's brother, Yecheskel Dovid, once acting like a rebbe, who had lived for a short time after the end of World War II in Palestine, had pretty much given up that vocation. Although when he arrived in New York he was known to some as the Pokshevenitza Rav, a title he had nominally inherited from his father-in-law, he decided instead to become a diamond merchant who lived on Manhattan's West Side. Manhattan in the mid-1940s certainly did not seem a place to reestablish a Hasidic court.

Shlomo's widowed sister Chumtche survived with two children, Samuel Yehuda and Shoshana Roiza. After living in Palestine they moved to London, where Chumtche married Yehoshua Meir Frishvasser (known in England as Osias Freshwater [1897–1976]), who had escaped from Poland to London in 1939. They had two more sons.

Freshwater became an extraordinarily wealthy property developer and helped, among other things, to underwrite the creation of Kiryat Bobov, a community of Bobovers, established in the early 1960s in Bat Yam, Israel.[48] But the Freshwaters did not live as Hasidim.

Could Shlomo do so? If he acceded to the continuing pressures placed upon him by other rebbes, most prominently the Sanzer and Satmarer, as well as the Bobover survivors who looked to him to replace the crown on his head, could he be successful in America? He had been a wartime rebbe; could he be one in peacetime? He was not sure. Changed by his experiences, he no longer embraced the zealotry that had been so associated with his predecessors. Could there be a Bobov that was kinder and gentler, one that made its peace with America or even with Israel? Only about three hundred Bobover Hasidim had survived the Holocaust, and who knew where they all were and how many were prepared to once again take up the life of Hasidism. The younger survivors had spent years trying to avoid death and demoralization that in the past they might have spent being molded into Hasidim . As a result they were largely ignorant of what it meant to be a Hasid—if they wanted to be one at all. The few older ones who had survived were often broken vessels. In a sense they mirrored their rebbe.

In the end, Shlomo understood that at the age of forty he was a refugee who lacked skills and educational certificates that might enable him to reinvent himself. More importantly, he and the surviving Hasidim needed one another. What they had both gone through had bonded them even more tightly and had made him a symbol of their survival. Nothing suited him more than his role as a rebbe; he could not escape who he had become. His postwar reluctance to be rebbe, the Hasidim believed, reflected a humility they valued. His suffering, still resonating in his person, mirrored their own feelings and ennobled him. His effort to rebuild his life inspired and echoed their own efforts. The smile and inner joy that he began to radiate as he gained his footing and confidence as a rebbe reflected Bobover growing confidence in their ability to restore the glory of the past in the New World. More than his philosophy or his teachings, his personal charisma and returning joy, which overcame his initial depression and wounded faith, became the essential spirit of Bobover resurrection. He was leader and icon in one.

The start was modest, a small congregation near where he lived in Manhattan. Yet if he was to restore Bobov, he would need to rebuild his own family first. In 1947, he reunited with Naftali, who for a long time had not known for certain the fate of his father. Now that his father was in America, Naftali believed that that was where Bobov was destined to rebuild its court. Next, in 1948, Shlomo remarried. His new wife was Frieda Rubin (d. 2008), a second cousin and the orphaned daughter of Aryeh Leib, the Rebbe of Cieszanów, who had died in 1942, and Chana Rachel Halberstam Rubin. Not terribly beloved by Shlomo's first family, including his mother, who was now living near him, she would bear Shlomo six children: five daughters and one son, Benzion Aryeh Leib (b. 1955), named after both his grandfathers and born when his father was forty-eight and his half brother Naftali was twenty-four.

The tension between Shlomo's first and second families was no secret within Bobov, and it would be one of the seeds of the conflict that would envelop the court in America. Not only was it the result of the natural rivalries that emerge when a man has two wives and sets of children, but it was exacerbated by the fact that many in Shlomo's first family were far more open to the surrounding culture—"modern," as insiders put it—than his second family, who lived in the far more religiously insular and conservative or *haredi* environment emerging in the second half of the twentieth century. Although her son was rebbe and her grandson his designated successor, Shlomo's mother, the dowager *rebbetzin* and a woman of Hasidic royalty, found herself relegated to a secondary position in America as Shlomo's new wife and children became the new royal family.

What would postwar Bobov be? The story is told of Shlomo's visit to Yoelish Teitelbaum, fellow Holocaust survivor and rebbe, who embraced zealotry, anti-Zionism, and culture war with America while rebuilding his court. Yoelish, who saw himself as a postwar Jewish leader, took a powerful interest in the resurrection and direction of Hasidic life, which he wanted in his ideological image. During the visit, Yoelish asked Shlomo about his small congregation on Manhattan's Upper West Side and asked why "you allow your Hasidim and even some of your family to *daven* for the *omud* [lead the prayers] without beards." The beard had after all become the sine qua non of Hasidism, and it (along with earlocks and the special clothes Hasidim wore) served to establish their life and identity apart in ways Yoelish deemed crucial in the open and seductive world of modern American society (figure 13). Indeed, a photo of a dinner during the 1950s held in support of the Bobover yeshivas in America shows most of the attendees clean-shaven and not looking at all like Hasidim.[49] Shlomo, perhaps recalling his own appearance during the war, replied: "I see beards on them."[50] Just as Hasidim during the war years could see him as their rebbe even though

13. Shlomo Halberstam (at right), the Third Bobover Rebbe, speaking with Moshe Teitelbaum, the Second Satmar Rebbe and nephew of Yoelish Teitelbaum, the First Satmar Rebbe. By permission of L. Trainer and Trainer Studio.

he was clean-shaven, he could see the Hasid in the apparently clean-shaven Jew, could perceive the possibilities for reviving the Bobover court out of people who were not yet Hasidim.

Some Bobovers tried to press Shlomo toward zealotry, to be more like Yoelish (who encouraged them). They were called "rebel Bobovers" (*Hasidim bogdim*) and ultimately either were expelled or left on their own. Although a few ultimately returned to the fold, most joined Satmar. The majority of the Bobovers, however, remained loyal to Shlomo and his moderate character.

Like most other rebbes who had started in Manhattan, Shlomo soon realized that if he did revive Bobov it would not be in his West Eighty-Sixth Street small location. He moved to Orthodox Brooklyn, first to Crown Heights, where he established a Bobover yeshiva on Brooklyn Avenue, between Bergen and Dean Streets. Schools, and later a summer camp, established in 1957 in the Catskills village of Ferndale, would become the pipelines for a new generation of Bobover Hasidim. There was even a trade school.[51] By 1967, Bobov had relocated to where they are today the largest Hasidic group: Borough Park, Brooklyn.

As he built his institutions, Shlomo saw that those who sent their youngsters to his schools would often become his Hasidim, or at least their children did. Gradually, people who were new to Bobov or even Hasidism outnumbered those descended from Bobover families in Europe. The newcomers often became even more enthusiastic, and their spirit energized the old Hasidim and the rebbe.

By 1963, Shlomo was already a public figure in New York, reported to have ten thousand followers; and when he left by ship for a trip to Israel, where he would also rebuild his group, his debarkation was deemed newsworthy and described by the *New York Times*.[52] A man whose smile could light up a room, whose eyes sparkled when he listened to his Hasidim sing and watched them dance, he had also learned how to urge them into livelihoods, which many made in the diamond trade, a business that Hasidim soon dominated in New York and that in the early postwar years flourished.

By his late eighties, Shlomo was described in the *Times* as "revered above all other Borough Park sages." [53] In his 1988 presidential bid, Al Gore began his tour of Brooklyn at Shlomo's home because the Bobovers were known as "the dominant Hasidic group" in the area.[54]

NAFTALI

Naftali, who in October of 1950 had married his cousin Hessa (Hessie) Paneth, became his father's chief aide. He became a key figure whose task was trying to put Bobov in a position of financial well-being, expanding the organization, and acting as his father's representative on travels and to outsiders and insiders alike. He saw to it that all the teachers in the yeshiva and functionaries in the court were paid on time and received living wages. He borrowed money to pay mortgage costs; and he established relationships of trust. To be sure, he was not always successful. Insiders described him as a poor administrator. He often blurred the financial lines between his private funds and those of the court, at one point leaving the Bobover *mesifta* (boys' secondary school) about $8 million in debt. Nevertheless, the fact that he busied himself with these sorts of financial matters freed his father to focus on spiritual matters and not sully his charisma with the often mundane business of handling the money, paying the bills, and finding benefactors. But it also meant that Naftali, although secure in his position as the successor select, became associated in some quarters with the more worldly, profane, and sometimes unsavory fiscal aspects of Bobover life.

Yet Naftali was not just aide, administrator, and fund-raiser. Like his father, he embodied continuity with the old world of Bobov, now illumined by sacred nostalgia as a result of its tragic end. Naftali's charisma was far more a product of his birth, suffering, his personal history, and later his office than a function of his personality or his activities in postwar Bobov.

When the Third Rebbe, Shlomo, described as "regal-looking" with "gentle charisma" in the obituaries that filled the press, died at age ninety-two in 2000, Naftali, who was then sixty-nine years old, and who had been treated from the earliest days of his life as next in the royal line, became the new rebbe.[55] In the symbolic transfer of authority, the Hasidim, barely hours after Shlomo's funeral, chanted, "Yechi adoneinu, moreinu, v'rabeinu" (Long live our master, our teacher, and our rebbe). This classic Hasidic version of "The king is dead, long live the king," proclaiming continuity and a new beginning in the face of death, was the formal expression of the Hasidim's acceptance of Naftali as their new rebbe.

While people had certainly recognized Shlomo as having succeeded his late father legitimately, the actual moment of *his* ascent to the throne, taking effect after the murder of his father, had not been celebrated and marked in any ceremonial way. But in the newfound stability in America and in a revitalized Bobov, there could be such a public marker of succession. Moreover, because Shlomo, whose obituary noted "his artful way of sidestepping the internal squabbles that plague other Hasidic sects," had effectively prepared the way for this transition, the moment was free of tension.[56] Everyone knew how Shlomo had kept Naftali close and saved his son time and again during the Holocaust and understood that all that was in order to enable Naftali to succeed him.

Living his entire life in the shadows of his two larger-than-life predecessors, Naftali at last stepped into the spotlight. In spite of half-serious comments that Naftali was reported to have made during his father's lifetime that he personally did not see himself as a likely successor to his father—comments that hearers took as expressions of his humility and unpretentiousness—there had been no question that upon Shlomo's passing Naftali would be the heir. Perhaps for this reason Shlomo had left no written *tzav'a* (will) that would have established who he wanted to follow him as rebbe. Everyone had known for years that Naftali, the only surviving son of Shlomo's first family, was next in line. As the *New York Times* remarked on the smooth transition at the time of Shlomo's death, Bobov Hasidism was "known for not emphasizing disputes."[57]

As inevitable as his coronation was to all Bobovers, for Naftali, who was trusted by and known to all, the transition from official and fixer to rebbe and *zaddik* was not simple. For the preceding year or so Shlomo had been sick, and the *rebistve* needed an infusion of new energy. Naftali, however, was not the ideal candidate for the role everyone expected him to take. His reputed reluctance to embrace his new position was not simply his humility, which many Hasidim found endearing. It was also the fact that like so many crown princes who follow a long-reigning and larger-than-life monarch, he was shaped by having spent his entire life as the crown prince in waiting, toiling in the background through the years when he was at his strongest.[58] Now he was no longer young and was suffering from Parkinson's disease.

For all the Hasidim, Shlomo was the only rebbe they had ever known. His life was a huge part of the history of Bobov, for he had led it longer than any of his predecessors. Naftali's reluctance was also a consequence of his realization that he was not as charismatic as his beloved father. In his unassuming manner, Naftali, often hen-pecked by his wife, even as a new rebbe, exhibited the character of a simple and plain-spoken person rather than the regal quality Shlomo had achieved. He still seemed the fellow who for years the Hasidim would find sitting in the *bes medrash* sipping a hot chocolate and schmoozing with people. Nor was he interested in the increasingly powerful expressions of religious fervency—the *haredi* element—taking over the Hasidic world. Over the years, he was content sometimes to come to prayers late and leave early, and he could often be seen chatting when he *was* there, in ways not becoming a rebbe or crown prince. Long after it was largely considered unacceptable in Orthodox Borough Park to do so, he would, for example, stop in the street and talk with the wives of his Hasidim and other women, eschewing the growing tendency, reflecting the religious rightward tilt of Orthodoxy, to rigidly separate public relations between men and women. While most rebbes embraced this norm as a sign of their attachment to *haredi* values, Naftali was comfortable challenging it. His authority flowed not from this sort of display but rather from his family heritage.

The Hasidim, who had just lived through Shlomo's physical decline during the final years of his life, understood that by the time Naftali became rebbe he would not usher in a new era of vigor, growth, and renewal. For about a year, Naftali tried as much as he could to play the part. The beginning of a reign is when the new rebbe must shape and then inhabit the imagination of his followers in order to make the office his own. He must find a way to connect to memories of his predecessor even as he dims those memories and makes the *rebistve* his own. If the predecessor was old and weakened or in obvious decline during his last years and the new rebbe is in contrast young, energetic and engaged, this is easier. But in Naftali's *rebistve,* everything was about the past.

On the other side, the future was also squeezing him. At the same time as the *gabbai* announced Naftali's ascent, his half brother, Benzion Aryeh Leib (who was young enough to be Naftali's son), was appointed *rav-tza'ir,* a title signifying not only that he would help the new rebbe as deputy but that he was the young crown prince. If some Hasidim looked upon Naftali as a pale substitute for his father, promising an extension of the sick years, Benzion Aryeh Leib represented their hope for the future, the potential of a *rebistve* that would be more imposing and representative of a new generation.

SIGNS OF TROUBLE

Not everyone, however, looked at the *rav-tza'ir* thus. Naftali's two sons-in-law, often at his side, also emerged, representing the same generation as Naftali's half brother. The deference and honor that each of these men showed the new Fourth Rebbe at first masked the competition and tension between the two sides. Naftali's wife, the new *rebbetzin,* Hessie, long ago had understood what was at stake in succession. Although once on warm terms with her father-in-law Shlomo's second wife, Hessie had soured on Frieda when she came to believe that her daughters and her family were not treated as equals with the offspring of the second *rebbetzin*'s family. Hessie's children were not rewarded with the same sorts of positions in the court or the Bobov organizations as the children of Frieda and their spouses were. Hessie felt as if her children were being pushed out, even though she knew that someday her husband would be rebbe. She tried to persuade Shlomo to provide prestigious positions for her daughters through appointments for their husbands, but without success. She became acutely sensitive to any perceived slights to her husband or children on the part of her father-in-law. Her sense of entitlement and disappointment embittered her and planted in her an abiding conviction that even when her husband Naftali became the rebbe the other family—of which Benzion Aryeh Leib was the scion—would in due course seek to retrieve and keep exclusive hold over Bobov, leaving her and her children out of the leadership she believed legitimately theirs. Hessie pushed hard for that not to occur and encouraged her sons-in-law to position themselves to be the natural successors of Naftali, rather than second-class members of the Bobov family. In contrast to the humility of her husband, Hessie was a strong-willed and dominating woman, more ambitious for her children and husband perhaps than they were for themselves. With the ascension of her husband, Hessie, who enjoyed driving about in her red town car, knew that if she and her offspring were to remain significant they had to plan for a future that kept them close to the *rebistve*.

As she and others who supported Naftali became aware of those in Bobov who seemed unable to wait for Naftali's reign to give way to Benzion Aryeh Leib's, they began to think the unthinkable: how to guarantee that succession would stay in Naftali's family. For that to happen, his sons-in-law would have to be visibly closer to Naftali than his half brother and apparent successor would be. Naftali's rapidly advancing infirmity provided that opportunity.

As Naftali began to falter because of his failing health and progressively debilitating sickness as well as the murmurings of Hasidim eager to champion the coming era of his younger and more vigorous half brother, the two sons-in-law raised their profile. All this took a dramatic turn in 2002, when they led the trembling Naftali to the pulpit on Kol Nidrei night, at the onset of Yom Kippur, when by Bobov tradition the rebbe chants the prayers. Shuffling to the front of the congregation, with them at his side, Naftali stood mute, unable or unwilling to utter a word. His silence was a painful reminder to the entire Bobov community of the loss of leadership and the diminished *rebistve* they were suffering.

For those who remembered the history of Bobov, Naftali's failure to chant the signature prayer that opens the Yom Kippur service might have recalled a moment during the war when his grandfather also expressed an inability to chant the service, a dramatic moment when his son Shlomo took over, as if ready to bear the religious and spiritual burden of the *rebistve*. But if the Kedushas Zion's silence came from the existential angst of his flight from the Nazis and the evil in the world that pierced his ability to arouse worshippers in prayer and served as a way to allow his son to share his burden and signal his ability to lead, Naftali's stillness, as he trembled before the ark, with thousands of his Hasidim looking on, seemed instead a frustration or maybe even anger at being forced to go on. Or perhaps it was simply feebleness. The Rebbe Naftali stood mute interminably, and many of those in the room were in tears, uncomfortable with what seemed a kind of mercilessness in the way that these two young men urged and almost seemed to force him forward to perform what he felt unable to do. When at last it became clear that Naftali could not do the service, the older son-in-law, fifty-year-old Yehoshua Rubin, stepped up to lead the prayers.

This drama of his son-in-law taking over from Naftali was not considered a template for a future passing of authority. Rather, it was fraught for many who witnessed it and evidence of a grab for power by the sons-in-law, who were effectively eclipsing Benzion Aryeh Leib. To those who believed that for Shlomo his oldest son from his second marriage was the only legitimate successor to his oldest son from his first marriage, this moment signaled the possibilities of a future conflict. At this dramatic moment, Benzion Aryeh Leib, present in the assembly, remained silent, reluctant to appear to rush to sideline or embarrass his half brother. His supporters among the Hasidim, however, fumed, realizing now they would need to plan for a future contest—something that had never happened in Bobov.

Naftali's half brother, Benzion Aryeh Leib, aware of the complexity of the situation, continued to insist that his proper stance was to hold himself back from actively asserting his role as heir apparent, always responding to requests for leadership from those who saw him as next in line and who pushed him to be more active even during Naftali's *rebistve* with the assertion that he was "not now the rebbe." To all importuning him to step forward, he demurred, confident that his time would come and he would get what he considered his birthright without pushing Naftali aside. Some Hasidim took his stance as standoffishness; others saw it as a tacit recognition that he could not compete with the take-charge attitude of the sons-in-law.

As the Rebbe Naftali's health continued to decline, his sons-in-law, Yehoshua Rubin and Mordechai Dovid Unger, took on more and more of his duties. To Benzion Aryeh Leib's Hasidim this was more of an unseemly seizing of both position and power, but others looked upon it as affirmation that Naftali and his family would control the future. The showdown would come two days before the holiday of Purim in 2005.

NAFTALI'S DEATH AND THE SPLIT OVER WHO WOULD BE THE FIFTH REBBE

On March 23, 2005, just before the joyous Jewish holiday of Purim, Naftali Halberstam, died at age seventy-four. If all of Bobov had been certain upon Shlomo's death that Naftali would be their rebbe, his age and infirmity made it clear from the outset that he was going to be more of a transitional figure than one who, like his long-reigning father, would brand Bobov with his personality and charisma. Though only five years in total, his reign, because it followed on his father's decline, nevertheless seemed to some to last too long. For about ten years, as the court grew in population, institutions, and complexity, it was led by two old and infirm rebbes. Now, the Hasidim looked forward to a new generation of leadership, born in America, in good health and with energy to lead the great court that Bobov had once again become. Bobov had reached unprecedented heights—in the early years of the twenty-first century it claimed (probably with exaggeration) a membership of over 120,000 worldwide.[59]

Even before the funeral of the Fourth Rebbe was over, supporters of Naftali's half brother, Benzion Aryeh Leib, moved to cut off the possibilities of a split over who would be the leader.[60] Considering him to be like Naftali, the only son of his father, though second in line after the Polish-born first son, and convinced that Shlomo had meant for him to succeed to the crown, they effectively ignored any expectations Naftali might have had about who would follow him and treated the succession as a continuation of the transition from Shlomo. The absence of Naftali's will (although some asserted they had seen a will, which quickly "disappeared") made "oral understandings" key.

But there were two opinions about what those were. One focused on Shlomo's understandings, and the other on Naftali's (and implicitly his wife's, now the dowager and ailing *rebbetzin,* who had great sway over him). For the former, Benzion Aryeh Leib was the successor, while for the latter, Naftali's son-in-law Mordechai Dovid Unger was. Each side made its case.

Benzion's Hasidim made much of a report that once, in Miami, Shlomo had told the Bobovers with him that he had always planned for Benzion Aryeh Leib to succeed his half brother (figure 14). But Mordechai Dovid's champions dismissed this as hearsay and irrelevant. Without written wills, there was no agreement as to what the expectations of either the Third or the Fourth Rebbe were.

Shlomo's succession had taken place without ceremony in the war. Naftali's, even in the absence of a written will, had been acknowledged in the synagogue by everyone, even before the funeral for his father. But now matters were not as unequivocal. While both sides insisted that unity was crucial for continuity, neither could agree on which man would bring about that unity and be the new rebbe.

Each group could claim that its candidate had the necessary family ties. Benzion Aryeh Leib was a holy seed and was the recognized *rav-tza'ir,* as well as the *ben-achar-ben,* son, grandson, and great-grandson of the First, Second, and Third Bobover Rebbes. Although he had no sons, Naftali, the Fourth Rebbe, had two daughters, and the husband of Rivka, Mordechai

14. An intimate moment between Shlomo Halberstam, the Third Bobover Rebbe, and his son Benzion, shortly before the former's passing. By permission of Duvid Singer.

Dovid Unger, was the challenger. He too was a holy seed, a son of the Dombrover Rebbe, scion of a distinguished Polish Hasidic lineage founded by his namesake. Having married into Bobov and served at Naftali's side, he was considered by some, particularly those who had studied under him in the yeshiva, as a legitimate claimant to the crown, which they argued had become Naftali's alone to pass on. As a challenger, Mordechai Dovid made himself more approachable than his more reserved rival.

Prominent among Mordechai Dovid's supporters was Benzion Dunner, who in 1986 had married Esther Stern, granddaughter of Shlomo's sister, Chumtche Stempel Freshwater. Dunner, who came from a prominent British Orthodox family, had amassed an enormous fortune and used much of it to support Bobov. The Freshwaters in London felt a special connection to Naftali, who was their full blood relative, and considered his children (who were their full relatives) to be no less the heirs of Shlomo than those of the new family he had created in America and whose prince was Benzion Aryeh Leib. For the last three years of Naftali's life, Dunner covered much of the cost of his medical care, including at the end round-the-clock nursing beyond what insurance provided.[61] Now he would supply the funds to Naftali's daughter and her husband as they reached for the Bobov crown.

As they jockeyed for control, each of Shlomo's two families under-stood that the side that gained the *rebistve* got everything, while the one who lost it got nothing. There would be no real place for the losing con-tenders in the court of the winners. Mordechai Dovid and his Hasidim claimed he had been his father-in-law's designated successor, while his older brother-in-law, Yehoshua Rubin, married to Naftali's daughter, Rachel, was the chosen *rav* and *av beit din,* a division of authority agreed to by both brothers-in-law and Naftali. How, supporters of the challeng-ers reasoned, could the branch and seeds of Naftali's family be com-pletely stripped from the Bobover leadership tree? And yet, what else would these sons-in-law do but remove the holy seeds by excluding Shlo-mo's son Benzion Aryeh Leib? Given that Mordechai Dovid had culti-vated a following as his ailing father-in-law's viceroy, he could not, many of his Bobover supporters believed, be denied a position of leadership.

For Benzion Aryeh Leib's Hasidim, Shlomo's first family's claims had died with the Fourth Rebbe. Naftali's sons-in-law would have to find another calling, especially since their behavior in the last years seemed to be more a naked grab for power than genuine preparation for ascen-sion to it. In no way could their usurpation be rewarded. In contrast, their candidate had shown proper humility in his refusal to make a pub-lic move that would undermine his half brother.

While events seemed to have turned the succession into a zero-sum game, it did not have to reach such a state. In his time, the Rebbe Shlomo had faced the problems of finding positions for *his* sons-in-law in the Bobover world, and he had done it: Chaim Tauber, married to Shlomo's daughter, Miriam Nechama, was made *dayan* in the Borough Park head-quarters; Yonasan Goldberger, married to Devorah Leah, became head of the *kollel* (yeshiva for married students); Boruch Horowitz, married to Esther Sheindel, led the yeshiva in Brooklyn; Yaakov Meisles, married to Sarah Chana, went to lead the Bobover settlement in Israel's Bat Yam; and Benzion Blum, married to Malka, was dispatched to serve as a *dayan* in the Bobover community in London's Stamford Hill. These positions, however, were not made available for Naftali's sons-in-law.[62] While the Bobover empire was growing and spreading, the conflict meant that any emerging positions would be for the new rebbe to distribute.

As the standoff became more tense in the brief interval before Naf-tali's funeral, attitudes that had once been incipient hardened. For Ben-zion Aryeh Leib's supporters, Mordechai Dovid had risen beyond his station during the last few years; for Mordechai David's supporters, he had risen too high to just be shunted off to some minor post or to drop out of the leadership. Whereas the founder of Bobover Hasidism had gone to another place to establish a new court, this was not possible for either of the two current contenders: there was no other place to go where sufficient Bobover Hasidim lacked a leader or where he could establish a court. Mordechai Dovid's father, Benzion Unger, remained the Dombrover Rebbe (living in Borough Park), and his son could not challenge him for leadership. Moreover, Bobov was a bigger and more prestigious community, and Mordechai Dovid was already part of its elite. He and his Hasidim stood their ground. Benzion Aryeh Leib and his Hasidim ignored them.

THE CROWNING OF A NEW REBBE

Because the death of one rebbe is, as with royalty of all sorts, followed almost immediately with the crowning of his successor, there was really no time for negotiations among the contenders—even if anyone had been prepared to enter into them. Normally, the transition would simply be by unanimous acclamation or the reading of the previous rebbe's will in public followed by the Hasidim handing the new rebbe petitions or *kvittlach* for blessing. Thus had gone the succession from Shlomo to Naftali. But everyone realized nothing like this was going to happen now.

To close off any challenge to their candidate, supporters of Benzion Aryeh Leib organized quickly. Immediately following the funeral of Naftali, and even as the shivah week of mourning began, they convened a group of Bobover Hasidic elders, led by Chaim Tauber, the Bobover *dayan* and Shlomo's (whom they pointedly referred to as the "rebbe") son-in-law. Assembling in Tauber's Borough Park home (since they had been warned by Mordechai Dovid and his supporters that they would not allow this to take place in the main Bobover *bes medrash*), they prepared a *hachturah* (crowning) of Benzion Aryeh Leib as the new rebbe. Crowded around a long wooden table were men, many of whom were among the senior and longest affiliated of Hasidim, or whose fathers and grandfathers were, including most prominently those who had attached themselves to Shlomo in his first years in America when he was taking his tentative first steps to resurrect Bobover Hasidism. There were also family members, many of whom had a powerful interest in ensuring that their branch of the Halberstam family retained control of the *rebistve*. They were hoping with their action to reverse the rising tide of dispute.

They jostled for position in the packed room. The more prominent among them sat at the table or stood near Tauber, who, looking at first a bit uncomfortable, sat down on a gold-colored armchair, and finally, as if overcome by the gravity of the situation, rose to address the Hasidim present.[63] Visibly overcome with emotion, he swayed back and forth, eyes closed, as if at prayer. Raising his hand to his forehead and then lowering it, he then swept it across the table as if wiping a slate clean, back and forth, left to right. A number of people were recording the event; a video of the proceedings would later be posted on the Internet. Murmuring filled the room. Wearing a black hat and a long buttoned *bekeshe,* Tauber seemed to search for the right words, as if not knowing where to begin. He turned his left hand palm up as if to say, What can I do, what can I say? Then he stroked his long gray beard. Finally, he pinched the bridge of his nose with his thumb and forefinger as if he were about to recite the great credo of Jewish liturgy, *Shema Yisrael* (Hear, O Israel).

At last he stood and began to speak, leaning on the table with his fingertips and still swaying back and forth, as the murmuring in the room diminished and all eyes turned to him.[64] Throughout his talk, he repeatedly paused, as if searching for the just the right words with which to continue.

"There are times," he said in Yiddish, the lingua franca of Hasidism, "for which we cannot prepare any speeches. It's distressing that we have come to such a time for which we could not prepare; we do not *want* to prepare for such a situation, and therefore we cannot prepare what we want to say. Each one of us is broken-hearted." He was of course referring to the feelings of loss that flood the hearts of the Hasidim when their rebbe has died, but he might also have been expressing the trepidation everyone felt about the imminence of a conflict that had the potential to tear them apart. For him it was also the loss of a brother-in-law with whom he had been close.

From the street outside, the blaring of horns and yelling could be heard, as the entire neighborhood was still in an uproar over the funeral, the ride back from the cemetery, and the disputes already breaking out among the Hasidim over what would happen next. Home from the funeral and having just put their rebbe into his grave, these men were now turning toward the future and to him to help them navigate their way in it.

Tauber continued, "Usually, when this sort of moment comes, many thoughts arise in one's mind, many subjects. We are a holy community. My father-in-law, of blessed memory, suffered for ten years with extraordinary self-sacrifice." Everyone knew what he was talking about; the last years of Shlomo had been difficult as he aged. But, Tauber reminded them all, he had done that with the "help" and "extraordinary selflessness" provided by "my brother-in-law, the *ruv,* may his memory be a blessing."

Throughout his life, and even after becoming rebbe, Naftali had lived and toiled in his father's shadow, yet he had remained resolute and uncomplaining. When at last he had become rebbe and had been overtaken by age and illness, he remained in his father's shadow. Now even after his death, as Tauber recalled him, he was still in that shadow.

What Tauber was about to say and do, he claimed, was neither to demean nor deny Naftali his rights or gainsay his contributions to Bobover Hasidism. Rather, as he now said, "It is our task and our responsibility—each and every one of us—to do what we can to assure our continuity, to preserve our community and to make it grow. But the leadership of our world has been taken from us."

He reminded them that they could not remain leaderless. "The orientation of our world is such that every congregation, every society, must have a leader." He quoted the Bible (Num. 27:16–17), repeating the words that Moses, when he was about to pass from the scene, had asked of the Almighty to guide the Children of Israel after him: "Let the Lord, the God of the spirits of all flesh, set a man over the congregation, who may go out before them, and who may come in before them, and who may lead them out and who may bring them in." But while Moses had received an answer from God, the Bobovers did not know how they would discover the Almighty's or even their rebbe's will.

"Perhaps," Tauber went on, there were "a few" who might have heard the wishes of the previous rebbes, "but by no means have all or most of the congregation ever heard what that was. So there are many people who live with and carry questions and doubts [about what the future of our leadership should be]. Yet I am convinced, having clearly heard from people that the will of my father-in-law, of blessed memory, was— without doubt or question—very simply, that he wanted, that he clearly revealed, that now and today in this situation my [other] brother-in-law, the *rav-tza'ir* [Benzion Aryeh Leib], should take over the leadership."

For Tauber and those in the room, the wishes of Shlomo were those mattered, and not what Naftali, his son, the rebbe they had just buried, might have wanted. Shlomo's will still dominated Bobov, even after five years of his son's reign. Shlomo was still the *tateh,* the father to all of the Hasidim. With great emphasis, Tauber declared what he "knew" the *tateh's* will to be.

Tauber acknowledged that what they were doing here might subsequently appear to some as a kind of secret cabal. He referenced the crowning of Naftali. "The truth is that when such an unfortunate situation occurred in the past, what we are doing here was done in full view of all the people." Regrettably, however, he explained, "I'm afraid that were we to do so today, there would be a *chillul hashem* [desecration of God's name]."

Tauber and all those in attendance recognized the schism developing in Bobov during the closing years of Naftali's life, and they fretted that it would come to a crisis now that he was dead. They had seen the uproar caused, just a few months earlier, by a *boteh* (an intimate gathering, something like a minor *tish,* lacking the full complement of food, and commonly held by future heirs to the throne) carried out by some Hasidim who gathered around Benzion Aryeh Leib at the back of the *bes medrash* on the first Sabbath after the High Holy Days in the days when Naftali was still alive but totally incapacitated and fading quickly. They knew about the efforts of Mordechai Dovid's supporters to have him lead, and about their conviction that no one else was suitable. The competing views and talk about who should be the next rebbe had accelerated in the previous year. Even the *New York Times* took note of the feud and headlined a story in the days after Naftali's passing on March 26, 2005—the holiday of Purim—"A Battle for Succession Takes No Holiday."[65]

Many of the men crowded around Tauber closed their eyes or gazed into space. A few covered their eyes with their hands. Speaking not simply as a son-in-law and brother-in-law of the two previous leaders but as the one appointed and affirmed by them as the *dayan,* with the authority inherent in that position, Tauber continued, turning his palms up as if again to say, What can we do?

"In the face of our many transgressions, we do not want all this in the streets or in the newspapers, with scuffling and fighting. I think there's nothing to be served by stretching this unfortunate and painful story out. In the end, I feel a personal responsibility, now, in *the present circumstances,*" he punched the air with his fists, "to avoid any upheaval, quarrel, or dispute, to ensure peace and brotherhood, and to see that all may be carried on in tranquility—for *that reason and only for that reason* and not, *heaven forbid,* for the opposite, as others might explain it—to take this step." The step was to declare Benzion Aryeh Leib as the new Bobover Rebbe.

Others might accuse the assembled of trying to "irritate, of trying to grab [power]," or of taking illegitimate initiative. "On the contrary," Tauber declared. "On the contrary," he repeated, "quite the opposite;

we seek peace and concord, and we do not want fights, and we do not want to spite anyone. Let us all remember well what we were taught, what our rebbes imparted to us day and night, what our mission is, and what we have been taught to serve. Because of all this I feel a personal responsibility to *take a stand* on this matter and to let the congregation know what was my father-in-law's will, and I believe we all want to fulfill that will completely." Again he paused, realizing he had asserted that Shlomo's will and not Naftali's was paramount.

"And lest anyone doubt or question or, heaven forbid, fight it, I remind you that we must not fight. We want no fights and no quarrels. We dare not fight. If there is anything we need to fix there are ordered ways that we can fix things.

"But the fundamental question of who shall take over leadership is in my humble opinion beyond question and doubt. As I said earlier, to prevent embarrassments and shame and heartache or other aggravations, we are going to do this before a large group. The crowd here," he assured them, speaking as a controlling legal authority, "this important group, senior Hasidim, notables, the foremost faces of our congregation, qualifies as *b'rov am* [the large assemblage]." As a judicial authority, he declared the actions taken before this group would have the same mandate as if they were carried out in the *bes medrash* (the large study hall of the yeshiva where the largest assemblage could gather) before everyone.

> If you who are assembled here understand that we must remain strong, then the Almighty will surely help us to ensure our continuity and to repair our broken forces and spirits and do what it is that we must do, to bring honor to Bobov, and to bring honor to my father-in-law, may he rest in peace, and the *ruv*, may he also rest in peace, to bring honor to my brother-in-law who today has sadly been torn away from us, and whose eternal desire was to foster peace and brotherhood.

By maintaining the will of their forebears, the community would remain in "touch with the world on high." The action they were taking, Tauber assured his listeners, would bring these former leaders "repose and gladness" and keep them on the path their rebbes had set for them to follow until "the day of redemption, may it come speedily and in our days. Amen."

When he was done, Moshe Hayim Mandelbaum, a son of one of those Hasidim who had been part of Shlomo's small circle on the Upper West Side, spoke up, affirming the need for this decision. Speaking for the "old-timers" who had helped rebuild Bobov in America, who had been there when Shlomo needed to be reawakened to his *rebistve* after the Holocaust, Mandelbaum reminded them that they, who filled the room, were "the faces [i.e., pillars] of the community. Here stands the *dayan;* here are the heads of the yeshivas." In the room were the people who "never went against what our father [Shlomo], may his memory be a blessing, wanted." It was essential to establish that those in the room had the authority, both moral, historic, and administrative, to affirm the identity of the next rebbe.

Like Tauber, Mandelbaum reassured them that what they were doing was what Shlomo wanted. It would be, moreover, a dishonor to Naftali, who throughout his life had been guided by his father's will, to do otherwise. Naftali's "will was his father's will." Let there be no doubt, no suggestion that there had been any other wishes on the part of their late rebbe. It was essential, he concluded, that there be "one leader, one head, one *memaleh makom* [successor]," and that all of them assembled here make certain that "the holy name 'Bobov' not be sullied—neither in public nor in private and not in the *bes medrash*. Let us all be agreed to hold ourselves back, not to go, heaven forbid, to war, or to engage in little disputes. Let us all agree to serve the will of our holy rebbe, which he made clear his entire life." And then he concluded with what effectively was the utterance by which the Hasidim proclaimed their rebbe: "Yechi adoneinu, moreinu, v'rabeinu [Long live our master, our teacher and our rebbe], mazel tov." The crowd echoed with waves of "Mazel tov."

Present were Yonasan Goldberger, Shlomo's son-in-law and, like Tauber, brother-in-law to Benzion Aryeh Leib; Leibush Landau, one of the *gabbaim;* Moshe Elias, the so-called "foreign minister" of Bobov, who made connections to and often dealt with the outside world; Duvid Singer, from the family of the Ba'al Shem Tov and an old-time Hasid; Zushe Follman, son of one of the Hasidim from Shlomo's Upper West Side days and among his first students; Asher Scharf, an important financial backer of the *rebistve* and Bobov; Nuchem Mayer German, dean of the *mesifta,* the Bobover Talmudical academy; and others. Next, they all marched across the street to Benzion's home on Borough Park's Forty-Eighth Street.

Wearing a plain black frock coat and hat, and bent over in his chair, Benzion Aryeh Leib was sitting shivah for his late half brother. In the midst of mourning, he put his right hand over his eyes. He knew very well what was about to happen. Speaking for them all, Zushe Follman stood to his right and declared: "May the Almighty help you to have many years of this reign, years of 'still waters' [Psalms 23:2]," where there might be no disputes and attacks against him. He wished that the new rebbe lead the court "until the advent of the Messiah, may he come speedily and in our days, amen." "Amen," everyone repeated, and again a wave of "Mazel tovs" spread through the room.

Almost imperceptibly the new rebbe nodded his head in acceptance. Standing to his right, Tauber reiterated the hopes that there would no *machlokes,* no disputes, no aggravation, no quarrels, and no grief in any way whatsoever. Of course, everyone knew that however much they wished and repeated these wishes, just outside the doors disputes were being hatched as another group of Hasidim were rushing to another place following the *mincha* (afternoon) service to be with Mordechai Dovid Ungèr and affirm him as the Bobover Rebbe.

The men with Benzion Aryeh Leib would have none of that. They saw themselves as the protectors of the continuity that they believed vital for the future of Bobov.

"And if we want to continue in these ways that we have received from our forebears," Tauber declared, *"and if we want our children to continue in these ways,"* for the young were the true guarantors of the future and if they saw that one could break with precedent and tradition then the future would never be assured, "then we must fortify ourselves to flee from all" disputes.

"And there was a king in Jeshurun, when the heads of the people were gathered," Tauber concluded, using the biblical words of the blessing Moses spoke as he was about transfer the leadership from himself to his successor Joshua. *Jeshurun* was a word derived from the Hebrew word for those who are "upright," the upstanding. The reference to themselves was not lost on the assembled, who also saw themselves is the upstanding members of the Bobov community, part of a long chain of Jewish being. Tauber quoted what he claimed was the Rashi commentary on the verse, which asserted that "where the heads of the people were gathered, there the spirit of God was present." In fact, what he perhaps meant to say was what Rashi, the eleventh-century French Jewish exegete, actually cited in commenting on the verse: "When they are gathered together in one group and when there is peace among them, He is their king, but not when there is strife among them." [66]

"May the kingship continue, may it bring honor to Bobov, an honor for our rebbe, may his memory be a blessing, and a way of honoring heaven," Tauber concluded. "With the Almighty may he have success, and may we see the rebuilding of our holy Temple and a full redemption speedily in our days, amen."

As if accepting on behalf of all the Hasidim, Leibush Landau, the *gabbai,* responded. "May we all agree together: *Yechi adoneinu, moreinu, v'rabeinu, shlit'a* [Long live our master, our teacher and our rabbi, may he live many long and good days]." [67] Everyone in the room repeated the phrase, effectively affirming their acceptance of the man whom they addressed as their new leader.

Benzion Aryeh Leib whispered a few words about his unworthiness, which of course the Hasidim took as evidence of the opposite. In confirmation of the fact that they believed him to be more than worthy, a number of men wrote *kvittlach,* the notes, petitions, and requests that Hasidim commonly bring to their rebbe, along with the offerings or *pidyonos* they give him in hopes that if the rebbe accepts them, they will be blessed with an answer to their prayers, ultimately with *bonei, chayei, and mzonei,* the children, health, and livelihood they all want. The would-be rebbe sat before a small wooden bench with the pile of notes before him, silent witnesses to what had just happened. With that, the *hachturah* was complete.

The next morning in the main Bobover *bes medrash* on Brooklyn's Forty-Eighth Street at Fifteenth Avenue, at the end of the prayers, the dean of the *mesifta,* Rabbi Nuchem Mayer German, stood up, still wearing his *talis* and *tefillin,* the prayer shawl and phylacteries, and holding his still open prayer book stood before the entire congregation. He swayed back and forth as he spoke, as if still in prayer, pausing often to find the right words, and announced: "In the name of the *dayan* [Chaim Tauber], I want to share with you his words that the leadership of this place, of our holy community, who yesterday did not have the time to call us all together, declared. We wanted to do everything quickly, just as it was set out in the will." German was talking about Naftali's will, which he was one of the few who claimed to have seen— a will that would "disappear" in the days ahead, and whose authenticity and even existence would be questioned in the whirl of controversy about who really was meant to be the Fifth Bobover Rebbe. What he really meant by "quickly" was of course to create a *fait accompli* before supporters of Mordechai Dovid could organize an alternative declaration of a new rebbe.

German continued his announcement with a quote from Deuteronomy (17:20) and the words in which the Bible warns the people about their kings and the would-be kings about how they must act. The king is warned "that his heart not be lifted up above his brethren, and that he turn not aside from the commandments." The grumblings among some of the Hasidim over the previous few years that the potential heirs to the succession were acting with a sense of entitlement or grabbing for power, accusations that were part of the brewing controversy over who was the right man to lead Bobov, were surely on the minds of many as he quoted this verse.

"May the Almighty help 'so that he prolong his days in his kingdom,'" German concluded, and may "his holy father stand at his right hand and help him." Only Benzion Aryeh Leib could refer to the Rebbe Shlomo as "his holy father." Understanding the consequences of his announcement, German added that the *dayan* had requested that "everyone help and give all their strength so that our group remain strong." Strength meant unity and acceptance of one leader.

Referring to the rebbe whom they had just buried a day earlier and for whom they were still in mourning, he assured them that he had along with his father labored to make certain there would be peace and unity. He recalled how just a few months earlier, on the eve of the Sukkot festival, he had been called in by Naftali, who had asked that he ensure there would never be any aggravation over the succession. Like the supporters of Benzion Aryeh Leib, German was trying to impress upon the Hasidim that the murmurings and disputes that had been the legacy of the bulk of Naftali's years as an incapacitated rebbe had to end now. There could only be one path forward.

THINGS FALL APART

German's earnest declaration was one more sign that things were actually falling apart. In Naftali's house, even before the funeral had taken place, both his sons-in-law had been tapped as his successors. This was announced in the presence of the lay leader of the Bobov community, Moshe Meir Einhorn. In Bobov tradition, the rebbe had always also been the *ruv*, an ordained rabbi who had the power to adjudicate law. At their installation, the two sons-in-law agreed that Mordechai Dovid would serve as rebbe, Yehoshua Rubin would be *ruv*, and there would be no *rav-tza'ir*. The crowning took place in the Bet Yaakov school on Forty-Fifth Street.[68] Bobov was now officially divided.

Whereas in the aftermath of Shlomo's death everyone had sat shivah together, now the two families sat in mourning separately. Benzion Aryeh Leib and his sisters were in what had been Shlomo's house, while Naftali's daughters and their husbands sat with Naftali's dowager *rebbetzin* in her house. This was not simply a dispute between two men who sought to be rebbes; it was about family claims and each family feeling it was being usurped by the other.

Many of the young boys in the *mesifta* were among Mordechai Dovid's most enthusiastic followers. Perhaps that accounted for the school's dean speaking out and calling for them to unite behind Benzion Aryeh Leib. He knew what was happening in the school. Among the *mesifta* students were newcomers to Bobov who had been attracted to the court as a result of their education in its schools rather than out of family traditions, so if they went with the challenger they were not necessarily rebelling against their roots. Many of these young Hasidim felt perhaps less attached to the dynasty of the Halberstams, whom Benzion represented. They knew that Benzion Aryeh Leib had been the *rav-tza'ir*, but they felt drawn to Mordechai Dovid, who seemed interested in creating a very personal relationship with them. In his court, they would not be juniors in the back or at the margins, newcomers, as they might be in Benzion Aryeh Leib's Bobov. In Mordechai Dovid's court, they would be among the founding members and maybe even in the inner circle, and that was no small matter to someone new to the Bobover way. They became very loyal soldiers to Mordechai Dovid, and often they were able to take their fathers and brothers along, who also were welcomed.

German's announcement was actually the coda to a scuffle that had occurred earlier that morning, when some of Mordechai Dovid's young supporters had entered the hall and a fistfight had broken out in the midst of the prayers between them and the backers of Benzion Aryeh Leib.[69] The New York City Police Department was called, and officers (including a woman) entered the men's section of the sanctuary to separate the fighters and try to restore order. While some Hasidim, still wrapped in their prayer garb, cried out their prayers, trying to ignore the scuffles, their sound was drowned out by the calls of the police repeatedly warning the disputants to "back off." Hasidim screamed at one another, "Don't be a *chochom* [wise guy]" or urged others to get out. Some jumped up on the tables, their feet dangerously close to the holy prayer books and volumes of Talmud lying there. The profanation of the prayer space was seen as inexcusable. Any hopes that the quarrels over who was rebbe would fade away were dashed.

Still looking for a counterargument that would undeniably cancel all alternate claims, Benzion Aryeh Leib's Hasidim hoped that his crowning by the *dayan* Tauber and those with him had accomplished that. But the morning's scuffle showed it had not. Ad hoc arguments broke out. Some of Benzion's supporters contended that had Naftali truly wanted a son-in-law to succeed him he would surely have appointed the older of the two, Yehoshua Rubin. Mordechai Dovid's Hasidim would have none of that.

In a crude display of force, some of those who held the keys to Bobov real estate—supporters of Benzion—locked the doors to many buildings to prevent any sort of an invasion or takeover. When after the end of the shivah Mordechai Dovid entered the main sanctuary and tried to move to the front to lead the prayers, some of those supporting Benzion tried to push him aside.

As the numbers for Benzion seemed to be larger, Mordechai Dovid and his people decided to withdraw from the Forty-Eighth Street headquarters. They set up a rival headquarters and *bes medrash* on the ground floor of a girls' school a few blocks away from the Bobov main building. On Purim, when the shivah was partially suspended, Mordechai Dovid led his Hasidim in singing, as a "big box of hamantaschen, the triangular pastries made in the shape of Haman's hat, made its way around the tables." [70] When it was over, he shouted "L'chaim," and sped off in a car.

But these were all little more than skirmishes in what would turn out to be a far longer and stubborn struggle. It would involve a search for Hasidim, financial supporters, and communal legitimacy from other rebbes. Charisma and tradition, family and history, money and even Jewish law would be invoked.

THE SEARCH FOR SUPPORTERS AND LEGITIMACY

The two sides raced to establish legitimacy and to demonstrate that their man had what it took to lead the Hasidim into the twenty-first century. With thousands of members, this Bobov court was much larger and more complex than it had been, and it would require more organization and control. As well, the ability to provide for Hasidim, service the court, and run its many institutions was not based only on the leader's charisma; it required financial backing. For that, anyone who would be rebbe needed help.

Mordechai Dovid had resources. Benzion Dunner, the London-based son-in-law of the Stern-Freshwaters, informed him that whatever it cost he was prepared to set him up as the next Bobover Rebbe. [71] He bought buildings for his new rebbe and his Hasidim and offered economic backing, critical during the initial period of the contest. However, when in August 2008, three years after Mordechai Dovid's challenge, the forty-five-year-old Dunner was killed after losing control of his speeding Bentley and crashing it into an embankment, the financial condition of the challenger was severely crippled.[72] By then, Mordechai Dovid had established a reputation as a rebbe, so when some supporters of his rival offered him a financial settlement if he dropped his challenge, he refused to accept it.

In the early days of the conflict, Benzion Aryeh Leib's Hasidim organized economic support their rebbe would need to control the reins of power. Supported on their side by, among others, the successful hedge fund manager Israel Englander, who had and would continue to give millions of dollars to help buy real estate or construct new buildings, and generally sustain the Bobovers who stayed with Shlomo's son, they appeared to be financially secure.[73] Englander, an Orthodox Jew and head of the multi-billion-dollar Millennium Management Fund, was the yeshiva-educated son of Polish refugees. His parents spent the war in a Soviet labor camp and came to the United States in 1947, about a year before his birth in Brooklyn, and he had gotten close to the Rebbe Shlomo. For him, Benzion Aryeh Leib was the undeniable choice.[74]

Besides Englander, Benzion Aryeh Leib had other backers with large financial resources, including the family of Haim Schlaff, based in Vienna; Solomon Obstfeld, based in New York; and Leibel Rubin, a real estate mogul.[75] Unlike his half brother and father, Benzion Aryeh Leib knew how to be a fund-raiser, an important skill in any contest over leadership. Of course, the financial needs of Mordechai Dovid were greater, since, unable to use the assets Bobov had, he and his Hasidim had to create a whole series of new parallel institutions, while his rival managed to hold most of those that were part of the established court.

As the two claimants shored up their funding, they sought public recognition of their position as Bobover Rebbe and thereby legitimacy from other Hasidic rebbes and from the community at large. For example, when Mordechai Dovid traveled to London in 2007 to attend the wedding of a member of the Freshwater family, he was—according to certain media reports—greeted by "thousands" as "the Bobover Rebbe" and shared the rostrum with members of the local Bobov leadership.[76] Similar reports accompanied Benzion Aryeh Leib's appearances. Pictures of each man with previous Bobover Rebbes or with prominent Hasidic leaders were posted in public places.[77] Generally, Mordechai Dovid seemed to have himself photographed in the role of rebbe and with other leaders more often, as if trying to create a pictorial record that affirmed his status; his rival often relied simply on his last name.[78] Indeed, to guard his dignity, Benzion Aryeh Leib shunned publicity photos, but there were still many around. Pictures with elected officials were ubiquitous, each man shown sitting with the governor, the mayor, or other public officials or candidates, who, for their part, eschewed taking sides and were often eager to be photographed with both leaders.[79]

When young men and boys chose to ally themselves with Mordechai Dovid, at times defying their fathers, he announced that he would provide the necessary clothing, the expensive *bekeshe* (kaftan) and suits, for anyone whose father refused to do this. If they wanted to register to study in *his mesifta,* they could do so on their own, rather than via their fathers, who normally would have been the ones to register them. Such offers were in effect encouragements to rebel. Those who went to him found that opportunities for returning to the other side disappeared. That too cemented their ties to him. In this way, he gained a loyal following in many cases being intimately involved in their lives.

THE SPLIT GOES TO COURT

The Bobover community realized the challenge for the *rebistve* was not going to go away. The break was formalized when the supporters of Mordechai Dovid began filing papers in a variety of secular courts. Both sides hired lawyers, and a case was brought before the Brooklyn Supreme Court. Justice Herbert Kramer, seeing this as a religious schism, persuaded both sides to take their dispute for arbitration before a Jewish religious court. In May of 2005, two months after the death of Naftali, the two sides initiated a *din torah*.[80] Because the quarrel had become so acrimonious, at first neither side accepted the legitimacy and summons from the *beit din* to which the other side had submitted its claims (this was why they had at first turned to a secular court with its power of subpoena). Accordingly, as is the case when the parties to a dispute cannot find a mutually acceptable Jewish court, a joint *beit din* was formed by a procedure called a *zabla*. In a *zabla,* each side picks one judge and those two go on to select the rest of the court, normally simply a third man. In this case, the two judges that were chosen together selected three more judges, and the five judges formed the *beit din* charged with resolving the case. Each side argued that Hasidic precedent supported its claim.

For eight years, the *zabla* court struggled with the question of who legitimately headed the Bobover Hasidic community, who owned its assets, and who could rightfully claim the title of Bobover Rebbe. The essential question the *beit din* considered was whether the legal concept of "inheritance" could be invoked at all with regard to a Hasidic dynasty or whether it was up to Hasidim to freely to decide whom they wished to lead them.[81] Even if the question of who was "rebbe" was beyond the court's decision, it was asked to reach some valuation of Bobov assets (should they have to be divided) and to make a judgment as to who could legitimately identify himself as a Bobover Hasid. The great question of who was a *zaddik,* once a matter of charisma, was now instrumentalized into a matter of trademarking: Who could possess the rights to the identifier *Bobov,* and how much was it worth?[82] Personal charisma had little to do with it; it was now all about the office.

Both sides believed that they had a sympathetic ear on the court, and that conviction moved them to agree to accept the ultimate verdict, even though no one could be sure that they would. But as the case ground on year after year, each side tried to create facts on the ground that would force the court to acknowledge its rights. After years of testimony the court explored paths to adjudicate the dispute, floating a variety of options of settlement. For example, in 2007, the idea was suggested that the followers of Mordechai Dovid Unger be willing to take the name "Sanz-Bobov" and allow the other side to call itself "Bobov" in return for the latter's dropping their claims to all the material assets associated with Bobov.[83] It went nowhere.

While family claims, financial resources, photos and meetings with public figures or other rebbes, and the court decision were important in the dynamics of the contest for succession, ultimately the Hasidim of each man, as well as recognition in the larger community of Hasidic rebbes, were what counted most.[84] Accordingly, around the time of the Jewish New Year in 2007, Bobovers tried to resolve the contest by acceding to the *zabla* court's demand for a survey, a poll that would serve almost like an election, to see which of the two men had the most support among the Hasidim.[85] The name *Bobov* (and the significant economic resources associated with it) remained at the heart of the contest, as insiders explained.[86] Anyone could call himself a rebbe if he had Hasidim; but as they saw it, only one man could call himself the Bobover Rebbe.

THE POLL

The *beit din* initiated its poll of the Hasidim, counting only the choice of every male (women did not vote) over the age of eighteen. To qualify as a voter, a man had to have made use of or celebrated an event in one of the Bobover-sponsored institutions (*mosdos*). Not only were voters asked with whom they allied themselves but also who they believed had a right to call himself the Bobover Rebbe and if that right was exclusive.

Both sides would have to agree to—literally sign off on—the results and lists that emerged. The results showed that approximately 24 percent affiliated with Mordechai Dovid and 76 percent with Benzion Aryeh Leib. By 2012, the court prepared to decree that the division was 70/30 and to issue a verdict. But when presented with these results, Mordechai Dovid and his Hasidim asked to have his lawyers and experts look at the poll details before signing their acceptance of it. The numbers mattered; however charismatic the challenger, if those who followed him were actually a minority, it would be inconceivable for him to wrest away legitimacy and nominal control over Bobov.

In the meantime, the two Bobover *rebistve*s carried on: one led by Benzion Aryeh Leib and holding on to the headquarters and buildings on Forty-Eighth Street, and the other led by Mordechai Dovid, with many venues of meeting but originally convening in a building on Forty-Fifth Street. In the Hasidic world, the two factions became known informally as Bobov 48 and Bobov 45. From a distance, the differences were hard to distinguish. Were the uninformed to walk into a gathering of either one, they would hardly be able to tell at first glance into which of the two Bobov camps they had entered. For example, on the interim days of the Sukkot holiday, when Bobovers traditionally convene a complement of Hasidic violinists at their rebbe's table, an observer would find two identical gatherings, along with the requisite fiddlers playing the same tunes, gathered in two remarkably similar sukkahs and simultaneously singing and eating with their rebbes, both of whom were called the Bobover Rebbe.

Given that most of the Hasidim remained attached to and allied with Benzion Aryeh Leib, Mordechai Dovid continued to be far more approachable, open to meeting whoever would acknowledge him as Bobover rebbe. Holding on to more of the Bobover cards, Benzion Aryeh Leib maintained his dignity, playing the more imposing and regal leader. He felt that the weight of Bobover history rested his shoulders, giving him a position and stature with which his arriviste rival could not really compete.

In February of 2013, after years of deliberation, the *beit din* again sought to issue its judgment, but the two sides were still not ready to accept this decision as final. Of course, as long as the *beit din*'s decision was not formally accepted by both sides, none of its verdicts would take hold. The process was stalemated; the questions of which group could call itself Bobov, which man was entitled to call himself the Bobover Rebbe, and which group owned the assets belonging to Bobov remained unanswered in any legal way.

THE VERDICT

At last, in mid-August 2014, seeking to lay these questions to rest, the *beit din* informed both sides that it was absolutely going to issue its final decision. Mordechai Dovid and his Hasidim, whose numbers remained largely unchanged, tried to postpone the event, but with no success. Everyone knew what was coming. On August 21, 2014 (25 Menachem Av, in the Jewish calendar), about nine years after the case was brought to it and after about $8 million in arbitration costs, the *beit din* published its decision:

- Only Benzion Halberstam, the son of Shlomo Halberstam, can be called the Bobov Ruv and Bobover Rebbe, so that when the term *Bobov* without any other identifying additions is used it will be understood as referring solely to Benzion Halberstam.

- Neither Mordechai Dovid Unger nor his brother-in-law Yehoshua Rubin may be called the Bobov Ruv and Rebbe, in any language. This applies to the United States and everywhere else in the world.

- It is the responsibility of Rabbis Unger and Rubin to make sure that they are not so called in any way, shape, or form. They must inform all newspapers and all others who are not among their Hasidim of this decision, and they must make sure that they are never so announced at weddings or anywhere else.

- It is further their responsibility to make sure that whenever someone refers to Bobov, it is understood unequivocally to mean the faction of Benzion Halberstam. In effect the Bobov "trademark" [the court used this English term] is awarded only to the Halberstams.

- Rabbis Unger and Rubin have the option to call themselves with an additional name of a town along with the name of Bobov, so long as the new town name of their Hasidic identity existed as part of their family heritage from a period historically prior to the time the name of Bobov was established (before 1905). For example, they could choose to be called Sanz Bobov, as they too were descended from the Divrei Chaim [the Sanzer Rebbe]. They also have the option to choose to call themselves Bobov45, but only if there is no space between the digits and the letters, which must all be in the same font size and on the same line. In short, there must be no confusing the name of the Unger faction with the Halberstam one. Nor may members of the Unger court or his Hasidim transgress these terms.

- They must quickly choose their name. Once their choice is made, that name will become final, and they may never change to a different name along with the name *Bobov*.

- The Unger faction may not call their *mosdos* [institutions] and corporations by any of the names being currently used by Bobov, including but not limited to Kehal Sharei Zion, Yeshivah Bnei Zion, Bnos Zion, Mesivta Eits Chaim, Kollel Zichron Chaim, Ameidei Zion, Camps Shalva and Gila.

- The Unger faction must change their emblems. And they may not use the same uniform for the girls as Bobov is currently using.

- Every single Bobov asset belongs to the faction of Rabbi Halberstam, including but not limited to the following buildings: New Beis Medrash, Old Beis Medrash, yeshiva buildings on Forty-Eighth and Forty-Second Streets, *mesifta* buildings, Bnos Zion Buildings, Kerem Shlomo Building, the *mesifta* camp in the Poconos, Camps Shalva, Kerem Shlomo, and Camp Gila.

- All of the property (both real estate and movable assets, including all Torah scrolls) that was in possession of Bobov at the time of the passing of the previous rebbe, Naftali Halberstam, belongs to and remains in the control of the Benzion Halberstam faction. The Unger faction shall receive $6.2 million—to be paid out over a period of five years. This is the grand total they will receive out of the Bobov enterprise.

Sensing from an earlier preliminary announcement of the verdict that Benzion's side had effectively won everything significant, Mordechai Dovid's side neither attended the decision nor signed the verdict. Yet once issued it was final. Throughout the process that led up to it and afterward, Mordechai Dovid and his side did not deny that Benzion Aryeh Leib was *a* Bobover rebbe. They just wanted to say he was not the only one and that their leader was one too. That of course was no longer a full-fledged challenge for the crown.

In effect, the court agreed only that they were Bobovers, but with a modifier—and that made all the difference. The Bobov45 group wanted the opportunity to continue to campaign for the name without the qualifier, to compete for and slowly build up a constituency in the hopes that someday their leader might one day eclipse all other claimants and effectively be the dominant one.

But the *beit din*'s decision—enforceable by New York State courts, which had sent it this case for binding arbitration—closed off that possibility. Bobov45 could grow, and its rebbe could gain stature, but he would never be called *the* Bobover Rebbe. The decision could be viewed only as an humiliating defeat for Mordechai Dovid and his Hasidim.

Trying to subtly undermine the *beit din*'s decision, some of the losers complained that even though it took about ten years of rabbinic consideration, it was presented like a profane document, lacking any references to the Torah on which it was presumably based. "So profane," as one blogger put it, "you could even read it while sitting on the toilet." [87] The specificity of the verdict, the level of detail in the court's directives, seemed demeaning. Others claimed that two of the five rabbinic judges were biased because they or their families had ties with Bobov, a fact long known and judged not to be significant.

One wag noted the inaccuracy and incompleteness of the Bobov45 label: by 2014 their synagogue was on Forty-Ninth Street, the rebbe lived on Fiftieth Street, the all-important income-generating matzah factory was at Sixty-Second Street while the water (*mayim shelanu*) used for it was on Eighteenth Avenue, the yeshiva was located on Fifty-Second Street, the primary school was on Fifty-Third Street, and so on.[88] The title Bobov45 was meaningless.

Many in Bobov devolved into an obsession with what Freud called the "narcissism of small differences," the phenomenon of "communities with adjoining territories, and related to each other in other ways as well, who are engaged in constant feuds and ridiculing each other." [89] Others called for a boycott of businesses that received kosher supervision from Rabbi Yechiel Babad of Tartikov, one of the judges in the court that had ruled against them.[90] In the end, the decision stood, and the rebels who were now to be known as Bobov45 seemed to admit their altered status.

ADMITTING DEFEAT

A bit over two months after the verdict in late November of 2014, Mordechai Dovid addressed his Hasidim with what seemed an acknowledgment of the result. This was clearly not an easy moment for him, as all those present (as well as those who later watched the video posted by Yeshiva World News) could see.[91] In an address marked by long pauses and obvious discomfort, the would-be Bobover Rebbe who now had to call himself the Rebbe of Bobov45, spoke. In the days after the verdict he and his Hasidim had complained that the decision had not offered a "peace plan," which he now framed as the purpose of the court case from the outset. He wanted "peace," he said, "but they want war." He announced that he was ready to sacrifice his honor on the altar of peace, and he urged his Hasidim to "hold themselves together." [92] In Israel, however, his group had filed a civil suit to claim Kiryas Bobov, an Israeli neighborhood near Bat Yam dominated by Bobovers.[93]

Like so many rebbe talks, this one began by referencing the Torah portion of the week. Mordechai Dovid cited the verse in which the patriarch Jacob awakens following his famous dream, recounted in Genesis 28:10–22, and declares: "Surely the Lord is in this place, and I was not aware of it." He too was awakening from a dream, one in which he had been the successor to the crown of Bobov. Like Jacob, he and his Hasidim needed to realize that where they were now God was present. Using an acrostic he had constructed from the preceding verse, Mordechai Dovid demonstrated how it spelled out the Hebrew word *tzibbur,* "congregation." Then he made the connection at which he had hinted even more explicit.

"A congregation that holds itself together with dedication and continues in the holy paths that our holy rebbes have blazed before us, the grandfather, may his memory be blessed [Shlomo], and the father-in-law, may his memory be blessed [Naftali], and when one looks upon such a congregation [meaning the Hasidim before him], one can truly declare 'Surely the Lord is in this place. . . .'" Referring to his predecessors in this way, Mordechai Dovid subtly reminded his audience of his direct family ties to those who had come before him. Concluding that "there is the spirit of the Divine Presence here," he asserted that God was with them.

The message? No matter what the court's decision, his congregation was still being led along pathways established by the previous rebbes, and it was a place in which the Divine Presence rested, and he, Mordechai Dovid, had brought them to this place. They would continue "to work together with a pure intention," and not with the less benevolent motives that others ascribed to them. "How awesome is this place! This is none other than the house of God; this is the gate of heaven," he repeated, reiterating the message that what he and his Hasidim had created was no less awe-inspiring than the other place that called itself "Bobov."

"After my father-in-law's death, it was not at all easy to keep ourselves together." Some had been drawn to his rival. But with "help from Heaven" they had held on to one another and had continued the holy customs of their rebbes in this new camp. Now they needed to consult with one another, to take stock of their situation.

Standing at a lectern, Mordechai Dovid spoke from a prepared speech held in his hands, but he broke from it repeatedly, nervously stroking his beard and swaying side to side, as if finding it hard to say words the court verdict now forced upon him. He reminded his audience that they themselves had initiated the case, had resolved to see what "the great men of Israel" would determine rather than to let the street decide, "and so it was." They now owned the result. Pausing again for what seemed an eternity, he finally admitted that "the verdict was not so simple to understand, everyone [looking at the facts] with a different emphasis." He wanted to frame the decision in his own terms.

Mordechai Dovid needed to save face, to explain the reason that, having sought a decision, he and his side had delayed acknowledging it. Some, he claimed, had urged him to ignore the verdict. But, he explained, out of this could come terrible and unintended consequences—"a *chillul hashem*," desecration of God's name. Rabbinic courts were not held in such high esteem these days, he said, making a subtle swipe at this one. He quoted a favorite Talmudic adage cited by the *Kedushas Zion* that all Bobovers knew: "Better that I be known as a fool all my life than to be an evil-doing transgressor against God for one moment in my life." If people heard that in Bobov a *beit din* verdict had been defied, then others might take this as an excuse to likewise ignore the courts. This subtly reminded the court that it was no less dependent on him than he on them and that he chose, at the sacrifice of his own interests, to be the defender of rabbinic courts.

Yes, there were "strong reasons" to ignore the verdict, including the difficulty so many had understanding it, the fact that it dishonored them and caused so much pain and humiliation, "the aggravation that so vexed our families." Again he paused for a long time. The room was hushed. He rubbed his eyes. "Both sides had strong arguments."

They needed, however, to heed the words of rabbis as set forth in Avot 3:1: "Reflect upon three things and you will not come to the hands of transgression. Know from where you came, where you are going, and before whom you are destined to give a judgment and accounting."

"We have reached the decision," he continued, "based on how my father-in-law would have responded had he been in this situation." Stressing the authority of Naftali rather than Shlomo was of course a way of putting emphasis on the rebbe from whom Mordechai Dovid and his followers drew their succession claims. Rocking back and forth, pulling his beard, and silent for nearly a half minute, he seemed unable to conclude. "His was the way closer to peace and farther from dispute." Again silence and swaying: "This is the decision."

Yet he never articulated the decision, never stated its restrictions and demands. Everyone knew them, and perhaps he could not bring himself to repeat them.

Mordechai Dovid's delivery grew increasingly punctuated by silence; he sniffled and he wiped his eyes. "This is not a disgrace. This is," he paused and then cried out, "the Bobover way, and its aim is, with the Almighty's help, that there be a total peace." Then he added that if there would truly be a total peace, the decision would be enforced—"Vehamavin yovin" (Those who understand know what I mean). He would be bound by the decision only if the other side stopped its attacks on them.

Addressing the ignominious demand that "45" be henceforth attached to the name of his *rebistve,* he asserted it was purely for "recognition," rather than diminution. He struck the lectern with his fist. "If someone says something to you, you don't always have to answer back. As my father-in-law once explained, if someone says something [unpleasant] to you and you remain silent, it is a way of praising God." He would remain silent about the "45."

Shuffling some papers in silence, he swayed again, as his audience shifted uneasily. No matter what he said, the ignominy of his defeat was undeniable. Nearly a minute passed as he groomed his beard, banged on the lectern, and seemed to search for a way to continue.

"We come back to the verse," he resumed at last. "'And Jacob awoke from his sleep. . . .' The time has come for us to take ourselves in hand, and with God's help build ourselves anew, with strength, increasing the honor of heaven." He closed his eyes now as he spoke, as if intoning words of prayer. He listed the places where he had Hasidim, including those "across the seas" and "in the Land of Israel." In all those places where they had congregations, they needed "to awaken." In those places they needed to demonstrate that "surely the Lord is in this place."

Finally, he thanked by name those who had economically supported his efforts and reminded the assembled that they too had made pledges of millions that he trusted would be fulfilled (the word on the street had been that the finances of his court were precarious). He reiterated his hope that in the near future they would be able to have their own place of prayer, a place that would be a "worthy" symbol of their growth and character. Once again he referenced the Torah portion of the week and quoted from it (Gen. 26:22): "And he removed from thence, and dug

15. Benzion Halberstam, the current Bobover Rebbe, presiding over a *tish*, serenaded by fiddlers. By permission of and copyright Stanley Weiss.

another well; and for that they strove not. And he called the name of it Rehoboth; and he said: 'For now the Lord hath made room for us, and we shall be fruitful in the land.'" Mordechai Dovid and his Hasidim would end their quarrels; they would be like the Patriarch and remove themselves from where they had encountered strife to a place where God would make room for them and would there grow mighty. They could trust that the Almighty would turn matters better for them: study houses would grow, in beautiful buildings with institutions of Torah that would honor Heaven. Like all rebbes, he promised his Hasidim that God would provide them a livelihood, for the merit of their holy forebears would hold them together and help bring the final redemption.

THE SITUATION TODAY

As things now stand, Benzion Aryeh Leib, who holds the lion's share of Hasidim, avoids being in the same room at the same time as Mordechai Dovid; the two do not attend events in the Hasidic world at the same time. They continue to vie for power, control, authority, and legitimacy. Each man issues decisions about what is prohibited or permissible behavior in the Bobover community. For example, in the name of Benzion Aryeh Leib, his *gabbaim* gave notice that any Hasid who "had in his possession any instrument connected to the Internet, without a superior filter," would be prohibited from "leading the services," and his yeshiva banned eyeglasses with a "designer" full black frame as not "in the spirit" of the community. In the name of Mordechai Dovid, it was announced that his Hasidim do not recognize the legitimacy of the *eruv,* the Jewish legal boundary meant to permit the carrying of objects and pushing of strollers in public spaces on the Sabbath.[94]

Because he is the upstart and holds a smaller group of Hasidim, Mordechai Dovid remains welcoming to anyone who wants to sit at his table and acknowledge him as a Bobover rebbe. He is happy to sit with any Hasid, even if that person also feels some sort of attachment to Benzion Aryeh Leib. Indeed, those who come from families close to his rival or with a long Bobov pedigree are treated, as one Hasid put it, "like foreign dignitaries" and are offered an especially warm embrace and access to the leader. Mordechai Dovid is more often willing to be photographed with politicians and power brokers.

Although more outgoing than he was before the court's verdict, Benzion Aryeh Leib remains far more demanding of complete and utter loyalty from his Hasidim, insistent they acknowledge him as *the one and only* Bobover Rebbe. While the larger family tries hard to avoid taking sides openly, those who imply that Mordechai Dovid's claims are *as* legitimate as Benzion Aryeh Leib's are held at arm's length by the latter but are welcomed with open arms by the former.[95]

Both men try to stress their continuity with the past, but Benzion controls the main institutions of Bobov (figure 15). During a week in January of 2014, when Bobovers celebrated the marriage of one of Benzion's daughters, signs were placed on his home and the nearby home of his late father, both of which are adjacent to the main sanctuary and *bes medrash* of Bobov on Forty-Eighth Street. In huge letters under the symbolic crown of Bobov they spelled out a well-known scriptural verse (1 Kings 8:57), spoken by King Solomon when he brought the Ark of the Covenant from where his father King David had left it to the Holy Temple in Jerusalem. Repeated in the liturgy regularly, the verse invokes the special relationship between the royal father and son and the theme of continuity. Over Benzion's doorway were the words: "The LORD our God be with us," while across the street over the father's was the second half of the verse: "as He was with our fathers." Everyone who read it knew the verse's final words, which were meant for every Bobover Hasid: "May he neither leave us, nor forsake us."

5

Satmar

Succession Charged with Conflict

Among those even slightly familiar with contemporary Hasidism, certainly in the United States, perhaps no group is more associated with a struggle over succession than the Satmar Hasidim. Generally considered the largest and most influential Hasidic group in America, it is headquartered in Williamsburg, Brooklyn, with about ninety-five thousand members, but with a large and growing settlement in Kiryas Joel in New York's Orange County (nearly twenty-two thousand people according to the US Census in 2013, a rise of 8.5 percent since the decennial census of 2010) as well as growing outposts elsewhere in New York State and in Canada, Israel, England, Belgium, and even Australia.[1] So quickly has the community grown that in late 2014 it announced the formation of a new Satmar outpost, Kiryas Yetev Lev, with four hundred apartments in the village of Bloomingburg in New York's Sullivan County.[2]

No present-day battle for a *rebistve* is more intense and widely known. But Satmar, which has had three generations of rebbes, has been marked by a series of difficult successions from the outset. Its founder, Yoelish Teitelbaum, established the Satmar dynasty when his father found no place for him at his own court in Sighet. After Yoelish's death, with no immediate heirs, his widow Feige sought unsuccessfully to hold the throne for herself and prevent his nephew, Moshe, from succeeding him. Finally, as Moshe's health declined, two of his sons, Aaron and Zalman, began a bitter struggle to succeed him that broke out full force upon his death. Since its inception in eastern Europe, Satmar

The Sighet/Satmar Dynasty

MOSHE TEITELBAUM (1758–1841): Known as the Yismach Moshe; Rebbe of Ujhel, Hungary

ELAZAR NISSAN TEITELBAUM (1786–1856): Rebbe of Drohobych, Ukraine; son of Moshe Teitelbaum

YEKUTIEL YEHUDAH TEITELBAUM (1808–83): Also known as Zalman Leib (Yiddish) and the Yetev Lev; Rebbe of Sighet, Hungary; son of Elazar Nissan

CHANANYAH YOM TOV LIPA TEITELBAUM (1836–1904): Known as the Kedushas Yom Tov; Rebbe of Tesh and later Sighet; oldest son of Yekutiel Yehudah

HAIM TZVI TEITELBAUM (1879–1926): Known as the Atzei Haim; Rebbe of Sighet; oldest son of Chananyah Yom Tov Lipa

YOELISH TEITELBAUM (1886–1979): Known as the Divrei Yoel; founder and First Rebbe of the Satmar dynasty; second son of Chananyah Yom Tov Lipa

ZALMAN LEIB (1912–44): Sigheter Rebbe; son of Haim Tzvi Teitelbaum

MOSHE TEITELBAUM (1914–2006): Known as the Beirach Moshe; Rebbe of Sighet and second rebbe of Satmar; second son of Haim Tzvi Teitelbaum and nephew of Yoelish

AARON TEITELBAUM (1947–PRESENT): rebbe of the Satmar community in Kiryas Joel, New York, and one of two claimants to the title of Third Rebbe of Satmar; first son of Moshe

ZALMAN LEIB (1952–PRESENT): Also known as Yekutiel Yehudah; rebbe of the Satmar community in Williamsburg, New York, and one of two claimants to be the Third Rebbe of Satmar; third son of Moshe

Hasidism thus has been marked by disputes over transition and leadership. One might even say that clashes and conflict are in its DNA, essential to it. I turn to Satmar and its stories of succession next.

THE ORIGINS OF THE DYNASTY

The roots of the dynasty begin with Moshe Teitelbaum (1758–1841), called the Yismach Moshe after his most famous book of homilies. Teitelbaum, who became a Hasid only after his marriage, is credited with bringing Hasidism to what we today call Hungary from Poland, where he had become a disciple of the famous Hasidic master Yaakov Yitzchak Horowitz, known as "the Seer of Lublin." In the northern Hungarian town of Ujhel (Újhely), where he took up a position, he became known for, among other things, his involvement in mystical matters but even more for his tenacious opposition to any modernizing or acculturating trends among the Jewry of his day—from decrees he made prohibiting mixed-sex dancing to minor "desecrations of the Sabbath" such as shampooing, and to the appointment of rabbis he viewed as "modern." [3]

Although in 1834 he tried to arrange the appointment of his son Elazar Nissan (1786–1856) as a rabbi in Sighet (Sighetu Marmației), a city about 240 kilometers to the east in Transylvania, where he hoped to establish a Hasidic court, his effort was unsuccessful. The locals refused to accept the son's authority, leading to Elazar's humiliating departure and return to Ujhel after six years. His father urged him to stay in Sighet and fight for his position, but Elazar went about 300 kilometers to the northeast to serve as a rabbi in Drohobych, Ukraine, his wife's hometown.[4] After his failure in Sighet, however, he never acted as a Hasidic master again, turning away any Hasidim who came to him in the hopes of persuading him to change his mind.[5]

Elazar's son, Yekutiel Yehudah (1808–83), sent to live with his grandfather Moshe, was greatly influenced by the larger-than-life older man, his worldview, and his religious behavior, more than by his reclusive father. He too followed the family profession, succeeding his grandfather in Ujhel in 1841 after the latter's death. However, he also ran into controversy when those who appointed him to the rabbinic position wanted him to act not as a Hasidic leader but simply as the town rabbi. Like his father, he was ignominiously expelled from his rabbinic position both in Ujhel and later in Drohobych, where he tried to take up his father's post.[6] Finally in 1858, after living on the outskirts of the city, Yekutiel Yehudah, taking advantage of political rivalries within it, established himself as a Hasidic leader in Sighet, where he was also appointed as a rabbi, largely on the strength of a eulogy he gave for a local Jewish philanthropist. This proved to be his most successful post.

In Sighet, known as the Yetev Lev for his commentary on the Torah, Yekutiel, like his forebears, embraced extremist antimodern positions. He closed a school that had been in Sighet for fifty years, replacing it with his own Hasidic yeshiva, while throughout the Hungarian district and in nearby Galicia he appointed as rabbis members of his family who echoed the extremist and insular Teitelbaum ideology, gradually forging a cadre of young followers who, in their antimodernist zealotry, contrasted sharply with those who were more accepting of the general culture, such as the many German Jews who had migrated into the area during the time.[7] Marrying off his daughter Pesel to a son of the influential Rebbe of Sanz, Chaim Halberstam (1793–1876), known as the Divrei Chaim, Yekutiel raised his profile, further enhancing his reputation and his extremist views.[8]

He arranged for his son Chananyah Yom Tov Lipa (1836–1904), a rabbi in the town of Tesh (Técső) for nineteen years, to succeed him. The son saw himself as a spiritual heir and follower more of the better-known and more widely respected Divrei Chaim than of his father. Lipa, as he was known, was no less controversial and for a time struggled politically to maintain his rabbinic position and even to protect the reputation of his late father. Some broke away from his authority and set up a separate Jewish community in the city, on which Lipa placed a ban. There are reports that he used thugs to settle accounts with his opponents, explaining in a commentary that

> there are times when even a leader of the Jewish people must show a bit of cruelty as a show of strength, grab a stick and beat them over the head. This springs from the quality of mercy, for he does it so that they will heed his voice and so that he will raise them up and lead them with the might of his hand to the wellsprings of Torah and good deeds. And here, whoever is fearful, that this leader does something that seems cruel, let it become clear to him that he is actually pursuing the opposite quality, while it is not pleasant or seemly to do what he does.[9]

Lipa had more success in handling conflict than his forebears and managed after a few years to get the secessionists to return, enhancing his status as a major Hasidic leader in Transylvania. His refusal to compromise on his extremist views seemed vindicated by this success in arresting the breakaway trend.

The yeshiva that Lipa inherited from his father became one of the largest in Hungary, growing to about three hundred students. This institution building added to his stature, since its graduates would forever see him as their spiritual guide. Dedicated to a "relentless fight against modern education," Lipa also opposed and harassed anyone "suspected of taking part in any sort of Zionist activity," which he saw as particularly heretical, both because of its largely nonreligious leadership and because of its goal of forcing an end to what Lipa and other Hasidic anti-Zionists considered a Jewish exile ordained by God.[10] He also actively opposed use of the "Gentile" (i.e., Hungarian) language in his schools and community, even minor changes to Hasidic and traditional dress or appearance, and any sort of modernization or acculturation, a view his Hasidim supported, turning opposition into part of their public collective persona.

Firmly ensconced as the Sigheter Rebbe, Lipa was, however, childless, having lost an only son in early infancy. That endangered the continuity of his court, and it troubled him. He understood that he needed to find a successor. Seeking the counsel of the Divrei Chaim, who tried to allay his concerns by telling him that many *zaddikim* "were childless," Lipa insisted on some sort of specific advice.[11] The elder rebbe finally suggested setting a definite date by which, if he failed to have a child, he could divorce and marry another woman in the hope of having heirs.[12]

After twenty years of marriage, Lipa's wife, Reitze, initially refused to accept a divorce (in 1876 she at last assented).[13] In the meantime, with the help of the Divrei Chaim, Lipa managed to secure a special decree, signed by a hundred rabbis, that according to Jewish law allowed him to take a second wife even without his first wife's accepting a divorce. At the age of forty-two, he married his first cousin Chana Ashkenazi Rubenstein, who divorced from Avraham Abba Rubenstein (with whom she had two children); Chana ultimately bore Lipa five children who survived childhood: two sons and three daughters.[14]

The eldest, Haim Tzvi (1879–1926), named for his father's mentor, was from the outset groomed to succeed his father in Sighet. He did in 1904 at the age of twenty-five. Known as the Atzei Haim (Trees of Life, a play on his name Haim, meaning life and after the name of his commentary), he was also brother-in-law of the Benzion Halberstam, the Second Bobover Rebbe, whose sad end at the hands of the Nazis we learned in the last chapter.

YOELISH TEITELBAUM AND HIS QUEST FOR A *REBISTVE*

Lipa's younger son, Yoel (1886–1979)—called "Yoelish"—was the last of the children. Born when his father was fifty-one years old and a powerful Hasidic leader, Yoelish was also judged to have the qualities necessary for leadership. He shared his father's views, showed intellect as a young student, and distinguished himself in his Torah studies, being able to review a folio of Talmud at age five.[15] Yet from an early age he knew that as the younger son he would not succeed his father.

This realization drove him to distinguish himself all the more. As the baby of the family and doted on by his mother and sisters, he developed a piety remarkable for a boy, studying for hours in a separate room, sleeping only briefly during the night, taking on a regimen of fasting, growing his earlocks longer than most, distributing alms on behalf of the family, and practicing a scrupulosity in Jewish rituals.[16] This scrupulosity in ritual behavior extended beyond religion and verged on obsessive-compulsive behavior. For example, he repeatedly and excessively rinsed his mouth, washed his hands, and sat on the toilet, often interrupting his prayers to evacuate his bowels in order, as he put it, to "purify himself." [17]

Although during his father's reign Yoelish served as his representative to a variety of communal organizations behind the scenes, an unsung role was not to his liking. He believed that he had the makings of no less a leader than his father or elder brother, and his mother encouraged this opinion. Like so many other *rebbetzin*s, she sought to assure the future of *all* her offspring, especially her beloved baby. She therefore asked Lipa, whose health was failing and who would be dead shortly, that when the time came her elder son might become the town chief rabbi (*rav*) while her younger one might be appointed to lead the Hasidic court (rebbe) or at least serve as a *dayan* (judge). At a minimum, she requested that he be made a circuit rabbi in a few of the villages where there were some of his father's Hasidim, hoping he would attract a following via the Sighet rabbinate.[18] But her husband refused, much to her consternation.[19]

Accordingly, even before his brother Haim Tzvi ascended to the crown of Sighet, Yoelish, still in his shadow, understood that if he was to distinguish himself in public or in the Hasidic world he would have to do it by himself elsewhere. First, he would need to get married, for no single man could ever be a full-fledged rebbe.[20] At seventeen, he wed Chavah Horowitz, a cousin to whom, at his father's demand, he had been betrothed when he was only seven years old.[21] Because Lipa's health was poor, Haim Tzvi presided at his younger brother's wedding in what must surely have made it clear to everyone that he was the heir apparent, serving *in loco parentis*. Following marriage, Yoelish received ordination.[22]

When shortly thereafter Lipa died, the title of Sigheter Rebbe, the headship of the yeshiva, and the rabbinic leadership in the town were all formally inherited by the elder brother, regardless of Yoelish's undeniable intellectual gifts and religious piety or his mother's wishes. For the baby brother, there was a minor and rather part-time rabbinic post about a hundred kilometers to the east in the village of Muzhijevo (Nagy Muzsaly), previously arranged by his father primarily to keep the boy from being drafted into the army. Unenthusiastic about this post, Yoelish barely visited, keeping his home in Sighet.

Yoelish's quest for a position with no less stature than his brother's convinced him to move to his father-in-law's house for a few months, returning to Sighet after the Succot holidays and remaining until September 1905. His mother and father-in-law tried to persuade him to serve as a Hasidic leader in nearby places. When his mother met the great Belzer Rebbe at the Marienbad Spa, a common vacation place for Hasidic royalty, and beseeched his help to find a situation for her baby, he suggested Szatmár (Satmar—more properly Szatmárnémeti); then in Hungary but after the First World War in Romania), about a hundred kilometers east of Sighet.[23]

The official town rabbi of Satmar, Yehuda Grünwald, happened to be at the baths as well and agreed that the seventeen-year-old Teitelbaum's arrival would not be seen as *hasagat gvul,* an incursion into his territory or an effort to undermine his authority. Indeed, he shared many of the antimodernist attitudes of the Teitelbaums and thought Yoelish would support his authority among Hasidim.

Although he would have no official position in Satmar, once he became resident the young Yoelish began to gather about himself a small group of Hasidim—not enough to build a court, and certainly nothing to rival what his brother had in Sighet.[24] Yoelish was not the only would-be Hasidic leader in Satmar; at least four other Hasidic masters had made Satmar their home at the time.[25] These four worried that the presence of a scion of the Sighet court would challenge *their* authority and livelihoods as Sigheter Hasidim gravitated toward him. In actuality, however, the Sigheter Hasidim in Satmar were not particularly enthusiastic about Yoelish, for seeing that he had not been kept at the court, they had no reason to believe attachment to him would bring them closer to his brother, the rebbe with whom they identified.

If Yoelish was to succeed, he would have to do more. The few students and followers he had were insufficient to sustain him financially now that he had two daughters. So in 1911, still looking for work, he was elected rabbi of the Subcarpathian town of Orsova (in Yiddish, commonly Orshiva), about 475 kilometers away to the south. Orshiva, however, was not a high-activity area of Hasidic life and was also surrounded by places with already-established rebbes. Serving in Orshiva until the eve of the First World War, Yoelish maintained a residence in Satmar, still hoping he could build a court and larger following there.[26] His Orshiva appointment was not without controversy and competition. Officially elected rabbis in a town, such as Yoelish had now become, had, among other duties, to approve the kosher certification of butchers and meat, potentially affecting people's pocketbook and arousing enmity if they were too punctilious and disqualified someone. Meat was expensive, and few butchers (as we learned in the case of Munkács, often among the affluent and influential laity in these places) could afford to have their supply prohibited by an official rabbi—and the latter rarely took them on. With his scrupulosity, however, Yoelish did just that, making him unpopular with many of the powerful laity. It would not be the last time he found himself in conflict because of his uncompromising stand and his scrupulously stringent interpretation of Jewish law.

The fact that he did not speak the vernacular well, preferring Yiddish or *loshn koydesh* (Hebrew), also put him in a weaker position with state authorities who formally had to approve officially elected rabbis. In the end, however, he did get the appointment, in the process learning how to handle the politics of controversy to his benefit as well as how to marshal supporters on his behalf.[27] Without great success and with some audacity, he tried to poach Hasidim from some of the surrounding communities as well, while hoping to appoint his own followers to the administrative staff, including a *dayan* whose judgments of Jewish law would comport with the same stringent views his father had. These views he made publicly known in sermons and notices, opening schools where they would be promoted and studied. The fortuitous flow of Jews into the area because of the dislocations of World War I meant more people were exposed to him, and his profile as a leader grew in spite of what might have otherwise become obstacles to his self-promotion.

When the Great War was over and international borders had shifted, the Jews of Austro-Hungary found themselves dispersed among a variety of new states and separated by new national boundaries. Orshiva ended up in Czechoslovakia, while Satmar was in Romania. A commute between the two cities was now more complicated. Luckily, Yoelish had returned to Satmar in October 1914, hoping to spend the war there.

Once again he gathered about him his few Hasidim in the city, remaining there until 1922 while slowly assembling more followers. He became a more public and political figure, serving on more rabbinic councils. During and after the war, rising nationalism sometimes accompanied by strident anti-Semitism became endemic. For some Jews taken up with nationalist fervor but unable or unwilling to find its expression in Europe, Zionism was the answer; for others it was acculturation as expressed by their use of the vernacular. But neither of these options suited the Yiddish-speaking, anti-Zionist, counteracculturationist

Yoelish and his ilk, who instead embraced a defiant insular Jewish Orthodoxy that defined their Hasidim.

In 1920, Yoelish, needing more income to support his family and cut off from his post in Orshiva, applied for a rabbinic position in Satmar. But opposition to his candidacy emerged, fueled both by those who felt he was too young or zealous and by those who objected to a Hasidic rabbinic appointment in a town where so many lived who did not see themselves as Hasidim. Remaining too was opposition by other Hasidic leaders who did not want him to outshine or try again to steal followers from them, and the fears by some more acculturative Jews that he was too extreme and insular in his views. The religious council in the city rejected his candidacy.[28] To add to his bad luck, in 1921 a scarlet fever outbreak in the city infected his middle daughter Esther, killing her at only ten years of age.

Although he did not receive the official rabbinic appointment in Satmar, some Hasidim who had broken with the organized Jewish community were impressed by his outspokenness and began to see Yoelish as their leader. They supported him privately, and some even claimed that he was their sole authority and religious leader. Gradually he became first choice to the more extremist groups seeking their own rabbi. While he did not discourage these people and endorsed their extremism and willingness to separate from the main Jewish Orthodox community, he still needed an official paid position and was not prepared to accept one from the tiny communities nearby.

Frustrated with his inability to get the posts he coveted, Yoelish returned to Orshiva in 1922, after an absence of about eight years. To get there, he had to cross the border into Czechoslovakia, which meant he could no longer serve actively on rabbinic councils in Romania or Hungary. Moreover, his long absence from the region of Orshiva had diminished his political clout and connections there.

Yoelish increased enrollment at his yeshiva to about one hundred students, building a following and looking for allies where he could find them. One of these was Chaim Elazar Shapira, the Munkács Rebbe. While Shapira and Teitelbaum shared some of the more extremist views of Hungarian Jewry as well as anti-Zionist sentiments, neither was ready to allow the other to lead this camp.[29] Their relationship, as we have already seen elsewhere in these pages, would remain shaky at best: they were both ideological allies and political competitors, an ambiguity that figured into relations between the Satmar Rebbe and the grandson of the Munkács Rebbe many years later in America.

Yoelish did manage his rabbinic authority as a district rabbi, finding his footing in the political machinations that went on around him. In 1924, just before Rosh Hashanah, he married off his daughter Chaya Roysaele to a cousin in a ceremony at which his brother, the Rebbe of Sighet, officiated.[30] His new son-in-law, who later became the Sassover Rav, served him as an aide. To some people, he even looked like a possible successor to Yoelish, often sitting close to him when he led a *tish* or at other public occasions. "That possibility, however, had soured" over time because some of Yoelish's Hasidim claimed that the young man had engaged in a "presumptuous grab for power" by sometimes leading the *tish* and offering words of Torah in his father-in-law's absence and that he had not been "sufficiently anti-Israel."[31] Such questions of succession to Yoelish would come much later; for now there was not much for an heir to inherit.

Whatever success Yoelish had in Orshiva, his abiding ambitions to stand out were not fulfilled there, even though he steadily stoked a reputation as one unafraid of arousing controversy and conflict. To Shaul Brach, the appointed rabbi and family friend in Nagykaroly ("Krole," in Yiddish), only about thirty-five kilometers away from Satmar, who had found a position elsewhere, this recommended Yoelish as a suitable replacement. Although unenthusiastic, he took the job when the influence of some well-to-do Jews tipped the vote in his favor.[32] In 1926, he relocated his yeshiva from Orshiva to Krole.[33] Recruiting students among all local Jews, Yoelish hoped they would ever after see him as their teacher and rabbi.

FAILURE IN SIGHET AND SUCCESS IN KROLE

Part of Yoelish's unhappiness in Krole came from the fact that the same year he arrived there his older brother suffered a massive stroke and died suddenly at the age of forty-six. Yoelish, who now had useful experience as a rabbi and was increasingly known in the Hasidic world, with ambitions to be a general leader, might have been his brother's natural successor in Sighet.[34] Only the accident of his younger birth and his father's refusal to find him a station there had made him leave. But Yoelish's selection as his brother's successor would have left the latter's widow (who ironically would herself die later in 1926) and her children out in the cold and without positions, to say nothing of leaving all of the administrative staff that his brother had assembled in Sighet also out of power. The weak personality of the late Sigheter Rebbe had allowed them all to accumulate power they did not want to give up. If the more assertive Yoelish took the crown now, he would surely eclipse them all and then perhaps retaliate for his effective exile from Sighet years before. Thus the new Rebbe of Sighet would be, not the surviving brother, but Haim Tzvi's then rather uncharismatic and inexperienced fourteen-year-old son, Zalman Leib (1912–44). That this undistinguished, unmarried youngster was preferred to his uncle was evidence of what we have already seen in these pages: *when it comes to succession, familial, social, economic, and political concerns trump almost all else.*

Yoelish settled in Krole, confirmed in his desire to eclipse Sighet and its Hasidic stature. Seeking to find unity, the family betrothed Yoelish's daughter, Rachel, to Zalman Leib (tragically she suddenly died in March of 1931).[35] The marriage gave her father some additional influence over the new young rebbe (and, as he thought then, the possibility that his daughter might bear the future heir to the Sighet crown). Ironically, many years later, Moshe, Zalman Leib's younger brother, would inherit both the Sighet and Satmar crowns—but that part of the story was unimaginable in 1926.

Dissatisfied with Krole, Yoelish campaigned for positions in a number of places he visited and also advised his nephew in Sighet, building a reputation that outshone that of his late older brother and his nephew, whose inherited charisma turned out to be limited at best. He also boosted his political power by networking, making him far more than a local leader in Krole and a larger target for his opponents.

THE SATMAR REBBE AND RAV AT LONG LAST

When the official rabbi (*rav*) of Satmar died in the spring of 1928, the vacancy this created attracted Yoelish and his supporters. Not only did he have a history in the city, but getting this post in the larger community with about ten thousand to fifteen thousand Jews would mean more income and influence in a more important locale. The fact that in Satmar at the time only a minority were Hasidim meant he could test his power here to battle quite a number of non-Hasidic, more acculturated, and powerful Jews and turn himself into an even more powerful force against the Zionist and assimilative trends that were seemingly ascendant.[36] The idea of being both a rebbe (head of Hasidim) and a *rav* (the religious authority for the whole Jewish community) appealed to him. That had been his father's situation in Sighet; Yoelish wanted no less for himself in Satmar.

He won election by a plurality of votes but was met by a powerful opposition claiming that his selection was fraudulent, since it was impossible that the minority Hasidim could have managed to dominate the vote and get one of their own appointed over the whole community.[37] A Jewish court was convened, letters were written, cases were made, and new elections were ordered. After the second set of elections—the result of many machinations, and held in a hall owned by one of Yoelish's great supporters—the results were even more one-sided in his favor.

In October 1928, Yoelish therefore received a formal letter of appointment as rabbi (rav) of Satmar.[38] But "fierce opposition to him" continued, with appeals to the non-Jewish official authorities to intervene.[39] In early 1929, the dispute went to another Jewish court. Accusations of bribery, fraud, undue pressure, and ballot stuffing surfaced. In the end, the court reaffirmed him as the official rabbi of Satmar. The losers refused to endorse the verdict, meaning that there was no full disposition of the beit din's judgment. That would mean yet another election, scheduled in a year's time. But those opposed to the results voted earlier, in April of 1929. In this election, Yoelish was defeated.

Feeling disenfranchised, Yoelish's supporters moved to secede from the general community and set themselves up as a separate congregation, with their chosen leader as both their rebbe and their rav. Such communal divisions carried economic consequences as well as political and legal ones. A recognition by the state authorities that the Orthodox Jews of the city of Satmar were divided would give this decision formal standing.[40] For more than two more years quarrels went on between supporters and opponents of Yoelish's formal appointment, each side absolutely convinced that only a total victory was acceptable to ensure the continuity of their way of living and the nature of Jewish life in Transylvania. Yoelish held off returning to Satmar. When in 1934 the disputes seemed to subside, as population and hence religious views and political changes within Satmar Jewry occurred, Yoelish felt increasingly secure that he would be able to fully "occupy the rabbinate."[41] He planned his return. When at last he arrived, he left Krole very early in the morning, with little or no fanfare, and moved into Satmar earlier than expected, also with little or no fanfare. While he served formally as the leader only of his Hasidim in the city, he also attended the main non-Hasidic synagogue at least once a month as a symbol of his ambition to be a rabbinic authority over all Jews in Satmar.[42]

For Satmar Hasidim conflicts served as a form of socialization and identity formation.[43] Satmar Hasidim always identified themselves relative to their and the rebbe's opponents. Extremism, a consciousness of difference, and fealty to the causes that Yoelish championed not only strengthened feelings of dissociation from those who were different but also energized and generated a powerful sense of solidarity among Yoelish's Hasidim.[44] As time went on, this relish for conflict, framed as a steadfast ideological purity, would become *the* essential identity of Satmar Hasidism. Almost every place he went, Yoelish found opponents. Fighting for certain Jewish ideas and practices became his trademark, a badge of honor or calling card. Wherever he went, he also created champions who saw him as a perfect foil for their zeal.

With the relocation of Yoelish's yeshiva from Krole, leading to an influx of more students and the growth of his influence, Satmar became increasingly "a bastion" of his particular version of Hasidism.[45] He established not only his yeshiva for boys but also institutions for girls.[46] These institutions, as well as serving educational and social functions, provided employment (*mzonei*) for his followers. Yoelish became an institutional fund-raiser.[47] He enhanced the appeal of the Jewish practices he advocated by lowering their financial burden, endearing him to the less affluent among his Hasidim. He advocated for a cadre of Hasidim who did not study Torah all day but who acquired trades. He wanted Hasidim who were *baaley batim*—home owners and earners— and not just *lomdim,* learners.[48] His yeshiva in Satmar became one of the largest in Transylvania, with 350 students generating a growing cadre of young, enthusiastic Hasidim and their families with whom he was particularly close.[49]

Gradually, Satmar and its rebbe overshadowed Sighet; many who had been Sigheter Hasidim and had once spurned his leadership began to think of themselves as *his* followers rather than those of his nephew the Sigheter Rebbe. In 1904, before his first departure from Sighet, when Yoelish was marrying Chava Horowitz, his older brother Haim Tzvi had presided over the wedding. In 1929, in a symbolic reversal, when Haim Tzvi's orphaned daughter, Chana, wed, it was Uncle Yoelish who was the honored rabbi at the marriage.[50] While there were many notables there, the Satmar Rebbe towered over the occasion. And when the next year the bride's brother finally married Yoelish's daughter, Rachel, it was Yoelish who, after the couple had lived for a time in his home and under his guardianship, brought the pair in 1930 back to Sighet, where the young man was formally crowned as the Sigheter Rebbe.[51]

The Satmar Rebbe—who had emerged when, as the younger son finding no opportunity to succeed his father in Sighet, he had left home and wandered from place to place developing his own reputation and *rebistve*—had now closed the circle and achieved a position and high status that ultimately outshone the *rebistve* he did not get. The successor in Sighet was his young son-in-law, whom Yoelish placed on the throne he once had sought. Even those who were not formally his Hasidim increasingly turned to him for blessings and petitions, even sending him telegraphed requests.[52] When in 1932 he visited the Holy Land, hoping to be selected as leader of the anti-Zionist Edah HaHaredis, supporters distributed leaflets in Jerusalem that heralded his arrival: "A wise man is coming to the city, the honorable, our master, teacher and rabbi, the light of the exile, the *zaddik* who is the foundation of the world, the light of Israel, son of the holy ones . . . our Rabbi Yoel Teitelbaum." [53]

When the king of Romania, Carol II, made a brief stop in Satmar in 1936, he saw fit to greet Yoelish first among the row of dignitaries assembled to meet him at the train station. That striking act, immortalized in a photo, ratified for the rebbe's followers and for those who read about it their leader's outsize importance and stature in the Jewish community.[54]

WIDOWHOOD, REMARRIAGE, AND SUCCESSION

While Yoelish's career as a Hasidic leader continued its success, his personal life suffered. He had lost two of his three daughters to fatal diseases, the second daughter who had become the wife of the Sigheter Rebbe, only a year and a half after her wedding. That misfortune took its toll on his wife, Chavah, and her health also deteriorated. By January of 1936, she too was dead.[55] Only his daughter Roysaele remained. As of 1936, after twelve years of marriage, she was still childless. Concerns about succession slowly heightened.

Following Passover in April of 1936, Yoelish, widowed for only four months, directed Roysaele to begin a search on his behalf for a new wife.[56] Reportedly, already at the end of the mourning week of shivah, he told someone close to him, "I want them to find me a *shidduch* [match] right away. The Torah says, 'It is not good for a man to be alone.' I don't want to be 'not good' even for a short time." [57] Hoping he might still father a male successor in spite of his childless first marriage, his daughter and others urged him to "choose a widow or divorcee who already had children, to ensure that she would be capable of bearing children." [58] But if he married a woman who had borne children before and failed to do so afterwards, it would be difficult to deny that any infertility came as a consequence of her far older husband. The rebbe rejected the advice.

By August 1937, less than a month before the Jewish High Holy Days, the nearly fifty-one-year-old Yoelish remarried. His new wife, Alte Feige Shapiro (1912–2001), the orphaned and never-married daughter of Poland's Tchenstechover (Częstochowa) Rebbe, was only half his age. Although old for a first-time Hasidic bride, she was young for a man like the Satmar Rebbe. Her youth recommended her as capable in principle of bearing him children and providing a successor.[59]

At the time of this second marriage, Roysaele, older than her father's new bride, was acting very much like a *rebbetzin,* and there was reputedly tension between the daughter and Feige. The latter did not appreciate having been vetted by her stepdaughter, especially after she acquired the higher status of being the rebbe's wife. Indeed, the relationship between the two was never good, and whenever the daughter took steps to get closer to her father her stepmother managed to rebuff them.[60] In her eyes, only one woman could be close to the rebbe: his wife. Ultimately Feige triumphed in making the role of *rebbetzin* her own and distancing Yoelish from Roysaele and her husband. Yet neither woman would have any children, a matter that deeply troubled Yoelish and his Hasidim.

At least two biographers recount that every Rosh Hashanah, following his sermon before the blowing of the shofar, Yoelish would quote the Torah reading of the day (Gen. 21:1–2), regarding Sarah, mother of the Jewish people, recalling how the Almighty had remembered her barrenness so that "Sarah conceived and bore Abraham a son in his old age." He would tell his congregants that the Lord was the one who "makes the barren woman of the house a joyful mother of children," and then would "beg the people to pray for him that he might be privileged to have children and descendants." The rebbe's "heartrending cries aroused everyone to tears," and it "was usually quite a while before the rebbe and the congregation composed themselves" so that the service could continue.[61] His wishes for a son were never fulfilled, although his publicly expressed hopes could not but disturb his wife and highlight her barrenness.

An heir was crucial for the continuity of the Satmar Hasidic court. After Roysaele's death in 1953 and the exclusion of her widowed husband (who sat shivah for her separately from her father) as a possible successor, the pressure grew to solve the problem of continuity.[62] Some in Satmar hoped to persuade Yoelish to divorce Feige in order to try to have children with yet another wife. Among these was reputedly the rebbe's nephew Moshe Teitelbaum, who at the age of eleven, after the death of his father and mother, had been partially raised in Yoelish's home and who could be considered a kind of adopted son and closest heir. In the feud between Feige and Roysaele, Moshe had remained loyal to his cousin, a fact the new *rebbetzin* would never forgive. Coupled with his suggestion about a divorce, this meant the relationship between Moshe and Feige was forever poisoned. She accused him of wanting her out in order to claim the throne of Satmar for himself, but he countered that if he had truly wanted to be heir he would not have encouraged his uncle to remarry and produce a more direct successor.[63] Reportedly unimpressed by his argument, Feige would spend her life making herself indispensable to her husband and in his declining years to many of his Hasidim. In spite of her childlessness and her inability to give him an heir, Yoelish consistently refused to divorce her. Nor did too many Hasidim press the issue, preferring to hope instead that the Messiah would come in time to solve all these issues.

THE YEARS OF THE HOLOCAUST

The very fact that Satmar had hopes for a successor was remarkable. Like so much of European Hasidism, it had faced the abyss and decimation as the Nazis and later the communists destroyed Jewish life. To be sure, Yoelish had always been convinced that European Jews were surrounded by enemies and that care should be taken not to arouse the anger of the anti-Semites. For all his fights with other Jews, Yoelish was far less ready to challenge the Gentile enemy, both the local rulers and later the Nazis.[64] He saw such efforts—even self-defense organizations, let alone revolutionary ones—as futile.[65]

The intensification of anti-Jewish activity during the decade and even the outbreak of war with the German invasion of Poland in 1939 left Hungarian Jewry relatively safe at first. In August of 1941, however, more than twenty thousand were expelled, many of them to their deaths.[66] Among these deportees were some of Yoelish's yeshiva students as well as his brother-in-law.[67] Only with the German occupation of Hungary in March of 1944, along with the rise of their Hungarian Arrow Cross Party allies whose rule began in October of that year, did the situation for Hungarian Jewry became as grim as it had been for most of the rest of European Jewry.

For any rebbe, whose relationship to his Hasidim was always based on a deep spiritual and material interdependence, the Holocaust—

referred to by many Hasidim as the *churban* (destruction), in line with generations of persecutions and attacks against Jews—was a religious and a leadership test: Could rebbes, interceding with God or influencing the powers that be, save their Hasidim?

As leaders, they, their families, and their staff, as we have seen in the case of Bobov, were often the particular targets of aggression. As many Hasidic leaders ran for their lives, those left behind thought: "The rebbes flee, and what will be with us?" [68]

Between 1938 and 1940, Yoelish did not flee. He traveled instead to many Jewish communities, building up and solidifying his influence, stressing the need for insularity from modern secular life—bans on attending the theater, reading newspapers, and secular literature were among his priorities. He continued his battle against Zionism and its supporters. In 1939, the rebbe asserted, "Those who seek to immigrate to the Land of Israel through the Zionists are grabbing onto a flame of fire!" [69] He also discouraged emigration to America.

Nevertheless, in September 1939, some of his supporters, fearing for his safety and for the future of Satmar Hasidism, tried to get him a tourist visa for a visit to Palestine.[70] His response was to condemn anyone who cooperated with them and to claim that the Zionists were ready to help only those Jews escape who "shared in their heretical Zionist ideology." [71] By the end of 1943, however, he sent his daughter Roysaele to Budapest to try to get certificates for him and his family to enter Palestine. She was unsuccessful.[72] Shortly afterward, using his political influence in Jewish circles, he tried himself, knowing it would not be easy to get Zionist leaders to provide the necessary papers for one who had so publicly opposed them. In fact, when his request reached those in the Jewish Agency empowered to procure the necessary papers from the British Mandatory authorities, the rebbe was by many accounts asked by them to sign a document publicly acknowledging his recognition of the Zionist Organization's authority. He refused.[73]

In the spring of 1944, as the Jews in Transylvania were herded into ghettos and as a rumor reached Yoelish that the Nazis were searching for him, he assented to an alternate plan to flee toward Romania, where the conditions of Jews were at the time not as dire.[74] He changed out of his clothes, wrapped a kerchief around his face to cover his beard and earlocks (so that he would not need to shear them off), and stepped into a Red Cross ambulance headed for Cluj (Klausenberg) on the Romanian border, and from there into Romania, where King Carol II was still resisting the Nazi pressure to send the Jews to death camps.[75] In Cluj, thirty kilometers short of the border, he was caught and sent to the Jewish ghetto being set up in the city. Here he tried to use his influence with the *Judenrat,* contacting among others Rudolf Kasztner, a Jewish Hungarian lawyer who was the father-in-law of the Jewish Agency's representative in Hungary and a member of the Budapest *Judenrat.*[76] Kasztner, working for the Zionist Jewish Agency, was engaged in negotiations with Adolf Eichmann to allow a trainload of Jews to receive safe passage through Switzerland en route to Portugal and on to Palestine in return for a large ransom payment. Kasztner was persuaded, after someone paid a "huge sum," to include Yoelish and some of those connected to him among the 1,670 in the train.[77]

On May 3, 1944, the rebbe and his wife, along with his *gabbai,* Yosef Ashkenazi, "were spirited out of the Cluj ghetto, and taken by a special car to Budapest" and housed in what had once been the Institute for Deaf Mutes.[78] From there on Friday night, the Sabbath, June 30, he left on the Kasztner train, which ultimately took them to the Bergen-Belsen concentration camp in Germany, where they arrived on July 9, 1944.[79] Remaining there while negotiations for more money went on, they finally boarded another train for Switzerland on the evening of December 4, a time when Germany was suffering from repeated Allied air attacks.[80] At last, three days later, they crossed the frontier and arrived in St. Gallen, Switzerland. The day—21 Kislev in the Hebrew calendar—became a Satmar day of thanksgiving, still celebrated today.[81]

Ignoring the contradictions between their rebbe's condemnation of the Zionists and his escape ride on a train they organized, the Hasidim looked at the rescue of their leader from mortal danger as a sign from heaven not only that he was subject to special consideration but that by virtue of their attachment to him they too might be miraculously protected and the future of Satmar assured.[82] As one Hasid put it, explaining the extraordinary concern for the safety of a rebbe: "I felt that if our crown—that is, the holy Rebbe—were trampled, Heaven forbid, our heads would not be safe either."[83]

The question has been asked: Why did the rebbe who "forbid his Hasidim to make use of the services of the Zionists in order to emigrate to the Land of Israel not impose on himself the same decree when his community standing was firm and the possibility of emigration to other countries was possible for him?"[84] Surely it was because he believed that the survival of Satmar, which he represented, was of supreme importance in that it represented the future of Hasidism, if not all observant Jewry.

SATMAR AT WAR'S END

With the war's end, Romania once again controlled Transylvania. In Satmar several thousand residents returned, opening synagogues and yeshivas as well as orphanages and even a burial society and *beit din*. Hasidim came back too, hoping Yoelish would join them. He, however, remained in Switzerland. But the Swiss, notoriously uninterested in opening their country to refugees or immigrants, wanted the Jewish exiles out. Rather than heading back to Satmar (where he might have faced criticism for his behavior during the Holocaust), the rebbe tried harder to get a certificate for Palestine.[85]

The response to his request for a certificate, as his son-in-law wrote in a letter, was that "all the parties on the right and on the left are opposed to his coming, knowing they will have no pleasure from him when he is here." The Zionists saw no reason to help one who even now saw their movement as "a tremendous danger for the Jewish people."[86]

Nevertheless, when at last the British sent papers for all the refugees on the Kasztner transport, the Satmar Rebbe, notwithstanding all his ideology, left for Italy to board a boat to Haifa in Palestine on August 19, 1945.[87] The forces he had so long fulminated against had both saved him and allowed him to get to the Promised Land, where his surviving daughter and her husband awaited him in Jerusalem.[88]

Arriving there, he visited the Western Wall (twenty-one years later in 1967, he would issue a "prohibition against visiting, let alone praying at, Jerusalem's newly liberated Western Wall").[89] He tried to establish himself in Jerusalem, creating a small yeshiva, but he "was hardly able to sustain" it.[90] Most of his Hasidim had been incinerated in the Nazi firestorm from which he had escaped; only about six thousand Jews from northern Transylvania survived, and few Satmarers went to Palestine.[91]

His yeshiva in Jerusalem started with ten students in a small building in the Meah Sherarim quarter.[92] If he was to build a new cadre of followers, he would have to make it grow quickly, even as he fought Zionism from within the land where it was dominant. But he had little or no success. By the Jewish New Year of 1946, about a year after his arrival in Palestine, he landed in the United States, ostensibly to raise funds for his institution in Jerusalem but perhaps in recognition of his inability to succeed as he wished in the Holy Land. He could also see that, at least in the immediate term, the Zionist project was headed for success and statehood.

SATMAR IN AMERICA

Yoelish's start in America was modest. His first residence was in a borrowed home on President Street in Crown Heights, Brooklyn. When he wanted to pray with a minyan, he "had to call Jews off the street" in order to assemble the minimum ten men.[93] Only when he relocated to the Williamsburg neighborhood would the growth of what would become the largest Hasidic court in America truly begin.

In America, he could once again forcefully take up his trademark tirade against Zionism. As Shaul Magid notes, "He knew that America was a place where Jews could practice their religion in relative safety. Hence, the dismantling of the Jewish state would not by definition put the Jewish people in grave danger."[94] Yet while he hoped America would be the final Diaspora, he worked hard to build a community. In so doing, he was guided by the prophetic vision of Jeremiah (29:4–7), who urged the Jews as they went into exile to build a life where they were going until the day the Lord chose to end the exile and bring them back. Until that day, which could not be hurried, they had to separate themselves from the evil that surrounded them, while waiting for the Redeemer, however long he might tarry.

His survival Yoelish attributed to God and "the religious Jews" who were the Almighty's "agents."[95] By no means did the Zionists have any part in it. On the contrary, he would argue later in the mid-1950s when his magnum opus *VaYoel Moshe* was written, "The Zionists themselves, who determined the number of permissions [i.e., certificates] that the English authorities issued each year, refused to give such permission except to those who followed their ways and held to their approach, the approach of Zionism and its sacrilege and heresy, God help us."[96] In his post-Holocaust theological reasoning, Yoelish held that Zionism was the original sin for which the destruction of European Jewry was the punishment. To him, the Zionists had both broken and forced others to break God's commandments about terminating "the Diaspora before the appointed end of time, [therefore] the Diaspora terminated them as punishment for forcing the end."[97] If some were saved through Zionists' efforts, that was more than offset by the many who were not saved because of them.

In America, Satmar Hasidism warned that contemporary culture, no less than anti-Semitism and modern Zionism, could terminate Jewry by swallowing it up and making Jews act like Gentiles. The rebbe would fight against Jews acting in even the most minor ways like the people around them. He endorsed passive resistance and cultural insulation as a strategy.

"We will only survive, he said, if you work and generate cash to nourish us. . . . Satmar men branched into real estate—buying up much of Williamsburg—and the diamond business," and later electronics, insurance, currency exchange, and other businesses, many located in midtown Manhattan.[98] Others learned blue-collar trades. All the same, with their large families, insistence on private education, and Jewish lifestyle, many Satmarers remained poor—65 percent of them, on average, were below the poverty line (at least according to the US census). All the while they created a firewall between their personal lives and values and their business pursuits. America learned to live with their stores closing before sunset on Fridays and on Jewish holidays and to interact with people dressed like Hasidim, whose English sounded as if they had just learned it.

The Satmar community Yoelish built in Brooklyn, starting in the late 1940s in Williamsburg, was along Bedford Avenue. Here the Satmar view dominated.[99] Yoelish was the magnet that drew and held his Hasidim there to "remain close to their Rebbe and the institutions that had shaped their lives." [100] The challenge of building a growing community and still remaining insulated from modern life in an urban neighborhood so close to "Sin City" was daunting. But the proximity of cultural "pollution" could be a source of strength because it made the culture war in which the Satmar community was engaged feel immediate and unrelenting enough to inspire the troops daily. To justify his choice of location, Yoelish liked to quote the Belzer Rebbe, who reputedly said, "If a city had no wicked Jews, it would be worthwhile to pay some wicked Jews to come and live there so that the good Jews would have someone to separate from." [101] This oppositional stance honed in Europe remained a core element of his and his followers' identity. "The very act of declaring separateness from the wicked strengthens the commitment of the righteous," as the rebbe explained.[102]

Inside his enclave, in contrast to building synagogues as the basis of a community, which he claimed had been the dominant Jewish American model and a doomed organizing principle that "did not give any thought to the education of their children," he would "build a Talmud Torah [primary Jewish school] and a yeshiva . . . so that we overcome the difficult trials here." [103] In Satmar, the idea of secular education—even though mandated by American law—was not of ontological value; it was a dangerous tool of acculturation and therefore would be offered at the barest minimal level. His schools, the rebbe asserted, would be "like those founded by our fathers, without any compromises or changes, Heaven forbid"; they would stand out as different, no less than the Hasidic clothes the rebbe insisted his followers wear on the street without shame, and in so doing would produce Jews who would be exactly like their forebears in Satmar even on the new soil of America.[104] This effort to graft the European past on the American present, he claimed repeatedly, "doesn't grow from compromises." [105]

While America, with its open society, democracy, and absence of institutionalized anti-Semitism, would be very different from Europe, Yoelish sought to continue the same spirit of separatism he had nurtured in Europe. Ironically, in America it would become far more aggressive, precisely because here society was open, so that the seductions of the host culture were greater and the opportunities to give way to them more numerous. A world free of restrictions was minutes away. When Jews could by law move and live wherever they chose and could afford to, residential and cultural insularity had to be reinforced by those *inside* the ghetto.[106] To discourage an exodus, the Satmar Rebbe first stressed the need to be publicly and uncompromisingly Hasidic—emphasizing distinctiveness at a time when the melting-pot ideal was still the norm in America and before the rise of the unmeltable ethnics and cultural pluralism made the Satmar sort of distinctiveness less unusual. The struggle to remain apart as well as distinctive and to argue that these positions were the only and authentic way of being Jewish not only made Yoelish's followers feel that they were part of a great cause and the true defenders of Jewry and Judaism but made Satmarism and its inventor a kind of model for what steadfast Orthodox Judaism was meant to be, a vanguard of contra-acculturation and authenticity. Second, he had to make sure that his educational system did not provide his Hasidim with the skills that would make leaving the enclave easy. Third, he had to demonize the world outside so that his followers would either be afraid of entering it or be confident that their own ways were infinitely superior.

The Satmar approach was the opposite of outreach—and Yoelish's Hasidim often fought with the Lubavitchers, who embraced outreach.[107] Believing that bringing outsiders near was a recipe for making insiders become distant from Judaism, Yoelish grew his community by inreach, encouraging early marriage and large families, shaping the young in his schools, and branding the uncompromising stance as the essential recipe for Jewish survival in the modern world. That meant emphasizing Yiddish over the vernacular, even in the post-Holocaust world (many

16. Yoelish Teitelbaum, the first Satmar Rebbe, meeting with John Lindsay, mayor of New York City (with hand on chin), one of many public officials paying tribute and visiting. By permission of Ichud Archives, Brooklyn, New York.

Satmar Hasidim could barely speak English); "Since conversing leads to friendship, it is proper for the Jew [not just the Satmar Hasid] to avoid speaking at all with one whose soul is not purified." [108] The latter were all those who did not share Yoelish's values and worldview.

At the front lines of the cultural war were Satmar children, who learned to be proudly different and limited in their knowledge of the outside world. Looking at them, he announced, "When the final redemption comes, we will have nothing to be ashamed of; we can point to these children and say, 'This is what we accomplished in the midst of the bitter exile.'" [109] In a relatively short time, the population that followed Yoelish, "along with its religious, educational, and communal institutions, quickly exceeded that of the combined prewar Hasidic communities of the entire Satmar and Sighet regions." [110]

After Robert Moses's Brooklyn Queens Expressway cut through the heart of the Williamsburg neighborhood in 1960 and led to the area's economic decline and the departure of many middle-class acculturating Jews, Yoelish found it easier to keep his people insular and oppositional. By remaining behind in the inner city as one community, they would be culturally protected. In the inner city, they were freed of the desire to assimilate into the surrounding society, and they could grow without importing outside values. Satmar became, as Israel Rubin called it in his eponymous book, "an island in the city," governed by Hasidic Jewish rules and regulations.[111] The rebbe became a power broker and a community leader that even influential politicians acknowledged.

This process started in 1948, when Yoelish set up a community structure and administration—Yetev Lev, he called it—with a set of regulations (promulgated in 1952 in Yiddish, the lingua franca of the enclave) that served as a template for Satmar Hasidism in the post-Holocaust world.[112] Effectively, however, all that went on in the Satmar enclave was ruled by the rebbe and his appointees who carried out his will. Whereas in Europe the entire community had had to vote on and accept him as their leader, in America Yoelish simply opened his doors and watched who came into his congregation. "When I was elected I had to do what you told me to. Here I'm not obligated to do any-thing."[113] In America, he could control every facet of his community.

This included Satmar institutions and services—from schools (the first Torah V'Yirah yeshivas opened in 1950–51) to butcher shops with their own certification of kashruth (the first opened in 1955) and matzah bakeries claiming to be better at guarding against even accidental leavening. In 1956 Satmar established its first summer camps in the Catskill Mountains, totally controlled environments.[114] As one woman, who had grown up in Williamsburg in those days as the daughter of immigrants, explained, "My mother felt extremely grateful to Rabbi Teitelbaum. He helped her raise her children Hasidic. She did not know if she would be able to raise them Hasidic in the United States of America without his work. There was nothing before he came. It's really priceless."[115]

Yoelish's ideology, religious views, ritual standards, and moral codes became normative. He demanded that married women cut off all their hair, permitting them "to place a piece of unthreaded silk, known as a *shpitzel,* in front" of a hat or kerchief covering their heads, which from afar might look a bit like hair.[116] He ruled that couples place their beds along the wall, in contrast to the modern style of bed perpendicular to walls, eschewing anything "in imitation of the gentiles," a prohibition he and others traced to scripture (Lev. 18:3).[117] He found excuses to visit his Hasidim's homes to check to see that they were compliant on this matter. Under his banner of "modesty" he demanded that women wear opaque stockings—something he sermonized about from the pulpit. In 1956 he made these stockings a special cause, and in 1958 he argued that the redemption of the Jewish people depended on the opacity of women's stockings.[118] To make sure such unstylish stockings would always be available, in 1978 the Hasidim prevailed on Lipa Brach, one of their own in the hosiery business, to design and manufacture an especially thick type of stocking with a seam. Named "Palm Stockings," a translation of the name Teitelbaum, they are still the norm in Satmar.[119]

Gradually, Satmar created more and more stringencies. They excluded television, with its window on the outside world through which the impure could enter to defile the home. Although Yiddish was their primary language, they restricted which of the Yiddish newspapers were to be read, ultimately buying one, *Der Yid,* and making it the semiofficial news source for the community. Through the school and the paper, they gradually built a growing following, all attracted by the special charisma of the rebbe and unified by his culture wars and codes of behavior and belief. The rebbe's repeated stress on his rules was "to make sure that I myself do not get swept up . . . in this whirlwind of sheer *minus* [heresy]" that characterized life among the rest of Jewry.[120] Yoelish believed he offered a new model for American Jewish life. His Hasidim called themselves *erlicher yidn,* fine Jews—as if to say those who did not live like them were not.[121]

A SATMAR VILLAGE AND KINGDOM

Williamsburg was growing because of Hasidic demographic expansion, driven by large families and the absence of persecution and assimilation. It also grew because the Hasidim successfully lobbied for "zoning changes—by turning an industrial area residential."[122] Ironically, those changes would at a later date help make Williamsburg a stylish extension of SoHo and a mecca for those the Hasidim called *artisten* (artists). Now culture contact became complicated. Much of the Williamsburg real estate that became gentrified belonged to Satmar landlords, and the lure of having high-paying tenants was difficult to block, even though the culture they brought with them seemed to threaten Satmar insularity and values. The insertion of bike lanes in the neighborhood, which would allow among others scantily dressed female bicyclists to pass before the eyes of Hasidic men, became a point of contention.[123] So did the barely dressed New York Marathon runners who passed through Williamsburg's streets.

As the Satmar community grew, Yoelish was convinced his people would be better off in a more remote place where they could truly live in a world apart and where the corrosive influences of American culture could be kept at bay. As he explained, "It would be better if each community lived in its own small town, around the big city. Then it would be easier to prevent assimilation." [124]

A visit in 1947 to the Nitra Yeshiva in Westchester County's Mount Kisco—then considered very far upstate—persuaded him that he could establish something similar.[125] In the meantime, in 1954 Skvir Hasidim under their rebbe, Yaakov Yosef Twersky (1899–1968), established a neighborhood in the city of Ramapo in New York's Rockland County. They started moving there in 1956 and incorporated themselves as the village of New Square in 1961. The Tasher Rebbe, Meshulem Segal-Loewy, established a similar settlement in Kiryas Tash north of Montreal in 1963. In Israel's B'nai B'rak, in 1948 the Vizhnitzer Rebbe, Hayim Meir Hager, organized Shikkun (the neighborhood of) Vizhnitz, a Hasidic quarter that concentrated all his Hasidim in a defined geographic area, where all the neighborhood's apartments were sold to his Hasidim, who would be required to sell them only to other Vizhnitzers. Yekutiel Yehudah Halberstam (1905–94), Yoelish's nephew by marriage, the Kalusenberg-Sanzer Rebbe, built Kiryat Sanz in Netanya, Israel, in the mid-1950s. The Belzer Hasidim built their neighborhood of Kiryat Belz in Jerusalem with a synagogue that dominated the skyline, rivaling even the golden dome on the Temple Mount. The demographic growth of Hasidism made all this possible.

After some false starts, Satmar established a village near Monroe, New York, about an hour's drive north of Brooklyn. In late 1974 and into 1975, the first Hasidim began to move into what would ultimately be incorporated in 1977 as Kiryas Joel Village in New York, often in the face of opposition from their new neighbors.[126] Here a virtual kingdom where his rules were the law developed, and here he would move.

THE SECOND SUCCESSION BATTLE: NEPHEW VERSUS *REBBETZIN*

By the time he was in Kiryas Joel, however, Yoelish was a broken vessel. In February of 1968 while at Friday night prayers, the then eighty-two-year-old rebbe suffered a devastating stroke. Unconscious for ten days, he woke up to find himself severely impaired in his speech and movement.[127] The question of succession arose again.

For two years after the stroke, Yoelish lived in semiseclusion from his Hasidim, staying at a summer house in Belle Harbor on Long Island and trying to recover. During this time, his wife, Feige, and his *gabbaim,* including prominently Yosef Ashkenazi but also Azriel Glick (who following the rebbe's death and at the unveiling of the tombstone would announce that the soul of the departed rebbe could not enter paradise until a successor to him had been selected) and the yeshiva head, Nosson Yosef Meisels, gradually took outsized roles acting as conduits for his messages and as de facto leaders of the community, sometimes even making speeches on his behalf.[128] The power of the *rebbetzin* loomed particularly large. Credited as founder of the Satmar Ladies Auxiliary and a prodigious fund-raiser for Satmar causes, she was also credited with creating the well-known and popular Bikur Cholim, an agency that provided support and help for any Jews hospitalized in the New York area by supplying them with kosher food, free housing for their loved ones near the hospitals, and other services; it became the goodwill side of Satmar that offset the sectarian and anti-Zionist causes that were far more alienating to many Jews.[129] Feige also had outsized power because of the absence of any direct heirs who could be eased into a position of leadership during what would be her husband's ten-year precipitous physical decline.

"With a small group of loyal assistants, she controlled access to her ill husband and often had a strong say in major decisions regarding the Satmar community."[130] Feige and the *gabbaim* maintained the fiction that they were taking direction from Yoelish, and all was as it had been. She even came into the men's section of the synagogue to distribute *shirayim*, the leftovers of the rebbe's food that he previously would have distributed himself at a *tish*.

When the ailing rebbe briefly returned to his Hasidim in early spring of 1970, they could see he was a shadow of himself. Although he would deliver a talk in the fall of 1971 at the yeshiva in Williamsburg, his slurred speech was difficult to understand. In 1972, he moved back to Williamsburg into a new house especially outfitted for his physical limitations, but by the spring he was back in Belle Harbor. In September of 1974, he moved to Kiryas Joel, choosing to live far from the center of the village.[131] Throughout these years, the invalid rebbe became a prisoner of his body, as his Hasidim anxiously watched and wondered how his court would sustain itself in the absence of his leadership.

While Feige and the *gabbaim* seemed in charge from day to day, Moshe Teitelbaum, Yoelish's nephew and nominally the Sigheter Rebbe, was quietly taking a growing role at the court. During his uncle's precipitous decline, Moshe was increasingly being brought into his room in ways that could be seen as setting the stage for a transition of leadership. Hasidim looked for signs from their ailing rebbe that he was ready to anoint Moshe as his successor. They took Yoelish's embrace of

Moshe as such a sign, and they reportedly engaged in wordplay and Satmar exegetic interpretation with a famous liturgical blessing recited each Sabbath and holy day, "Al kiso lo yeshev zar" (On his throne shall no stranger sit), seeing this as a reference to their rebbe and his possible successor, since a nephew was no stranger.[132] But the *rebbetzin,* recalling how Moshe had been among those urging his uncle to divorce her, and realizing that Moshe's succession would leave her irrevocably separated from the center of power, resisted this effort as much as she could. Whereas a dowager *rebbetzin* has a son or son-in-law who takes over as a rebbe and who still looks upon his mother (or mother-in-law) with respect and because of her continuing family tie cannot cut her off from her royal station, Feige realized Moshe would have no incentive to empower her. Only Yoelish tied her to the *rebistve.*

Though she had tacit control over his *gabbaim,* they would likely be replaced almost immediately by any new leader. She also had the force of her personality and a long history with the Hasidim, particularly her high profile as a fund-raiser for charities, and these might support her after her husband was gone. As hard as she could, Feige worked to build up credit and authority, using the nearly ten years of her husband's decline for the purpose. For a long time maintaining a close relationship with some of the most generous Satmar financial supporters, she disbursed funds (on one trip to Israel reputedly carrying "three million dollars to distribute to charity"); this was perhaps her strongest card, for it was critically important for the Hasidim, reminding them that she, no less than the rebbe, was the source of their sustenance (*mzonei*). She did favors, looked to make alliances, and generally acted as a powerful stand-in for her ailing husband, even at times speaking from the lectern and taking *pidyonos* for and delivering blessings from her husband.[133] All this was freighted with symbolic meaning and was normally limited to a rebbe. With her stepdaughter, Roysaele, dead and the latter's widowed husband out of the picture, Feige became a near rebbe. But of course, she could not lead a *tish,* nor could she give out her own blessings; and when all the other rebbes came together at public occasions, she could never be among them—for women, even powerful ones like the *rebbetzin,* could not mix with the men in this highly gendered social order (although in March 1979, she remarkably appeared as the only woman at a gathering of Hasidic rabbis in Felt Forum in Manhattan, seated behind her husband and listening to his nephew Moshe addressing the crowd [figure 17]).[134] Even if she could somehow find some modus vivendi that would allow her to make peace with Moshe's

17. Feige seated behind her husband, Yoelish, on the dais—the only woman among the men and rabbis. Copyright and permission of L. Trainer, Trainer Studios.

taking over her husband's *rebistve,* she knew that Moshe's oldest son, Aaron, his apparent heir, would take up all the available extra power and leave her with nothing. To Aaron, she was even a greater threat because he could leave her no space if he was to assure himself of a future.[135]

After a lifetime as a *rebbetzin,* Feige believed that because so many Hasidim had seen her late husband as a larger-than-life figure, almost messianic in character, they might be persuaded he was irreplaceable. She convinced herself they might be willing simply to have a *rav,* someone who would serve as an appointed rabbi but without all the mystical and intercessionary powers with heaven that a rebbe had. She hoped, as did some of the *gabbaim* with whom she was allied, that after his passing his gravesite and memory would serve as the spiritual base, almost like a kind of extension of the incapacitated rebbe. She even had a plan to bring other great rabbinic forebears and have them reburied in the new cemetery in Kiryas Joel where her husband would be interred, imagining a kind of holy place that would serve in place of a living rebbe and would leave her space to act as its living guiding spirit.[136] As the appointed rabbi she would have a man who was respected as a legal authority but lacking charisma of his own. Because some of the older members of the community from Hungary had in their origins not been Hasidim—recall that Satmar had been a mixed community, which had been one of the sources of resistance to Yoelish's appointment as its head—she presumed that they might be satisfied with a respected rabbinic authority and with a *rebistve* left in a kind of suspended animation and in the care of herself, the dowager *rebbetzin,* and her retinue.

But the younger Hasidim, with no memories of Hungary, having lived in the atmosphere of absolute hands-on rule that marked their experience, wanted a full-fledged rebbe and not a powerful *rebbetzin.* A number of other Hasidim worried that if Moshe were not appointed as Satmar Rebbe he would simply continue in his role as Sigheter Rebbe and slowly attract more and more of the Satmar Hasidim, for whom a return to the Sigheter affiliation would simply be an acknowledgment of their own Hasidic history and roots. To avoid that real possibility, they moved to make Moshe the rebbe and crown him as the Satmar Rebbe.[137]

Feige also had made enemies over the years who resented her power and who could not see a woman as the crown and scepter of their Hasidic glory.[138] These enemies, many of whom were coalescing around Moshe and his heir apparent Aaron, reminded everyone that she had no heirs of her own. Of course, her gender made it clear that however powerful she was in these closing years of her husband's life, Feige would have to step aside if Satmar was to continue after Yoelish and to maintain its position as the largest and most powerful Hasidic group in America (or, as they claimed, in the world).

All this concern with continuity was of course not only about symbolic, charismatic, or spiritual leadership; it was also about economic power and resources. The growth of Satmar had led to "a portfolio of shuls, yeshivas, no-interest-loan associations, meat markets, and charities" valued in millions of dollars, and in addition there was "a social-service empire" with access to "millions of public dollars for health, welfare, food stamps, and public housing."[139] For all the putative poverty in Satmar, and there was lots of evidence of it, as a Hasidic group it was an economic powerhouse, and the rebbe stood at the apex of that power.

During the late summer of 1979, Yoelish's condition worsened. Present before his Hasidim in the synagogue in Kiryas Joel on what would be the final Sabbath of his life, he was watched intently. Later the Hasidim reflected on his every move and gesture as having been fraught with significance. Late on Saturday night, August 18, he developed fluid in his lungs and was rushed to Mount Sinai Hospital in New York, while his anxious followers frantically recited psalms for his recovery—convinced now that he needed their entreaties if he were not to be called to the "yeshiva on high."

"Those on high and those on earth" were said to be pursuing him; the cosmic battle was now in its most intense stage, as the Hasidim saw it.[140]

By the early morning, just before seven, his heart stopped. The *New York Times* reported that one hundred thousand people gathered for his funeral and created a monumental traffic jam on New York Route 17, the road leading to Kiryas Joel and the cemetery.[141] In keeping with his aspirations to be more than simply the Satmar Rebbe, Yoelish was referred to in *Der Yid,* the semiofficial organ of the Satmar community, as "the rabbi of all Israel" or "the Rabbi of all the Diaspora," and his death was described as having "orphaned" the entire Jewish people.[142]

The fact that all this had occurred on the eve of the Hebrew month of Ellul, the start of the season of atonement and the so-called "Days of Awe," infused the occasion with a kind of solemnity that only enhanced the sense of the significance of the events—this was after all the time when Hasidim always sought to be close to their rebbe in the hopes that he would intercede on their behalf on high in order to assure the acceptance of their prayers for forgiveness of sins and blessings in the coming year. But now their rebbe would not be with them "to open the gates of mercy."

Questions like "What will be? What must we do? Where are we headed?" filled the air.[143] Obviously some leaders had made plans, but others were not enthusiastic about those plans. The moment of truth had arrived.

MOSHE TEITELBAUM AND THE TRANSITION TO LEADERSHIP

By 1979, Moshe Teitelbaum (1914–2006), the Sigheter Rebbe, had been for many years totally eclipsed by his Satmar uncle. Living in nearby Borough Park, he hardly focused all of his energies on his small court, instead spending much of his time running a number of small businesses, managing real estate, and overseeing the kosher certification of the Meal Mart food chain rather than being a full-time *zaddik.*[144] But now Moshe was the likely successor to claim the leadership of Satmar. Some other names had been briefly floated in internal discussions, but none really were serious contenders.[145] By blood, Moshe stood above the rest, part of the stock of Sighet Hasidic holy seed.

His Holocaust survival story was no less dramatic than his uncle's, although far less contentious. Orphaned and shuttled between his maternal grandfather and his uncle, while his older brother took on the crown of Sighet, Moshe married at twenty-one to Leah, a cousin and daughter of the Karacscka Rebbe. He was appointed head of his father-in-law's yeshiva for the next five years until in 1941 he moved to Zenta, then in Hungary, to be designated rabbi. Within a few years, as the situation of Hungarian Jewry deteriorated, Moshe's wife and their three small children were murdered in Auschwitz. At war's end, he was in Theresienstadt, recuperating from typhus. On April 9, 1945, still weak, and unlike his uncle, who had never gone back home, Moshe returned to Sighet to try to revive the rabbinical seat of his martyred older brother. In the summer of 1945, he remarried, this time to another cousin, Pessel Leah (1922–2010), daughter of Aaron Teitelbaum (1881–1944), the Nirbator Rav.

Under communism, any hopes he might have had for a revival in Sighet came to naught, and he made plans to reach America. Unable to exit through proper channels, Moshe paid $500, a fortune at the time, to be smuggled, with his wife, through the border blockades. In the fall of 1946, after a brief detour to Brazil, he arrived at 500 Bedford Avenue in Williamsburg, where he met his uncle, Yoelish, who had come from Palestine.

Jews from Sighet who reached Brooklyn before World War II established their own congregation at 152 Hewes Street in Williamsburg. Moshe was invited to serve as their *rav* and to live there. That synagogue served as the center of the resurgence of the transplanted community of Sighet on American soil. At first, Moshe seemed to develop his court more quickly than his uncle, who was still imagining himself returning to Jerusalem with funds from America.[146] But quite soon after that idea died, the Satmar Rebbe outshone his nephew in attracting followers, as he had done in Europe before the war. In April 1965, Moshe relocated to Fifteenth Avenue and Fiftieth Street in Borough Park, hoping to emerge from the Satmar shadow and create some space for himself. A few years later he appointed his oldest son Aaron (1947–), rav of the Sigheter congregation that he had left behind in Williamsburg.

One of the six children Moshe had with his second wife, Aaron, would, if his father became the new Satmar Rebbe, be his likely heir, presumably solving the looming concerns about the future of Satmar. That was not a happy possibility for those supporting Feige, and they looked to undermine him. At Aaron's June 1966 wedding to Sasha, daughter of the Vizhnitzer Rebbe Moshe Hager of Israel, they made much of his ties with a man who seemed to have made his peace with the Zionists and whose daughter had attended the insufficiently Orthodox and anti-Zionist (by Satmar standards) Bais Yaakov schools, where instruction was in Hebrew rather than Yiddish. Indeed, Satmar Hasidim in Israel, many of whom considered Vizhnitzers as unredeemably Zionist, had been warned against attending the wedding, and few did so.[147] Feige expressed concern about putting Aaron in line for the Satmar crown, arguing that anyone who married into such a "Zionist" family was not worthy of leading Satmar. Her motives may not have been purely ideological. Thirteen years later, when Moshe was emerging as the odds-on choice of successor to Yoelish, these arguments came up again.

On the last day of Yoelish's life, Moshe—already identified in the Yiddish press as "the probable candidate" to take his uncle's place—was in Los Angeles.[148] Learning of the rebbe's death, he rushed back to New York immediately after Sabbath's end on the red-eye flight. Given the time difference and the nearly six-hour journey, Moshe arrived near the end of the nearly five-hour Sunday funeral that began in the afternoon. His keenly awaited entrance near 6:30 p.m. (just before the 7:49 sunset) was quite spectacular. After landing at Kennedy Airport, he boarded a waiting helicopter that flew him straight to Kiryas Joel and dramatically dropped down from the heavens.[149] The symbolism was not lost on the assembled. Following his brief eulogy, the last from among a long line of prominent rabbis, before the mandatory burial by sunset, *he* would be the one to recite Kaddish for his uncle, a ritual normally performed by a surviving son.[150]

Although she did not speak at the funeral—women were never expected to do so—the widowed *rebbetzin* found a way to be noticed. She was described in newspaper accounts as "breaking out in heart-rending tears" for all to see and hear as she turned to the coffin and asked for forgiveness (as was customary) from her late husband and prayed that he would be an "advocate on high" for all of the Jewish people.[151] But this tableau did not provide her with the same platform as Moshe. As for the late rebbe's will, the press reported it would be read only after the monument over his grave was unveiled.[152] In fact, no will was ever read.[153]

By the following Sunday, a tombstone had been erected, providing yet another occasion for the Sigheter Rebbe, Moshe Teitelbaum, to offer tears and a eulogy. This time he spoke *before* the speeches of all the others. While one of the Yiddish papers still described him only as the one who "*could possibly* be the replacement for the deceased" (perhaps in deference to the resistance from Feige's supporters), it was obvious to all that he *was* the one.[154]

At the same time, one newspaper account reported that the dowager *rebbetzin*, Feige, was "not healthy," having suddenly become "unwell," and that a "big doctor from Mount Sinai Hospital was called." According to the report, she had recently suffered a "light heart attack." Her doctor had advised that "she cease her community activities" and be put under a nurse's care, and she was "unable to see anyone during the coming weeks," even though during the preceding week of shivah for her husband she had—rebbe-like—received *pidyonos* that she brought to the rebbe's grave, perhaps as the start of her desperate campaign to turn it into her vehicle for holding on to power.[155] The announcement of her incapacitation, however, was an effective face-saving way to halt that plan. At the same time, it was reported that many of the older Hasidim—the elite who would serve as a signal of where the allegiance of the court was headed—already had handed *kvittlach* (petitions for blessing) to the Sigheter Rebbe, as a sign that they wanted him to take over.[156]

In yet another signal of the transition to a new rebbe, Rabbi Yitzchak Yaakov Weiss, newly appointed *av beit din* of the Edah HaHaredis in Jerusalem, announced that if Moshe took over the *rebistve* he, Weiss, would give up his new position in favor of the Satmar leader.[157] In fact, Weiss remained in his position, while Moshe, like Yoelish before him, would be named "president," a largely symbolic role.

In spite of all this, a continuing dispute over succession lingered. Leaflets were distributed on which, under unflattering images of Moshe, were the words: "Is this the man who is worthy of inheriting the place of our holy rebbe?" At the all-important third meal of the Sabbath, one of the late rebbe's *gabbaim*, Azriel Glick, rather than Moshe recited a prayer normally recited by the Satmar Rebbe.[158] Later Glick and the other *gabbai*, Yosef Ashkenazi, and Sender Deutsch, publisher of the Yiddish paper *Der Yid*, would negotiate with Moshe over the *rebistve*.[159]

Moshe appeared to some Hasidim painfully inferior to his uncle.[160] Even as the inevitability of his succession gathered strength, these people continued to paint him as unworthy, supporting Feige's idea to have the rabbis and *dayanim* run the day-to-day affairs and religious matters, while she would be the paramount leader. This plan would distribute greater power to the religious virtuosi and would turn the paramount leader into a symbol who reigned but did not rule.

In the midst of all this, a letter purporting to be from Yoelish surfaced.[161] It claimed that Shulem Halpert, one of the young *gabbaim* who had served him, should be his replacement. The idea that their late rebbe would have wanted as his successor a man with neither family ties to Hasidic royalty (*yichus*) nor acknowledged Torah scholarship shocked thousands of Hasidim. Turning to the *dayanim*, whose judgments they respected, they quickly received a verdict. Yecheskel Roth, a respected *dayan* in the Borough Park Satmar Bes Medrash, called the letter a forgery, and the succession moved forward to the less charismatic but inevitable nephew, Moshe Teitelbaum.

By September 14, 1979, reports in the paper made it official: "The Sigheter Rav is the new *rav* of the Satmar community." [162] A front-page story in *Der Yid* identified him as "the famous genius rabbi and *zaddik* Moshe Teitelbaum." [163] He was made guardian of Satmar assets and rabbi of Yetev Lev, the formal name of the Satmar congregation. The appointment had been made at a meeting of the administration and officers of the community, the elite Hasidim. Seven of the most prominent leaders had come to his residence to inform him of his selection. Even though he would immediately take over administrative and leadership decisions, he would formally be crowned only at the conclusion of the year of mourning. Moshe deferred all expressions of "Mazel tov" until then.

That same day Feige was "taken to the hospital where she was placed in intensive care." [164] Some people—no doubt among her supporters—had urged a postponement of the decision and meeting to appoint Moshe because of her condition, as if to suggest that his ascension to the throne could cost the *rebbetzin* her life. But in a news report four days later, Feige was quoted as saying that the meeting should go ahead. Her challenge was essentially over.

A limited number of diehard opponents broke from the main branch of Satmar and came to be known as the B'nai Yoel (sons of Yoel). [165] Others derisively called these people "the *rebbetzin*'s Hasidim" (since she helped economically support many of them) or the *misnagdim* (opponents), a term with a double meaning, since it not only referred to their opposition to Moshe's selection purely by blood but had been used in the early years to refer to opponents of Hasidism in general. [166] These opponents echoed what Yoelish had written: "The ways of the Ba'al Shem Tov have been forgotten." By that they believed he meant that just because someone had royal blood he should not automatically succeed to the crown. Those mystical notions of holy seed should not the governing principles any longer. What mattered more, as the B'nai Yoel and their sympathizers understood it, was one's zeal for continuing Yoelish's ways, and Moshe did not have it. [167]

But although they built their own schools and institutions, the B'nai Yoel led by Yossel Waldman remained a small minority. However much a giant Yoelish may have been in the eyes of his Hasidim, his declining years had been troublesome and anxious for most. The shift from a debilitated rebbe and a court run by a *rebbetzin* to one taken over by a younger, albeit less charismatic relative, the Beirach Moshe, as he was called, after the commentary he had written, promised a new energy in the court—if only those who still opposed the succession could be controlled. Hoping this would happen within less than a month's time, the leadership planned for their new rebbe's appearance in the main synagogue in Williamsburg at the start of the *slichot* prayers for forgiveness that would begin in the week leading up to Rosh Hashanah.

The new leader continued to defer all wishes of "Mazel tov" to his ascension and even frustrated the hopes of about a hundred Hasidim who had come to his synagogue in Borough Park expecting a chance to "toast a *l'chaim*" to the new chief.[168] Instead, he told stories about his predecessor and about their mutual forebears, tales that would remind his listeners of his family heritage and credentials as a worthy successor.[169] As Moshe lingered in the shadow of the man who had preceded him, his strategy of reminding them that he too was scion of the royal family was his strongest way to stake his claim for legitimacy. Showing a reluctance to accept "Mazel tovs" demonstrated humility.

THE NEW SATMAR REBBE IS CROWNED, THE *REBBETZIN* FADES AWAY

On Saturday evening, following the year of mourning for Yoelish and in the *melave malka* ceremony during which the Sabbath is mystically ushered out, the coronation in Kiryas Joel of Moshe as the Second Satmar Rebbe was set to take place.[170] In the preceding weeks, Moshe had been in Europe, collecting funds among Satmar supporters for the institutions he would lead. In a practice made in other Hasidic successions, he had also gone to visit the graves of his forebears in Hungary and Romania, as if asking for their endorsement, before making his way back for the coronation. As the Sabbath ended, by Jewish law the date changed and year of mourning ended; the ceremony could begin. It climaxed a series of observances begun the previous Wednesday. With a reported crowd of over twenty thousand Hasidim in attendance, Moshe was formally called to be the replacement (*memaleh makom*) of the rebbe identified as "the rabbi of all the Diaspora, the holy of holies." [171] From then on he would be referred to simply as "the Satmar Rebbe."

For three days and nights, Hasidim (including "women and children") by the thousands visited, recited psalms, prayed for their livelihoods and for spiritual comfort for themselves and all the Jewish people, and reviewed the writings of Yoelish at his gravesite. A massive feast and gathering on Thursday evening marking the ultimate ascension of the rebbe's soul to paradise served as the onset of the first *yarzheit*.

The New York State Police had been present since midweek to help control the crowds who overwhelmed the narrow roads and byways of the little hamlet. The Hasidim were always excited and proud when they could point to their considerable numbers and the fact that even the authorities of the state could not ignore them. This was a sign of the success of their rebirth after their near death in the Holocaust.

On Thursday night the synagogue was filled with Hasidic elders at long tables, and the bleachers that circled the room were packed with younger Hasidim. There was barely enough space to stand on them and almost none to breathe. At around 11 p.m., Moshe walked in from a side doorway directly to the dais. Late entrances that made the Hasidim wait added to the sense of anticipation so crucial for such an occasion. All of those who were still sitting rose to their feet and strained to see the rebbe-select's every move. A moment earlier the din of thousands talking rumbled through hall, but with his entrance silence filled the room. Sitting at the center of the head table, the rebbe opened a large volume of the Talmud set before him. Throughout the year, the entire thirty-seven volumes had been reviewed in Yoelish's honor and memory. By midnight, Moshe began to recite the last words of the final volume, after which he recited a special grand Kaddish and inaugurated the festive meal of completion. The new rebbe offered a Hasidic *ma'amar*, reviewing a lesson learned from his predecessor and combining it with his own new teaching. It was an intellectual exercise overladen with the symbolism of continuity and progress. He reminisced about the man whom he was replacing, concluding with a promise to hold fast to his ways and especially his struggle against Zionism—the trademark cause of Satmar identity.

Many Jews at the time were debating the question of Israel's evacuating the conquered territories, he noted, but the real question was the unacceptable fact and original sin of Israel's heretical establishment and its continued existence before the coming of the Messiah, and the great and unacceptable religious rebellion that this signified. By 2:00 a.m. Moshe was done and the gathering dispersed, some returning to the grave to recite more psalms before the morning prayers commenced at daybreak.

Later in the morning Yoelish's gravesite was mobbed. The paths to the tomb in the new cemetery built for the rebbe's remains were filled not only with pilgrims but with little tables manned by those collecting money for all sorts of Satmar causes and institutions. Taking advantage of the belief that charity given at auspicious times and places redounded with special merit for the giver and that it could put off the angel of death, these collectors had a banner day. At the grave, *kvittlach* and *pidyonos* were placed on the grave, in hopes that the dead rebbe would grant petitioners last favors and promote their cause before the heavenly throne. Then as the sun set and the Sabbath commenced, all the visits to the grave ceased and mourning was suspended—a pause between the reign of the First Satmar Rebbe and the Second.

As the day gave way to night, Satmarers turned toward their new leader, who had already sworn "to lead the holy community in the ways of the previous rebbe, may the memory of that *zaddik* be a blessing, and of his forefathers." The meal began around midnight, and the new rebbe entered an hour later. His every move was presumed by the Hasidim to be filled with deep meaning. While the soul of Yoelish was ascending to a higher spiritual plane, it made space for his nephew to inhabit the lower realms on earth.

Sender Deutsch, administrative head of the Satmar institutions, whose newspaper *Der Yid* chronicled it all, began the proceedings and said that they could all be grateful to God that "following our terrible misfortune that had occurred last year on this day" he had not "destroyed our chance for a redeemer," and had instead brought the Hasidim "the leader of Israel from the House of our Rebbe." The "tree will not be cut down" until the coming of the Messiah.[172] That was the promise of succession. Whoever was the Satmar Rebbe was more than a local *zaddik;* he was the "rabbi of the world," or—at the very least—of all the Diaspora, the leader-in-waiting for the Messiah.[173]

As the ornate document that affirmed Moshe's *rebistve* was read aloud, everyone listened intently. The ceremony was like a wedding, in which the two parties—the Hasidim and their rebbe—committed and contracted themselves to one another and to the venture of building their joint house. Leibish Lefkowitz, head of the Yetev Lev congregation and financially instrumental in the founding of Kiryas Joel, handed the document of appointment to the new rebbe. Rabbi Weiss of the Edah HaHaredis handed the new rebbe the first *kvittel*.[174] At the conclusion, as many Hasidim reportedly wept, all those in the hall sang together from Psalms 61 and 91: "May Thou add days unto the King's days, may his years be as many generations. With long life will I satisfy him and let him behold my salvation." Then they concluded with "Long live our master, our teacher, and our rabbi." With that the new covenant between leader and led was established. Various notables from both the Diaspora and the Land of Israel, from other Hasidic courts and from the Edah HaHaredis, offered their congratulations and wishes for the Almighty's help and the rebbe's long life.[175]

By the time it was Moshe's turn to speak he suggested that the hour was too late for him to offer a long and complex Torah address and said he would therefore speak only briefly. He began by again recalling his younger years, telling his hearers of the days when he was orphaned and how he moved into his uncle Yoelish's home, knowing that recalling his family ties at this time would be a useful reminder of his legitimate succession claims. Quoting Genesis 44:30, he suggested that he and his uncle were souls bound together no less than Jacob and his son Benjamin in the Bible.

"We had always been certain that the Rebbe would lead us to the days of the righteous Messiah," he said, "and I never dreamed for a moment that things would be otherwise," though many likely recalled the animosity of the dowager *rebbetzin* toward him and how she had claimed that for years he had been positioning himself to take over.[176] While he assured them that he knew he was "not worthy of leading this holy community," repeating the mantra that expressed a belief in the steady diminution of the generations following the great men of the past, his voice broke and he paused to weep. He concluded that he would "follow in the footsteps of his uncle." Then he was escorted by crowds of singing Hasidim to his residence in the village.

THE FIRST CROWN PRINCES

Moshe moved quickly now to take possession of the crown and to assure Satmar's future. By the afternoon of the day following the coronation, an announcement was made that Moshe's second-born child and oldest son, Aaron, "the rabbi and outstanding scholar," was to be appointed head of the yeshiva in Kiryas Joel. Less than a month later, Moshe's third son, Yekutiel Yehudah, known as Zalman Leib (1952–), took over the Atsei Haim Community of Sighet in Brooklyn that had been his father's base.[177] The new rebbe's second son, Lipa, married to the daughter of Yoelish's *gabbai,* Yosef Ashkenazi, who had been in the diamond business, found work in the Satmar office, and the youngest, Shulem Eliezer, was named a rabbi in another Satmar synagogue on Fifteenth Avenue in Borough Park. A son-in-law was named a chief rabbi of the Satmar community in Montreal, yet another became a Satmar rabbi in the main Satmar synagogue in Borough Park, and a third did so in Monsey in New York's Rockland County.[178] Nosson Yosef Meisels, for years head of the yeshiva but now an opponent of the new rebbe, was sent off to London. A new rebbe and a new family were now firmly in positions of authority.

By late October, Moshe was effectively in control, even signing directives about how the Hasidim were to vote in the upcoming primary for state assembly.[179] The succession seemed complete, and his sons and sons-in-law were situated in the Satmar empire. In time there would be some moving around, but that would come later as part of the next generation of Satmar upheaval. The "free hand" that Moshe had been awaiting for the last year was now his.[180]

In her Kiryas Joel redoubt Feige was still a force to be reckoned with, and Moshe showed her the honor due to a dowager *rebbetzin*—especially one who had been as powerful and unique as her. Her home adjacent to the large synagogue there made it easy for many Hasidim to visit her on Sabbaths and other occasions to wish her well or even to ask for her help in some personal matter, much as they might to a rebbe. She handed out candies to young children, like a grandmother; but she tried also to exert influence, like a rebbe, which of course put her on a collision course with Aaron, the crown prince, who also lived in the village. Her authority, based only on her being a dowager *rebbetzin,* could not compete with his scholarship and religious expertise and his role as heir apparent.

In 1984, Aaron's profile was again raised. Although Aaron was not the rebbe's eldest child, as the eldest son in the family he effectively held the prerogatives of the firstborn son.[181] On a Monday in October, during the intermediate days of the festival of Sukkot, a group of Hasidim on the board of the community met with Moshe in his glamorous sukkah in Williamsburg and urged him to appoint Aaron as *rav* and *mara d'asrah* (rabbi and formal head of the entire community) in Kiryas Joel in virtual charge of all the institutions in the rapidly growing village.[182] At the end of a festive Sabbath in an elaborate public ceremony on the night of November 10, in the presence of his father and many other distinguished leaders and rabbis, a crowning ceremony was held at which Aaron was given a certificate of appointment.[183] The evening was filled with symbols of continuity, and Aaron was clearly presented as the chosen son and heir. Never before in Sighet/Satmar had such an appointment of a son been made during his father's lifetime.

This news was momentous; for the first time since the court was reestablished in America, its future leadership was clear and assured. Stability of this sort was unprecedented for a Hasidic court that had reached historically massive proportions and wealth but had been forced for as long as anyone could recall to defer a sense of certainty about the future in favor of vague hopes about the Messiah's arrival.[184]

When Aaron and his father Moshe walked into the packed hall, the Hasidim began to sing, "Hasdei Hashem Lo Tamnu," a song that played on a phrase generally understood to mean that the goodness of the Lord is unending but that in another reading could be pronounced to mean that the Hasidim of God—the Satmarers of course—had not been "finished off" and that their continuity was assured.[185] The speeches recalled dynastic pasts and the "merit of the fathers," and the rebbe spoke of studying with one's children and assuring Judaism for the coming generations, particularly in a place like Kiryas Joel, where this could be accomplished without the corrosive influence of "foreign elements." After Aaron was handed his certificate of appointment and the crowd sang about "the sound of joy and salvation in the tents of *zaddikim*" and shouted "Mazel tov," the new crown prince spoke and prayed, "May the Lord our God be with us as he was with our fathers." For the first time in Satmar history there was a clear path to succession.

The newly empowered Aaron considered Feige's lingering influence in his territory as an intolerable challenge, though he framed his opposition to her and her supporters as driven by his desire to protect the honor of his father, which he saw undermined by her continuing bid for influence and power and the lingering objections of her supporters, the B'nai Yoel. He framed Feige and the B'nai Yoel as stoking efforts at "dethronement."[186] The B'nai Yoel were not the true sons of Satmar; he was. The tension between the supporters of each side intensified, and Aaron's Hasidim came to blows with Feige's. It was then that a split became irreconcilable.

Once at the head of Satmar in all but name, Feige was now completely associated with the B'nai Yoel, who remained a marginal presence in Kiryas Joel, continuing to maintain that the previous rebbe had never expressly accepted his nephew as his successor. The dowager *rebbetzin* visited Williamsburg at least once a week and held an open house in the late rebbe's and her old residence on Bedford Avenue for people who needed assistance.[187] She demanded respect, but even when she received it from the new rebbe's supporters—as she did in a full-page ad in *Der Yid* of July 10, 1981, that congratulated her on the marriage of her grand-nephew—it echoed with a reminder that she really had no heirs who were among the new leadership of Satmar. Gradually her battle against Moshe and Aaron became quixotic. While members of B'nai Yoel were banned as a rebellious community, Feige was simply outflanked and increasingly cut off from being able to maintain a following. There was a stream of litigation, often argued in state courts rather

18. Moshe Teitelbaum, the Second Rebbe of Satmar (seated in the center, with a white beard). By permission of Ichud Archives, Brooklyn, New York.

than rabbinical ones (because neither side could agree on the rabbinic judges), as well as mass protests, violence, and attacks on property.[188] Attempts at reconciliation ended.

There were also tests of Moshe's ability to marshal the power of Satmar. As he beat back all challenges, Moshe's authority became recognized by nearly everyone. Since he was less imposing and with a far lower profile than his predecessor, his charisma flowed primarily from the office he held and secondarily from the fact that he was a Teitelbaum of the generation who came from Europe. But his continuing ability to fight off opponents also enhanced his personal power. And his institutional successes were significant. After years of political and legal negotiations, in July 1984 he convinced the government to officially designate his Hasidim as "a disadvantaged minority," making them eligible for a wide array of economic and welfare benefits that helped effectively to subsidize Satmar growth and existence (and to an extent also to lessen his group's dependence on other Jews, with whom Satmar's relations were often fraught).[189] Thus, through a food grant program, Satmar students, though in private schools, received free hot breakfasts and lunches. Other welfare subsidies flowed. Money from the public coffers was more easily accessed than donations from other Jews. The population exploded; the yeshivas expanded with budgets topping $20 million annually. This was a rebbe who could provide for his flock (figure 18).

Generally described as a "self-effacing and humble" personality (a contrast to his predecessor's fiery confrontational one), Moshe created conditions that allowed Satmar to grow to unprecedented size. As Yoelish became a subject of hallowed memory, the birth of new generations of Hasidim who had never seen him or experienced his charisma helped transform Moshe into the face of Satmar. The charisma that came to him with his office became increasingly attached to his person. Although not as public a figure as Feige, Moshe's wife increasingly filled the role of *rebbetzin.* In 1987 on a trip to Jerusalem, it was she who was "given the royal treatment" once given Feige.[190] A relatively calm period of growth with a clear future settled on the court. All seemed well.

MOSHE'S DECLINE AND A THIRD BATTLE OVER SUCCESSION

For all of his success, Moshe was not the attention-grabbing figure his uncle had been, and he did not stand out in the Hasidic pantheon by virtue of a dominant personality. In the public American imagination of what a Hasidic leader was, he was eclipsed by Menachem Mendel Schneerson, the Lubavitcher Rebbe of nearby Crown Heights, who seemed to have the world marching to his door, his name constantly in the press, and his picture on the cover of the *New York Times Magazine* for influencing Jews beyond the borders of his court. Moshe, however, was still the leader of the largest group of Hasidim in America and maybe the world.[191] When a skirmish broke out between the Lubavitcher and Satmar groups in which the latter accused Schneersohn's followers of trying to poach their Hasidim, Moshe beat back Lubavitch, who always had fewer Hasidim than he did.[192]

He could not, however, beat back time. Like his predecessor, Moshe, who was sixty-five when his predecessor died, had now begun to enter a period of steep physical decline that troubled his followers and seemed to sap the energy of his court. Although they had grown in numbers, at least some missed the vitality of the many conflicts and battles that had so often been part of the Satmar life during Yoelish's reign. Under Moshe, the fight was missing. Even the trademark war against Zionism so ingrained and associated with Satmar seemed muted. Throughout Moshe's years of leadership, the state of Israel became more powerful and became firmly accepted as a fact of Jewish life and in the Middle East, even tacitly in Hasidic circles that were generally anti-Zionist. With the rebbe's health in decline, esprit de corps among the Satmar Hasidim also diminished.

Unsurprisingly, increasing attention was paid to Moshe's projected heir, Aaron.[193] Speculation grew about what his coming reign might be like. Like many a crown prince, he had "an especially high evaluation of power" and often acted as if he were already a full-fledged rebbe.[194] Apparently, his father did not object. In 1996, after a stay in the hospital for kidney surgery, the eighty-two-year-old rebbe, perhaps feeling especially mortal, reputedly called in all of his sons and reiterated his intention to have Aaron serve after him, suggesting that he himself was merely a bridge between his great predecessor and the son whom he saw as the worthy successor.

But Aaron was also subject to criticism, fomented in part by the residual effects of his contest with Feige and her supporters. Unable to target the rebbe, some of these critics projected their lingering resentment about his treatment of Feige onto the heir apparent. They spread the opinion that Aaron led the village in a high-handed manner, and they labeled him a usurper who exerted power not yet his. That imperious reputation reached from Kiryas Joel to Williamsburg.[195] Old criticisms that had been submerged for decades resurfaced. Yoelish's objection to Aaron's marriage into a "Zionist-sympathizer" family, ignored for years, was recalled again. Complaints about what some considered exorbitant remunerations he received for his services were voiced. Various people bristled when Aaron moved to consolidate power by appointing more of his own people to positions of authority in the village, as it continued to grow.[196] Quiet efforts to diminish his authority if not to altogether dethrone him began in some quarters.

In Williamsburg, Moshe's weakness in 1996 and his growing confusion (a sign of the dementia to come) raised Aaron's authority even more. Hasidim who in the past had automatically gone to his father for blessings, counsel, or help began to turn toward the son. In the winter of 1999, Moshe, recognizing this trend, reportedly telephoned Aaron in Kiryas Joel and asked if he would relocate to Williamsburg for some extended period in order to help in running the court. Supposedly, the two agreed on a one-day-a-week visit as well as a few Sabbaths during the winter.

The veracity of this story was challenged by some in Satmar. As proof they pointed to an event just a few months later during Passover when Aaron and some of his Hasidim gathered in the synagogue in Williamsburg, hoping to celebrate his formal appointment as *rav-tza'ir*, the formal crown prince. Son and father had met earlier in the rebbe's home. During the tête-a-tête, Aaron, catching wind of a report that some were trying to convince his father to reorganize the *rebistve*, reportedly had raised the possibility of his moving to Williamsburg to help his father run the court and to preposition himself for the succession.

In this version of events, his father had been cool to the idea and had told Aaron that there was surely enough for him to do in Kiryas Joel. If true, this version of events would suggest that he probably had not asked him to come to Williamsburg a few months earlier—or if he had, something or someone had changed his mind. After waiting in vain in the synagogue for a long time for Moshe to arrive and give his blessings to the appointment, Aaron's supporters dispersed when the rebbe's assistant entered and told them there would be no such event. A succession that for years had seemed a foregone conclusion was suddenly in question.

Apparently, the weakened rebbe had been persuaded by some of his *gabbaim,* most forcefully by Moshe Friedman (known popularly as "Moshe Gabbai"),* first among equals, that he could no longer manage the community by himself given the huge growth in numbers, which by some estimates was up to 120,000 members. Even for a vigorous rebbe, many of whose activities require face-to-face meetings with his Hasidim at all hours of the day and night as well as decision making about institutions and collective action, dealing with so many followers would be overwhelming. In his late eighties and after almost twenty years on the throne, the rebbe was no longer up to the task. *Der Yid* echoed the sentiment: "It has long been necessary that there be a *rav* standing at the holy right hand of our rebbe, may he live many good years." [197]

Convinced that something had to be done, Friedman and other key supporters were not persuaded that Aaron was the one to do it. Moreover, the *gabbaim* and staff understood from Aaron's appointments in Kiryas Joel that his ascent would ultimately lead to their own political decline as the future rebbe would bring his own staff from Kiryas Joel to quickly assert control, lest his father's *gabbaim* try to manipulate him.

In June 1999, at Friedman's suggestion, Moshe's third son, Zalman Leib (named for the rebbe's late brother), was installed to be the *av beit din* and head of the yeshiva in the Yetev Lev congregation in Williamsburg and to remain at his father's side.[198] In a front-page story, *Der Yid* reported that the appointment had taken place in a "small gathering of community leaders" (but that there would be "a large reception in the days to come") and described the appointee not only as a "genius and the *zaddik*" but also as a "beloved son." The full text of the rebbe's letter was reprinted, noting that Zalman Leib was appointed as "the *rav* in our

---

* Friedman, a classmate of Lipa Teitelbaum, the brother of Aaron and Zalman, had been a bit of troublemaker as a boy but with Lipa's support had been turned into a formidable success as a *gabbai.*

community in Williamsburg" and that "his hand is like my hand"; his authority with regard to heading all the institutions of Torah (the schools) would be an extension of the rebbe's.[199] This added a dramatic new twist to Zalman's history. The "exiled" brother sent to the Satmar hinterland in Israel was back in the Satmar heartland bigger than ever, and his elder brother Aaron appeared about to be impeded from succession.

Zalman had not been in line for such a prominent place. In 1980, after his father's ascension, he got only the small congregation in Borough Park that had been his father's.[200] Later, even that was taken away as he was all but banished to lead the small Satmar community in Jerusalem, reportedly at the urging of Aaron.* Satmar in Jerusalem was tiny, overshadowed by other bigger and more prominent Hasidic groups like Ger and Belz.

So now the personable Zalman was back at Satmar headquarters, and his new role was described as parallel to what Aaron was doing in Kiryas Joel. At forty-eight years old, Zalman was young enough to be energetic but old enough to take on the many responsibilities that his father held. "It is for others to describe," wrote *Der Yid*, "the amazement and expression of the Satmar community in Williamsburg." [201]

On Thursday evening, June 17, Zalman's formal appointment took place in his father the rebbe's residence before an audience that included lay leadership and the elite of the Williamsburg community. Yaakov Kahana, a major financial supporter, announced that this decision had actually occurred during the intermediate days of Passover (precisely at the time that Aaron and his Hasidim had convened their unsuccessful gathering to crown him *rav-tza'ir*).[202] Had Aaron's failed gambit speeded Zalman's successful ascent?

Whatever the answer, the new appointment was greeted not simply with "great joy by the members of the community" in Williamsburg, as the paper wrote, but also with shock and anger by Aaron and his Hasidim.† The younger Zalman was unexpectedly in a higher-profile position and perhaps ahead in line as the "heir apparent of his father's position." [203] As if to underscore this possibility, the report of his appointment made no mention of Aaron.

---

* In a sense this was a replay of what had happened years before when Yoelish was exiled from Sighet.

† This came to be known as "apple cider night," when some of Aaron's Hasidim who ministered to the rebbe learned about the plan to bring Zalman in to challenge Aaron, in anger they filled the wine bottles at the rebbe's seder with apple cider in a dirty trick meant to signal that they would fight any effort to dethrone Aaron.

"The impact of dethronement should not be underestimated," Henry Abramovitch reminds us. When an older sibling perceives a younger sibling as having displaced him, a "deep sense of wounding" often leaves "a lasting sense of injustice," leading to the older child to feel surrounded by enemies and rivals.[204] The more popular and prominent Zalman became, the more resentful Aaron and his Hasidim became.

For those opposed to Aaron and what they considered his high-handed ways, who still smarted from his ignominious dispatch of Feige and her supporters, Zalman presented a happy alternative; even the B'nai Yoel could and did find a reason to support him. In the guise of supporting the alternative to Aaron, they found a vehicle to give revenge to Feige. They joined Zalman's enthusiastic supporters in Kiryas Joel, and he in turn found a way to welcome them back into Satmar and his heart, ignoring the extent to which they had opposed his father. He managed this by suggesting that they always had held a "hidden love" for Satmar, even as they had temporarily wandered away.* For Aaron's supporters any alliance with the B'nai Yoel was painted as an attack on the rebbe Moshe.

According to *Der Yid*, the rebbe, when speaking at Zalman's formal appointment, recognized, in a lucid moment, the implications of his decision. He again explained the need for a vigorous leader for the growing community in Williamsburg, asked the *dayanim* to appoint Zalman to lead the community "as it should be led," and added that he hoped there would be "no disputes" that would tear apart his Hasidim, since it was all too easy to destroy a great community with quarrels and much harder to rebuild or to retain what was there. If people were worried about a fight over the succession, Moshe assured them that he "was certain that the Almighty would help and the Messiah would come soon and in our days." That, of course, would obviate the necessity of any succession, as everyone knew the Messiah's arrival presaged the resurrection of the dead. Of course, the invocation of the Messiah (as always) was a sign that the question of succession no longer had an unequivocal answer.

After some singing, Zalman spoke briefly. Claiming that he had "never asked my father for any power," a subtle reminder that his elder brother had, he added that he'd been "happy with what I had." When he had gotten the call on Passover, he had asked no questions. Williamsburg was now a very great community, but, he insisted, he was not

---

* The name "Hasidim of Hidden Love" (i.e., secret admirers) is still used by some of Aaron's Hasidim to identify some of Zalman's supporters.

its leader, only an emissary and a helpmate of his father, and he would do only what his father asked of him, for the sake of heaven. The crowd toasted him with "*L'chaim*" and "Mazel tov." Once again Aaron was not mentioned, nor does the news account even say he was present.[205]

It was difficult at first for most Hasidim to completely reverse their expectations that Aaron would be the next in line—so long had this been accepted thinking. Zalman, in contrast, unencumbered by any expectations, was helped by the fact that he had never been seen as a likely successor to his father, a fact that had allowed him to develop less imperious ways, as reflected in his brief remarks. Even after he suddenly found himself in a new position of authority, Zalman, in contrast to Aaron, remained more approachable, as any challenger to entrenched authority has to be.* For Hasidim who yearned to be close to their rebbe, approachability was of singular importance, and it would make some look forward to his ascent more than to his brother's.

"Firstborns understand power and often use it to buttress their special status"[206] Aaron marshaled all his power to fight back against his younger brother. But the challenge to Aaron from within the family increasingly emboldened those who were dissatisfied with the status quo and strengthened Zalman.

Slights to Aaron now occurred more publicly in Williamsburg, which fast became Zalman territory. At the September 2000 Williamsburg bar mitzvah of Aaron's grandson, the first of Moshe's great-grandchildren to reach this milestone, and in the presence of the rebbe, a quarrel and fighting broke out because some of the supporters of Aaron were troubled at the failure of the rebbe's *gabbai,* a Zalman supporter, to allow the boy to be called to the Torah, a clear affront to the boy's father. This slight to Aaron in his father's presence so soon after Zalman's elevation was seen as an attack on Aaron's honor and authority and as an effort to separate and alienate his children from the rebbe and the court.

The Aaronis, as Aaron's Hasidim became known, struck back. Their response to Aaron's rejection and humiliation included physical and verbal violence. They also claimed that Zalman's wife, the daughter of Moshe Shpitz, was one of the B'nai Yoel sympathizers and the initial opponents of Moshe. In fact Zalman's wife had had her problems with her father-in-law during the years that her husband was in exile because she resented his having been put in a weak position, but after his 1999 recall to Williamsburg she had not been at all sympathetic to those who

---

* Not unlike Mordechai Dovid Unger in Bobov.

opposed her father-in-law, since she now viewed Moshe as a patron and supporter of her husband and family position.

For their part, the Zalis, Zalman's Hasidim, claimed that Aaron had brought all his troubles upon himself. They asserted that he had started using family celebrations for political ends and to enhance his standing and that he should therefore not be surprised when his opponents turned them into opportunities to strike back. They resurrected the whispering campaign that he was not anti-Zionist enough, that when he was at home with his Israeli wife he spoke the forbidden Modern Hebrew rather than Yiddish. The anti-Zionist theme, so deeply a part of the Satmar brand, now turned inward in the war between Aaron's and Zalman's Hasidim; no hint of compromise on this matter could be tolerated in a future Satmar Rebbe. The fact that Zalman was not the oldest son, they counterargued, meant nothing. The great Yoelish himself had been a younger son like Zalman.

In Yiddish newspaper reports, Aaron was referred to as "the genius and *zaddik av beit din* of Kiryas Yoel," but no longer as a crown prince; in some cases he was even called "Kiryas Yoeler Rav." [207] These titles, of course, removed the all-important Satmar label. The energy of conflict was back in Satmar, and the Hasidim were now charged up by it. This time, however, it was turned inward rather than toward external enemies.

When in his continuing physical and mental deterioration the rebbe ceased making public speeches, leading prayers, and officiating at weddings and was no longer able to even to have face-to-face talks with his Hasidim without getting confused, attention to his sons intensified, and so did the conflict. When the old rebbe stopped attending events that might be interpreted as favoring one son over the other in order to prevent outbreaks of violence and dispute, this actually exacerbated the tension between the two sides. Without the rebbe present, a contest ensued over which brother's event was attended by more notables, whose pronouncements deserved greater attention, and so on. Everything became a referendum on leadership and a zero-sum game; one brother's receiving support was based on the other's losing it.

When the rebbe Yoelish had gotten sick, his *rebbetzin* Feige along with his *gabbaim* had taken on the role of serving as "acting rebbe." Even though she had broken many taboos, her unchallenged control had provided stability during this troubled period. Only when her husband died did that all fall apart. During the rebbe Moshe's decline, however, as both Zalman and Aaron and their Hasidim contested the future succession, the result was far more unstable. Moshe's sons knew that the winner of *their* contest *would* be the next rebbe, so they fought even harder. No one imagined the fight would go on beyond their father's death. At first, most people still believed Aaron would win, tradition being on his side. But growing numbers looked to Zalman.

THE FUNCTIONS OF THE CONFLICT

The competition between sons, while no doubt adding confusion and tension, also injected the energy of a contest into what had become a routinized Satmar. As the Hasidim chose between competing camps, they were forced to stress all the positive qualities of their choice and demonstrate their loyalties. The opposition between the groups hardened and toughened them, as each person took a side.[208] Each group mobilized funds and resources to make certain their candidate could point to these as signs of his strength. Everyone was galvanized as members of each faction bonded powerfully to one another, "strengthening group consciousness."[209] Even though there was a large enough population to sustain two courts or "identity groups," few seemed prepared to let the two brothers rule simultaneously with equal authority. The intramural competition infused everything, strengthening each side's awareness of its distinctiveness as well as its victories.[210] The longer the conflict went on, the more care and energy went into making and amplifying even the smallest of distinctions. Neither side was willing to give up. Therefore, instead of finding things they did not like about the brother they sided with, the Hasidim deflected any hostility they might have felt away from their own group and onto those they opposed.[211] Whereas Satmar Hasidim had remained unified in the past by directing hostility outwards toward Zionists and modernizers, now they directed it toward one another in the internal war between the "Aaronis" and the "Zalis."[212]

Often the conflict took the form of litigation in the New York courts. There were fights over property, especially if it was of symbolic importance. Thus, for example, a dispute broke out over the ownership of the cemetery in Kiryas Joel in which Yoelish was interred and also over *batei medrash* (study halls), Talmud *torahs* (primary schools), yeshivas, girls' seminaries, ritual bathhouses, summer camps, and matzah bakeries—assets with a value of around $500 million. Each faction conducted separate elections of the board of directors and of officers for Congregation Yetev Lev D'Satmar in Williamsburg and contested the legitimacy of the other side's election.

The judges hearing the cases recognized that "all the civil legal disputes were ultimately ancillary issues used to dress and color the core issue," and that was one of religious legitimacy.[213] The court affirmed that these were not really property but "ecclesiastical" issues that the "members of the congregation" and not the courts had to decide. But of course, the "members of congregation" were so divided that they could not.

As the battles between the brothers intensified in the closing years of Moshe's life, one of the factions even petitioned the court to have the aging rebbe declared incapacitated and to have co-guardians appointed for his personal needs and property management. Reportedly the rebbe turned on Aaron at a public occasion around this time. "You *rushe ben rushe* [evil person]," the rebbe shouted. "You think I'm already *kaleching* [mentally declining]? You think I don't know what's going on?"[214]

This effort was fought vigorously by the *gabbaim* and Zalman, for whom the weakened rebbe was a ticket to power. The dispute galvanized both sides, even as it clearly diminished the rebbe's honor and stature. How could a rebbe who was declared incompetent be looked upon as a holy intermediary between the Hasid and the Almighty, or even as a provider of *chayei, bonei,* and *mzonei?* To do this to a *zaddik,* one who by definition Hasidim considered a figure of extraordinary powers, was unheard of; it denied the very charisma that was at the core of what defined a rebbe. Some looking on from the outside saw this as a particularly low point for Satmar.[215]

THE DEATH OF THE REBBE MOSHE

In the days before Passover 2006, as the ninety-two-year-old Moshe lay in critical condition in Manhattan's Mount Sinai Hospital, the Hasidim declared a world day of prayer on his behalf. The fact that he had not really been acting as a rebbe for years was acknowledged, but the Hasidim were buoyed by "being able to see the rebbe's face and form."[216] Whatever the resistance to his leadership when he first assumed the crown, twenty-seven years later by the end of his life he was described as the *ateres tiferes* (mantle of glory) and as one of the "princes" of the Satmar "holy institutions," standing "at the right hand" of the saintly Rebbe Yoelish, of blessed memory, and one of the few remaining "shepherds of Israel of the previous generation," most of whom were already in "the treasuries on high."[217] In Kiryas Joel, there were twenty-four-hour watches at Yoelish's tomb, where psalms were recited to beg for his intercession on high on behalf of his ailing successor.[218]

When the inevitable end came on April 24, 2006, the battle for succession became frantic. The two pretenders lacked the talismanic character that post-Holocaust Hasidism had projected upon the European-born survivor rebbes, and their ongoing disputes had tarnished both of them. They embodied the principle of declining generations, each seeming to be a diminished version of his forebears.*

At the end, as one reporter noted, "Not even sitting shivah has muted the war."[219] Instead, the immediate concern was discovering conclusively what had been the late rebbe's will; that would be determinative. Citing a verbal will dated with the Hebrew year 5756 (1996), Aaron's Hasidim claimed that Moshe had declared his eldest son alone would be the new Satmar Rebbe. Witnesses were brought to corroborate this fact, even though no document was produced.

For their part, Zalman's Hasidim arranged for a public reading of a subsequent will. Really a letter signed in 2002 declaring Zalman as the successor to his father, this text began: "Insofar as I have appointed my dear son, the scholar and *zaddik,* Yekutiel Yehudah, as *rav* and *av beit din* of our congregation, Yetev Lev here in Williamsburg. . . ." It concluded that Zalman was "to stand at the helm of our holy institutions here" in Williamsburg.[220]

In rebuttal, the Aaronis argued that this document had been signed after the late rebbe was afflicted with dementia and could therefore not be considered reliable. Moreover, they added that Moshe had been over eighty when it was signed and that according to a Jewish ruling, to which the late leader adhered, wills written after one was eighty could not be considered valid. Finally, they claimed that in any event the 2002 letter had been cajoled out of an infirm rebbe by his *gabbai* Moshe Friedman and that therefore the wish to have Aaron reign expressed in 1996 was final.[221]

In making their claims Aaron and his Hasidim were effectively attacking the *gabbaim* (and particularly Moshe Friedman, Zalman's champion) who surrounded the rebbe and his son Zalman and who, many believed, increasingly controlled things, turning the rebbe and later Zalman into little more than figureheads. Because Aaron refused

---

* This attitude was exemplified when in response to my asking for a "biography of the rebbe" in Williamsburg bookstores, I was always given one of Yoelish Teitelbaum. When I said that I wanted the current rebbe, they showed me one of Moshe Teitelbaum, who at the time was also dead. No, I objected, I meant the men who were actually now claiming to be the Satmar Rebbe. With a wave of the hand or a shrug of the shoulder, I was told there was nothing to be found.

to be a figurehead and wanted control of everything, the *gabbaim* considered him imperious and an adversary. Zalman, whose position was the result of their intercession, might reasonably be more disposed to maintaining at least some of their authority to which he was beholden. He also supported the idea of using *dayanim* and religious virtuosi to control much more while he remained symbolic leader (a plan not so different from Feige's).

For readers of *Der Yid,* owned in 2006 by among others the *gabbai* Moshe Friedman, there was no doubt who was to be the new rebbe. On its front page under a banner headline announcing Moshe Teitelbaum's death was a second headline only slightly smaller that began with the line from scripture (Num. 27:17) "And the congregation of the Lord shall not be like sheep that have no shepherd" and continued in large letters: "The Yetev Lev Congregation of Satmar has appointed our master, teacher, and rabbi, the genius and *zaddik,* the Hasid Rabbi Yekutiel Yehudah Teitelbaum . . . to be the successor of his honor our teacher and rabbi, the genius and *zaddik* of blessed memory . . . to serve in holiness as the *av beit din* of the holy community of Satmar until the coming of the just Redeemer [the Messiah]." [222]

Beneath was a reproduction of the signed letter of 2002, appointing Zalman, whose authority was "from that day forward and forever," including "after the length of my days and years." [223] In the baroque language of the document, the late rebbe asked "all who have issued forth from my loins," as well as the "holy community," to "stand at his right hand" and neither object nor do anything to undermine this appointment.

Cognizant of the controversial nature of their role in now extending Zalman's authority from Williamsburg to all of Satmar, even before the funeral procession for Moshe had taken place, the Hasidim doing so claimed to be acting in the best tradition of generations of leaders, noting that it was especially important to act expeditiously in America, where the "destruction of religion" was rampant. "The trusted captains of the community" as well as the "true aides" of the late rebbe, men who understood "the path that had to be followed and the actions that needed to be taken," made the only "responsible" move to maintain the continuity of leadership.[224] They were "thankful to the blessed Lord that their rebbe had left them a son" to be his successor, and that son was not Aaron but rather Zalman.[225]

For seven years they had watched this son help his father lead the community. The announcement catalogued all that Zalman had done that perhaps was not widely known, particularly his role in "providing for the poor and the many charitable organizations that he handled," stressing one of the three main aspects of any rebbe's role. In case anyone missed the subtlety here, a huge ad on the same page announced that anyone who wanted to come to share the coming Sabbath with "our teacher the rebbe, may he live many good years," and who wanted to have "food, drink, and a place to sleep" arranged for him should simply call the posted phone number and all would be provided.

Max Weber once postulated that in large organizations there should be a clear separation between politics and administration and that those appointed by political or charismatic leaders should not be able to acquire or hand over the power of those who appointed them to another. Yet he also observed that after the death of a charismatic leader those who were his closest disciples were often endowed with the residual charisma of that leader. A dowager *rebbetzin* and a *gabbai,* as we have seen repeatedly, often inhabit that complex social space. Moreover, at a time of generational change, they may represent a link between the past and the future, especially important when the future rebbe is not fully tested or when he is challenged over his succession. With the dowager *rebbetzin* out of the picture in the last years, the role of the *gabbaim* loomed larger.[226]

That some, like Joseph Ashkenazi, married into the rebbe's family or that others, like Moshe Friedman, took over the Satmar newspaper and manipulated events only underscores how powerful they had become. In the end, however, the administrative staff and the *gabbaim* did not manage to completely control the succession. Instead they watched the conflict become institutionalized.

The crowning ceremony of Zalman was carried out hurriedly in a small room and was not at all like the drama of his father's coronation.[227] The Aaronis and the large number of their Hasidim were not present and did not acquiesce to what was happening there.

The event included a public rereading of the 2002 letter along with the testimony of several men who had witnessed its signing. These men swore that they were absolutely certain that Moshe wanted Zalman as his successor and that he fully understood the consequences of his choice. Perhaps none of the speakers was more important at that moment than Lipa, the son born after Aaron and before Zalman, who spoke just before the end.

"Gentlemen," he began, "I feel I must here reveal something that I have held within me all these years." He went on to recall the events of 1999 when his father brought his younger brother Zalman back from

Jerusalem to Williamsburg. He detailed how his father had asked him how he felt about this decision, whether he was for or against it. After all, if his father was moving away from his older brother, he, Lipa, was next in line and not Zalman. His reaction at the time, he now claimed, had been "You are the general and I am only a soldier." Then, as Lipa was about to leave the room with all the others, his father called him back and said, as the son now recalled, "I know that you are three years older [than Zalman] and it will perhaps be difficult for you, but I pray give me your hand that you will stand by him." Lipa gave him his hand and word that he would do what he could to support the institutions. "I know that it was his will," he concluded, "and I will do all I can, for my father wished it 'with a full heart,' and anyone who says otherwise is 'a liar and a deceiver.'" Turning now toward his about-to-be-crowned brother, he wished him mazel tov and asked the Almighty to help him lead Satmar until the coming of the Messiah and the resurrection of the dead.[228] Lipa, who would become a fund-raiser for Satmar and the Zalis, had just sworn public allegiance to Zalman. The following week Lipa was given leadership of the new Satmar congregation, Kehal Berach Moshe of Zenta.[229] After Lipa concluded, there were shouts of "Mazel tov" and the collective cry "May our master, teacher, and rabbi live."

With visible tears, Zalman began to speak. Comparing himself to the high priest at the Holy Temple in Jerusalem as he was about to enter the Holy of Holies and begin the divine service, he said that like him he needed to concentrate on where exactly he was going. That place was where his illustrious forebears who burned "with the flame of holiness" had stood. He prayed that their merit and the collective power of the congregation would redound to his benefit and allow him to lead. He would be an icon, but a far more modest one, of a diminished generation who he hoped would not have to sit long on the throne, in the confidence that the Messianic redemption would soon come. These expressions of modesty, whether truly felt or not, were his effort perhaps to distinguish himself from his brother Aaron.

During the week of shivah, Zalman and his brother Lipa mourned in Williamsburg with their mother. Aaron sat in Kiryas Joel. Hasidim came to each son with kvittlach, as well as pidyon money, as if he were the only one to whom such missives could be brought.[230] Even though the emphasis was on continuity, the fact was that there was no consensus on who exactly represented it.

On the first Sabbath after Moshe's death, when everyone in Satmar looked to who would lead the all-important first tish, both Aaron and

Zalman led separate gatherings in Williamsburg. Each ignored the fact that the other was acting as if his were the only true assembly and as if he were the true and only heir. Aaron whose home base was in Kiryas Joel, gathered his Hasidim under a huge white tent set up in a public school playground. Zalman and his people used the Yetev Lev Bes Medrash on Rodney Street, the same hall in which the late rebbe had held court. Much was made of the fact that they were gathering in this "same holy place, where his father had served," the same "place where the [Satmar] forefathers had prayed," a location freighted with meaning.[231] The contrast to Aaron's temporary tent was striking, no matter how many supporters gathered beneath it.

Not long afterward, the Aaronis marched into the Williamsburg synagogue "less than a month after the Zalis repulsed a similar attack. This time, the Aaronis brought a platoon of bouncers from a nightclub. The bouncers climbed onto the dais that leads to the Torah scrolls," hitting several Satmar men in the face and knocking them down.[232] But recognizing that they had lost Rodney Street and the main Satmar redoubt to the Zalis, the Aaronis built their own large synagogue space in an astonishing fourteen days on nearby Hooper Street, gradually expanding their presence in Zali territory.[233]

THE LINES OF DISPUTE

As the future unfolded, the lines of the Satmar dispute hardened. Aaron sought to claim definitively what he considered his birthright, demanding to be the only Satmar leader. Zalman held on to the major Satmar institutions in Williamsburg and moved to assert authority elsewhere. Neither brother was prepared to bow to the supremacy of the other, as Lipa had (figures 19 and 20).

Votes were held in a variety of Satmar communities over who would be on the controlling boards of the communities and the *mosdos* (institutions). In some places Zalis won, in others Aaronis. At stake were considerable property, assets, real estate—in short, a fortune. The victory of one side led to the formation by the other of parallel competing institutions. This was an extraordinarily expensive option, but with a battle joined, both sides seemed fired up as they had not been for years. Often they described this as "broadening the borders of holiness."[234]

As with political campaigns, success was measured in numbers, often those of fund-raising.[235] The more successful a gathering was, the more funds were collected. So headlines screamed about the "thousands"

19. Zalman Teitelbaum (center, with cane), one of the sons of the late Grand Satmar rebbe Moses Teitelbaum, leaves a fund-raiser in Lawrence, Long Island, 2006. Photo by Anthony DelMundo for *New York Daily News*.

20. Aaron Teitelbaum (in white caftan), one of the two Satmar Rebbes, surrounded by his Hasidim. By permission of and copyright Moshe Indig.

who gathered with one or the other of the competing rebbes and about "great crowds," "colossal successes," and "soul-raising" experiences.[236]

In the evolution of a highly conservative Hasidic world, insiders increasingly found "little room for variation" in the sorts of behavior tolerated in the community. People dressed the same, lived only within the boundaries of Hasidic enclaves, were educated in essentially the same ways, and generally adhered to a "one-size-fits-all" principle of social and cultural uniformity.[237] But the conflict between the Aaronis and Zalis now gave Satmar Hasidim an opportunity to differentiate themselves. To be sure, as one wag put it, "The theological differences between the brothers are thin as a page in the Talmud." [238] But the narcissism of small differences made the strengths of one brother and the weaknesses of the other loom large. Each man's Hasidim pointed to what Weber might have referred to as his personal "gift of grace." [239] The contest goes on, and the numbers grow.

ChaBaD Lubavitch

A Rebbe Who Never Dies

ChaBaD, founded by Schneur Zalman of Lyadi (Liozna, in the Vitebsk region of Belarus) (1745–1812), one of the first generation of Hasidic leaders following the Besht, is today among the best-known Hasidic groups, largely because of its nearly obsessive concern and involvement with Jewish outreach and messianism. These interests actually derive from its particular history of succession and are a unique solution to its complexity.

At its outset, as already detailed in these pages and elsewhere, and throughout its history, ChaBaD Hasidism faced complex and often difficult successions.[1] The death of its founder threw his Hasidim into turmoil about who would lead them next, and we have already reviewed how they handled the complications of that first transition, navigating between the competing claims of a top disciple, Aaron Hurwitz, and DovBer Schneuri (1773–1827), son of the founder. The victory of the son over the disciple helped establish the importance of the principle of "holy seed," the crucial role of the family, and the influence of the dowager *rebbetzin* (the widow) in Hasidic succession. It is therefore appropriate that we should complete our consideration of the subject with a return to ChaBaD.

We have found references to the Messiah's arrival emerge among Hasidim when the trajectory of succession is in question. That is what happened to ChaBaD when it faced a dearth of successors. Its solution, a decision to ignore the need for a successor by believing their rebbe was

---

The ChaBaD Lubavitch Dynasty

SCHNEUR ZALMAN (1745–1812): Known as the Alter (Old) Rebbe; First ChaBaD Rebbe in Lyadi, Belarus

DOVBER SCHNEURI (1773–1827): Known as the Mittler (Middle) Rebbe; first rebbe in Lubavitch and second in the ChaBaD dynasty; son of Schneur Zalman

MENACHEM MENDEL SCHNEERSOHN (1789–1866): Known as the Zemach Zedek; second rebbe in Lubavitch and third in the ChaBaD dynasty; nephew and son-in-law of DovBer

SHMUEL SCHNEERSOHN (1834–82): Known as the Maharash; fourth in the ChaBaD dynasty (by now the Chabad and Lubavitcher titles were used interchangeably); seventh son of Menachem Mendel

SHALOM DOVBER SCHNEERSOHN (1860–1920): Known by the acronym RaSHaB; Fifth Lubavitcher Rebbe; second son of Shmuel

YOSEF YITZCHAK SCHNEERSOHN (1880–1950): Known by the acronym RaYaTZ; Sixth Lubavitcher Rebbe; only son of Shalom DovBer

MENACHEM MENDEL SCHNEERSON (1902–94): Known by the acronym RaMaM; Seventh Lubavitcher Rebbe; son-in-law and cousin of Yosef Yitzchak

---

not really dead but simply had withdrawn to higher realms and could continue to guide them in his afterlife before his return in the flesh as Messiah, is the story of this chapter.

FROM CHABAD TO LUBAVITCH: DOVBER TO THE ZEMACH ZEDEK

The resolution of the conflict of succession after the death of the founder of ChaBaD Hasidism was, as we have seen, that some of Schneur Zalman's Hasidim, who embraced the ChaBaD philosophy, followed his disciple Aaron while others remained with his son DovBer.[2] Thus for a while there was no definitive ChaBaD successor. Eventually, DovBer left Lyadi and established himself in the town of Lubavitch, becoming in effect the First Lubavitcher Rebbe of ChaBaD. Here he built a yeshiva and attracted his own new followers, shaping a version of his father's Hasidism in his own image.[3]

Although DovBer had a son, Menachem Mendel, and a daughter, Menucha Rachel, at the end of his fifteen years of leadership he was not succeeded by a son. While one ChaBaD source claims that DovBer's brother Chaim Avraham was a contender, the successor turned out to be Schneur Zalman's grandson, the son of Devorah Leah, daughter of the founder.[4] Also named Menachem Mendel (1789–1866), he had been wed at the age of fourteen to Chaya Moussia, his predecessor's daughter, making him DovBer's son-in-law as well as his nephew. Even more important was the fact that when he was only three and after his mother's death, Menachem Mendel had been raised in his grandfather's home. At the extraordinarily young age of twelve he reportedly had written many treatises on Jewish law, and by the age of twenty he held a position of communal responsibility at his grandfather's court. He was thus *both* heir and stellar student or disciple.

When his uncle DovBer became his grandfather's successor, Menachem Mendel, according to ChaBaD sources, "commenced a period of fourteen years of seclusion."[5] Although the official accounting of these years was that he was engaged in study, one can imagine that while his uncle was in a contest over who would succeed the founding rebbe, the presence of another challenger from within the family like his brilliant nephew who, only sixteen years younger than DovBer, had played such a prominent role at the court could not have been welcome. Indeed, some reports indicate Menachem Mendel's "consideration for succession."[6] There are also stories about tension between DovBer and his nephew and son-in-law, who was so tightly bound to his grandfather that the idea of accepting his uncle as a worthy successor might have been difficult.[7] "Seclusion" is a far more elegant way to account for what might have been a tacit exile.

In 1826, however, a year before his uncle's passing, when DovBer was accused by state authorities of subversive activities, Menachem Mendel appeared as his father-in-law's public defender. No doubt this reemergence at a time of crisis impressed the Hasidim and stressed his role in the family as well as his value for ChaBaD. With the idea of succession seemingly limited to members of the family after the drama of DovBer's competition with Aaron Hurwitz, the fact that Menachem Mendel was kith and kin (and possibly a previous candidate) as well as a scholar and disciple strengthened his position as potential successor. By the time his father-in-law died shortly thereafter in 1827, Menachem Mendel was the leading if not completely unopposed choice as next rebbe.

Known as the Zemach Zedek after a volume of his writings, Menachem Mendel seemed to have everything, and his ascension to the crown would effectively resolve lingering questions of merit versus birth as grounds for succession, since he could make the claim on the basis of both. Some even went so far as to argue that his father-in-law's selection as the leader of ChaBaD "was made because it would eventually pave the way for his [nephew and] son in law . . . when older and more experienced to succeed him."[8] But since such stories are often projected on the past after a new leader is selected to reinforce the inevitability of his succession, one cannot really be certain.

DovBer's brother, who had served at times as a stand-in for the rebbe when Hasidim wanted a personal audience, and the rebbe's two sons could each have made a claim. Yet none of these men seemed particularly attractive to the Hasidim. Either they were too self-effacing or too familiar; the assistant often cannot make the leap to chief, as we have already seen. In contrast, the Zemach Zedek's absence from the court for a while made him more intriguing. And when it comes to charisma, mystery is always helpful.

Yet in spite of his attractiveness, the Zemach Zedek's succession was not immediate. For three years following DovBer's passing there was an interregnum, as according to the ChaBaD sources the Zemach Zedek tried to persuade his brothers-in-law, Menachem Nachum and Chaim Abraham, the second rebbe's sons, to take on the crown. How sincere this desire was we cannot know. The interregnum might also have been a time during which he worked to make his ultimate succession seem inevitable. His apparent reluctance to take on the role actually made him more appealing.

There was yet another reason to select the Zemach Zedek. Since Aaron Hurwitz, with whose approach to ChaBaD the Zemach Zedek was known to identify, died around this same time, his succession rather than that of one of DovBer's sons or his brother could also appeal to Aaron's followers. He might draw them back to the fold without their having to appear defeated by DovBer and his progeny.[9] A subtle thinker and leader, the Zemach Zedek understood that he could draw legitimacy as both scholar and beloved grandson to Schneur Zalman, whose authority no one, including Aaron's followers, in ChaBaD could question. A unified ChaBaD under the leadership of Lubavitch would be a commanding succession.

At last acquiescing to mounting entreaties from the Hasidim, which he had played very subtly, the now thirty-eight-year-old Zemach Zedek agreed to take on the leadership so long as they did not trouble him endlessly with petitions for their personal material welfare but looked to him only for spiritual guidance. It was an audacious request given the expectations that Hasidim had of their rebbe, but it was not unlike what Schneur Zalman, the first rebbe, had demanded too. Indeed, Schneur Zalman's book *The Tanya* was really a series of discourses that he hoped his Hasidim would study for the personal spiritual guidance they might otherwise seek from him directly.

The Zemach Zedek understood too that keeping some personal distance from his Hasidim would enhance his charisma and actually make him a stronger presence in their lives. Not surprisingly, he marked his ascendance by offering a discourse based on one given by his grandfather, dazzling his audience and not incidentally reaffirming his connection to the traditions and spirituality of the original ChaBaD of Schneur Zalman. Aaron's group indeed did melt back into the Zemach Zedek's followers. Now there was only ChaBaD Lubavitch.

For thirty-eight years, more than twice the length of his predecessor's reign, and until his death in 1866, the Third ChaBaD Rebbe (and Second Lubavitcher Rebbe—though no one actually counted things that way, for that would have reminded everyone of the earlier schism) ruled, establishing a powerful reputation as a scholar, especially knowledgeable in matters of Jewish law, a mystic, and a Jewish leader far beyond the boundaries of Lubavitch. Many of his Hasidim came from Belarus, but his reputation grew, and he attracted followers from "farther afield," gaining respect even among opponents of Hasidism.[10] The fact that he cultivated a relationship with the czar's court physician also gave him influence among Russian Jewry in general. Likewise, his concern with such issues as Jewish boy soldiers ("Cantonists") drafted into the czar's army and their subsequent alienation from Judaism, which he combated by sending his Hasidim to do outreach among them, helped transform him into more than a local Hasidic rebbe.[11] Furthermore, he employed emissaries, or *shluchim,* as they were called in ChaBaD, to reach an unprecedented number of people and spoke in venues outside the court, stressing his intellect and Talmudic knowledge, a quality that impressed and may even have endeared him to Jews generally not open to Hasidic masters. By the time of his death at seventy-six, he had established communities of Hasidim as far away as the Holy Land and had made Lubavitch a well-known brand. He was a hard act to follow.

THE DEATH OF THE THIRD REBBE AND THE BREAKUP OF CHABAD

The Zemach Zedek had seven sons—Boruch Shalom (1804–68), Yehuda Leib (1811–66), Chaim Shneur Zalman (1813–79), Yisrael

Noah (1816–83), Yosef Yitzchak (1822–77), Yaakov (1826?–38), and Shmuel (1834–82)—and two daughters, Rada Frieda and Devorah Leah. Upon his death, ChaBaD, whose unification had been so important an accomplishment for him, fell apart in some measure because he presented such a formidable model as rebbe. Unlike the sons of DovBer, almost all of the Zemach Zedek's sons wanted to follow their illustrious father into a *rebistve*. Most did, setting up courts not terribly far from one another, but at the same time creating alternate versions of what it meant to be a ChaBaD rebbe.

That they should have wanted to follow their father was not unexpected. He had often used them as his emissaries, and with their borrowed charisma, they, his holy seed, were sought after in many Hasidic circles during his lifetime. Those born after their father took the crown particularly considered themselves "rebbes-in-training."

In contrast, Boruch, born while his father was seventeen and still in "seclusion" and not yet headed for the *rebistve,* was never groomed to become crown prince and never saw himself as one. Instead, for the first twenty-one years of his life, during which his father was living a private life, Boruch explored other interests, ultimately pursuing a business career. After his father took the *rebistve,* Boruch continued his own interests. Finally, when his father, now the famous Zemach Zedek, died, Boruch, in his late fifties, was not about to abandon the life he had made for himself.[12]

Many years later, Boruch would be returned to the orbit of the *rebistve* when, unexpectedly, his great-grandson, Menachem Mendel, named after the Zemach Zedek, became the Seventh Lubavitcher Rebbe, the very leader whose followers claimed him to be the Messiah.[13] By then, the story of why Boruch had not pursued the *rebistve* had to be revised. In this new revision of ChaBaD history, Boruch was understood to have had held himself back from claiming his birthright "as a supreme act of humility"—not because of any "blemish," or any other interests or emotional weakness, but because of "his saintly qualities."[14]

Given Boruch's lack of interest in following in his father's path, Yehuda Leib, the Zemach Zedek's second son, was effectively for most of his father's *rebistve* considered the crown prince and even held court at his own *tish* during his father's lifetime. Indeed, the latter sent many of his elder Hasidim to hear talks that his son gave, presumably to allow them to spread the word of his abilities, assimilate the inevitability of his becoming their next rebbe, and tacitly endorse that eventuality. No less important, in the year preceding his father's death, Yehuda Leib "set out on a tour of various communities in Russia," where he reportedly "impressed many audiences with his scholarship and charisma," presumably paving the way for what he imagined would be his inevitable ascension to power.[15]

Nevertheless, as the Zemach Zedek aged and grew infirm, he grew closer to his youngest son, Shmuel, born when his father was forty-five. Shmuel and "his family had been living in his father's house for the past few years," and his wife, Rivkah, had taken on many of the *rebbetzin*'s responsibilities at the court after the death of her mother-in-law.[16] While his older brothers were attempting to enhance their reputations abroad, Shmuel and his wife remained in a strategically important position at court on what would be the eve of his father's passing and the inevitable transition that would follow.

Simultaneously, disputes among the brothers as to who would succeed their father were developing; the younger brothers did not want to be left out in the cold after their father's passing. But whom had the Zemach Zedek really chosen as his successor? By no means was the answer unequivocal.

Upon the father's death and during the period of mourning the brothers did not sit shivah together; instead, each of them convened and led his own minyan (prayer service) made up of his supporters, and each added his own special customs, allowing Hasidim to visit each son to sample and compare the religious experience.[17] This also made it clear to everyone that they were asserting their independence and displaying their leadership qualities.

Behind the scenes, efforts to prevent a breakup were ongoing. Shortly after the week of mourning, a document purporting to be the late rebbe's will surfaced. To the surprise of many, it tapped the youngest son, Shmuel, and not his older brother Yehuda Leib, as first among equals.[18] Shmuel, known to be his father's favorite son, at least in his later years, had a reputation according to some for being sharp, witty, and a bit of a prankster, fond of regal ways, including "riding in a heraldic horse-drawn carriage," and getting involved in "inside matters and royal affairs" at the court. Insiders who had watched what was happening at the court during the last years and months guessed that the ambitious young man who was effectively acting on his father's behalf would, upon his death, "make a 'revolution' at the court."[19] Others (presumably Hasidim preferring another brother) considered him "a rather uncharismatic and apparently dull person."[20] The will took aim at the putative crown prince and declared that thenceforward Yehuda Leib was no longer authorized to give Hasidic discourses in Lubavitch and that if he transgressed his father's moral will, the Zemach Zedek would take his revenge from "the world beyond." [21]

Understanding their options, most of the brothers would need to go elsewhere to set themselves up as rebbes if they wanted to continue in the family business. Yet the will had purportedly cut that possibility off by adding that they were all prohibited from leaving Lubavitch and should together stay and lead the Hasidim as one. The will stipulated, however, that Shmuel, who had "an especially holy soul," would guide his brothers, for they would then be blessed from the treasury of heaven.[22]

No young pretender to the throne could have asked for more in a will. Could Shmuel have helped his aging father compose it? The idea that the rebbe, although dead, could continue to direct affairs at court and in the world of the living was not unheard of. Faith in the powers of a rebbe bordered on the magical, and his ability to influence heaven and earth was a given, in death no less than in life.

Many ChaBaD elders, still certain that Yehuda Leib was to be the next leader, expressed doubts about the will's authenticity. So too did nearly all of Shmuel's brothers, each of whom found "his own supporters." [23] Everyone agreed that the idea of having all the sons acting as rebbes in the same place would not work. Tensions among the brothers became quite heated.[24] Suddenly the question of succession in ChaBaD became a kind of open competition, as Hasidim continued to visit "all the different brothers to compare and contrast qualities." [25] Some Hasidim tried to crown Yehuda Leib as their rebbe. But others among the younger, more worldly and outward-looking Hasidim in Lubavitch, who saw in the youngest son a man who shared their sympathies or at least would not hamper them and had acquired knowledge beyond the purely Hasidic, supported the authenticity of the will and Shmuel.[26]

With the forces favoring Shmuel carrying the day and "fulfilling the will of his father," leaving him in charge in Lubavitch, the older brothers established themselves elsewhere.[27] Given the reputation of their father and the shared charisma they were used to having, they could and did find receptive communities happy to have one of his holy seeds as their local rebbe.[28]

Yehuda Leib found a robust following in Kopust (Kopys, Belarus), holding on to many Lubavitchers. When, however, he unexpectedly died within the year at age fifty-five, a fact that Shmuel's supporters in Lubavitch saw as the fulfillment of the threat in his father's will warning him against doing this, this only helped Shmuel consolidate his position.

Yehuda Leib was succeeded by his oldest son, Shlomo Zalman, while another of Yehuda Leib's sons, Shalom, moved *his* court to Rechitsa (Rečyca, Belarus), and a third son, Shmaryahu Noah, went to Babruysk (Belarus).

After remaining in Lubavitch for three years, Chaim Schneur Zalman, the Zemach Zedek's third son, moved to the cradle of ChaBaD Hasidism, Lyadi, where he served as a *zaddik* and was succeeded by his son Yitzchak DovBer. Yisrael Noah, the fourth son, left for Nezhin in Ukraine, where his grandfather, the Second ChaBaD Rebbe, DovBer, was buried. A *zaddik*'s tomb is part of his legacy, since at it one can gain access to his soul, pay one's respects, or even commune with the late rebbe, so Yisrael Noah's decision to set up a court could be seen as a symbolic challenge to his brother Shmuel by controlling access to an earlier rebbe.[29] Yosef Yitzchak, a fifth son, went to Ovruch, an area that belonged variously to Ukraine, Russia, and Poland. His daughter Shterna Sarah would become the wife of the Fifth Lubavitcher Rebbe, Shalom DovBer, and his grandson and namesake would become the sixth rebbe.

The sixth son of the Zemach Zedek, Yaakov, married to his brother Yehuda Leib's daughter, moved to Orsha, Belarus, about 140 kilometers away from Lubavitch, but did not pursue a ChaBaD *rebistve*. In 1838 he died young, predeceasing his father, in Tolocin, about fifty kilometers to the west. Only the court of the Zemach Zedek's youngest son, Shmuel, would remain in Lubavitch, where he could call himself both a ChaBad and a Lubavitcher rebbe. Each of the other brothers who established a *rebistve* and took the name of the place in which he established himself remained attached to and variously interpreted ChaBaD Hasidic ways, texts, ideas, and traditions.[30] Lubavitch had lost its ChaBaD monopoly.

At the age of thirty-two and in sole possession of the Lubavitcher succession, Shmuel had to come to terms with the fact that ChaBaD was no longer a unified *rebistve* and that its various branches were growing in directions over which he had nothing like the control that his predecessors had. In a number of ChaBaD communities during Shmuel's brief reign, Hasidim were divided between Lubavitcher and other customs, and in some cases fights broke out among the different groups.[31]

At the same time, the expansion of the number of rebbes associated with ChaBaD helped promulgate its philosophy, expand its influence, and attract followers, adding to its overall prestige and numbers in the long run. Since all of its rebbes had some sort of following, ChaBaD became more than simply its local Lubavitcher version.[32]

As frequently occurred in royal families, marriage was used to create alliances and mitigate the tensions of rivalry and competition. Marriages were complex. Before he became a rebbe, Shmuel was married to the daughter of his older brother Chaim Schneur Zalman. But when she got sick during the first week of their marriage and died only months later—an inauspicious sign—he remarried.[33] This time his bride was a cousin, the aforementioned Rivkah, a granddaughter of the Second Rebbe, DovBer, a match that would in some ways help him more in any ambitions he had of succeeding his father. After Chaim Schneur Zalman's death, most of the Hasidim transferred their loyalty to Shmuel, but this was only shortly before his own death about two years later.[34]

No less important than this marriage and being situated in Lubavitch, the primary seat of the dynasty for about half a century, was the fact that Shmuel "managed to retain possession of the considerable collection of manuscripts of Ḥabad [ChaBaD] Hasidic teachings left by his father, comprising the latter's own voluminous writings along with those of Shneur Zalman and DovBer."[35] Possession of these items served as symbols of leadership, authority, and the right of succession in Hasidic life, and for subsequent Lubavitcher Rebbes (especially after they left the town of Lubavitch to relocate elsewhere) these objects remained the symbolic keys to the kingdom.

In spite of his hold on Lubavitch, Shmuel found that following an illustrious father is hard, especially when one's older brothers are busy setting up competing courts. His relatively brief sixteen-year reign (1866–82)—during which he was reportedly sickly—also took place at a particularly stormy time for Jews in Russia, with outbreaks of pogroms and the continuing impact of an early draft of young Jews into the czar's army as well as ferment within the Jewish population leading to secularization, increasing Jewish modernization, and Zionism.[36] Many Jews emigrated from Russia and the Pale of Settlement, while others were drawn away from Jewish tradition. Shmuel was unsuccessful in dealing with many aspects of this change. Little from his reign stands out even in Lubavitcher lore. Nor did he outshine his brothers, even though he controlled Lubavitch—indeed, there is no official ChaBaD image left behind of how he looked.[37]

Perhaps as a reflection of his charismatic limitations, Shmuel established the role of *mashpi'a,* or spiritual guide, as an appointed official in his Hasidic court, separate from the role of the rebbe. The task of the *mashpi'a* was to offer Hasidic discourses, mentor individual Hasidim, and, it seems, to conduct Hasidic gatherings, complete with stories and melodies.[38] This new position freed the rebbe to do other things, while getting help in matters spiritual.[39] Shmuel effectively outsourced some of the essential characteristics expected of a rebbe, thus making sure that the Hasidim were supplied with them, even if not by him.

To be sure, his late father had already established the principle of allowing prominent Hasidic elders to offer discourses (*ma'amar*), something that had generally been only the rebbe's prerogative. But he realized that the Hasidim, particularly those older than him, who had powerful links to the past, and later those who had their own charisma, "could easily command followers" of their own. Better to allow them a higher profile, which they would have anyway, in return for their loyalty, then to create schisms.[40] Shmuel's appointment of a *mashpi'a*, however, seems to have been driven more by a desire to supplement his weaknesses, while his father's strategy might be understood more as a way of controlling his court and keeping it unified.

FROM THE FOURTH TO THE FIFTH LUBAVITCHER REBBE: WHO REALLY WANTS TO BE A REBBE?

Although the rebbe Shmuel had four sons and two daughters, for most of them (or in the case of the daughters, for their husbands) the pursuit of the crown was not an ambition. The world they inhabited in the late nineteenth century, even around Lubavitch, offered other attractions and opportunities. Moreover, the *rebistve* Shmuel had established, no longer as lustrous as his father's and plagued by competition from his brothers, did not make that much use of his children, so they were not as actively integrated into its life.

The oldest son, Schneur Zalman Aaron (1858–1908), married twice (first in 1873, when he was fifteen, to his cousin Shterna, daughter of Yisrael Noah, the Rebbe of Nezhin) and died at the relatively young age of fifty. There are accounts describing his close but troubled relationship with his younger brother, Shalom DovBer (1860–1920), who two years later in 1875, when *he* was fifteen, also married a cousin named Shterna, this one the daughter of his uncle, Yosef Yitzchak. There are reports of sexual irregularities involving the two brothers and their young wives that exacerbated these tensions.[41]

In fact, Shalom DovBer had suffered sexual abuse from one of the Hasidim assigned to mentor him. It began when he was "five or six" and lasted until his marriage.[42] (Later in life, Shalom DovBer, by then the Fifth Lubavitcher Rebbe, was so anxious and desperate psychologically that he would consult with Sigmund Freud and be treated by Wilhelm Stekel for a variety of emotional issues and what was diagnosed as psychosomatic paralysis and a variety of neuroses.)[43]

A third brother, Avraham, had died at the age of eight in 1882, and a fourth, Menachem Mendel (1867–1942), who married three times, showed no interest in Jewish Orthodoxy in general or Hasidism in particular. He traveled the world, living in Paris and ultimately dying in Corsica. Only after his death did the Lubavitchers retrieve his body and bring it to the Holy Land and "holy city" of Safed, burying him among the holy men of Jewish mysticism.

Shmuel's daughter Devorah Leah married Aryeh Leib Ginsburg, and his daughter Chaya Moussia married Moshe Horensztajn. Neither of their husbands were candidates for the *rebistve* nor did they play a role in their father-in-law's court.

When the rebbe Shmuel died at the young age of forty-eight, there was no clear path to succession. Reportedly he had, like his own father, requested that his children rule together in Lubavitch and not go into any other business.[44] But they resisted. At the time, some Lubavitchers believed this was the end of the line of succession. At last, Schneur Zalman Aaron, the eldest but not particularly interested in the role, became the provisional leader. Those who urged it upon him saw his selection as a natural expression of primogeniture. For more strategic thinkers, he offered a way to bring back the Nezhin branch of ChaBaD, from which his wife came, under the Lubavitch banner. Moreover, his troubled and emotionally fragile younger brother, Shalom DovBer, whom he dominated psychologically during their youth, appeared too young and perhaps not spiritually ready to take on a *rebistve,* while the youngest, Menachem, wanted none of it.[45]

Signs of Shalom DovBer's difficulties surfaced when in 1883, just at the end of the year of mourning for his father (during which he refused to receive Hasidim or respond to their requests, the basic expectation of one who would be a rebbe), he simply left his wife, Shterna, his two-year-old son, and the town and court of Lubavitch, heading for the seaside in the South of France and later to other "warm climates," including the baths in Yalta, Germany, Austria, Italy, and elsewhere, ostensibly to "cure" his nervous ailments.[46] He remained away for nearly two years, with only brief reappearances at home. According to his only son, who years later wrote a journal entry about his recollections of the time, when his father finally returned the then nearly four-year-old did not even recognize him.

These journeys reflected neither an interest in nor an enthusiasm for family life, the *rebistve,* or matters Hasidic. There were few if any ChaBaD Hasidim where Shalom went, although he reportedly saw some in Kharkov during one of his sojourns. That he should go off alone like this for a "cure" was certainly dramatic. Coupled with his refusal to act at all like a rebbe, this affirmed his older brother as the default if reluctant successor to their father. Why had Shalom, who would ultimately become the next Lubavitcher Rebbe, left?

There are no definitive answers, and one can only speculate what went through his mind. His need for a "cure" is vague enough and can cover a wide range of maladies both emotional and physical. While in retrospect the getaway could always be explained as a kind of spiritual retreat (a similar argument would later be made about the Seventh Rebbe's departure from the Hasidic inner circle to cosmopolitan Berlin and Paris), on their face the extended departures seem a clear effort to escape a life he did not want or at best felt unprepared to take on as his own. These getaways might be understood as the desperate actions of a man with a series of psychosomatic problems, a history of troubled relations with his wife and brother, and what would ultimately diagnosed as a "traveling neurosis," a condition that obsessively drove him to leave home.[47]

In that account of his father's time away, the son—whose penchant for writing and even revising history is well documented—recalled a feud at a gathering of the Hasidim (*fabrengen*) when his father returned.[48] The dispute between his father and his brothers, Schneur Zalman Aaron and Menachem Mendel, focused on their future roles. Clearly, their late father's request that they rule together was not working. Could it be that they were arguing not about *who* would inherit the *rebistve* but over the fact that *none* of them really wanted it? Could it be that after having been saddled with the job for the last two years, the oldest brother wanted out, resenting Shalom's time away, while at the same time the other two, each for his own reasons, also wanted out? Menachem Mendel, who, as we know, would ultimately run away from Hasidism, his wife, Lubavitch, and Orthodoxy of any sort, surely could not be arguing to succeed to the crown. Shalom had already shown his readiness to abandon the court. And Schneur Zalman Aaron had other interests, as the Hasidim were discovering to their chagrin. But whatever the argument, apparently no final decisions were made at the time.

For nearly ten years Schneur Zalman Aaron and Shalom DovBer nominally shared duties in leading Lubavitcher Hasidism, with the older brother being first among equals, as he had been throughout their childhood.[49] Generally in the joint leadership, "the older brother took on responsibilities for the movement's administration," hoping to gradually move out of the rebbe role, while his younger brother (barely twenty-two years old) focused on Hasidic matters.[50] In the meantime, Menachem Mendel left the scene. Even Hasidic princes were affected by the progressive loosening of the bonds of religious life and chose paths other than those offered them by virtue of their birth, seeking their own destinies.

Ultimately, Schneur Zalman Aaron abdicated or at the very least got out of town and moved to Vitebsk, where he took on "the business affairs of his father," fulfilling his true desire to be a businessman.[51] His more worldly interests were increasingly unacceptable to the more Orthodox Hasidim who gradually dominated the Lubavitchers. As more worldly Hasidim joined the stream of Jews leaving traditional Jewish life, those resisting the lure of the modern became more religiously conservative. The rebbes they respected were those who reflected their views.

The shared leadership for those ten years after Shmuel's death must have been a rather diffident and uncertain rule, a period of social turmoil presided over by sons who did not seize the reins and refused to reign. Perhaps that was why it aroused concerns among the most loyal Lubavitchers about continuity and why many "wondered whether there would ever be another true Lubavitcher *rebbe*."[52] But after Schneur Zalman's and Menachem Mendel's departures, a more pious Shalom DovBer became by default sole successor to the Lubavitcher crown. In no hurry to take responsibility for it, he dawdled and continued traveling.

When he *did* return home, he studied in a yeshiva, intensifying concerns about the possible eclipse of the Lubavitcher brand.[53] Thoughts of messianic solutions filled the air. At last in 1894 on the eve of Rosh Hashanah, the now thirty-four-year-old took up the position, marking the occasion by moving from his own seat to his late father's in the synagogue in Lubavitch.[54] This subtle shift laid to rest any possibility that Schneur Zalman Aaron, of whom Shalom DovBer was still in awe if not in dread, would be the Lubavitcher Rebbe.

Unsure if the younger brother was up to the task, one of Shlomo Zalman Aaron's acquaintances reportedly asked him if he thought him worthy. In something less than a ringing endorsement, he was reported to have replied, "There is no intermediate between a rebbe and a regular man; he is either a rebbe or a fraud, and my brother is certainly no fraud."[55]

Whatever his previous doubts and misgivings, Shalom DovBer embraced the concerns of his Hasidim and began the process of consolidating power and determining the direction of the movement he now headed. Continuing to suffer from psychosomatic illnesses, he traveled endlessly looking for cures (and perhaps escapes), turning this into a hallmark of his *rebistve*.[56]

Meanwhile, his cousins who had established the other ChaBaD courts were also finding continuity difficult, turning this into a good time for the Lubavitch brand to once again make ChaBaD all its own. This, however, would require outshining the cousins, the other ChaBaD rebbes, a task that would be completed by Shalom's only child and successor, Yosef Yitzchak, the future Sixth Lubavitcher Rebbe, whom Shalom DovBer had by 1895 at the age of fifteen appointed as his secretary.[57] An important part of this would also be taking full possession of the ChaBaD manuscripts, a spiritual and financial asset that his son would guard jealously. Schneur Zalman Aaron was still interested in the economic power of ChaBaD, and control over the manuscripts, an important resource, would remain a source of tension within the family.

Increasingly, Lubavitcher Hasidim imposed on Shalom DovBer their *kvittlach* (supplications), which he would take to his father's grave, as if the true authority over the Hasidim were still there with the dead rebbe and as if the connection to the Almighty were still exclusively his father's (this sort of procedure would reappear in the days of the Seventh Rebbe).[58]

A MOBILE MESSIANIC MISSION

In the turbulent times in which Shalom DovBer lived, he would have to become more than a local leader in Lubavitch, for the ChaBaD brand had expanded beyond its boundaries, and he was soon to become its prime representative. His "oppressive restlessness" and "traveling neurosis," the condition "in which he was seized by a desire to travel at night by train and to walk in forests by day," could now be sublimated and rationalized by his need to see Jews wherever they were to be found.[59] His obsession to be away "frequently and for long periods of time" abetted an increasingly universal mission not just to other ChaBaD Hasidim but to all Jews throughout Europe, whose cultural assimilation and Zionism he hoped to prevent.[60] But his wandering took its toll on his family life. For a rebbe to have only one child was unprecedented among Lubavitchers.

An inveterate student, Shalom DovBer established a yeshiva in Lubavitch that he called Tomchei Temimim (Supporters of the Unblem-

21. Shalom DovBer Schneersohn, the Fifth Lubavitcher Rebbe. Collection of the author.

ished), where he included as subjects of study not only the traditional Talmudic and rabbinic texts and commentaries but also Hasidic writings, discourses, and even letters, many from the ChaBaD library. Like all Hasidic yeshivas, it would be an important vehicle for expanding his authority and the number of his Hasidim, as well as for making Lubavitch a magnet for learning. The "Temimim" (the unblemished ones), as its students were called, would be not only scholars but also foot soldiers in the ChaBaD movement, which all succeeding rebbes would make an increasingly mobile one for all Jews.

The only remaining competitor for control over ChaBaD was Shmaryahu Noah of Bobruisk, older than Shalom DovBer and descended from a more famous son of the Zemach Zedek. But Shmaryahu's son and heir was killed in the Russian civil war, inevitably shifting the center of ChaBaD gravity to Shalom DovBer (figure 21).

Disturbed by the ferment that he perceived among Jewry, the ideological and social drift as well as the political changes that appeared to be reordering the world as he knew it, and perhaps still looking for a way to give up being a rebbe, Shalom DovBer began to think and speak as if his were the days before the messianic redemption. These were days of darkness and disaster— world war and revolution, the popularity of Zionism, growing secularism, waves of migration away from the areas where tradition was valued—interspersed with rays of light and hope—the success of his yeshiva and the enthusiasm of his followers. His ChaBaD, he concluded, represented hope and a future redemption.

At the same time he vehemently opposed the idea of trying to hasten that redemption by encouraging Jews, certainly not his Hasidim, to move to the Land of Israel as the Zionists were doing. In his opinion, as he wrote in a letter, "Even if the Zionists were God-fearing Torah true Jews, and even if we had reason to believe that their goal was achievable, we are nevertheless not permitted to listen to them and bring our redemption with our own strength. We are not even permitted to force a premature redemption by insistent entreaties to the Almighty." Rather, he believed that Jewish redemption from exile was dependent on "a hope for the Almighty Himself to bring us the Messiah, and bring about the redemption," not through the hands of one of flesh and blood, "but by the Holy One Blessed be He by Himself." As for the Zionists, "All their plans are built upon fantasies, for their aims can never be achieved." [61]

At the core of the Fifth Rebbe's embrace of a universal mission and messianic beliefs was a well-known story of an encounter between the Besht, the legendary eighteenth-century progenitor of modern Hasidism, and the Messiah. [62] According to the story, which we have already reviewed in an earlier chapter, the Besht, engaging in one of his periodic spiritual exercises of unification with the Kingdom of Heaven, this time "met" with the Redeemer himself, who told him that when those he encountered would "be able to make 'unifications' and ascents like you,'" he would come. [63] Lubavitch had for generations promoted this narrative as their mandate to pass ChaBaD ideas to the Jewish people in order to prepare the ground for messianic redemption. [64]

But why did they believe redemption was imminent? The conviction that there is a Messiah who will come to redeem his people is of course a central tenet of Judaism. [65] Generally, the advent of the Messiah is not something Hasidim cling to because, in effect, they believe that their rebbe can accomplish much that others might look for in a Messiah. [66] While he deals with their daily concerns and guides them in many aspects of their lives (something no one expects from the Messiah), he, no less than the Messiah, is seen as a charismatic political and religious leader—someone who leads the faithful into the future and can intercede on their behalf with God, who has near-divine powers to effect miracles, who knows how cosmically to move worlds, both above and below, and who can redeem the sinner and raise even the most mundane acts so that they are endowed with religious, mystical meaning. For the most part, the *zaddik* can do all this while still remaining very much in this world. Someday the Messiah will surely arrive, and the Hasidim and their rebbes "will gather in Jerusalem around him, the Holy Temple will be rebuilt, and the full redemption will come," as Joseph Dan puts it. "But until then, things are not so bad, as long as there is certainty in the continuity of the *zaddik*'s dynasty." [67]

However, as already noted, when Hasidim are worried about their leader's and hence their own continuity as a group, when there is no clear successor to their rebbe, then they, and sometimes their rebbe as well, invoke the Messiah, hoping for a swift fulfillment of the promise of redemption and the end to history associated with messianism to obviate a need for succession.

According to Jewish tradition, just before the Messiah's arrival, "audacity" will increase and the "enemies of the Lord" will gather strength, Shalom DovBer told his Hasidim.[68] Around him, he perceived this happening. His Temimim would help him fight back by spreading the message of ChaBaD. As Menachem Friedman has noted, it was "no coincidence that the [Tomchei Temimim] yeshiva was established less than a month after the First Zionist Congress in 1897. The popularity of Zionism and its leader, Herzl, was then at its peak in the Russian Pale of Settlement," where the Lubavitcher Rebbe was competing for influence.[69] It was also a time when Russian revolutionary ideas were in the air.[70]

In addition to his messianic outreach via the yeshiva and his opposition to Zionism, the rebbe became troubled a few years later by the advance of German troops during World War I toward his town, Lubavitch. German culture was to him subversive, seductive, and the ultimate evil, so he fled, moving his court in October 1915 to the Russian controlled Rostov-on-Don, a place that had no real Hasidim among its one hundred thousand residents and where a merchant class and anticommunism were still dominant. Although in Rostov-on-Don the rebbe was far from his origins and uncertain about the future, he continued to identify himself as the *Lubavitcher* Rebbe, transforming his title to one independent of place.

His universalizing tendencies and wanderlust turned out to be perfectly fitted to this time when Jews in the area engaged in large-scale migration. Only if he could find ways of communicating with his Hasidim, who also moved throughout the region, would Shalom DovBer be able to hold Lubavitcher Hasidism together. In his self-imposed exile in Rostov, with its overwhelmingly secular population, he could not be expected to stay put. He traveled to his Hasidim and kept in touch with them via his emissaries. Although after the First World War the Schneersohns returned to Lubavitch, it was only briefly.

By the end of Shalom DovBer's reign, Lubavitcher Hasidism had effectively become defined as driven by three principles: (1) the present era heralded the coming of the Messiah; (2) the Messiah's coming was contingent on "dispersing the wellsprings" of ChaBaD Hasidism among all Jews; (3) this outreach was the main function of the rebbe and his "unblemished" students and Hasidim.[71] Succession was moot; the Messiah was coming any day now.

But the Messiah did not come, change was endemic, and as time would show the Zionists' goals were not fantasies. In November 1917, the United Kingdom's foreign secretary Arthur James Balfour wrote to Baron Rothschild, leader of the British Jewish community, asking him to inform the Zionist Federation that "His Majesty's government view with favour the establishment in Palestine of a national home for the Jewish people, and will use their best endeavors to facilitate the achievement of this object."

By March 21, 1920, at the end of the Sabbath, when Shalom DovBer passed away in Rostov, the situation for ChaBad looked bleak. Within the thirty days after his death, the home that he had abandoned in Lubavitch burned to the ground. Whatever it now meant to be a Lubavitcher Rebbe or a Hasid, it no longer had anything to do with being in the actual town of Lubavitch. When the Fifth Rebbe died in Russia, the country was in the midst of the Bolshevik revolution, and Hasidism in what was to become the Soviet Union was about to enter its most precarious situation. If ever the future was unclear, it was now. A yearning for messianic redemption grew, and Shalom DovBer's only son and successor Yosef Yitzchak embraced it.

THE SIXTH LUBAVITCHER REBBE, YOSEF YITZCHAK SCHNEERSOHN: LEADING AT A TIME OF CHANGE

Yosef Yitzchak (1880–1950) was very connected to his father and the *rebistve*. Throughout his father's peripatetic reign, Lubavitcher Hasidim

22. Yosef Yitzchak Schneersohn, the Sixth Lubavitcher Rebbe, and son of the Fifth Rebbe. Collection of the author.

grew accustomed to the idea that the boy, and later young man, knew perhaps even better than his father how things worked at the court. To ease the expected succession, his father had married him off to Nechama Dina, his cousin and granddaughter of Yisrael Noah of ChaBaD Nezhin, hoping this marriage would someday unite the Nezhin and Lubavitch courts under Yosef's leadership. Avraham, the bride's father, had not pursued the Nezhin *rebistve*. Indeed, some Nezhin family members moved far from Hasidism, as reflected in the fact that a great-great grandson was the famous violinist Yehudi Menuhin.[72] Many of the Nezhin Hasidim attached themselves to the older Shmaryahu Noah (1842–1924) of Babruysk of Kapust/ChaBaD, who had been a rebbe for thirty-six years, rather than to Shalom DovBer, who was eighteen years his junior. To his dying day, however, Shalom remained convinced that ultimately *his* son would alone inherit all ChaBaD Hasidim when he ascended to the crown.[73] He was right.

In 1920, following his father's reign of twenty-seven years as an active leader and an earlier ten (or eight if we deduct his years away), Yosef Yitzchak easily became Sixth Lubavitcher Rebbe (figure 22), hoping to become the sole ChaBaD rebbe, something not seen since the days of the Zemach Zedek. He was the latter's only great-grandson to become a rebbe. Although there was some talk about selecting Itsche Gurevitz, "the *masmid*" (diligent student), a particularly respected senior Hasid, or Schneur Zalman, a son of the Rechitsa (Rečyca) Rebbe, both of whom appealed to a small conservative segment of the Hasidim who considered Yosef Yitzchak's bibliophilic passions a sign of hidden secular tendencies (not all the books in his private library were "holy") and who were troubled by the fact that he was not known as a scholar, Yosef Yitzchak became the preferred choice, especially by the family. No serious challengers for the *nesiut* (presidency), as the Lubavitchers referred to their position of leadership, emerged, especially after the death of Shmaryahu Noah in 1924.[74]

Yosef Yitzchak inherited his position during perhaps the most difficult time ChaBaD had ever faced. Prepared over years, heading the yeshiva since he was eighteen (though he had never had the luxury of being a student there), and responsible for creating a network of its alumni, he took full control of Lubavitch at the age of forty. While a transition from being his father's assistant and amanuensis, as we have already seen in the case of Naftali of Bobov, is never simple, he succeeded at least in part because ChaBad Hasidism was in such crisis that it needed a smooth transition. Intensifying Jewish cultural assimilation in eastern Europe, the triumph of communism in the heartland of Lubavitcher Hasidism, the growing appeal of Zionism, emerging Nazism and the Holocaust, and continuing mass Jewish migration all presented an enormous challenge to ChaBaD. That the new rebbe enthusiastically became possessed by messianic convictions in the face of all this was no surprise.

At the start of his reign, he faced a newly empowered Bolshevism. Initially, the end of the czarist empire seemed good; it allowed Jews who so desired to pursue a free, active cultural life in the new Russia.[75] During what someone called "the halcyon decade following the Bolshevik Revolution," when the new rebbe took his position, there was a period of idealism and cultural flowering, and some Hasidim thought they might be able to grow their courts at this time, although they recognized—and certainly the Fifth and later Sixth Lubavitcher Rebbes did—that given the outward-looking interests of Jews, it would be not be easy to draw them to Hasidism.[76] The revolution, after all, freed those who wanted to assimilate and become fully Russian to do so, and of course there were those who embraced Bolshevism, quite of few of them former Hasidim. Many held the view that the Jews did not constitute a nation or nationality and that religion was an opiate to be prohibited and removed from society.

Others ran away to America, and still others followed the dream of Zionism to Palestine.

Hoping to find a larger stage for his efforts, Yosef Yitzchak relocated his court from the backwater of Rostov to Leningrad (formerly the capital, St. Petersburg). He soon understood that the Soviets were no friends of Judaism. Not only had they "eliminated the Jewish political parties, suppressed Zionism and Hebrew, driven religion into the remote corners of Soviet life or underground and gained a monopoly of power 'on the Jewish street,'" but they also had created the Yevsektsiya (a contraction of *Yevreyskaya sektsiya,* or Hebrew section) of the Bolshevik Party.[77] Directed by Semion Dimanstein, a former student at the Telshe, Slobodka, and Lubavitcher yeshivas, its mission was to undermine and end all forms of Jewish religious behavior and organization, which it saw as an obstacle to the total assimilation of Jews into the new communist society.[78] No Jewish activity was too minor to attract attention and be stamped out. The yeshiva, the synagogue, and rites like circumcision were "put on trial," often by Jewish communists who wanted to demonstrate that they were more communist than anyone else.[79] In the face of these conditions, a significant number of Hasidic leaders fled to places beyond the reach of these authorities. They did so not only because of perceived dangers to their physical welfare but also because their economic situations were rapidly worsening under the socialist revolution. Once-wealthy supporters of rebbes were stripped of resources to sustain themselves, let alone the Hasidic leaders they had once helped support.

The presence of former Hasidim in the Yevsektsiya's ranks would prove useful for knowing where and what needed to be attacked. Between January 1923 and March 1924, 120 out of 320 Yevsektsiya campaigns were against religion. Between 1922 and 1923, over one thousand traditional Jewish schools (*cheder*s) were closed, and during the decade nearly 650 synagogues were shuttered.[80] All this was of course bad news for Hasidim and Hasidism, which were seen as part of "debris of a civilization whose day had passed."[81]

To the Yevsektsiya, Yosef Yitzchak's activities, aimed at maintaining, if not heightening, Jewish religious identity and involvement, were anathema, and any successes he had, however limited, represented a threat.[82] His activities became even more important when the new young rebbe became one of the few Hasidic and traditional Jewish leaders who did not flee the Bolsheviks, running his network of Temimim from his headquarters in Leningrad. The Soviets targeted ChaBaD's emissaries, or *shluchim,* whom they considered hostiles.[83]

Jews outside the Soviet Union regarded their kinsmen in the communist lands as a trapped Jewish minority targeted by brutality. This served indirectly to enhance Yosef Yitzchak's stature and ambitions as a Jewish leader who stayed behind with them. In the absence of almost all other Russian rabbinic leaders of importance, Jewish organizations worldwide that wanted to help and support Soviet Jewry looked increasingly to Yosef Yitzchak and his network. He became the go-to man to reach Soviet Jewry. For the rebbe, the repression of Soviet Jewry and his opportunity to play a role in its survival had cosmic significance. He saw all this as a sign of the "birth pangs" of the Messiah and his leadership as helping to hasten redemption in fulfillment of his father's prophecy.[84]

In 1914, American Jews—the very Jews whose sins Yosef Yitzchak would later hold responsible for the travails of European Jewry—founded the Joint Distribution Committee (JDC), originally organized to aid Palestinian Jewry during the First World War.[85] Beginning in the 1920s the JDC began coming to the aid of Soviet Jewry, in dire straits after having lost their private property, stores, and factories, and also suffering from the famine that had struck Russia. Seeking someone inside the country to distribute the funds they were collecting, they concluded that with his network of ChaBaD emissaries, no one was better positioned to reach large numbers of Jews than the Lubavitcher Rebbe. Control over these funds entrusted to him enhanced his power, while making him a larger target for the communist authorities. Some Jews accused him of using the funds for his sectarian purposes, but he also could now claim that he and ChaBaD were leading *all Jews* in the Soviet Union.

Denounced by the Yevsektsiya, he was labeled a foreign agent heading a counterrevolutionary network imperiling the Soviet state. Near midnight on June 14, 1927, a detail of the Soviet secret police, headed by two former Lubavitcher Hasidim, came to the rebbe's home and, after searching the entire premises and interrogating him and others in the apartment, including two of his daughters, arrested him.

Fearing for his life, the forty-seven-year-old rebbe reportedly approached the crib of his only grandchild, Shalom DovBer Gourary, son of his eldest daughter, Chana, and her husband, who shared the rebbe's apartments. Before being taken away by the police, he offered a blessing "that this child grow to be the greatest of his brothers, and stand firmly on the same basis on which his grandfather is standing," and asked that God "grant that he tread the same path that was boldly trodden by my holy forebears, for in his veins flows holy blood that is bequeathed from a father to his son, to his grandson, and to his great-grandson."[86] Since the boy had no actual brothers (and would remain Yosef Yitzchak's only grandchild), the blessing clearly implied the rebbe's hopes that, should the Messiah tarry, this grandson would take on the mantle of Lubavitcher leadership in the future.[87] Until the infant reached majority and followed in the steps of his forebears, the boy's father, Shmaryahu Gourary, would naturally act as regent.[88]

After a brief arrest, however, Yosef Yitzchak returned home, concluding that like so many other rebbes he needed to leave Russia and the reach of the Soviets. Although unhappy to abandon the bulk of his Hasidim to their fate in the increasingly dangerous Bolshevik state without some explanation, he sent a missive *after* his departure for neighboring Latvia, which was not yet under Soviet control.[89] In it he assured them: "Know that I shall be with you always. . . . Know that what you are seeing [referring to himself] is a *neshamah* [soul], as it exists in *Gan Eden* [paradise] clothed in a body."[90] *It was a hint of a belief that he and the Messiah might be one and the same and that redemption was near.*

He still imagined that he could continue to run his network of *shluchim* and serve as JDC representative from his new home in Riga. For a while, he continued to send letters, remit money, and generally try to tend to the needs of his flock and work for the betterment of all Jews left under Soviet rule.[91] The rebbe, however, would never see his Hasidim in the USSR again.

In Riga, much as his father had from Rostov, Yosef Yitzchak, abetted by JDC support, emphasized a universal mission and echoed his father's messianic message, meeting not only with his Lubavitcher emissaries but also with all sorts of Jews. After a year, he realized Riga was not an optimal location. Moreover, his connections to the Soviet Union gradually weakened.

Warsaw, and Poland in general, remained a powerful center of Hasidic life; Yosef Yitzchak explored the idea of moving there. But Poland was dominated by its own homegrown Hasidic leaders who did not look kindly on the Lubavitcher trying to establish himself in their territory.[92] Nevertheless, he tested the waters there when in November 1928, barely a year after his arrival in Riga, he threw a large wedding in Warsaw for his second daughter, Moussia, and her cousin and bridegroom, Menachem Mendel Schneerson. No doubt he hoped that this large affair would impress the Hasidic world and perhaps segue into his establishing himself there. But the fact that a number of the important rebbes in Poland, including most prominently the Gerrer, snubbed the wedding and that his new son-in-law, not one of the important or well-known princes of the Hasidic world, was studying at university undermined Yosef Yitzchak's ambition to make Warsaw his new home.

Returning to Riga after the wedding, he continued to seek a new location. A trip to the Holy Land in the summer of 1929, and in particular to the Cave of the Patriarchs in Hebron, might have been part of this exploration. But when a few days after his visit Arab riots broke out in Hebron (stimulated, some believed, by Yosef Yitzchak's insistence on visiting the tombs in the Cave of the Patriarchs located in the city) and resulted in the murder of nearly seventy Jews, among whom were students of a newly established yeshiva in the city, he concluded that Hebron and Palestine were not the place for him to settle.

Later that year, he made his first trip to the United States, likely also part of his quest to find a new base of operations. For ten months he "visited Jewish communities in New York, Philadelphia, Baltimore, Chicago, Detroit, Milwaukee, St. Louis, Boston and several other communities, and was even received by President Hoover at the White House." [93] His extended visit enhanced his public profile and affirmed the possibility that America was now a conceivable destination for Hasidic life. Yet he returned to Europe.

In 1934, he moved to Poland, on the pretext that his yeshivas there were gaining "momentum" and that his presence would help.[94] But with all the Hasidic competition there, he settled in Otwock, about forty kilometers from Warsaw, where his cousin and youngest son-in-law, Mendel Horensztajn, came. Like Rostov, Otwock was not really a center of Hasidic life. Although there was a Tomchei Temimim yeshiva in town, even his son-in-law did not attend it.[95] Almost immediately, Yosef Yitzchak realized this was not the best place to rebuild his court in order to guarantee its continuity. Even his own family did not want to stay there. Of his three sons-in-law, only the oldest, Shmaryahu Gourary, along with his wife and son, remained with him at this court. The other two, Mendel Schneersohn and Mendel Horensztajn, married respectively to Moussia (Chaya) and Sonya (Shayna), the rebbe's younger daughters, were by then both studying engineering in Paris at a technical school, their tuition paid by the rebbe.[96]

By now in his midfifties, the overweight and heavily smoking rebbe was stricken with multiple sclerosis. In 1936, he also suffered a stroke. Soon he was spending extended time at sanatoria and mineral baths. Between December 1937 and March 1938 he stayed at a sanatorium near Vienna. The question of succession, unspoken, hung heavily in the air. The Messiah still tarried.

A DEARTH OF SUCCESSORS AND A CALL FOR THE MESSIAH

During much of the period of its last two leaders, ChaBaD, as we have seen, found itself with a diminishing reserve of leadership. All the other ChaBaD courts had disintegrated except for Lubavitch, and even the latter was facing a very limited set of choices for the crown. After some misgivings and alone among his brothers, Shalom DovBer had provided a long-term leader for ChaBaD. He had only one son. That son had only the three daughters. Of these, the younger two had married cousins whose interests had led them to secular education and European cities like Berlin and Paris, where they were largely distant from Hasidic life and engagement, a path that both their wives approved.[97] Yosef Yitzchak's only grandson lived with his parents at the court. While years earlier his grandfather had indicated that the crown of succession would rest upon the boy, the youngster was increasingly uninterested in a life like his grandfather's. As he would later admit in America, the young man (now known as "Barry") was not attracted to the *rebistve*, an all-absorbing vocation that he had learned about from his years of assisting his grandfather. He eschewed a position that involved fundraising as well as endless dealings with the personal problems and lives of the Hasidim and others who approached the rebbe for help and counsel. Years later he would explain: "I decided that was not the kind of life I wanted to lead. I wanted a life more like that which was being led by Mendel Schneersohn, the hard sciences life," referring to his uncle's early plans to study mathematics and engineering.[98] Unsurprisingly, as he aged, the Sixth Rebbe spoke more and more about the imminence of the Messiah.

Then came September 1, 1939, and Yosef Yitzchak was cut off in Nazi-occupied Poland. In a story amply described elsewhere, he was ultimately snatched from under the bombs and out of the inferno with the help of American Jewry, the US State Department, and ChaBaD connections.[99] The complex escape ended when Yosef Yitzchak, his wife, his widowed mother, his oldest daughter Chana and her husband Shmaryahu Gourary, his grandson Barry, his librarian Chaim Lieberman, his faithful Hasid Chaim Hodakov, and his twenty-three-year-old nurse Sheina Locs arrived late on March 18, 1940, at Pier 97 on Manhattan's Hudson River.[100] The next morning, he stepped onto Manhattan's shore, wearing his *shtreimel*, with Shmaryahu Gourary in a top hat at his right, and was taken by a delegation of Lubavitchers to the Greystone Hotel.[101] After a short stay, on September 12, 1940, the rebbe moved his headquarters to Brooklyn.[102] He was weak, overweight, a heavy smoker, and troubled by a variety of sicknesses, and his messianic beliefs now became almost frantic.

Looking at the precariousness of his situation and that of Jewry in general, Yosef Yitzchak repeated his father's messianic pronouncements, sharing his conviction with anyone who would listen that Jewry was living in the days that necessarily precede the coming of the Messiah. Messianism became key to his making sense of the events of his life, of modern Jewish history as well as the vicissitudes of the ChaBaD dynasty. "We are standing ready in our uniforms to greet Mashiach [Messiah], and it only remains for us to polish our buttons," he announced to all who would listen.[103]

Sensing time was running out for him, his new motto became "L'altar l'tshuvah, l'altar l'geula" (The sooner repentance comes, the sooner redemption comes). Even though his Hasidim were still reeling from a destructive and apocalyptic Holocaust and Stalinism, worried about the ailing rebbe, and not at all certain who if anyone could succeed him, he assured them that divine redemption and the Messiah were the answer. He warned American Jewry that if they wanted to be among the redeemed rather than among those who had burned like the Jews in the Holocaust, they had to raise their lax level of Jewish observance and repent now.[104] This Holocaust survivor who had been saved in the midst of the war by these very American Jews and their friends in government warned them that what was still happening in Europe would happen in America too.[105]

His Hasidim posted stickers with this slogan around his neighborhood, but it was a message whose significance at the time was not always clear to everyone, nor to those who got it was it very persuasive: after all Yosef Yitzchak and his observant followers had been the ones in the firestorm while liberal American Jewry remained in relative safety.[106]

Yosef Yitzchak neither perfected nor even clearly articulated his idea of outreach to the unbelieving. Few American Jews even registered his presence. To his Hasidim, however, his promises of messianic redemption were beyond question. So while they watched their increasingly invalid leader, concerned about his future and the succession, they were comforted by his promises of redemption.

Then, on the Sabbath morning of January 28, 1950, their hopes crashed. The sixty-nine-year-old rebbe, who two months earlier had suffered what his physicians called a mild heart attack, now had a fatal one. By 8:07 a.m., he was pronounced dead.

Not only had the Hasidim lost their leader; they also had to confront the fact that his messianic assurances remained unfulfilled. The double shock left them facing the question of continuity as never before in their memory. If the Messiah was not here to lead them, who could guide them into the future? Was the promised redemption still imminent, or would they encounter the fire that their rebbe had warned would come if the repentance he had called for did not materialize? For truly faithful Lubavitcher Hasidim these were critical questions.

The last years had changed so much in the situation of Lubavitch Hasidism that no one really knew what continuity meant. The leadership of Lubavitch had departed from what was now the Soviet Union, leaving the great bulk of its Hasidim caught behind the Iron Curtain in a place that sought to stamp out religion. Then, after a brief respite, had come the horror of the Holocaust, the decimation of Hasidic life, and the migration of those outside Soviet control to America and to the new Zionist state of Israel. All this had upended so many expectations and predictions by the rebbes. What were continuity and succession supposed to mean under such conditions? In January 1950, there were no easy answers.

A SEVENTH REBBE

Without a Messiah, the Hasidim necessarily looked for a successor or at least someone who could tell them what was coming next. Only Yosef Yitzchak's two daughters and their husbands remained among the living: the eldest, Chana Gourary, and her husband Shmaryahu, who were at 770 Eastern Parkway, the late rebbe's residence, and Moussia and her husband Menachem Mendel, who lived a few blocks away at 1304 President Street. Mendel and Moussia, snatched from their life and dreams in France and brought to America in the midst of the war with the aid of the Sixth Rebbe, American Jewry, and the State Department, were the lucky ones. The youngest daughter, Sheina, and her husband Mendel had also been living and studying in France, but despite desperate efforts by her father and those who helped him they became trapped in Poland, where they perished, unable to take advantage of the escape route that the others had found.[107]

There were unsubstantiated rumors that Yosef Yitzchak had left a will naming Barry, his beloved grandson, as successor, but it could not be found; perhaps it had been eliminated intentionally. Barry was no longer considered a candidate for the crown, at least by the Hasidim. Still unmarried and with interests increasingly elsewhere, he was making life choices taking him further away from Hasidism rather than closer. While that trend was not at odds with what other immigrant modern Orthodox Jews were trying to do in this new world, it was, as we have already seen, counter to what the Satmar Rebbe, Yoelish Teitelbaum, who lived not far away, was demanding: that Hasidim should publicly display their steadfast unwillingness to assimilate into America, eschewing acculturation and Americans' dream to be like everyone else around them.

While Satmarers chose the in-your-face approach of zealotry, which ultimately dominated much of Hasidism, the Lubavitchers had begun with zealotry but because of their messianism began adding elements of outreach, seeing themselves as instruments of penitence who would thereby bring redemption to the world. In his last years, Yosef Yitzchak had started sending his Hasidim to help Jews return to God. Less than a month before his death, he dispatched a couple of his Hasidim, Shlomo Carlebach and Zalman Schachter, out to college campuses to reach Jewish students.[108]

But even this less confrontational Hasidism, a counter-Satmar approach, could not be handed to Barry, even if he wanted it, which he did not. He was not looking to bring ChaBaD and its message of redemption to the American world of Jewry; rather, he was looking to become part of that world. Who, then, could take up the task, the messianic missionizing Hasidism of Lubavitch, rather than the confrontational Hasidism of Satmar, to keep the campaign to bring the Messiah alive? That question remained acute during the year of transition and mourning for Yosef Yitzchak. Effectively, the only choice was either Shmaryahu Gourary or his brother-in-law, Menachem Mendel Schneerson.

That Shmaryahu would want the job was obvious. Handpicked as husband of Chana by her grandfather, the Fifth Rebbe, he had dedicated his life to serving his father-in-law, Yosef Yitzchak. He had literally sat at his right hand and lived in the same house. Ultimately, however, he was unable to transition from son-in-law and amanuensis to leader, despite being the choice of the dowager *rebbetzin* and a significant minority of Lubavitchers.[109] After losing out to his brother-in-law, he accepted the new reality and become a minor official in the administrative labyrinth of ChaBaD, albeit with an important pedigree. His mother-in-law, wife, and son, who refused to acknowledge the full extent of his dethroning and of their own diminished position, were gradually marginalized and even attacked when they tried briefly to reassert their share in the crown in a symbolic war over property, keys, books, and money.[110]

Menachem Mendel, the chosen successor, had held many hopes for a career as an engineer, living in Paris. He and Moussia had moved away from the court even before their marriage in 1928, living as university students and situating themselves where Hasidim and Lubavitchers in particular were neither their neighbors nor an active presence in their lives.[111] In spite of Yosef Yitzchak's repeated efforts to interest his middle son-in-law in becoming more engaged in the life of the court or even taking a position leading a Parisian Hasidic congregation, Menachem Mendel remained focused on his dream of becoming an engineer.[112] Even as the Nazis were preparing to change the face of Europe, Menachem Mendel, in February 1938, a month before receiving his diploma, wrote to his father about his search for a job and confided his "many dreams regarding a position or possibly a partnership with my specialist," referring to the engineer with whom he had been interning.[113] As late as 1939, he repeated in a letter to his parents that he still harbored "dreams about a job or a partnership in his profession" but recognized that their likelihood of coming true was small, noting, "At least part of these are *only a dream*." [114]

By 1950 and the death of the Sixth Rebbe, those young man's dreams were forgotten and the refugee Menachem Mendel was rerooting himself in Brooklyn's Lubavitch. The change in orientation from a cosmopolitan life in France to one anchored in ChaBaD was already visible while he and his wife waited in Marseilles for papers that would allow them to escape to America. In Marseilles, he contacted his cousin Zalman, who like him had abandoned Nazi-occupied Paris and now lived on the rue des Convalescents. There in January 1940 at Zalman's invitation on the holiday of Tu B'Shvat, engineer Mendel Schneersohn, in a trim-looking beard and a gray suit, tie, and fedora, addressed a small group of Lubavitchers in Yiddish. In the gloom of the war, he shared his ideas about messianic redemption with the young refugees gathered around the table. The talk reflected his changing consciousness.

At least some of those who heard him at the time had no idea who he was, even after his talk. Nevertheless, as those terrible days closed in on him, he was thinking, as were so many who looked into the dark abyss of what would turn out to be the Holocaust, about the hope of ultimate redemption and was beginning to talk very much like a disciple of his father-in-law.[115] He too saw the Messiah's advent as the key to the future.

By June 23, 1941, when he and his wife docked in Manhattan, met by a delegation of Lubavitchers and whisked to Brooklyn, they realized nothing would be as it had been for them. In a short time, the erstwhile engineer had made himself an integral part of the newly reconstituted world headquarters of ChaBaD Lubavitch.

After receiving his US citizenship on November 14, 1946, Menachem Mendel returned briefly to Paris in the early spring of 1947 (his only trip away from America after his arrival in 1941). Flying from New York, he arrived just before the Passover.[116] His now-widowed mother, who had managed to escape the Soviet Union, was in Paris, staying with her cousin Zalman Schneersohn in his home. Reuniting with her after a twenty-year break, her son would bring her back with him to New York. According to at least one report, he publicly noted how saddened he was by fact that "he could not perform the commandment of honoring his parents for a long period," and, weeping, he compared himself to the biblical Joseph, who had left home as a young man and likewise had been separated from his parents and people while he became a great leader in Egypt. According to rabbinic commentary, with which Menachem Mendel was surely familiar, Joseph felt guilty for his long separation.[117]

Menachem Mendel did too. But more than about separation from his mother, he might have been referencing his years of separation from his Hasidic roots. When he arrived in Brooklyn and Lubavitch, he replanted himself in the Hasidic life and never again left the confines of the court, except for a brief trip to a Lubavitcher summer camp in the Catskills and later his regular visits to his predecessor's grave in neighboring Queens.

Convinced that the Sixth Rebbe had been correct about the possibility of redemption and religious return, he believed he could continue to lead such a movement. First, he would have to engineer his ascendancy and outflank his brother-in-law, who was ahead of him in line. He would have to give the Hasidim a sense of hope about the future and a way to connect it to their past. He had the year of mourning to accomplish it.[118]

Since his arrival, Menachem Mendel had sat at his father-in-law's left side on public occasions while his brother-in-law sat on the symbolically more important right. But those who looked to the younger son-in-law as a successor began to claim that even during his years in Germany and France he had remained involved with ChaBaD and Hasidism, carrying out "important" unheralded missions and tasks for his rebbe.[119] These accounts aided the reintegration of the "outsider" son-in-law into the public life of the court. Unlike Moussia, his wife, who in Brooklyn kept her distance from active involvement in the Lubavitcher world, he plunged into it.

As we have learned, Hasidic transitions are handled best when a rebbe leaves clear instructions for his succession, by naming a successor either during his lifetime or in an uncontested will. In such a case the new leader shares the charisma of his predecessor, in addition to the charisma inherent in the office he enters. In time, of course, the abilities (or lack thereof) of the new head lead either to the consolidation of his leadership or to its decline. The former is marked by growth in numbers, the latter by Hasidim who move to someone else. In Lubavitcher succession, we have seen that being a son or son-in-law of a rebbe has been the sine qua non of leadership, even though it has not always led to smooth transitions.[120]

But with Yosef Yitzchak's death, there was no unequivocal designation, and no accepted will was found. Whereas at the time of his arrest by the Yevsektsiya he had made his implicit will known with his blessing of his infant grandson, now nothing was clear. Discombobulated by the failure of their rebbe's messianic predictions to come true, the Lubavitchers had to decide what to do in the face of a failed prophecy in an American cultural environment where an openness to their message and way of life was not at all assured. With only two sons-in-law to choose from, an insider and an erstwhile outsider, the choice was far from obvious.

Although Menachem Mendel, the erstwhile outsider, had found his way back, his elder brother-in-law was more involved, and his wife, Chana, the eldest sister, unlike Moussia, was part and parcel of the court. Perhaps most important, the dowager *rebbetzin* favored the son-in-law who had lived at the court and been the rebbe's right-hand man. But to many of the Hasidim, familiarity with Shmaryahu Gourary had bred contempt; one Hasid, who had been a modern Orthodox Jew and had joined the Lubavitchers as a follower of Menachem Mendel early in his reign, explained his attraction to a man he felt "had a global perspective, and that's what got me." [121]

In postwar America, being worldly and cosmopolitan was valued more than it had been in the traditional eastern European Jewish world. Undoubtedly, that ethos had seeped into the thinking of the Lubavitchers; as they endeavored to reconstruct themselves in the postwar new world, Shmaryahu Gourary seemed yesterday's man. Menachem Mendel, in contrast, was new to them and from their perspective someone who knew the brave new world into which they were moving. More familiar with the culturally open environment in which ChaBaD now found itself, having spent so much time in it, he, more than his parochial and sheltered elder brother-in-law, seemed a better fit for the future.

For a while even before Yosef Yitzchak's death, Menachem Mendel had led *farbrengen*s or gatherings of Hasidim at the end of Sabbath morning prayers once a month. His father-in-law's illness and decline had made these gatherings even more exciting as the contrastingly youthful forty-nine-year-old leader they were just learning about took the stage. He captured the enthusiasm of the crowds.[122] Menachem Mendel, who while becoming an engineer had never studied in a Lubavitcher yeshiva, turned out to the Hasidim's amazement to be knowledgeable in ChaBaD wisdom and Jewish sources.[123] As he spoke, he seemed to observers to undergo "an internal transformation" reflecting *pnimius,* a charismatic and deep spirituality.[124] He also led Merkos L'Inyonei Chinuch, the Lubavitcher educational publication arm, and seemed to have the intellectual heft that the other contender lacked.

With the emergence of Menachem Mendel as a serious candidate for succession, tension between him and his brother-in-law as well as those who supported each man rose throughout the year of mourning. As early as the shivah week, the traditional start of mourning, the strains surfaced when both daughters and their husbands sat mourning in separate rooms at 770 Eastern Parkway and each son-in-law led independent prayer services and recited Kaddish, a practice continued throughout the year of mourning.[125] As was customary at such gatherings, each son-in-law offered words of Torah and Hasidism (*sichos*). In doing so, each man implicitly competed with his rival over whose words revealed greater insight, erudition, and acumen, as well as who could draw a more enthusiastic, larger, and engaged audience. It was an uncanny replay of what had happened years earlier following the death of the Zemach Zedek, Menachem Mendel's namesake.

Hasidim claimed they found Shmaryahu's talks to be derivative repetitions of *sichos* that Yosef Yitzchak had once given, whereas Menachem Mendel's were novel, thought-provoking, surprising. The fact that this Menachem Mendel was both a direct heir of his namesake, the Zemach Zedek (whose wives *also* shared names), was not lost on them. He was doubly endowed with holy seed, as a Schneersohn by both birth and marriage, and also seemed like the most informed disciple. Shmaryahu was neither an intellectual disciple nor a holy seed. And the holy seed he had fathered now seemed distant from holiness.

Menachem Mendel and Moussia were childless and at the end of their forties were not likely to be blessed with offspring. Shmaryahu and Chana had a son, but he was no longer a suitable heir. Hence whichever one of the two was chosen, his succession would only put off the inevitable. There was no one to follow them. The Messiah was still going to have assure the future. Menachem Mendel would stress that point throughout his *rebistve.*

As more Hasidim felt drawn toward Menachem Mendel, they concluded that his late father, Levi Yitzhak, with whom he studied and corresponded even after leaving for Berlin, had transmitted to him scholarship and Kabbalistic knowledge. He had also been instructed by the previous rebbe. No detail was too trifling for him, and he often wrote to Yosef Yitzchak with questions.[126] Since coming to New York in 1941 he had spent much time in the library at his father-in-law's court delving into its esoterica, and he had published a calendar that served as a kind of manual for ChaBaD daily practices and customs. People said he had absorbed ChaBaD so deeply that even when he spoke extemporaneously he displayed great erudition.

Individual Hasidim began to send Menachem Mendel letters asking for counsel and blessing, indicating a readiness to be led by him.[127] As early as a month after the previous rebbe's passing, some asked him outright to be their rebbe, adding the wish, as one man did, "that we should have a rebbe, that you should be that rebbe, and that you should be blessed with children." [128] While the last wish would have required him to find a new wife—a most unlikely prospect—these sorts of importuning increased, and commonly Menachem Mendel waved them off. Of course nothing so encouraged more requests as these refusals. In the closing months of the year of mourning, they increased, much to the chagrin of the dowager *rebbetzin* and those who held on to the hope that Shmaryahu would inherit the crown.

Although dowager *rebbetzin*s have power, as we have seen, Lubavitch was now headquartered in America, where change was the order of the day and seemed inevitable, at least to the Lubavitchers (in contrast to Yoelish Teitelbaum's Satmarers, who for a time would be the most active opponents of ChaBaD in America), and in this atmosphere the *rebbetzin*'s power quickly declined. Caught in the past, she watched helplessly as ChaBaD moved to a new reality. Menachem Mendel's widowed mother, Chana, whom he had brought to New York, became the more prominent woman of the previous generation—and she of course championed her son.

THE LIVING AND THE DEAD REBBE LEAD TOGETHER

As the year of mourning came to an end, the momentum was clearly with Menachem Mendel. Already during the High Holy Days of Rosh Hashanah and Yom Kippur of the year of mourning, he had begun accepting *pidyonos* on behalf of his father-in-law.[129] Rising to the pulpit before the afternoon prayers on Rosh Hashanah with his prayer shawl over his head, he read them there, as part of the petitions to heaven.[130] The unmistakable message was that God and Yosef Yitzchak would answer them. It was an idea that soon would be raised to the level of doctrine. A few weeks later when Menachem Mendel was called to the Torah with the title nominally reserved for leaders, "Arise, our teacher and rabbi," he did not object as he rose to the occasion. Everyone knew the Talmudic (B.T. Yebamot 87b) principle that "silence is tantamount to acknowledgment."

On Sundays, Tuesdays, and Thursdays from 8:00 p.m. until well after midnight, he met with individuals, some of them Lubavitchers, but also quite a few who were not. Shmaryahu met with people at the same time, but not in the increasing numbers who came to Menachem Mendel.[131] The fact that so many wanted to consult him was not lost on the Hasidim, particularly the younger ones whose loyalties were up for grabs. People began testifying to his power to affect them and his ability to provide answers; there were even reports of how he had helped miraculously in matters of health and welfare.

While the transition to him was not universally accepted, growing numbers of Lubavitchers pledged their allegiance to Menachem Mendel. On the evening of the anniversary of the previous rebbe's passing, several of the most senior Hasidim brought *pidyonos* to Menachem Mendel, much as they would in the past have brought them to Yosef Yitzchak. At first, Menachem Mendel ostentatiously refused to read them, as if to say that he was not the one to whom petitions were to be brought. Gradually, however, he began to open and read them and, weeping, went to place them on the grave, as if passing them on to his predecessor. This highly symbolic act echoed a practice that the Sixth Rebbe himself had performed repeatedly in his own lifetime, explaining, "It was clear to me that it was my prayer at the resting place of my holy forebears that had aroused God's loving kindness and compassion."[132] That in turn was an echo of Shalom DovBer's own act of bringing notes of supplication to *his* father's grave. In Lubavitch, the tomb of one's predecessor turned out to be quite important, a tool for easing or even authorizing the process of succession.

At about 9:45 p.m. on Yud Shvat, the anniversary of Yosef Yitzchak's death, Menachem Mendel arose to offer a Torah talk.[133] However, in light of the fact that he had received the *pidyonos* earlier, after about an hour of this, one of the elders among the Hasidim stood up and shouted something like "*Sichos* are fine, but the congregation wishes a *maymer khsides.*" [134] This request was for an address that is also called a *Divrei Elohim Chayim* (*DACh,* in its Hebrew acronym), the "words of a Living God," a talk that seemed to continue the topic of the last such *maymer* given by the previous rebbe, filled with ChaBaD philosophy and thought that is recited in a distinctive and unmistakable singsong, punctuated by the singing of the Hasidim in the congregation, and that in Lubavitcher practice can be offered only by a rebbe.[135] It followed upon an extraordinary claim that he had made in the preceding months, a claim that seemed at one and the same time to solve the question of succession and answer the question about the failure of the Messiah to appear.

THE REBBE DID NOT DIE

In a brilliant solution to the Lubavitchers' dilemma, Menachem Mendel explained his predecessor's death and the apparent false prophecy of the imminence of the Messiah by asserting that while to the uninformed it might appear that their rebbe was dead and gone, to those who recognized a deeper level of reality (that is, those who believed in his message), it was clear that he had simply moved from one plane of existence to another. He assured them that Yosef Yitzchak was now closer to God and was still advocating for them before the Heavenly Throne. He knew this was true, he said, because when he visited the tomb he was able to communicate with the previous rebbe, who reported all this to him. Throughout his *rebistve,* Menachem Mendel returned regularly to commune and consult with his father-in-law.

But Yosef Yitzchak's presence was not limited to the gravesite. His successor would tell the Hasidim that he was with them "in this room," still working to ensure that what he foresaw would happen: the Messiah was coming. Those who understood this would be his emissaries working to complete his mission to hasten the coming of the Messiah by changing the consciousness of Jewry.

Menachem Mendel had not invented this idea of talking to a dead rebbe and claiming he was not really gone. Recall that after the death of the Third Rebbe, the Zemach Zedek, his youngest son and successor, announced to his followers, "Know that Father did not die, and whoever wants to make any requests [of him] can still do so. I too have done so." [136] Yosef Yitzchak had gone to the grave of his own father to speak to him and claimed to have gotten replies. For all these rebbes, however, such encounters with the dead were infrequent. For Menachem Mendel, in contrast, this communion with his father-in-law became a regular occurrence and the *professed basis of his legitimacy*. Perhaps it was why he would never stray further than a short car ride away from the cemetery for the rest of his life.

In effect, the man who became the Seventh Rebbe would assert from the outset of his *rebistve* that he was only a *stand-in* for a still active Yosef Yitzchak.* He was simply an emissary between the rebbe and his Hasidim. Although over the years Lubavitchers would forget this detail as the stand-in loomed larger in their lives and allegiances, Menachem Mendel always saw himself as an appendage to Yosef Yitzchak—two bodies wearing one crown, both of them still working to hasten the coming of the Messiah—and that was why there was no need to worry about succession.[137]

Menachem Mendel concluded his inaugural *maymer* with the words: "We are now very near the approaching footsteps of Messiah, indeed, we are at the conclusion of this period, and our spiritual task is to complete the process of drawing down the Shechinah [Divine Presence]—moreover, the essence of the Shechinah—within specifically our lowly world."

MAKING THE CROWN HIS OWN

At the evening's end, it was clear that the relatively small crowd present believed that with the *maymar* Menachem Mendel had offered he had effectively accepted and acknowledged his new role. It would take longer for everyone in Lubavitch to acknowledge it. At a large Lubavitcher banquet the following Sunday where Menachem Mendel was notably absent but Shmaryahu was center stage, the crowning of a new rebbe went unmentioned. Although Lubavitchers today mark the previous Wednesday as the date on which Menachem Mendel formally succeeded his father-in-law, there remained some resistance to his ascendance, particularly from the dowager, Shmaryahu, and his dwindling supporters.

A few months later, in March 1951, Menachem Mendel's Hasidim sent a letter to the dowager complaining that Shmaryahu, for whom they had "the greatest respect," had "refused to agree" to relinquish control over all the "ChaBaD institutions" and to assent to the complete authority of his brother-in-law, whom each day they felt "attached to more and more" and who they believed "with full faith" (although with little or

---

* In time, that word would be carved on his own tombstone.

really no documentary evidence) was the previous rebbe's chosen heir. They wanted her to tell her elder son-in-law to defer to the new rebbe, who in the eyes of "all the Hasidim and Temimim [Lubavitcher yeshiva students] in all lands" as well as the lay leadership (*bale-batim*), was now in command of "all institutions." They expressed regret that Shmaryahu "had not [yet] agreed" and accused him of wanting "to disturb everything." They laid blame on him for walking out of the Sabbath prayers in protest rather than being present when his brother-in-law was called to the Torah reading with the title "Our master, our teacher, our rebbe." The walkout was a symbolic act of public defiance that they found disturbing and even sacrilegious, as well as embarrassing, especially in the face of the outsiders, who often attended these services. They also expressed fear that this continuing resistance would, "heaven forbid, cause everything to fall apart and the entire structure of Lubavitch to crumble," and avowed that this was something they "[would] not permit." [138]

Angered by this letter, the dowager, who favored the son-in-law who had lived in her house and had constantly been by her husband's side in his waning years, and the daughter who had helped care for her and had borne her only grandchild, responded in a letter of her own by calling them *chutzpahnikes* (arrogant). In the letter, she "refused entry into her house to those who had mocked" Shmaryahu and claimed to consider herself the "only Lubavitcher *Rebbetzin*." [139] Significantly, in an act of widely recognized symbolism, she refused to transfer her husband's distinctive *shtreimel* to Menachem Mendel. This was the fur hat that the rebbe wore on every Sabbath and holy day and on other festive occasions and in which he was famously photographed. [140] Menachem Mendel reacted by abandoning *shtreimels* from ChaBaD practice and was forever after seen only in his trademark snap-brim black fedora.

In time Shmaryahu bowed to the overwhelming support his brother-in-law had achieved and recognized him as the successor. Recounting how once he had been troubled over an important decision he had to make, he decided that since "my brother in law, Menachem Mendel was here, [I thought,] why not consult with him?" The latter deliberated deeply about the matter and replied that the question was so weighty that he did not deign to give counsel on his own, but that as he was going that day to the tomb, "he would speak to and confer with our father-in-law, the holy Rabbi Yosef Yitzchak, may his memory preserve us, and bring an answer. And indeed, upon his return from the *tsiyen* [tomb] he brought me a wondrous reply."

Then Shmaryahu added, according to the author of this account, "My brother-in-law, may he be well, is not given to exaggeration. If he says he will consult with the father-in-law at the *tsiyen,* then he will surely speak to him there." Finally, as if to explain why he, once heir apparent, had deferred to Menachem Mendel, he added, "I know that *I myself cannot converse with my father-in-law*. . . . If he can, then I am bound to him." [141]

AN IMMORTALITY SYSTEM

When the childless forty-nine-year-old Menachem Mendel, with a wife a year older than him, took over, everyone realized, though no one mentioned, that with this man at their helm there would be no holy seed to succeed him. The Messiah was still the solution for the future. The new rebbe knew it too.

Menachem Mendel and the Lubavitchers therefore developed an "immortality system," a series of strategies that would mitigate if not altogether deny their awareness of the mortality and vulnerability of their leaders as the solution to the problem of succession.[142] It worked for them after the death of Yosef Yitzchak, and it would work for them again forty-four years later, when Menachem Mendel himself died.

Before that day, Lubavitchers grew obsessed by messianism, galvanized by a series of outreach campaigns initiated by their rebbe. The involvement in these campaigns would become an essential element of this immortality system. The Messiah's arrival would do away with the worries about succession and would even deny death.

But as the Lubavitcher Rebbes had explained, this required mankind to prepare the conditions, a task the Hasidim took on by "spreading the wellsprings," the necessary preliminary work the Besht had been told would lead to spiritual ascent and hasten the Messiah.[143] No Lubavitcher leaders had believed this more than the Fifth and Sixth Rebbes, who had universalized the mission of their Hasidim, until the advent of the Seventh Rebbe, for whom it became the keynote of his *rebistve* from start to finish.

As he explained, he and his generation had the destiny and responsibility to complete the mission of their antecedents and at last bring God back to the people and "into this lowly world." [144] They did this not because they were especially suited to the task but by virtue of being the generation of the Messiah's arrival and the one living in the spiritual abyss. What vested him with authority was not his previous service or his desire to be the leader but simply his destiny, as it was also the destiny of those in his generation.[145] This explained Menachem Mendel's own understanding of how he had, despite his earlier dreams and his hopes to be an engineer living in Paris, ended up as Lubavitcher Rebbe.

He and his predecessor along with their emissaries would fulfill their destiny by persuading and helping the rest of their Jewish generation to mend its ways and reattach to Judaism, and then they, the Lubavitchers, would lead all Jews to the true Promised Land of the messianic age, supplanting the false messiahs of materialism, communism, and Zionism. Whether they wanted to or not, he and his generation could not flee from their religious responsibility, even if they were reluctant to take it on.

The new rebbe would ultimately engineer a revolution with the language and ideas contained in Jewish Kabbalistic tradition and ChaBaD Hasidism. He would do it with the help of the young Hasidim but would couch it in terms that would enable even the most conservative of elders to accept it. He would be revolutionary but would seem to be in harmony with the past.

As if to illustrate this, he added perhaps the most revolutionary idea to his inaugural talk's conclusion: "May we be privileged to see and meet with our rebbe [Yosef Yitzchak] here in this world, in a physical body, in this earthly domain, and *he* will redeem us." The previous rebbe, he implied, was not just pleading with God; he was the Redeemer Messiah himself, and he was returning.

This claim that his predecessor was immortal and the Messiah, coupled with his own place as the one destined to see the messianic redemption to its completion, effectively sealed Menachem Mendel's succession. Moreover, it solved the problem of the Sixth Rebbe's apparent mortality (as well as his own mortality and lack of children). Menachem Mendel never abandoned this belief. In his final years, particularly after the death of his wife in 1988, he went ever more frequently to the grave of his predecessor in the Old Montefiore cemetery in Queens, as his followers (and he, perhaps as well) became desperately anxious about the future and ever more frantic in their messianism. Traveling with only a small coterie of aides, he would sit behind a closed door inside a small antechamber adjoining the tomb. Indeed, it was here that he suffered his first devastating stroke in 1992, after which he never spoke a word again.

A KINDER AND GENTLER MESSIANISM

In his own version of the messianic campaign, Menachem Mendel seemed to continue Yosef Yitzchak's project but in fact totally changed its tone. Yosef Yitzchak's increasingly insistent messianism, inherited from his father, had been tinged with disappointment bordering on contempt for nonobservant Jews, to whom he addressed threats that without repentance they were doomed and were dooming world Jewry. This message carried a powerful criticism of broad swaths of modern Jewry, whose laxity in Jewish observance, he argued, had defiled the world and brought about catastrophe and ruin, including most recently the Holocaust. Fifteen months after his arrival as a refugee in his adopted country with the help of Jews who were not at all Orthodox in their observance, Yosef Yitzchak had asserted that American Jews' "coldness and indifference . . . toward Torah and religion" were no less destructive than the fire in Europe that threatened "to annihilate more than two-thirds of the Jewish people." [146] Only immediate repentance would ensure the Messiah's coming.

For Menachem Mendel, however, modern Jews could be inspired to change not by contempt or threats that they were going to burn and doom the world if they did not change but rather by a "devotion to the cause of spreading kindness and goodness." He saw this as part of his role in "awakening in everyone the potential that he has," as he explained to a *New York Times* reporter.[147] His emissaries would not go around warning Jews to repent but rather would seek ways to attract them to ChaBaD with goodwill and friendship. This distinguished the Lubavitcher Rebbe from most of the other rebbes, who like the Satmar and other *haredi* Jews kept the nonobservant at a distance. The Lubavitcher Rebbe could be a champion of Hasidism, but he downplayed ultra-Orthodoxy. His emissaries could be stringently observant in their own Jewish behavior while seeming tolerant and even pluralist in their approach to those whose Jewish consciousness they wanted to raise. While this might distinguish and even alienate them from other Hasidim, it also made them more comfortable traveling through the modern world and living in settings far from their Hasidic enclaves while they were on their mission. They believed their rebbes' assurances that they were living in premessianic times and would succeed in inaugurating the messianic era, so that they need not worry that their methods would lead to their own spiritual harm.

Menachem Mendel's approach did not offer answers to the questions that his father-in-law's approach implicitly raised: Why was suffering a prerequisite for redemption? Why had so many religious Jews who held on to tradition, including many of his own Hasidim, been burned in the Nazi crematoria? Why had the "sinful" Jews in America survived? If exile was a punishment by God, how could mankind be allowed to hasten its end? What about those who did repent? Why had some of them also been victimized?

Menachem Mendel simply asserted that redemption did not require any further death and suffering as a prerequisite, any more birth pangs or martyrdom. His was a messianism not of pain and catastrophe but of promise. He stressed the ability of the converted sinner to change the cosmic balance and bring about redemption.[148] The evidence of the Messiah's imminence was not in the torment that preceded his arrival but rather in the Jewish revival that in the course of his *rebistve* was breaking out all over, a revival he and his emissaries would be part of, if not lead. It was in the insistence of his followers that they wanted "Moshiach [Messiah] Now."

In Menachem Mendel's last years, before his debilitating stroke, he had been disconcerted by the tarrying of the Messiah in spite of all the Lubavitcher efforts to hasten his coming. Shortly after Passover, the holy day of redemption, when so many of his followers were convinced the Messiah was about to come, the rebbe, in bewilderment, went on 27 Nisan (April 11, 1991) to his father-in-law's gravesite for a "conversation." He stayed there for a very long time. We do not know what he said or what he heard. But when he came out, the world appeared unchanged and the earth was as it was. The utter sameness must have been crushing for one who wanted the "Moshiach now."

Returning to his headquarters and after the evening prayers that night, he began to address his flock: "How can it be that until this moment, we have not been able to bring about the coming of the Messiah?" With no alternative answer, he put the blame on his Hasidim, concluding that if those who truly wanted the Messiah to come would sincerely "plead and cry," the Redeemer would come. They had to really mean it. "How can it be," he continued in desperation and perplexity, "that you have not yet succeeded in this time of grace to actualize the coming of the righteous Messiah?"[149] Echoing the sentiment he had expressed nearly a half century earlier when he had accepted their call to be their leader, he declared: "In ChaBaD the Rebbes have always asked their Hasidim to act on their own initiative."[150]

At last, sounding like Moses coming down from Sinai, he cried out, perhaps out of a sense of frustration and even failure: "What else can

I do so that the Children of Israel will cry out and *demand* the Messiah come, after all else that was done until now has not helped since we are obviously still in exile, and even more so in an internal exile from truly serving God?" [151] Then, sounding almost like Abraham pleading before the destruction of Sodom and Gomorrah, he added, "May it be God's will that at least there be found ten Jews who will persist in demanding of the Holy One" to bring the Messiah immediately, and he concluded, "I have to hand over the task to you: Do all you can to bring the righteous Moshiach, *mamesh*." [152]

They had by then all come to believe that Menachem Mendel—not Yosef Yitzchak—was the Messiah and that *he* was to bring the redemption. Maybe he even believed it himself. *Mamesh* meant "in fact," but it also was a Hebrew acronym for "Menachem Mendel Schneerson."

"As for bringing the redemption," he went on, visibly rising to the occasion, "*I know* myself well what to do, and I am doing all that is in my hands to do." He concluded, "And in any event, rather than using this opportunity to find new tasks for me, it would be better that each of you decides what is upon *you* to do." [153]

His followers would continue to press him to reveal himself as the Redeemer and to inaugurate the messianic age. "Long live our master, our teacher, and our rebbe, the King Messiah forever and ever," they sang repeatedly.

It never happened. Instead, after 1992, when he suffered his stroke at the tomb, he remained silent and paralyzed. Later, the rebbe suffered another stroke in 1994. As he lay dying in the hospital, the Hasidim, who had been carrying "Moshiach beepers" they'd expected to sound when the Messiah revealed himself, signed petitions to him and to God demanding the Messiah appear. It was to no avail.

DISPERSED CHARISMA: THE CHARISMATIC FELLOWSHIP

With the Seventh Rebbe dead and buried alongside his predecessor, Lubavitchers refused to choose a successor, arguing that as long as they, his Hasidic representatives, remained on his messianic mission, he would be alive, as would his predecessor (figure 23). The messianic campaign, which they continued, was the engine of the immortality system. The future would take care of itself. As Binyomin Klein, longtime secretary of the Seventh Rebbe, was reported to have said after the latter's death, "Continue in all of the things of the Rebbe that you have done until now *and even more so*." [154]

23. An advertisement on an Israeli public bus with the image of Menachem Mendel Schneerson, the late Seventh Lubavitcher Rebbe and son-in-law of the Sixth Rebbe, identifying him as the Messiah and offering a phone number to call to connect to him and the marvels of the redemption. Photo and copyright by Samuel Heilman.

"The key to our tomorrow is our constant striving to be true *shluchim* of our dear rebbe," as one of his emissaries put it, twelve years after Menachem Mendel's death.[155] If the messenger deviated even slightly from the aims of the one who sent him, "he ceased being a *shaliach*," and if he was no longer an emissary then the one who sent him was gone.[156]

The Hasidim understood that they alone would have to succeed where he did not. For some this meant praying for his speedy resurrection and return as Messiah. Lubavitchers now believed in a Second Coming, a dogma once thought to be limited to Christians.

But as time passed with no Messiah in sight, the Hasidim gradually dispersed their dead rebbe among themselves. As he had argued when his predecessor died, so too they now claimed. He was not dead; he was still leading them, sending them messages and alive for them. They were on his mission; their Lubavitch identity was defined by it.

This became the answer to the question of succession. Menachem Mendel's Hasidim refused to recognize his mortality and channeled him, as he had channeled his predecessor. Reinvoking his own solution to his predecessor's death, the Hasidim saw themselves as stand-ins for the missing rebbe. They revivified him and themselves not only by coming and remaining together as his Hasidim but also by invoking a basic principle of Jewish law, one that became the official theme of their annual gathering in 2006: *shlucho shel adam kamoso* (B.T. Kiddushin 41b), which means that a person's *shaliach* or emissary is like himself and the *shaliach*'s actions and accomplishments are attributed to the

24. The Lubavitcher world headquarters in Crown Heights, Brooklyn, since the Seventh Rebbe's death has become dominated by the messianist Hasidim. Photo and copyright by Samuel Heilman.

one who empowered him to act in his stead.[157] Some even claimed to be getting messages from him. The rebbe had enunciated this principle when he first sent them far away from the court, assuring them that they would not fail in their mission because they carried his power as a rebbe with them. It was repeated frequently in many of the missives and publications that Lubavitchers sent out to their supporters, youth, and *shluchim,* the answer to how and why they must keep going on.

Some Hasidim saw hidden messages in his published letters, which in an act of bibliomancy they opened at random for answers to all their questions after his passing. Other times they watched the endless supply of videos of him (he was forever on reruns) and discovered relevant messages from him in them. Events in their lives offered evidence to them of his hidden presence.[158] In spite of his demise, the basic direction on which he had set them oriented them. When they had succeeded in bringing the redemption, having aroused the Jews and the world, the Messiah would come. Whether that Messiah was Yosef Yitzchak or Menachem Mendel would remain to be seen, but surely, they all believed, it would be the Lubavitcher Rebbe. Until that time, there was really no need for a successor (figure 24).

In practice, the *shluchim* in their many ChaBaD houses and other posts where they were carrying out their mission were acting as rebbe stand-ins, *shtikel rebbes.* They quoted him and served as leaders for the unaffiliated or the marginally attached to Judaism as well as for those who were attaching themselves to Judaism through Lubavitch, allowing them to defer ultimate leadership to their rebbe, whether he was in his court in Crown Heights or leading them from the afterlife. In effect, the ChaBaD model allowed almost every Hasid to become a rebbe for someone, even if that someone did not think of himself as a Hasid. It became a movement for all Jews, Hasidic or not.

For ChaBaD the Hasidim shared in "a charismatic fellowship" as together and separately they became the incarnation of their leader and his will. The "gifts of divine grace felt to be extraordinarily powerful, spontaneous, and humanly unpredictable were now dispersed" among the Hasidim, albeit unevenly, with those who had known the rebbe during his lifetime having a greater share in the charisma, and those who had been his intimates or contemporaries being endowed with the most.[159] Since the death of their last rebbe, ChaBaD has sustained itself with this dispersed charisma, and as well by their annual gathering in New York, during which they share "moments of ecstatic, egalitarian fellowship, moments of an extra-ordinary high in passionate religious experience," and reiterate their attachment to their departed rebbe, around whose messianic mission they still find meaning in their lives and activities.[160] While they regularly visit his grave to commune with him or pass him notes—as he himself did with his father-in-law—this is not a cult of the dead. Just as he saw himself and his predecessor as two bodies but a single rebbe, so they can imagine themselves as extending his life by their personal activities and continuing to carry out and spread his message of imminent redemption, religious revival, and a return to Judaism, or at least the ChaBaD version of it.

Often by speaking of their rebbe in the present tense—"That is why the rebbe says to us"—they display how he continues to be a living presence for them. As one Hasid, referring to Menachem Mendel Schneerson, recently put it, "We believe the Rebbe is even today the one and only *Zaddik Yesod Olam* [who serves as the foundation of the world]. . . . There are no others that can fill this role."

Final Thoughts

In this last chapter, I want to recall briefly some of the central lessons learned about contemporary Hasidic succession. These highlights are meant to help distill what the cases we have considered are meant to teach.

The central organizing theme of these pages has been that when a rebbe passes from the scene or even in anticipation of that moment, the question of who might possess the necessary qualities to succeed him becomes a central concern for his Hasidim, crucial for their continuity as a distinct group. This is because a rebbe is essential to Hasidic identity and their sense of who they are. They are always Hasidim *of* someone, supporters and devotees who cleave (feel *dvekut*) to a special charismatic man whom they regard as holy. They want—need—to be with him and expect him to take care of them and provide them with blessings that guarantee their own continuity, fertility, and prosperity. He in turn lives for and off them. As we have seen, this mutual bond has led to dynastic succession.

The very idea of dynasties has forced Hasidism always to look to the past as essential to the present. To be a successor rebbe today, one needs to show how one is tied to the past. Even those who have come from far afield or have wanted to make radical changes, like the Seventh Lubavitcher, who turned his attention to the unaffiliated modern Jews even more than to Hasidim, or the current Boyaner, retrieved from a modern life in New York, or the Munkácser, who broke with his father, or both current claimants to the crowns of Bobov and Satmar, all had to root themselves in a dynastic past and reframe their newness by stressing their continuity with it. They have accomplished this in a variety of ways: being designated or blessed by a predecessor, making trips to his grave, invoking loyalties of the family, imparting past teachings as part of their own, celebrating time-honored customs, and of course by marriage. Ultimately, successors thus share in the charisma of their predecessors.

Contemporary Hasidic successions, as we have seen, have been affected by the mass migration of Jewry and the relocation of Hasidim to a much smaller and more concentrated area than the one in which they first flowered as well as their placement in modern open, largely democratic welfare states that serve as the cultural and social background for their current attempts to ensure their continuity. Although Hasidim have handled the transition remarkably well, they also find that if they do not, their rebbes may lose Hasidim to another court with another, possibly more charismatic leader. In a world where movement is easy and rebbes rub shoulders in sometimes uncomfortable ways with their neighbors, invidious comparisons are common and brand loyalty can only go so far. Successions are often the most precarious times.

We have seen how the Holocaust has played in a part in enveloping the Hasidic past in a kind of sacred nostalgia and those rebbes who survived it with a special appeal, while also making the assurance of continuity a sacred obligation. Of course, each rebbe stamps the office he assumes with his own character and unique life experience. Personalities matter along with biographies.

CHARISMA

Hasidim consider their rebbes not only as matchless and religiously attractive but also as "holy seed," exceptional because they were conceived by holy predecessors and were thereby endowed with a numinous character and spiritual gifts. But if all children of a rebbe are holy seed, what happens to those not chosen as successors? We have seen that birth alone does not account for someone's selection. Social dynamics, personal relationships, family considerations, and political manipulation enter into the mix. Leaders can be cultivated nearly from scratch or can be on the thinnest of branches of the family tree.

Sometimes simply winning a contest for succession by itself endows a winner with charisma, as Hasidim rewrite history to prove that the ultimate successor was always destined to lead. Charisma and holiness thus are as much in the eye of the beholder and subject to collective ratification as they are personal characteristics. One group's holy rebbe may turn out to be another's false pretender. "For us Aaron is holy, for them Zalman is," as one Satmar Hasid explained in a recent debate about the difference between him and supporters of Zalman.

Succession does not play out in a vacuum. The question of who will lead matters to a large body of others, many of whose lives and fortunes have become intertwined into the process. Family matters. As we have also discovered, the way democratic societies choose leaders is not foreign to contemporary Hasidic life, even as it seems to be organized on traditional and somewhat authoritarian lines, with power going from the top down. The led select and bestow on the leader the power to govern their spiritual and personal lives. But after they have done so, they come to believe it is inherent and inborn, bow to and ask it for blessings. Hasidim effectively decide who is holy, bestowing charisma on him in return for the recipients' agreeing to act as if he has always had it.

Rebbes are this-worldly leaders who nonetheless invoke otherworldly powers that are claimed as the basis of their charismatic authority. Those otherworldly powers, however, are subject to recognition, ratification, and legitimation by persons very much in this world. Having the office helps, but the new rebbe must persuade his Hasidim that what was once solely his predecessors' is truly his own. When there are no other claimants to the office this is easier. When there is a competition, the rivalry absorbs everyone.

BECOMING THE REBBE

As we have discovered, long life for a rebbe, a wish repeated by all Hasidim, can have a powerful impact on succession. Extended life gives everyone time to consider who should be successor. Nevertheless, being "a successor-in-waiting" too long can make one lose rather than gain stature because serving as a subordinate takes its toll on one's reputation and character. One is seen as either too much in a hurry to take over or better suited to be second-in-command than leader.

A successor is often expected to display humility and express reluctance to become rebbe. Hasidim see this as evidence of his deservedness. An overeager crown prince may find that his effort to share charisma, head off a challenge, or assume power too quickly actually undermines and stains his ultimate succession, especially if he is following a longtime leader. The successful successor must find a way to play for time and nurture his shared charisma until he can make it his own. Ultimately time and the emergence of a new generation that has known only him as their rebbe allow this to happen. The new generation, the yeshiva boys and their families (the *yunger leit,* as they are called in Yiddish) who grow up during his reign (and with early marriages and high birthrates this can happen in as little as ten to fifteen years), ultimately determine his success.

Succeeding one who was because of his long reign viewed as larger than life makes a smooth transition harder while those who recall the old rebbe's greatness are still around. Much depends on the comparisons made between predecessor and successor.

If, however, a rebbe lives into his dotage and needs help carrying out his role, being next in line can offer a successor a chance to ease into his future role. If the crown prince does not fulfill the Hasidim's expectations during that time and there are other potential competitors, this can create conditions leading to the emergence of another candidate and a battle over succession. Of course, where there are no competitors, following an aged and infirm predecessor can be beneficial, especially if the new rebbe is contrastingly energetic and engaged.

MESSIANISM AND DISPERSED CHARISMA

When no clear successor seems to be on the horizon, we have seen that talk of the Messiah becomes common among Hasidim. This posits an end of history that will obviate the need of a successor. Of course, this solution has never ultimately proven itself in history. Hence, without a successor, we have seen the emergence of "dispersed charisma."

This concept refers to the ability of certain Hasidim to reflect some of the charisma of a rebbe as if it were dispersed among them. Some of the senior or oldest Hasidim, those who were especially close to the departed leader, may have such dispersed charisma, as we have seen in Munkács and Boyan. In ChaBaD, all the Hasidim today have it (though some of the older ones more than others), in light of their rebbe's long absence. They have mixed this with messianism, arguing that by working to hasten the Messiah's coming, as their late rebbe urged them, they will bring about redemption and find the leadership they so earnestly seek. Lubavitchers have persuaded themselves that the Messiah and their late leader are one in the same and that dispersing charisma is their mission.

MOSDOS AND PIDYONOS

As we have seen, contemporary rebbes have increasingly built and expanded their institutions, *mosdos*. While the nominal justification for these institutions is to "spread the word of Torah" and disperse the wisdom of the particular rebbe, they are also his political and economic assets, as well as domains where his authority is as close to absolute as it can be.

Foremost are schools that provide a reliable supply of new Hasidim. There are also real estate and other pecuniary resources. Everything from the group's matzah factory to its kosher certifications or publications brings in money. The group most likely will have a charitable arm, a *g'mach* (*gemilas chesed* [kindness committee]), effectively a free loan society fund that provides interest-free loans and can serve as a kind of bank or community chest.

To compete successfully with others in the Hasidic world, these institutions require financial support. Of course, tuitions and grants from a variety of sources that many yeshivas get, sometimes even from the welfare state, are part of that. But many other institutions generate income, giving some of the rebbes heading large courts control over multi-million-dollar empires.

As the financial resources of a Hasidic group grow, they not only give the Hasidim and the rebbe a concrete measure of their own success (often demonstrated in the conspicuous wealth and consumption of the rebbe as well as his stable of philanthropists who pay him tribute), but also serve the Hasidim as a confirmation of their having made the right choice in a successor. Competition over the crown is thus also competition for control of *mosdos,* which is why conflicts over a *rebistve* are so economically significant and costly.

Mosdos also provide placements for members of rebbe's family and potential rivals. Among the primary staff decisions a rebbe makes is whom he will put in charge of the yeshiva and other institutions, roles that he may use to head off challengers.

Pidyonos, donations accompanying blessings, and *ma'amad,* a set endowment that a rebbe receives from each Hasid, are also among a rebbe's material assets, and often succession is affirmed by their ceremonial receipt. The pile of *kvittlach* accompanying the *pidyonos* a new rebbe receives upon his crowning symbolize the Hasidim's acknowledgment of his authority. The higher the pile, the greater his acceptance and hope of success. *Kvittlach* are almost like ballots that allow everyone to see if the man they are following is popular. Of course, charisma matters, but numbers count.

KEEPING UP THE NUMBERS

Hasidic growth has benefited from an unprecedented period during which Jews have not been persecuted, economic boom times, and growth of the welfare state that effectively subsidizes Hasidic existence in both America and Israel. Sustained by high fertility and assisted by improved medical care and a knowledge of how to move the levers of political power, Hasidic communities have grown beyond anything previous generations of leaders ever imagined possible in the Promised Land or the Land of Promise. Larger courts have grown exponentially, and even some of the more obscure small courts have attracted followers.

A desire to increase their overall population remains among Hasidic core values. After the Holocaust, this drive took on a kind of moral imperative as they sought to rebuild. Making more Hasidim in the bedroom(and also driving up numbers by attracting those not born to Hasidism) became a holy mission because it was a way of making up for the many lost to the Nazis and Stalinists as well as to assimilation. This demographic expansion—perhaps greater among Hasidim than anywhere else in the Jewish world—helps increase the political and social empowerment that contemporary Hasidim seek, out of the ideological conviction, among many rebbes, that the Hasidim should chart the direction of Jewish history and thrive.

Increasingly rebbes feel they are not only local leaders of their Hasidim but also international voices heard beyond their courts. Getting many Hasidim is seen as a groundwork for this. While every Hasid claims, "There are other rebbes, but none who can match my rebbe," when he is one of a very large group this assertion becomes more convincing. Rising numbers enhance a rebbe's leadership while also affirming it. The Satmar Rebbe became an important leader in direct proportion to the number of Hasidim who saw him as their rebbe. A successful succession is thus one in which the number of Hasidim increases, as do the rebbe's reputation and clout.

LEADERSHIP

While the role of chief Hasidic rebbe has never been formalized, to Boruchel Rabinovich's eternal disappointment, those heading the largest or best-known Hasidic groups have increasingly tried to present themselves in that position. Indeed, in one or another respect, all of the groups considered here have tried to demonstrate that their rebbe can act or speak for all Hasidim, that he is a leader above all others. Only the ones who have many followers can convincingly make that claim.

The more followers a rebbe has, the more "pilgrimages" not only Hasidim but also politicians and officials, especially those in elective office, make to consult with or to be with him. While these visits by the latter are often for the purposes of an endorsement and attracting the Hasidic bloc of votes, the arrival of the representatives of power is often a Hasidic point of pride and an iconic moment that reminds everyone that the powers-that-be in the outside world recognize the stature of the rebbe and his followers. Indeed, the ability of Hasidim and their rebbes to serve as icons or symbols of Jewry in such encounters, covered frequently by the media and photographed, has no doubt exaggerated their influence in their own eyes as well as in the eyes of those who desire, publish, or view these photos. Of course, the photos that are most important are those that show rebbes surrounded by a sea of Hasidim who ecstatically attach themselves to them.

Mass media that make these images ubiquitous have effectively given these rebbes more importance than they have ever had in their history and made them public representatives of the growing political, cultural, and social influence of the ultra-Orthodox sector in world Jewry. Located today in or near large cities, in countries where they are especially noticeable and at a time when their every move and statement can reverberate throughout the world, rebbes can each seem like a "Grand Rabbi," a term that in English has become a synonym for Hasidic rebbe.

Because the last Lubavitcher Rebbe knew well how to manipulate the media and his successful outreach campaign, he was able to convince many that he had many more Hasidim than an actual count of his followers revealed.

Hasidim often count the victories of public officials who have visited their rebbe as measures of *his* influence or a sign of his blessing. Indeed, proxy battles between various courts as well as within them are often fought in the elections for local offices and even at times for state and federal ones in the United States or for the Knesset in Israel. Today, the provision of livelihood (*mzonei*) may be seen in the rebbe's ability to demand and receive political favors, maintain a good connection to officialdom, and access power.

When many Hasidim are drawing on public assistance, rebbes find an important ally in the welfare state. A rebbe is often assessed by his ability (commonly through his handpicked staff) to find support from government programs his Hasidim can access. These include block grants, grants for families with dependent children, housing subsidies, tuition assistance, health care benefits, and so on. His capacity to attract funds is ultimately seen as an expression of blessings and power. There is room for fraud in the effort to get the aid, and some have fallen afoul of the law. In such cases, the rebbe himself will be protected from the consequences, and where punishments are meted out someone else will take the blame.[1]

Indeed, if there is anything that unites all the rebbes described in these pages—including the challengers in a succession battle—it is their abilities to manipulate and draw benefits from officialdom and the government: their comfort with democracy, their ability to influence the voting behavior of their Hasidim, and even their capacity to place their own followers in administrative or elective positions at the local level. In 2016 a Hasidic woman was elected as a civil court judge (ironic, since in Jewish law and a Jewish court [*beit din*] as a woman she would not qualify as a judge or even as a valid witness).[2] In an interview she acknowledged the help she had received from a rebbe. For rebbes the power to be kingmakers and governmental rainmakers is no small testament to their enhanced power and leadership. The men described in these pages have been acknowledged to be achievers in this regard. That too has often helped them deflect challenges to their positions and legitimacy.

HASIDISM AS ULTRA-ORTHODOXY

Situating themselves within ultra-Orthodox Judaism, and embracing its Manichean notions that one is either an insider or on the road to perdition, contemporary Hasidim have become socially blocked from doing anything not Hasidic by the threat of stigma and ultimately expulsion. They experience pressures to remain insulated from what they consider the corrosive culture of mainstream society. General knowledge and secular education are denigrated. Even languages other than Yiddish, the consecrated lingua franca of Hasidism, are avoided.

Consequently, those in line for succession no longer even entertain the thought that they might pursue a life beyond the boundaries of their insular world. They not only see a life embracing modern culture as off limits but also lack the educational and cultural competence to pursue it.* As we have seen, even a generation ago that was not always the case. Today, the sons and sons-in-law of rebbes seek habilitation overwhelmingly inside Hasidism, leading to more seeking the top job. Because they emerge from their insular and increasingly religiously conservative environment, the contest is often fought by contenders stressing how opposed they are to integrating with the outside world and modernity.

DECLINING GENERATIONS

A belief widely shared by Hasidim is the concept of *hiskatnus hadoros*, the decline of the generations, an increasingly normative stance of ultra-Orthodox Jewry. In proud opposition to the modern attitude that associates the new with the improved, this principle asserts that those who preceded us were greater than us. The old is always better than the new.

This necessarily valorizes predecessors over successors, who are inherently disappointing. A dead rebbe, as we have seen, can continue to be venerated and consulted by a successor and may even compete with him.[3] The tragedy of the Holocaust intensified all this by turning those who perished or went through it into eternal saints bathed in a sacred nostalgia, who became hard if not impossible acts to follow. All that has made postwar rebbes easier to challenge. Even a new rebbe therefore venerates his predecessor before asserting his own powers.

CONFLICT

We have seen that internal conflict is a feature of contemporary Hasidic succession. It is a function of competition, and competition *can* lead to excellence as each claimant tries to outshine the other and offer more to the Hasidim, and as the Hasidim commit more of themselves to the contest and to their favorite.

One might, however, also see conflict as a source of instability. Indeed, upon its initial outbreak, most groups fear it as destabilizing. Yet both the Bobover and Satmar cases demonstrate that as groups learn to manage a lasting conflict they reach some sort of stasis. They begin to draw on the energies the conflict generates, as each side in the

---

* In some recent cases, daughters of rebbes have escaped, but they were never really in the running for succession.

dispute over who is the true successor rebbe builds itself up and develops new strategies to defeat or humble its competitors. As each side scores successes—building bigger and better institutions, increasing its influence in the community, and so on—these actually both intensify the conflict and demonstrate its benefits.

The heightened identification of each Hasid with the successor he prefers and the "team" of Hasidim who share his sympathies invigorates all of them and the rebbe. People contribute more readily to their rebbe's coffers in order to outdo the other side. They sing the praises of their man over the other and force each of the competing rebbes to show more attention to them. The weaker challenger, as we have seen, is likely to be more open to newcomers and to increase recruitment and outreach, offering Hasidim a chance to get closer to him (the winning side can afford to appear more regal). This makes the challenger seem more approachable. The stronger contender pays more attention to holding on to what he has. In both cases the individual Hasid gets an extra boost spiritually and socially from his attachment to his rebbe. The conflict often leads to double the number of institutions and may even increase the overall size of the brand, as each side seeks to recruit more followers and to demonstrate the great attraction of its candidate for rebbe.

Paradoxically, even as it seems to be a sign of a troubled succession, continuing conflict may enhance group strength. We may be entering an era where multiple *rebistve*s and internal contests over who is the first among equals become normative. The examples in these pages give some hint of how this might play out in the future.

In conflicts, the narcissism of small differences looms large.[4] The actual differences among Hasidic groups and their rebbes, certainly from the outsider's point of view, may be hard to distinguish. In internal conflicts, the differences may be even smaller. Appearances seem deceptively similar, as do patterns of social behavior. A *tish* is pretty much the same, whichever rebbe leads it, especially within the same group. Hasidic men more or less dress and groom themselves the same, and the same could be said of the boys. The girls and women are a bit harder to identify, although their "modest" attire—high necklines, low hemlines, subdued colors, and, for the married, hair covering—makes them easier to recognize with a bit of orientation. Communal norms tend to emphasize conformity to religious custom and powerful loyalty to the brand and the rebbe. Even many of the Hasidic attitudes toward mainstream culture and contemporary society have much in common across the different groups, as already noted. The contests make even the smallest distinctions into major differences as these similar people seek out and even exaggerate the differences that justify the conflict.

The psychic and social energy that often drives the competition within and between Hasidic groups is at least in part a product of the conviction on each side that a time will come when the other side will have to admit that *they were wrong* and that the candidate of their opponents or competitors *is indeed the superior* rebbe. The anticipated satisfaction that such an admission will bring spiritually vitalizes the conflict.

Conflict is of course not an unadulterated benefit. Although rebbes are considered remarkable personalities, holy seed endowed with great power, the internal conflicts over who should be the rebbe can turn the sacred rebbe into a profane personality. The attacks of the other side occasionally hit their target. Doubts creep in, and both men may become diminished by their conflict. This is exacerbated, as we have discovered, when the competition becomes institutionalized. As the members of the group supporting the competitor promote his superiority (and through it their own, for following him), they necessarily demote the personality and diminish any sense of sanctity claimed by his rival and his Hasidim. Since both sides in the conflict do the same, enthusiasms generated for one successor are matched with disparagements that lessen the stature of the other. Thus both claimants to the throne become associated with criticisms and profanations that diminish them in the larger Hasidic community,

Such profanation limits contenders' ability to enhance their dignity and sense of the holy because the Hasidim of the challenger do all they can to tear the opposing rebbe down and show him to be a humbug, unable to truly act as an intermediary before God or as a source of blessing. When all this occurs in the same neighborhood or nearby, the impact is harder to ignore.

As illustrated in the case of Munkács, when the two brothers resolved their competition and one moved out of the proximity of the other and found a new name for himself, both of them enhanced their positions and gained greater dignity, both among their Hasidim and in the Hasidic community at large. Their stature grew as their conflict diminished. On the contrary, the intense and ongoing conflict between the Satmar brothers Aaron and Zalman Teitelbaum has diminished both of them in the eyes of their opponents, and, as we have seen, has enhanced the appeal and enlarged the following of the Dynover Rebbe, a man who at one time called himself the Flatbush Rebbe of Munkács, who, now located in Williamsburg and cleansed of his conflict with his brother, stands tall outside the squabble.

THE SOCIETY OF REBBES: MENTORSHIP AND ENDORSEMENT

Those who have been designated as successors during their predecessor's lifetime can often learn by watching and helping him over the years. Successors who were unexpectedly selected for the role of rebbe often need special help transitioning to the position. The rebbes of both Munkács and Boyan needed such help. Their situations highlight the role of mentors and the fellowship of rebbes in succession. Mentors are usually established rebbes who counsel and support a new successor, creating alliances with him and by transitivity with his Hasidim. These alliances may become enhanced by marriages of their offspring or by their willingness to acknowledge in public the stature of the new rebbe. The wedding between the Kopczynitz and Boyan families undoubtedly helped the young new rebbe in his transition from American modern Orthodoxy to Hasidic leadership.

Endorsements empower a new rebbe but also boost the prestige, political influence, and stature of the patron. Often the patron's ideas and positions are embraced by the rebbe he has supported, making them more broadly held and enhancing his charisma in the Hasidic world. We have seen how Yoelish Teitelbaum used this approach.

Visits between rebbes—ostensibly a way for the visitor to honor the visited—likewise serve to create alliances, political and social, that enlarge the power not only of those involved in the association but also of the Hasidic world in general. We have seen how this encourages rebbes to welcome neophytes into their club—at least so long as the newcomer does not break with or try to usurp the mentor's position of dominance. We have seen how the challenger in Bobov has tried to use such visits to bolster his challenge.

The emergence of mentors and encouragement from other rebbes for a languishing *rebistve* or one in search of an incumbent is in part a reflection of a continuing feeling among Hasidim that, despite their numerical growth and great success in reestablishing themselves after the Holocaust, in a world dominated by secularity and nonobservant Jewry, Hasidism is still fragile and insecure. Mentorship and the encouragement to fill all available *rebistve*s remind them that they are part of a movement, distinct, networked, and self-referential. This has served as an incentive to encourage dynasties to assure their continuity when they were facing extinction because of a dearth of possible successors.

What ties together the various succession narratives detailed in this book is that they have occurred in a place and time when all the accepted wisdom suggested Hasidism as a way of life would be impossible. As we know, most pre-Holocaust Hasidim deemed neither modern, largely secular America nor the modern Zionist and also predominantly secular state of Israel hospitable to their community. Some Hasidim made their way to the Holy Land to await the Messiah there, and some came to the New World, predicting it would turn out to be the last, brief stop of the long Jewish Diaspora. No less a Hasidic giant than Chaim Halberstam, the Rebbe of Sanz (1793–1876), although never leaving Europe, claimed that the final era of Jewish exile would begin in America and would end with the arrival of the Messiah. Although few Hasidic rebbes repeated this message or urged Hasidim in Europe to leave even as Nazi and Soviet persecution intensified (a failure that would have fatal consequences for many of them and their followers), during the last years of the war and immediately afterward the theme began to emerge more powerfully.

Yet for all the talk about the Messiah, to most Hasidim who found themselves in America and Israel after the Holocaust, redemption did not appear imminent. So they set about rebuilding, assuring succession and guaranteeing continuity even where they had once thought they would not be able to do so. That effort serves as the background against which so much described here takes place.

Hasidim have by now abandoned their reservations about both Israel and the United States and seek now instead to demonstrate to themselves and everyone else how successful their rebuilding has been (even if it has been accompanied by internal conflicts over who should lead and be considered responsible for it). And even in post-Soviet Russia, Lubavitcher Hasidim are ubiquitous. Hasidim have turned the places once deemed dangerous to their survival into lands of opportunity for the fulfillment of their continuing dreams of growth. They and their leaders have fought back against whatever they considered dangerous to their continuity and their communities. This has given them a sense of confidence perhaps unprecedented in their history, and certainly greater than anything they experienced in the closing years of their European existence.

That confidence is generally projected onto their rebbes. They are a source of blessings and strength. Perhaps no group in the modern, largely urbanized world that Hasidim inhabit (and even when they live in suburban villages, they urbanize them or maintain an ongoing tie to an urban base) invests a single individual like a rebbe with so much of their sense of identity and hope. Both as individuals and as families, they are absorbed within his life and what goes on around it, they organize their lives so that they may be near him or at least in touch with what he wants, and they implicate the rebbe's life in their own and vice versa. When he succeeds, they do; when they do, he shares in their successes. The path between the leader and the led is bidirectional: they cannot exist as Hasidim without him, nor can he be a rebbe if they abandon him.

But this relationship cannot be taken for granted; it requires repeated reanimation, moments of what Emile Durkheim called "collective effervescence." [5] Those occur when rebbe and Hasidim are together, perhaps no more palpably than at the celebration of succession when a renewed sense of communion between Hasidim and their new leader is expressed and experienced.

Long after many people in the modern world stopped thinking that particular individuals held miraculous or extraordinary powers, in an environment that, as Max Weber described it, is effectively "disenchanted," Hasidim still hold on to the conviction that their rebbe has the power to move heaven and earth on their behalf, affecting their well-being and cosmic order; for that alone they remained beholden if not in thrall to him. [6] Whether rebbes themselves believe they have these powers or are convinced of it via their experiences with their Hasidim is hard to know for certain. What is clear is that beneath the black-and-white exterior of Hasidism is a colorful spirit that continues to animate them, and the question of "Who will lead us?" remains as compelling or even more compelling to them in these days than it was in the past.

Notes

PROLOGUE

1. Egon Mayer, *From Suburb to Shtetl* (Philadelphia: Temple University Press, 1979), 3.

2. Shimon Schwab, *Selected Writings* (Lakewood, NJ: CIS Publications, 1988), 234.

3. Cf. Marc B. Shapiro, *Changing the Immutable* (London: Littman Library, 2015), 10.

4. "Opinion and Comment: On Writing Biographies of Gedolim," Dei'ah veDibur, n.d., accessed November 10, 2015, http://chareidi.org/archives5765 /bechukosai/obiogrphbck65.htm.

1. SUCCESSION IN CONTEMPORARY HASIDISM

1. See Moshe Rosman, *Founder of Hasidism: A Quest for the Historical Ba'al Shem Tov* (Berkeley: University of California Press, 1996), 13–26.

2. Max Weber, *The Theory of Social and Economic Organization,* trans A.M. Henderson and Talcott Parsons (1947; repr., Glencoe, IL: Free Press, 1964), 358.

3. Ibid., 358–59.

4. Max Weber, *The Sociology of Religion* (New York: Beacon Press, 1963), 168. See also Max Weber, *Economy and Society: An Outline of Interpretive Sociology* (New York: Bedminster Press, 1968), 1:544–50.

5. The fact that Abraham, the son of the Maggid of Mezherich, was called *malach* (angel) perhaps reflects the transition from the name *maggid* to *zaddik* and later *rebbe*.

6. NSW Board of Jewish Education, "Hitboded: A Chassidic Concept," n.d., accessed December 31, 2013, http://bje.org.au/course /judaism/jewish-prayer

/hitboded.html. See also Zvi Mark, *Mysticism and Madness: The Religious Thought of Rabbi Nachman of Bratslav* (London: Continuum, 2009), 132.

7. Stephen Sharot, *Messianism, Mysticism, and Magic: A Sociological Analysis of Jewish Religious Movements* (Chapel Hill: University of North Carolina Press, 1982), 162. See also Rosman, *Founder of Hasidism.*

8. See Immanuel Etkes, "The Hasidic Court in Its First Stages," in *Text and Context: Essays in Modern Jewish History and Historiography in Honor of Ismar Schorsch,* ed. Eli Lederhendler and Jack Wertheimer (New York: Jewish Theological Seminary, 2005), 157–86.

9. This was especially the case of Yisrael Friedman of Ruzhin and his Hasidim. See David Assaf, *The Regal Way: The Life and Times of Rabbi Israel of Ruzhin* (Stanford, CA: Stanford University Press, 2002). For Lubavitcher Hasidim today, it can be done via videos. See Samuel Heilman, "Still Seeing the Rebbe," *Killing the Buddha,* September 5, 2001, http://killingthebuddha.com/mag/dogma/still-seeing-the-rebbe/.

10. Yehoshua Bar Yossef, *MiZefat l'Yerushalayim* [From Safed to Jerusalem] (Jerusalem: Mossad Bialik, 1972), 106.

11. Mendel Piekarz, *The Hasidic Leadership: Authority and Faith in Zaddikim as Reflected in the Hasidic Literature* [in Hebrew] (Jerusalem: Bialik Institute, 1999), 36. The translation is my own.

12. Emile Durkheim, *The Elementary Forms of the Religious Life* (New York: Macmillan, 1915).

13. Solomon Maimon, *Solomon Maimon: An Autobiography,* trans. J. Clark Murray (Urbana: University of Illinois Press, 2001), originally published as *Solomon Maimons Lebensgeschichte* (Berlin, 1792–93).

14. Etkes, "Hasidic Court," 162. While Maimon's enthusiasm for Hasidism ultimately waned, enough other Jews retained their initial excitement and became changed persons.

15. See Haviva Padaya, "On the Development of the Social-Religious-Economic Model in Hasidism: Pidyon, the Society, and the Pilgrimage," in *Zaddik and Devotees: Historical and Sociological Aspects of Hasidism* [in Hebrew], ed. David Assaf (Jerusalem: Zalman Shazar, 2001).

16. Another word for *rebistve* was *rebbeschaft.*

17. I thank Zalman Alpert for pointing this out to me.

18. Etkes, "Hasidic Court," 157.

19. Ibid., 158.

20. See Max Weber, "Politics as a Vocation," in *From Max Weber: Essays in Sociology,* ed. H.H. Gerth and C. Wright Mills (New York: Routledge, 1948), 77–128.

21. Elimelech Weisblum of Lyzhansk (1717–87), *Noam Elimelech,* sec. Bo, p. 72.

22. Piekarz, *Hasidic Leadership,* 17–18.

23. Rivka Schatz-Uffenheimer, ed., *Magid Devarav Le-Ya'akov of the Maggid Dov Baer of Mezhirech: Critical Edition with Commentary* [in Hebrew] (Jerusalem: Magnes Press, 1990), 219; Piekarz, *Hasidic Leadership,* 42.

24. Piekarz, *Hasidic Leadership,* 35.

25. Ibid., 18.

26. Etkes, "Hasidic Court," 163.

27. Piekarz, *Hasidic Leadership*, 17.

28. That there were some Christian undertones in this thinking seemed to some undeniable. See Ada Rapoport-Albert, "Hasidism after 1772: Structural Continuity and Change," in *Hasidism Reappraised*, ed. Ada Rapoport-Albert (London: Littman Library, 1997), 84–85.

29. See Benjamin Mintz, *Sefer Ha-Histalkut* [The book of leaving] (Tel Aviv: Ketubim, 1930).

30. A case in point: the Hasidim of Elimelech Weissblum of Lyzhansk upon his death in 1787 studied his book *Noam Elimelech*.

31. Rapoport-Albert, "Hasidism after 1772," 77n2.

32. Ibid., 76.

33. Nehemia Polen, "Rebbetzins, Wonder-Children, and the Emergence of the Dynastic Principle in Hasidism," in *Shtetl: New Evaluations*, ed. Steven Katz (New York: NYU Press, 2007), 54.

34. Rapoport-Albert, "Hasidism after 1772," 90.

35. Ibid., 103.

36. Uriel Gellman, "Discipleship: The Foundation of Spiritual Legacy in Early Hasidism," paper presented at the annual meeting of the Association for Jewish Studies, Boston, December 2015.

37. See Rapoport-Albert, "Hasidism after 1772," 104, 107; Salo W. Baron, *The Jewish Community* (Philadelphia: Jewish Publication Society, 1942).

38. Rapoport-Albert, "Hasidism after 1772," 97.

39. Richard Werbner, "New World Revival, African Reprise," paper presented at the conference "Religion on the Global Stage: Social Scientific Perspectives," Indiana University, Bloomington, November 14–16, 2014, 2–3.

40. Immanuel Etkes and David Assaf, "On Ada Rapoport-Albert's Scholarly Work," in *Studies in Hasidism, Sabbatianism and Gender*, ed. Ada Rapoport-Albert (Jerusalem: Zalman Shazar, 2015), 8–10.

41. Sharot, *Messianism, Mysticism*, 170. See also Piekarz, *Hasidic Leadership*.

42. Polen, "Rebbetzins, Wonder-Children," 56.

43. *Shivchei HaBesht*, quoted in Marc Shapiro, *Changing the Immutable: How Orthodox Judaism Rewrites Its History* (Oxford: Littman Library, 2015), 77.

44. Polen, "Rebbetzins, Wonder-Children," 56; J. L. William Whiston, *The Short History of the Regal Succession* (London, 1731), 27.

45. Gadi Sagiv, "King Lear's *Einiklach*: Inheritance Disputes in Nineteenth-Century Hasidism," paper presented at the annual meeting of the Association for Jewish Studies, Boston, December 14, 2015.

46. Gellman, "Discipleship."

47. Through Menachem Nachum's daughter, Malka, he would also become the great-grandfather of Yisrael Friedman of Ruzhin. See Gadi Sagiv, *Dynasty: The Chernobyl Hasidic Dynasty and Its Place in the History of Hasidism* [in Hebrew] (Jerusalem: Shazar, 2014).

48. Polen, "Rebbetzins, Wonder-Children," 58.

49. Ibid., 58–60.

50. Ibid., 60. This was something the aforementioned Chava Friedman, mother of Abraham and Yisrael, understood.

51. See Immanuel Etkes, *Ba'al Ha-Tanya: Rabbi Shneur Zalman of Liady and the Origins of Habad Hasidism* [in Hebrew] (Jerusalem: Shazar, 2011), 421.

52. Ibid., 425 (my translation).

53. Ibid., 426.

54. Hayim Meir Heilman, *Beit Rabbi* (Berditchev, 1902), 2:185.

55. Rapoport-Albert, "Hasidism after 1772," 111. See also Shmuel Ettinger, "The Hasidic Movement: Reality and Ideals," in *Jewish Society throughout the Ages,* ed. Haim Hillel Ben-Sasson and Shmuel Ettinger (New York: Schocken Books, 1973), 251–66, and Rabbi Boruch of Medzibezh, *Butsina dinehora hashalem, mekor baruch,* sec. 94 (Bilgoray, Poland: Kroneburg, 1753). Rapoport-Albert ("Hasidism after 1772," 112–13) persuasively claims that this particular conversation never actually took place (see below), but the tradition reflects how the dynastic principle infected even the idea of discipleship as a basis of succession.

56. Etkes, *Ba'al Ha-Tanya,* 427.

57. Ibid., 428.

58. Ibid., 417. See also H. Heilman, *Beit Rabbi,* 2:189–90.

59. Ibid., 428. The conflict over who was worthy of carrying on the leadership of Schneur Zalman's Hasidim focused on how to pray, but all this was, as Etkes demonstrates (*Ba'al Ha-Tanya,* 430–34), simply a vehicle for expressing the contest between the two would-be successors. To be sure, in some smaller courts disciples have been able to take over, but this still is very largely the exception rather than the rule.

60. See Rapoport-Albert, "Hasidism after 1772," 117, citing a Breslov Hasidic volume *Avaneihah barzel,* chap. 34, sec. 46. See also Etkes, *Ba'al Ha-Tanya,* 67–70.

61. See Rhonda Berger-Sofer, "Political Kinship Alliances of a Hasidic Dynasty," *Ethnology* 23, no. 1 (January 1984): 49–62, esp. 55–56. See also Gellman, "Discipleship."

62. Jerome Mintz, *Hasidic People: A Place in the New World* (Cambridge, MA: Harvard University Press, 1992), 126.

63. Rapoport-Albert, "Hasidism after 1772," 118; A. Grossman, "Yichus mishpacha umekomo bechevra hayehudit be'Ashkenaz hakedumah," in *Perakim BeToledot HaChevra Hayehudit Biyemei Habeinayim uva'et Hachadasha,* ed. Immanuel Etkes and Yosef Salmon (Jerusalem: Magnes Press, 1980), 9–23.

64. Etkes, *Ba'al Ha-Tanya,* 442.

65. This letter, which the Ba'al Shem Tov, Israel Ben Eliezer, founder of Hasidism, wrote to his brother-in-law, Gershon Kitover, exists in different versions. See Naftali Loewenthal, *Communicating the Infinite: The Emergence of the Habad School* (Chicago: University of Chicago Press, 1990), 221n43. On the relatively recent adoption of this exchange between the Besht and the Messiah as one of ChaBaD's outreach slogans, see Naftali Loewenthal, "The Baal Shem Tov's *Iggeret Ha-Kodesh* and Contemporary HaBaD Outreach," in *Hasidim and the Musar Movement,* vol. 1 of *Let the Old Make Way for the New:*

Studies in the Social and Cultural History of Eastern European Jewry Presented to Immanuel Etkes, ed. David Assaf and Ada Rapoport-Albert, 2 vols. (Jerusalem: Shazar Institute, 2009), English section, 69–101, esp. n2. On unifications, see chapter 2.

66. See Loewenthal, *Communicating the Infinite,* 6, 14. See also Mor Altshuler, *The Messianic Secret of Hasidism* (Boston: Brill, 2006), esp. 3–13.

67. See Samuel Heilman, "What's in a Name? The Dilemma of Title and Geography for Contemporary Hasidism," *Jewish History* 27, nos. 2–4 (2013): 221–40.

68. Rapoport-Albert, "Hasidism after 1772," 111n115. See also Etkes, *Ba'al Ha-Tanya,* chap. 3.

69. Werbner, "New World Revival," 5–6.

70. Cited in Ben Ezra, *ha-"Yanuka" mi-Stolin* [The infant of Stolin] (New York: A. Ben-Ezra, [1950/51]), 19–24. Ben Ezra titles the first will "the Family's Will" and the second "the Hasidim's Will" (in line with the content in each of the texts); Zev Rabinovitch, *HaHasidut HaLita'it: Me reshita v'ad yameinu* [Lithuanian Hasidism: From its origins to the present] (Jerusalem: Bialik, 1961), 88–89;Aharon Hoyzman, *Divrei Aharon* (Jerusalem: HaTechiya, 1962), 122. Thanks to Benjamin Brown for providing this reference.

71. I thank Zalman Alpert for this information.

72. So powerful was the charisma of the rebbe that he could even "purify" the name of the town of Gura-Kalvarya (Calvary Hill), which after all recalled a place in the Christian New Testament but now became associated with the holy *zaddik,* the Gerrer Rebbe. Thanks to Yoram Bilu for pointing this out to me.

73. See Yisroel Friedman, *The Golden Dynasty: The Lives and Times of the Rizhniner Rebbe* (Jerusalem: Girsa, 1997), chap. 15, "The Bohusher Rebbe, Reb Yitzchok zt"l," Nishmas Chayim, The Chassidic Library, www.nishmas.org/gdynasty/chapt15.htm.

74. Weber, *Economy and Society,* 1:1139.

75. Rapoport-Albert, "Hasidism after 1772," 126.

76. See ibid., 127, for a fuller consideration of this point.

77. David N. Myers, "'Commanded War': Three Chapters in the 'Military' History of Satmar Hasidism," *Journal of the American Academy of Religion* 81, no. 2 (March 2013): 3.

78. Sharot, *Messianism, Mysticism,* 155.

79. Weber, *Economy and Society,* 1:1139.

80. See, for example, George Vecsey, "Hasidim in Brooklyn Feuding over Israel and Neighborhood Sanctity," *New York Times,* June 1, 1977. Sometimes the tensions were between Hasidim in Israel and America; see, for example, Ari Goldman, "Guard Set for Belz Rabbi as Hasidic Tension Grows," *New York Times,* March 3, 1981.

2. MUNKÁCS

1. See "The History of the Munkács Community before the Holocaust: Religious Life. The Hasidic Rabbis of Munkács," Yad Vashem, n.d., accessed October 15, 2012, www1.yadvashem.org/yv/en/exhibitions/communities/munkacs/rabbis.asp.

2. See Motti Inbari, "Messianic Activism in the Works of Chaim Elazar Shapira, the Munkács Rebbe, between Two World Wars" [in Hebrew], *Katedra* 149 (October 2013), http://libres.uncg.edu/ir/uncp/f/Messianic%20Activism%20in%20the%20Works%20of%20Chaim%20Elazar%20Shapira,%20the%20Munkacz%20Rebbe.pdf, 82.

3. "History of the Munkács Community before the Holocaust. Religious Life. The Hasidic Rabbis of Munkács."

4. See ibid.

5. He was given the name Chaim, which means "life," when he contracted a childhood disease. Adding names that can be understood as blessings for long life (*Alter* for a male or *Alte* for a female, meaning "old one" in Yiddish, was another common appellation given to sick people) was a common practice among European Orthodox Jewry.

6. "History of the Munkács Community before the Holocaust. Religious Life. The Hasidic Rabbis of Munkács." One paper reports that the certificate turned out to be inauthentic and that only after a reapplication in 1904 did Shapira receive the appointment. See Yitzchak Raphael and Yitzchak Alfassi, eds., *Hasidic Encyclopedia,* series II [in Hebrew] (Jerusalem: Mossad HaRav Kook, 1986), 1:568. See also David Kahane, *Toldos Rebeinu* (Brooklyn, NY: Munkács Publishers, 1998), 81b, which claims that after a dream Shapira went for a retest and received certification.

7. Allan Nadler, "Munkatsch Hasidic Dynasty," in *YIVO Encyclopedia of Jews in Eastern Europe,* ed. Gershon David Hundert, 2010, www.yivoencyclopedia .org/article.aspx/Munkatsh_Hasidic_Dynasty#author.

8. See Motti Inbari, *Jewish Radical Ultra-Orthodoxy Confronts Modernity, Zionism, and Women's Equality* (New York: Cambridge University Press, 2016), 94–130, and Inbari, "Messianic Activism."

9. See, for example, "Rabbi Chaim Elazar Shapiro, Munkaczer Rebbe, Author of *Minchas Elazar* (1871–1937)," True Torah Jews, n.d., accessed April 21, 2015, www.truetorahjews.org/munkacz.

10. Levi Cooper, "The Reactionary Rebbe," *Segula,* no. 20 (January 2014): 44, www.academia.edu/6266217/Munkatch_The_Reactionary_Rebbe.

11. The "miracle" of the Russian failure to invade boosted the authority Shapira had in getting Jews to follow his counsel but also would emotionally affect many Jews years later when the fear of an invasion of the Nazis seemed possible; those who remembered how they had been saved by the rebbe's advice that no invasion would occur believed that history would once again repeat itself and spare Munkács.

12. According to his grandson Chaim Elazar Rabinovich, the opposition to Zionism was secondary to his animosity to all ideologies that were connected with emancipated and enlightened Jewry (interview by author, June 21, 2012).

13. *Munkatch Rebbe,* 1933 footage, uploaded May 19, 2007, www.youtube .com/watch?v=CbfC949G17U. See also Nadler, "Munkatsch Hasidic Dynasty."

14. Family member, personal communication to author, October 16, 2012. See also Kahane, *Toldos Rebeinu,* 69; Levi Cooper, "The Mukatch Rebbe Chaim Elazar Shapira the Hasidic Ruler—Biography and Method" [in Hebrew] (PhD diss., Bar Ilan University, 2011); Levi Cooper, "Against the Flow of the

Raging Waters: The Hasidic Master of Munkács Rabbi Chaim Elazar Shapira"
[in Hebrew], in *The Gdoilim: Men Who Shaped the Haredi Community in
Israel,* ed. Benjamin Brown and Nissim Leon (Jerusalem: Magnes Press, forth-
coming).

15. Family member, interview by author, November 5, 2011.

16. Kahane, *Toldos Rebeinu,* 29–30. Tzvi Rabinowicz, *Hasidism in Israel: A
History of the Hasidic Movement and Its Masters in the Holy Land* (Northvale,
NJ: Jason Aaronson, 2000), 258, puts the date as 1907, but most sources mark
it as 1906.

17. "Rochel Peri Spira," Geni, n.d., accessed October 18, 2012, www.geni.com
/people/Rochel-Shapira-Spira-Munkatcher-Rebbetzin/6000000006712206335#
/tab/timeline. See also Kahane, *Toldos Rebeinu,* 48.

18. Family member, interview by author, November 5, 2011.

19. *Jewish Life in Munkatch—March 1933—Complete Version,* uploaded
March 17, 2009, www.youtube.com/watch?v=rp1OeIfoDow&feature=BFa&li
st=FLwoB_r56EBFCzAa9fIOM7xQ.

20. The marriage had its problems, and for a time the couple was separated,
with Boruch living in Warsaw and his wife returning to her parents.

21. Harry Rabinowicz, *The Rebbes of Munkacz* (London: Valentine Mitch-
ell, 1998), 18.

22. Family member, interview by author, November 5, 2012.

23. Inbari, "Messianic Activism," 86–90.

24. See Boruch Rabinovich's introduction to his memoir *Binat Nevonim*
[The understanding of the wise], 2nd ed. (Petach Tikvah: published by the family, 2012), 13.

25. Ibid., 15.

26. Ibid., 15n10.

27. Chaim Elazar Rabinovich, interview by author, August 19, 2012

28. See Esther Farbstein, "Miracle upon Miracle: Rabbi Baruch Rabinowitz
Rav of Holon," in *The Forgotten Memoirs: Moving Personal Accounts from
Rabbis Who Survived the Holocaust* (Brooklyn, NY: Shaar Press, 2011), 319.

29. Family member, interview by author, November 5, 2012.

30. See Samuel Heilman and Menachem Friedman, *The Rebbe: The Life and
Afterlife of Menachem Mendel Schneerson* (Princeton, NJ: Princeton University
Press, 2011), 77 ff., 131.

31. Kahane, *Toldos Rebeinu,* chap. 182.

32. Family member, interview by author, October 16, 2012.

33. Zvi and Hirsch are the same name; *Zvi* is the Hebrew and *Hirsch* the
Yiddish for "deer."

34. The reason for the custom is to differentiate the shofar blasts of the preceding month of Elul and those of Rosh Hashanah that begin the new month
and mark the New Year (see Mishneh Berura 24). The story, repeated by Boruch
on a later occasion, is posted on the well-known blog *Circus Tent* as "Belated
Yet Timely," November 16, 2008, http://theantitzemach.blogspot.com/2008/11
/belated-yet-timely.html:

> In the final year of his life the *Minchas Elozor* took the *shofar* on *Rosh Chodesh Elul*
> and tried the horn to see if it was in OK condition. Hershelle was in the room then and

was very visibly excited with the *shofar* and its sounds; he asked his *zeide* [grandfather] for *"noch ein blooz,"* one more blast, which his *zeide* gladly obliged. From then on, for the next month, this became a ritual; the Rov blowing once for little Hershelle. On Erev Rosh Hashonoh Hershelle was there awaiting his daily blast, but he was disappointed. *"Haynt iz Erev Rosh Hashoone, Haynt bloozt men nisht, morgen vet men bloozen asach mool in shil"* [Today is the eve of Rosh Hashanah and we do not blow, tomorrow we shall blow many times in the synagogue], his *zeide* told him. The child knew no *Chochmes* [rationalizations]. He kicked and screamed, telling his zeide *"Nor Ein Blooz! Nor Ein Blooz!"* [Only one blow!]. After a while his *zeide* had *rachmones* [pity] on his favorite *eynikel* [grandchild] and took the *shofar* and blew one *blooz* [blow].

On *Rosh Hashoneh* before *Tekios* [the shofar blasts] the *minhag* [custom] in *Munkács* was that the *Rov* spoke. That year the *Rov* went up before the *aron kodesh* [holy ark], opened the ark and said: *"Ribono Shel Olam, Ich darf tshiveh tuhn, ich hub over geven af an halochoh* [Master of the Universe, I must repent, I have transgressed a law]. It's written that on *ERH* [Rosh Hashanah eve] one mustn't blow *shofar*, yet I did." He began to sob uncontrollably and called out: *"Ribono shel olam,* do you know why I transgressed that *halochoh?* it was because my young (grand)child lay on the floor and begged me and cried that I should only blow one *blooz* for him. My heart melted, I couldn't bear to watch him cry like that, so I blew once for him, despite the fact that I shouldn't have. *Tatte* [Father], how can you stand by and see how millions of your children are down on the floor and cry out to you, *Tatte eyn blooz—TeKa BeShofar Godol LeChayruseynu* [Father one blow— Blow on the great shofar for our redemption]. Even if the time is not right for it yet, the time for *Moshiach* [Messiah] has yet to arrive, but your children cry out to you, how can you stand idly by?!"

When *Reb Baruch* told the story he cried, and recounted how at that time the crowd cried along with the *Rov*, the *Tekios* were delayed, and for a long time they could not "come to themselves, loud wailing was heard throughout the shul."

The story was confirmed by Binyomin Wulliger, who was there at the time (interview by author, December 10, 2012).

35. See B. Rabinovich, introduction to *Binat Nevonim*.

36. Binyomin Wulliger, interview by author, December 10, 2012. See also Farbstein, "Miracle upon Miracle," 324.

37. Chaim Elazar Rabinovich, interview by author, June 21, 2012.

38. Binyomin Wulliger, interview by author, December 12, 2012.

39. Chaim Elazar Rabinovich, interview by author, June 21, 2012.

40. In 1930, the yeshiva opened amid great celebration in Jewish Poland. Marshall Pilsudski himself, the head of the Polish government, came to the opening.

41. See B. Rabinovich, *Binat Nevonim*, as well as a protocol in late summer of 1944, testimony 03/3822 at Yad Vashem Archives and in E. Y.M. Levin, *Derech Budapest: Hatzalah B'Hungaria* (Jerusalem: Yad Vashem, 1976).

42. B. Rabinovich, *Binat Nevonim*, and Farbstein, "Miracle upon Miracle," 327–29.

43. Boruchel would later try a variety of means to save Hungarian Jewry. See Levin, *Derech Budapest*.

44. B. Rabinovich, *Binat Nevonim*; see also Yitzchak Frankfurter, "Unsung No More," *Ami*, September 24, 2015, 176.

45. B. Rabinovich, *Binat Nevonim,* and Farbstein, "Miracle upon Miracle," 333.

46. B. Rabinovich, *Binat Nevonim,* and Farbstein, "Miracle upon Miracle," 334.

47. See Frankfurter, "Unsung No More," 164–78.

48. Esther Farbstein, "Father of the Refugees," *Ami,* September 24, 2015, 198.

49. Frankfurter, "Unsung No More," 172.

50. Family member, interview by author, October 16, 2012.

51. B. Rabinovich, *Binat Nevonim,* 14. See also Farbstein, "Miracle upon Miracle," 340–41.

52. Farbstein, "Father of the Refugees," 188.

53. Nadler, "Munkatsch Hasidic Dynasty"; B. Rabinovich, *Binat Nevonim,* 15.

54. Letter from the collection of Israel Guttman.

55. "History of the Munkács Community: During the Holocaust. The Munkács Ghetto," Yad Vashem, n.d., accessed October 15, 2012, http://www1 .yadvashem.org/yv/en/exhibitions/communities/munkacs/ghetto.asp.

56. Farbstein, "Father of the Refugees," 188.

57. "History of the Munkács Community: During the Holocaust. The Liquidation of the Jewish Community," Yad Vashem, n.d., accessed October 15, 2012, http://www1.yadvashem.org/yv/en/exhibitions/communities/munkacs /liquidation.asp.

58. See "History of the Munkács Community: Before the Holocaust. Religious Life. The Hasidic Rabbis of Munkács."

59. Chaim Elazar Rabinovich, interview by author, June 21, 2012.

60. B. Rabinovich, *Binat Nevonim,* 6 (translation mine, punctuation in original).

61. Family member, interview by author, October 16, 2012.

62. Binyomin Wulliger, interview by author, December 10, 2012.

63. Peska Friedman, *Going Forward* (New York: Mesorah Publications, 1994), 77, 159.

64. Chaim Elazar Rabinovich, interview by author, June 21, 2012. Rabinovich claims that his father told him that after the second such meeting Charlap, discovering who the young man was, told him that they could not meet again because "it's dangerous for you and for me."

65. Nadler, "Munkatsch Hasidic Dynasty."

66. B. Rabinovich, *Binat Nevonim.* See also Akiva Weisinger, "Miracles in the Life and Thought of Rabbi Barukh Rabinowicz," *Kol HaMevaser* 6, no. 1 (2012): 16.

67. Farbstein, "Father of Refugees," 198.

68. Chaim Kugel, "Hayitachen?" [Can it be?], *Davar,* no. 6343, May 30, 1946, my translation. Chaim Kugel was born in 1897 in Minsk to parents active in the Hovevei Zion movement. He acquired his doctorate in economics and philosophy at the Czech University in Prague. He arrived in Munkács as an emissary from the Jewish-Zionist students' union in Prague, in order to lecture to the Zionist youth movements in the town. See "The History of the Munkács Community before the Holocaust: The Munkács Zionist Movement in the Interwar

Period. Chaim Kugel," Yad Vashem, n.d., accessed October 31, 2012, http://www1.yadvashem.org/yv/en/exhibitions/communities/munkacs/kugel.asp.

69. See Nosson Dovid Rabinovich, *Sefer Ve'Eleh HaDevarim She Ne'emru L'Dovid* [And these are the words spoken to David] (Jerusalem: The grandchildren of the author, 1983). See also Weisinger, "Miracles," 16–17.

70. Binyomin Wulliger, interview by author, December 10, 2012.

71. Chaim Elazar Rabinovich, interview by author, December 4, 2012.

72. Binyomin Wulliger, interview by author, December 10, 2012.

73. Family member, interview by author, November 5, 2012.

74. Chaim Elazar Rabinovich, interview by author, January 6, 2013.

75. Family member, interview by author, November 5, 2012.

76. Frankfurter, "Unsung No More," 174.

77. See S. A. Pardes, "Orchim G'Dolim v'Chashuvim b'Chicago" [Great and important guests in Chicago], *HaPardes: A Rabbinical Monthly Journal* 22, no. 1 (October 1947): 5.

78. In the end, the powerfully anti-Zionist Teitelbaum would leave Palestine and reestablish the bulk of his court in Williamsburg, Brooklyn, and later in Kiryas Joel, New York. On Kasztner, see the website Kastzner Memorial, n.d., www.kasztnermemorial.com/r.html, accessed November 1, 2012. Peska Rabinovich, Boruch's sister, was one of those saved by Kastner.

79. He would learn it later and try to publicize it. See Frankfurter, "Unsung No More," 175.

80. Jeanette Friedman, interview by author.

81. Farbstein, "Father of the Refugees," 200.

82. Family member, interview by author, May 16, 2012. Many of the facts of Boruch's life come from this interview.

83. Family member, interview by author. There is a story of the Menachem Mendel Schneerson having a dog, but that was when he was a boy and long before anyone imagined he would become a rebbe. See "The Rebbe's Dog," Farbrengen Stories, May 2013, http://stories770.blogspot.co.il/2013/05/the-rebbes-dog.html.

84. See "K'Hal Adat Munkatch Mechadeshet N'ureha" [The Munkács community renews its past], *Hamaor* 3, no. 4 (April 1952):, 19–20.

85. Letter from collection of a family member.

86. Letter from a private collection.

87. Weisinger, "Miracles," 16; Boruch Rabinovich, "Einei haEdah" [Eyes of the community], in *Kuntres Divrei Torah ve-Hiddushim mi-Kevod Dodi ha-Ga'on Rabbi Barukh Yehoshua Yerahmiel Rabinowicz* [The collection of words of Torah and novellae from the Honorable My Uncle the Genius Rabbi Barukh Yehoshua Yerahmiel Rabinowcz] (B'nai B'rak: Bar Nadri, 1980), cited in Natan David Rabinowitz, *Sefer Be'erot Natan* [The book of the springs of Natan] (B'nai B'rak: Bar Nadri, 1980).

88. Family member, interview by author, and Jeanette Friedman, interview by author; see also Dov Kesselman, "Baruch Rabinowitz, Wandering Rabbi," *Segula,* January 2014, 53, www.academia.edu/6266217/Munkatch_The_Reactionary_Rebbe.

89. Katz had been in the United States during the early years of World War II raising funds for the school and was thus in position to help reestablish the yeshiva there in the face of the collapse of European Jewish life.

90. Jeanette Friedman, interview by author.

91. Binyomin Wulliger, interview by author, December 10, 2012, at the time about ninety-one years old. He had come to America three years after his bar mitzvah. As for Wulliger's brother Herschel, he would be this author's fifth-grade teacher.

92. Chaim Elazar Rabinovich, interview by author, August 19, 2012.

93. Chaim Elazar Rabinovich, interview by author, August 19, 2012.

94. Chaim Elazar Rabinovich, interview by author, January 6, 2013.

95. Jeanette Friedman, interview by author.

96. Binyomin Wulliger, interview by author, December 10, 2012.

97. For the truth about Schneersohn's secular education, see Heilman and Friedman, *The Rebbe.*

98. Family member, interview by author, October 16, 2012.

99. When the Minchas Elazar lay dying in 1937, Teitelbaum wanted to visit him and end the bad feeling that had arisen between the two after reports of his comment about heirs had reached the former. But while the dying rebbe agreed to meet, the Satmar would not come without a formal invitation, something Boruch, without telling his father-in-law, would not offer, believing that it would be demeaning and that the Satmar needed to swallow his pride as part of any visit. The reconciliation and meeting never occurred, something Boruch told his sons he later regretted very much, wishing he had been more flexible.

100. Some might argue more cynically that since Satmar had absorbed so many ex-Munkács Hasidim during the postwar period, Teitelbaum simply wanted to dominate their young future rebbe as well, to make his court a satellite of his own.

101. Jeanette Friedman, interview by author, June 2015.

102. Strzyżów, in Poland, was where the Minchas Elazar was born and where the man who married Boruch's widowed mother had come from.

103. Another witness to the events, a young cousin of the Rabinovich family, after half a century recalled matters differently. A fourteen-year-old at the time, she watched as the newly married couple was being danced down from the chuppah into the hall and saw Chaim Ber knock into Boruch, toppling the *shtreimel* from his head and shouting in Yiddish, with barely concealed contempt, "*Di bist ois Rebbe,*" you are no longer the rebbe. Jeanette Friedman, interview by author.

104. "David's Next Move?," *New York Post,* October 15, 2009, www .nypost.com/p/news/local/brooklyn/david_next_move_ZlajhrnkpbWKwQp-fioeGAO. See also "Munkacs Renewal," *Circus Tent* (blog), December 21, 2009, http://theantitzemach.blogspot.com/2009/12/munkacs-renovation.html.

105. Chaim Elazar Shapira, *Sefer Chaim v'Shalom* [The book of life and peace] (Jerusalem: Emes, 1999), http://munkatcherseforim.org/pdf/mincheaelazer/chaim% 20veshalom.pdf, 274. Whether the Minchas Elazar actually followed his own advice in his *rebistve* has been a matter of some debate.

106. "Every Month" [in Hebrew], *Chodesh B'Chodsho,* Kislev 5756, no. 21 (1995): 3.

107. "Hasidim Y'kablu P'nai HaRav Rabinovich Mi Munkatch" [The Hasidim greet Rabbi Rabinovich of Munkács], *Maariv,* April 11, 1962, 7.

108. Gershon Tannenbaum, "Historical Dinov," *5 Towns Jewish Times,* November 30, 2013 http://5tjt.com/historical-dinov/.

109. A photo of the letter is available at www.facebook.com/933862036 715381/photos/a.965816680186583.1073741829.933862036715381/9658 16386853279/?type=3&theater.

110. Obituary of Chaim Ber Greenfeld, *Der Yid,* November 9, 1984, 13.

3. BOYAN AND KOPYCZYNITZ

1. DovBer Rabinowitz, *Mishkenot HaRo'im* (Tel Aviv: Rabinowitz, 1984), 36.

2. Ibid., 52.

3. Andras Whittam Smith, "In Viennese Painting of the Early 20th Century, You Get a Sense of Horrors to Come," *Independent,* Thursday, November 14, 2013, www.independent.co.uk/voices/comment/in-viennese-painting-of-the-early-20th-century-you-get-a-sense-of-horrors-to-come-8940166.html. See also Deborah Holmes and Lisa Silverman, eds., *Interwar Vienna: Culture between Tradition and Modernity* (Rochester, NY: Camden House, 2009).

4. Yad Vashem Archives, PKA/E-6.

5. Rabinowitz, *Mishkenot HaRo'im,* 60.

6. Ibid., 61.

7. Ibid., 14, 47. He was also the brother-in-law of the Kopyczynitzer Rebbe, Avraham Yehoshua Heschel (199). On exactly where Bukovina was, see Paul Robert Magocsi, *A History of Ukraine* (Toronto: University of Toronto Press, 1996), 420.

8. Rabinowitz, *Mishkenot HaRo'im,* 63n18.

9. See "This Day in History: 5 Adar, Harav Mordechai Shlomo Friedman of Boyan, *zt"l,*" *HaModia,* February 17, 2013, http://hamodia.com/features /this-day-in-history-28/.

10. Jerome Mintz, *Hasidic People* (Cambridge, MA: Harvard University Press, 1992), 14.

11. See "This Day in History: 11 Kislev/December 3, Harav Yitzchak Friedman of Sadigura-Rimanov, *zt"l,*" *HaModia,* December 2, 2014, http:// hamodia.com/features/day-history-11-kislevdecember-3/. The year listed as 1925 is probably wrong given that his tombstone says 1924.

12. For a picture of his gravestone with the date, see "Rebbe Yitzchok Friedman," n.d., accessed March 11, 2015, http://kevarim.com/rebbe-yitzchok-friedman/#more-16.

13. Unpublished eulogy provided by the rebbe's grandson, Mr. Yitzchak Friedman.

14. See "15,000 Jews Pay Tribute to Rabbi of Sadigora." Jewish Telegraphic Agency, December 10, 1924.

15. Rabinowitz, *Mishkenot HaRo'im,* 63.

16. Ibid., 63n18.

17. See Samuel Heilman and Menachem Friedman, *The Rebbe: The Life and Afterlife of Menachem Mendel Schneerson* (Princeton, NJ: Princeton University Press, 2011).

18. Haskel Lookstein, "The Public Response of American Jews to the Liberation of European Jewry, January–May 1945," in *Why Didn't the Press Shout: American and International Journalism during the Holocaust*, ed. Robert Moses Shapiro (New York: Ktav, 2003), 140. See also Edward Kaplan, *Spiritual Radical: Abraham Joshua Heschel in America, 1940–1972* (New Haven, CT: Yale University Press, 2007), 52.

19. See David Assaf, *The Regal Way: The Life and Times of Rabbi Israel of Ruzhin* (Stanford, CA: Stanford University Press, 2002).

20. Mintz, *Hasidic People,* 77–79.

21. Ibid., 19.

22. Yisroel Friedman, *The Golden Dynasty: The Lives and Times of the Rizhniner Rebbe* (Jerusalem: Girsa, 1997), foreword, Nishmas Chayim, The Chassidic Library, www.nishmas.org/gdynasty/frame.htm.

23. Yisroel Besser, "Miracle on the Lower East Side," *Mishpacha,* October 10, 2011, 114–28.

24. Abraham Heshel, "The Chasidic Group of Kopyczynitz," JewishGen KehilaLinks, 2003, http://kehilalinks.jewishgen.org/suchostaw/sl_kopyczynce_chasidic_group.htm.

25. Zushe Heshel, son and brother of the Kopyczynitzer Rebbes, father-in-law of the current Boyaner Rebbe, quoted in Mintz, *Hasidic People,* 72.

26. Avraham Y. Heschel, "Vienna, 1938: From Royal Shelter to Lion's Den," *HaModia* March 12, 2013, D10, http://hamodia.com/2013/03/12/vienna-1938-from-royal-shelter-to-lions-den/.

27. See "This Day in History: 16 Tammuz/July 14, Harav Avraham Yehoshua Heschel of Kopycznitz, zt"l," *HaModia,* July 13, 2014, http://hamodia.com/features/day-history-16-tammuzjuly-14/.

28. "Rabbi Abraham Heschel, Agudist Leader, Dead at 79," *Jewish Telegraphic Agency,* July 26, 1967, www.jta.org/1967/07/26/archive/rabbi-abraham-heschel-agudist-leader-dead-at-79.

29. "This Day in History: 16 Tamuz/June 24, Harav Avraham Yehoshua Heschel of Kopycznitz, zt"l," *HaModia,* June 23, 2013, http://hamodia.com/features/this-day-in-history-16-tammuzjune-24/.

30. Kaplan, *Spiritual Radical,* 81. See also Avrohom Raynitz, "Rabbi Shneur Zalman Gurary, A'H: Minister of the Courtyard," *Bes Moshiach,* no. 435, 5 Marcheshvan 5764, 14–24, http://beismoshiach.org/_pdf/435.pdf. See also "Scion of Chernobyl Dynasty, Dead at 74," *Israel National News,* November 6, 2001, www.israelnationalnews.com/News/Flash.aspx/4733#.VOdwrvnF-So; Yitzchak Meir Twersky, *Mi Yarenu Tov* (New York: self-published, 2002), 65 (photo).

31. Heshel, "Chasidic Group of Kopyczynitz."

32. Mintz, *Hasidic People,* 75.

33. Ibid.

34. Ibid.

35. See B. Moses, "The Kopyczynitzer Rebbe: Reb Moshe Mordechai Heschel, Zt'l," *Yated Ne'eman,* n.d., https://ja.scribd.com/document/128075393/Famous-Rabbies.

36. Mintz, *Hasidic People,* 73.

37. Ibid., 81.

38. Ibid., 82.

39. Yosef Grossman, "A Collection of Thoughts on the Passing of a Gentle and Humble Giant—Rabbi Zyshe Heschel Z'L," *Daf HaKashrus* 12, no. 5 (February 2004): 17, https://oukosher.org/content/uploads/2013/02/Daf-12-5.pdf.

40. See Heshel, "Chasidic Group of Kopyczynitz."

41. Raynitz, "Rabbi Shneur Zalman Gurary," 19.

42. Ibid., 19, 23.

43. A.Z. Rand, *Toldot Anshei Shem,* 1:28, www.hebrewbooks.org/pdfpager.aspx?req=6562&st=&pgnum=28.

44. "Scion of Chernobyl"; see also Zalman Alpert, "A Chassidic Court Comes Alive," *Jewish Press,* November 24, 2004, www.jewishpress.com/sections/a-chassidic-court-comes-alive/2004/11/24/?print; Twersky, *Mi Yarenu Tov,* 65 (photo).

45. Family member, personal communication to author. See also Friedman, *Golden Dynasty,* chap. 17, "The Kapischnitzer Rebbe: Reb Avrohom Yehoshua Heschel zt'l," www.nishmas.org/gdynasty/chapt17.htm.

46. Heshel, "Chasidic Group of Kopyczynitz."

47. Yosef Katz, "Ha'Admor Ha'Itonai" [The reporter rebbe], *BaKehila,* 9 Shvat 5775 [2015], 37–41.

48. Menachem Brayer, *The House of Rizhin* (New York: Artscroll, 2003), 443–44; and Besser, "Miracle."

49. Kaplan, *Spritual Radical,* 26. See also "This Day in History: 5 Adar, Harav Mordechai Shlomo Friedman of Boyan, *zt"l,*" and "U.S. Orthodox Convention Asks Jewish Federations to Support Yeshivoth," Jewish Telegraphic Agency, November 16, 1965, www.jta.org/1965/11/16/archive/u-s-orthodox-convention-asks-jewish-federations-to-support-yeshivoth.

50. Friedman, *Golden Dynasty;* family member, interview by author, September, 2012.

51. Rabinowitz, *Mishkenot HaRo'im,* 213–20. The wife of the younger son managed to escape on a ship to Palestine, but the vessel sank before its arrival in the Holy Land and she was drowned (227).

52. On Nathalie, see "Paid Notice: Deaths, Friedman, Dr. Nathalie," *New York Times,* October 7, 2001, www.nytimes.com/2001/10/07/classified/paid-notice-deaths-friedman-dr-nathalie.html; "Series B: Rabbi Joseph H. Lookstein Records, 1910, 1928–1979, 1997," Yeshiva University Libraries, Finding Aids Database, accessed March 4, 2015, http://libfindaids.yu.edu:8082/xtf/view?docId=ead/kehilathjeshurun/kehilathjeshurun.xml;query=;brand=default.

53. Mintz, *Hasidic People,* 77.

54. Charles S. Liebman, "Extremism as a Religious Norm," *Journal for the Scientific Study of Religion* 22, no. 1 (1983): 75–86.

55. Mintz, *Hasidic People,* 78.

56. Ibid., 78–80.

57. "A Prince Has Passed," *Circus Tent* (blog), December 23, 2009, http://theantitzemach.blogspot.co.il/2009/12/prince-has-passed.html#links.

58. Mintz, *Hasidic People,* 80.

59. Ibid.; Brayer, *House of Rizhin.*

60. Nachum Dov Breyer, interview by author, January 2013.

61. Mintz, *Hasidic People*, 80.

62. Yair Ettinger, "A Hasid—and a Professor," *Haaretz*, February 7, 2007, www.haaretz.com/print-edition/features/a-hasid-and-a-professor-1.212259.

63. Family member, interview by author, September, 2012. This quotation and others come from this interview.

64. Yerucham Yitzchak Landesman and Aryeh Ehrlich, "Majesty and Mystery in Boyan," *Mishpacha*, March 20, 2013, 51.

65. Quotations, unless otherwise identified, come from my interviews with Nachum Dov Brayer in January 2013.

66. Landesman and Ehrlich, "Majesty and Mystery," 52.

67. Ibid., 52.

68. The first Rebbe of Vizhnitz, Menachem Mendel Hager (1830–84), had been a son-in-law of Yisrael Friedman, the Rebbe of Ruzhin.

69. Psalms 37:23.

70. Nachum Dov Brayer, interview by author.

71. Emile Durkheim, *The Elementary Forms of the Religious Life,* trans. J. W. Swain (New York: Free Press, 1965), 216–19, 226.

72. See ibid., 236.

73. Interview by author, January 2013. Unless otherwise noted all quotations from Schneid are from interviews by the author.

74. Interview by author, January 15, 2014.

75. David Landau, *Piety and Power* (New York: Hill and Wang, 1993), 55.

76. Ibid.

77. Ibid., 57.

78. Ibid., 61.

79. Ibid., 67.

80. To be sure, the fact that about 64 percent of the working-age men and 46 percent of the working-age women were unemployed according to the 2010 census suggests that economically supporting those neighborhoods will be a significant challenge for the Boyaner community. See Paul Rivlin, *The Israeli Economy from the Foundation of the State through the 21st Century* (Cambridge: Cambridge University Press, 2011), 169.

81. Dovid Rossoff, *Kedoshim asher B'Aretz* [The Holy Ones in the earth] (Jerusalem: Machon Otzar HaTorah, 2005), 316. See also Rabinowitz, *Mishkenot HaRo'im*, 136.

82. Yair Ettinger, "Dr. Brayer and the Admor of Boyan," *Haaretz*, February 6, 2007, www.haaretz.co.il/misc/1.1384019.

83. "Majesty and Mystery," 56.

4. BOBOV

1. Many of the details in this chapter come from many hours of interviews with insiders to Bobov who asked to remain unacknowledged and anonymous.

2. Mayer Amsel, "Eleh Toldos Admorei Bobov" [These are the generations of the leaders of Bobov], in *Hamaor* (Brooklyn, NY: Balshon, 1974), 81, www.hebrewbooks.org/pdfpager.aspx?req=36015&st=&pgnum=81.

3. Hirshel Tzig, "Read This Book and You'll See Why What's Happening in Bobov Today Is a Crying Shame," *Circus Tent* (blog), November 4, 2014, http://theantitzemach.blogspot.com/search?q=Bobov.

4. Antony Polonsky, "Tarnów," in *YIVO Encyclopedia of Jews in Eastern Europe,* ed. Gershon David Hundert, 2010, www.yivoencyclopedia.org/article .aspx/Tarnow, and Sean Martin, "Kraków: Kraków after 1795," in Hundert, *YIVO Encyclopedia,* www.yivoencyclopedia.org/article.aspx/Krakow/Krakow_ after_1795.

5. On the mix of Hasidic rebbes and more cosmopolitan Jews in Marienbad, see Mirjam Zadoff, *Next Year in Marienbad: The Lost Worlds of Jewish Spa Culture* (Philadelphia: University of Pennsylvania Press, 2012).

6. Amsel, "Eleh Toldos Admorei Bobov," 83.

7. Devora Gliksman, *Nor the Moon by Night* (New York: Feldheim, 1997), 33, 123.

8. Amsel, "Eleh Toldos Admorei Bobov," 89.

9. Ibid., 94.

10. Esther Farbstein, *Hidden in Thunder,* trans. Deborah Stern, vol. 1 (Jerusalem: Mossad Harav Kook, 2007), 104.

11. Amsel, "Eleh Toldos Admorei Bobov," 97.

12. Gliksman, *Nor the Moon by Night,* 104–7.

13. "19 km from Auschwitz: The Story of Trzebinia," the section "Before the War: Religious Life. The Bobover Rebbe, Rabbi Ben Zion bar Shlomo Halberstam (1874–1941)," Yad Vashem, n.d., accessed October 9, 2013, www.yadvashem .org/yv/en/exhibitions/communities/trzebinia/religious_life_halberstam.asp. A film purporting to show this execution is posted on YouTube, *Bobover Rebbe Ben Zion Halberstam at the Last Moments of His Life?,* uploaded September 22, 2009, www.youtube.com/watch?feature=player_embedded&v=jbBGjG6cMcY.

14. Amsel, "Eleh Toldos Admorei Bobov," 118; Gliksman, *Nor the Moon by Night,* 34.

15. "19 km from Auschwitz."

16. Gliksman, *Nor the Moon by Night,* 101.

17. Amsel, "Eleh Toldos Admorei Bobov," 119.

18. Gliksman, *Nor the Moon by Night,* 130.

19. Ibid., 144.

20. "Koprzywnica," Virtuelles Schtetl, n.d., accessed October 9, 2013, www.sztetl.org.pl/de/article/koprzywnica/6,demografie/. See also Amsel, "Eleh Toldos Admorei Bobov," 120.

21. Gliksman, *Nor the Moon by Night,* 149.

22. Ibid., 150.

23. She was the daughter of Shulem Halberstam, the Ratzferder Rebbe.

24. Amsel, "Eleh Toldos Admorei Bobov," 123–24.

25. Maier Orian, *Madregot be'olama shel hasidut* [Ranks in the Hasidic world] (Jerusalem: Masada, 1975), 128–29.

26. See, for example, Gliksman, *Nor the Moon by Night,* 130, 149, 195.

27. Amsel, "Eleh Toldos Admorei Bobov," 127.

28. Ibid.

29. Ibid., 128.

30. Ibid., 129.

31. Ibid., 132.

32. Quoted in ibid., 133. See also Yated Ne'eman, "Borough Park, NY: The Life and Legacy of Rabbi Shlomo Halberstam, Zt'l, The 'Tzadik' That Rebuild the 'Bobov' Dynasty in America," *Vos Iz Neias,* August 1, 2008, www.vosizneias .com/18763/2008/08/01/borough-park-ny-the-legacy-and-life-of-rabbi-shlomo-halberstam-zt%E2%80%9Dl-the-tzadik-that-rebuild-the-bobov-dynasty-in-america/.

33. Gliksman, *Nor the Moon by Night,* 257.

34. Amsel, "Eleh Toldos Admorei Bobov," 137.

35. It is estimated that approximately 15,000 Jews were deported from Bochnia, with at least a further 1,800 killed in the town and its surroundings. "Bochnia Ghetto," updated May 28, 2006, www.deathcamps.org/occupation /bochnia%20ghetto.html.

36. Gliksman, *Nor the Moon by Night,* 348.

37. Radu Ioanid, *The Ransom of the Jews: The Story of the Extraordinary Secret Bargain between Romania and Israel* (Chicago: Ivan R. Dee, 2005), 23.

38. Amsel, "Eleh Toldos Admorei Bobov," 150.

39. Ibid.; Ioanid, *Ransom of the Jews,* 15.

40. Gliksman, *Nor the Moon by Night,* 376–77.

41. "Only 30,000 Aged Jews Remain in Budapest, Says Refugee Who Fled City Last Week," Jewish Telegraphic Agency, January 16, 1945, www.jta .org/1945/01/16/archive/only-30000-aged-jews-remain-in-budapest-says-refu-gee-who-fled-city-last-week. See also Kristian Ungvary, *Battle for Budapest: One Hundred Days in World War II* (2002; repr., London: I.B. Tauris, 2011), 137.

42. Gliksman, *Nor the Moon by Night,* 456.

43. For a family tree, see "Halberstam Family Tree," n.d., accessed March 3, 2013, www.loebtree.com/halbs.html.

44. Gliksman, *Nor the Moon by Night,* 458.

45. See more at Susanna Kokkonen, "Jewish Displaced Persons in Postwar Italy, 1945–1951," *Jewish Political Studies Review* 20, nos. 1–2 (Spring 2008), Jerusalem Center for Public Affairs, http://jcpa.org/article/jewish-displaced-persons-in-postwar-italy-1945–1951.

46. Amsel, "Eleh Toldos Admorei Bobov," 157.

47. Pinny Dunner, interview by author, March 10, 2013.

48. William Rubenstein et al., eds., *The Palgrave Dictionary of Anglo-Jewish History* (London: Macmillan, 2011), 299.

49. Gliksman, *Nor the Moon by Night,* 466–67.

50. Family member, interview by author, November 13, 2013. Many of the details of the Bobovers in America come from this source.

51. See Adam Bartosz, "From the House of Chaim," Muzeum Okregowe w Tarnowe, n.d., accessed January 20, 2014, www.muzeum.tarnow.pl/artykul .php?id=61&typ=5.

52. "500 Orthodox Jews Wish Leader Bon Voyage at Pier," *New York Times,* October 24, 1963.

53. Peter Hellman, "The Devout Raise a City within a City and Prosper," *New York Times,* September 15, 1995, www.nytimes.com/1995/09/15/arts

/the-devout-raise-a-city-within-a-city-and-prosper.html?pagewanted= all&src=pm.

54. Bernard Weinraub, "In Brooklyn, Shadow of Jackson Follows Gore," *New York Times,* April 11, 1988, www.nytimes.com/1988/04/11/us/in-brooklyn-shadow-of-jackson-follows-gore.html.

55. Blaine Harden, "Grand Rabbi Shlomo Halberstam, 92, Is Dead," *New York Times,* August 3, 2000, www.nytimes.com/2000/08/03/nyregion /grand-rabbi-shlomo-halberstam-92-is-dead.html.

56. Ibid.

57. Ibid.

58. See, for example, Jane Ridley, *The Heir Apparent* (New York: Random House, 2013), on how waiting shaped the life and reign of Edward VII.

59. Lawrence Joffe, "Rabbi Shlomo Halberstam: After Escaping the Nazis He Revived an Entire Jewish Sect," *Guardian Leader,* September 2, 2000, 22.

60. Naftali was the son of Shlomo and his wife (also his cousin) Bluma Teitelbaum, who perished in the Holocaust. Ben Zion was the son of Shlomo and his second wife, Friedel Rubin (also a cousin).

61. Pinny Dunner, personal communication to author, March 11, 2013.

62. Joffe, "Rabbi Shlomo Halberstam," 22.

63. For the text and video, see *K"K Admor'Bobov Shlita Hachtura,* May 29, 2007, www.consultmi.com/bobov/hachtura.html.

64. The translation is the author's. Some minor adjustments have been made to conform with English syntax and speech.

65. Andy Newman, "A Battle for Succession Takes No Holiday," *New York Times,* March 26, 2005, www.nytimes.com/2005/03/26/nyregion/26rabbi .html?_r=0.

66. *The Pentateuch and Rashi's Commentary,* ed. Abraham Ben Isaiah and Benjamin Sharfman (Brookline, MA: S. S. & R, 1949).

67. The term *Shlita* is actually an acronym and stands for the words "Shey-ichye L'orech Yamim Tovim Aruchim" (May he live many long and good days).

68. See "Mordechai David Unger," n.d., accessed December 30, 2016, www .worldlibrary.org/articles/mordechai_david_unger.

69. See, for example, "After 8 Years, Warring Bobov Hasidic Factions Settle Half of Dispute," *Failed Messiah* (blog), February 13, 2013, http://failedmessiah .typepad.com/failed_messiahcom/2013/02/after-8-years-warring-bobov-fac-tions-settle-half-of-dispute-456.html. For a film clip, see *Bobov Fights Yid Bies Uder in 48 Shul with Police,* YouTube, uploaded August 24, 2010, www .youtube.com/watch?v=DF3iUrPUX80.

70. Newman, "Battle for Succession."

71. Pinny Dunner, interview by author, March 10, 2013. There were a variety of explanations for his support. Some suggested that he represented Shlomo's first family, who believed that once the *rebistve* went to Benzion Aryeh Leib it would leave that family out in the cold. Others suggested that Dunner had been insulted by a request from Benzion that a dinner in Dunner's honor in 2004 that had been planned on the anniversary of the passing of the Third Rebbe should be canceled because it was unseemly to use that day as time for fund-raising and

because the event had been instigated as an act of personal pique supporting Benzion's rival. That dinner, planned in the last year of Naftali's life, when his health prohibited him from attending, would have also made his sons-in-law, who often stood in for Naftali, appear to be the heirs apparent, something those supporting Benzion Aryeh Leib did not want to allow.

72. Luke Salkeld, "'God's Postman' Who Gave Away Millions Snorted Cocaine before He Died in 80mph Bentley Smash," *Daily Mail,* August 6, 2008, www.dailymail.co.uk/news/article-1041830/Gods-postman-gave-away-millions-snorted-cocaine-died-80mph-Bentley-crash.html.

73. "Englander Foundation: Total Gifts over Time," Million Dollar List, n.d., accessed January 14, 2014, www.milliondollarlist.org/donors/englander-foundation. Money is of course a key element in maintaining a *rebistve* and a court. Bobov has had its share of problems on this front: perhaps the most troubling was an accusation of money laundering against the Shaarei Zion Synagogue, Bobov 48's main headquarters. See Josh Margolin, "B'klyn Hasid Temple a $inagogue: FBI," June 18, 2012, http://nypost.com/2012/06/18/bklyn-hasid-temple-a-in-agogue-fbi/.

74. See Benzion dancing with Englander in *Bobov Rebbe 48 Dances with Duddy Roth & Izzy Englander on Purim,* YouTube, uploaded March 8, 2015, https://www.youtube.com/watch?v=3h-89ht-wTE, and the *Ah Blick* magazine tweet "Philanthropist billionaire Izzy Englander flew to Miami this morning to Daven Rosh Chodesh with C"k Admo"r M'Bobov," November 23, 2014, https://twitter.com/ahblicklive/status/536553215916253184.

75. On Schlaff, see Gidi Weitz, "The Schlaff Saga," *Haaretz,* September 7, 2010, www.haaretz.com/weekend/2.283/the-schlaff-saga-the-mysterious-billionaire-who-shuns-the-media-1.312798. Obstfeld became the subject of negative news stories when he was found to have plunged from the nineteenth floor of the posh Essex House in Manhattan. See Alison Gendar and Kerry Burke, "Shady, 'Thuggish' Mogul Solomon Obstfeld Ran with Powerful Pals, No One's Buying Suicide Story," *New York Daily News,* June 18, 2010, www.nydailynews.com/new-york/shady-thuggish-mogul-solomon-obstfeld-ran-powerful-pals-buying-suicide-story-article-1.180707.

76. "London: Thousands Attend Kabolas Ponim," YeshivaWorld.com, January 3, 2007, www.theyeshivaworld.com/news/uncategorized/4466/london-thousands-attend-kabolas-ponim.html.

77. Bobov website, photo gallery, accessed January 17, 2014, www.consultmi.com/bobov/photo.html.

78. See, for example, FrumPics, www.frumpics.com/, accessed January 17, 2014; "Video—Bobover Rebbe, Rav Bentzion Halberstam at Simchas Bais HaShoeva," YeshivaWorld.com, October 26, 2008, www.theyeshivaworld.com/news/category/bichatzros-hakodesh/page/23; "Photos: Bobover Rebbe Visits Lakewood," *Lakewood Scoop,* June 17, 2013, www.thelakewoodscoop.com/news/2013/06/photos-bobover-rebbe-visits-lakewood.html.

79. See, for example, "Politicians Paying Their Respects of Bobover Rebbe Z"tl," *Chaptzem* (blog), March 31, 2005, http://chaptzem.blogspot.com/2005_03_01_archive.html, and "Photos: NYC Mayoral Candidate Bill

Thompson Visiting the Bobover Rebbe (45)," YeshivaWorld.com, September 3, 2013, www.theyeshivaworld.com/news/nyc/184293/photos-nyc-mayoral-candidate-bill-thompson-visiting-the-bobover-rebbe-45.html.

80. Shlomo Greenwald, "Bet Din on the Clock," *Jewish Press,* March 21, 2012, www.jewishpress.com/indepth/interviews-and-profiles/bet-din-on-the-clock-nathan-lewin-wants-jewish-courts-to-run-more-efficiently/2012/03/21/0/?print. See also Trademark Trial and Appeal Board, Congregation Talmud Torah D'Chasidei of Monsey v. United Bobov International, Inc., filed April 21, 2005, for the mark BOBOV, published September 12, 2006, www.likelihoodof confusion.com/wp-content/uploads/2007/04/bobov-78614126-monsey .pdf.

81. "Bobov Dispute Heads into Final Stage at Din Torah, Not Secular Court," *Vos Iz Neies,* November 23, 2009, http://archive.is/ya3CT.

82. See Trademark Trial and Appeal Board, Congregation Talmud Torah D'Chasidei of Monsey v. United Bobov International, Inc.

83. Behadrei Haredim forum, "Din Torah Zeit aus gut fir Bobov" [The court case looks good for Bobov)], www.bhol.co.il/forum/topic.asp?topic_id=2300219& forum_id=13951, posted October 24, 2007.

84. See the comments at *Bobov Fights,* accessed December 19, 2013, www .youtube.com/watch?v=DF3iUrPUX80.

85. Shlomo Shamir, "A Hasidic Sect Discovers Democracy," *Haaretz,* September 24, 2007.

86. See, for example, Trademark Trial and Appeal Board, Congregation Talmud Torah D'Chasidei of Monsey, v. United Bobov International, Inc.; and "First Round of Bobover Din Torah Commences," *Chaptzem* (blog), June 26, 2005, http://chaptzem.blogspot.com/2005/06/first-round-of-bobover-din-torah .html.

87. "B'Olomom shel Haredim," *The World of the Ultra-Orthodox* (blog), August 26, 2014, http://bshch.blogspot.com/2014/08/blog-post_4908.html?m=1, accessed August 29, 2014.

88. The water used in matzah baking must be left to stand overnight (to ensure that it is allowed to cool). This water is then referred to as *mayim shelanu* (water that has "slept"). Rabbi Yaakov Horowitz, "Getting to Know Your Matzah," n.d., accessed January 8, 2014, http://oukosher.org/passover/articles /getting-to-know-your-matzah/.

89. Sigmund Freud, *Civilization and Its Discontents,* ed. and trans. James Strachey (1930; repr., New York: W. W. Norton, 1961), 60.

90. "Bobov 45 Launches Boycott of Businesses That Receive Kosher Supervision From Beit Din Judge Who Ruled against It," *Failed Messiah* (blog), August 31, 2014, http://failedmessiah.typepad.com/failed_messiahcom/2014/08 /bobov-45-launches-boycott-of-businesses-that-receive-kosher-supervision-from-beit-din-judge-who-rule-123.html.

91. *Rebbe of Bobov 45 We Will Assume the Distinction of "Bobov 45,"* YouTube, uploaded November 24, 2014, https://www.youtube.com/watch?v= LcBJOw4IjWg&feature=youtu.be.

92. *Powerful Speech by the Bobov Rebbe after Latest Ruling,* YouTube, uploaded August 27, 2014, https://www.youtube.com/watch?v=iatPf1SptVc.

93. "Bobov 45 Sues Bobov 48 in Israeli Secular Court," *Failed Messiah* (blog), August 25, 2014, http://failedmessiah.typepad.com/failed_messiahcom /2014/08/bobov45-sues-bobov-48-in-israeli-secular-court-234.html.

94. "New Bobov Bans and Legal Maneuvering," *Failed Messiah* (blog), June 3, 2013, http://failedmessiah.typepad.com/failed_messiahcom/2013/06/new-bobov-bans-and-legal-maneuvering-234.html. A photograph of a poster in Yiddish reviewing these bans is shown within the post.

95. For a testimony of a Hasid about his attraction to Bobov, see Hadad ben Badad's post "Nisht kein bari u'nisht kein shema: mein einige meinung" [Neither a certainty nor a possibility: My own interpretation], to the forum Kave Shtiebel, December 11, 2013, www.kaveshtiebel.com/viewtopic.php?f=5&t= 5402.

5. SATMAR

1. US Census Bureau, Quick Facts, accessed October 6, 2014, http:// quickfacts.census.gov/qfd/states/36/3639853.html. The 8.5 percent growth rate in the Satmar community of Kiryas Joel compares with a 1.4 percent rise in New York State as a whole in the same period. "The House of Satmar," *Jerusalem Post*, September 6, 2007, www.jpost.com/Local-Israel/In-Jerusalem/ The-house-of-Satmar. Families or households may have nine or more children.

2. *Der Yid*, October 8, 2014, http://satmarnews.files.wordpress.com/2012/03 /d791d79cd795d79ed799d7a0d792d791d795d7a8d792.pdf. See also "Bloomingburg will Hold Dissolution Vote Today," *Times Herald-Record*, September 30, 2014, www.recordonline.com/apps/pbcs.dll/article?AID=/20140929/NEWS /14092973; Eva McKend, "Court Order Will Delay Results of Bloomingburg Dissolution Vote," *TWC News*, October 1, 2014, www.twcnews.com/archives /nys/hudson-valley/2014/09/30/court-order-will-delay-results-of-blooming burg-dissolution-vote-NY_773111.old.html; Andrew Beam, "Bloomingburg Dissolution Revote Possible," *Times Herald Record*, January 5, 2015, www .recordonline.com/article/20150105/NEWS/150109729.

In 2007, when Skvir Hasidim tried to establish a village named Kiryas Square in the same Mamakating area, the opposition was successful. Joseph Berger, *The Pious Ones* (New York: Harper, 2014), 288.

3. Menachem Keren-Kratz, "Rabbi Yoel Teitelbaum: The Satmar Rebbe, 1887–1979, A Biography" [in Hebrew] (PhD diss., Tel Aviv University, 2012), 36n6.

4. Ibid., 37. See also Yekutiel Yehudah Greenwald, *Matzevas Kodesh* (New York: Hadar, 1952), 29.

5. "This Day in History: 8 Tishrei/September 12, Harav Elazar Nissan Teitelbaum of Drobich, zt"l," *HaModia*, September 11, 2013, http://hamodia .com/features/this-day-in-history-8-tishreiseptember-12/.

6. See Michael Silber, "'There Are No Yeshivot in Our Country—for Several Good Reasons': Between Hasidim and Mitnagdim in Hungary" [in Hebrew], https://www.academia.edu/3219774/There_are_no_Yeshivot_in_our_Coun try_for_Several_Good_Reasons_Between_Hasidim_and_Mitnagdim_in_Hun gary_Hebrew_.

7. Keren-Kratz, "Rabbi Yoel Teitelbaum," 39.

8. This is the same man from whom the Bobover Rebbes also traced their origins.

9. Chananya Yom Tov Lipa of Sighet, *Kedushat Yom Tov* (Brooklyn, NY: Yerushalayim, 2001), Shemot 42c. Thanks to Benjamin Brown for this reference.

10. Menachem Keren-Kratz, "Marmaros: The Cradle of Extreme Orthodoxy," *Modern Judaism* 35, no. 2 (2015): 147–74.

11. Shlomo Yaakov Gelbman, *Moshian shel Yisrael* [Savior of Israel] [in Hebrew] (Kiryas Joel, NY: Ohel Torah, 1989–2008), 1:42. See also Dovid Meisels, *The Rebbe: The Extraordinary Life and Worldview of Rabbeinu Yoel Teitelbaum,* trans. Yirmiyahu Cohen, 3rd ed. (Lakewood, NJ: Israel Book Shop, 2011), 17.

12. See the discussion on Munkács in chapter 2 of this book.

13. Meisels, *Rebbe,* 19.

14. Keren-Kratz, "Rabbi Yoel Teitelbaum," 42. See also "Moshe HaCohen Rubinstein," Geni, n.d., accessed February 5, 2014, www.geni.com/people/Moshe-HaCohen-Rubinstein/6000000006712229228?through=6000000006712229223.

15. Keren-Kratz, "Rabbi Yoel Teitelbaum," 44.

16. Ibid.

17. Meisels, *Rebbe,* 23–25. See also Allan Nadler, "The Riddle of Satmar," *Jewish Ideas Daily,* February 17, 2011, www.jewishideasdaily.com/824/features/the-riddle-of-the-satmar/.

18. Keren-Kratz, "Rabbi Yoel Teitelbaum," 47.

19. According to one source, she threw a kitchen knife at her older son in her anger. See ibid., 47n106, citing Chaim Lieberman, *Der Rebbe und der Satan: Satmar und di Neturei Karta und Zayer Milchama oyf Medinas Yisrael* [The rebbe and the Satan: Satmar and the Neturei Karta and their war against the state of Israel] (Jerusalem: Committee for Israel, 1959).

20. See above, the discussions on Munkács and Boyan in chapters 2 and 3 respectively.

21. Keren-Kratz, "Rabbi Yoel Teitelbaum," 45.

22. Ibid., 46. For a list of the rabbis who conferred the title upon him, see n101.

23. On the role of Marienbad in Hasidic life, see Mirjam Zadoff, *Next Year in Marienbad: The Lost Worlds of Jewish Spa Culture,* trans. William Templer (Philadelphia: University of Pennsylvania Press, 2012).

24. Keren-Kratz, "Rabbi Yoel Teitelbaum." See also Allan Nadler, "Satmar Hasidic Dynasty," in *YIVO Encyclopedia of the Jews in Eastern Europe,* ed. Gershon David Hundert, 2010, www.yivoencyclopedia.org/article.aspx/satmar_hasidic_dynasty.

25. Keren-Kratz, "Rabbi Yoel Teitelbaum," 49.

26. Ibid., 55.

27. Ibid., 58.

28. Ibid., 68.

29. Ibid., 174–77.

30. Ibid., 82–83.

31. Jerome Mintz, *Hasidic People: A Place in the New World* (Cambridge, MA: Harvard University Press, 1992), 88–89.

32. Keren-Kratz, "Rabbi Yoel Teitelbaum," 86.

33. Chaim Moshe Stauber, *The Satmar Rebbe* (New York: Feldheim, 2011), 53. Levi Yitzchak Greenwald, who replaced Yoelish in Orshiva, carried on his predecessor's emphasis on stringency in observance and instituted such observances as *Cholov Yisrael* (all kosher dairy products must come from kosher animal species, but this requirement adds that dairy products must derive from milk that has been milked under the supervision of an observant Jew) and the more demanding standards of *Glatt Kosher*.

34. Keren-Kratz, "Rabbi Yoel Teitelbaum," 87–88.

35. Ibid., 88–89.

36. Ibid., 94.

37. Ibid., 99–100, and Stauber, *Satmar Rebbe*, 66.

38. Keren-Kratz, "Rabbi Yoel Teitelbaum," 101.

39. Nadler, "Satmar Hasidic Dynasty."

40. Keren-Kratz, "Rabbi Yoel Teitelbaum," 106.

41. Ibid.

42. Stauber, *Satmar Rebbe*, 76–77.

43. See Lewis Coser, *The Functions of Social Conflict* (New York: Free Press, 1956), 31.

44. J.C. Turner, "Social Identification and Psychological Group Formation," In *The Social Dimension: European Developments in Social Psychology*, ed. Henri Tajifel (Cambridge: Cambridge University Press, 1984), 2:530.

45. Stauber, *Satmar Rebbe*, 79.

46. Ibid., 164.

47. See Menachem M. Friedman, *Society in a Crisis of Legitimization: The Ashkenazi Old Yishuv—1900–1917* [in Hebrew] (Jerusalem: Mossad Byalik and Israeli Academy of Science 2001), 31–50.

48. I thank Menachem Friedman and Menachem Keren-Kratz for opening my eyes to this.

49. Keren-Kratz, "Rabbi Yoel Teitelbaum," 149.

50. Ibid., 207.

51. Stauber, *Satmar Rebbe*, 73–74.

52. See, for example, Yehoshua Bar Yossef, *MiZefat l'Yerushalayim* [From Safed to Jerusalem] (Jerusalem: Mossad Bialik, 1972), 107.

53. Keren-Kratz, "Rabbi Yoel Teitelbaum," 128–29.

54. Stauber, *Satmar Rebbe*, 75, 86.

55. Ibid., 82.

56. Menashe Koenig, *Zichronos Rambach* [Memoirs of Rabbi Menashe ben Chaim Koenig] (Jerusalem: self published, 1998), 92; Meisels, *Rebbe*, 57.

57. Elimelech Ozer Bodek, *Tifferes Yoel* (Brooklyn, NY: Z. Berman Books, 2003), 3:68; Meisels, *Rebbe*, 57.

58. Koenig, *Zichronos Rambach*, 91; and Meisels, *Rebbe*, 57.

59. She was known generally as "Feige."

60. Mintz, *Hasidic People*, 88.

61. Meisels, *Rebbe*, 60; Koenig, *Zichronos Rambach*, 97.

62. Keren-Kratz, "Rabbi Yoel Teitelbaum," 36, 235. Roysaele died and was buried in New York. Her body was later transferred for burial in Israel, against her father's wishes. When he visited Israel, he refused to visit her grave there.

63. Mintz, *Hasidic People,* 383n2.

64. Menachem Keren-Kratz, "Hast Thou Escaped and Also Taken Possession? The Responses of the Satmar Rebbe—Rabbi Yoel Teitelbaum—and His Followers to Criticism of His Conduct during and after the Holocaust," *Dapim: Studies on the Holocaust* 28, no. 2 (2014): 97–120.

65. See, for example, Yoel Teitelbaum, *Chidushei Torah u'Drashot* [Torah novellae and sermons] (Brooklyn, NY: Yerushalayim, 1977), 227–38.

66. Keren-Kratz, "Rabbi Yoel Teitelbaum," 186; Randolph Braham, *The Destruction of Hungarian Jewry: A Documentary Account,* 2 vols. (New York: Pro Arte, 1963).

67. Stauber, *Satmar Rebbe,* 90. See also "Hungary before the German Occupation: Hungary after World War I," in *Holocaust Encyclopedia,* ed. US Holocaust Memorial Museum, n.d., accessed February 20, 2014, www.ushmm.org/wlc/en/article.php?ModuleId=10005457. See also Jürgen Matthäus and Mark Roseman, *Jewish Responses to Persecution,* vol. 2, *1938–1940* (Lanham, MD: AltaMira Press, 2011), 285–86.

68. Yisachar Shlomo Teichtal, *Eim Habanim Smeicha* [Happy is the mother of sons] (Katzberg: Budapest, 1943), 212. See also Yitzchak Hershkovits, "Elbon HaTorahHaGadol Halozeh: Giluim Chadashim al Pulmus Brichat HaRabanim mi Budapest 1944" [The great Torah affront: New revelations regarding the escape of Great Rabbis from Budapest, 1944], Yad Vashem Archives, 37–1 2009 110–89.

69. Meisels, *Rebbe,* 93; Gelbman, *Moshian shel Yisrael,* 7:132.

70. Gelbman, *Moshian shel Yisrael,* 6:418.

71. Meisels, *Rebbe,* 94, and Yoel Teitelbaum, *Vayoel Moshe* (Brooklyn, NY: Yerushalayim, 2005), 1:111. See also Keren-Kratz, "Rabbi Yoel Teitelbaum," 162n544.

72. J.L. Jacob, *Sefer Derech HaMelech* [The king's road] (Jerusalem: self-published, 2007), 1:435. See also Keren-Kratz, "Rabbi Yoel Teitelbaum."

73. Gelbman, *Moshian shel Yisrael,* 7:518–21. A similar request was made of Boruch Rabinovich, the Rebbe of Munkács, who likewise refused.

74. Esther Farbstein, *Hidden in Thunder,* trans Deborah Stern, vol. 1 (Jerusalem: Mossad Harav Kook, 2007), 98.

75. Stauber, *Satmar Rebbe,* 95–97; Meisels, *Rebbe,* 106–7.

76. Stauber, *Satmar Rebbe,* 102.

77. Meisels, *Rebbe,* 115, citing an item in *Der Yid,* November 6, 2006.

78. Stauber, *Satmar Rebbe,* 104. See also Zvi Hersh Friedman, *Sefer Me'Afela L'Or Gadol* [From darkness to great light] (Kiryas Joel, NY: self-published, 2004), 1:148–49, and Meisels, *Rebbe,* 114.

79. Stauber, *Satmar Rebbe,* 110–17.

80. Meisels, *Rebbe,* 115–16, 120; Stauber, *Satmar Rebbe,* 107–9.

81. Farbstein, *Hidden in Thunder,* 1:100.

82. Meisels, *Rebbe,* 122–23; Stauber, *Satmar Rebbe,* 118–27.

83. Farbstein, *Hidden in Thunder,* 1:102.

84. Keren-Kratz, "HaRabbi MiSatmar v'Rakevet Kasztner," unpublished ms.

85. Yoel Teitelbaum, *Letters* (privately published by Satmar for themselves, n.d.), 1:192–94. Thanks too to Menachem Keren-Kratz for suggesting this second reason for the rebbe's decision to avoid Satmar after the war.

86. Meisels, *Rebbe*, 124, 67; cf. Gelbman, *Moshian shel Yisrael*, 9:165.

87. Gelbman, *Moshian shel Yisrael*, 9:214–21.

88. Meisels, *Rebbe*, 93.

89. Stauber, *Satmar Rebbe*, 39; Nadler, "Riddle of Satmar."

90. Stauber, *Satmar Rebbe*, 139n166.

91. *Der Morgan Djurnal*, July 11, 1945, 8.

92. Meisels, *Rebbe*, 127.

93. *Algemeiner Journal*, August 24, 1979, 13.

94. Shaul Magid, "'America Is No Different,' 'America Is Different': Is There an American Jewish Fundamentalism? Part II. American Satmar," in *Fundamentalism: Perspectives on a Contested History*, ed. S.A. Wood and D.W. Harrington (Columbia: University of South Carolina Press, 2014).

95. See "No Thanks to Kastner," *True Torah Jews* (blog), November 6, 2009, www.truetorahjews.org/kastner.

96. Yoel Teitelbaum, *VaYoel Moshe*, § 111, p. 124.

97. See Pinchas Peli, *Agudat ha-sofrim ha-Ivrim be-Yisrael* (Jerusalem: Snif Yerushalayim, 1979), 11–12, 105–25. See also Steven T. Katz, ed., *Wrestling with God: Jewish Theological Responses during and after the Holocaust* (New York: Oxford University Press, 2007), 251, n35; Teitelbaum, *VaYoel Moshe*, 5.

98. Michael Powell, "Hats On, Gloves Off," *New York Magazine*, May 8, 2006, http://nymag.com/news/cityside/16864/. See also Harry Gersh, "Satmar: A Zealot Community," *Commentary*, November 1, 1959.

99. See, for example, Michael Idov, "Clash of the Bearded Ones," *New York Magazine*, April 11, 2010, http://nymag.com/realestate/neighborhoods/2010/65356/.

100. George Kranzler, *Hasidic Williamsburg: A Contemporary American Hasidic Community* (Northvale, NJ: Jason Aronson, 1995), 164.

101. Meisels, *Rebbe*, 148, quoting Shlomo Yaakov Gelbman, *Retzon Zaddik* [Desires of a *zaddik*] (Kiryas Joel, NY: Executive Printers, 1998), 5–6.

102. Meisels, *Rebbe*, 159; Gelbman, *Moshian shel Yisrael*, 3:247.

103. Meisels, *Rebbe*, 148, quoting Gelbman, *Retzon Tzaddik*, 5–6.

104. Meisels, *Rebbe*, 148, quoting Gelbman, *Retzon Tzaddik*, 6.

105. Meisels, *Rebbe*, 150. Cf. Ben Zion Yakobovitch, *Zechor Yemos Olam* [Remember the days] (B'nai B'rak: self-published, 1997).

106. Kranzler, *Hasidic Williamsburg*, 106.

107. Ironically, many years later, Satmar Rebbes would, on their vacations in Palm Springs, actually hold their own prayers in the ChaBaD Lubavitch synagogue there. See Hirshel Tzig, "Ahhh, vi geshmak iz tsu zitsen skhs sansu in falm sfring," *Circus Tent* (blog), January 8, 2013, http://theantitzemach.blogspot.com/2013/01/blog-post_8.html.

108. Meisels, *Rebbe*, 150. To this day, Satmar neighborhoods are marked by people for whom Yiddish is the primary language. See "Language Barrier

Continues to Thwart Victims of Crimes," *New York Times,* May 12, 2014, www.nytimes.com/2014/05/12/nyregion/language-barrier-continues-to-thwart-victims-of-crimes.html. The map shows Hasidic Williamsburg as over-whelmingly Yiddish-speaking.

109. Meisels, *Rebbe,* 154.

110. Nadler, "Satmar Hasidic Dynasty."

111. Israel Rubin, *Satmar: An Island in the City* (New York: Quadrangle Books, 1972).

112. See "Satmar Chasidim," Religion Case Reporter, n.d., accessed May 29, 2014, www.paradigmpub.com/Subscriber/NonSubscriberViewIndex.aspx?indexCode=satmar.

113. Mintz, *Hasidic People,* 29.

114. Stauber, *Satmar Rebbe,* 182; Meisels, *Rebbe,* 486.

115. Berger, *Pious Ones,* 42.

116. Meisels, *Rebbe,* 349.

117. Ibid., 350–51.

118. Ibid., 358.

119. Ibid., 356–59.

120. Stauber, *Satmar Rebbe,* 195, quoting Divrei Yoel, *Letters,* vol. 1, pt. 1, letter 69.

121. Solomon Poll, *The Hasidic Community of Williamsburg* (New York: Free Press, 1962), 135.

122. Idov, "Clash of the Bearded Ones."

123. For an interesting account of the issues, see "My Experimental Phase," a documentary in the series *This American Life,* episode 268, June 25, 2004, about a Hasid who became a rock musician named Curly Oxide; www.thisamericanlife.org/radio-archives/episode/268/my-experimental-phase. See also Idov, "Clash of the Bearded Ones."

124. Meisels, *Rebbe,* 532.

125. Ibid., 531.

126. Stauber, *Satmar Rebbe,* 176. See also "Brooklyn Hasidim Believed Planning Large Colony at Upstate Resort Site," *New York Times,* September 16, 1974, and Meisels, *Rebbe,* 546–48.

127. Stauber, *Satmar Rebbe,* 287.

128. See, for example, Meisels, *Rebbe,* 561; Mintz, *Hasidic People,* 85; *Algemeiner Journal,* August 31, 1979, 1.

129. Keren-Kratz, "Rabbi Yoel Teitelbaum," 307.

130. Zalman Alpert, "Faige Teitelbaum, 1912–2001," in *Jewish Women: A Comprehensive Historical Encyclopedia,* Jewish Women's Archive, n.d., accessed May 19, 2014, http://jwa.org/encyclopedia/article/teitelbaum-faige.

131. Meisels, *Rebbe,* 557–58.

132. Ibid., 562. See also *Algemeiner Journal,* August 31, 1979, 9.

133. Mintz, *Hasidic People,* 134.

134. *Algemeiner Journal,* March 23, 1979, 6.

135. Powell, "Hats On, Gloves Off." There was a case of a woman who sought to be a rebbe—Edel, the daughter of Aharon Rokach, the Fourth Belzer

Rebbe—but this is a whole different kind of story. See Yitzchak Buxbaum, *Jewish Tales of Holy Women* (San Francisco: Jossey Bass, 2002).

136. *Algemeiner Journal,* August 31, 1979, 9.

137. I thank Zalman Alpert, who in a personal communication offers this analysis and these facts.

138. Mintz, *Hasidic People,* 90.

139. Powell, "Hats On, Gloves Off."

140. *Der Yid,* August 31, 1979, 2.

141. "Rabbi Joel Teitelbaum Dies at 92; Leader of Satmar Hasidic Sect," *New York Times,* August 20, 1979, http://query.nytimes.com/mem/archive/pdf?res=F30913FD385D12728DDDA90A94D0405B898BF1D3.

142. *Der Yid,* August 31, 1979, front page.

143. *Der Yid,* August 31, 1979, 2.

144. *Der Yid,* December, 5, 1969.

145. Laura Deckelman and Chana Rubin, *The Final Solution Is Life: A Chassidic Dynasty's Story of Survival and Rebuilding* (New York: Mesorah, 2000).

146. Keren-Kratz, "Rabbi Yoel Teitelbaum," 308. See also *Der Yid,* March 11, 1966, 9.

147. Keren-Kratz, "Rabbi Yoel Teitelbaum," 309.

148. *Algemeiner Journal,* August 24, 1979, front-page headline.

149. *Der Yid,* August 24, 1979, 14.

150. *Der Yid,* August 31, 1979, 2.

151. Ibid.; *Algemeiner Journal,* August 24, 1979, 14.

152. *Algemeiner Journal,* August 24, 1979, 1.

153. Keren-Kratz, "Rabbi Yoel Teitelbaum," 361.

154. *Algemeiner Journal,* August 31, 1979, 1.

155. *Algemeiner Journal,* August 31, 1979, 9.

156. Ibid.

157. Ibid.

158. Keren-Kratz, "Rabbi Yoel Teitelbaum," 361; *Algemeiner Journal,* August 31, 1979, 9.

159. *Algemeiner Journal,* September 7, 1979, 1. See also Keren-Kratz, "Rabbi Yoel Teitelbaum," 358.

160. Mintz, *Hasidic People,* 136.

161. The letter was subsequently determined to be a forgery.

162. *Algemeiner Journal,* September 14, 1979, front-page headline.

163. "The Great Scholar and Rabbi of Sighet Has Been Appointed as Av Besdin of the Yetev Lev Community of Satmar," *Der Yid,* September 14, 1979, 1.

164. *Algemeiner Journal,* September 14, 1979, 1.

165. Kranzler, *Hasidic Williamsburg,* 140.

166. Mordechai Wilensky, *Hasidim u Mitnagdim* (Jerusalem: Mossad Bialik, 1970).

167. See Yechezkel Roth, *Emek HaT'Shuva: Pischa D'Aggedta B'Inyan Toras HaBesht* [The valley of repentance: A legend in the teachings of the Besht] (Brooklyn, NY: Shaarei Zion Karslburg, 2004), 4:18–20, www.otzar.org

/wotzar/Book.aspx?152863&+%D7%A2%D7%9E%D7%A7%20%D7%94%D7%AA%D7%A9%D7%95%D7%91%D7%94&page=22.

168. *Algemeiner Journal,* September 14, 1979, 17.

169. *Der Yid,* September 14, 1979, 3.

170. *Algemeiner Journal,* August 8, 1980, 5.

171. "Thousands of Hasidim and Hundreds of Rabbi at the Coronation [Hachtura] of His Holy Honor, the Admor, Shlita," *Der Yid,* August 8, 1980, 1.

172. *Der Yid,* August 8, 1980, 33. Referring to the new rebbe as the "redeemer" was a reminder that for hasidim a rebbe is a stand-in for the Messiah, the ultimate redeemer.

173. *Der Yid,* August 8, 1980.

174. *Algemeiner Journal,* August 15, 1980, 1.

175. *Der Yid,* August 8, 1980, 34, and *Algemeiner Journal,* August 15, 1980, 1. Much of what follows and is quoted below can be found in both these sources.

176. Mintz, *Hasidic People,* 128.

177. *Der Yid,* October 17, 1980.

178. Mintz, *Hasidic People,* 384n9.

179. *Der Yid,* October 31, 1980.

180. *Algemeiner Journal,* September 7, 1979, front-page headline.

181. Henry Abramovitch, *Brothers and Sisters: Myth and Reality* (College Station: Texas A&M University Press, 2014), 32–33. Aaron was preceded by a sister.

182. *Der Yid,* October 26, 1984, 1.

183. *Der Yid,* November 16, 1984, 2.

184. The court was wealthy even though many, if not most, of its Hasidim were among the poorest citizens in New York State, with a median household income of $24,430 compared to $58,003 for the state as a whole (US Census, 2009–13, American Community Survey 5-Year Estimates).

185. *Der Yid,* November 16, 1984, 27.

186. "When a younger sibling displaces an older one, this process is called 'dethronement,'" writes Abramovitch (*Brothers and Sisters,* 33). See also Mike Levine, "How Bitter the Tyranny in K.J.," *Times Herald-Record,* January 15, 2007, www.recordonline.com/article/20070115/NEWS/70115783.

187. Kranzler, *Hasidic Williamsburg,* 114.

188. See, for example, "Borough Park, NY—Appellate Court Revised Lower Court Ruling in Satmar Real Estate Dispute," *Vos Iz Neias,* November 14, 2008, www.vosizneias.com/22535/2008/11/14/borough-park-ny-appellate-court-revised-lower-court-ruling-in-satmar-real-estate-dispute/.

189. Kranzler, *Hasidic Williamsburg,* 51, 181. To be sure, Satmar did continue to receive significant money from the Jewish Community Relations Council of New York and the Metropolitan Council on Jewish Poverty; Josh Nathan-Kazis, "Did Satmars Bite Hand That Feeds Them with Anti-Israel Message at Draft Rally?," June 12, 2013, http://forward.com/articles/178568/did-satmars-bite-hand-that-feeds-them-with-anti-is/?p=all.

190. Kranzler, *Hasidic Williamsburg,* 114.

191. See Samuel Heilman and Menachem Friedman, *The Rebbe: The Life and Afterlife of Menachem Mendel Schneerson* (Princeton, NJ: Princeton University Press, 2011).

192. Mintz, *Hasidic People,* 154–65.

193. S. Gottlieb, "A Talmid's Recollections: The Beirach Moshe, Rav Moshe Teitelbaum of Satmar Zt'L upon His Fifth Yahrzeit," *Yated Ne'eman,* May 4, 2011,https://yated.com/a-talmidaes-recollections-the-beirach-moshe-rav-moshe-teitelbaum-of-satmar-ztae%C2%9Dl-upon-his-fifth-yahrtzeit/.

194. Abramovitch, *Brothers and Sisters,* 35.

195. Kranzler, *Hasidic Williamsburg,* 115.

196. Mintz, *Hasidic People,* 210. See also Kranzler, *Hasidic Williamsburg,* 115.

197. "Controversial Legendary Satmar Gabbai in First-Ever Interview: Two Chassidic Courts? Of Course It's Good," *Voz Iz Neias,* October 1, 2009, www.vosizneias.com/39238/2009/10/01/williamsburg-ny-controversial-legendary-satmar-gabbai-in-first-ever-interview-two-chassidic-courts-of-course-its-good/.

198. *Der Yid,* June 4, 1999, front-page headline.

199. *Der Yid,* June 4, 1999, 1, 4.

200. See ads announcing this and welcoming him in *Der Yid,* October 17, 1980, 12, 15.

201. *Der Yid,* June 4, 1999, 4.

202. *Der Yid,* June 18, 1999, 3, 63.

203. "Satmar Chasidim."

204. Abramovitch, *Brothers and Sisters,* 33.

205. *Der Yid,* June 18, 1999, 63.

206. Abramovitch, *Brothers and Sisters,* 35.

207. "Impressive Gathering in Satmar Bes Medrash in Monsey on the Previous Saturday Night," *Der Blatt,* October 15, 1999, 52.

208. See Edward A. Ross, *The Principles of Sociology* (New York: Century, 1920), 162.

209. Coser, *Functions of Social Conflict,* 34.

210. Kurt Wolff, ed., *The Sociology of Georg Simmel* (Glencoe, IL: Free Press, 1950).

211. See also Coser, *Functions of Social Conflict,* 41.

212. Daniel Wakin, "The Heir Apparent," *New York Times,* January 24, 2002, www.nytimes.com/2002/01/24/nyregion/the-heir-unapparent-brothers-feud-fractures-a-hasidic-community.html.

213. "Satmar Chasidim."

214. Powell, "Hats On, Gloves Off," quoting HasidicNews.com.

215. Ibid.

216. *Der Yid,* April 7, 2006, 1.

217. *Der Yid,* April 12, 2006, 1, and *Der Yid,* April 7, 2006, 9.

218. *Der Yid,* April 7, 2006, 71.

219. Powell, "Hats On, Gloves Off."

220. Signed 20 Adar 5762 (March 4, 2002).

221. "The House of Satmar," *Jerusalem Post,* September 7, 2007. This in itself was striking in light of the principle among Hasidim that the living rebbe's words and commands are inviolable. To say that he was demented and his words were not to be taken seriously could be seen as heretical. Indeed, making

such medical/psychiatric claims would have been unthinkable in the early years of Hasidism, when rebbes were generally unchallengeable—and certainly not by their Hasidim.

222. *Der Yid,* April 30, 2006, 1.

223. *Der Yid,* April 30, 2006, 3, 61.

224. *Der Yid,* April 30, 2006, 3.

225. *Der Yid,* April 30, 2006, 63.

226. Max Weber, *Economy and Society: An Outline of Interpretive Sociology* (New York: Bedminster Press, 1968), 956–1000; See also Robert Michels, *Political Parties* (New York: Free Press, 1968), 342ff.

227. *Der Yid,* April 30, 2006, 63.

228. *Der Yid,* April 30, 2006, 65.

229. *Der Yid,* May 5, 2006, B1. In 1939, Moshe Teitelbaum had briefly taken on the title of Rabbi of Zenta in then Yugoslavia; this title was now being resurrected for Lipa as a reward for his loyalty to Zalman.

230. *Der Yid,* May 5, 2006, B45.

231. *Der Yid,* May 5, 2006, B50.

232. Powell, "Hats On, Gloves Off."

233. Patrick Gallahue, "It's a House of 'Gosh!'—B'klyn Jews Slam Up Temple in 14 Days," *New York Post,* October 2, 2006, http://nypost.com/2006/10/02/its-a-house-of-gosh-bklyn-jews-slam-up-temple-in-14-days/.

234. *Der Yid,* May 5, 2006, B64.

235. See, for example, *Der Yid,* May 12, 2006, B23, and May 31, 2006, B31.

236. See, for example, *Der Yid,* May 26, 2006, B1–3, and June 1, 2006, B1.

237. Kranzler, *Hasidic Williamsburg,* 133.

238. Powell, "Hats On, Gloves Off."

239. Max Weber, *The Theory of Social and Economic Organization,* trans A.M. Henderson and Talcott Parsons (New York: Free Press, 1947), 328.

6. CHABAD LUBAVITCH

1. Perhaps the fullest consideration of this topic is to be found in M. Avrum Ehrlich, *A Critical Evaluation of HaBaD Leadership, History and Succession* (Northvale, NJ: Aronson, 2000). Menachem Friedman and I have also written about the last succession in its chain; see Samuel Heilman and Menachem Friedman, *The Rebbe: The Life and the Afterlife of Menachem Mendel Schneerson* (Princeton, NJ: Princeton University Press, 2011).

2. The acronym ChaBaD, denoting the dominant Hasidic philosophy of Lubavitchers, is formed from the words *Chochma* (wisdom), *Bina* (understanding), and *Da'as* (knowledge) and refers to Kabbalistic elements of the divine that play a part in defining the special nature of the Jewish soul. That soul, members of ChaBaD believe, is protected by the Torah and its commandments and is endangered by knowledge and practices that come from elsewhere.

3. Naftali Lowenthal, "Schneuri, Dovber," in *Encyclopedia of Hasidism,* ed. Tzvi Rabinowicz (London: Aronson, 1996).

4. Hayim Meir Heilman, *Beit Rabbi: Toldot Ha'Admore Haemtzai* (Berditchev: Sheftel, 1902).

5. "Rabbi Menachem Mendel—the Tzemach Tzeddek: Becomes Rebbe," n.d., accessed June 26, 2015, www.chabad.org/library/article_cdo/aid/110451/jewish/Becomes-Rebbe.htm.

6. Ehrlich, *Critical Evaluation*, 122.

7. Ibid., 143–47.

8. Ibid., 123.

9. Ehrlich speculates on this (ibid., 145; see also 147).

10. Naftali Loewenthal, "Lubavitch Hasidism," in *YIVO Encyclopedia of Jews in Eastern Europe*, ed. Gershon David Hundert, 2010, www.yivoencyclopedia.org/article.aspx/lubavitch_hasidism. See also Chaim Tchernowitz, *Pirkei Chaim* [Autobiography] (New York: Bitzaron, 1954), 104, and Naftali Lowenthal, "Schneersohn, Menachem Mendel," in Rabinowicz, *Encyclopedia of Hasidism*.

11. Lowenthal, "Schneersohn, Menachem Mendel"; Larry Domnitch, *The Cantonists: The Jewish Children's Army of the Tsar* (New York: Devora, 2003), 57.

12. Ehrlich, *Critical Evaluation*, 160.

13. See Heilman and Friedman, *Rebbe*.

14. Ehrlich, *Critical Evaluation*, 160.

15. Ibid., 161.

16. DovBer Avtzon, "Tzemach Tzedek's Final Years," Chabad On Line, April 5, 2012, www.collive.com/show_news.rtx?id=19468.

17. Raphael Nachman Hacohen, *Shmues v'Sipurim* [News and stories], 3rd ed. (Chmol: [Hotza'ah Shlishit], 1990), 1:63.

18. Tchernowitz, *Pirkei Chaim*, 105.

19. Ibid.

20. Ehrlich, *Critical Evaluation*, 158. See also Yanki Tauber, *Once upon a Chassid* (Brooklyn, NY: Kehot, 1995), 51.

21. Tchernovitz, *Pirkei Chaim*, 105.

22. Zvi Har-Shefer, "Recollections," *Kfar Chabad*, no. 613, Iyar 5754 (April 1994): 14–18.

23. Ehrlich, *Critical Evaluation*, 157.

24. H. Heilman, *Beit Rabbi*, 61.

25. Ehrlich, *Critical Evaluation*, 159.

26. Tchernowitz, *Pirkei Chaim*, 105. According to one eyewitness, the "shy" Shmuel read German and Russian newspapers. See Hacohen, *Shmues v'Sipurim*, 1:69.

27. Tchernowitz, *Pirkei Chaim*, 105.

28. Ehrlich, *Critical Evaluation*, 158.

29. See Gadi Sagiv, "King Lear's *Einiklach*: Inheritance Disputes in Nineteenth-Century Hasidism," paper presented at the annual conference of the Association for Jewish Studies, Boston, December 14, 2005; Ehrlich, *Critical Evaluation*, 165.

30. David Assaf, *The Regal Way: The Life and Times of Rabbi Israel of Ruzhin* (Stanford, CA: Stanford University Press, 2002), 666.

31. Tchernowitz, *Pirkei Chaim*, 106.

32. See Menachem Friedman, "Habad as Messianic Fundamentalism: From Local Particularism to Universal Jewish Mission," in *Accounting for Funda-*

mentalisms, ed. Martin Marty and R. Scott Appleby (Chicago: University of Chicago Press, 1994).

33. Yosef Yitzchak Kaminsky, *Dates, Personalities, and Events in the History of Chabad* (Kfar Chabad: Kehot, 1994), 17.

34. H. Heilman, *Beit Rabbi,* 62.

35. Loewenthal, "Lubavitch Hasidism."

36. See H. Heilman, *Beit Rabbi,* 61. "All recruits, including Jews, had to serve 25 years in the army, and, if they married, their offspring, as children of Russian soldiers, became the patrimony of the military and were destined to attend schools for soldiers' children entitled *kantonistskie uchebnye zavedenia* (cantonists' institutions). . . . Jews were required to provide conscripts between the ages of 12 and 25, whereas for others the conscripts were between 18 and 35." "The Ministry of Interior argued against Jewish equality and triggered, especially during the term of war minister Petr Vannovskii (1881–1897), the introduction of discriminatory regulations regarding Jewish military service. The military required a disproportionately large number of Jewish recruits and introduced the collective responsibility of Jews for draft arrears." Yohanan Petrovsky-Shtern, "Military Service in Russia," in Hundert, *YIVO Encyclopedia,* www.yivoencyclopedia.org/article.aspx/Military_Service_in_Russia.

37. One website purports to show a photo of him ("Shmuel Schneersohn," n.d., accessed September 11, 2015, www.snipview.com/q/Hasidic%20rabbis%20in%20Europe), but nowhere have I found a Lubavitcher source that confirms this to be a true picture. In fact the many posters and images that depict the rebbes generally show only the first, third, fifth, sixth, and seventh. See, for example, "Lubavitch Dynasty 1 #9058," photo by Carl Braude, n.d., Gift of Judaica Art Gallery, accessed September 11, 2015, http://giftofjudaica.com/?sid=122&articles_id=11289&act=artist5&artist=668&collection=0.

38. Loewenthal, "Lubavitch Hasidism."

39. Tzvi M. Rabinowicz, "Schneersohn," in Rabinowicz, *Encyclopedia of Hasidism,* 430.

40. Ehrlich, *Critical Evaluation,* 151.

41. Maya Balakirsky Katz, "An Occupational Neurosis: A Psychoanalytic Case History of a Rabbi," *AJS Review* 34, no. 1 (April 2010): 1–31, and "A Rabbi, a Priest, and a Psychoanalyst: Religion in the Early Psychoanalytic Case History," *Contemporary Jewry* 31, no. 1 (2011): 3–24.

42. See Katz, "Occupational Neurosis" and "Rabbi, a Priest," as well as Hacohen, *Shmues v'Sipurim,* 1:81.

43. See Maya Balakirsky Katz, "Occupational Neurosis" and "Rabbi, a Priest."

44. Yosef Yitzchak Schneersohn, *Sefer HaMa'amarim* (Brooklyn, NY: Kehot, 1951).

45. See Katz, "Occupational Neurosis," 4.

46. ChaBaD, *Chanoch L'Naar,* booklet, 10, 11. The booklet claims that his "health" required this long trip.

47. See Katz, "Rabbi, a Priest."

48. On Yosef Yitzchak Schneersohn's tendency to rewrite history, see, for example, Marc B. Shapiro, *Changing the Immutable: How Orthodox Judaism Rewrites Its History* (Portland, OR: Littman Library, 2015), 27.

49. See Katz, "Rabbi, a Priest," 15.

50. Ehrlich, *Critical Evaluation,* 179.

51. Ibid., p. 180. See also Yosef Yitzchak Kaminetzky, ed., *Dates and Events in Chabad* (Kfar Chabad: Kehot, 1994), 20.

52. Ehrlich, *Critical Evaluation,* 177.

53. Ibid., 180.

54. Kaminetzky, *Dates and Events,* 20. See also ChaBaD, *Chanoch L'Naar,* 12.

55. Hacohen, *Shmues v'Sipurim,* 73.

56. ChaBaD, *Chanoch L'Naar,* 12–13.

57. Ibid., 13.

58. Ehrlich, *Critical Evaluation,* 181. See also S. Heilman and Friedman, *Rebbe,* xii, 15–17, 20.

59. Katz, "Occupational Neurosis," 5.

60. Ehrlich, *Critical Evaluation,* 183.

61. Menachem Mendel Schneerson, *Igros Kodesh Maharshav,* vol. 1, letter 86, in S. Z. Landau and Y. Rabinovitch, *Or L'yesharim* (Warsaw: Halter, 5660 [1900]), 57–58.

62. On the Besht, see chapter 1 above.

63. *Ben Porat Yosef,* 128a. There are versions of this letter that the Baal Shem Tov, Israel Ben Eliezer, founder of Hasidism, wrote to his brother-in-law Gershon Kitover. See Naftali Loewenthal, *Communicating the Infinite: The Emergence of the Habad School* (Chicago: University of Chicago Press, 1990), 221n43. On the relatively recent adoption of this exchange between the Besht and the Messiah as one of ChaBaD's outreach slogans, see now Naftali Loewenthal, "The Baal Shem Tov's *Iggeret Ha-Kodesh* and Contemporary HaBaD Outreach," in *Let the Old Make Way for the New: Studies in the Social and Cultural History of Eastern European Jewry Presented to Immanuel Etkes,* ed. David Assaf and Ada Rapoport-Albert, 2 vols. (Jerusalem: Shazar Institute, 2009), vol. 1, *Hasidism and the Musar Movement,* English section, 69–101. On "unifications," see above, chapter 2.

64. See Loewenthal, *Communicating the Infinite,* 6, 14. See also Mor Altshuler, *The Messianic Secret of Hasidism* (Boston: Brill, 2006), esp. 3–13.

65. See Joseph Dan, "Modern Jewish Messianism: From Safed to Brooklyn" (Tel Aviv: Ministry of Defense, 1999); also Gershom Scholem, *The Messianic Idea in Judaism and Other Essays* (New York: Schocken, 1971).

66. See Joseph Dan, "Kefel Ha'Panim shel Ha'Meshichiyut b'Chasidut" [The two-sidedness of messianism in Hasidism], in *B'Maagaley Hasidim,* ed. Emanuel Etkes, David Assaf, Yisrael Bartal, and Elchanan Reiner (Jerusalem: Bialik, 2000), 299–315.

67. Dan, "Kefel Ha'Panim," 306.

68. A. H. Glitzenstein, "Rabbi Shalom Dov Ber Schneersohn of Lubavitch, the Meharshav," in *Sefer Hatodaot,* 2nd ed. (Kfar Chabad: Kehot, 1976), 227–36.

69. See Friedman, "Habad as Messianic Fundamentalism," 328–60, esp. 335.

70. On the appearance of a new revolutionary party, Narodnoye Pravo, see V. I. Lenin, *Collected Works* (Moscow: Progress Publishers, 1960–78), 2:323–52, https://www.marxists.org/archive/lenin/works/1897/dec/31b.htm.

71. Friedman, "Habad as Messianic Fundamentalism," 336.

72. See Menachem Mendel Schneerson to R. Moshe Menuchin [father of Yehudi Menuchin], letter 588, 26 Nisan, 5710, TheRebbe.org, www.chabad.org/therebbe/letters/default_cdo/aid/2277990/jewish/Letter-No-588-The-connection-of-the-Menuchin-family-to-the-Lubavitch-Rebbeim.htm.

73. Naftali Lowenthal, "Schneersohn, Shmaryahu Noah," in Rabinowicz, *Encyclopedia of Hasidism.*

74. See Ehrlich, *Critical Evaluation,* 190–92. I also thank Zalman Alpert for alerting me to the initial challenges to Yosef Yitzchak's leadership.

75. Zvi Y. Gitelman, *Century of Ambivalence: The Jews of Russia and the Soviet Union, 1881 to the Present* (Bloomington: Indiana University Press, 2001), 60.

76. Allan Nadler, "Hidden Master," *Jewish Ideas Daily,* August 25, 2011.

77. Gitelman, *Century of Ambivalence,* 86.

78. Abba Ahimeir and Shmuel Spector, "Dimanstein, Simon," in *Encyclopaedia Judaica,* ed. Michael Berenbaum and Fred Skolnik, 2nd ed. (Detroit, MI: Macmillan Reference USA, 2007), 5:662. Dimanstein was ultimately arrested during the Stalin purges and died in prison, probably in 1937. On the Yevsektsiya, see Mor Altshuler, *Reshit ha-Yevsektsiya, 1918–1921* (Jerusalem: Ha Aguda l'Cheker Tefutzot Yisrael, 1966). See also Abraham Greenberg, "The Rabbinic Conference at Korostin 1926," *Shvut* 4, no. 20 (1996): 53–58; Michael Beizer, "The Leningrad Jewish Community: From the NEP through Its Liquidation," *Jews in Eastern Europe* (Hebrew University of Jerusalem, Center for Research and Documentation) 3, no. 28 (Winter 1995): 16–42; Zvi Gitelman, *Jewish Nationality and Soviet Politics* (Princeton, NJ: Princeton University Press, 1972).

79. Gitelman, *Century of Ambivalence,* 79.

80. Ibid., 81.

81. Ibid., 73.

82. There were also concerns about a planned conference of Orthodox rabbis (the so-called LERO or Jewish Community of Leningrad), supported by Zionists and other so-called "enlightened" Jews, which Rabbi Yosef Yitzchak opposed because he believed it would be used by the Yevsektsiya to infiltrate itself into religious matters (something other rabbis did not believe) and also feared it would be dominated by unbelievers and Zionists. See Zalman Alpert, letter to *Counterpoint* (Yeshiva University newsletter), Summer 2000. See also Hacohen, *Shmues v' Sippurim,* 1:207–9, as well as Shalom DovBer Levin, *Toldot ChaBaD b'Russia Hasovietit 5678–5710* [1918–1950] (Brooklyn, NY: Kehot, 1989), 78–96.

83. Many of the details of Sixth Rebbe's and later his successor's responses to the situation of their *rebistve* are described and analyzed in S. Heilman and Friedman, *Rebbe,* and I will not repeat them in these pages.

84. See Menachem Friedman, "Messiah and Messianism in Chabad-Lubavitch Hasidism" [in Hebrew], in *The War of Gog and Magog: Messianism and Apocalypse in Judaism—In the Past and Present,* ed. David Ariel-Yoel et al. (Tel Aviv: Yediot Aharonot, 2001), 199–201, www.biu.ac.il/SOC/so/Chabad-Mashi'ach.pdf; and Yosef Yitzchak Schneersohn, *Sichos Kodesh, 5680–5700* [1919–39] (Kfar Chabad: Kfar Chabad Publishing, 5741 [1980]), 95.

85. Its founding fathers were the very successful German Jewish immigrants ambassador Henry Morgenthau and financiers Jacob Schiff and his brother-in-law, Felix Warburg, probably among the more assimilated American Jews. They sent the Russian-born agronomist Joseph Rosen to handle relief missions to the famine-starved regions, having made a deal with the Soviets to aid all Russians, but Rabbi Yosef Yitzchak was going to handle specifically Jewish needs. See Sara Kadosh, "American Jewish Joint Distribution Committee," and Yehuda Bauer, "Joseph A. Rosen," in Berenbaum and Skolnik, *Encyclopaedia Judaica,* 2:59–64 and 14:269 respectively.

86. See Yosef Yitzhak Schneersohn, *A Prince in Prison: The Previous Lubavitcher Rebbe's Account of His Incarceration in Stalinist Russia in 1927,* trans. Uri Kaploun (Brooklyn, NY: Sichos in English, 1997), the section "The Imprisonment of 1927," www.sichos-in-english.org/books/prince-in-prison/04 .htm, and Zalman Alpert, review of *The Heroic Struggle: The Arrest and Liberation of Rabbi Yosef Y. Schneersohn of Lubavitch in Soviet Russia,* by Yosef Yitzhak Schneersohn (Brooklyn, NY: Kehot, 1999), *Jewish Action* 60, no. 4 (Summer 2000). See also S. Heilman and Friedman, *Rebbe.*

87. See Schneersohn, *Prince in Prison,* the section "The Imprisonment of 1927"; Alpert, review of *The Heroic Struggle.* The relationship between Barry and his grandfather was discussed by Barry Gourary in an interview by Bryan Rigg, May 2003. We thank Dr. Rigg for sharing his interview tapes with us.

88. See Schneersohn, *Prince in Prison,* and Alpert, review of *The Heroic Struggle.* See also S. Heilman and Friedman, *Rebbe,* 18–20.

89. See S. Heilman and Friedman, *Rebbe,* 115–16, for details about how he managed to get to Latvia.

90. Yosef Yitshack Kaminetsky, *Days in Chabad: Historic Events in the Dynasty of Chabad-Lubavitch* (Brooklyn, NY: Kehot, 2002), 25–26.

91. See Levin, *Toldot Chabad.*

92. David Assaf, "Hasidism: Historical Overview," in Hundert, *YIVO Encyclopedia,* www.yivoencyclopedia.org/article.aspx/Hasidism/Historical_ Overview#idowrx.

93. "Sunday, September 3, 2017: Sixth Lubavitcher Rebbe Visits US (1929)," Chabad.org, Jewish Calendar, accessed September 24, 2015www.chabad.org /calendar/view/day_cdo/aid/156770/jewish/Sixth-Lubavitcher-Rebbe-visits-US .htm.

94. "Rabbi Joseph Isaac Schneersohn, the Rebbe Rayatz: World War II Erupts," Chabad.org, Jewish History, n.d., accessed September 24, 2015, www.chabad.org/library/article_cdo/aid/110491/jewish/World-War-II-Erupts .htm.

95. See the City of Otwock's archives of the Gymnasium, 1933–36.

96. See S. Heilman and Friedman, *Rebbe.*

97. For a full discussion of their life choices, see ibid.

98. Gourary, interview by Rigg, May 2003. Barry would add that it was ironic that his Uncle Mendel would end up choosing the life that he himself would spurn, almost as if the two had exchanged futures.

99. Bryan Rigg, *Rescued from the Reich: How One of Hitler's Soldiers Saved the Lubavitcher Rebbe* (New Haven, CT: Yale University Press, 2004).

100. See Avraham Chenoch Glitzenstein, ed., *Sefer Toldos RaYaTZ* (Brooklyn, NY: Kehot, 5747), 4:69–71; National Archives in Washington, DC, 20408/Immigration and Naturalization, roll 6451, beginning March 16, 1940.

101. Kaminetsky, *Days in Chabad,* 136.

102. Nissan Mindel, *Rabbi Joseph I. Schneersohn: A Short Biography* (Brooklyn, NY: Kehot, 1961), 15.

103. See Haggadah of Passover (Brooklyn, NY: Kol Menachem, 2008), 62.

104. Gershon Greenberg, "The Rebbe's Response to the Holocaust," paper presented at New York University, November 6–8, 2005. Chaim Elazar Shapira, the Minchas Elazar, had issued a similar warning.

105. See Friedman, "Messiah and Messianism," 208–14.

106. Zalman Schachter, interview by author, May 10, 2008. Schachter was one of those posting these stickers. See also Yosef Yitzchak Schneersohn, "Tevet, the Month of Collective Soul-Searching," *Machane Yisrael B'Eretz Yisrael* (Jerusalem), May 1943, 6. See also Yosef Yitzchak Schneersohn, *Kovetz Michtavim v'Sichos* (Brooklyn, NY: Machane Yisrael, Sivan 5701 [1941]), 10–12. Repentance did not bring redemption—the Messiah would come anyway. Repentance simply put one among the saved.

107. See S. Heilman and Friedman, *Rebbe,* 121–22, and chap. 5 for a detailed account of these events.

108. See ibid., 168–71.

109. See ibid., 74–80.

110. See ibid., 53–56.

111. See ibid., esp. 65–129.

112. See ibid., 118–19.

113. *Kovetz Chof Menachem-Av* (Brooklyn, NY: Kehot, 2004), 54–56.

114. Ibid.

115. Zalman Schachter, interview by author, May 12, 2008. Schachter was present in Marseille on this occasion. See S. Heilman and Friedman, *Rebbe,* 134–36.

116. See Mordecai Menasheh Laufer, *Yemei Melech* (Brooklyn, NY: Kehot, 5751 [1991]), 2, 937.

117. Ibid., 939.

118. See S. Heilman and Friedman, *Rebbe,* chap. 2.

119. See M. M. Laufer, *Yemei Melech* (Brooklyn, NY: Kehot, 1991), 2:948.

120. In ChaBaD Hasidism as we saw above after the death of the First Rebbe (when matters of succession were still fluid). See Emanuel Etkes, "Controversy over Inheritance in ChaBaD Hasidism," paper presented at the Institute for Advanced Studies of the Hebrew University, July 10, 2008. It occurred as seen above in the case of the Third Rebbe, several of whose sons established courts that ultimately withered: Yehuda Leib in Kapust (Kopys) Belarus, Chaim Schneur Zalman in Lyadi, and Yosef Yitzchak in Ovruch (Ukraine). See Ehrlich, *Leadership.*

121. Rabbi Shmuel Lew, interview by author, June 20, 2007.

122. Zalman Schachter, interview by author, May 18, 2008.

123. Shaul Shimon Deutsch, interview by author, April 2008.

124. See Loewenthal, *Communicating the Infinite,* 5, who explains that this is the way knowledge was expected to affect a Hasidic master.

125. Barry Gourary, interview by Menachem Friedman, September 1, 1991, Menachem Friedman Archives, Mazkeret Batya, Israel. The practice of Jewish mourning lasts a year. See Samuel Heilman, *When a Jew Dies* (Berkeley: University of California Press, 2001).

126. See, e.g., Menachem Mendel Schneerson, *Torat Menachem: Reshimat HaYoman* [Diary notes] (Brooklyn, NY: Kehot Otzar Hasidim, 2006). These notes are filled with everything from a story he heard about the Rebbe Shalom DovBer while walking on a Saturday night with the Rebbe Yosef Yitzchak in the summer of 1930 (156) to the importance of being "sanctified" at the time of intercourse (174).

127. Laufer, *Yemei Melech,* 1151.

128. Zalman Schachter, the Hasid in question, interview by author, May 27, 2008. See also Laufer, *Yemei Melech,* 1159.

129. See Ehrlich, *Leadership,* 351n110, who cites the unpublished diary of Lubavitcher Hasid Eli Gross (New York, 1950–53).

130. Kahan Diaries, 11 Tishrei 5711 (September 22, 1950). Much of what follows in this page comes from Kahan's diaries. See Yoel Kahan, "Excerpts from a Diary," in a newsletter published by Kfar ChaBaD between January and September 1981.

131. Allon Dahan, "Maavakei HaYerusha B'Chasidut ChaBaD," *Kivunim Chadashim* 17, January 2008, 212.

132. *Likkutei Dibburim,* 4:244–45, www.chabad.org/library/article_cdo/aid/2632808/jewish/Likkutei-Dibburim-Volume-4.htm. See also Rigg, *Rescued from the Reich,* 25.

133. Kaminetsky, *Days in Chabad,* 119.

134. Ibid.

135. For a fuller description, see S. Heilman and Friedman, *Rebbe,* 47–49.

136. Yosef Yitzchak Kaminetzy, *Dates in the History of ChaBaD: Persons and Events in the History of ChaBaD* (Kfar Chabad: Kehot, 5754 [1994]), 153 [in Hebrew].

137. In a way, he acted in a manner that Moshe Idel describes in his study of Hasidism as being shamanistic, mediating between the sacred dead rebbe and the community. See Moshe Idel, *Ascensions on High in Jewish Mysticism* (Budapest: Central European University Press, 2005), 154.

138. Letter to Nechama Dina Schneersohn, 26 Adar I 5711 (March 14, 1951) (collection of Menachem Friedman). In the letter they also refer to the aggravation (*agmes nefesh*) Shmaryahu Gourary caused Rabbi Yosef Yitzchak "when once he sought to grab all the affairs of Lubavitch into his hands," suggesting thereby that the previous rebbe had not wanted to cede control and leadership to this son-in-law.

139. Ehrlich, *Leadership,* 399.

140. The handing over of this hat is in many circles "an indication of succession." See Shaul Shimon Deutsch, *Larger Than Life,* 2 vols. (New York: Chasidic Historical Productions, 1997), 1:156.

141. Shalom DovBer Wolpe, "Two Stories and a Conclusion," *Kfar Chabad*, 4 Cheshvan 5750 (October 2, 1989) (italics added; translation by Samuel C. Heilman).

142. Ernest Becker uses this concept to refer to the strategies used to mitigate our awareness of mortality and vulnerability in his book *The Denial of Death* (New York: Simon and Schuster, 2007).

143. See chapter 1.

144. Yosef Y. Schneersohn and Menachem Mendel Schneerson, *Basi L'Gani*, ed. Uri Kaploun (Brooklyn, NY: Kehot, 1990), 88.

145. To be sure, in 1926, on 2 Nisan (March 17), the anniversary of the passing of his father, Yosef Yitzchak had given a talk entitled "All Sevens Are Dear to God," noting that his father had been the seventh generation after the Ba'al Shem Tov, the man whom the Messiah had told about spreading the wellsprings in order to hasten the Messiah's return. Menachem Mendel undoubtedly knew that talk, as he knew so much about the Lubavitcher past. Menachem Mendel, however, had a different set of seven in mind.

146. *HaKri'ah Vehakedusha* (ChaBaD monthly published in New York), August 1941, 2. See also Yosef Yitzchak Schneersohn, *Igros Kodesh* [Holy letters] (Brooklyn, NY; Kehot, 1982), 6:170–73; Friedman, "Messiah and Messianism," 208–15; and Rigg, *Rescued from the Reich*, 181.

147. Israel Shenker, "Lubavitch Rabbi Marks His 70th Year with Call for 'Kindness,'" *New York Times*, March 27, 1972.

148. See, e.g., Schneersohn, *Sichos Kodesh* [Holy talks], 5720 (Brooklyn, NY: Kehot, 1960), 175, for a description and summary of the events on 10 Shvat 5720 (February 2, 1960).

149. "Messiah Plain and Simple," *Yom HaShishi*, 3 Iyar 5751 (April 17, 1991), 10.

150. Kaminetsky, *Days in Chabad*, 119.

151. Leaflet, 27 Nisan 5751 [April 11, 1991], Menachem Friedman Archives, Mazkeret Batya, Israel.

152. Yori Yanover and Nadav Ish-Shalom, *Rokdim V'Bochim* [Dancing and crying] (New York: Meshi, 1994), 74–75. See also "3 Tammuz 1994: Transmission," TheRebbe.org, n.d., accessed July 4, 2008, www.chabad.org /therebbe/timeline_cdo/aid/62185/jewish/3-Tammuz-1994-Transmission.htm.

153. "Messiah Plain and Simple."

154. "Rabbi Binyomin Klein, 79, OBM," Chabad On Line, June 5, 2015, www.collive.com/show_news.rtx?id=35758.

155. Yossi Bryski, "Kinus haShluchim," Keynote address, 2006, http:// chabadinfo.com/video/kinus-hashluchim-keynote-speech/.

156. "An Emissary Like Him—Like Him Literally," missives to Tzierei ChaBaD Youth Organization, no. 487, November 11, 2003, translated by Samuel C. Heilman.

157. See Menachem M. Schneersohn, *Likkutei Sichot* [Collected talks], 39 vols. (Brooklyn, NY: Kehot, 1980–), 35:113–19, and sources cited there.

158. For a particularly striking example, see Samuel Heilman, "Still Seeing the Rebbe," *Killing the Buddha*, September 5, 2001, http://killingthebuddha .com/mag/dogma/still-seeing-the-rebbe/.

159. Richard Werbner, "New World Revival, African Reprise," paper presented at the conference "Religion on the Global Stage: Social Scientific Perspectives," Indiana University, Bloomington, November 14–16, 2014, 3.

160. Ibid., 7. Werbner is describing itinerant Pentecostal preachers and missionaries of the Holiness Movement, but he might as well have been talking about ChaBaD emissaries (*shluchim*).

FINAL THOUGHTS

1. See, for example, "Bobov Shul Laundered Massive Amounts of Money, FBI Was Told," *Failed Messiah* (blog), June 18, 2012, http://failedmessiah .typepad.com/failed_messiahcom/2012/06/bobov-shul-laundered-massive-amounts-of-money-fbi-was-told-234.html, and Josh Nathan-Kazis, "$20M Hasidic Fraud Suspects Claimed to Be Millionaires and Paupers—at Same Time," *Forward*, November 13, 2014, http://forward.com/news/209156 /20m-hasidic-fraud-suspects-claimed-to-be-milliona/.

2. "In First, Hasidic Woman Elected to Serve as Civil Court Judge in NY State," Jewish Telegraphic Agency, September 14, 2016, www.jta.org/2016/09 /14/news-opinion/united-states/in-first-hasidic-woman-elected-to-serve-as-civil-court-judge-in-ny-state. See also Esty Mendelowitz, "Despite the Odds: An Interview with Ruchie Freier," *Jewish Press*, May 26, 2015, www.jewishpress .com/indepth/interviews-and-profiles/despite-the-odds-an-interview-with-ruchie-freier/2015/05/26/0/.

3. See Mendel Piekarz, *The Hasidic Leadership* [in Hebrew] (Jerusalem: Bialik, 1999), 73.

4. Sigmund Freud, *Civilization, Society and Religion* (New York: Penguin, 1991), 131, 305.

5. Emile Durkheim, *The Elementary Forms of the Religious Life* (New York: Macmillan, 1915), 245–51.

6. Max Weber, "Science as a Vocation," in *From Max Weber: Essays in Sociology*, ed. H.H. Gerth and C. Wright Mills (New York: Routledge, 1948), 77–128.

Index

Contents

Introduction

You have been shopping for a particular home furnishing and just can't seem to find what you want, or you have found it but it is poorly made and overpriced. Why deal with these frustrations when you can have beautiful and well-made furnishings that exactly meet your needs—and save you money, too? In *Home Woodworking Projects, Volume 1* you'll find a showcase of projects that will help you create a more attractive, functional and satisfying home environment.

Using just a few simple tools, you can build a pine futon frame the whole family can snuggle into; a poker table for evenings full of congenial competition; a desk, table and chairs, and picnic table sized to fit your childrens' needs—as well as a delightful playhouse; an oak stepladder for reaching top shelves in your den; a writing desk, drafting stool and secretary topper that can be made individually or as a set; and many other furnishings to give rooms in your home personal charm and functional appeal.

For each of the creative, practical building projects in *Home Woodworking Projects, Volume 1*, you will find a complete cutting list of parts, a materials-shopping list, a detailed construction drawing, full-color photographs of the major construction steps and easy-to-follow directions that guide you through every step of the building process.

The information in this book gives do-it-yourselfers of all skill levels the power to build beautiful wood projects, and the satisfaction of creating well-made pieces inexpensively. Every project in this book can be built using only basic hand tools and portable power tools that you probably already own. And you won't need to spend hours scouring specialty woodworking stores for the materials and hardware you'll need. We used only products that are sold in most building centers and corner hardware stores to make these items.

Organizing Your Worksite

Portable power tools and hand tools offer a level of convenience that is a great advantage over stationary power tools. But using them safely and conveniently requires some basic housekeeping. Whether you are working in a garage, a basement or outdoors, it is important that you establish a flat, dry holding area where you can store tools. Set aside a piece of plywood on sawhorses, or dedicate an area of your workbench for tool storage, and be sure to return tools to that area once you are finished with them. It is also important that all waste, including lumber scraps and sawdust, be disposed of in a timely fashion. Check with your local waste disposal department before throwing away any large scraps of building materials or any finishing-material containers.

Safety Tips
•Always wear eye and hearing protection when operating power tools and performing any other dangerous activities.
•Choose a well-ventilated work area when cutting or shaping wood and when using finishing products.

Tools & Materials

At the start of each project, you will find a set of symbols that show which power tools are used to complete the project as it is shown (see below). You will also need a set of basic hand tools: a hammer, screwdrivers, tape measure, a level, a combination square, C-clamps, and pipe or bar clamps. You will also find a shopping list of all the construction materials you will need. Miscellaneous materials and hardware are listed with the cutting list that accompanies the construction drawing. When buying lumber, note that the "nominal" size of the lumber is usually larger than the "actual size." For example, a 2 × 4 is actually 1½ × 3½".

Power Tools You Will Use

Circular saw *to make straight cuts. For long cuts and rip-cuts, use a straight-edge guide. Install a carbide-tipped combination blade for most projects.*

Drills: *use a cordless drill for drilling pilot holes and counterbores, and to drive screws; use an electric drill for sanding and grinding tasks.*

Jig saw *for making contoured cuts and internal cuts. Use a combination wood blade for most projects where you will cut pine, cedar or plywood.*

Power sander *to prepare wood for a finish and to smooth out sharp edges. Owning several power sanders (½-sheet, ¼-sheet, and belt) is helpful.*

Belt sander *for resurfacing rough wood. Can also be used as a stationary sander when mounted on its side on a flat worksurface.*

Router *to cut decorative edges and roundovers in wood. As you gain more experience, use routers for cutting grooves (like dadoes) to form joints.*

Guide to Building Materials Used in this Book

•Sheet goods:
PLYWOOD: *Basic sheet good sold in several grades (from CDX to AB) and thicknesses. BCX is well-suited for outdoor projects.*
BIRCH PLYWOOD: *An alternative to pine or fir plywood, has smooth surface excellent for painting or staining. Moderately expensive.*
OAK PLYWOOD: *Oak-veneered plywood commonly sold in ¼" and ¾" thicknesses. Fairly expensive.*
LAUAN PLYWOOD: *Usually ¼" to ½" thick, found in cabinetry and furniture, and used as a flooring underlayment. Inexpensive.*
HOUSE SIDING: *Cedar or fir based exterior plywood, usually with vertical grooves 4"or 8" on center. Most is ⅝" thick.*
HARDBOARD: *Dense particleboard used for backing. Inexpensive. Made from cedar or pressure-treated pine.*
PEGBOARD: *Perforated hardboard. Inexpensive.*

•Dimension lumber:
PINE: *A basic, versatile softwood. "Select" and "#2 or better" are suitable grades. Requires a water-resistant finish.*
RED OAK: *A common hardwood that stains well and is very durable. Relatively inexpensive.*
ASPEN: *A soft, workable hardwood. Available at building centers in standard sizes and in extra-wide glued panels. Moderately expensive.*

Guide to Fasteners & Adhesives Used in This Book

•Fasteners & hardware:
WOOD SCREWS: *Brass or steel; most projects use screws with a #6 or #8 shank. Can be driven with a power driver.*
NAILS & BRADS: *Choose galvanized or brass.*
CARRIAGE BOLTS: *Like lag bolts, but with round heads: ⅜ to ⅝".*
LAG SCREWS: *Heavy-duty fasteners for extra holding strength.*
MISCELLANEOUS HARDWARE: *Use galvanized, brass, or plastic hinges, door pulls, and specialty hardware as required.*

•Adhesives:
WOOD GLUE: *Yellow glue is suitable for all projects in this book.*
MOISTURE-RESISTANT WOOD GLUE: *Any exterior wood glue, such as plastic resin glue.*
TILE ADHESIVE: *An adhesive specially designed for ceramic tile.*

•Miscellaneous materials:
Wood plugs (for filling counterbores); ceramic tile & grout; trim moldings; dowel rods; wood putty; others as required.

Finishing Your Project

Glue precut wood plugs into visible screw counterbores and sand them until smooth; fill nail holes and countersunk screw holes with wood putty, then sand smooth. Sand all surfaces to remove rough spots and splinters, using medium-grit (120- to 150-grit) sandpaper, then finish-sand (150- to 180-grit) all surfaces. Wipe the wood clean with a rag dipped in mineral spirits, then prime and paint with enamel paint, or apply a wood-staining agent to color the wood. Topcoat with several coats of tung oil, polyurethane or other products as desired. Mask or remove hardware before applying finishing products.

PROJECT
POWER TOOLS

Library Table

This oak library table features a clean, sophisticated appearance that suits any family room or study.

CONSTRUCTION MATERIALS

Quantity	Lumber
1	¾" × 4 × 8' oak plywood
1	½" × 2 × 4' oak plywood
2	1 × 2" × 8' oak
3	1 × 4" × 8' oak
2	1 × 6" × 6' oak
2	2 × 2" × 8' oak

High-quality, stylish furniture doesn't need to be overly expensive or difficult to make, and this library table is the proof. We used a traditional design for this old favorite. The simple drawer construction, beautiful oak materials and slender framework add up to one great-looking table.

Consider the possibilities for this table in your family room or study. These areas of the home call out for a simple yet elegant table to support a lamp or books, or just to add a decorative accent. We applied a two-tone finish. But no matter how you finish it, this library table serves many needs—and it looks great in the process.

6

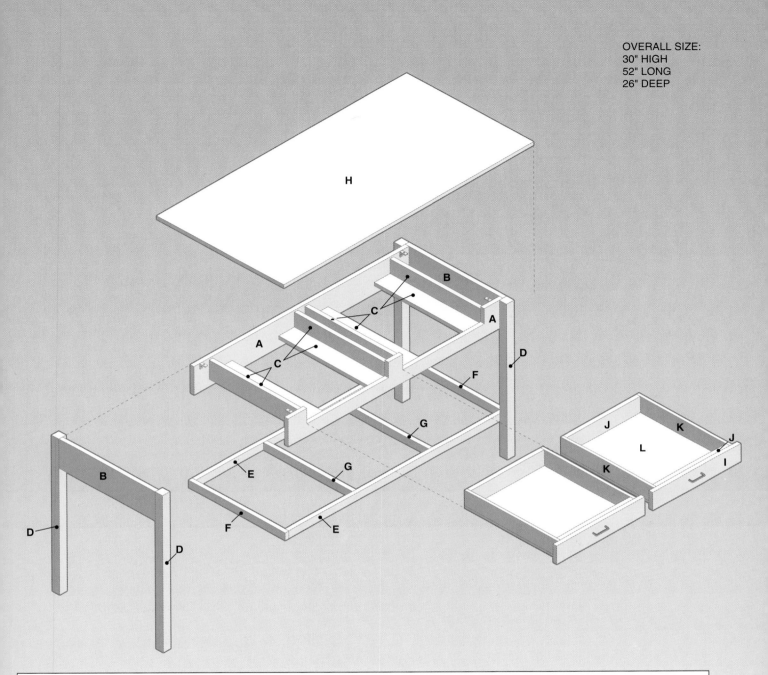

OVERALL SIZE:
30" HIGH
52" LONG
26" DEEP

Cutting List

Key	Part	Dimension	Pcs.	Material
A	Side	¾ × 5½ × 44½"	2	Oak
B	End	¾ × 5½ × 20"	2	Oak
C	Guide	¾ × 3½ × 18½"	8	Oak
D	Leg	1½ × 1½ × 29¼"	4	Oak
E	Side rail	¾ × 1½ × 44½"	2	Oak
F	End rail	¾ × 1½ × 20"	2	Oak

Cutting List

Key	Part	Dimension	Pcs.	Material
G	Cross rail	¾ × 1½ × 18½"	2	Oak
H	Top	¾ × 26 × 52"	1	Plywood
I	Drawer front	¾ × 3½ × 18"	2	Oak
J	Drawer end	¾ × 2⅜ × 15⅞"	4	Oak
K	Drawer side	½ × 2⅜ × 19"	4	Plywood
L	Drawer bottom	½ × 16⅞ × 19"	2	Plywood

Materials: #6 × 1", 1⅝" and 2" wood screws, 4d and 6d finish nails, 2" corner braces with ⅝" screws (4), 4" drawer pulls (2), ⅞"-dia. rubber feet (4), tack-on furniture glides (4), ¾" oak veneer edge tape (15'), ⅜"-dia. oak plugs, wood glue, finishing materials.

Note: Measurements reflect the actual size of dimension lumber.

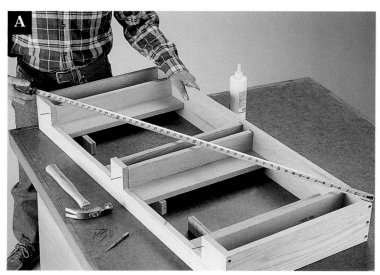

Measure the diagonals, and adjust the apron frame as needed until it is square.

Tape 8"-long blocks of scrapwood to the legs to hold the rail assembly for installation.

Directions: Library Table

MAKE THE APRON ASSEMBLY. The apron section of the library table holds the drawers. It is made by attaching the sides, ends and guides. Start by cutting the sides (A) and ends (B) to size, and sand them smooth. Choose which side you want to be the front, and draw the two 3"-deep × 17"-long rectangular outlines for the drawer cutouts on it. The outlines should start 3¾" in from each end of the front. Use a jig saw and a straightedge guide to make the cutouts. Drill counterbored pilot holes, and attach the sides between the ends with glue and #6 × 1½" brass wood screws, driven through the ends and into the sides. Make sure the outside faces of the sides are flush with the ends. Cut the guides (C) to length. The guides are attached in pairs to form supporting corners on either side of the drawer notches. Fasten the guides together in right-angle pairs: butt one guide's long edge against the face of an-

other guide, making sure their ends are flush, and attach the guides with glue and wood screws. Position the guide pairs between the sides so the inside faces are flush with the bottom and sides of the rectangular cutouts. (Set the guide pairs on spacers to keep them aligned with the cutouts as you work.) Before fastening the guides, check for square by measuring from corner to corner **(photo A)** and apply glue to the end of the guide. If the measurements

are not the same, adjust as needed. Drill pilot holes, and drive 6d finish nails through the sides and into the guides. Use a nail set to set the nail heads below the surface of the wood.

MAKE THE RAIL ASSEMBLY. The rail assembly is a frame that provides stability to the legs. Start by cutting the side rails (E), end rails (F) and cross rails (G) to size. Position the side rails on edge. Drill counterbored pilot holes, and attach the end rails with glue

Support the drawer with a ½"-thick scrap to center the drawer front correctly. Clamp the front to the drawer before driving screws.

and #6 × 2" wood screws—the resulting rectangular frame should sit flat on your worksurface. Attach the cross rails between the side rails, 14" in from the inside edges of the end rails. Fill all counterbores with ⅜"-dia. wood plugs. Sand the rail assembly smooth.

ASSEMBLE THE TABLE. Begin by cutting the legs (D) to size. Sand the legs to smooth out any rough spots and sharp edges. Use glue and 2" wood screws to fasten the legs to the apron so the top edges and outside faces are flush. Be careful not to drill into the screws connecting the sides and ends. Stand the table up, then clamp or tape 8"-long scrap blocks to the inside edges of the legs, flush with the bottom leg edges. These scrap blocks hold the rail assembly in place as you attach it. Apply glue, and fasten the rail assembly to the legs, making sure the end rails are flush with the outside edges of the legs **(photo B).** Cut the top (H) to size. Clean the edges thoroughly, then cut strips of ¾" self-adhesive veneer edge tape slightly longer than all four

edges of each top. Attach the tape by positioning it over the edges, then pressing it with a household iron set at a medium-low setting. The heat will activate the adhesive. Sand the top, and choose which side of the top you want to face up. Choose the smoothest, most attractive side to face up. Draw reference lines on the underside of the top, 3¾" in from the long edges. Fasten two 2" corner brackets on each line, 5¼" in from the top ends. Attach the top to the apron with ⅝" screws driven through the corner brackets and into the top and apron.

MAKE THE DRAWERS. Start by cutting the drawer ends (J) and drawer sides (K) to size. Sand them to smooth out any rough spots, and fasten the drawer ends between the drawer sides, using glue and 4d finish nails. Make sure the outside faces of the drawer ends are flush with the ends of the drawer sides, and set all the nails with a nail set. Cut the drawer bottoms (L) to size. Center a bottom over each drawer. Drill pilot holes for 4d finish nails, and attach the bottom to the drawer ends

and sides, driving the nails through the bottom and into the edges. Do not use glue to attach the drawer bottoms. Cut the drawer fronts (I) to size. To attach the drawer fronts, first set the drawers on a ½"-thick piece of scrap. This piece of scrap will make sure the top-to-bottom spacing is correct when you attach the drawer front. Check to make sure there is an equal distance between the ends of the drawer fronts and the drawer sides on both ends of the drawer fronts **(photo C).** Clamp the drawer fronts in place, and fasten the drawer fronts to the drawers with countersunk, #6 × 1" wood screws, driven through the drawer ends and into the drawer fronts. Test-fit the drawers in the apron. Adjust the fronts if they are uneven on the front of the apron.

APPLY FINISHING TOUCHES. Fill all screw counterbores with glued oak plugs, and fill all nail holes with wood putty. Finish-sand the entire project with 180-grit sandpaper, and apply your choice of finish. We applied a mahogany-colored stain to the apron and rubbed a natural oil finish on the drawer fronts and top. We also applied three coats of paste wax to the tabletop for extra protection. When the finish has dried, install the drawer pulls on the drawer fronts, and wax the top faces of the guides with paraffin. Insert the drawers, and set the table on its back edges. Attach ⅞"-dia. rubber feet to the bottom of the drawers to prevent them from being pulled out of the table **(photo D).** Attach furniture glides to the leg bottoms.

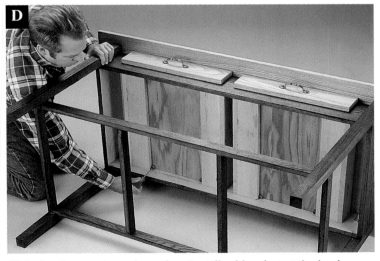

Slide the drawers into place, then install rubber feet at the back corners to serve as drawer stops and keep the drawers centered.

Sideboard

This elegant sideboard has plenty of room to hold everything from a meal with all the trimmings to stacks of important files.

The sideboard is an attractive, multipurpose fixture that can be used as a food serving counter, file holder—anything that requires shelf or counter space. The sideboard is a traditional home fixture, adding low-profile storage to just about any area of the home. Positioned against a wall or behind a desk, the sideboard is out of the way, yet is perfect for storing games, photo albums and other items you want to keep close at hand.

We made the sideboard out of oak and oak plywood. The construction is simple and sturdy. Two long interior shelves span the length of the project, giving you a surprising amount of storage space for such a small unit. The top shelf is concealed by two plywood doors, while the bottom shelf is left open for easy access to stored items. Cove molding fastened around the edges of the top and the curved profiles of the legs add a touch of style to this simple project.

CONSTRUCTION MATERIALS

Quantity	Lumber
1	¾" × 4 × 8' oak plywood
2	1 × 4" × 8' oak
2	¾ × ¾" × 8' oak cove molding

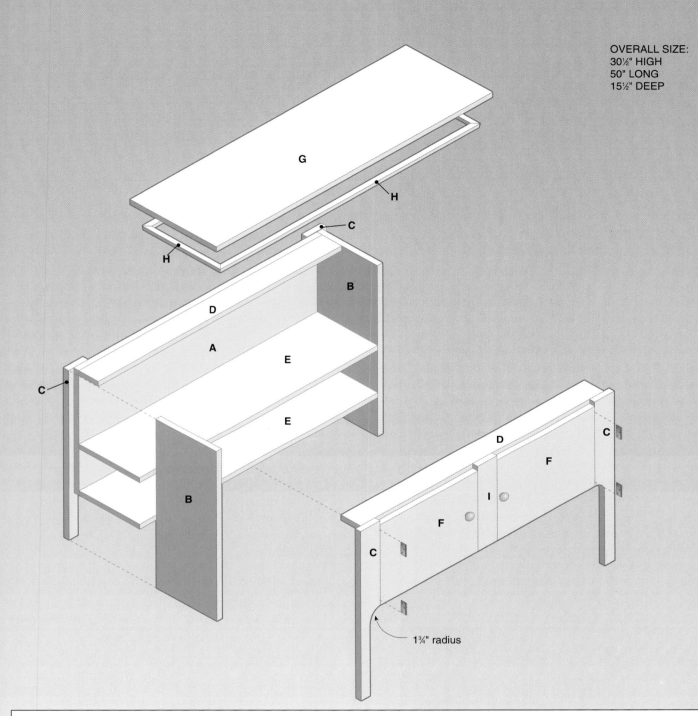

OVERALL SIZE:
30½" HIGH
50" LONG
15½" DEEP

G

H

C

B

D

A

E

E

C

B

D

F

C

I

F

F

C

1¾" radius

Cutting List

Key	Part	Dimension	Pcs.	Material
A	Back panel	¾ × 20 × 44"	1	Plywood
B	End panel	¾ × 11 × 29¾"	2	Plywood
C	Leg	¾ × 3½ × 29¾"	4	Oak
D	Cleat	¾ × 2½ × 44"	2	Plywood
E	Shelf	¾ × 10¼ × 44"	2	Plywood

Cutting List

Key	Part	Dimension	Pcs.	Material
F	Door	¾ × 13⅛ × 17⅜"	2	Plywood
G	Top panel	¾ × 15½ × 50"	1	Plywood
H	Top trim	¾ × ¾ × *"	4	Cove molding
I	Stile	¾ × 3½ × 14"	1	Oak

Materials: #6 × 1" and 2" wood screws, 16-ga. × 1¼" brads, 1½ × 3" brass butt hinges (4), ⅞"-dia. tack-on furniture glides (4), 1"-dia. brass knobs (2), roller catches (2), ¾" oak veneer edge tape (35'), ⅜"-dia. oak plugs, wood glue, finishing materials.

Note: Measurements reflect the actual size of dimension lumber.
*Cut to fit.

Directions: Sideboard

MAKE THE CARCASE. The carcase for the sideboard is the basic cabinet formed by the back, end and top panels. Start by cutting the back panel (A) end panels (B) and shelves (E) from ¾"-thick plywood. We used oak plywood. Use a household iron to apply oak veneer edge tape to one long edge of each shelf. Trim the edges with a utility knife. Sand all the parts smooth, and set the back flat on your worksur-

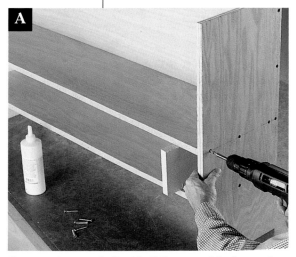

Support the top shelf with 5¼" spacer blocks on the bottom shelf before fastening it.

face. Position one face of an end panel against each short edge of the back panel. With the top edges flush, mark and drill pilot holes through the end panel and into the back. Use glue and #6 × 2" brass wood screws to attach the back panel between the end panels, keeping the top edges flush. Position the shelves between the end panels, making sure the edge with the veneer tape is facing away from the back panel. Position the bottom face of the bottom shelf flush with the bottom edge of the back. The top shelf should be 5¼" up from the lower shelf. Attach the bottom shelf with glue and #6 × 2" wood screws, driven through the end panels and into the shelves. Set the carcase upright, and position 5¼"-wide spacer blocks on the bottom shelf. Set the top shelf on the spacer blocks. Attach the top shelf with glue and wood screws **(photo A)**. Cut the cleats (D) to size. After sanding them smooth, use glue and wood screws to fasten one cleat between the end panels so one long edge is flush with

the front edges of the end panels. Position the remaining cleat with one long edge squarely against the back panel, and fasten the cleat with glue and wood screws.

MAKE THE LEGS. The legs for the sideboard are cut from 1 × 4" oak. They feature curves near the top, tapering downward to 1¾" in width. Cut the legs (C) to length. Designate a top and bottom of each leg. To draw cutting lines, first draw a centerline from top to bottom on each leg. Then, draw reference lines across the legs, 14" and 15¾" up from the bottom. Set a compass to draw a 1¾"-radius semicircle, and position it on the lower reference line. The point of the compass should be on the reference line, as close to an edge as possible. Draw the semicircle to complete the curved portion of the cutting line. Clamp the legs to your worksurface, and use a jig saw to cut the legs to shape, starting at the bottom and following the centerline and semicircle all the way to the end of the top reference line **(photo B)**. Sand the legs smooth.

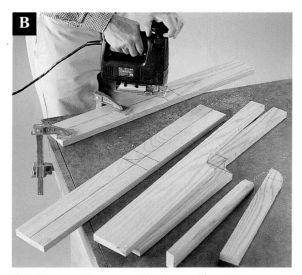

Cut the curved tapers in the legs with a jig saw.

Fasten the legs to the front edges of the end panels. Make sure the outside edges of the legs overhang the end panels by ¼".

Measure the front and back overhang to make sure the top panel is centered on the carcase.

Miter-cut cove molding to cover the seam between the top and the carcase.

ATTACH THE LEGS & STILE. Position two legs against the front edges of the end panels. The cutout sections of the legs should be the inside edges of the legs. Make sure the legs are flush with the end panels at the top and bottom edges, and that they overhang the end panels by ¼". Drill pilot holes, and attach the legs to the ends and shelves with glue and #6 × 2" wood screws **(photo C).** Cut the stile (I) to length. Place it between the legs so it spans the gap between the cleat and top shelf. Center the stile between the legs. Make sure the bottom edge of the stile is flush with the bottom of the top shelf, and attach it with glue and wood screws. Turn the project over, and fasten the remaining legs to the back and ends. Keep the top and bottom edges flush.

INSTALL THE TOP PANEL. Begin by cutting the top panel (G) to size. Apply veneer edge tape to all four edges of the top, and sand the surfaces smooth. Lay the top on a flat surface with its better face facing down. Center the carcase over the top. The

top should extend 1½" beyond the front and back of the legs **(photo D),** and 2¼" beyond the outside faces of the end panels. Fasten by driving countersunk, #6 × 1" wood screws through the cleats and into the top. Cut the top trim (H) to fit around the underside of the top, miter-cutting the ends at 45° angles so they fit together at the corners. Attach the top trim with glue and 1¼" brads, driven through the top trim and into the top panel. Set the brads with a nail set **(photo E).**

ATTACH THE DOORS. Cut the doors (F) to size. We cut the doors so the grain runs in an opposite, contrasting direction from the carcase. Apply oak veneer edge tape to all four edges of each door. Attach 1½ × 3" brass butt hinges to one short edge of each door, starting 2" in from the tops and from the bottoms. Mount the doors on the carcase by attaching the hinges to the legs. Make sure the bottom edges of the doors are flush with the bottom of the top shelf.

Attach each door to a leg, using 1½ × 3" butt hinges.

APPLY FINISHING TOUCHES. Fill all brad holes with untinted, stainable wood putty. Glue ⅜"-dia. oak plugs into all counterbored screw holes. Finish-sand all the surfaces smooth, remove the door hinges and apply your finish of choice—we used two coats of clear polyurethane. When the finish has dried, reattach the doors. Fasten 1"-dia. brass knobs to the door fronts, and mount roller catches on the doors and stile, 5" down from the top of the stile. Tack furniture glides to the leg bottoms.

13

Drafting Stool

Simple and sturdy, this oak beauty keeps your posture perfect as you work at your drafting table or writing desk.

Proper seating is the key to comfort and productivity at a writing desk, drafting table or any workstation. An ultra-soft reclining or swiveling chair can sometimes make you drowsy, resulting in poor sitting posture and sore muscles. On the other hand, an unsupportive, rigid chair with a low back-rest can make working at your desk uncomfortable and unpleasant. This drafting stool offers firm support without lulling you to sleep.

We designed this solid oak stool for use with the writing desk (page 18). The style and scale of the stool match those of the writing table, but you'll find there are many additional uses for this versatile project. You may want to use it as a bar stool in your den, or place it in the kitchen to provide seating at your breakfast counter.

We used oak lumber, but you can select building materials to match your desk or room decor. For a finished look, we filled the screw holes in our chair with oak plugs, but contrasting plugs would provide an interesting design element. There certainly are many options for building and using this drafting stool. Best of all, this piece is much easier to build than its appearance suggests.

CONSTRUCTION MATERIALS

Quantity	Lumber
3	1 × 2" × 8' oak
2	1 × 4" × 6' oak
2	2 × 2" × 8' oak

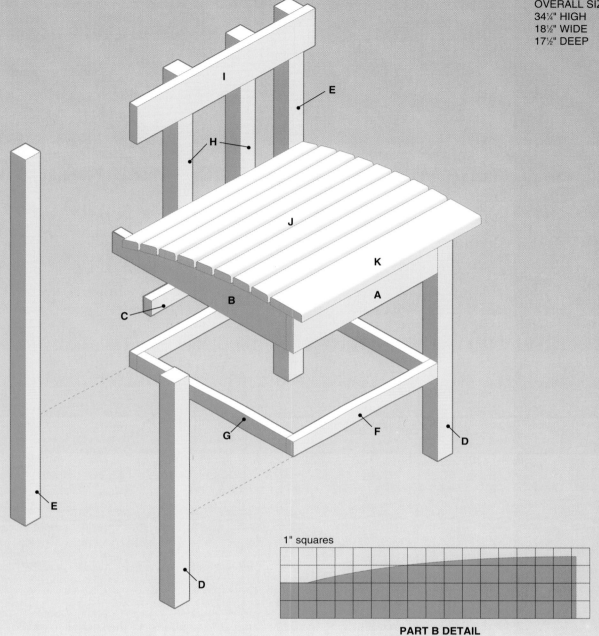

1" squares

PART B DETAIL

		Cutting List		
Key	**Part**	**Dimension**	**Pcs.**	**Material**
A	Front	¾ × 3½ × 15"	1	Oak
B	Side	¾ × 3½ × 16¼"	2	Oak
C	Back	¾ × 2 × 13½"	1	Oak
D	Front leg	1½ × 1½ × 21¼"	2	Oak
E	Rear leg	1½ × 1½ × 34¼"	2	Oak
F	End rail	¾ × 1½ × 15"	2	Oak

		Cutting List		
Key	**Part**	**Dimension**	**Pcs.**	**Material**
G	Side rail	¾ × 1½ × 15½"	2	Oak
H	Back brace	1½ × 1½ × 16½"	2	Oak
I	Backrest	¾ × 3½ × 18½"	1	Oak
J	Slat	¾ × 1½ × 18½"	8	Oak
K	Front slat	¾ × 3½ × 18½"	1	Oak

Materials: #6 × 1⅝" wood screws, 10d finish nails, ⅜"-dia. oak plugs, wood glue, finishing materials.

Note: Measurements reflect the actual size of dimension lumber.

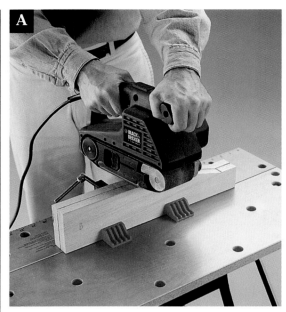

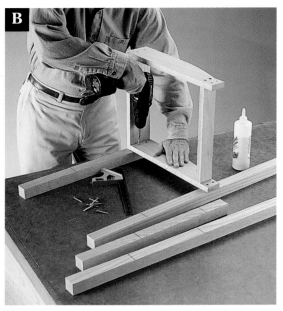

Gang-sand the sides with a belt sander, making sure their profiles are identical.

Align the seat frame on the top reference lines, and fasten it to the legs.

Directions: Drafting Stool

MAKE THE SEAT FRAME. The seat frame is the central structural element in the drafting stool. The frame is sloped from front to back, forming the seat shape. This slope is made by transferring cutting lines from a grid pattern on page 15 to the sides of the frame. Start by cutting the front (A), sides (B) and back (C) to size. Sand the parts to smooth out any rough edges. Draw a grid with 1" squares onto a face of a side board. (Use the *Part B Detail* from page 15 as a guide for drawing the side contour.) Cut the side to shape with a jig saw, and sand the edges. Trace the finished side onto the uncut side board, and cut it to shape. Clamp the sides together and gang-sand them with a belt sander **(photo A),** making sure their profiles are identical. Position the front board (A) against the front ends of the sides. Drill counterbored pilot holes, and fasten the front to the sides

with glue and #6 × 1⅝" wood screws. Make the counterbores deep enough to accept a ⅜"-dia. wood plug. Position the back board (C) between the sides so the rear face is 1½" in from the ends of the sides. Make sure the bottom edges of

the parts are flush, and fasten the back with glue and #6 × 1⅝" wood screws.

ATTACH THE LEGS. Two legs are attached to the front and back of the seat frame. Before attaching the frame and legs, draw accurate reference lines

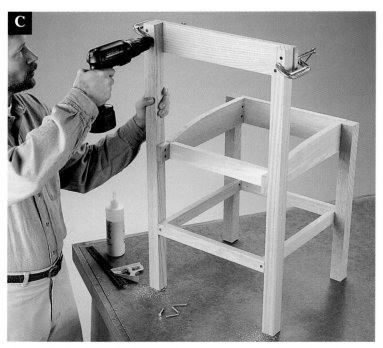

Clamp the backrest in place at the tops of the rear legs, then fasten with glue and wood screws.

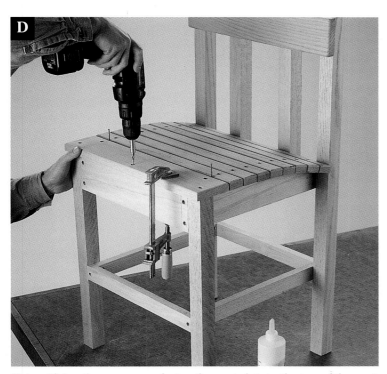

Using 10d nails as spacers, fasten the seat slats to the top of the seat frame, ending with the front slat.

to mark the position for the legs. Otherwise, the legs will be uneven. Start by cutting the front legs (D) and rear legs (E) to size. Sand the parts, then draw reference lines 8" and 17¾" up from the bottom ends. Position one front leg and one rear leg on your worksurface. Set the seat frame on the legs so the bottom edge is flush with the top reference lines. Apply glue and fasten the seat frame to the rear leg, keeping the ends flush and the frame square to the leg. Use counterbored #6 × 1⅝" wood screws, driven through the seat sides and into the leg. Make sure the seat frame is flush with the front edge of the front leg and with the top reference line. Drill pilot holes **(photo B),** and fasten the frame to the front leg with glue and wood screws. Turn the assembly over, and attach the remaining front leg

and rear leg, using the same methods.

ATTACH THE RAILS. The rails are joined together to form a simple frame. This frame is then attached between the legs to strengthen the stool. Cut the end rails (F) and side rails (G) to length. Position the side rails between the end rails so their top and bottom edges are flush. Drill counterbored pilot holes through the end rails, and use glue and #6 × 1⅝" wood screws to fasten the end rails to the side rails. Position the rail assembly between the posts so its bottom edges are flush with the bottom reference lines. Drill countersunk pilot holes through the side rails, and attach the rail assembly with glue and #6 × 1⅝" wood screws, driven through the side rails and into the legs. To avoid hitting the screws in the rail assembly, these screws must be

slightly off center. The front and rear edges of the rail assembly should be flush with the front and rear leg edges.

ATTACH THE BACK BRACES & BACKREST. Begin by cutting the back braces (H) and backrest (I) to size. Clamp the backrest to the fronts of the rear legs so the top edges are flush. The backrest should extend ¼" past the rear legs on both sides. Check the back of the legs for square, and drill staggered pilot holes with ½"-deep counterbores through the legs. Apply glue, and fasten the backrest to the rear legs with glue and #6 × 1⅝" wood screws **(photo C).** Attach the back braces to the back and backrest with glue and wood screws. Use a piece of 1 × 4 scrap as a spacer to maintain equal distance between the rear legs and back braces.

ATTACH THE SLATS. Cut the slats (J) and the front slat (K) to size. Sand the slats, slightly rounding the top edges with a belt sander. Starting at the rear of the seat, attach the slats with glue and counterbored #6 × 1⅝" wood screws. Maintain a ⅛"-wide gap between slats— 10d finish nails make good spacers. Clamp the front slat to the front of the seat frame with its front edge overhanging the front by ½" at the front and ¼" at each side. Attach the front slat with glue and counterbored screws **(photo D).**

APPLY FINISHING TOUCHES. Glue ⅜"-dia. wood plugs into all counterbores, and sand the plugs smooth so they are flush with the surface. Finish-sand all the surfaces with 180-grit sandpaper, and apply your finish of choice. We used three coats of tung oil.

Writing Desk

Build this practical, attractive writing desk for a fraction of the cost of manufactured models.

CONSTRUCTION MATERIALS

Quantity	Lumber
1	¾" × 4 × 8' oak plywood
2	1 × 2" × 6' oak
2	1 × 4" × 6' oak
1	1 × 6" × 8' oak
1	1 × 10" × 6' oak
2	2 × 2" × 8' oak
1	¼" × 2 × 4' acrylic sheet
2	¾ × 1⁵⁄₁₆" × 6' oak panel molding
2	⅜ × 1¹⁄₁₆" × 6' oak stop molding

A beautiful piece of furniture, this writing desk is based loosely on popular Shaker styling. With its hinged top, you have access to a storage area for keeping important papers organized and out of the way. We built the writing desk out of red oak, an attractive and durable hardwood, so the project would to look great for a long time. Designed to match the drafting stool and secretary topper (pages 14, 24), the writing desk also works well as a stand-alone piece. And, it can be built for a fraction of the cost of similar furnishings, even those sold by catalog. The worksurface is covered with a sheet of clear acrylic, giving you a hard, smooth surface for writing. When the acrylic gets scratched or worn, just slip it out of the top frame and turn it over.

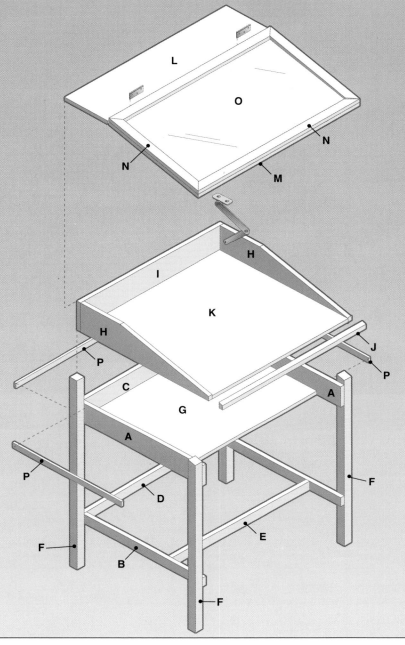

OVERALL SIZE:
37¼" HIGH
34" WIDE
30½" DEEP

Cutting List

Key	Part	Dimension	Pcs.	Material
A	Apron side	¾ × 3½ × 24¾"	2	Oak
B	Side rail	¾ × 1½ × 24¾"	2	Oak
C	Apron back	¾ × 3½ × 30"	1	Oak
D	Back rail	¾ × 1½ × 30"	1	Oak
E	Kick rail	¾ × 1½ × 28½"	1	Oak
F	Leg	1½ × 1½ × 35¾"	4	Oak
G	Shelf	¾ × 20 × 28½"	1	Plywood
H	Desk side	¾ × 5½ × 26½"	2	Oak

Cutting List

Key	Part	Dimension	Pcs.	Material
I	Desk back	¾ × 5½ × 30"	1	Oak
J	Desk front	¾ × 1 × 30"	1	Oak
K	Desk bottom	¾ × 26½ × 28½"	1	Plywood
L	Desk top	¾ × 9¼ × 34"	1	Oak
M	Worksurface	¾ × 21 × 34"	1	Plywood
N	Top molding	¾ × 1⁵⁄₁₆ × *"	4	Panel molding
O	Top protector	¼ × 19⅛ × 32⅛"	1	Acrylic
P	Side trim	⅜ × 1¹⁄₁₆ × *"	3	Stop molding

Materials: #6 × 1⅝" and 2" wood screws, #6 × 1" brass wood screws, 16-ga. × ¾" and 1" brass brads, 1½ × 3" brass butt hinges, 6" heavy-duty lid-support hardware, ¾" oak veneer edge tape (25'), ⅜"-dia. oak plugs, wood glue, finishing materials.

Specialty tools: Block plane, plastic cutter.

Note: Measurements reflect the actual size of dimension lumber.   * Cut to fit.

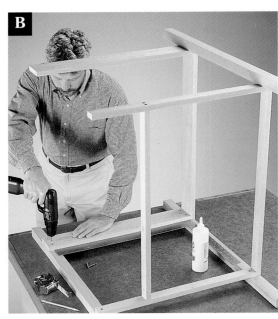

Fasten the apron assembly between the back legs with glue and wood screws, driven through the apron sides and into the legs.

Attach the front legs to the free ends of the aprons and rails.

Directions: Writing Desk

JOIN THE LEGS & APRON. Start by cutting the legs (F) to length. Sand the parts smooth. Set the legs together edge to edge with their ends flush. Draw reference lines across the legs, 8" and 30½" up from one end. These lines mark the positions of the apron and rail assemblies. To build the apron assembly, start by cutting the apron sides (A) and apron back (C) to length. Attach an apron side to each end of the apron back with glue and counterbored #6 × 2" wood screws, driven through the apron back and into the apron sides. Make sure the outside faces of the apron sides are flush with the ends of the apron back. To attach the apron assembly to the legs, first set a pair of legs on your worksurface, about 30" apart, with the reference lines facing each other. Position the assembly between the legs so the top edges of the assembly are flush

Use a block plane to trim the desk front to match the slanted profiles of the desk sides.

with the reference lines 30½" up from the bottom. Apply glue, and drill two counterbored pilot holes through the sides. Drive #6 × 1⅝" wood screws through the sides and into the legs **(photo A).** Avoid the screws already driven in the apron assembly.

INSTALL THE FRAME RAILS. The frame rails are 1 × 2 oak strips that fit between the legs to stabilize the desk. Cut the side rails (B), back rail (D) and kick rail (E) to length. Drill counterbored pilot holes, and attach the side rails to each end of the back rail with glue

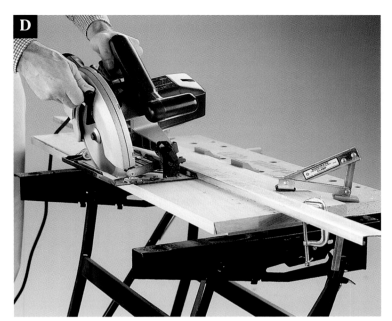

Use a circular saw and straightedge guide to make a slight bevel on the front edge of the desk top.

Trace the angles of the desk sides onto the front legs, then trim the legs to follow the sides.

TIP

When planing hardwood, always plane with the grain. If you find your planing strokes are resulting in ragged cuts, rather than smooth shavings, switch the direction of your planing strokes.

bored pilot holes, and attach the rail assembly with glue and wood screws. Fasten the front legs to the fronts of the apron sides and side rails, making sure the reference lines are flush with the edges **(photo B).**

MAKE THE SHELF. The shelf fits within the apron assembly, flush with the bottom edges. Cut the shelf (G) to size. Sand the shelf to smooth out any rough edges. Apply oak veneer edge tape to one long edge of the shelf, using a household iron. Trim and sand the edges of the tape. Position the shelf between the apron sides so it butts against the inside face of the apron back. The front edge will be recessed 4¾" in from the front legs. Drill counterbored pilot holes, and attach the shelf to the aprons with glue and wood screws, driven through the apron sides and apron back. Make sure the taped edge of the shelf faces front. The shelf should be flush with the bottom edges of the apron assembly.

BUILD THE DESK BOX. The desk box is built as a unit, then installed on top of the aprons. Start by cutting the desk sides (H) to length. The desk sides are cut with slanted top edges. To make the slanted cuts, mark points on one long edge of each desk side, 8¼" in from one end. This long edge will be the top edge. Then draw reference lines on the opposite end of each side, 1" up from the bottom edge. Draw straight cutting

and #6 × 2" wood screws, driven through the back rail and into the side rail ends. Make sure the outside faces of the side rails are flush with the ends of the back rail. Position the kick rail between the side rails so its front face is 7" in from the front ends of the side rails. Make sure the top and bottom edges are flush, and attach the kick rail with glue and #6 × 2" wood screws. Position the rail assembly between the legs so the bottom edges are flush with the reference lines 8" up from the bottom of each leg. Drill counter-lines connecting the marks, and cut along the lines with a circular saw and straightedge cutting guide. Cut the desk back (I) to length from oak 1 × 6. Cut the desk bottom (K) from ¾"-thick plywood. To cut the 1"-thick desk front (J), use a straightedge cutting guide to rip-cut a 1"-thick strip from a 1 × 4 or 1 × 6. Sand to smooth out any rough spots. Drill counterbored pilot holes through the desk back, and use glue and #6 × 2" wood screws to fasten a desk side at each end, flush with the top, bottom and side edges of the desk back. Set the desk bottom between the desk sides, and attach it with glue and wood screws, driven through the desk sides and back and into the bottom. Drill counterbored pilot holes in the desk front, and fasten it to the front edge of the desk bottom. To trim the desk front to match the slanted profiles of the desk sides, first draw reference lines on each end of the desk front, extending the slanted profiles of the desk sides. Use a combination square to draw a reference line across the front face of the desk front, connecting the ends of the end reference lines. Use a block plane to trim the profile of the desk front to match the angles of the desk sides **(photo C).** To avoid damaging the desk sides with the plane, start the trimming with the block plane and finish with a pad sander.

MAKE THE DESK TOP. Cut the desk top (L) to size. The desk top has a bevel cut along one long edge where it meets the worksurface (M). To make this bevel, adjust the sole plate setting on a circular saw until it

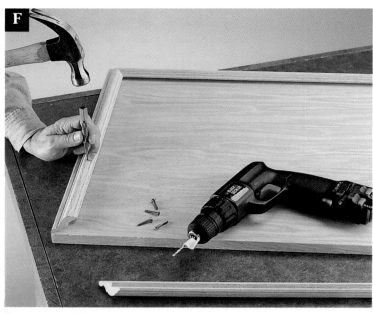

Permanently fasten the top and side pieces of the frame around the worksurface.

cuts a ⅛"-deep bevel on the front edge of the desk top. First make test cuts on scrap pieces. Clamp a straightedge guide to the desk top, and make the bevel cut on one long edge of the workpiece, removing a ⅛"-thick strip **(photo D).**

INSTALL THE DESK BOX. Stand the leg assembly up, and slide the desk assembly into place on top of the side aprons, making sure the back edges are flush. In order for the worksurface to sit flat on the desk sides, the front legs are cut to match the slanted profiles of the desk sides. First, trace the angles of the desk sides onto the front legs **(photo E).** Remove the desk assembly, and use a circular saw to cut the front legs along the cutting lines. Replace the desk, and make sure the front legs are cut at or slightly below the desk side profiles. Fasten the desk assembly with glue and #6 × 2" wood screws, driven through the desk sides and into the legs. Remember to

drill counterbored pilot holes before attaching the assemblies. Position the desk top on the flat section of the desk sides so the back edge of the desk top overhangs the back of the legs by ⅛". Make sure the beveled edge faces forward and slants in from top to bottom. Attach the desk top with glue and wood screws. Because there is a visible seam where the desk assembly meets the aprons, make the side trim (P) pieces that fit between the legs on the sides and back. Tack the side trim over the seam, using ¾" brass brads.

MAKE THE WORKSURFACE. The worksurface is a flat plywood board framed with molding. A sheet of clear acrylic is inserted in the molding frame to create a smooth writing surface. One piece of the molding is removable, allowing you to replace the acrylic if it gets worn and scratched. Cut the worksurface (M) to size. Apply veneer edge tape to all four

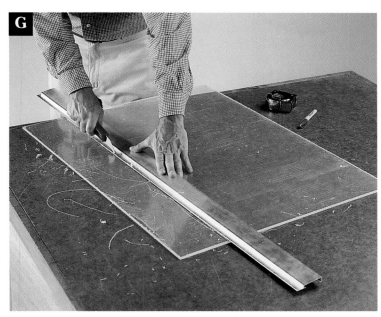

Score the acrylic sheet repeatedly, using a utility knife and a straight-edge guide.

edges of the board. Sand to smooth out any rough edges. Cut the top molding (N) from ¾ × 1⁵⁄₁₆" panel molding to fit around the edges of the work-surface. Miter-cut the corners of the molding pieces to make miter joints. Use glue and ¾" brads to attach the top molding to the sides and top of the worksurface **(photo F).** Drive 1" brass brads through one molding piece and into the other at each joint, lock-nailing the pieces. To secure the unat-tached piece of top molding, first clamp it in place on the worksurface. From underneath the worksurface, drill counter-sunk, 1¼"-deep pilot holes, ⁹⁄₁₆" in from the front edge. Use a piece of tape on your drill bit as a depth guide, making sure you don't drill through the face of the molding. Drive #6 × 1" brass wood screws through the pilot holes and into the mold-ing. Remove the clamps.

MAKE THE TOP PROTECTOR. Cut the top protector (O) to size from ¼"-thick clear acrylic. Acrylic sheets can be cut with a knife. Using a board or other straightedge as a guide allows you to make repeated cuts to score the material deeply **(photo G).** Then use light pres-sure to bend and break the ma-terial along the score line, leav-ing the straightedge in position next to the line. Remove the screws holding the front top molding piece, and insert the top protector into the frame.

APPLY FINISHING TOUCHES. Glue and insert ⅜"-dia. oak plugs into all the counterbored holes. Fill all nail holes with wood putty. Sand all the sur-faces smooth, and finish the project. We used three coats of clear tung oil to preserve the natural wood tones. Attach 1½ × 3" brass butt hinges to the top edge of the writing top, and fasten it to the desk top **(photo H).** Because the work-surface is fairly heavy, you may need to support it from behind as you fasten the hinges. To support the worksurface, fasten a 6" heavy-duty lid support near the top of the worksurface and one desk side, inside the storage compartment.

Attach the worksurface to the beveled edge of the desk top with evenly spaced hinges.

Secretary Topper

Transform a plain table, desk or cabinet top into a fully equipped secretary with this box-style topper.

In the furniture world, a secretary is a free-standing, upright cabinet with a drop-down worksurface that conceals numerous storage cubbies when raised. The traditional secretary also has two or three large drawers at the bottom. With this secretary topper, we zeroed in on the cubbyhole feature, creating a simple storage unit that will convert just about any flat surface into a functioning secretary.

The fixed shelves are designed to accommodate papers up to legal size, while the adjustable shelf can be positioned to hold address and reference books. The vertical slats with the cutout dividers are good for storing incoming or outgoing mail. And the handy drawer is an ideal spot to keep stamps, sealing wax and other small desktop items.

We made this simple wood project from oak and oak plywood. If you are building a secretary topper to complement an existing piece of furniture, try to match the wood type and finish of the piece.

NOTE: This secretary topper is sized to fit on top of the Writing Desk featured on pages 18 through 23.

CONSTRUCTION MATERIALS

Quantity	Lumber
1	¼" × 2 × 3' oak plywood
2	1 × 10" × 8' oak
1	½ × 8" × 6' oak
1	¼ × 2" × 7' oak mull casing

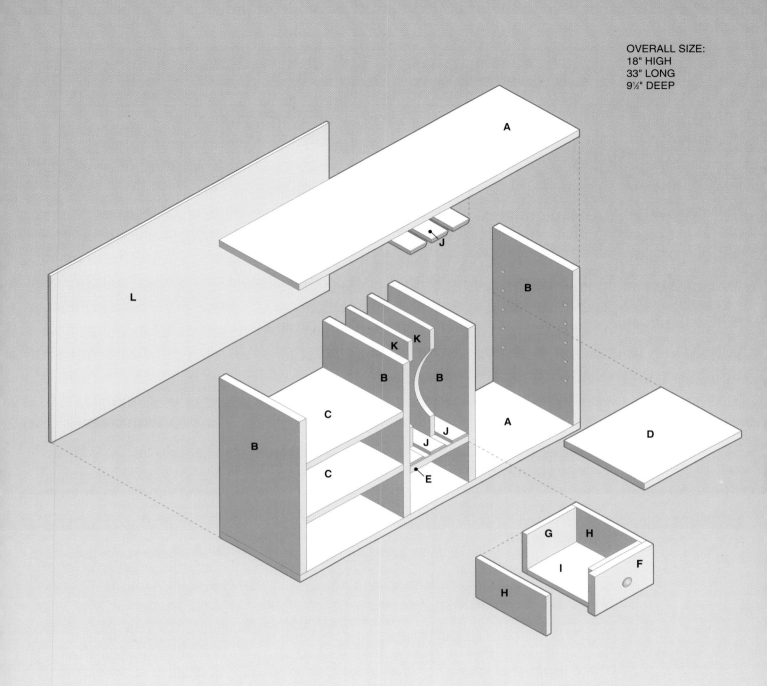

OVERALL SIZE:
18" HIGH
33" LONG
9½" DEEP

Cutting List				
Key	**Part**	**Dimension**	**Pcs.**	**Material**
A	Top/bottom	¾ × 9¼ × 33"	2	Oak
B	Partition	¾ × 9¼ × 16½"	4	Oak
C	Fixed shelf	¾ × 9¼ × 11½"	2	Oak
D	Adjustable shelf	¾ × 9¼ × 11¼"	1	Oak
E	Bin top	¾ × 9¼ × 7"	1	Oak
F	Drawer front	¾ × 4⅛ × 6¾"	1	Oak

Cutting List				
Key	**Part**	**Dimension**	**Pcs.**	**Material**
G	Drawer end	½ × 4⅛ × 5¾"	2	Oak
H	Drawer side	½ × 4⅛ × 8¼"	2	Oak
I	Drawer bottom	½ × 5¾ × 7¼"	1	Oak
J	Bin spacer	¼ × 2 × 9"	6	Mull casing
K	Divider	½ × 7¼ × 11½"	2	Oak
L	Back panel	¼ × 17⅞ × 32¾"	1	Plywood

Materials: #6 × 1⅝" wood screws, 16-ga. × ¾" and 1" brads, ¼"-dia. shelf pins (4), ¾"-dia. brass knob (1), ⅜"-dia. oak plugs, adhesive felt pads (6), wood glue, finishing materials.

Note: Measurements reflect the actual size of dimension lumber.

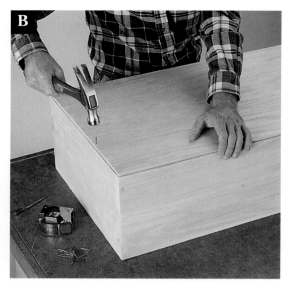

Use pegboard as a drilling template to make sure shelf pin holes in the partitions align.

Fasten the back panel to the secretary cabinet with wire brads, squaring as you go.

Directions: Secretary Topper

MAKE THE SHELF FRAME-WORK. The shelf framework is made by attaching two shelves and a bin top between three vertical partitions. Start by cutting the partitions (B), fixed shelves (C) and bin top (E) to size. Sand the parts after cutting to remove any saw marks or rough spots. Draw reference lines across the faces of two partitions, 5" in from one short edge and 5¾" in from the other short edge. Drill counterbored pilot holes, and use glue and #6 × 2" wood screws to fasten the shelves between the two partitions with their bottom edges flush with the reference lines. Draw reference lines on the outside face of one of the attached partitions, 4¼" up from the bottom edge. Use glue and wood screws to fasten the bin top to the partition, with its bottom edge on the reference line. Make sure the front and rear edges are flush, then fasten an unattached partition to the

free end of the bin top with glue and wood screws, keeping the edges flush. The final section contains an adjustable shelf. To drill holes in the partitions to hold the shelf pins, clamp a piece of pegboard to one face, and use it as a drilling template **(photo A)** to drill ¼"-dia. × ⅜"-deep holes into the partitions. After you drill holes in one partition, mark the locations of the pegboard holes you used with tape, and repeat with the opposing partition. Keep the same end up and the same edge in front. Wrap masking tape around your drill bit as a bit stop to keep you from drilling through the partitions. Sand the assembly smooth.

COMPLETE THE CABINET. The top and bottom panels, a back panel and an outer partition are added to wrap the shelf framework, forming a cabinet. Cut the top/bottom panels (A) to size. Attach a panel to the ends of the partitions at the top and at the bottom of the frame-work. Fasten the remaining partition between the top and bottom panels, making sure the

outside face is flush with the ends of the shelf framework. Cut the back (L) to size. Sand the edges, and then fasten the back to the cabinet with ¾" brads **(photo B).** Fasten one end of the back first, then check for square. Adjust if needed, then finish attaching the back panel.

MAKE THE DRAWER. The drawer parts are made from ½"-thick oak stock and are cut to size by rip-cutting a ½ × 8"-wide board. Start by cutting the drawer ends (G), drawer sides (H) and drawer bottom (I) to size. Sand the edges, and fasten the drawer ends between the drawer sides with glue and ¾" brads, driven through the drawer sides and into the drawer ends. Make sure the outside faces of the drawer ends are flush with the ends of the drawer sides. Position the drawer bottom inside the drawer ends and drawer sides. Drill pilot holes, and fasten the drawer bottom with ¾" brads **(photo C).** Do not use glue to attach the bottom. Cut the

The drawer is made from ½"-thick wood, so be sure to drill pilot holes for the nails.

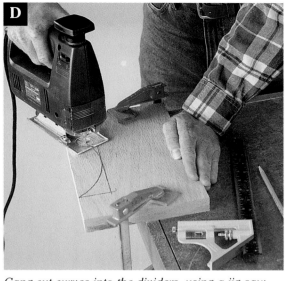

Gang-cut curves into the dividers, using a jig saw.

drawer front (F) to size from 1 × 10 stock, and center it on one drawer end. With the edges flush, attach the drawer front with glue and 1" brads, driven through the end and into the front. Sand all the edges, and test-fit the drawer into the bin.

INSTALL VERTICAL DIVIDERS. Cut the bin spacers (J) and dividers (K) to size. The bin spacers are made from ¼"-thick × 2"-wide oak mull casing, which is frequently used with patio doors. Draw a curve on the front edge of one divider: start the curve 2¼" in from the top and bottom edges, and make the curve 2" deep at the center. Clamp the dividers together with their edges flush, and gang-cut them along the curved cutting line with a jig saw **(photo D).** Sand the dividers while they are still clamped, using a drum sander attachment on an electric drill. The bin spacers have bevels sanded into their front edges. A belt sander mounted on its side grinds bevels quickly. Clamp a scrap guide to your worksurface to stabilize the parts as

you grind them, making sure the sanding belt is perpendicular to the surface. Use the scrap as a guide to steady the workpieces as you grind bevels on the front edges of the spacers **(photo E).** Use ¾" brads to fasten two of the bin spacers to the bin top, flush against the partitions. Fasten two more bin spacers to the top. Insert the dividers, and fasten the last bin spacers between them. Remove the dividers for finishing.

APPLY FINISHING TOUCHES. Cut the adjustable shelf (D) to size. Fill all counterbored holes with glued oak plugs. Finish-sand all wood surfaces. Apply a finish of your choice. We used linseed oil. When the finish is dry, attach a ¾"-dia. brass knob to the drawer front. Insert the shelf pins and adjustable shelf. Attach adhesive-backed felt buttons to the bottom of the secretary topper to prevent scratching your desk.

A belt sander mounted on its side grinds bevels quickly and easily.

Mug Rack

Your everyday coffee mugs become decorative kitchen items when displayed on this original mug rack.

A mug rack gives you a great way to combine storage and decoration. Just put your mugs in this simple, convenient frame to display them on your kitchen countertop or hang them on a wall. The mugs will always be there when you need them, and instead of taking up valuable shelf space, they will become decorative kitchen items for all to see. Colorful mug designs look great against the beaded siding board backing on the rack. Paint the project to match your kitchen, or cover it with a clear finish to preserve the natural look of the wood. You can hang your mugs on Shaker pegs, which are easy to install with some glue and a portable drill. Fit the bottom and back of the mug rack with rubber bumpers for increased stability. With a minimum of work or cost, our mug rack will give you a decorative home accent you can be proud of.

CONSTRUCTION MATERIALS

Quantity	Lumber
1	1 × 4" × 10' pine
1	1 × 8" × 8' beaded siding board

OVERALL SIZE:
18½" HIGH
3½" DEEP
31" LONG

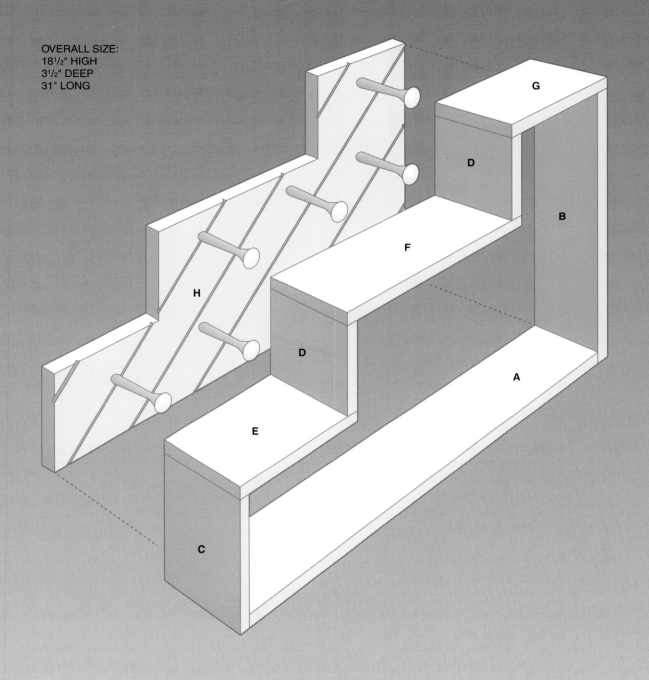

Cutting List

Key	Part	Dimension	Pcs.	Material
A	Frame bottom	¾ × 3½ × 29½"	1	Pine
B	Tall end	¾ × 3½ × 17¾"	1	Pine
C	Short end	¾ × 3½ × 9¾"	1	Pine
D	Divider	¾ × 3½ × 3¼"	2	Pine

Cutting List

Key	Part	Dimension	Pcs.	Material
E	Lower shelf	¾ × 3½ × 7"	1	Pine
F	Middle shelf	¾ × 3½ × 15"	1	Pine
G	Top shelf	¾ × 3½ × 10½"	1	Pine
H	Backing	¾ × 7½ × *"	3	Siding

Materials: Wood glue, 4d finish nails, Shaker pegs (8), rubber feet (4), finishing materials.

Note: Measurements reflect the actual thickness of dimensional lumber.

*Cut to fit

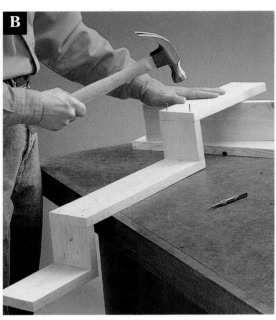

Use glue and finish nails to attach the dividers to the tops of the lower and middle shelves.

Fasten the top shelf to the middle shelf divider.

Directions: Mug Rack

ASSEMBLE THE FRAME. The mug rack frame is assembled completely with glue and finish nails. After you drive the finish nails into the wood, use a nail set to set the head below the wood surface. Remember to fill all the nail holes with wood putty. Start by cutting the frame bottom (A), tall end (B), short end (C), lower shelf (E) middle shelf (F), top shelf (G) and dividers (D) to size from 1 × 4 pine. Sand out any rough edges with medium-grit (100 or 120) sandpaper, then finish-sand with fine grit (150 or 180) sandpaper. Fasten the ends to the bottom with glue and 4d finish nails, driven through the ends into the frame bottom edges. Make sure the

edges are flush. Next, attach the dividers to the tops of the lower and middle shelves with glue and finish nails **(photo A).** The end of each shelf should be flush with the end of each divider. Use support blocks to help you keep the pieces stationary on the worksurface. Once the dividers are attached, fasten the middle shelf to the top of the lower shelf divider. Make sure the divider edges and middle shelf edges are flush. Fasten the top shelf to the

> TIP
>
> *Siding is available in many different patterns such as tongue-and-groove, shiplap, or channel groove. Each pattern has a different joint pattern and appearance. These siding styles all cut easily with a circular saw or jig saw, but be careful of kick back, which can cause the material to jump off the table with dangerous force.*

middle shelf divider, once again keeping the edges flush **(photo B).** Finally, use glue and finish nails to fasten the shelves flush with the tall and

short ends to complete the mug rack frame.

BUILD & ATTACH THE BACKING. The backing (H) fits into the frame and holds the Shaker pegs. Make the backing from pieces of your favorite beaded siding. Join the pieces together as necessary to create an 18½ × 31½" panel that is treated as a single workpiece. Cut the backing, and place the mug rack frame on the pieces so their grooves run diagonally at about a 60° angle. The space inside the frame should be completely filled with the backing. Trace the cutting lines onto the back panel, following the inside of the frames **(photo C).** Glue the backing pieces together and let them dry. Next, turn the backing over, face down. Turn the frame face down on top of the backing,

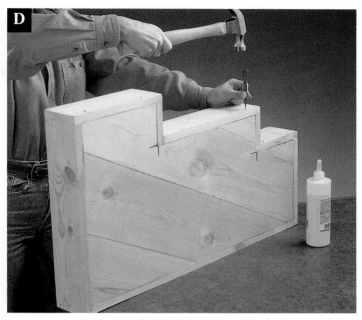

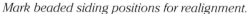
Mark beaded siding positions for realignment.

Fasten the backing into the frame with finish nails, then set the nail holes.

and trace the inside of the frame. Remove the frame, then use a straightedge or square to retrace or straighten the lines. Cut the backing to shape with a straightedge guide and a jig saw. Test-fit the backing into the mug rack frame. If needed, trim it to fit the frame, and fasten the backing with 4d finish nails **(photo D),** driven through the frame and into the edges of the backing panel. Set and fill all the exposed nail holes.

ATTACH THE MUG PEGS. The main section of the project is now complete. For the final construction steps, you need to attach the mug pegs. The peg locations must be measured and marked carefully before any drilling is done. Start by measuring and marking a vertical line 4½" from the tall end, then draw three more vertical lines spaced 7¼" apart. Mark the peg centerpoints along the

lines. The first centerpoint should be 5½" from the bottom. The second should be 11" from the bottom. The third peg centerpoint should be 16½" from the bottom shelf. Use a power drill to make ½ × ⅝"-deep holes for the mug pegs at these centerpoints **(photo E).** Glue the pegs, and insert them into the holes. Wipe away any excess glue.

APPLY THE FINISHING TOUCHES. Make sure all the surfaces are sanded smooth, then paint or finish the mug rack as you see fit. We used a linseed oil finish on our mug rack. When the finish has dried, hang the mug rack on the wall, or install rubber bumpers on the bottom for stable countertop placement.

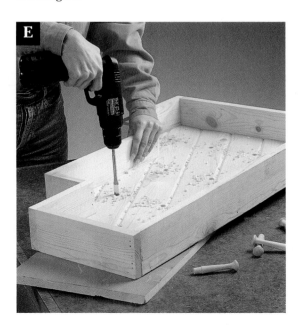

Measure and mark peg locations on the backing, then drill peg holes with a spade bit. Do not drill all the way through the backing.

Butcher Block Knife Box

*Slice and dice on the oak-strip butcher block top, then store your
kitchen knives in the handy drawer below.*

The beauty of butcher block and the grace of simple design come together in this knife box. Strips of red oak are pinned and glued together to form a solid butcher block cutting board that functions as the top of the knife box. The low-profile drawer that fills the base of the box is sized to store a wide selection of kitchen knives in one convenient spot.

In this project, we show you how to glue and pin oak strips to create a butcher block surface—it's not as difficult as you may think. But if you aren't quite that ambitious, you may prefer to purchase a prefabricated butcher block panel cut to size. Or, you can even trim down a common cutting board to fit. If you choose to purchase the cutting board premade, try to find one that is made of red oak to match the wood used for the base and drawer. Other-

wise, you can purchase any top you want, but you'll get the best results if you change the wood type for the box and drawer, as well. Making your own butcher block panels is a valuable skill. Even if you are a little hesitant, we suggest that you give it a try. You can use the same techniques to create a multitude of handy kitchen accessories that are custom-designed to meet your needs. And after a few small projects, you may even want to tackle the ultimate butcher block project—making your own custom countertops.

CONSTRUCTION MATERIALS

Quantity	Lumber
6	1 × 2" × 8' oak
1	1 × 2" × 2' oak
1	1 × 3" × 2' oak
1	1 × 4" × 4' oak
1	¼ × 2' × 2' plywood
1	½ × 2" × 4' oak

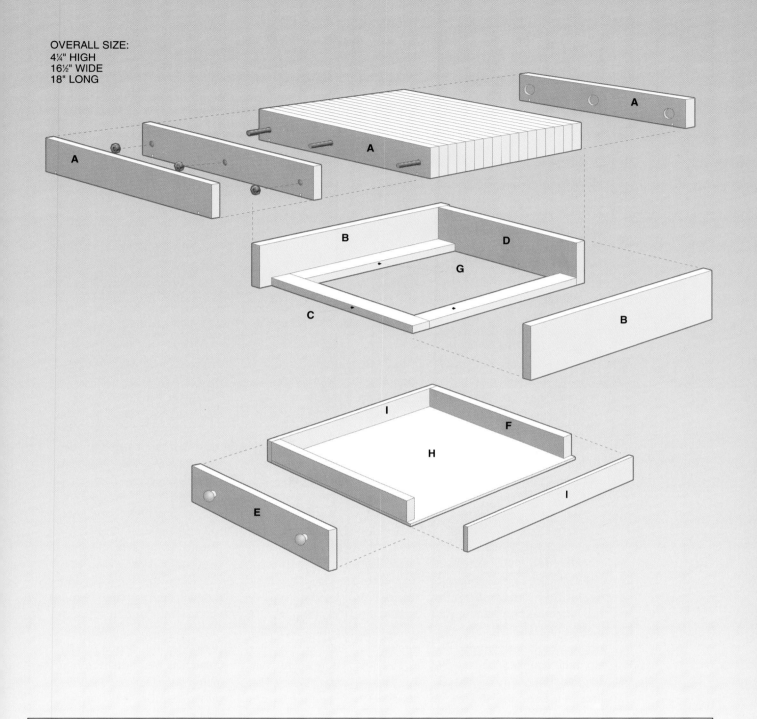

OVERALL SIZE:
4¼" HIGH
16½" WIDE
18" LONG

Cutting List				
Key	**Part**	**Dimension**	**Pcs.**	**Material**
A	Slat	¾ × 1½ × 18"	22	Oak
B	Side	¾ × 2¾ × 15½"	2	Oak
C	Front rail	¾ × 1½ × 15⅜"	1	Oak
D	Back	¾ × 2¾ × 15⅜"	1	Oak
E	Drawer front	¾ × 2½ × 15⅛"	1	Oak

Cutting List				
Key	**Part**	**Dimension**	**Pcs.**	**Material**
F	Drawer end	¾ × 1½ × 14⅛"	2	Oak
G	Drawer glide	¾ × 1½ × 12"	2	Oak
H	Drawer bottom	¼ × 15⅛ × 13½"	1	Plywood
I	Drawer side	½ × 1½ × 13½"	2	Oak

Materials: Glue, brass wood screws (#6 × 3", #6 × 2", #6 × 1¼"), 1" wire brads, ⅜"-dia. × 16" threaded rods (3) with nuts and washers, 1"-dia. wooden knobs (2), rubber bumpers, ⅜"-dia. oak plugs, finishing materials.

Note: Measurements reflect the actual size of dimensional lumber.

33

Directions:
Butcher Block Knife Box

PREPARE THE OAK SLATS. The butcher block cutting board is made from 22 oak slats that are glued together. The inner slats have three holes bored through them, positioned 2" from each end and at the center of each slat. During the gluing process, threaded rods are inserted into these holes and secured with nuts and washers to draw the slats together. The edge slats fit along the front and back of the butcher block, covering the ends of the threaded rods. Begin by cutting the slats (A) to length from 1 × 2 oak. Mark points 2" from both edge slat ends, and at each center. Use a drill fitted with a 1" spade bit and a portable drill guide to bore 1"-dia. × ½"-deep stopped holes at these points—on the inside face of each edge slat. Since you cannot use a depth stop with a spade bit, you should put a piece of tape ½" up on the bit to achieve the correct hole depth. If the point of the spade bit pokes through the slat, drill ⅜"-dia. holes through the slat holes. You can plug them later in the assembly process. Mark these corresponding points on one inner slat, and drill ⅛"-dia. pilot holes through this inside slat. You

With an inside slat on the dowels, slide the threaded rods into place and apply a thin coat of glue to the inside face.

will use this slat as a drilling template for the remaining inner slats. It is extremely important to maintain accuracy during this portion of the process. Carefully clamp the drilled inner slat over an undrilled slat with their edges flush. Drill ⅛"-dia. holes through the holes in the drilled slat, into the undrilled slat. Remove the drilled inside slat and set it aside. Repeat these steps with the rest of the inner slats, then use a drill and portable drill guide to drill ½"-dia. holes through all the pilot holes at the centerpoints.

PREPARE THE WORKSURFACE. Since you will be gluing extensively as you assemble the cutting board, make sure your worksurface is adequately prepared. Start by taping two 1 × 2 spacers (we used 1"-dia. × 18"-long dowels) to a level worksurface, 12" apart. These pieces keep the cutting board off the worksurface as you assemble. Cover the worksurface with wax paper to prevent sticking and glue damage. Have the

threaded rods, washers and nuts ready.

ATTACH THE INNER SLATS. Place an inner slat on the dowels. Cut the three threaded rods to 16" lengths with a hacksaw. Use a grinding wheel or file to remove any burrs. Thread a nut and washer onto one end of the rod, and insert a threaded rod into a hole in the slat **(photo A).** Apply a thin coat of glue on the inside face. Apply glue to another inner slat and slide it over the rod and against the first slat. Continue the gluing process, gluing slats on both sides until all the inside slats are in place. Insert the remaining two rods into their holes. To ensure a flat surface, set a straight, square scrap piece across the slats. Tap the top of the piece with a hammer to make sure the slats are flat against the dowels or spacers on the underside. Slip the washers and nuts into place and tighten them until the glue squeezes out between the slats. Scrape the excess glue off the inner slats with a putty knife.

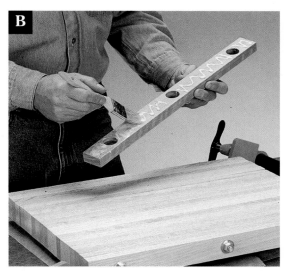

The two outer slats of the cutting board have 1"-dia. x ½"-deep holes to cover the ends of the rods.

Use a belt sander with a 100-grit sanding belt to create a smooth, even surface.

Use a circular saw and an edge guide to cut ⅛"-deep drip grooves ¼" from each bottom edge of the butcher block.

Let the glued-up assembly sit for ten minutes, then tighten the nuts.

ATTACH THE EDGE SLATS. The two edge slats fit over the front and back of the cutting board to cover the washers and nuts. They are attached with glue. Apply glue to the inside faces of the edge slats. Place the edge slats against the front and back of the inner slat assembly, making sure the holes cover the ends of the threaded rods **(photo B).** Clamp the slats together with a bar clamp until the glue is dry. Make sure bottoms of the slats are flush and even. Don't worry if the top of the butcher block surface is slightly uneven—you will probably need to sand this surface smooth. Allow the butcher block to dry for at least two days before continuing to the next step.

COMPLETE THE CUTTING BOARD. Use a belt sander with a 100-grit sanding belt to remove excess glue and smooth out the surface of the cutting board **(photo C).** If you don't own a belt sander, you can use a plane or finish sander to smooth out the cutting board. Use a circular saw with an edge guide to cut drip grooves on the bottom of the cutting board **(photo D).** Set the saw to cut ⅛"-deep grooves, ¼" from each edge of the block. Drip grooves help to protect the drawer section from spills because liquid trickling over the cutting board gets stopped. Sand the butcher block surfaces with 120-grit sandpaper and smooth out any rough edges.

MAKE THE BASE. The base fits under the butcher block cutting board. It includes a small drawer for convenient knife storage. Start by cutting the sides (B), front rail

TIP

Let glued-up wood dry for two or more days before you sand or shape it. The moisture in glue causes wood to swell temporarily. If you sand it before the swelling has diminished, you will get uneven results.

Drive counterbored wood screws through the sides to secure the drawer glides to the bottom inside edges of the frame.

Use a portable drill guide to make sure the pilot holes in the sides are straight.

(C) and back (D) to size. Rip-cut the sides and back to a 2¾" width with a circular saw and cutting guide. Drill pilot holes through the sides (B) in position to fasten the back and front rail with #6 × 2" wood screws. Position the back between the two sides, inset ¼" from the back edges. Position the front edge of the front rail 1" from the front ends of the sides. Drill centered pilot holes in the front rail, ⅜" above the bottom edges of the sides. Drill centered pilot holes for the back ⅝" from the back ends of the sides. Sand the pieces with medium (100- or 120-grit) sandpaper to smooth out any rough spots, then finish-sand with fine (150- or 180-grit) sandpaper. Fasten the sides, front rail and back with glue and wood screws, making sure their bottoms are flush. Cut the drawer glides (G) to fit between the back and front rail. Finish-sand the pieces, then apply glue to their edges. Position the glides

To attach the drawer bottom, drive brads through the drawer bottom into the drawer sides and ends.

against the inside faces of the sides, flush with the bottom side edges. Secure the drawer glides by driving evenly spaced, counterbored #6 × 1¼" wood screws through the sides and back into the drawer glide edges **(photo E).** Finally, use a

drill with a portable drill guide to bore two evenly spaced pilot holes through the bottom edges of the sides. These pilot holes will be used later to fasten the bottom to the butcher block **(photo F).**

BUILD THE KNIFE DRAWER PARTS. We used a simple drawer design that requires few

Attach the drawer front to the drawer end with glue and wood screws driven through the drawer end.

To attach the base to the cutting board, drive wood screws through the pilot holes in the sides and into the cutting board.

parts. Start by cutting the drawer front (E), drawer ends (F), drawer sides (I) and drawer bottom (H) to size. Drill two evenly spaced pilot holes through one drawer end for attaching the drawer front. Sand the parts to smooth out any rough edges.

ASSEMBLE THE KNIFE DRAWER. Apply glue to the drawer ends, and attach the drawer sides by driving 1" brass brads through the sides and into the drawer ends. Apply glue to the bottoms of the drawer ends and drawer sides, then fasten the drawer bottom with 1" brass brads driven into the drawer sides and ends **(photo G).** Next, draw a line across the inside face of the drawer front, ½" from the bottom edge. This line will help you align the drawer front against the drawer box. Center a drawer end on the drawer front, with the bottom of the drawer end on the guideline. Drive evenly spaced,

counterbored #6 × 1¼" wood screws through the drawer end and into the drawer front to complete the drawer assembly **(photo H).** Smooth out the sharp edges with sandpaper, then attach drawer knobs on the drawer front, centered top-to-bottom, 4" from each end.

APPLY THE FINISHING TOUCHES. Fill all counterbored screw holes with ⅜"-dia. red oak plugs. Sand all the surfaces with medium (100- or 120-grit) sandpaper to smooth out rough spots, then finish-sand with fine (150- or 180-grit) sandpaper. Apply a food-safe finish to all the parts. We used salad bowl oil, a nontoxic finish good for any surface that comes in contact with food. In addition, the finish can be renewed easily as the butcher block surface becomes worn—simply sand out any knife marks, and reapply the salad-bowl oil. To improve the operation of the drawer,

apply several coats of beeswax to the tops of the front rail and drawer glides. Renew this wax as needed. Finally, fasten the base section to the butcher block by driving #6 × 3" wood screws through the pilot holes in the sides into the butcher block **(photo I).** Attach rubber bumpers to the bottom of the base section for stability and to protect your kitchen counter surfaces.

TIP

Line the bottom of the drawer with felt to protect both the knives and the drawer. Just cut a piece of felt to fit on the drawer bottom, and glue it in place.

Pine Pantry

*Turn a remote corner or closet into a kitchen pantry
with this charming pine cabinet.*

CONSTRUCTION MATERIALS

Quantity	Lumber
2	1 × 10" × 10' pine
3	1 × 8" × 8' pine
1	1 × 8" × 10' pine
1	1 × 6" × 8' pine
1	1 × 4" × 8' pine
5	1 × 3" × 8' pine
1	1 × 2" × 10' pine
1	¾" × 4 × 8' plywood
1	¼" × 4 × 8' plywood

This compact pantry cabinet is ideal for keeping your kitchen organized and efficient. It features a convenient turntable shelf, or "Lazy Susan," on the inside of the cabinet for easy access to canned foods. A swing-out shelf assembly lets you get the most from the pantry's space. Its roominess allows you to store most of your non-refrigerated food items.

But the best feature of the pantry is its appearance. The rugged beauty of the cabinet hides its simplicity. For such an impressive-looking project, it is remarkably easy to build, so even if you don't have a traditional pantry in your home, you can have a convenient, attractive storage center.

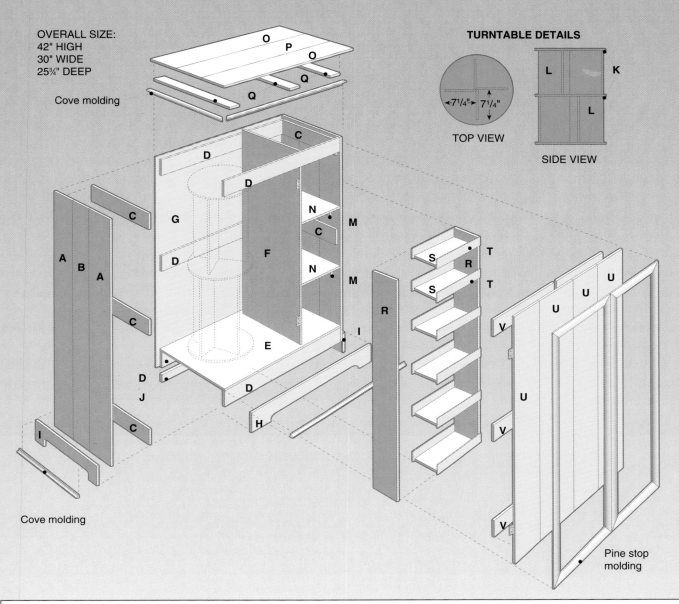

OVERALL SIZE:
42" HIGH
30" WIDE
25¾" DEEP

Cove molding

Cove molding

TURNTABLE DETAILS

←7¼"→ ←7¼"→

TOP VIEW

L K

L

SIDE VIEW

Pine stop molding

		Cutting List		
Key	Part	Dimension	Pcs.	Material
A	Side board	¾ × 9¼ × 39¼"	4	Pine
B	Middle board	¾ × 5½ × 39¼"	2	Pine
C	Panel cleat	¾ × 2½ × 22½"	6	Pine
D	Stretcher	¾ × 2½ × 26½"	5	Pine
E	Floor	¾ × 24 × 26½"	1	Plywood
F	Divider	¾ × 22½ × 36"	1	Plywood
G	Back	¼ × 28 × 39¼"	1	Plywood
H	Base front	¾ × 3½ × 29½"	1	Pine
I	Base side	¾ × 3½ × 24¼"	2	Pine
J	Base back	¾ × 1½ × 28"	1	Pine
K	Turntable shelf	¾ × 16"-dia.	3	Plywood

		Cutting List		
Key	Part	Dimension	Pcs.	Material
L	Supports	¾ × 7¼ × 12"	8	Pine
M	Shelf cleat	¾ × 1½ × 22"	4	Pine
N	Fixed shelf	¾ × 9 × 23"	2	Plywood
O	Top board	¾ × 9¼ × 30"	2	Pine
P	Middle board	¾ × 7¼ × 30"	1	Pine
Q	Top cleat	¾ × 2½ × 22¼"	3	Pine
R	Swing-out end	¾ × 6 × 32"	2	Pine
S	Swing-out shelf	¾ × 6 × 10"	6	Pine
T	Swing-out side	¼ × 2 × 11½"	12	Plywood
U	Door board	¾ × 6⅝ × 35"	4	Pine
V	Door cleat	¾ × 2½ × 11"	6	Pine

Materials: #6 × 1¼", 1½" and 2" wood screws, 2d, 4d and 6d finish nails, 16-ga. × 1" wire nails, turntable hardware, cabinet handles, 3 × 3" brass hinges (2), cabinet door hinges (4), ¾" cove molding, ⅜ × 1¼" stop molding, glue, finishing materials.

Note: Measurements reflect the actual size of dimension lumber.

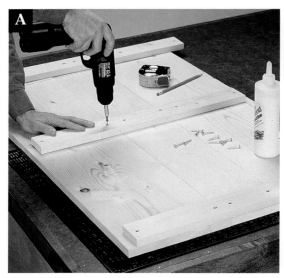

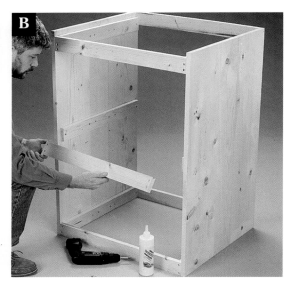

Use cleats to fasten side and middle boards, forming the cabinet sides.

Attach front and back stretchers at the top and bottom, and a middle stretcher at the back.

Directions: Pine Pantry

MAKE THE CABINET SIDES. Each cabinet side is made from three pine boards fastened together with three 1 × 3 cleats. Start by cutting the side boards (A), middle boards (B) and panel cleats (C) to size. Sand all parts with medium-grit sandpaper to smooth out any rough edges after cutting. Position a middle board between two side boards, making sure all top and bottom edges are flush. As you assemble the sides, butt the boards against a framing square to keep them in line. Position a panel cleat widthwise across the boards so the bottom edge of the cleat is flush with the bottom edges of the boards. The ends of the cleat should be ¾" from the outside edges of the side boards. Fasten the cleat to the boards with glue and #6 × 1¼" wood screws. Attach the next panel cleat to the boards so its top edge is 21½" up from the bottom edge of the first cleat **(photo A).** Maintain a ¾" distance from the cleat ends to the board edges. Install the top panel cleat with its top edge 1" down from the board tops. Repeat these steps to make the other cabinet side.

ATTACH THE SIDES. Connect the two sides by attaching side stretchers (D) between them. Attach the stretchers by driving screws through them into the ends of the panel cleats. Start by cutting the stretchers to length. Attach them at the front and back of the cabinet along the bottom, making sure their top and bottom edges are flush with the top and bottom edges of the panel cleats. The top two stretchers are positioned a little differently—while the back stretcher is flush with the tops and bottoms of the panel cleats, the front stretcher is positioned flush with the top edges of the cabinet sides. Finally, attach one stretcher at the back of the cabinet, flush with the panel cleats on the middle of the cabinet sides **(photo B).**

ATTACH THE FLOOR. The floor (E) of the pantry organizer is attached to the tops of the bottom stretchers and panel cleats. Start by cutting the floor to size from ¾"-thick plywood. Fill any voids in the front edge of the floor with wood putty. Glue the parts and fasten the floor between the cabinet sides by driving wood screws through the floor into the stretchers and panel cleats.

ATTACH THE DIVIDER. The divider fits inside the cabinet, and has shelf cleats attached to it to hold the cabinet shelves in place. Begin by cutting the divider (F) and shelf cleats (M) to size. Draw a line across the floor, 9" from the right-hand cabinet side (this line marks the position of the divider's inside face). Measure and mark shelf cleat position lines on the right-hand cabinet side 10" and 20¾" up from the cabinet floor. Draw corresponding lines on the divider. These lines mark the top edges of the shelf cleats. Use glue and wood screws to fasten the shelf cleats

Install the divider 9" in from the right-hand side of the cabinet.

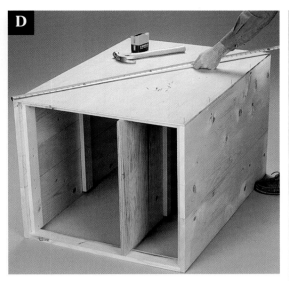

Check for square by measuring diagonally between the corners to make sure the distances are equal.

to the divider and side with their top edges at the lines. Insert the divider into the cabinet with its cleated face facing the cleated cabinet side. Apply glue to the bottom edge of the divider. Drive wood screws up through the cabinet floor into the bottom divider edge, and drive 6d finish nails through the top stretchers and into the divider edge **(photo C).**

ATTACH THE BACK. The back (G) is made from ¼"-thick plywood and is tacked to the cabinet side edges and stretchers with 1" wire nails. Cut the back to size, and drive evenly spaced nails into one side edge. Measure diagonally across the opposite corners on the back to check if the cabinet is square **(photo D).** If the two diagonal measurements are different, your cabinet isn't square. Square up the cabinet, if needed, by applying pressure to the opposite corners. Drive evenly spaced nails into the stretchers and edges to secure the back to the cabinet.

ATTACH THE FIXED SHELVES. The fixed shelves (N) fit between the divider and cabinet side. They are fastened permanently to help keep the cabinet square. Cut the fixed shelves to size from ¾"-thick plywood, and attach them to the cleats with glue and wood screws.

MAKE THE BASE. The base is made of four pine boards that are scooped out on their bottom edges to create a foot at each corner. Start by cutting the base front (H), base sides (I), and base back (J) to size. Sand the parts, then use a compass to draw 1¾" radius semi-circles, centered 7¼" from each end of the base front. Using a straightedge, draw a straight line connecting the tops of the circles. Repeat these steps on

the base sides, only center the semicircles 4¾" from the front and 5½" from the back. Cut along the lines with a jig saw. Mark lines ½" from the bottom edge on the rear edges of the base sides. These lines mark the position of the bottom edge of the base back. Glue the parts, then attach the base sides to the base front by driving 4d finish nails through the base front into the base side edges. Attach the base back between the base sides along

Cut the round turntable shelves with a jig saw. Each turntable shelf has an 8" radius.

Assemble the turntable supports in three pairs, joined at right angles.

Using 4d finish nails, attach the swing-out shelf side.

the marked lines. The bottom edge of the base back should be ½" from the bottom edges of the base sides. Set the nails.

ATTACH THE CABINET & BASE. With the cabinet on its back, slide the base over its bottom edges until the base back is flush with the bottom cleats. The base should extend 2" below the pantry's bottom edges. Drive counterbored #6 × 1¼" wood screws through the pantry sides into the base sides, and through the front stretchers into the base front.

BUILD THE TURNTABLE SHELVES. The turntable shelves are made by cutting three circular plywood parts from square stock. They are attached to each other with pine supports. Once these parts are assembled they are mounted on a turntable, or "Lazy Susan." Start by cutting the turntable shelves (K) and turntable supports (L) to size. To cut the turntable shelves into their final, circular shape, mark the center of the turntable shelves, and use a compass to draw the turntable shelves' guidelines. Each shelf should have an 8"

radius. Cut the shelves to size with a jig saw **(photo E).** Attach pairs of turntable supports at right angles by applying glue and driving 1½" counterbored screws through one support's face into the other support's edge **(photo F),** forming simple butt joints. To attach the turntable supports to the turntable shelves (see *Diagram*, page 27), use a straightedge to scribe a line on the shelves, directly through their centerpoints. Place one pair of supports along the line with the joint at the centerpoint. Make sure the support pair forms a right angle, then outline the supports on the shelf. Position another support pair on the other side of the line and draw the outline. Drill pilot holes for #6 × 1½" wood screws centered within the outlines, and fasten the turntable shelves to the turntable supports with glue and wood screws. The supports should have their spines meeting at the centerpoint of the turntable. Attach the turntable hardware to the bottom face of the bottom turntable shelf,

following manufacturer's directions. It is critical to center the turntable on the shelf, or the assembly will not rotate smoothly. Insert the turntable assembly after you apply the finish to the pantry organizer.

BUILD THE SWING-OUT RACK. Six swing-out shelves are attached between two shelf ends to make the rack. When completed, the rack swings on hinges to give you easy access to cans or dry goods. Cut the swing-out shelves (S), swing-out ends (R) and swing-out sides (T). Starting from one end, mark lines 6" apart up the swing-out ends. These lines mark the positions of the swing-out shelves. Apply glue to the shelf edges, then attach them to the swing-out ends by driving wood screws through the ends into the shelf edges. The bottom shelf should be flush with the bottom of the end edges. Finally, attach the swing-out shelf sides (T) on the edges of the shelves with glue and 4d finish nails **(photo G).** Set the swing-out rack aside until you have applied the finish.

Use a circular saw with a straightedge guide to rip-cut the door boards to size.

Tack pine cove molding frame around the edges of the assembled doors.

MAKE THE TOP. Cut the top boards (O), middle board (P) and top cleats (Q) to size. Sand them, and join the top boards and middle board by attaching a top cleat across the inside faces of the boards, 1¾" from each end. Fasten the third top cleat so its right-hand edge is 11½" from the right-hand edge of the top. When the top is placed on the cabinet, the right edge of this middle cleat should touch the divider. Position the top onto the cabinet, and fasten it by driving 4d finish nails into the cabinet sides and through the middle cleat, into the divider edge.

BUILD THE DOORS. Each door is made from two boards, held together with three cleats. The outside faces of the doors are framed with stop molding. Cut the door boards (U) and door cleats (V) to size **(photo H).** Use glue and counterbored wood screws to attach the top and bottom door cleats; the top edges of the top cleats should be 2" down from the tops of the boards. The bottom edges of the bottom cleats should be 3½" up from the bottoms of the

boards. Center and attach the final door cleat on the inside faces of the door panels. Miter-cut ⅜"-thick stop molding to frame the front faces of the doors. Fasten the molding with glue and 2d finish nails **(photo I).**

APPLY FINISHING TOUCHES. Miter-cut ¾"-thick cove molding to fit around the base and top (see *Diagram*, page 27). Attach the molding with 2d finish nails and glue. Fill all nail holes, and finish-sand the pantry organizer with fine (150- or 180-grit) sandpaper. We applied a clear poly-

urethane finish to the outside and inside surfaces. Attach two evenly spaced 3 × 3" butt hinges to the edges of the swing-out rack, and mount it on the divider **(photo J).** Position ¼"-thick spacers between the rack and divider to create a clearance for the shelf to swing. Attach the turntable assembly to the floor of the pantry organizer—check to make sure the turntable rotates freely. Attach hinges and handles to the doors, then mount the doors to the cabinet sides.

With ¼"-thick spacers in place beneath the swing-out rack, attach the rack to the divider with 3 × 3" butt hinges.

China Cabinet

This tall, sleek fixture displays and stores fine china and other housewares without occupying a lot of floor space.

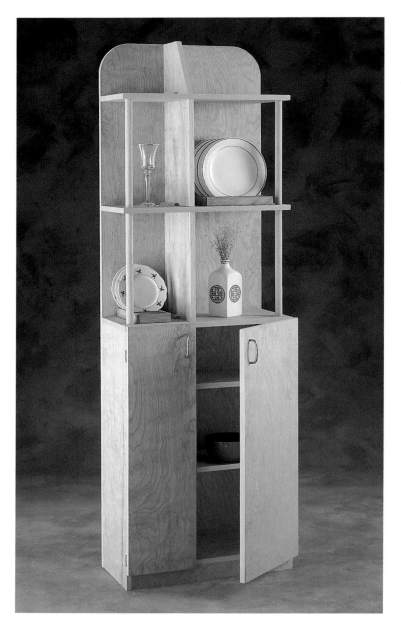

This modern-looking china cabinet features a snappy, efficient design to showcase and store all types of china and dishware with equal elegance. The bottom half of the cabinet is a simple cupboard for storing everyday serving trays, napkins, silverware and miscellaneous houseware.

CONSTRUCTION MATERIALS

Quantity	Lumber
2	¾" × 4 × 8' birch plywood
2	1"-dia. × 3' dowel
1	½ × ½ " × 3' quarter-round molding

The upper half is an open rack for displaying your favorite porcelain statues, china, vases and collectibles.

Among the more interesting features of this china cabinet are the 1" dowel columns that support the shelves in the rack area. The asymmetrical design allows you to store and display a wider range of items than if the cabinet was equally weighted on the right and left. And the overall slenderness of the cabinet means you can fit it

into just about any room, whether it's tucked into a corner or featured prominently along the center of a wall.

Plates and other items that are displayed in the rack area of the cabinet can be accentuated with plateholders. Or, you can do as we did and build a few custom-sized plate holders from scraps of molding. Just cut the molding into strips about the same width as the plates, and inset the strips at ¼" intervals in a plain wood frame.

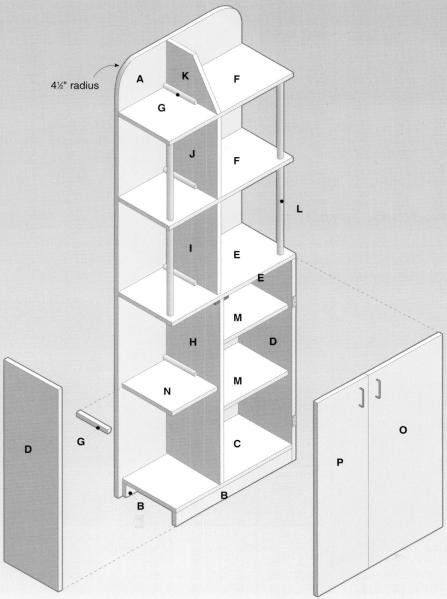

OVERALL SIZE:
75" HIGH
24" WIDE
12" DEEP

4½" radius

Cutting List

Key	Part	Dimension	Pcs.	Material
A	Back	¾ × 24 × 75"	1	Plywood
B	Bottom rail	¾ × 2¼ × 22½"	2	Plywood
C	Cupboard bottom	¾ × 10½ × 22½"	1	Plywood
D	Cupboard side	¾ × 10½ × 35¼"	2	Plywood
E	Cupboard top	¾ × 10½ × 24"	1	Plywood
F	Rack shelf	¾ × 10 × 24"	2	Plywood
G	Cleat	½ × ½ × 6"	6	Toe molding
H	Cupboard divider	¾ × 10½ × 32¼"	1	Plywood

Cutting List

Key	Part	Dimension	Pcs.	Material
I	Rack divider	¾ × 10 × 15⅛"	1	Plywood
J	Rack divider	¾ × 10 × 14¾"	1	Plywood
K	Rack divider	¾ × 10 × 7½"	1	Plywood
L	Column	1 × 30⅝"	2	Dowel
M	Cupboard shelf	¾ × 13¼ × 10"	2	Plywood
N	Cupboard shelf	¾ × 8½ × 10"	1	Plywood
O	Large door	¾ × 14⅜ × 33¾"	1	Plywood
P	Small door	¾ × 9½ × 33¾"	1	Plywood

Materials: Wood glue, wood screws (#6 × 1¼", #6 × 2"), birch veneer edge tape (50'), ⅜"-dia. birch wood plugs, 1¼" brass butt hinges (4), 1¼" brads, magnetic door catches (2), 2½" brass door pulls (2), finishing materials.

Note: Measurements reflect the actual size of dimensional lumber.

Attach the cupboard bottom by driving screws through the cupboard sides and into the edges.

Carefully sand the wood plugs to level, using a belt sander or power hand sander.

Directions: China Cabinet

MAKE THE BACK PANEL. With its rounded top, the back panel runs the entire height of the china cabinet, anchoring both the rack and cupboard units. Start by cutting the back (A) to size. Sand this and all parts to smooth out rough spots after cutting. Use a compass to draw a semicircle roundover with a 4½" radius at each top corner of the back panel. Cut the curves with a jig saw. Use a household iron to apply birch veneer edge tape to the side and top edges of the back. Trim the excess tape with a sharp utility knife, then sand the edges smooth. As a guide for installing the rack shelves, mark reference points 51⅛" and 66⅝" up from the bottom edge, 9¼" in from one side edge of the workpiece (this side should become the left side when facing from the front).

MAKE THE CUPBOARD. Start by cutting the bottom rails (B) and cupboard bottom (C) to size. Apply edge tape to one long edge of the cupboard bottom. Position the bottom rails beneath the cupboard bottom, flush with the edges. Drill counterbored pilot holes through the cupboard bottom and into the tops of the rails, then attach the parts with glue and #6 × 2" wood screws. Cut the cupboard sides (D) to size, and apply edge tape to the front edges. Position the cupboard bottom between the cupboard sides. Drill counterbored pilot holes, then apply glue and drive wood screws through the sides and into the edges of the cupboard bottom **(photo A).** Cut the cupboard top (E) to size, and apply edge tape to the front and side edges. Attach it to the tops of the cupboard sides with glue and screws driven down through the cupboard top and into the tops of the sides.

ATTACH CUPBOARD SHELVES & DIVIDER. Cut the cupboard divider (H) and cupboard shelves (M, N) to size. Apply veneer tape to the front edges

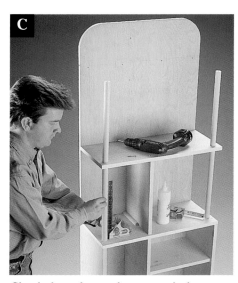

Check the columns for square before attaching them to the cabinet top.

of the shelves and dividers. Draw reference lines on the cupboard bottom and cupboard top, 9¼" in from the left cupboard side, for positioning the divider between them (these lines should align with the marks you made earlier on the back panel). Set the divider between the cupboard top and bottom, so the left face is on the reference lines. Attach the divider with glue and wood screws, driven through the top and bottom and into the divider. Draw reference lines on the right side and right face of the divider, 12" and 24" up from the bottoms, for positioning the larger cupboard shelves (M). Draw reference lines for the smaller cupboard shelf (N) 16" up from the bottoms on the left side and left face of the divider. Apply glue to the side edges of all three shelves and position them between the cupboard sides and the divider, with their bottoms on the reference lines. Make sure the back edges of the shelves are flush with the back edges of the sides. Fasten the shelves with #6 × 2" wood screws, driven through the sides and the divider, and into the edges of the shelves. Glue ⅜"-dia. birch wood plugs into all the exposed counterbores in the cupboard. When the glue has dried, sand the plugs down to the surface of the plywood with a belt sander and a medium sanding belt **(photo B).** Be careful not to scar the surrounding wood. Attach the back panel to the cupboard with glue and #6 × 2" wood screws.

MAKE & MARK THE RACK PARTS. Cut the rack dividers (I, J, K) to full size. The lower rack dividers (I, J) are left square. The upper divider is trimmed off at an angle on the front edge. To make the angled cut in the upper divider, mark a point on one long edge, 5¼" from one end. Draw a straight line from that point to the bottom corner on the opposite end. Cut along the line with a jig saw or circular saw. Cut the two rack shelves (F) to size, sand smooth, then attach veneer edge tape to the front edges of the rack dividers, and to the front and side edges of

the rack shelves. With the taped edges facing you, draw reference lines on the shelves, 9¼" in from the left sides. Next, drill two 1"-dia. holes for the columns (L) all the way through one shelf. The center of each hole should be 1¾" in from the front edge and 1¼" in from the side edge of the shelf. This shelf will become the lower rack shelf. Cut the columns (L) to length.

INSTALL THE RACK. When installing the rack, alternate between shelves and dividers. Use glue and #6 × 2" wood screws, driven through counterbored pilot holes in the back panel, to fasten the lower rack divider (I) in position at the marks on the shelf and back panel. Use a square to make sure the divider is perpendicular to the back panel. Cut cleats from quarter-round molding (G) to size, and use glue and 1¼" brads to attach the cleats on each side of the divider, flush against the back. Apply glue to the top edge of the lower divider, and position the shelf with the 1"-dia. holes on top of the divider, so the holes are in front. Attach the shelf to the divider with wood screws, driven through the back and into the shelf, and through the shelf and into the lower divider. Apply glue to the bottom of each column, and slide them through the holes in the shelf. Use a square to make sure they are straight **(photo C),** then drive a #6 × 1¼" wood screw up through the cabinet top and into the bottom of each column. Next, position the middle rack divider (J) on the shelf. Fasten it with glue, screws and cleats. Attach the upper shelf to the middle

divider and back panel with glue and wood screws, then drive #6 × 1¼" wood screws through the shelf and into the tops of the columns. Finally, apply glue to the back and bottom edges of the upper divider, and attach it with wood screws and cleats.

INSTALL THE DOORS. Start by cutting the doors (O, P) to size. Apply edge tape to all edges of each door. Make sure all the surfaces are sanded smooth. Attach 1¼" brass butt hinges to the doors, 3½" down from the top edges, and ½" up from the bottom edges. Fasten the doors to the cupboard sides, flush with the cabinet top **(photo D).** Install magnetic door catches on the cupboard divider and doors. Attach door pulls to the outside faces of the doors, 1½" down from the top edges of the doors, and 1½" in from the inside edges—we used plain, 2½" brass door pulls. Give the project a final finish-sanding, wipe clean with a rag dipped in mineral spirits, then apply your finish of choice (we simply applied two coats of polyurethane over unstained wood).

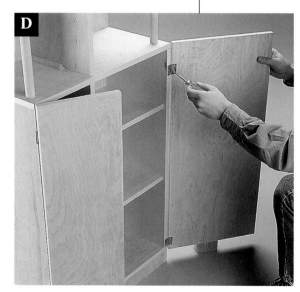

Hang the doors with brass butt hinges.

47

Liquor Locker

Store spirits of all varieties safely under lock and key in this beautiful oak cabinet.

Compact and elegant, this liquor locker provides protected storage for liquor or cordials, without looking like a bank safe. Made from oak and oak plywood, this functional furnishing has a formal style that features arched cabinet doors. A simple cylinder lock installed in one of the door frames keeps your alcohol products away from curious young hands.

The main compartment in the liquor locker is sized to hold several full-size bottles of your favorite liquors, cordials and aperitifs. A narrow shelf in the back of the compartment is perfect for storing mixers that usually come in smaller bottles, like bitters, vermouth or lime juice. Or, you can stow glassware on the shelf. The top of the cabinet is made from oak plywood. It is large enough to provide ample surface area for preparing or serving after-dinner drinks in your den.

To accentuate the natural tones of the red oak, we did not stain the wood but applied a clear topcoat of water-based polyurethane. When choosing a topcoat product, note that alcohol will dissolve products like shellac and paste wax.

CONSTRUCTION MATERIALS

Quantity	Lumber
1	¾" × 4 × 8' oak plywood
1	½" × 2 × 4' oak plywood
1	1 × 2" × 8' oak
1	1 × 4" × 6' oak
2	2 × 2" × 8' oak
1	¾ × ¾" × 6' cove molding
2	⅜ × ¾" × 8' base shoe molding

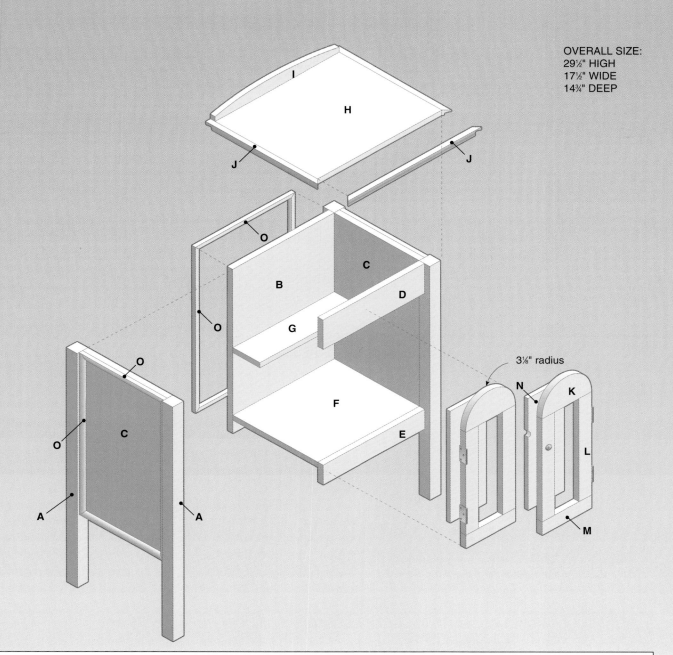

OVERALL SIZE:
29½" HIGH
17½" WIDE
14¾" DEEP

3⅛" radius

Cutting List				
Key	**Part**	**Dimension**	**Pcs.**	**Material**
A	Leg	1½ × 1½ × 27¼"	4	Oak
B	Back panel	¾ × 13 × 19¼"	1	Plywood
C	Side panel	¾ × 11 × 19¼"	2	Plywood
D	Top rail	¾ × 3½ × 13"	1	Oak
E	Bottom rail	¾ × 2 × 13"	1	Oak
F	Bottom panel	¾ × 11 × 13"	1	Plywood
G	Shelf	¾ × 3½ × 13"	1	Oak
H	Top panel	¾ × 14 × 16"	1	Plywood

Cutting List				
Key	**Part**	**Dimension**	**Pcs.**	**Material**
I	Backsplash	¾ × 1½ × 16"	1	Oak
J	Top molding	¾ × ¾ × *"	3	Cove molding
K	Top door rail	¾ × 3½ × 6¼"	2	Oak
L	Door stile	¾ × 1½ × 12"	4	Oak
M	Lower door rail	¾ × 1½ × 6¼"	2	Oak
N	Door panel	½ × 4¼ × 13"	2	Plywood
O	Side trim	⅜ × ¾ × *"	12	Base shoe molding

Materials: #6 × 1¼", 2" and 2½" brass wood screws, 8d finish nails, 16-ga. × ¾" and 1¼" brass brads, 16-ga. × 1" wire nails, 2" brass corner braces (6), 1½ × 3" brass hinges (4), cylinder lock hardware, elbow catches (2), ⅜"-dia. oak plugs, wood glue, finishing materials.

Note: Measurements reflect the actual size of dimension lumber.
*Cut to fit.

Directions: Liquor Locker

MAKE THE CABINET SECTION. The legs are the main structural members for the cabinet. We used oak plugs to conceal the screw holes, so we counterbored all visible pilot holes. Start by cutting the legs (A), back panel (B) and side panels (C) to size. Arrange the legs in pairs, and position a side panel between the legs in each pair. One short edge of each side

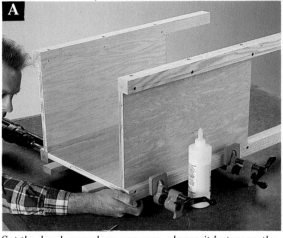

A

Set the back panel on spacers, clamp it between the rear legs and fasten it with glue and wood screws.

panel should be flush with the tops of the legs and the inside of the side panel is flush with the inside of the legs. Drill pilot holes, and attach the sides between the legs with glue and countersunk #6 × 2½" brass wood screws, driven through the legs and into the edges of the side panels. Set the back panel on your worksurface, supported by ¾"-thick scraps. Butt the leg pairs against the edges of the back panel, making sure the tops are flush. Apply glue, and clamp the leg pairs to the back panel with bar or pipe clamps. Attach the legs to the back with countersunk #6 × 2½" brass wood screws **(photo A).** Cut the top rail (D), bottom rail (E) and bottom panel (F) to size. Fasten the top rail between the legs with glue and #6 × 2½" wood screws, with the top and inside edges flush. Attach the bottom rail to the front edge of the bottom panel with the top edges flush. Apply glue to the edges of the bottom panel and bottom rail, and insert them into the cabinet: the top edge of the bottom rail should be 10¼" up from

the bottoms of the legs. Drill pilot holes, and fasten the bottom panel and bottom rail with #6 × 2" wood screws. Like the sides, back and top rail, the front face of the bottom rail should be ¾" back from the outsides of the legs. Measure diagonally from corner to corner to make sure the cabinet is square **(photo B).** If the measurements are the same, the frame is square. Cut the shelf (G) to size, and position it so the bottom face is 7" up from the bottom panel. Attach the shelf with glue and wood screws, driven through the back and side panels.

MAKE THE TOP. The top is made from plywood and edged with oak cove molding. Begin by cutting the top panel (H) and backsplash (I) to size. The peak of the curved backsplash, located at the midpoint, should be 1½" up from the bottom edge. To draw a smooth, even curve onto the backsplash, drive a finish nail part-way into the board at the peak of the curve, then drive nails at the starting points of the curve, ½" up from the bottom edge of the backsplash. Slip a flexible

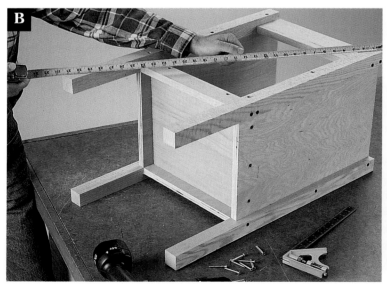

B

Measure from corner to corner to check for square. If the project isn't square, apply pressure to one side or the other until it is square.

C

Apply glue, clamp the backsplash in place, and attach it to the top.

straightedge behind the nails at the starting points and in front of the nail at the peak to create a smooth curve. Trace along the inside of the straightedge to make a cutting line. Cut the curve with a jig saw, and sand it smooth. Clamp the backsplash to the top panel so the side and back edges are flush. Drill pilot holes, apply glue, and fasten the backsplash to the top with #6 × 1¼" brass wood screws **(photo C).** Cut the top molding (J) to size, miter-cutting the front ends of the side pieces and both ends of the front piece. Apply glue to the top molding, and attach it with 1¼" brads, forming miter joints at the front corners. Drill pilot holes to avoid splitting the molding. Center the top panel over the cabinet, with the back edges flush. Clamp the top in place, and secure it with six 2" brass corner braces, spaced evenly on the inside faces of the side and back panels.

MAKE THE DOORS. The cabinet doors are frame-and-panel style. The frames feature an arched rail at the top, and the door panels are attached to the backs of the frames. Start by cutting the top door rails (K) to length. Use a compass to draw a 3⅛"-radius semicircle on each rail, centered ⅜" up from the bottom edge of the rail. The tops of the semicircles should just touch the top edges of the boards. Cut along the semicircles with a jig saw, and gang-sand both arches smooth with a belt sander to remove any saw marks. Cut the door stiles (L) and lower door rails (M) to size. After sanding them smooth, drill pilot holes, and attach the door rails to the bottoms of the door stiles with

glue and #6 × 2" wood screws, driven through the bottom edges of the door rails and into the door stiles. To complete the door frames, position the semi-completed frame on your worksurface, and butt the arched rails against the free ends of the door stiles. Apply glue, and clamp the frame together with bar clamps. Check the frame to make sure it is square. Drill pilot holes, and attach the arched top rails to the door stiles with 8d finish nails, driven through the tops of the rails and into the door stiles **(photo D).** When the glue has dried on the frame, drill a hole for a cylinder lock through the front face of one door stile, using a backing board to prevent splintering when the bit exits the door stile on the other side. The lock hardware we used required a ⅞"-dia. hole, 3½" below the top of the arched rail. Cut the door panels (N) to size. Draw reference lines on one face of each door frame, ½" in from the inside edges. Position the panels within these lines. To accommodate the lock hole on one frame, cut a notch in the panel with a jig saw. Sand the panels, then attach them to the frames with glue and 1" wire nails.

APPLY FINISHING TOUCHES. Cut the side trim (O) pieces to length from ¾" base shoe molding. Miter-cut the ends at 45° angles to make miter joints at the corners. Use glue and ¾" brads to attach the trim so it butts against the sides and legs, and along the top and bottom edges of each side. Also frame the back panel with base shoe molding. Set and fill all nail holes. Fill all screw holes with wood plugs, and

finish-sand the project. Install two brass 1½ × 3" hinges on each door, 1" in from the ends of the stiles. Fasten the hinges to the legs, making sure the doors overlap the bottom rail by ¾". Install the lock. Fasten elbow catches at the top and bottom to secure the door that does not contain the lock **(photo E).** Cover the hardware with masking tape, and apply your finish of choice. We used clear polyurethane.

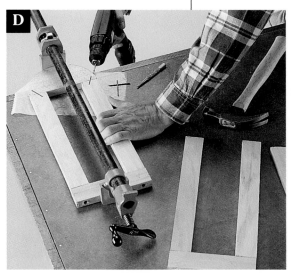

Drill pilot holes for 8d finish nails, and drive them through the joint between the arch and stiles.

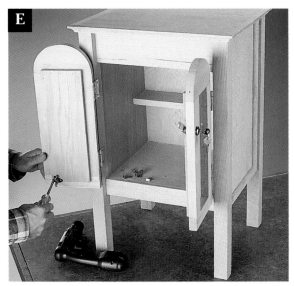

Attach elbow catches to the door that does not contain the lock.

Tile-top Coffee Table

The dramatic, contrasting textures of floor tiles and warm red oak will make you forget that this table is designed to create storage.

CONSTRUCTION MATERIALS

Quantity	Lumber
1	¾" × 4 × 8' oak plywood
2	1 × 2" × 8' oak
2	1 × 4" × 8' oak
1	⅛ × ⅞" × 8' oak corner molding

Functionally, the trim size and the amply proportioned storage shelf are the two most important features of this tile-top coffee table. But most people won't notice that. They'll be too busy admiring the striking tile tabletop and the clean oak lines of the table base.

Measuring a convenient 45" long × 20¼" wide, this coffee table will fit nicely even in smaller rooms. The shelf below is ideal for storing books,

magazines, newspapers, photo albums or anything else you want to keep within arm's reach when sitting on your sofa.

We used 6 × 6" ceramic floor tiles for our coffee table, but you can use just about any type or size of floor tile you want—just be sure to use floor tile, not wall tile, which is thinner and can fracture more easily.

After you've built this tile-top coffee table, you may like it so much that you'll want to build a tile-top end table to match.

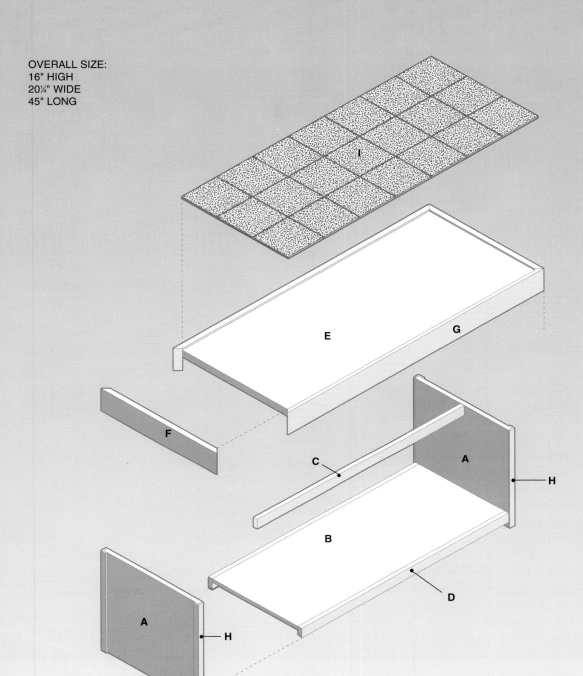

OVERALL SIZE:
16" HIGH
20¼" WIDE
45" LONG

Key	Part	Dimension	Pcs.	Material
A	Side panel	¾ × 16 × 15"	2	Plywood
B	Shelf panel	¾ × 14½ × 35"	1	Plywood
C	Stringer	¾ × 1½ × 35"	1	Oak
D	Shelf edge	¾ × 1½ × 35"	2	Oak
E	Top panel	¾ × 18¾ × 43½"	1	Plywood

Key	Part	Dimension	Pcs.	Material
F	End skirt	¾ × 3½ × 20¼"	2	Oak
G	Side skirt	¾ × 3½ × 45"	2	Oak
H	Corner trim	⅞ × ⅞ × 15"	4	Corner molding
I	Table tiles	¼ × 6 × 6"	21	Ceramic

Cutting List

Materials: #6 × 1½" wood screws, 3d and 6d finish nails, ⅜"-dia. oak plugs, wood glue, finishing materials, ceramic floor tiles (21), ceramic tile adhesive, tinted grout, ³⁄₁₆" plastic tile spacers, silicone grout sealer.

Specialty tools: V-notch adhesive trowel, rubber mallet, grout float.

Note: Measurements reflect the actual size of dimension lumber.

Fasten the shelf edges to the shelf panel with glue and 6d finish nails.

Secure the stringer in place with glue and screws.

Directions:
Tile-top Coffee Table

ASSEMBLE THE TABLE BASE. The base for this tile-top coffee table is made up of a plywood shelf panel with oak edging that is fitted between two plywood side panels. Start by cutting the side panels (A) and shelf panel (B) to size from oak plywood using a circular saw and straightedge cutting guide. Then, cut the shelf edge (D) to length from 1 × 2 oak. Sand the edges and surfaces of the components with medium-grit sandpaper. Fasten the shelf edges to the shelf panel with glue and 6d finish nails **(photo A).** Be sure to drill pilot holes for the finish nails so you don't split the wood. Keep the top surfaces of the shelf edges and shelf panel flush when fastening. Next, set the shelf panel upright on ¾"-thick spacers. Stand a side panel upright on its bottom edge, against the end of the shelf panel, and fasten the side panel to the shelf panel with glue

Miter-cut and mount one skirt board at a time to ensure proper fit.

and 1½" wood screws driven into counterbored pilot holes. Keep the edges of the side panel flush with the outside surfaces of the shelf edging. Fasten the other side panel to the shelf panel. Cut the stringer (C) to length, and position it between the side panels, flush with the top edge and centered in the middle of the side panels. Clamp in place with a bar clamp or pipe clamp. Drill counterbored pilot holes through the side panels into the stringer. Remove the clamps and secure the stringer with glue and screws **(photo B).**

MAKE THE TABLETOP FRAME. The tabletop frame is a plywood panel framed with 1 × 4 oak. The frame extends above the plywood slightly to create a lip that covers the edges of the tile when it is installed on top of the plywood. The joints in the 1 × 4 frame are mitered— most hand-operated miter boxes can be used to cut a 1 × 4 when it's inserted on edge, but if you own a power miter box, making these cuts is an excellent time to use it. Start by cutting the top panel (E) to size from ¾"-thick oak plywood, using a circular saw and a straightedge cutting guide.

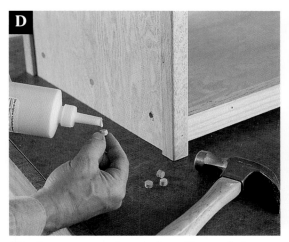

Fill all open counterbore holes with wood plugs.

Tap the tiles lightly with a rubber mallet to set them firmly in the adhesive.

Fasten the top panel to the side panels and stringer in the table base, using countersunk screws and glue. Be sure to leave an equal overhang on the ends and sides. Cut the end skirts (F) and side skirts (G) from 1 × 4 oak. Although the Cutting List on page 53 gives exact dimensions for these parts, your safest bet is to cut the first part slightly longer than the specified length, then custom-cut it to fit. Cut all the other skirt boards to length, using the first skirt board as a guide **(photo C).** Fasten the skirt boards to the edges of the top panel with glue and 6d finish nails.

FASTEN THE CORNER TRIM. Next, cut the corner trim (H) to length from oak corner molding. Fasten the corner trim to the side panel edges with glue and 3d finish nails—be sure to drill pilot holes for the nails.

FINISH THE WOOD. For cleanest results, perform the finishing steps on the table prior to installing the ceramic tile. Start by filling all open counterbore holes with ⅜"-dia. oak wood plugs **(photo D).** Finish-sand

the entire coffee table and apply sanding sealer to all exposed surfaces, except the top panel. Let the sealer dry thoroughly, then lightly sand the sealed surfaces with 180- or 220 grit sandpaper. Apply stain to the sealed oak surfaces, if desired, then apply two or three light coats of polyurethane to the wood.

INSTALL THE CERAMIC TOP. Once the finish has dried, the ceramic tiles can be installed. Start by masking off the top edges of the skirts to further protect the finished surfaces. Test-fit the table tiles (I), then apply a ⅛"-thick layer of tile adhesive over the entire table surface, using a V-notched adhesive trowel. Line the borders of the table surface with plastic spacers (we used ³⁄₁₆" spacers with 6" ceramic floor tile to make a tabletop surface that fits inside the tabletop frame). Begin setting tiles into the adhesive, working in straight lines. Insert plastic spacers between tiles to maintain an even gap. Rap each tile lightly with a rubber mallet to set it into the adhesive **(photo E).** Once the tiles have been set in

place, remove the spacers and let the adhesive set overnight. Then, apply a layer of grout (we used pretinted grout that matches the color of the tile we chose) to the tile surface so it fills the gaps between tiles **(photo F).** Wipe any excess grout from the tile faces. Let grout dry for about 30 minutes (check manufacturer's directions first), then wipe off the grout film from the tiles with a damp sponge, wiping diagonally across the grout lines. Let the grout set for at least a week, then apply silicone grout sealer to the grout lines.

Use a grout float to apply tile grout in the gaps between tiles in the tabletop.

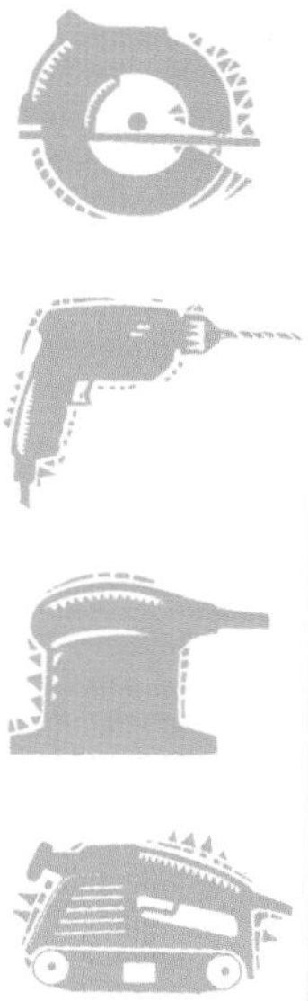

Corner Bar

*Slide the corner bar into an unobtrusive corner of your basement
or den to create a low-profile liquor cabinet.*

CONSTRUCTION MATERIALS

Quantity	Lumber
2	¾" × 4 × 8' birch plywood
1	¾" × 4 × 4' clad board
1	1 × 2" × 6' aspen
1	½ × ¾" × 4' shelf edge molding

This corner bar is perfect for a finished basement or study. It has plenty of room for all your wine and liquor bottles, plus a sturdy bin for mixed drink supplies and a convenient stemware rack for goblets and wine glasses. Both the bin and stemware rack are hinged on the inside of the corner bar to swing out for easy access.

The corner bar has plenty of room for supplies, but it doesn't call attention to itself. The triangular shape makes it easy to position in a corner of any room. The top is made with vinyl-clad particleboard for easy cleanup, and the storage bin and stemware rack are hinged so they swing out for easy access.

56

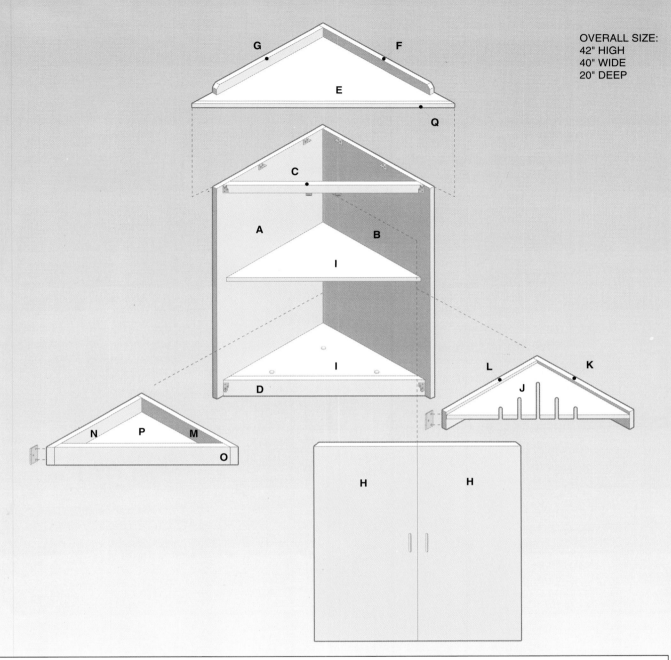

OVERALL SIZE:
42" HIGH
40" WIDE
20" DEEP

Cutting List				
Key	Part	Dimension	Pcs.	Material
A	Long side	¾ × 24 × 41¼"	1	Plywood
B	Short side	¾ × 23¼ × 41¼"	1	Plywood
C	Top rail	¾ × 1½ × 31¼"	1	Plywood
D	Bottom rail	¾ × 3 × 31¼"	1	Plywood
E	Top	¾ × 28 × 28"	1	Clad board
F	Long splash	¾ × 1½ × 24"	1	Aspen
G	Short splash	¾ × 1½ × 23¼"	1	Aspen
H	Door	¾ × 16⅜ × 39"	2	Plywood
I	Shelf	¾ × 21⅛ × 21⅛"	2	Plywood

Cutting List				
Key	Part	Dimension	Pcs.	Material
J	Stemware rack	¾ × 20 × 20"	1	Plywood
K	Long rack support	¾ × 3½ × 20"	1	Plywood
L	Short rack support	¾ × 3½ × 19¼"	1	Plywood
M	Long bin side	¾ × 5¼ × 20"	1	Plywood
N	Short bin side	¾ × 5¼ × 19¼"	1	Plywood
O	Bin front	¾ × 5¼ × 27"	1	Plywood
P	Bin bottom	¾ × 18⅛ × 18⅛"	1	Plywood
Q	Edge cap	½ × ¾ × 40"	1	Shelf edge

Materials: Wood glue, #6 wood screws (¾", 1½", 2", 2½"), 4d finish nails, small corner braces (6), 3 × 1½" zinc hinges (2), pin hinges (4), ⅞"-dia. domed nylon glides (3), wire pulls (2), magnetic catches (2), finishing materials.

Note: Measurements reflect the actual size of dimensional lumber.

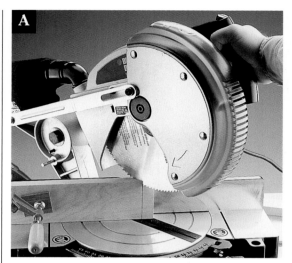

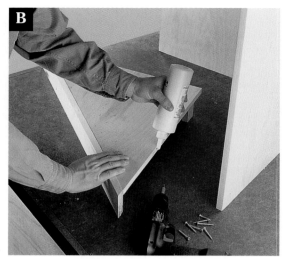

Use a miter saw to cut the top rail and bottom rail to fit between the cabinet sides.

Apply glue to the back of the bottom shelf and position it between the sides.

Directions: Corner Bar

MAKE THE CABINET SIDES. The cabinet sides form a "V" and fit flush with the walls in your room when the bar is positioned in a corner. Made from plywood, the exposed edges of the sides are covered with veneer edge tape so they can accept a clear finish (if you plan to paint the corner bar, you can simply fill the voids in the edges with putty, then sand them smooth). When the sides have been edge-taped and attached to each other at a right angle, rails are miter-cut and fastened between them on what will be the front of the bar. Start by cutting the long side (A) and short side (B) to size. Always sand parts after cutting to smooth out any rough spots and remove splinters. Use a household iron to apply adhesive-backed veneer edge tape to one long edge of the long and short sides—these edges will face the front of the unit. Fasten the long side to the short side with glue and #6 × 1½" wood screws, driven through the long side and into

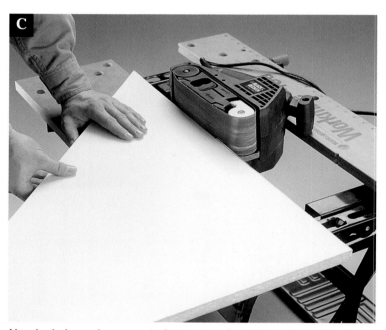

Use the belt sander as a grinder to smooth out the edges of the top.

the short side edge. Make sure the top and bottom edges are flush. Countersink the holes so the screw heads will be recessed.

MAKE THE RAILS & SHELVES. The top and bottom rails are miter-cut to fit between the long side and short side. Cut the top rail (C) and bottom rail (D) to size. Use a power miter saw or miter box and backsaw to miter-cut the ends of the top

rail and bottom rail at 45° angles **(photo A).** Both ends should be cut facing in, allowing the rails to fit flush between the sides. Apply veneer edge tape to the bottom of the top rail and the top of the bottom rail. Cut the shelves (I) to size. The shelves are made easily by cutting a square piece of plywood in half along a diagonal line to form two triangles. Apply edge tape to the long edge of one shelf. Position the bottom rail against the long edge of the un-taped shelf. Make sure the top edges are flush, and attach the bottom rail to the shelf with #6 × 1½" wood screws, driven through the bottom rail and into the shelf. Counterbore the pilot holes to accept ⅜"-dia. wood plugs. Prop up the back corner of the shelf with a 2¼"-high piece of scrap wood, and push the bottom rail and shelf against the sides. Apply glue to the bottom rail and shelf **(photo B),** and attach them between the sides with wood screws. (Drive #6 × 2" wood screws to secure the sides to the shelf, then drive a #6 × 1¼" wood screw through each side and into the bottom rail.) Position the top rail between the sides. Make sure the taped edge of the top rail is facing down and the top edges are flush with the top edges of the sides. Attach the top rail with glue and #6 × 1¼" screws, driven through the sides and into the ends of the top rail.

MAKE THE TOP. The triangu-lar top is cut to size and fitted with a piece of shelf-edge molding along its front edge. We used clad particleboard to make the top. Clad board is a type of particleboard that is coated with vinyl or hard enamel to resist moisture. (Clad board is usually not suit-able for painting.) If you are unable to find any of this mate-rial, you can either cut a piece of ⅛"-thick tile board and at-tach it to the top with panel ad-hesive, or simply use plywood and paint it with several coats of hard enamel paint. The top is attached with corner braces, which are installed on the sides and front rail. Start by cutting

the top (E) to the full size listed in the *Cutting List* on page 57. To cut the triangular shape, clamp a straightedge cutting guide to the square workpiece so the blade of your circular saw will cut just outside of a di-agonal cutting line. Carefully make the cut, then clamp a belt sander to your worksurface, with the belt perpendicular, and use the belt sander like a grinder to even out any rough spots or saw marks **(photo C).** Cut the edge cap (Q) from a piece of shelf-edge molding to fit on the front (long) edge of the top. Sand the edge cap to smooth out the edges, and paint it with several coats of enamel paint to match the top. Attach the edge cap to the top with glue and 4d finish nails driven through pilot holes **(photo D).** Set the nails with a nail set, and fill the holes with wood putty. Touch up the holes with paint as needed. Drill pilot holes for #6 × 1¼" wood screws along the side

edges of the top. These pilot holes will be used when you at-tach the splash rails to the top. Attach two small corner braces on each side, and on the inside face of the top rail. Set the top in place so the sides are flush to the top edges, and attach the top to the corner braces with #6 × ¾" wood screws.

ATTACH THE SHELF. The re-maining shelf fits between the sides, about halfway up from the bottom. Draw a line across the long and short sides, 22⅜" from the bottom. Drill pilot holes through the outside faces of the sides, spaced every 3" to 4", centered on the lines. Coun-tersink the pilot holes enough

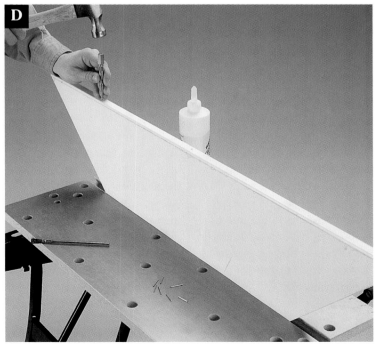

Attach the edge cap to the front edge of the top.

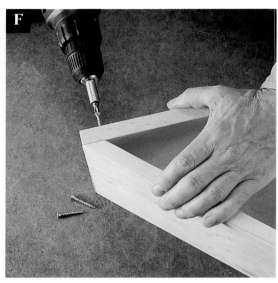

Attach the rack supports to the stemware rack with glue and screws.

Drive countersunk wood screws through the bin sides and into the bin front.

so the screw heads will be recessed. Cut 3 pieces of 19"-long
scrap wood to use as spacers
when installing the shelf. Position the spacers inside the
cabinet, and tape them against
the inside faces of the sides.
Apply glue to the nonveneer-
taped edges of the shelf, and
slide it into place on the spacers. Hold the shelf securely,
and drive #6 × 1¼" wood
screws through the sides and
into the shelf edges.

MAKE THE STEMWARE RACK.
The stemware rack is cut to
size and notched to hold wine
glasses, goblets and other types
of stemware. Cut the stemware
rack (J), long rack support (K)
and short rack support (L) to
size. Apply veneer edge tape to
the front edge of the rack, and
the top edges of the supports.
The rack has evenly spaced, 1"-
wide slots cut into it. We cut
two 2½"-long slots, two 5"-long
slots and one central 10"-long
slot. Lay out the slots for
stemware, starting on the front
edge of the stemware rack, and
cut the slots with a jig saw.
Sand the rack and supports to

The bin rests on nylon glides and is hinged to the cabinet back.

smooth out any roughness. A
round file is an excellent tool
for smoothing out the slots. Or,
if you prefer, cut the slots with
a ½"-dia. straight router bit. Drill
pilot holes through the long
and short rack supports, 1⅛"
down from the top (taped)
edges. Apply glue to the side
edges of the stemware rack,
then fasten the rack between
the long and short rack sup-

ports with wood screws **(photo
E).** It will help to position spacers beneath the stemware rack
as you fasten it to the supports.
Countersink the holes enough
so the screw heads will be
recessed.

MAKE THE BIN. The triangular bin is made to fit at the bottom of the corner bar. We also
hinged the bin for access, but
you may choose to fasten this

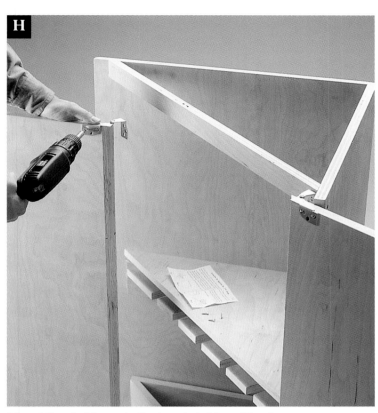

Mount the pin hinges to the beveled sides of the doors.

Mount another 3×3" hinge on one corner of the stemware rack, and attach it in the cabinet so the rack supports are 1" down from the shelf.

MAKE THE DOORS. Start by cutting the doors (H) to size. Bevel-cut one long side of each door with a circular saw set at a 45° cutting angle and a straight-edge cutting guide. When the doors are shut, the bevels will face inward, allowing the doors to swing wide instead of contacting the long and short sides. Edge-tape the three non-beveled edges of each door.

APPLY THE FINISH. Remove all hardware and the top. Glue ⅜"-dia. wood plugs into all counterbores, and sand to level. Finish-sand all surfaces with 180- or 220-grit sandpaper. Apply your selected wood finish—we used a light penetrating wood stain with two coats of polyurethane. When the stain has dried, reinstall the hardware.

INSTALL THE BACKSPLASH. Cut the long splash (F) and short splash (G) to size. Attach the short splash to the long splash with glue and wood screws, forming a "V." Clamp the splash assembly to the top so the sides are flush. Drive #6 × 1¼" wood screws through the predrilled pilot holes in the top and into the bottom edges of the backsplash. Reinstall the top. Mount pin hinges to the top and bottom of each door along the bevel-cut edges **(photo H).** Attach the doors to the cabinet so the bottoms overhang the bottom rail by ½". Attach pulls and magnetic catches to the doors. The magnetic catches should fit on the top and bottom rails.

permanently as well if you prefer. Domed nylon glides are installed on the bottom shelf to prevent the bin from dragging across the bottom of the cabinet. Cut the long bin side (M), short bin side (N), bin front (O) and bin bottom (P) to size. Apply edge tape to the top edge of the bin sides and front. Use a power miter saw to cut both ends of the bin front at a 45° angle. The miter cuts on the bin front should face in, allowing it to fit flush against the long and short bin sides. Use glue and wood screws to fasten the short bin side to a side edge of the bin bottom. Make sure the short bin side is flush with the rear and bottom edges of the bin bottom. Fasten the long bin side to the bin bottom and short bin side. Attach the bin front to the bin bottom with glue and wood screws.

Counterbore the pilot holes for wood plugs. Fasten the ends of the bin front to the bin sides by driving countersunk, #6 × 1¼" wood screws through the bin sides and into the bin front **(photo F).** Center the screws ⅝" in from the front of the bin sides to avoid tearing through the bin front.

INSTALL THE STEMWARE RACK & THE BIN. Drive three ⅝"-dia. nylon glides into the bottom of the cabinet, spaced evenly apart (see *Diagram,* page 61). Test-fit the bin on the glides to make sure it rests evenly **(photo G).** Attach a 3×3" hinge to one corner of the bin. With the hinge in the closed position, position the bin in the cabinet, and trace the hinge position where it contacts the side. Install the bin hinge and check for smooth operation.

Room Divider

*Crafted from cedar boards and lauan plywood, this portable
room divider makes it easy to create a new living space.*

CONSTRUCTION MATERIALS

Quantity	Lumber*
3	1 × 4" × 8' cedar
3	¾ × ¾" × 8' mahogany cove molding
1	¼" × 4 × 4' lauan plywood

*Materials for a single room divider section.

Strips of lauan plywood are woven together and set in rustic cedar frames to make this room divider. Held together with brass hinges, the sections of the divider can be arranged to fit almost any room. Use it as a partition to make a romantic dining nook in a large living area. Or, position the room divider near a sunny window to establish a tranquil garden retreat without adding permanent walls. There are many creative uses for this versatile decorative barrier.

The instructions for building the room divider show you how to make one section. Add as many additional sections as your space needs require.

OVERALL SIZE:
72" HIGH
3½" WIDE
24" LONG

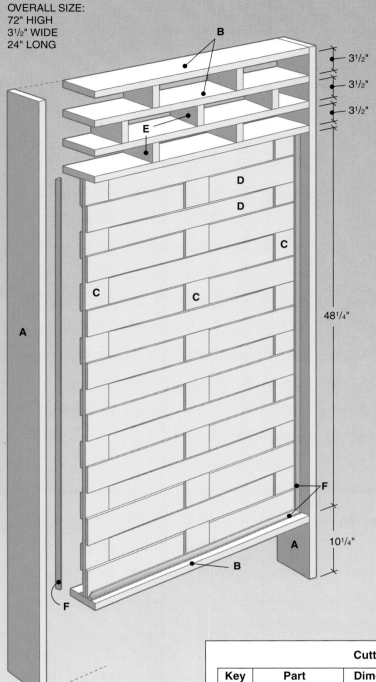

| Dimension labels in figure |
| 3½" |
| 3½" |
| 3½" |
| 48¼" |
| 10¼" |

Cutting List

Key	Part	Dimension	Pcs.	Material
A	Leg	¾ × 3½ × 72"	2	Cedar
B	Stretcher	¾ × 3½ × 22½"	5	Cedar
C	Vertical slat	¼ × 3 × 48"	3	Plywood
D	Horizontal slat	¼ × 3 × 22½"	16	Plywood
E	Divider	¾ × 3½ × 3½"	7	Cedar
F	Retaining strip	¾ × ¾" × *	8	Cove molding

Materials: 2" deck screws, 2d finish nails, 2" brass butt hinges, wood glue, finishing materials.

Note: Measurements reflect the actual size of dimension lumber.

*Cut to fit.

Directions: Room Divider

MAKE THE FRAME. Each frame consists of two legs and five stretchers. Four of these stretchers are positioned along the upper section of the frame. Start by cutting the legs (A) and stretchers (B) to size. Once these pieces are cut, measure and mark the positions for the stretchers on the inside faces of the legs. To make sure the measurements are exactly the same on both legs, tape the pieces together, edge to edge. Make sure the top and bottom edges are flush. Measure and mark a line 10½" from the bottom ends of both legs. These lines mark the top edge of the bottom stretcher. Next, measure and mark lines 48" up the legs from the bottom stretcher's top edge **(photo A).** These lines mark the bottom edge of the next stretcher. The top stretcher should be positioned between the legs, flush with the top ends. Mark the remaining stretcher positions as desired. We positioned them equally between the top and middle stretchers, approximately 3½" apart. To fasten the stretchers, drill holes for two counterbored 2" deck screws through the legs at each stretcher center position. Once the holes have been completed, glue the joints and fasten the stretchers to the legs, completing the room divider frame.

Tape the legs together with their edges flush, and gang-mark the stretcher positions on the inside faces.

Weave the 16 horizontal slats through the three vertical slats to make the divider panel.

MAKE THE DIVIDER PANEL. The divider panel is made from 19 strips of ¼"-thick lauan plywood, woven together without any fasteners or glue. This step is easy to complete if you work on a flat, even surface. Begin by cutting the vertical slats (C) and horizontal slats (D) to size. Sand the edges with 120-grit sandpaper until they are com-

pletely smooth. Lay the vertical slats on the worksurface. Weave the horizontal slats between the vertical slats in an alternating pattern to form the panel **(photo B).**

INSERT THE DIVIDER PANEL. The divider panel is held in the frame by retaining strips (F), which are fastened along the inside faces of the legs and stretchers. Use a power miter

Attach the retaining strips with 2d finish nails.

Join the divider panels and frames with butt hinges.

box or gang-cut the retaining strips to size from ¾"-thick mahogany cove molding. Attach the retaining strips on both sides of the panel to hold it in the frame, between the stretchers and legs. Use a power miter box to miter-cut the retaining strips to fit the inside of the frame. Measure and mark 1⅜"

from one side edge for the first line of retaining strips. Attach the retaining strips to one side of the frame with 2d finish nails **(photo C),** and set the nails with a nail set. Place the woven panel against the retaining strip frame, and secure the panel in the frame by attaching retaining strips on the opposite face of the panel. Fill all the visible

screw holes on the outside edges of the legs, and sand all the leg surfaces until they are completely smooth.

APPLY THE FINISHING TOUCHES. Inserting the dividers is the final construction step for the divider panels. These small pieces of cedar are purely decorative and can be spaced apart in any pattern. Since they fit snugly in between the top stretchers, you don't need to fasten them. Friction holds them in place and gives you the option of repositioning them when you see fit. Begin by measuring the distance between the top stretchers, and cut the dividers (E) to size. Sand the dividers until they are completely smooth. Just push them between the stretchers and position them as desired. Once you have made two or three room divider panels, brace the pieces with C-clamps for stability, then attach them with evenly-spaced 2" butt hinges **(photo D).** When clamping the frames, use a cardboard pad to prevent the clamps from damaging the relatively soft wood. Cedar lumber, mahogany trim and lauan plywood do not require a protective finish, so we left them unfinished. If you prefer a glossier, more formal look, apply a coat of tung oil to the parts before assembly.

Library Ladder

Self-standing, safe and stable, this oak stepladder is truly a top-shelf furnishing.

Floor-to-ceiling bookcases will cease to be unreachable and changing light bulbs in your ceiling fixtures will be less threatening once you've built this charming library ladder. Offering all the safety and convenience of a stepladder, this three-step, rung-style ladder surpasses just about any store-bought climbing structure in style and design. When extended, the runged stepladder sides pro-vide sturdy support for the lad-der treads. When not in use, the ladder folds together so it can be stored up against a wall and out of the traffic flow.

Designed for efficiency in use and in construction, this oak stepladder can be built with only three 8'-long 1 × 4 boards and a few feet of oak doweling. The treads are fas-tened to the sides of the ladder with oak through dowels for long-lasting joints that stand up to repeated use.

SAFETY NOTICE: When using any ladder, always exercise good judgment and safety prac-tices. Make sure the legs of the ladder are firmly planted on a level floor before use. Do not use the dowel rungs as steps. Do not carry heavy objects while using the ladder. This ladder is suitable for light-duty, indoor use only.

CONSTRUCTION MATERIALS

Quantity	Lumber
3	1 × 4" × 8' red oak
2	1"-dia. × 4' oak dowel
1	⅜"-dia. × 4' oak dowel

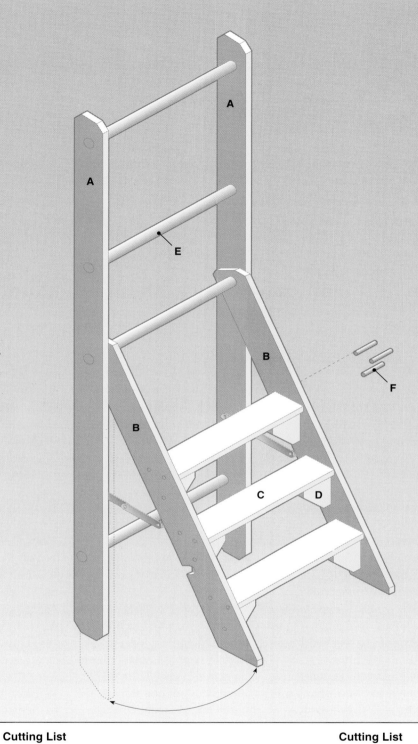

OVERALL SIZE:
58½" HIGH
19⅜" WIDE
25¼" DEEP

Cutting List				
Key	**Part**	**Dimension**	**Pcs.**	**Material**
A	Ladder side	¾ × 3½ × 58½"	2	Red oak
B	Step rail	¾ × 3½ × 40¼"	2	Red oak
C	Step tread	¾ × 3½ × 15½"	3	Red oak

Cutting List				
Key	**Part**	**Dimension**	**Pcs.**	**Material**
D	Tread brace	¾ × 3½ × 3½"	6	Red oak
E	Cross dowel	1"-dia. × 19⅜"	4	Oak dowel
F	Through dowel	⅜"-dia. × 2"	18	Oak dowel

Materials: 4d finish nails, wood glue, 10" chest lid supports (2), finishing materials.

Note: Measurements reflect the actual thickness of dimensional lumber.

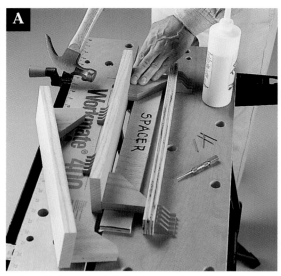

Attach the tread braces ½" in from the front edge of the step rails.

Draw reference lines for positioning the treads parallel to the bottoms of the step rails.

Directions: Library Ladder

MAKE THE LADDER STEPS. The steps for the library ladder consist of flat treads with triangular braces on each end. They are assembled first, then attached to the ladder sides with oak through dowels. Cut the step treads (C) to length from 1 × 4 oak, then cut the tread braces (D) to 3½" square. Mark points 2½" in from one of the corners of each tread brace, then connect the points to make cutting lines. For maximum brace strength, mark the cutting lines so the wood grain in each brace runs vertically when the brace is installed. Make the cutoffs with a jig saw or miter saw, then sand the edges smooth. Attach a brace to each end of each tread **(photo A),** so the outer face of each brace is recessed ½" from the front edge of the tread— use glue and 4d finish nails driven through pilot holes to attach the treads.

MAKE THE STEP RAILS. The step rails support the ladder treads. They are trimmed at one end so they lie flat on the floor when the ladder is set up. Each rail also contains a U-shaped cutout to fit over the bottom rung on the ladder sides. Cut the step rails (B) to length from 1 × 4 red oak. Mark points ¾" in from each corner on one end of each rail, then connect the points to make cutting lines for the triangular cutoffs at the top ends of the rails. Make the cutoffs with a jig saw. On the square end of one rail (this will be the bottom), mark points ⅝" in from one corner, in each direction. Mark another point on the edge, 2" up from the opposite corner. Connect the 2" point to the mark on the bottom to make a 35° cutoff line, then cut with a jig saw or miter saw. Sand the cut smooth, then use the first rail as a template for tracing a matching cutoff onto the other rail— this helps ensure that the legs will be uniform in shape. Cut and sand the second cutoff. Now, mark reference lines for positioning the tread assemblies onto the rails. Measuring up from the bottom, mark points on the shorter edge of each rail at 7½", 15½" and 21½". Set a T-bevel (if you have one) to match the angle on the bottoms of the rails, then use the T-bevel to extend reference lines out from the reference points on the rails—the reference lines should be parallel to the bottoms of the rails **(photo B).** If you don't own a T-bevel, set a 1 × 4 scrap onto one of the rails so the edges are flush and the scrap extends slightly past the bottom end. Trace the bottom cut onto the scrap, extending the line so it runs straight across the scrap board. Cut along the cutting line, then use the 1 × 4 as a guide for tracing the correct angle onto the rails.

ASSEMBLE THE TREADS & RAILS. Attach the tread assemblies between the rails, at the reference lines, using glue and clamps. The fronts of the treads should be flush with the front edges of the rails, with the tops flush up against the reference lines on the rails. When the glue has dried, carefully unclamp the assembly, then drill

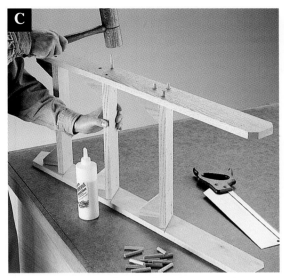

Drive three glued, 2"-long dowels into each step tread joint after the glue in the joints has set.

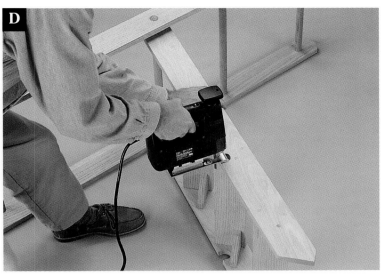

Cut U-shaped notches into the back edges of the step rails so they will lock over the bottom dowel rung.

three ⅜"-dia. × 1½"-deep dowel holes through the rails and into the tread assemblies at each joint—two of the holes should extend into the end of the tread, and one should extend into the brace. Cut eighteen 2"-long dowel rods from ⅜"-dia. oak doweling (or use ⅜"-dia. dowel pins). Make sure the guide holes are free of sawdust, then apply glue to the ends of each dowel, and insert them into the dowel holes. Drive the dowels all the way into the dowel holes with a wooden mallet, being careful not to break the glue bonds at the joints **(photo C).** Use a saw to trim the ends of the dowels so they are nearly flush with the rails, then sand the ends flush.

MAKE THE LADDER SIDES. Cut the ladder sides (A) to length. Mark and cut triangular cutoffs with ¾" legs at each corner of each end. Drill 1"-dia. holes through the sides at points centered (edge to edge) at 31", 41½" and 55½" up from the bottoms of the sides. Mark another centerpoint 1¼" in from the back edge of each side, 7½" up

from each bottom. To ensure that these 1"-dia. guide holes for the ladder rungs are aligned, clamp the sides together with all edges and ends flush, and drill through both boards at the same time.

JOIN THE RAILS & LADDER SIDES. The rail/tread assembly is attached to the ladder sides with a 1"-dia. dowel rung that passes through the tops of the rails and is seated in the lowest centered holes in the ladder sides. Drill 1⅛"-dia. guide holes at the top of each step rail, centered from edge to edge and with centerpoints that are 1½" down from the top ends. Set the step assembly between the ladder sides so the holes are aligned with the lowest centered hole in each ladder side. Drive a 1" dowel through all four holes, then slip the ends of the dowel out of the sides in turn, apply glue inside the guide holes in the sides, then reinsert the ends of the dowel. Drill pilot holes, then drive a 4d finish nail through an edge of each ladder side and into the ends of the dowel (this keeps

the dowel from spinning). Also install 1"-dia. dowels in the top two holes. Position the ladder so the rails are flush with the edges of the ladder sides, and trace the lowest holes in the sides onto the outer faces of the rails. Swing the ladder and sides apart, then drill 1¼"-dia. holes through the rails. Draw lines perpendicular to the back edges of the rails, connected to the top and bottom of the hole in each rail. Cut along the lines with a jig saw to make the notches **(photo D)** so the rails will lock over the bottom rung when closed. Install a 1" dowel in the bottom holes in the ladder sides. Install a chest lid support about midway up from the bottom of each rail, then attach the free ends to the ladder sides so the lid support locks into position when the ladder is set up (make sure the ends of the rails and sides all are flush against the floor). Finish-sand the exposed surfaces, then apply your finish of choice—we left the wood uncolored, and applied three coats of water-based polyurethane.

Bookcase

This open-back bookcase combines straight, simple lines with a few graceful curves for an effect that is at home in any room.

PROJECT
POWER TOOLS

The spacious shelves and open-backed design of our bookcase give it an impressive style all its own without making it an overwhelming element in the room. The decorative arches on the sides and rails provide style without sacrificing strength or stability. The bookcase is built simply from one sheet of plywood. We used birch, but you can use oak or any other plywood you choose. The bookcase is dressed up and finished off with the use of self-adhesive

veneer tape which, when applied to the plywood edges with a household iron, gives the bookcase the appearance of expensive solid hardwood instead of plywood.

The simple look and style will suit almost any room in your home, from bedroom to living room, and the project can easily support a full load of

your favorite hardcover volumes. Our bookcase clearly proves that book storage doesn't have to be overly expensive, ornate or cumbersome. With a few quick and easy jig saw cuts, some edge tape and screws, you can build a long-lasting bookcase for your home that is as effective as it is attractive.

CONSTRUCTION MATERIALS

Quantity	Lumber
1	¾" × 4 × 8' birch plywood

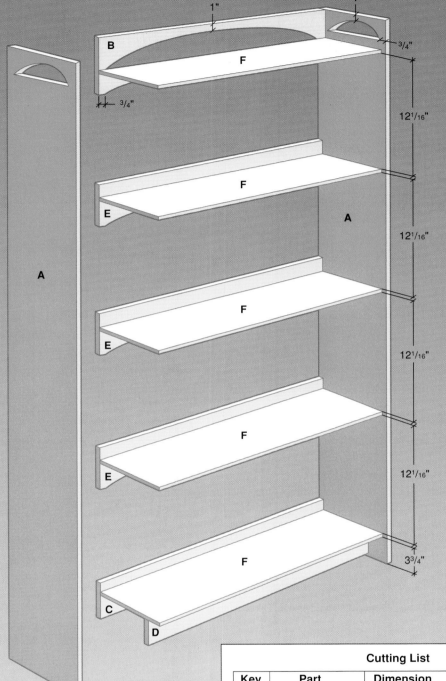

OVERALL SIZE:
58" HIGH
12" WIDE
28" LONG

1"

1"

3/4"

3/4"

12¹/₁₆"

12¹/₁₆"

12¹/₁₆"

12¹/₁₆"

3³/₄"

B

F

E

F

E

F

E

F

C

D

A

A

A

Cutting List

Key	Part	Dimension	Pcs.	Material
A	Side	¾ × 12 × 58"	2	Plywood
B	Top rail	¾ × 6¼ × 26½"	1	Plywood
C	Bottom rail	¾ × 4½ × 26½"	1	Plywood
D	Front rail	¾ × 2¾ × 26½"	1	Plywood
E	Mid rail	¾ × 3¾ × 26½"	3	Plywood
F	Shelf	¾ × 11 × 26½"	5	Plywood

Materials: Wood glue, #8 × 2" wood screws, birch plugs, finishing materials.

Note: Measurements reflect the actual size of dimensional lumber.

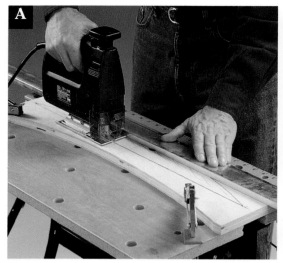

Cut the arch cutout in the top rail using a jig saw and a straightedge guide.

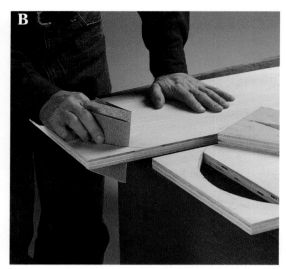

Wrap sandpaper around a piece of tin to create a sanding block that reaches into the cutout corners.

Directions: Bookcase

CUT THE PARTS. Begin by cutting the top rail (B), bottom rail (C), front rail (D) and mid rails (E) to size using a circular saw and straightedge. Cut the sides (A) to size from plywood material. Lay out the arches on the sides, three middle rails and the top rail. The arches are all centered on the rails, with the apex 1½" above the bottom edge. An easy way to draw the arches is to use a thin, flexible piece of metal, plastic or wood as a template, or tracing guide.

Use a heat gun to soften the adhesive on the veneer tape, then apply the tape to the inside edges of the cutout using a putty knife.

TIP

Veneer tape is often available in different types of wood species. Be sure to match the wood tape to the type of plywood you're using.

Measure and mark points ¾" from each side edge. Tack a casing nail into the center of the rails, 1½" above the bottom edge. Also tack casing nails lightly into the marks at each end to hold the strip in place as you trace along it to draw the arch. Hook the flexible guide over the center nail, then flex each end to the marked points. Trace the arches, and then remove the nails. Cut along the guidelines with a jig saw to make the arches. Unlike the other rails, the top rail also has an arch cutout on the top. The top arch starts 3¼" from the top edge and extends upward to 1" from the top edge. Drill a pilot hole for the saw blade, then cut the arch cutout with a jig saw. Make the arch cutouts in the sides to match those in the top rail, using the same methods to draw the arches. Use a straightedge guide to cut the straight portion of the arches on the top rail and sides **(photo A)**. A straightedge guide will ensure accurate, straight cuts once the arches have been cut. Sand the parts to 150-grit smoothness. Use a thin piece of metal or plastic backing to reach the corners of the arches when you sand the edges **(photo B)**.

ATTACH THE VENEER STRIPS. We used adhesive-backed birch wood edge tape veneer along the visible edges on the bookcase. Apply the edge tape to the top edges of the top rail,

Use bar clamps to keep the top rail and shelf in place when you drive the screws. Keep the back and top edges flush with the sides.

Plug all screw holes prior to finishing. You can make the plugs or buy them at hardware or woodworkers' stores.

TIP

Although you can buy veneer edge trimmers in hardware stores, a block plane may work just as well. If you use a plane to trim the edges, however, remember to trim with the grain to avoid damaging the wood.

mid rails and sides with a common household iron. Also apply veneer tape on the arches and to the front edges of the sides. Apply veneer tape to the top rail arches and side arches by softening the veneer tape with a heat gun, and then use a putty knife to fit the tape into the arch corners **(photo C).** Cut the shelves (F) to size from plywood using a circular saw and straightedge, and apply veneer tape to the front edges of the shelves. When the tape is fully

applied and cooled, trim and sand it to finished smoothness.

BUILD THE SHELF ASSEMBLIES. Begin this step by fastening the rails to the shelves with glue and wood screws. The top of the shelves should be ¾" from the top edge of the mid rails, with 3" separating the top shelf and the top edge of the top rail. The top edge of the bottom shelf is 1" from the top edge of the bottom rail.

ATTACH THE SHELVES. Use #8 × 2" counterbored wood

screws to fasten the top rail and shelf to the sides **(photo D),** making sure the top and back edges of the rail are flush with the side top and edges (see *Diagram*, page 67). When properly assembled, the front edges of the shelves should be positioned ¼" from the sides' front edges. Next, attach the bottom shelf, front rail and bottom rail to the sides. Once again, keep the back edges flush, and position both rails so that their bottom edges are ¼" above the bottom side edges. This gap between the rails and the floor allows the bookcase to adapt slightly to an irregularity or curve in the floor, increasing its stability. Set the front rail 2¼" back from the front side edges. To make sure the project is square, measure diagonally from corner to corner. To use bar clamps to draw the frame to square, position a bar clamp diagonally across the bookcase, and adjust it until the frame is pulled into square. Attach the remaining shelves and rails(see *Diagram*).

APPLY THE FINISHING TOUCHES. Fill all the screw holes by applying glue to the wood plugs and tapping them in with a mallet **(photo E).** Finish-sand the project with fine (150- or 180-grit) sandpaper, and finish it as desired. We applied two light coats of polyurethane.

Armoire

*With a simple, rustic appearance, this movable closet
can blend into almost any bedroom.*

CONSTRUCTION MATERIALS

Quantity	Lumber
3	¾" × 4 × 8' birch plywood
1	¼" × 4 × 8' birch plywood
1	1 × 2" × 8' pine
6	1 × 3" × 8' pine
1	1 × 6" × 4' pine
1	1½"-dia. × 2' fir dowel

Long before massive walk-in closets became almost standard in residential building design, homeowners and apartment-dwellers compensated for cramped bedroom closets by making or buying an armoire. The trim armoire design shown here reflects the basic styling developed during the heyday of the armoire, but at a scale that makes it usable in just about any living situation. A mere 60" high and only 36" in width, this cute little armoire still boasts plenty of interior space. Five shelves on the left side are sized to store folded sweaters and shirts. And you can hang dozens of suit jackets or dresses in the closet section to the right.

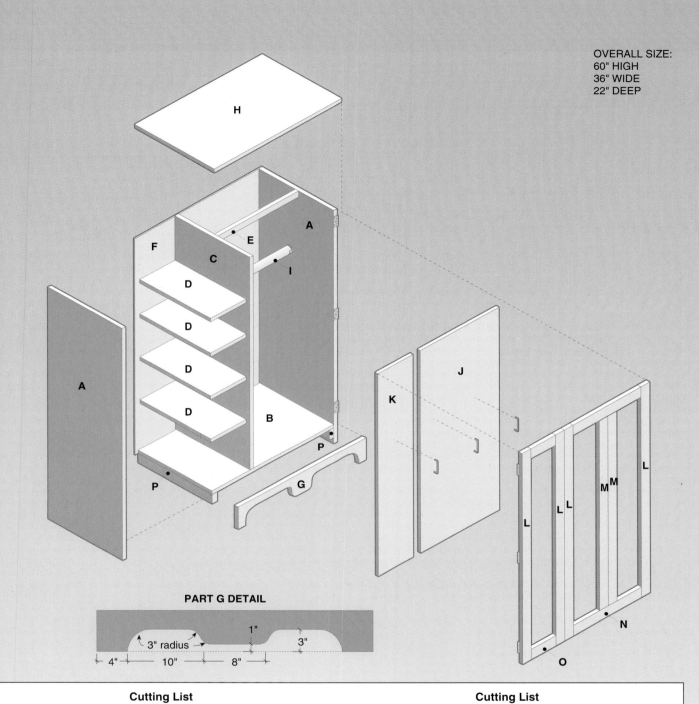

OVERALL SIZE:
60" HIGH
36" WIDE
22" DEEP

PART G DETAIL

1"
3" radius
3"
4" 10" 8"

Cutting List

Key	Part	Dimension	Pcs.	Material
A	Side panel	¾ × 21 × 59¼"	2	Plywood
B	Bottom panel	¾ × 21 × 34½"	1	Plywood
C	Center panel	¾ × 21 × 53¾"	1	Plywood
D	Shelf	¾ × 10⅞ × 20¼"	4	Plywood
E	Stringer	¾ × 1½ × 22⅞"	1	Pine
F	Back	¼ × 36 × 54½"	1	Plywood
G	Front skirt	¾ × 5½ × 36"	1	Pine
H	Top panel	¾ × 22 × 36"	1	Plywood

Cutting List

Key	Part	Dimension	Pcs.	Material
I	Closet rod	1½ × 22⅞"	1	Fir
J	Closet door panel	¾ × 22⁷⁄₁₆ × 52⅛"	1	Plywood
K	Shelf door panel	¾ × 10⁷⁄₁₆ × 52⅛"	1	Plywood
L	Door stile	¾ × 2½ × 53⅝"	4	Pine
M	False stile	¾ × 2½ × 48⅝"	2	Pine
N	Closet door rail	¾ × 2½ × 18¹⁵⁄₁₆"	2	Pine
O	Shelf door rail	¾ × 2½ × 6¹⁵⁄₁₆"	2	Pine
P	Cleat	¾ × 1½ × 21"	2	Pine

Materials: #6 × 1¼" wood screws, 3d and 6d finish nails, closet rod hangers (2), wrought-iron hinges and pulls, magnetic door catches, ¾" birch veneer edge tape (50'), wood glue, finishing materials.
Note: Measurements reflect the actual size of dimension lumber.

Apply veneer edge tape to the exposed plywood edges so they can be stained. Trim off excess tape with a sharp utility knife.

Directions: Armoire

PREPARE THE PLYWOOD PANELS. Careful preparation of the plywood panels used to make the sides, bottom, top and shelves is key to creating an armoire with a clean, professional look. Take the time to make sure all the parts are precisely square, then apply self-adhesive veneer edge tape to all plywood edges that will be visible (if you plan to paint the armoire, you can simply fill the edges with wood putty, then sand them smooth before you apply the paint). Cut the side panels (A), bottom panel (B) center panel (C), and shelves (D) to size from ¾"-thick plywood, using a circular saw and straightedge cutting guide. We used birch plywood because it is easy to work with and takes wood stain well. Smooth the edges and surfaces of the panels with medium sandpaper. Apply self-adhesive veneer edge tape to the front edges of the center panel, side panels and shelves. An effective way to apply self-adhesive edge tape is to cut it into strips, position the strips over the edges, then press them with a household iron set on low-to-medium heat setting. The heat from the iron activates the adhesive. Press all the edge tape strips into place. When the adhesive has cooled and set, trim the excess edge tape with a sharp utility knife **(photo A).** Sand the trimmed edges and surfaces of the edge tape with medium sandpaper.

ASSEMBLE THE CARCASE. The *carcase* for the armoire (or any type of cabinet) is the main cabinet box. For this project,

Clamp the bottom panel between the sides and fasten to the cleats with 6d finish nails and glue.

Fasten the shelves between the side panel and center panel with glue and 6d finish nails.

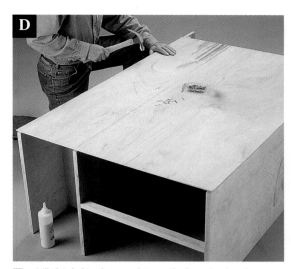

The ¼"-thick back panel is nailed to the back edges of the carcase to help keep it in square.

Lay out the decorative cutout at the bottom of the front skirt board using a compass to make the curves, then cut with a jig saw.

the carcase includes the sides, bottom and center panel. The panels are fastened together with wood glue and finish nails. Make sure all the joints are square and the edges are flush. Start by laying out the cleat positions on the lower sections of the side panels. Measure up 4¾" from the bottom edges of the side panels and draw a layout line across each side panel. Cut the cleats (P) to length from 1 × 2 pine, place them just below the layout lines, and secure them in place with glue and 3d finish nails driven through the cleats and into the side panels. Then, stand the side panels upright on their bottom edges and apply a bead of wood glue to the top of each cleat. Place the bottom panel between the side panels on top of the cleats, then clamp in place. Make sure the taped front edges of the side panels are flush and in alignment. Drive 6d finish nails through the bottom panel and into each cleat, then drive nails through the side panels and into the edges of the bottom panel. Fasten the bottom panel

to the cleats and side panels with 6d finish nails **(photo B).** Set all nail heads with a nail set. Next, lay the assembly on its back edge. Use a pair of shelves as spacers to set the correct distance between the center panel and the left side panel (as seen from the front of the carcase). Make sure the taped panel edges are at the front of the project. Fasten center panel to the bottom panel with glue and finish nails.

INSTALL THE SHELVES. Mark shelf position reference lines on the inside face of the left side panel and on the left face of the center panel. Measure up from the top of the bottom panel and draw lines at 13", 23⅜", 33¾", and 44⅛". Use a carpenter's square to make sure the lines are perpendicular to the front and back edges of the panels. Arrange the shelves (D) so the tops are just below the reference lines, flush with the back edges of the carcase (creating a recess in front of each shelf). Attach the shelves with glue

and 6d finish nails driven through the side panel and center panel, and into the edges of the shelves **(photo C).** Brace each panel from behind as you drive the nails. Set all nail heads.

ATTACH THE STRINGER & BACK PANEL. Cut the stringer (E) to length from 1 × 2 pine and fasten it between the center panel and side panel with glue and 6d finish nails. The stringer should be centered between the fronts and backs of the panels, and flush with the tops. Cut the back panel (F) to size from ¼" birch plywood. Measure the distances between opposite corners of the carcase to make sure it is square (the distances between corners should be equal). Adjust the carcase as needed, then position the back panel over the back edges of the carcase so the edges of the back panel are flush with the outside faces of the side panels. Fasten the back panel by driving 3d finish nails through the back and into the edges of the side, center and bottom panels, using 3d finish nails **(photo D).**

Mount the top panel so it covers the top edge of the back panel, and overhangs the front edges of the side panels by ¾".

Strips of 1 × 3 are attached to the fronts of the door panels to create a frame.

MAKE & ATTACH THE FRONT SKIRT. The front skirt serves as a decorative accent at the bottom of the armoire, and also conceals the empty space below the bottom panel. Start the skirt construction by cutting the front skirt (G) to length from 1 × 6 pine. To lay out the curves that form the ends of the decorative cutouts on the skirt board (see *Diagram*, page 75), start by measuring in 7" from each end and using a compass to draw a 3"-radius curve at each point to make the outside end of each cutout. Then, measure 11¾" in from each end of the skirt board and draw a 3"-radius curve to mark the top, inside end of each cutout. Measure 16⅜" in from each end of the skirt board, and mark points that are 1¾" down from the top edge of the board. Set the point of your compass at each of these points and draw curves that mark the bottom, inside ends of the cutouts. Then, at the middle of the bottom edge of the board,

measure up 1" and draw a line parallel to the bottom edge, intersecting the inside ends of the cutout lines. Finally, draw lines parallel to the bottom edge of the board, 3" up, to create the top of each cutout. Make the cutout on the skirt board, using a jig saw **(photo E).** Smooth the jig saw cuts with medium sandpaper. Position the skirt board against the front of the armoire carcase to make sure that the ends of the skirt are flush with the outside surfaces of the side panels, and the top of the skirt is flush with the top of the bottom panel. Fasten the front skirt to the front edges of the side panels and bottom panel with glue and 6d finish nails.

MAKE & ATTACH THE TOP PANEL. Stand the armoire upright, and measure the distance between the outside faces of the side panels (it should be 36"). Cut the top panel (H) so it matches that distance in length, and is 22" wide. Test-fit the top panel to make sure the

edges are flush with the outside faces of the side panels. The back edge should be flush with the back panel, and the front edge of the top should overhang the front of the carcase panels by ¾". Apply veneer edge tape to all four edges of the top panel (see *Prepare the Plywood Panels*, page 76). Fasten the top panel to the center panel, side panels and stringer with glue and 6d finish nails **(photo F),** making sure it is in the same position as it was when you test-fit the part.

BUILD THE DOORS. The doors are designed for easy construction, durable service and attractive appearance. They are simply plywood panels with pine trim surrounding the perimeter of each door panel. Start the door construction by cutting the closet door panel (J) and shelf door panel (K) to size from ¾"-thick plywood. Sand the edges and surfaces of the door panels to smooth out the saw blade marks and any rough spots. Apply edge tape to

Hang the armoire doors with pairs of hinges attached to the door stiles and to the front edges of the side panels.

the edges of each door panel, then trim off the excess and sand the edges smooth. Next, cut the door stiles (L), false stiles (M), closet door rails (N) and shelf door rails (O) to length from 1 × 3 pine (*rails* are the horizontal frame pieces, *stiles* are vertical frame pieces). Position the rails and stiles on the door panels so they overhang the door panels by ¾" at all edges of the panels. Tack the rails and stiles in place on both door panels with glue and 3d finish nails. Turn the door panels over on a worksurface, then reinforce the joints between the stiles and rails and the door panels with countersunk #6 × 1¼" wood screws driven through the countersunk pilot holes in the door panels, and into the stiles and rails **(photo G).** To hang the doors, first mark points along the outside edge of each outer door stile, 8" down from the top and 8" up from the bottom. Mount door hinges to the edges

of the stiles at these points (we used wrought-iron hinges). With the hinges mounted to the doors, position the doors in place against the side panels and fasten the hinges to the side panels **(photo H).** Be sure to adjust the hinges to allow for ⅛"-wide gaps between the door frames and the top panel, and between the doors.

APPLY THE FINISH. It is easier if you finish the parts of the armoire before you attach the rest of the hardware. Start by filling all nail holes and screw countersink holes with untinted wood putty, then sand the dried putty so it is smooth and even with the wood surface. Sand all the wood surfaces with medium (150-grit) sandpaper. Finish-sand the surfaces with fine sandpaper (180-or 220-grit), using a hand-held power sander. Wipe the wood clean, then brush on a coat of sanding sealer so the wood will accept the wood stain more evenly—be sure to read the directions and warnings on the

can label before applying any finishing products. Apply wood stain (if desired, you can also leave the wood unstained and simply apply a protective topcoat). Let the stain dry completely, then apply several coats of topcoating product—we used two thin coats of water-based, satin polyurethane.

INSTALL THE HARDWARE. The final step in finishing the armoire is installing the door catches and door pulls and the closet rod. Install door pulls on the door panels, 25" up from each bottom rail and centered between the stiles—we used hammered wrought-iron pulls for a nice rustic look. Mount closet-rod hangers to the sides of the closet compartment, 11" down from the top panel. Cut a 1½"-dia. closet rod (I) to length, and slip it into the closet rod hangers (applying finishing materials to the closet rod is optional). Finally, install magnetic door catches and catch plates on the upper corners of the doors and the corresponding areas on the bottom of the top panel to keep the doors closed tightly when not in use. For extra holding power, install catches at the bottoms of the doors as well.

TIP

An armoire is basically a free standing closet, but with a few modifications it can become a custom furnishing that meets a variety of specific needs. To bolster its use as a dressing cabinet, attach a full-length dressing mirror to the inside of one of the doors, rearrange the shelf positions and drill a few holes in the back, and you've got a beautiful entertainment center; or, add more shelves and tuck the armoire in your kitchen to become a portable pantry.

Cedar Chest

This compact cedar chest has the potential to become a cherished family heirloom.

CONSTRUCTION MATERIALS

Quantity	Lumber
3	1 × 2" × 8' cedar
1	1 × 3" × 10' cedar
1	1 × 6" × 8' cedar
3	1 × 8" × 8' cedar
1	2 × 2" × 8' cedar
1	¾" × 2 × 4' plywood

The cedar chest has a long history as a much-appreciated graduation gift. The appreciation will be even greater for a cedar chest you have built yourself. And short of a packing crate, you won't find a simpler chest to build anywhere.

Despite its simplicity, this cedar chest has all the features of a commercially produced chest costing hundreds of dollars. The framed lid is hinged in back and can be locked open with an optional locking lid support. A removable tray fits inside the chest for storing delicate items. The main compartment is fitted with aromatic cedar panels to keep sweaters or your favorite linen treasures safe from moth damage and musty odors.

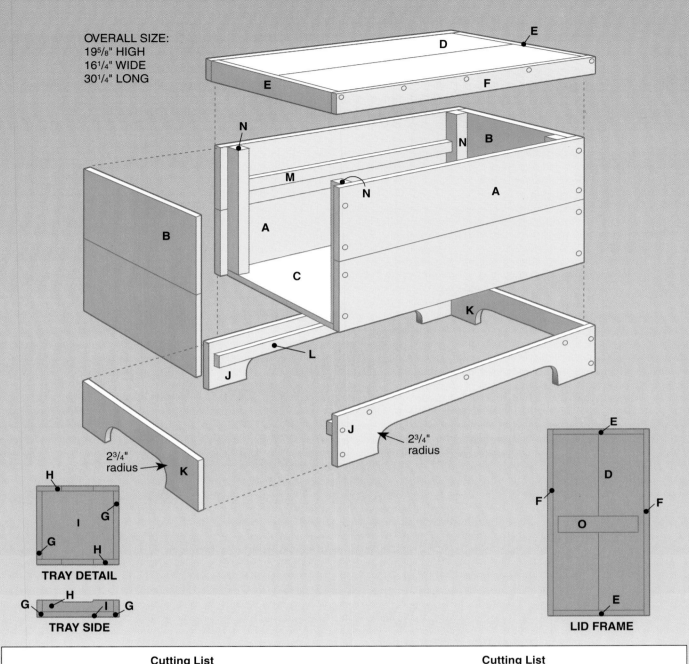

OVERALL SIZE:
19⅝" HIGH
16¼" WIDE
30¼" LONG

2¾" radius

2¾" radius

TRAY DETAIL

TRAY SIDE

LID FRAME

Cutting List						Cutting List				
Key	Part	Dimension	Pcs.	Material		Key	Part	Dimension	Pcs.	Material
A	Side	⅞ × 7¼ × 28"	4	Cedar		I	Tray bottom	⅞ × 2½ × 12¾"	4	Cedar
B	End	⅞ × 7¼ × 12½"	4	Cedar		J	Side plate	⅞ × 5½ × 29¾"	2	Cedar
C	Bottom	¾ × 12½ × 26¼"	1	Plywood		K	End plate	⅞ × 5½ × 14¼"	2	Cedar
D	Top	⅞ × 7¼ × 28½"	2	Cedar		L	Base cleat	⅞ × 1½ × 28"	2	Cedar
E	End lip	⅞ × 1½ × 14½"	2	Cedar		M	Chest cleat	⅞ × 1½ × 23¼"	2	Cedar
F	Side lip	⅞ × 1½ × 30¼"	2	Cedar		N	Corner post	1½ × 1½ × 13¾"	4	Cedar
G	Tray side	⅞ × 2½ × 12¾"	2	Cedar		O	Top cleat	⅞ × 2½ × 12"	1	Cedar
H	Tray end	⅞ × 2½ × 11¾"	2	Cedar						

Materials: 1¼" and 2" deck screws, 2d finish nails, 1½ × 2" brass butt hinges (2), lid support, optional hardware accessories, aromatic cedar panels, panel adhesive, ⅜"-dia. cedar plugs, wood glue, finishing materials.

Note: Measurements reflect the actual size of dimension lumber.

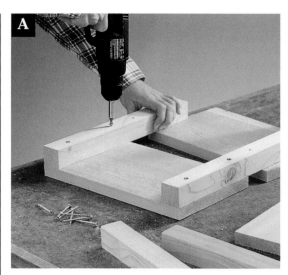

Drive screws through the posts into the ends.

Install the bottom onto the corner posts and fasten it to the sides and ends of the chest.

Directions: Cedar Chest

BUILD THE BOX FRAME. Start by cutting the chest sides (A) and chest ends (B) to size from 1 × 8 cedar. Cut the corner posts (N) to length from 2 × 2 cedar. Sand the chest ends, chest sides and corner posts with medium (100- or 120-grit) sandpaper to smooth out rough areas, then finish-sand with fine (150- or 180-grit) sandpaper. Use glue and counterbored 2" deck screws to fasten two chest ends to each pair of corner posts, with their tops and side edges flush **(photo A).** When using cedar that is rough on one side, which is fairly typi-

Attach the top cleat to undersides of the tops, making sure it is centered between the ends and the sides.

cal unless you are using select, clear cedar, be sure that exposed surfaces are consistent in texture. For this project, make sure all the rough sides are facing inside. Once the chest ends and corner posts are attached, apply glue to the outside edges of the corner posts and fasten the chest sides to the chest ends by driving 2" deck screws through the chest sides into the edges of the

chest ends. Make sure the top and side edges are flush. If the box frame is assembled correctly, there will be a ¾"-wide space between the bottom of the corner posts and the box frame's bottom edges. Cut the bottom (C) to size from ¾"-thick plywood. Turn the box frame upside down and fasten the bottom to the corner posts, ends and sides with glue and deck screws **(photo B).** Seal

Smooth out the jig saw cuts on the radius cutouts using a drum sander attachment and drill.

Set the box frame into the base, and fasten it with evenly spaced screws.

tops with glue and counter-bored #6 × 2" deck screws. Make sure the top edges of the lips and tops are flush.

BUILD THE BASE. Start by cutting the side plates (J) and end plates (K) to size from 1 × 6 cedar. Use a compass to lay out a curved cut with a 2¾" radius on each side plate and end plate. Start the cuts 4" from each side plate end and 3⅛" from each end plate end. Measure and mark carefully, then make the cuts with a jig saw. Finish-sand the side plates and end plates. Use a drill and drum sander attachment to smooth out the radius jig saw cuts **(photo D).** Fasten the side plates to the end plates with glue and counter-bored 2" deck screws driven through the front faces of the side plates into the ends of the end plates. Cut the two base cleats (L) to length from 1 × 2 cedar, and fasten them to the inside faces of the side plates, 2¾" from the bottom edges, flush with the top of the cutouts.

ATTACH THE BOX FRAME & BASE. Test-fit the box frame into the assembled base, and trim as necessary. Glue the joints, then attach the base to the box

the inside surfaces with an oil finish or sealer to prevent warping and splitting.

BUILD THE TOP ASSEMBLY. Begin by cutting the tops (D) to size from 1 × 8 cedar. Then cut the end lips (E) and side lips (F) to length from 1 × 2 cedar. Cut the top cleat (O) to length from 1 × 3 cedar. Finish-sand the pieces. Apply bar clamps to hold the tops together, with their ends flush.

Use a combination square to measure and mark the top cleat position on the inside faces of the tops. Make sure the top cleat is centered, with its side edges 13" from the outside ends of the tops and with its ends centered between the edges of the tops. Attach the cleat to the tops with glue and #6 × 1¼" deck screws **(photo C).** Attach the side lips and end lips to the edges of the

Tape the tray ends together, then draw a slot across the joint to mark even handle cutouts.

Attach the tray ends to the tray bottom and tray sides with glue and counterbored wood screws.

frame by driving evenly spaced, 1¼" deck screws through the end plates and side plates into the box frame **(photo E).** Sand all the surfaces until they are smooth to the touch. Smooth out all sharp edges with a sander.

MAKE THE TRAY. Cut the tray sides (G), tray ends (H) and tray bottom (I) to length from 1 × 3 cedar. Lay out the tray handles by placing the tray ends side by side, with the ends flush. Mark a 1½"-wide × 5"-long slot with ¾"-radius curves centered on each end of the cut where the two pieces meet **(photo F).** Make the cut with a jig saw, then finish-sand the pieces. Use a drum sander attachment on a drill to smooth out the radius cuts. Attach the tray sides to the tray ends with glue and 2" deck screws. Finally, fasten the tray bottoms between the tray sides and ends with glue and screws **(photo G).** Finish-sand the en-

tire tray, and smooth out any sharp edges.

INSTALL AROMATIC CEDAR PANELS. Start by cutting aromatic cedar liner panels to fit the inside of the chest. Attach the liner panels to the sides, ends, and bottom with panel

> **TIP**
>
> *Aromatic cedar panels have a strong cedar scent that keeps away pests, like moths, that will damage the contents of your cedar chest. The aromatic panels can be purchase in packages (usually 14 square feet), often described as "closet liner." Or, you can buy aromatic cedar in thin sheets that resemble particleboard.*

adhesive and 2d finish nails **(photo H).**

MAKE & INSTALL THE CHEST CLEATS. Cut the chest cleats (M) to size from 1 × 2 cedar, and finish-sand the cleats. Install the chest cleats so their top edges are 3½" from the top of the chest sides. They should fit snugly between the corner posts.

INSTALL THE TOP ASSEMBLY. Place the top assembly over the chest and use masking tape to mark where the lower edge of the lip contacts the back side. Install two 1½ × 2" brass butt hinges on the chest box, spaced 6" in from each end of the chest box. Mount the hinges so the barrels fall below the contact line. Next, place the chest and top assembly on a flat worksurface and prop the chest box against the top so the unfastened sides of the hinges rest on the inside of the lip of the top assembly. Insert spacers (ordinary wood shims work well for this) equal to the thickness of the barrel, between the chest and lip. Fasten the hinges on the lip using the screws provided with the hinge hardware **(photo I).** Test the lid assembly and hinges for proper operation and fit. Install a locking lid support between the lid assem-

H

Install aromatic cedar lining panels to the sides, ends and bottom, using panel adhesive and 2d finish nails.

bly and the chest box to hold the lid in an open position during use. For just a little more money, you can purchase hardware accessories called soft-down supports, which let the lid close gently instead of slamming down. Install chest handles and brass corner protectors if desired.

APPLY FINISHING TOUCHES. Fill all exposed counterbore holes with cedar plugs. Apply glue to the edges of the plugs and tap in place with a hammer. Sand the plugs smooth until they are level with the wood surface. Finish-sand all outside surfaces lightly. Sand all exposed edges and surfaces of the tray. Set the tray on the chest cleats and slide it back and forth to test the fit. Adjust the fit if necessary with a belt sander or palm sander and coarse (60-grit) sandpaper, then go through the previous sanding steps to remove any sanding scratches and roughness. There are various finishing options you have with the cedar chest. We chose a traditional clear finish to provide a rustic, natural appearance. To apply the finish, we first brushed on a coat of sanding sealer to even out the absorption (a good idea with soft wood like cedar). Then we applied two light coats of tung-oil finish and buffed the surface to a medium gloss with a buffing pad. We also applied a coat of tung oil to the tray and exposed inside surfaces. If one side of a board is left uncoated, the sides will absorb moisture at different rates, and warping is a likely result. After the finish is applied, dried and buffed, you may want to stencil a design or monograms onto the chest—especially if you are building the chest as a gift. If you choose to monogram the chest, look for plain stencils that are 1" to 2" tall, to keep in scale with the size of the chest. Very ornate type styles are hard to stencil, and are generally not in tune with the rustic look of a cedar chest (see *Tip*, above). If you are interested in stenciling a design or emblem onto the chest, also look for a simple pattern. Almost any nature motif (like pinecones) is a good fit.

I

Install brass butt hinges on the chest box and lid assembly. Use a wood shim as a spacer to help align the hinges.

Step Stool

Exceptionally stable and designed to be just the right height to help your toddler reach the countertop or sink, this step stool also features a ladder-style back with rungs for drying dish rags.

Whether you're trying to clean the back of a cupboard or changing a light bulb, our step stool is handy and reliable. You'll reach for this step stool when it comes time to do the household chores. It's small enough to fit in a corner of your kitchen, or even in a nearby closet, so it will always be there when you need it. With a sturdy step stool around the house, you won't have to use a chair to reach that next level. Although it's a practical home accent, our step stool is an attractive addition to any kitchen or pantry. Cover all the countersunk screw heads with contrasting plugs to give it an interesting finished appearance.

Assembling our step stool is an easy process. The entire project is built around a four-piece frame beneath the slats. Once this frame is built, just attach the posts, legs, slats and rungs—and the step stool is ready for action.

CONSTRUCTION MATERIALS

Quantity	Lumber
1	1 × 4" × 6' pine
2	1 × 3" × 8' pine
2	⅞" × 3' dowel

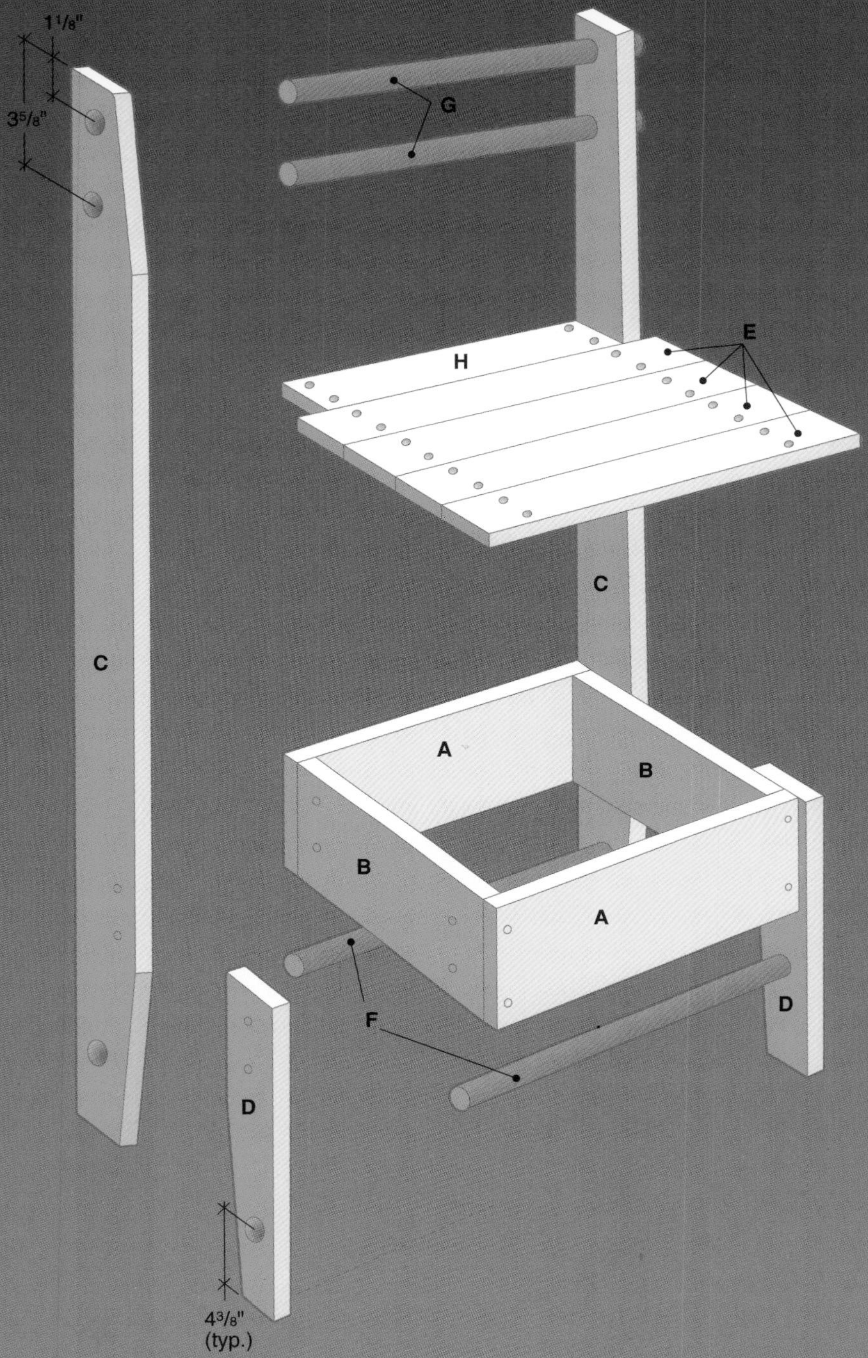
1 1/8"
3 5/8"
G
E
H
C
C
A
B
B
A
F
D
D
4 3/8"
(typ.)

OVERALL SIZE:
32" HIGH
12 1/2" WIDE
16" LONG

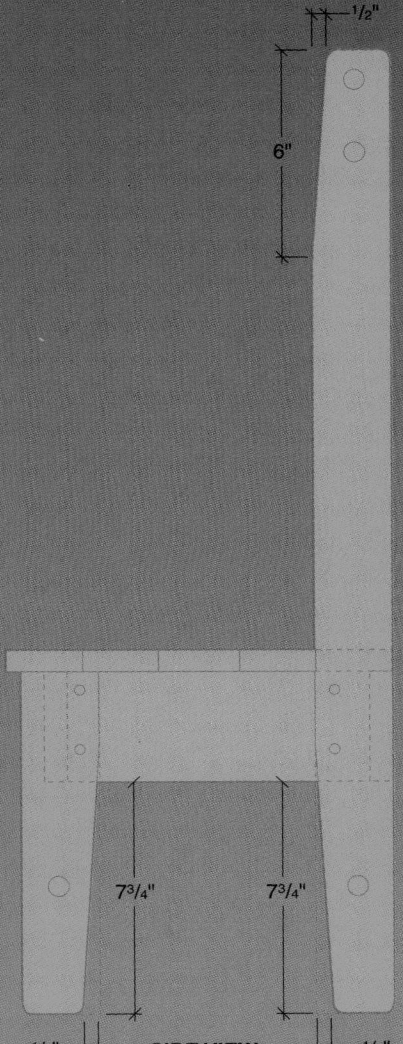
1/2"
6"
7 3/4"
7 3/4"
1/2"
1/2"

SIDE VIEW

Cutting List

Key	Part	Dimension	Pcs.	Material
A	Side	¾ × 3½ × 12"	2	Pine
B	End	¾ × 3½ × 9¾"	2	Pine
C	Post	¾ × 2½ × 32"	2	Pine
D	Leg	¾ × 2½ × 11¼"	2	Pine

Cutting List

Key	Part	Dimension	Pcs.	Material
E	Slat	1½ × 2½ × 16"	4	Pine
F	Rung	⅞ × 13½"	2	Dowel
G	Rail	⅞ × 16"	2	Dowel
H	Short slat	1½ × 2½ × 12"	1	Pine

Materials: Wood glue, wood screws (1¼", 2"), 4d finish nails, finishing materials.

Note: Measurements reflect the actual size of dimensional lumber.

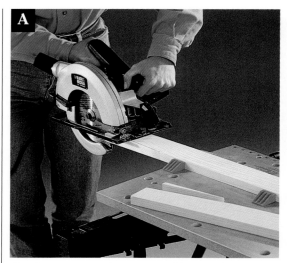

Cut the tapers on the posts and legs with a circular saw.

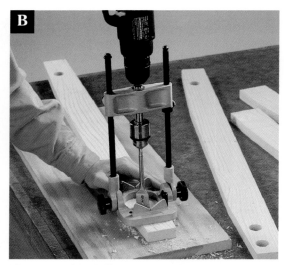

Use a portable drill guide to make straight holes for the rungs and rails.

Attach the posts to the frame so that their back edges are flush with the back edges of the frame.

Directions: Step Stool

BUILD THE FRAME. The step stool is built around a supporting frame. This frame consists of four pieces: two ends and two sides. Start by cutting the ends (A) and sides (B) to size.

Fasten the pieces by driving #6 × 2" wood screws through the sides into the end edges. Make sure all the corners are square and the edges are flush, then sand the pieces with 150-grit sandpaper until they are completely smooth.

MAKE THE LEGS & POSTS. Cut the posts (C) and legs (D) to size. Each leg has a slight taper cut from the back bottom edge. The posts have tapers cut from the front edges on their tops

and bottoms (see *Diagram*, page 9). To draw the taper guidelines, measure and mark points as follows: 7¾" from the bottom leg and post edges, 6" from the top post edges and ½" along the ends. Draw a line connecting the points to form a taper shape. Use a circular saw to make the taper cuts, forming the finished shapes of the legs and posts **(photo A).**

DRILL HOLES IN LEGS & POSTS. The legs and posts must be prepared to hold the dowel rungs (F) and rails (G). The rungs and rails provide stability to the step stool and help give the project a decorative touch. Though they are attached at the very end of the project's construction, you should drill the holes in the legs and posts now, before you attach them to the frame. For the rungs on the legs and posts, measure and mark centered points 4⅜" from the bottom edges on the pieces. For the rails on the upper posts, measure and mark centered points 1⅛" and 3⅜" from the top post edges. Use a

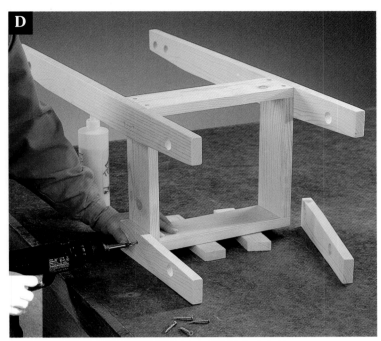

Use ¾" spacers under the frame to create a recess when attaching the legs.

the posts on each side. Fix the rungs and rails in place by driving a 4d finish nail through the legs and posts into each dowel piece.

APPLY THE FINISHING TOUCHES. Make sure all the surfaces are sanded smooth, and fill all the exposed screw holes with glued matching or contrasting plugs. You can make or purchase the plugs to match the stool, or decorate the project with contrasting pieces. We applied a clear tung-oil finish to the step stool.

drill with a portable drill guide to bore a ⅞"-dia. hole through each marked point on the posts and legs. Set a piece of scrap wood beneath the pieces when drilling the holes **(photo B).**

ATTACH THE LEGS & POSTS TO THE FRAME. Before attaching the legs and posts, sand them to finished smoothness, breaking the sharp edges and corners. It's easier to sand the pieces before they are attached to the frame. When the pieces are smooth to the touch, attach them to the step stool frame with glue and counterbored #6 × 1¼" wood screws. Center the screws 8½" and 10½" from the bottom of the legs and posts. When attached correctly, the back edges of the posts should be flush with the back of the frame **(photo C),** and the front edges of the legs should overlap the front of the frame by ¾" **(photo D).** The bottom edges of the frame should be 7¾" from the bottoms of the posts.

ATTACH THE SLATS, RAILS & RUNGS. Cut the stool slats (E) and short slat (H) to size. Cut the rungs (F) and rails (G) from the ⅞" dowel rod. The rear slat is 4" shorter than the other slats to allow it to fit in between the posts. Attach the slats to the frame with wood screws, starting with the short slat that fits between the posts. The short slat should be flush with the back of the frame. Simply bore two evenly-spaced counterbored holes on each end of the slats for the screw holes **(photo E).** Drill the counterbored holes 2⅜" from each edge. The counterbored holes on the short slats should be ⅜" from the side edges. Apply glue to the sides of the rung and rail holes, and install the rungs and rails. The rails should extend 1¼" beyond

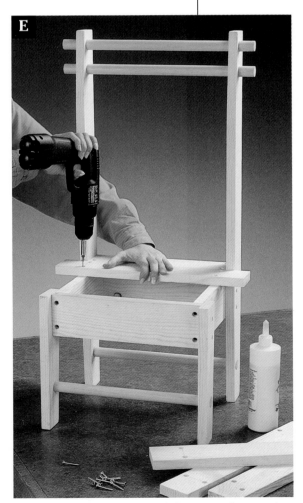

Attach the short slat between the posts, then work your way forward with the other slats.

Kids' Playhouse

New on market: spacious 1 rm playhouse, cheerful decor, many windows, folds up for storage. Take immediate possession.

CONSTRUCTION MATERIALS

Quantity	Lumber
4	¼" × 4 × 8' plywood
30	1" × 2 × 8' premium furring
3	1" × 4 × 8' pine

Kids of all ages long for a place of their own: a tree house, a backyard fort; a seldom-used shed; anything with four walls, a roof and a door. The problem is, most of these would-be retreats are either eyesores or they are well outside of a parent's field of supervision. By building this charming little playhouse with walls that have more window than wood, you can give a child the private space that he or she longs for, but still keep the little one within your sight.

Made from lightweight ¼" plywood, this playhouse is easy to move around and store. The walls are hinged together and will fold flat against a wall when the lift-off roof is removed. You can even set the playhouse up in the backyard on a pleasant afternoon to give your child a room with a view.

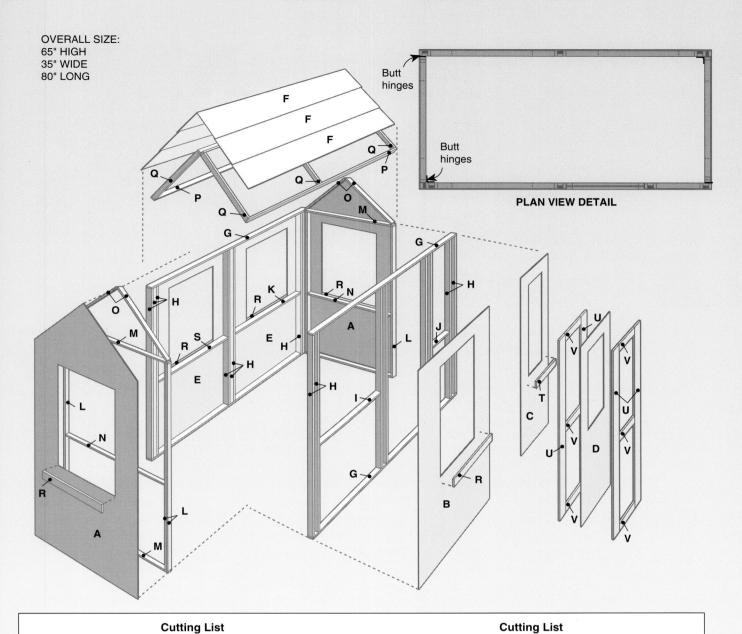

OVERALL SIZE:
65" HIGH
35" WIDE
80" LONG

PLAN VIEW DETAIL

Butt hinges

Butt hinges

Cutting List				
Key	**Part**	**Dimension**	**Pcs.**	**Material**
A	House end	¼ × 31½ × 59⅞"	2	Plywood
B	House front	¼ × 36 × 48"	1	Plywood
C	House side	¼ × 16 × 48"	1	Plywood
D	Door	¼ × 19½ × 46"	1	Plywood
E	Rear panel	¼ × 48 × 72"	1	Plywood
F	Roof panel	¼ × 7⅞ × 80"	6	Plywood
G	Side plate	¾ × 1½ × 72"	4	Pine
H	Wall stud	¾ × 1½ × 46½"	23	Pine
I	Front sill	¾ × 1½ × 28½"	1	Pine
J	Side sill	¾ × 1½ × 10"	1	Pine
K	Rear wall sill	¾ × 1½ × 31½"	1	Pine

Cutting List				
Key	**Part**	**Dimension**	**Pcs.**	**Material**
L	Corner stud	¾ × 1½ × 47¼"	6	Pine
M	End plate	¾ × 1½ × 31½"	4	Pine
N	End sill	¾ × 1½ × 29¼"	2	Pine
O	Gable frame	¾ × 1½ × 18¼"	4	Pine
P	Roof frame	¾ × 1½ × 80"	4	Pine
Q	Roof frame	¾ × 1½ × 19¾"	6	Pine
R	Window ledger	¾ × 1½ × 22"	5	Pine
S	Rear wall sill	¾ × 1½ × 30"	1	Pine
T	Window ledger	¾ × 1½ × 12"	1	Pine
U	Door stile	¾ × 3½ × 46"	4	Pine
V	Door rail	¾ × 3½ × 12½"	6	Pine

Materials: Glue, wood screws (#6 × 1", #6 × 1½", #6 × 2"), 4d finish nails, 3 × 3" butt hinges (14), 1½ × 3" butt hinges (3), nonlocking doorknob set, finishing materials.

Note: Measurements reflect the actual size of dimensional lumber.

Make window cutouts with a jig saw.

Mark the 1 × 2 wall stud positions on the side plates with a combination square and a pencil.

Directions: Playhouse

MAKE THE PANELS. The panels are lightweight skins that are fastened to the structural framework of the playhouse. Begin construction by cutting the house end panels (A), house front panel (B), house side panel (C), door (D) and back wall panel (E). To economize on material, lay out cutting guidelines carefully before cutting the parts. Sand all the parts smooth after cutting. To cut the angles on the end panels, measure 15¾" across the top end of the panel and place a mark. Measure 48¾" up from the bottom end on the sides and mark points. Use a straightedge to connect the points to the centerpoint on the top end. Cut along the diagonal lines with a jig saw to form the gable profile on the tops of the end panels. To make the window cutouts on the end panels, draw a line from side to side, 24" up from the bottom. Mark another line 45" up from the bottom. Mark points along

each line, 5¾" in from each side. Draw guidelines connecting the points to form a rectangle. Drill pilot holes in the corner of the layout and cut along the guidelines with a jig saw to form the 20"-wide × 21"-high window cutouts on the end panels **(photo A).** Make similar window cutouts on the house front panel, house side panel and back wall panel by finding the center of each panel and drawing lines 24" and 45" up from their bottom edges. On the front panel, make the sides of the window cutout 10" on each side of center. On the side panel, make the side of the window cutout 5" on each side of center. Unlike the other panels, the back wall panel has two cutouts, so mark centerpoints 18" from each end, and make the sides of the cutouts 10" to each side of those centerpoints. On the door, draw window cutout lines 23" and 44" up from the bottom, and mark their centerpoints. Mark points 6½" to each side of the centerpoints to form the cutout shape. Sand the edges smooth.

MAKE THE SIDE PLATES & WALL STUDS. The frames at the front and rear of the playhouse are made by attaching ¾"-thick wall studs between two pairs of side plates. Building this part of the playhouse is very similar to frame carpentry, if you've ever built a stud wall before. The frame for the front panel and the frame for the rear wall panel are the same, except for the door and small window on the front. Start by cutting the side plates (G) and wall studs (H) to size. Lay the side plates in pairs on a flat worksurface. Before attaching the studs between the side plates, you must carefully lay out the stud positions. Hook your measuring tape on one end of a front side plate. Mark lines 1½", 3¾", 33", 35¼", 56", 58¼" and 69" from one end on the face of the side plate. These marks show the stud positions on the front side plates, and are in order, left to right, if you are facing the front of the finished playhouse. Using a combination square, draw lines across the plates, ¾" to the right

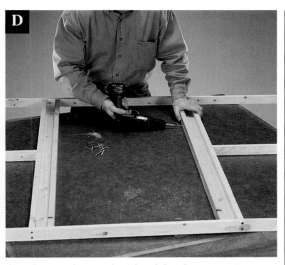

Drive countersunk wood screws through the frame sections into the door-frame studs.

Attach a stud to each side of the door opening to create a solid door frame.

of each mark, showing the position of each ¾"-thick stud **(photo B).** To mark the stud positions on the rear side plates, measure and mark lines at 2¼", 33", 35¼", 67½" and 69¾" from one end of the rear side plate. These markings are in sequence, left to right, if you are facing the front of the playhouse. At each end of the side plate pairs, use glue and counterbored #6 × 2" wood screws to attach a stud between the side plates.

MAKE THE FRONT FRAME. The front frame is made up of wall studs and sills that fit horizontally between the studs, just behind the bottom edges of each window cutout. These sill and stud assemblies are attached between side plate pairs with glue and #6 × 2" wood screws. Cut the back wall sills (K, S), front sill (I) and side sill (J) to size from 1 × 2 pine. Use glue and counterbored wood screws to fasten the front sill and side sill between the stud pairs, 22½" up from the bottoms of the studs—these frame parts fit behind the front panel. Position the front sill and its studs

between the side plates, starting at the second stud position lines on the left-hand side of the side plates (drawn previously on the side plate faces). Fasten the studs with glue and counterbored wood screws, driven through the side plates and into the ends of the studs. Insert a stud in the gap between the front sill assembly and the stud at the end of the frame. Make sure the inserted stud butts against the front sill assembly—the face should be flush with the inside edges of the side plates. Fasten it with glue and counterbored wood screws. Position the side sill and its stud pair on the right-hand side of the front frame, making sure the studs are aligned with their designated position lines. Attach these studs with glue and counterbored wood screws. Insert a stud in the gap between the side sill assembly and the stud on the end of the frame. Make sure the inside face of the inserted stud is flush with the inside edges of the side plates, and fasten it with glue and

wood screws. Now, make the door frame. To make a secure anchor for the door and its hinges, you need to attach two support studs on either side of the opening that was formed when you attached the side sill assembly and front sill assembly. Butt the studs against the assemblies, edge first, and fasten the studs so their faces are flush with the inside edges of the wall. Attach the parts with glue and counterbored wood screws, driven through one stud face and into the other stud side **(photo C).** Complete the door frame by attaching the two remaining studs, face first, to the door-frame support studs. Make sure the inside edges are flush, and attach the parts with glue and counterbored #6 × 2" wood screws **(photo D).**

MAKE THE REAR FRAME. The rear frame is similar to the front frame, but it has no door space. Start by attaching the rear wall sill (S) between two studs with glue and counterbored wood screws, 22½" from the stud bottoms. Fasten the rear wall sill between two studs at the same height. Fasten the sill (K) and studs between the plates, starting at the second stud position line on the right-hand side of the side plates (drawn previously on the side plate faces). Insert a stud in the gap between the wall sill assembly and the stud at the end of the frame. Make sure the inserted stud butts against the sill assembly—the face should be flush with the inside edges of the side plates. Fasten it with glue and counterbored wood screws. Fasten the second back wall sill (S) and studs between the side plates, starting at the first stud position lines on the left-hand side of the side plates. Insert a stud in the gap between the shorter wall sill assembly and the stud at the end of the frame. Attach it with glue and wood screws. Fasten a stud in the gap between the two frame assemblies at the center of the wall. Position this stud so the inside face is flush with the inside edges of the side plates. Use glue and counterbored wood screws to attach the stud.

MAKE THE END FRAMES & ROOF FRAMES. Start by cutting the corner studs (L) and end plates (M) to size. Use glue and counterbored wood screws to attach two corner studs between the two end plates. Position the corner studs so their outside faces are flush with the

Attach the roof frames with butt hinges.

Install a nonlocking doorknob set in the door.

end plate ends, and drive screws through the end plates into the corner stud ends, forming two rectangular frames. Cut the end sills (N) to size, and attach them to the remaining corner studs with glue and wood screws. The end sills should be 22½" from the corner stud bottoms. Position the attached end sills and studs into each rectangular end frame, and attach

them with glue and wood screws. To make the roof frames, cut the roof frame boards (P, Q) to size. Use glue and counterbored wood screws to attach the shorter roof frame boards between the longer roof frame pairs at each end and at their centers. When both sections are assembled, attach them with evenly spaced, 3 × 3" butt hinges (photo E).

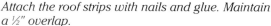

Attach the roof strips with nails and glue. Maintain a ½" overlap.

Position the finished roof onto the playhouse.

ATTACH THE PANELS & FRAMES. Attach the house end panels to the end frames with glue and counterbored wood screws, driven through the end panels and into the end frames. Attach the panels to the end frames so that one end frame has the double-end stud at the front, and the other at the back—when the frames are attached this will be very important for hinge placement. Make sure the bottom and side edges are flush. Cut the gable frames (O) to size, and use glue and wood screws to attach them along the top of the panels, flush with the top edges. Use glue and wood screws to attach the rear wall panel to the rear frame, making sure the window cutouts are unobstructed by the frame and the edges are flush. Attach the front and side panels to the front frame. Cut the door stiles (U) and door rails (V) to size. Glue the door stiles, and sandwich the door panel between stile pairs on the panel edges. Drive wood screws through the

inside stiles and into the outside stiles. Attach the door rails along the top and bottom edges of the door panel in the same manner. Attach the final door rails on the bottom edge of the door panel's window cutout. Drill the holes for the doorknob and latch, and hang the door in the frame with 1½ × 3" butt hinges. Install non-locking doorknob hardware **(photo F).**

ATTACH THE FRAMES. The front, rear and end frames are connected to each other on both sides with two evenly spaced 3 × 3" butt hinges. To ensure effective fold-up of the playhouse, the hinge barrels on the end frame sides with two end posts should face out. The hinge barrels on the single end post sides should be attached facing in (see *Diagram*, page 17).

MAKE THE ROOF & LEDGERS. Cut the roof panels (F) to size. Fold the roof frames in half, and fasten the roof panels to the frames with 4d finish nails, starting at the bottom edges.

(Keep the bottom edge flush with the frame.) Overlap the next roof panel by ½" on top of the first **(photo G),** and again with the final roof panel. Turn the roof over, and repeat the procedure with the remaining roof frame. The top panels will overhang the roof peak by about 1½". Set all the nails, and position the roof on the playhouse **(photo H).** Cut the window ledgers (R, T) to size. Center them on the outside, bottom edge of each window cutout, and fasten them with glue and wood screws to strengthen the window edges.

APPLY FINISHING TOUCHES. Fill screw holes with wood putty, then sand all surfaces. Cover all the surfaces with a washable, semi-gloss enamel paint. We used a fairly fancy paint job with our playhouse. We painted the walls one color, then painted the trim a contrasting color. We even chose to paint the roof and door another color.

Kid-size Oak Desk

This little oak desk gives new meaning to the three R's:
Red oak, Right angles, and Really easy to build.

CONSTRUCTION MATERIALS

Quantity	Lumber
1	¼" × 2 × 4' hardboard
1	½ × 2" × 4' red oak
1	½ × 3" × 2' red oak
1	¾" × 2 × 4' oak plywood
1	1 × 2" × 4' red oak
1	1 × 3" × 2' red oak
2	1 × 4" × 8' red oak
2	2 × 2" × 8' red oak

Here's a nice alternative to the scores of plastic and particleboard novelty desks that are sold as childrens' furniture. Made of oak and oak plywood, this small-scale version of an old-style school desk makes a great work and study area for your youngster. The spacious desktop provides plenty of workspace for drawing and reading.

The roomy "childproof" drawer has a built-in stop so it can't be pulled all the way out.

The simplicity of this desk design makes it easy to build, but it also gives it a timeless beauty that will blend into just about any decorating scheme. And best of all, you can save hundreds of dollars over comparable furnishings you might buy at a store.

96

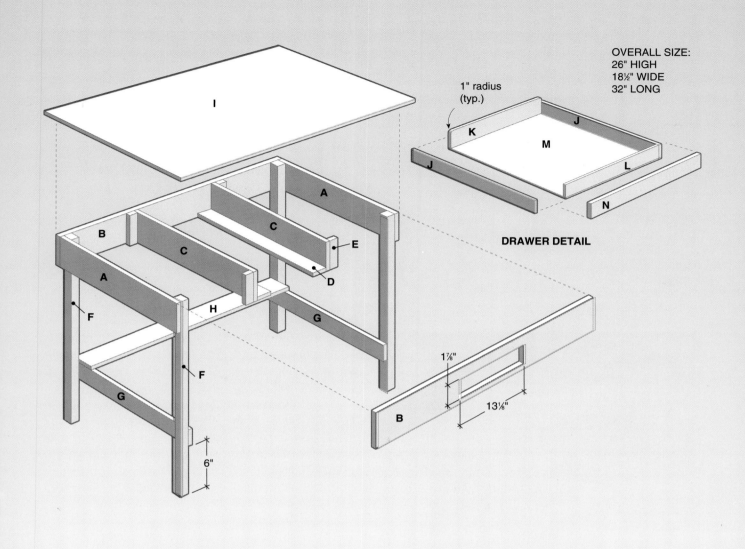

OVERALL SIZE:
26" HIGH
18½" WIDE
32" LONG

1" radius (typ.)

DRAWER DETAIL

1⅞"

13⅛"

6"

Cutting List				
Key	**Part**	**Dimension**	**Pcs.**	**Material**
A	End rail	¾ × 3½ × 14½"	2	Oak
B	Side rail	¾ × 3½ × 30"	2	Oak
C	Slide side	¾ × 3½ × 14½"	2	Oak
D	Slide bottom	¾ × 1½ × 14½"	2	Oak
E	Slide cleat	¾ × 1½ × 3½"	4	Oak
F	Leg	1½ × 1½ × 25¼"	4	Oak
G	Leg stretcher	¾ × 3½ × 14½"	2	Oak

Cutting List				
Key	**Part**	**Dimension**	**Pcs.**	**Material**
H	Stringer	¾ × 3½ × 25½"	1	Oak
I	Desktop	¾ × 19 × 33"	1	Oak plywood
J	Drawer side	½ × 1½ × 14"	2	Oak
K	Drawer back	½ × 2½ × 12"	1	Oak
L	Drawer front	½ × 1½ × 12"	1	Oak
M	Drawer bottom	¼ × 13 × 14"	1	Hardboard
N	Drawer faceplate	¾ × 2½ × 14"	1	Oak

Materials: Wood glue, brass wood screws (#6 x 1", #6 x 1¼", #6 x 1½"), brass corner brackets (8), oak wood plugs, oak drawer knob, wood putty, oak veneer edge tape (9'), finishing materials.

Note: Measurements reflect the actual size of dimensional lumber.

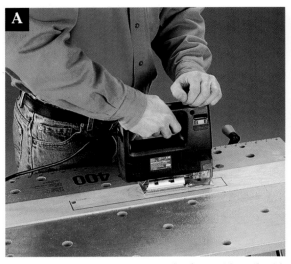

Cut out the drawer opening in the front side rail with a jig saw—drill starter holes at the corners.

Position the slides on the marks and secure in place with wood glue and screws driven through the cleats and into the side rails.

Attach the stringer to the leg stretchers with wood glue and countersunk screws.

Directions: Oak Desk

BUILD THE FRAME & DRAWER SLIDE. Cut the end rails (A) and side rails (B), and sand them smooth. Lay the side rails edge to edge and measure 8⁷⁄₁₆" in from each. Draw a line that spans both side rails. On one side rail (this will become the front rail), measure ⅞" down from the top edge and ¾" up from the bottom edge and draw lines to form a 13⅛ × 1⅞" rectangular cutout for the drawer. Drill a ⅜"-dia. starter

hole at each corner, and make the rectangular cutout with a jig saw **(photo A).** Smooth the edges with a sanding block. Cut the slide sides (C) and slide bottoms (D), and sand smooth. Position a slide bottom flush against the bottom of each slide side, and fasten with wood glue and #6 × 1½" brass wood screws. Drill pilot holes for the screws, countersunk just enough so the screw heads will be recessed. Cut the slide cleats (E) and fasten them to the ends of the slide sides with glue and countersunk screws. Position the slide assemblies so the inside faces of the slide sides are even with the sides of the drawer cutout and the matching lines on the back rail. The tops of the slide bottoms should be level with the bottom of the drawer cutout. Secure the slide assemblies with glue and countersunk screws driven through the cleats and into the side rails **(photo B).** Next, place the end rails between the side rails, flush with the ends, to form a rectangular frame. Clamp the frame, then

drill counterbored pilot holes (make sure the counterbores are sized to accept oak wood plugs) through the side rails and into the end rails. Unclamp the frame, apply glue to the joints, then reassemble it and drive #6 × 1½" brass wood screws into the pilot holes.

BUILD & ATTACH THE LEGS, STRETCHERS & STRINGERS. These support elements add stability to the desk. Cut the legs (F) to length from 2 × 2 oak and sand with medium-grit sandpaper. Turn the rail and slide assembly upside down on your worksurface. Clamp a leg in each corner, with the top of the leg flush with the top edge of the frame. Drill counterbored pilot holes through the end rails and into the legs. Unclamp the legs, apply glue to the joints, then secure the joints with screws driven into the pilot holes. Set the assembly in an upright position. Cut the leg stretchers (G) and stringer (H). Measure up from the bottom of each leg 6" and place a reference mark on the inside surface of each leg. At-

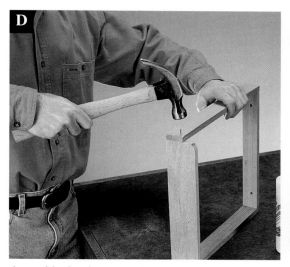

Assemble the drawer with glue and 3d finish nails. Be sure to drill pilot holes for the finish nails.

Trim the veneer edge tape with a sharp utility knife, then sand the desktop edges and surfaces.

tach the leg stretchers to the legs, just above the reference lines, so the ends of the stretchers are flush with the outside faces of the legs. Position the stringer on top of the stretchers, against the inside faces of the back legs. Attach the stringer to the leg stretchers with glue and counterbored screws **(photo C).**

BUILD THE DRAWER. The drawer construction is simply a box with an attached faceplate. We used ½"-thick oak for the drawer frame—you can find ½" oak with the shelving and molding at most building centers. Cut the drawer sides (J), drawer front (L), drawer back (K) and drawer bottom (M). Draw roundover cutting lines with a 1" radius at the top corners of the drawer back, and cut with a jig saw. Position the drawer front and back between the drawer sides, flush with the ends of the drawer sides. Assemble the drawer with glue and 3d finish nails **(photo D).** Be sure to drill pilot holes for the finish nails. The pilot holes should be thinner than the finish nails. Place the drawer frame upside down, and attach

the drawer bottom with glue and 3d finish nails. Turn the drawer unit over and place it on two pieces of ½"-thick scrap wood. Cut the drawer faceplate (N) to length from 1 × 3 oak. Place the faceplate upright on edge against the drawer front so it overhangs the drawer front by ½" on all sides. Fasten the faceplate to the drawer front with #6 × 1" brass wood screws, driven through countersunk pilot holes in the inside face of the drawer front, and into the back face of the faceplate. Tip the front of the drawer up, and insert the back edge into the drawer opening in the front rail. Test the drawer.

BUILD & ATTACH THE DESK-TOP. Cut the desktop (I) to size from ¾"-thick oak plywood. Sand the edges and surfaces with medium-grit sandpaper. Apply self-adhesive wood veneer edge tape to the edges by pressing with a household iron (the heat activates the glue). Trim any overhanging edges with a utility knife **(photo E).** Fasten the desktop to the desk with a brass corner bracket (or L-brace) at each side of all four

corners. The desk top should overhang all sides by 1½" **(photo F).**

APPLY FINISHING TOUCHES. Fill nails holes with oak-tinted wood putty, and glue oak plugs into screw counterbores. Sand the plugs so they are flush with the surface, then finish-sand all surfaces with 180-grit sand-paper. Apply stain (we used light oak wipe-on stain) and topcoat (we used three coats of polyurethane on the desk top, and two coats on the rest of the desk).

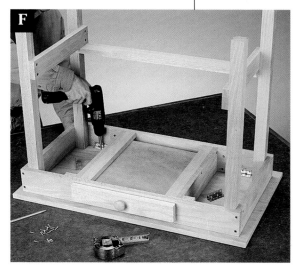

Fasten the desktop to the side rails with corner brackets, leaving a 1½" overhang on all four sides.

Kid-size Oak Table & Chairs

*Build a durable, attractive table-and-chair set just for the kids,
and watch them enjoy it for years to come.*

CONSTRUCTION MATERIALS

Quantity	Lumber
6	1 × 2" × 8' oak
2	1 × 3" × 8' oak
1	1 × 10" × 4' oak
1	¾" × 4 × 4' oak plywood
2	¾ × ¾" × 8' corner molding

A table-and-chair set just for kids, this project is great for games, puzzles or snack time. The tabletop features a convenient rim around the edges, which curbs messy spills and keeps all the pieces of a jigsaw puzzle or board game off the floor. The chairs are very nearly tip-proof and blend nicely with the table style. Though this project is made for children, the attractive styling and beautiful oak construction make it suitable in any decor. There is no doubt about the sturdiness of this solid oak project—it's truly built to last. In fact, it just might become a cherished family heirloom that is handed down from generation to generation.

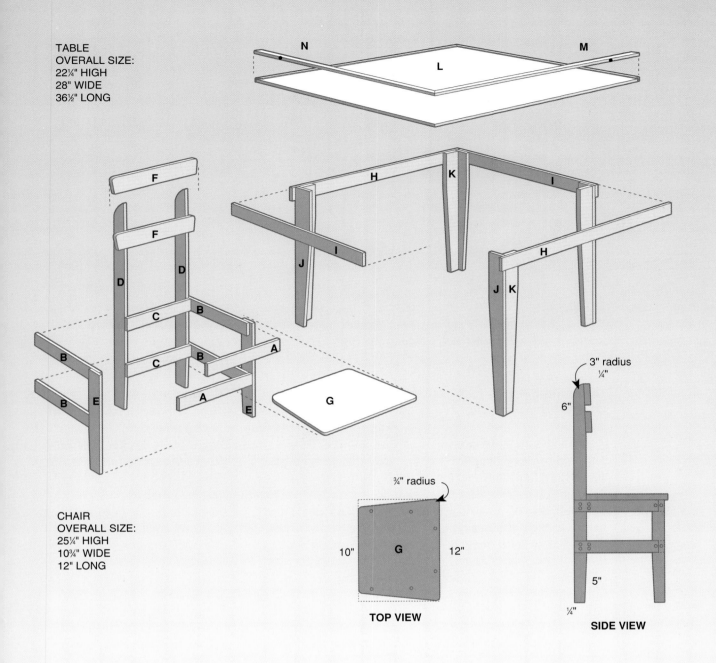

TABLE
OVERALL SIZE:
22¼" HIGH
28" WIDE
36½" LONG

CHAIR
OVERALL SIZE:
25¼" HIGH
10¾" WIDE
12" LONG

¾" radius

10" G 12"

TOP VIEW

3" radius
¼"

6"

5"

¼"

SIDE VIEW

Key	Part	Dimension	Pcs.	Material
A	Front	¾ × 1½ × 9½"	4	Oak
B	Side	¾ × 1½ × 9¾"	8	Oak
C	Cross rail	¾ × 1½ × 8"	4	Oak
D	Post	¾ × 1½ × 25¼"	4	Oak
E	Leg	¾ × 1½ × 12"	4	Oak
F	Slats	¾ × 2½ × 12"	4	Oak
G	Seat	¾ × 9¼ × 12"	2	Oak

Cutting List

Key	Part	Dimension	Pcs.	Material
H	Apron side	¾ × 1½ × 32"	2	Oak
I	Apron end	¾ × 1½ × 23½"	2	Oak
J	Outside leg	¾ × 2½ × 21¼"	4	Oak
K	Inside leg	¾ × 1½ × 21¼"	4	Oak
L	Top	¾ × 27½ × 36"	1	Oak plywood
M	End nosing	¾ × ¾ × 28"	2	Oak molding
N	Side nosing	¾ × ¾ × 36½"	2	Oak molding

Materials: Glue, brass wood screws (#6 × 1¼"), wire brads, finishing materials.

Note: Measurements reflect the actual size of dimensional lumber.

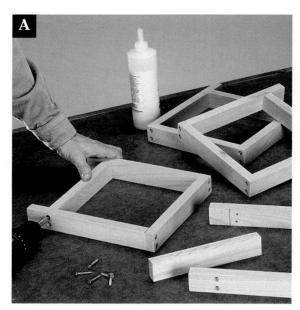

Attach the cross rails between the frame sides with glue and screws.

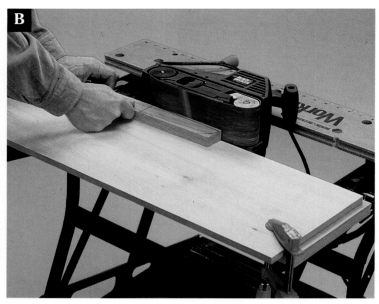

Sand the tapers into the posts and legs with a belt sander mounted sideways on your worksurface.

Directions: Oak Table & Chairs

BUILD THE CHAIR FRAMES. The *Cutting List* on page 101 shows the material needed for two small chairs, but you can build as many as you want or need with the directions provided. Start with the chair frames. Each chair contains two frames, which are made from four pieces of ¾"-thick oak. When the chair is completed, the top frame is located directly under the seat. The remaining frame is positioned 7" up from the bottoms of the legs. The entire chair assembly is built around the top frame, which serves as a kind of structural anchor for the seat and legs. Start by cutting the fronts (A), sides (B) and cross rails (C) to size. Sand all parts with medium-grit sandpaper to smooth out any rough edges after cutting. Drill a pair of counterbored pilot holes for #6 × 1¼" screws on the front

face of each front, centered ⅜" from each end. Drill pilot hole pairs for #6 × 1¼" wood screws on each side, centered ¾" and 1⅞" from one end of the sides. Fasten the fronts to the sides with glue and wood screws, driven through the pilot holes in the fronts and into the side ends—position the sides so that the ends with the pilot holes are facing away from the front. The top and side edges of the front and sides should be flush. Next, draw reference lines across the inside faces of each side, 1½" from the ends with the pilot holes. Glue the cross rail ends, and position them between the sides. Make sure the cross rails are lined up with the reference lines, and drive #6 × 1¼" wood screws through the pilot holes into the cross rail ends to secure them **(photo A).** Use sandpaper to smooth out the top and bottom edges of the frames.

BUILD THE POSTS & LEGS. The posts and legs must be cut to shape before they can be at-

tached to the chair frames. Both the posts and the legs have narrow tapers on their edges. Since the tapers are only ¼" deep, use a belt sander to remove the material. Start by cutting the posts (D) and legs (E) to length. To cut the tapers in the posts and legs, you must measure and mark the guidelines carefully. Draw lines across the outside face of each leg and post, 5" up from their bottoms. Draw similar lines 6" down from the top of the posts. On the bottoms of the legs and posts (and the top of the posts), mark lines ¼" in from one edge, then connect these end lines to the face lines to form the shape of a narrow wedge. Set a compass to a 3" radius, and draw an arc on the rear edges of the posts. The arc should start at the top, tapered corner and extend 1" down the rear edge. Mount a belt sander sideways on your worksurface, and sand down the tapers and

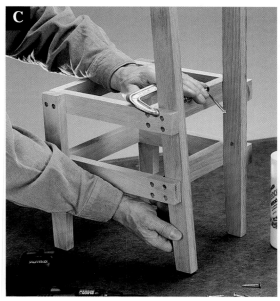

Clamp the posts in position on the back of the frame, and attach them.

Use the finished seat as a tracing pattern before cutting the slats to shape.

arcs on the legs and posts to finished shape **(photo B).** To make sure the chairs don't wobble, do not remove any excess material from the bottom ends of the legs or posts.

ATTACH THE LEGS & POSTS. The legs are positioned at the front of the chairs, flush with the frames. The posts are located at the backs of the chairs, fitted between the sides and butted against the cross rails. When attaching the posts and legs, make sure the tapered edges are facing inward (see *Diagram*, page 101). Before you attach the legs and posts, clamp them in place to make sure they do not wobble. Apply glue to the legs, and position them against the frame sides so their front and top edges are flush with the front and top of the frames. Clamp the legs to the frames—use a combination square to check to make sure the legs are positioned on the frames at right angles. Drive evenly spaced counterbored wood screws through the legs

and into the frames. Use glue and wood screws to fasten the second frame between the legs so the top edge of the frame is 7" up from the bottoms of the legs. Clamp the posts to the sides **(photo C).** The top edge of the upper frame should be 12" above the bottoms of the posts. The lower frame should be 7" above the bottoms of the posts. Make sure the posts are butting flat against the cross rails, and fasten the posts to the sides with glue and counterbored wood screws. Drive the wood screws through the sides and into the posts. Use a sander to smooth over the edges of the posts and legs.

MAKE THE SLATS & SEAT. The seat is made from a 1 × 10 piece of oak. When you cut the seat to shape, the seat will have a 12"-long front edge and a 10"-long rear edge (see *Diagram*). Do not attach the seat immediately to the frame when you cut it to shape—you can use the finished seat shape as a tracing pattern for the slats. Cut

the seat (G) to size. To cut the seats to shape, mark points on one edge, 1" in from each side. Use a straightedge to draw diagonal lines from the opposing corners to these edge points. Cut along these diagonal lines with a jig saw, forming a seat with a 12"-long front edge and a 10"-long rear edge. Use a compass to draw ¾" radius semicircles on each seat corner. Cut along the curves with a jig saw to complete the seat. Use the finished seat as a pattern to cut the slats (F) to rough size. Position the top slat under the front of the seat so the edges are flush. Position the lower slat under the back of the seat with the edges flush. Trace around the seat with a

TIP

When attaching two small pieces of oak, you should drill holes for the screws through both pieces. Extend the pilot holes through the first piece into the second to avoid splitting. Lubricate the screws with beeswax for easy insertion.

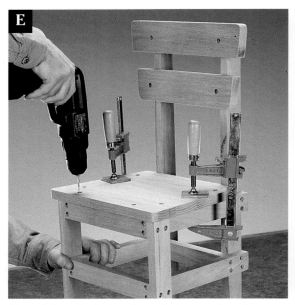

Extend the pilot holes through the seat into the frame to prevent splitting.

Smooth out the sharp edges on the apron with a power sander.

pencil **(photo D),** and cut along the traced lines with a jig saw to complete the slats. Sand the edges with medium-grit sandpaper.

ATTACH THE SLATS & SEAT. The slats and seat are centered on the posts and frame, respectively, and attached with glue and wood screws. Before you attach the parts, however, drill pilot holes for the screws. Once you have the slats and seat clamped in position, extend the pilot holes through the slats and seat into the frame and posts to prevent splitting. Draw a center line down the slats, and drill two evenly spaced, counterbored pilot holes through each slat. The pilot holes should be centered $3\frac{5}{8}$" from each side of their centers. Clamp the top slats to the posts so the top edges are flush. The top slat should extend 2" past the posts on each side. Fasten the slat with glue and #6 × $1\frac{1}{4}$" wood screws. Clamp the lower slat to the posts, $21\frac{1}{4}$" from the post bottoms, and fasten it to

the posts with glue and wood screws. Once the slats are attached, center the chair frame upside down on the seat top. Lightly trace the frame outline on the seat. Using the outline as a guide, drill evenly spaced, counterbored pilot holes through the seat for #6 × $1\frac{1}{4}$" wood screws. Center the seat over the frame, and clamp it in place. After extending the pilot holes into the frame **(photo E),** attach the seat with glue and wood screws. Glue and insert oak plugs into all the screw holes. When the glue has dried, sand the surfaces smooth, then finish-sand the entire chair with 180-grit sandpaper.

MAKE THE TABLE APRON. The table apron is a rectangular frame that anchors the legs and tabletop. Cut the apron sides (H) and apron ends (I) to size. Mark two evenly spaced centers for counterbored pilot holes at each end of the sides, $\frac{3}{8}$" from each end. Drill pilot holes at each center for #6 × $1\frac{1}{4}$" wood screws. Fasten

the apron ends between the sides with glue and wood screws, driven through the pilot holes and into the apron ends. Smooth out the corners and edges with a sander to remove any rough spots or splinters **(photo F).**

MAKE THE LEGS. Each corner of the apron has an outside leg and inside leg. These legs are attached to each other in a butt joint. Both legs are tapered on one long edge. Start by cutting the outside legs (J) and inside legs (K) to length. Mark a point on one long edge of the outside and inside legs, 16" from the bottom—mark a point on the bottom, $\frac{3}{4}$" from the same long edge. Draw a diagonal line connecting both marks, and cut along the line with a jig saw to create a taper on each leg **(photo G).** Drill four counterbored pilot holes on the outside legs, $\frac{3}{8}$" from the untapered edge of the outside legs. The pilot holes should be $6\frac{1}{2}$" apart, starting 1" from the bottoms of the outside legs. At-

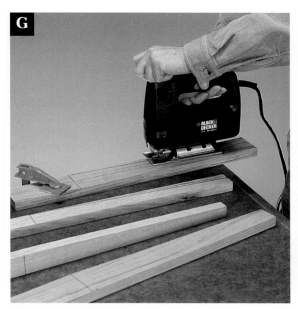

Use a jig saw to cut the tapers in the table legs.

Attach a leg in each corner of the apron frame with glue and screws.

Attach the end nosing and side nosing with glue and finish nails.

side legs with glue and wood screws. Make sure that the un-tapered edges are flush. Apply glue to the legs and attach them to the table apron by driving counterbored wood screws through the apron and into each leg. Keep the tops of the legs flush with the top edges of the apron so the legs are even on their bottoms **(photo H).** When all the legs are attached, fill the screw holes with glued oak plugs and sand the surfaces to smooth out any rough spots.

MAKE THE TABLETOP. The tabletop is made from a solid piece of ¾"-thick oak plywood and is framed by the end nos-ing and side nosing. The nosing pieces are cut to fit around the tabletop from ¾" oak corner molding. Cut the tabletop (L), end nosing (M) and side nosing (N) to size. Use a miter box to miter-cut the ends of the nosing to fit around the tabletop. Cen-ter the tabletop over the apron, and attach it with evenly spaced, counterbored wood screws, driven through the tabletop into the top edges of the apron. Fill the counter-bored screw holes with glued oak plugs, and sand the table-top with medium-grit sand-paper. Fasten the end nosing and side nosing to the tabletop with glue and 1" wire brads **(photo I).** Drill pilot holes be-fore driving the nails to avoid splitting the nosing. Set the nails and fill the holes with wood putty.

APPLY FINISHING TOUCHES. Finish-sand the table and chairs with fine (150- or 180-grit) sand-paper. Finish the project with two or three coats of satin-finish water-based polyurethane to protect the wood.

Kid-size Picnic Table

*This picnic table is loaded with sturdiness and charm,
but in a small package designed just for kids.*

CONSTRUCTION MATERIALS

Quantity	Lumber
11	1 × 4" × 8' cedar
4	2 × 4" × 8' cedar

A scaled-down version of an adult picnic table, this project is sure to appeal to all children. But with its stylish lines and warm, attractive appearance, you may want to build a scaled-up version for yourself.

But don't worry that your kids will outgrow this table too quickly. Although it is kid-size,

it is large enough to provide comfortable seating for kids of all ages.

Made completely from dimensional cedar lumber, this kid-size picnic table is lightweight despite its strength and durability. With a protective finish like linseed oil, it will maintain its warm cedar tones for many seasons.

OVERALL SIZE:
26" HIGH
48" WIDE
48" LONG

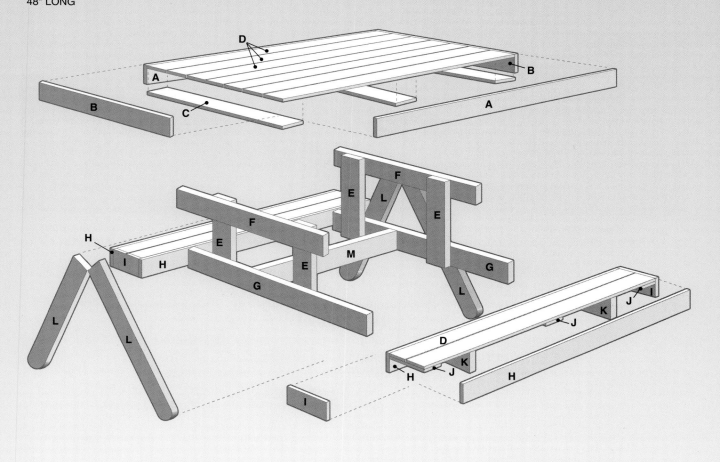

Cutting List

Key	Part	Dimension	Pcs.	Material
A	Table side	$\frac{7}{8} \times 3\frac{1}{2} \times 48$"	2	Cedar
B	Table cap	$\frac{7}{8} \times 3\frac{1}{2} \times 25\frac{1}{4}$"	2	Cedar
C	Table stringer	$\frac{7}{8} \times 3\frac{1}{2} \times 25\frac{1}{4}$"	3	Cedar
D	Slat	$\frac{7}{8} \times 3\frac{1}{2} \times 46\frac{1}{4}$"	11	Cedar
E	Temporary post	$1\frac{1}{2} \times 3\frac{1}{2} \times 15\frac{3}{4}$"	4	Cedar
F	Top rail	$1\frac{1}{2} \times 3\frac{1}{2} \times 25\frac{1}{4}$"	2	Cedar
G	Seat rail	$1\frac{1}{2} \times 3\frac{1}{2} \times 46\frac{1}{4}$"	2	Cedar

Cutting List

Key	Part	Dimension	Pcs.	Material
H	Seat cap	$\frac{7}{8} \times 3\frac{1}{2} \times 48$"	4	Cedar
I	Seat end	$\frac{7}{8} \times 3\frac{1}{2} \times 7\frac{1}{4}$"	4	Cedar
J	Seat stringer	$\frac{7}{8} \times 3\frac{1}{2} \times 7\frac{1}{4}$"	6	Cedar
K	Seat cleat	$\frac{7}{8} \times 3\frac{1}{2} \times 7\frac{1}{4}$"	4	Cedar
L	Leg	$1\frac{1}{2} \times 3\frac{1}{2} \times 31$"	4	Cedar
M	Stretcher	$1\frac{1}{2} \times 3\frac{1}{2} \times 26\frac{1}{4}$"	1	Cedar

Materials: Moisture-resistant wood glue, galvanized deck screws (1¼", 2", 2½").

Specialty items: Combination square.

Note: Measurements reflect the actual size of dimensional lumber.

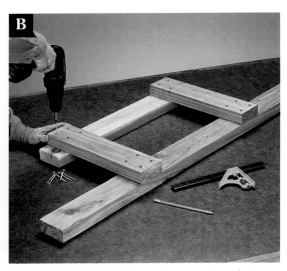

Slip a pair of slats under the table stringers as spacers, then drive deck screws to attach the side caps to the stringers.

Temporary posts hold the rails in position during assembly. Remove them when assembly is over.

Directions:
Kid-size Picnic Table

BUILD THE TABLETOP. The tabletop is formed by attaching seven cedar slats inside a 1 × 4 cedar frame. Cut all 11 1 × 4 cedar slats (D)—four will be used to make the seats—as well as the side caps (A), table caps (B) and table stringers (C). Sand all parts smooth. Set four slats aside. Position the table caps between a pair of side caps to form a rectangular frame. Fasten the rails between the side caps with moisture-resistant wood glue and 2½" deck screws, driven through the side caps and into the ends of the rails. Drill pilot holes before driving all screws, countersinking the pilot holes slightly so the screw heads will be recessed. With the frame lying flat on your worksurface, lay slats just inside each side cap to use as spacers while you attach the table stringers. Arrange the stringers inside the frame, so the two end stringers are flush against the inside faces of the table caps. The middle stringer should be centered between the outer stringers. Drive deck screws through the side caps into the ends of the stringers **(photo A).** Turn the frame over on your worksurface, and arrange seven slats on top of the stringers, keeping a ⅛"-wide gap between slats (use 10d nails as spacers). Make sure the ends of the slats are butted against the inside faces of the table caps (if the slats are a little short, that's okay; just try to keep the ends even on each side). Clamp a board across each end of the tabletop to hold the slats in place, and turn the assembly facedown on your worksurface. Drive two 1¼" deck screws through each stringer and into each slat.

BUILD THE TABLE SUPPORTS. The table is supported by two cross rails that are attached temporarily to posts during assembly, then fastened permanently to the legs (the posts are then removed). A second pair of rails below these cross rails extend out past the tabletop to help support the seats. The lower rails are connected with a stretcher. Cut the posts (E), top rails (F), seat rails (G) and stretcher (M) to size. Draw guidelines across the seat rails, 11¾" from each end. Use deck screws to fasten two posts to each seat rail, so their outside edges are on the guidelines, and their ends are flush with the outside edges of the rail. Fasten a top rail to the free ends of the posts, so the outside edge of each post is 1½" from the ends of the top rail **(photo B).** Turn the tabletop facedown on your worksurface, and position the top rails inside the tabletop frame, so the inside face of each top rail is 10" from the nearer table cap. Make sure the posts are inside the top rails. Apply glue, then drive two 1¼" deck screws through the side caps and into both ends of each top rail **(photo C).** Cut the stretcher (M) to size and position it between the two seat rails. Make sure the posts are perpendicular to the slats and the stretcher is centered end to end on the seat rails, then fasten it with glue and 2½" deck screws, driven through the seat rails into the ends of the stretcher.

*...ne inside face of each top rail is 10"
...letop ends, and fasten the parts.*

The seat rails fit through notches in the seat frames and are attached to the seat cleats.

...E SEATS. The seats ...much the same way ...etop. Cut the seat ...eat ends (I), seat ...) and seat cleats (K) ...u'll also need the ...D) you set aside ear-...ge the seat caps in ...and position a seat ...en both ends of ...so their edges are ...ch the seat ends to ...aps with glue and 2" ...ws, forming two seat ...rrange three seat ...acedown within each ...a stringer is flush with ...end and the third ...s centered between ...Use slats as spacers ...the stringers (see ..., and attach the ...with glue and 2" deck ...riven through the seat ...l into the ends of the ...Slip two slats in each ...ush against the seat ...th a gap between slats. ...he slats with glue and ...k screws driven through ...gers and into the slats. ...u'll need to cut ...s into the inside faces of

the inner seat caps to fit around the seat rails. Mark two 1½"-wide × 2⅝"-high notches for the seat rails on the face of each inner seat cap, starting 9⅜" in from the seat ends. Attach a seat cleat between the seat caps at the outside edge of each notch (see *Diagram*, page 57). Use glue and 2½" deck screws driven through the side caps and into the ends of the seat cleats. This completes the preparation of the seats. Slip the notches in each seat over the seat rails, so the seat rails butt against the inside faces of the outer seat caps. Attach the seat rails to the seat cleats with glue and 2½" deck screws **(photo D).**

MAKE THE LEGS. Cut the legs (L), then use a compass to draw a curved cutting line with a 1¾" radius at one end of each leg. Cut along the cutting lines with a jig saw. Stand the table on end, and draw a line to mark the center of each top rail. Position the legs on the outside faces of the rails, so the top inside corner of each leg touches the centerline, and the top outside corner of each leg is pressed against the under-

side of the tabletop. Each leg should also fit against the outer face of a seat rail and press against the inside bottom edge of the seat cap. Fasten the legs in these positions with glue and 2½" deck screws **(photo E).** Remove the posts.

APPLY FINISHING TOUCHES. Sand all the wood edges and surfaces, then apply a non-toxic protective finish (we used linseed oil). Refresh the finish annually.

Each leg should fit against the underside of the tabletop and the lower inside edge of the seat cap.

109

Gardening Center

This combination worksurface and cabinet lets you centralize your gardening tools & supplies in one convenient location.

CONSTRUCTION MATERIALS

Quantity	Lumber
1	¼" × 4 × 4' hardboard
1	1 × 2" × 8' pine
2	¾" × 4 × 8' AC plywood
1	4"-dia. × 4' PVC drain pipe

This gardening center eliminates the spread of gardening supplies, while doing double duty as a functional gardening workstation. Positioned at a comfortable working height, the plywood worksurface lets you repot plants or blend soils without straining your back. The main cabinet is large enough to hold most of your fertilizers, seeds, and other supplies. A soil cart housed in the cabinet rolls out to make transporting heavy materials a snap. The tubes at the sides of the cabinet organize your long-handled gardening tools. And the high shelves at the top of the cabinet are perfect for storing pesticides and other products that should be kept out of the reach of children.

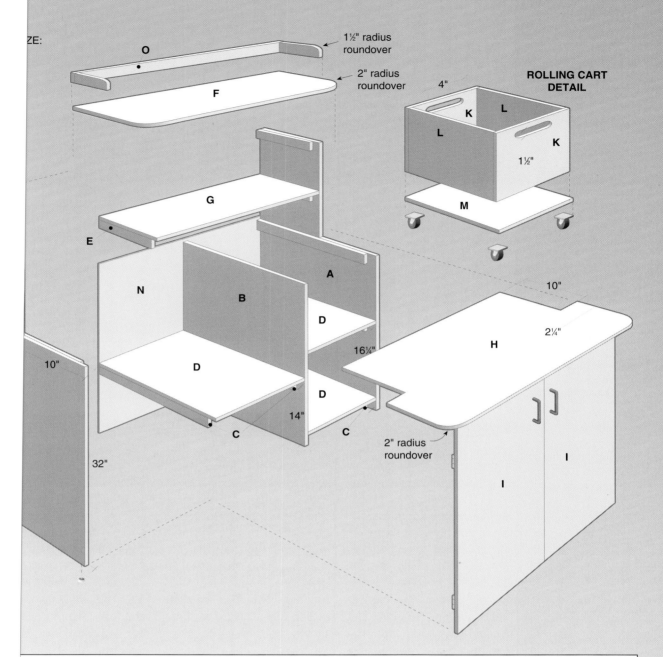

ZE:

1½" radius roundover

2" radius roundover

ROLLING CART DETAIL

4"

1½"

10"

2¼"

16¼"

14"

2" radius roundover

32"

10"

	Cutting List		
Part	**Dimension**	**Pcs.**	**Material**
e panel	¾ × 20 × 48"	2	Plywood
nter divider	¾ × 20 × 32"	1	Plywood
elf cleat	¾ × 1½ × 18"	8	Plywood
binet shelf	¾ × 13⅞ × 20"	3	Plywood
elf cleat	¾ × 1½ × 8"	4	Pine
p shelf	¾ × 13 × 33"	1	Plywood
ddle shelf	¾ × 10 × 28½"	1	Plywood
rksurface	¾ × 23 × 33"	1	Plywood

	Cutting List			
Key	**Part**	**Dimension**	**Pcs.**	**Material**
I	Door	¾ × 14¾ × 31⅞"	2	Plywood
J	Tool holder	4"-dia. × 24"	2	PVC
K	Box end	¾ × 12 × 10"	2	Plywood
L	Box side	¾ × 16 × 10"	2	Plywood
M	Box bottom	¾ × 12 × 17½"	1	Plywood
N	Back panel	¼ × 30 × 32¾"	1	Hardboard
O	Shelf skirt	¾ × 1½ × *	3	Pine

Wood glue, #6 × 1¼ wood screws, ¼"-dia. × 1½" carriage bolts with nuts and washers (4), glide feet (4), 2½"-dia.), self-closing cabinet hinges (4), door pulls (2), wood putty.

asurements reflect the actual size of dimensional lumber.

111

Cut along the straight cutting lines on the side panels with a circular saw, then use a jig saw or hand saw to finish the cuts at the corners.

Measure up from the bottom cabinet cle mark positions for the other cabinet she

Directions: Gardening Center

MAKE THE SIDE PANELS. The L-shaped plywood side panels for the gardening center support shelf cleats and the work-surface. Cut the sides (A) to size. Mark a point on one side edge of one plywood panel, 32" up from the bottom, to set the worksurface height. Draw a line perpendicular to the side edge at this point, then mark a point on the line 10" in from the edge. Mark another point 10" in from the top corner, at the same side, and connect the two 10" points to form the cutout area for the panel. Using a jig saw or circular saw, make the cutout. If you use a circular saw for the cutouts, you'll have to finish the corners of the cuts with a hand saw or a jig saw. Sand the edges smooth, then use the cut panel as a template to draw a matching cutout on the other side panel. Cut out the second side panel **(photo A).**

INSTALL THE SHELF CLEATS. The cabinet shelves are supported by 1 × 2 cleats mounted on the inside faces of the cabinet sides and on a center divider panel. Cut the divider (B) to size from ¾"-thick plywood. Then, cut the cabinet cleats (C) and shelf cleats (E) to size from 1 × 2 pine. Sand the plywood surfaces and edges with medium-grit sandpaper and a power sander. Attach a cleat to the inside face of one side panel, flush with the bottom and the back edge (the 2" set-back between the cleats and the front edges of the panels is to conceal the front end of the cleat). Use wood glue and #6 × 1¼" wood screws to attach the cleat. Also attach a cleat on one side of the divider, flush with the bottom and back. Mark points 16¼" up from the top of the cleats on the right side panel and on the cleated side of the divider **(photo B).** Also mark points 14" up from the bottom edge of the left side panel, and on the unmarked face of the di-

vider. Draw lines cor the points on the ins of the sides and on b of the divider. Attach just below the lines, the back edges of the and the divider. On t panels, attach cleats edges are flush with toms of the cutouts, ends are flush with th ends of the panels. M for the lower shelf cle area above the works above the tops of the the worksurface cuto the shelf cleats (E) ju the lines, flush with tl edges of the sides. Als cleats flush with the t side panels to help su upper shelf.

INSTALL THE SHELVE the cabinet shelves (D middle shelf (G) to siz the side panels in an (position, about 33" ap their cleated surfaces Attach the middle she area above the works using glue and #6 × 1 screws—counterbore

shelves and upper shelves are attached to the sides and o give the gardening center side-to-side strength.

e screws so the
be covered with
. Prop the divider
n the sides, making
eats are lined up cor-
the matching cleats
panels. Attach the
elves, making sure
nd back edges are
he edges of the side
oto C).

HE TOP SHELF. Cut the
F) to size from ply-
w cutting lines for
s on the front cor-
shelf, using a com-
r a 2" radius. Cut the
s with a jig saw. Use
nder to smooth out
or decorative appeal
vent items from slip-
e top shelf, we added
ls (O) to the back and
e shelf. First, cut a
e same length as the
t, cut two pieces of
in length. Draw a
s roundover at one
ch piece (see *Dia-
e* 111). Cut the
rs and sand smooth.
e back skirt board to

the back of the shelf, on edge
and flush at the ends. Use glue
and #6 × 1¼" wood screws
driven up through the shelf and
into the skirt board. Fasten the
side skirts to the ends of the
shelf, with the square end of
each piece butted up against
the back skirt board **(photo D).**
Fasten the top shelf to the top
cleats on the side panels.

TIP

Plywood, even sanded cabinet-grade material, usually has one side that is in better condition than the other. This is very true of the lower grades of plywood, which often have one side sanded and filled, with the other side left rough and full of knotholes and checks. Always make plywood building parts so the better face is facing out.

BUILD & ATTACH THE WORK-
SURFACE. The worksurface is
notched to fit around the top
shelf sections of the side panels. Rounded over at the front
corners, it overhangs the lower
sections of the side panels on
the front and sides. Cut the
worksurface (H) to size from
¾"-thick plywood. Mark 10"-
deep × 2¼"-wide notches at the
back corners to fit around the
sides (see *Diagram*, page 111).
Use a compass set for a 2" radius to mark roundover cutting
lines at the front corners of the
worksurface. Make the cutouts
with a jig saw, then smooth out
with a sander **(photo E).** Test-

The 1 × 2 skirt that frames the top of the upper shelf keeps items from falling off. Screw the skirt pieces in from below.

113

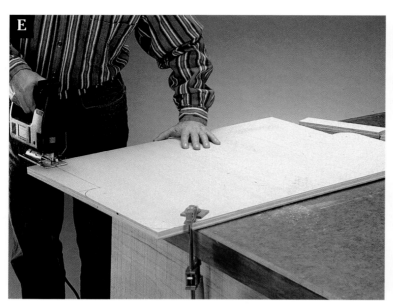

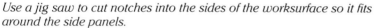

Use a jig saw to cut notches into the sides of the worksurface so it fits around the side panels.

Insert a pen or pencil into the guide hol‹ side panel and mark drilling points on t

fit the worksurface, checking to make sure the cabinet assembly is square at the same time. Set the worksurface onto the horizontal arms of the side-panel cutouts, with the notches fitting around the sides and the overhang equal from side to side. Attach the worksurface to the cleats with glue and screws.

MAKE & ATTACH THE TOOL HOLDERS. We mounted 2'-long sections of PVC drainpipe to the outside faces of the side panels to create holders for long-handled garden tools. Cut a section of 4"-dia. PVC drainpipe into two 24" lengths to make the tool holders (J). A hacksaw is a good tool choice for cutting PVC. Smooth out the cuts with emery paper or very fine sandpaper. If you plan to paint the PVC tool holders, buff the pipes with medium-grit sandpaper to create a better bonding surface for the paint (this activity is called scarifying). Draw reference lines for hanging the tool hold-

ers on the outer faces of the side panels. The lines should be parallel to the back edges, 7" in. On the reference lines, mark drilling points 4" and 24" up from the bottom edges of the side panels. Drill ¼"-dia. guide holes for carriage bolts at these points. Mark matching guide holes on the tool holders by positioning the pipes on the centerlines so the holes in the side panels fall 2" in from the top and bottom of each pipe. Insert a pen into the guide holes, from the inside, and mark the hole locations onto the surface of the pipes **(photo F).** Drill ¼"-dia. holes at these points. Place the pipes in position, with the guide holes aligned, and insert carriage bolts from inside each pipe, threaded through so the ends project out past the inside faces of the side panels. Attach washers and nuts to the ends of the carriage bolts and tighten securely—do not overtighten.

ATTACH THE BACK
the back panel (N) t‹
¼" hardboard using a
saw. Position the bac‹
the back of the cabin‹
bly, and attach it witl
mon (box) nails. Kee‹
edges of the back pa‹
with the outside surfa‹
side panels and the t‹
worksurface. If the ca‹
pears to be out of squ‹
check it by measuring
onal measurements a‹
back to make sure the
same. Do not attach tl
panel until you are ce‹
cabinet is square (one
main jobs of the back
to keep the cabinet fr‹
ping out of square).

ATTACH THE DOORS
cabinet doors (I) to si‹
¾"-thick plywood. Atta‹
hinges (we used self-c‹
cabinet door hinges si‹
¾"-thick wood) to the ‹
back faces of the door‹
G). The hinges should
tioned 2" down from tl
edge of each door, an‹

114

cabinet doors with self-closing cabinet hinges to keep the
swinging open.

bottoms. Position the
er the front of the cabi-
a ⅛" gap between
ark the hinge screw
s onto the inside faces
de panels, then remove
rs and drill pilot holes
crew locations. Hang
rs.

THE SOIL CART. The
soil cart lets you trans-
ended potting soils from
rk area to the garden
it creating back strain.
y cutting the box sides
ox ends (K) and box bot-
M) to size from ¾" ply-
. Mark hand-grip cutouts
e box ends: the bottom of
cutout should be 3½"
from the top edge of the
end; the top should be 2"
n; the ends of the cutouts
uld be 4" in from the side
es. Draw roundovers at the
ds of the cutouts, then make
e handgrip cutouts with a jig
w (you'll need to drill a
arter hole inside the cutout
ine first). Sand the edges

smooth. Attach the box ends
to the box sides with glue and
screws driven to form butt
joints (see *Diagram,* page 111).
Check to make sure the four-
piece frame is square when assembled, then attach the box
bottom to the sides and ends.

Attach casters to the underside
of the box bottom **(photo H).**
The casters (we used 2½"-dia.
casters) should be positioned
an inch or two inside each corner. If the screws that come with
the casters are more than ¾" in
length, substitute shorter screws
with the same shank size.

APPLY FINISHING TOUCHES.
Attach nail-on glide feet to the
bottom edges of the side panels to minimize ground contact. Fill all screw counterbores
with wood putty, sand smooth,
then finish-sand all wood surfaces. Apply a finish (we used
green exterior paint). You may
wish to remove the door before
applying the finish. Also paint
the tool holders, if you wish.
Once the finish is dry, attach
door pulls to the doors—we
used 3" plastic pulls mounted
about 3" down from the top of
each door.

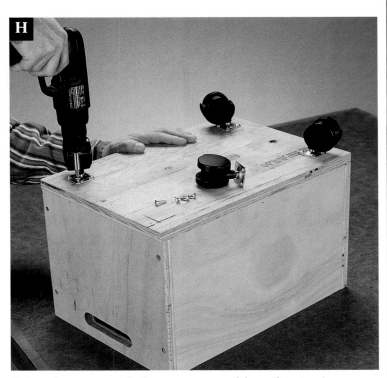

Fasten the casters to the bottom corners of the soil cart, using screws
that are no more than ¾" long.

115

Portable Workbench

Turn a few square feet of floor space into an efficient workshop with this portable, fold-up workbench.

CONSTRUCTION MATERIALS

Quantity	Lumber
4	2 × 4" × 8' pine
1	¾" × 4 × 8' plywood
1	¾" × 4 × 4' plywood

If your desire to build things is bigger than the space you have to work in, then an expandable, portable workbench may be just the solution you're looking for. Tucked away in a basement, garage or any spare room, this workbench keeps a low profile, while giving you a place to store all of your tools. When the weekend rolls around, roll out the workbench, flip up the extension leaves at the ends of the worksurface, and you've got a workbench large enough to handle full 4 × 8 sheets of plywood and other big-scale building materials. Built from plywood, 2 × 4s and a few pieces of hardware, this workbench is quick and easy to make.

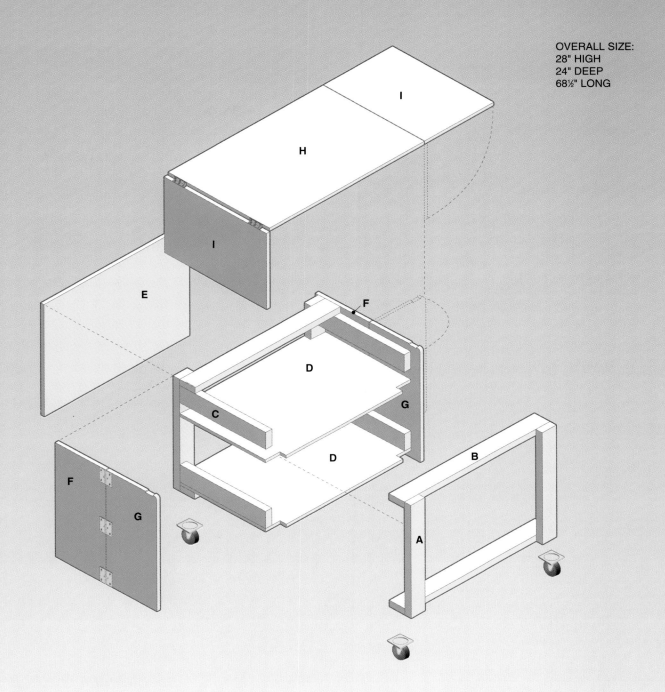

OVERALL SIZE:
28" HIGH
24" DEEP
68½" LONG

Cutting List				
Key	**Part**	**Dimension**	**Pcs.**	**Material**
A	Leg	1½ × 3½ × 24¼"	4	Pine
B	Side rail	1½ × 3½ × 34½"	4	Pine
C	End rail	1½ × 3½ × 20¼"	4	Pine
D	Shelf	¾ × 23¼ × 34½"	2	Plywood
E	Back	¾ × 24¼ × 34½"	1	Plywood

Cutting List				
Key	**Part**	**Dimension**	**Pcs.**	**Material**
F	End	¾ × 12 × 24¼"	2	Plywood
G	Door	¾ × 12 × 24¼"	2	Plywood
H	Top	¾ × 24 × 36½"	1	Plywood
I	Leaf	¾ × 16 × 24"	2	Plywood

Materials: Wood glue, wood screws (#6 × 1½", #6 × 2", #6 × 2½"), steel utility butt hinges (3 × 1½", 3 × 3"), 3" fixed casters (2), 3" swivel casters with brakes (2), finishing materials.

Note: Measurements reflect the actual size of dimensional lumber.

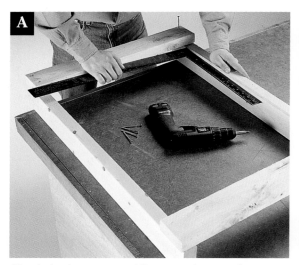

Check the frame assemblies to make sure they are square before you fasten them together.

Slide the shelf into place on the clamped spacers, 15¼" up from the bottoms of the legs.

Directions:
Portable Workbench

MAKE THE FRONT & BACK FRAMES. The front and back of the workbench is made from two identical 2 × 4 frames, which are made by attaching side rails to the top and bottom of a pair of legs. Start by cutting the legs (A) and side rails (B) to size. Sand all parts to smooth out rough spots after cutting. Set a pair of side rails on edge on your worksurface. Position a leg on each end of the side rails, face up. The edges of the legs should be flush with the ends of the side rails. Use a framing square to make sure the legs are square to the side rails, and apply glue to the mating surfaces. Attach the legs to the side rails with #6 × 2½" wood screws, checking to make sure the parts are square as you work **(photo A).**

ATTACH THE END RAILS & SHELVES. The end rails and shelves fit between the front and back frames to form the cabinet section of the workbench. Each shelf is notched to fit between the legs. Cut the

Before attaching the top, make sure it overhangs the ends by ¼".

end rails (C) and shelves (D) to size. Use a jig saw to cut a 1½"-wide × 3½"-long notch at each corner of the shelves. For the notches to properly accommodate the legs, they should run lengthwise down the long edges of the shelves. Stand the leg sections up, and position a shelf between them on the bottom side rails. Make sure the

legs fit snugly in the shelf notches. Attach the shelf with #6 × 1½" wood screws, driven through the shelf and into the side rails. Set one end rail on edge at each end of the shelf, flush with the outside edges of the legs. Attach the end rails with wood glue and #6 × 2½" wood screws, driven through the legs and into the end rails.

Dip wood screws in epoxy to fortify the holding power when the screws are being driven into the edges of plywood.

Position the unattached end rails underneath the top side rails, flush with their outside edges (see *Diagram*, page 31). Attach the end rails with glue and wood screws. Mark reference lines on the inside faces of the legs, 15¼" up from the leg bottoms. Clamp scrap blocks to the inside faces of the legs on the reference lines, and slide the remaining shelf into place so it rests on the scrap blocks **(photo B).** Use a combination square to make sure the shelf is square with the legs. If the shelf isn't square with the legs, adjust the height of the scrap blocks as needed. Secure the shelf by driving 2½" wood screws through the legs and into the shelf. Remove the scrap blocks.

ATTACH THE BACK, ENDS & TOP. Start by cutting the back (E), ends (F) and top (H) to size. Position the back against one long side of the assembled frame. The edges of the back should be flush with the edges of the legs. Attach one end of the back to one leg, using #6 × 2" wood screws. Check the workbench frame to make sure it is square. Drive evenly

spaced, #6 × 1½" wood screws through the back and into the middle shelf. Position an end on each side of the workbench, flush with the bottoms of the rear legs. The back and ends should meet at the corners, with the rear edge of each end flush with the rear face of the back. Fasten the ends with #6 ×1½" wood screws. Center the top onto the workbench, and check to make sure it overhangs each end by ¼" **(photo C).** Apply glue to the tops of the side rails, then secure the top by driving #6 × 2" wood screws through the top and into the side rails. Countersink the screws in the top to recess the screw heads.

ATTACH THE DOORS & LEAVES. The workbench doors are attached to the ends with hinges. The doors swing out to support the leaves, which are attached to the top with hinges. Begin by cutting the doors (G) and leaves (I) to size. To allow the doors to swing clear of the hinges for the leaves, make a 3½"-long notch on the top edge of each door with a jig saw. Start each notch 1¼" from the

front edge of the door (the notches only need to be about ¼" deep). Smooth over the front corners and edges of the doors with a sander. Attach 3 × 3" steel utility hinges at the top and bottom of each door, then attach them to the ends, keeping the top and bottom edges flush. Next, fasten 3 × 1½" steel utility hinges to one long edge of each leaf, 1½" in from the front and back ends. The barrels of the hinges should hang slightly below the bottoms of the leaves. Attach the leaves to the edges of the top with the hinges. When driving screws into the end grain of plywood, apply epoxy glue to the screws before driving them **(photo D).** The epoxy glue creates a very strong, permanent bond for the screws. Because the bond is permanent, make sure you dry-fit the parts before applying the epoxy glue.

APPLY FINISHING TOUCHES. For ease of steering, use a combination of fixed and swivelling casters (this is a little like the wheels on a car: the rear wheels are fixed parallel to the car frame, and the front wheels pivot to steer the car). Attach heavy-duty, 3" fixed (non-swiveling) casters to the bottoms of the legs at one end of the workbench. Attach 3" swiveling, locking casters to the legs at the other end of the workbench. Center the casters on the legs. Fill the screw holes in the top with wood putty, and paint all surfaces with primer and enamel paint.

> **TIP**
>
> *Epoxy glue is a two-part product that is usually sold in pairs of tubes that look a little like a syringe. To use epoxy, squirt a little of the material from each tube onto a mixing surface, then blend them together with a small stick. Use the blended epoxy immediately.*

Paint Center

Keep your painting equipment and supplies in one convenient location with this paint center.

Painting supplies have an amazing ability to create a mess in your basement or garage. Half-full paint cans, crusty brushes and sleeves, stirring sticks, drop cloths, roller trays, cans of solvent and cleaners…the tools and supplies used in painting seem to multiply every time you start a new project, and if they are left unchecked they will take over your work spaces in a hurry.

The solution? An efficient paint center that lets you store all your equipment and supplies in one spot.

The paint center shown here is composed of two main elements: a work area where you can mix the paint and clean up brushes and other equipment; and a roomy can rack that is designed specifically for paint can storage.

The main worksurface on this paint center contains a square cutout that allows you to wipe up spills easily, and is sized to frame a standard dishpan (set it on the shelf below) for cleaning up brushes and roller sleeves. The broad storage areas below the worksurface are spacious enough to hold drop cloths, roller trays, and oversized paint or solvent containers. The can rack at the side of the work area is sized to hold 1-gallon paint cans efficiently —no more stacking cans or searching for the right supplies every time you start a project. Drying rods for rags and a pegboard back panel for hanging paint brushes are bonus features that you will find very handy.

CONSTRUCTION MATERIALS

Quantity	Lumber
6	2 × 4" × 8' pine
3	1 × 10" × 8' pine
2	1 × 2" × 8' pine
1	¾" × 4 × 8' plywood
2	⅛" × 4 × 8' pegboard
2	½" × 6' quarter-round molding
1	1"-dia. × 6' dowel

120

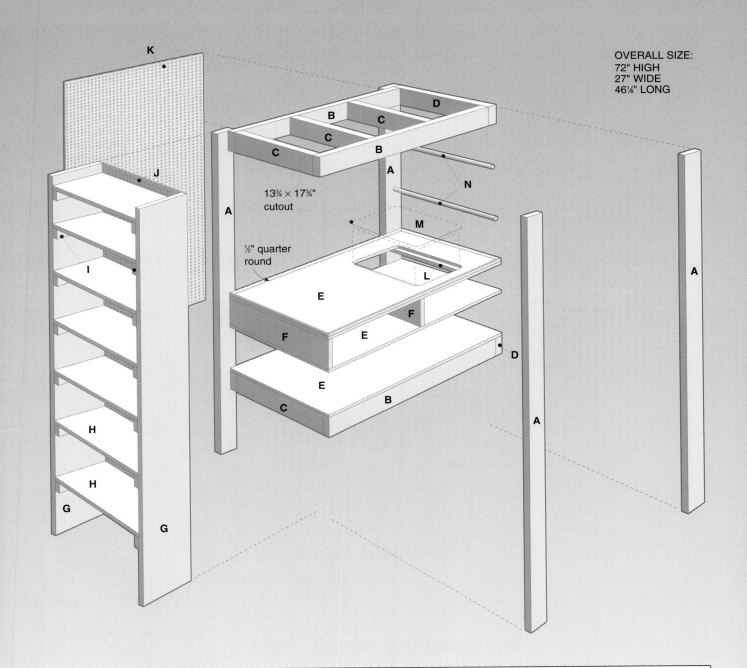

OVERALL SIZE:
72" HIGH
27" WIDE
46⅛" LONG

13¾ × 17¾"
cutout

½" quarter
round

Cutting List

Key	Part	Dimension	Pcs.	Material
A	Post	1½ × 3½ × 72"	4	Pine
B	Cross rail	1½ × 3½ × 35¼"	4	Pine
C	Short rail	1½ × 3½ × 21"	4	Pine
D	End rail	1½ × 3½ × 24"	2	Pine
E	Work area shelf	¾ × 24 × 36"	3	Plywood
F	Divider	¾ × 7 × 24"	2	Plywood
G	Can shelf side	¾ × 9¼ × 72"	2	Pine

Cutting List

Key	Part	Dimension	Pcs.	Material
H	Can shelf	¾ × 9¼ × 22½"	7	Pine
I	Shelf cleat	¾ × 1½ × 9¼"	14	Pine
J	Can shelf back	⅛ × 24 × 72"	1	Pegboard
K	Work area back	⅛ × 30¾ × 72"	1	Pegboard
L	Cover cleat	¾ × 2 × 16"	2	Plywood
M	Cutout cover	¾ × 13¾ × 17¾"	1	Plywood
N	Drying rod	1"-dia. × 27"	2	Dowel

Materials: Glue, wood screws (#6 × 1¼", #6 × 2", #6 × 2½"), 1" wire brads, finishing materials.

Note: Measurements reflect the actual size of dimensional lumber.

Complete the top section of the work area frame by attaching the end rail to the ends of the cross rails with #6 × 2½" wood screws.

Connect the top section and the shelf frame to the posts to assemble the work area frame.

The 2 × 4 framework for the work area section is the backbone of the paint center. Smooth out any sharp edges after it is assembled.

Directions: Paint Center

BUILD THE WORK AREA FRAMEWORK. The work area of the paint center is supported by a four-post 2 × 4 framework with a top section and a shelf support frame. The top section and the shelf support frame fit between the posts to give the framework its structure and keep it in square. The top section and the shelf frame are nearly identical 2 × 4 frames— the main difference is that the top section contains two short rails in the center for extra strength. Start by cutting the 2 × 4 cross rails (B), short rails (C) and end rails (D). Sandwich a short rail between each pair of cross rails, at one end only. Attach the short rails between the cross rails with glue and countersunk #6 × 2½" screws driven through the cross rails and into the ends of the short rails. Select one assembly to use for the top section, and install a pair of evenly spaced short rails between the cross

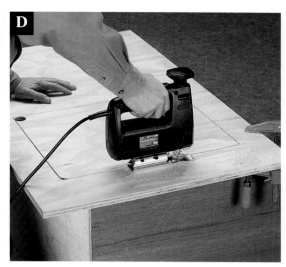

Drill a 1"-dia. starter hole at the front inside corner, then make the worksurface cutout with a jig saw.

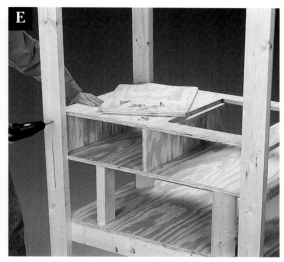

Install the lower work area shelf first. Use 2 × 4 spacers to support the middle shelf while you work.

rails (about 12" from the ends of the cross rails). Attach an end rail to the ends of each cross rail pair with glue and screws driven through the end rail and into the cross rails **(photo A).** Cut the 2 × 4" posts (A), and arrange them around the outside corners of the top section and the shelf support frame. The top section should be flush with the post tops, and the bottom of the shelf support frame should be 16½" up from the post bottoms. Adjust the parts so the posts overhang the frames by 1¾" on one side to create a recess for the can shelf to fit between the posts. Clamp the parts together with bar clamps or C-clamps **(photo B).** Check to make sure the assembly is square, then fasten the parts together with glue and screws driven through the posts and into the top section and frame. To make assembly easier, start the screws in the offset posts before squaring everything up. Stand the assembly upright and smooth out any sharp edges with a sander **(photo C).**

MAKE THE WORK AREA SHELVES. The work area has three shelves that are identical in size. The top shelf serves as a worksurface, and features a square cutout on the right side. The middle shelf and lower shelf are separated by dividers. They create storage and a resting place so a dishpan can be set below the cutout in the worksurface. The worksurface and middle shelf are attached with screws driven through the posts. The lower shelf rests on the shelf support frame of the work area framework. Start by cutting the work area shelves (E) to size from ¾"-thick plywood. Mark a 13¾ × 17¾" cutout 4½" from the right edge of one shelf, centered front to back. Use a 1"-dia. spade bit to drill a starter hole at the front, inside corner of the cutout. Use the hole as a starter for the jig saw blade as you cut out the rectangle **(photo D).** Cut carefully and save the waste to use for the cover for the cutout (M). The 1"-dia. hole will form a finger grip for removing the cover. Sand the edges of the cover and the cutout smooth.

INSTALL THE WORK AREA SHELVES. Install the lower shelf first by setting it on the shelf support frame and attaching with glue and screws. Cut four pieces of 2 × 4 to 11¾" in length to use as spacers, and set them on end on the lower shelf. Set the middle shelf onto the spacers, and drive counterbored screws through the posts and into the edges of the shelf. Drive two screws at each joint. Cut the dividers (F) and cover cleats (L) to size from plywood. Fasten the cleats to the underside of the worksurface shelf to create a 1" ledge inside the cutout (the ledge will support the cutout cover). Set the dividers on the middle shelf—one should be between the offset posts, flush with the edge of the shelf, and the other should be 20" in from the right edge of the shelf, flush with the front edge. Attach the dividers to the middle shelf with glue and screws driven up through the underside of the middle shelf and into the bottom edges of the dividers. Set the worksurface shelf on the top edges of the dividers, and drive screws through the posts and into the edges of the dividers and the worksurface shelf **(photo E).**

INSTALL THE WORK AREA BACK. Cut the work area back (K) to size from ⅛"-thick pegboard. Fasten the work area back to the back edges of the shelves and to the cross rails with #6 × 1¼" screws, making sure the work area frame is still square.

BUILD THE CAN SHELF. The can shelf part of the paint center is a cabinet-style shelf system with a pegboard back and plywood sides. It is designed to fit between the offset posts on the left side of the work area. Start building it by cutting the can shelf sides (G), can shelves (H) and the shelf cleats (I). Lay the shelf sides next to one another, with their tops and bottoms flush. Mark layout lines for the shelf locations onto the inside faces of the shelf sides, at 9¼" intervals,

The can shelf unit should fit snugly between the offset posts on the left side of the work area.

starting at the bottom. Marking both sides at the same time ensures that the shelves will be properly aligned. Attach shelf cleats to the shelf sides, butted up against the layout lines and flush with the back and front edges of the side panels. Use glue and two #6 × 1¼" screws to attach each cleat. Drill two pilot holes through the shelf sides, ⅜" above the top of each cleat. Set the shelf sides upright, with the inside faces facing one another, and install shelves that rest on the top cleats and the bottom cleats. Next, cut the can shelf back (J) from ⅛" peg board, and attach it to the rails between the posts. Before installing the rest of the can shelves, test-fit the assembly in the recess between the posts on

the left edge of the work area **(photo F).** If the shelf assembly is too wide, you will need to remove the top and bottom shelves, then trim all the shelves to fit. Fasten the rest of the can shelves, resting on the cleats, with glue and screws.

INSTALL THE CAN SHELF. Set the can shelf assembly between the offset posts on the left side of the work area. Attach the shelf to the posts by driving #6 × 2" wood screws through the shelf sides and into the shelf posts **(photo G).**

G

*Attach the can shelf unit between the posts with glue and #6 × 2"
screws driven through the shelf sides into the posts.*

H

*Use 1" wire brads to secure a quarter-round mold-
ing frame around the edges of the worksurface.*

FRAME THE WORKSURFACE.
We designed this paint center
with a frame made from trim
molding tacked around the
perimeter of the worksurface.
The frame helps contain small
paint spills so the paint does
not run off the surface and
onto the floor. We used ½"
quarter-round molding to make
the frame. To frame the worksurface, use a miter box
(power or hand operated) to
make a 45° miter cut at the end
of a piece of quarter-round
molding and set it on the back
edge of the worksurface. The
outside corner of the cut end
should be flush with the edges
of the worksurface. Make a
mark onto the molding at the
opposite end of the worksurface, and cut another 45° miter

cut that points in the opposite
direction of the first cut. Attach
the piece of molding to the
back of the worksurface with
1" wire brads. Butt the mitered
end of the molding piece next
to the molding you have installed, so the two make a
square corner. Mark a cutting
line on the quarter-round
piece, and miter-cut to fit. Continue cutting the remaining two
pieces of the frame in this fashion, then install them with glue
and wire brads to complete the
worksurface frame **(photo H).**

APPLY FINISHING TOUCHES.
Add a towel and rag drying
rack to the paint center by
drilling 1"-dia. holes through
the front and back posts on the
right side of the work area—we

positioned the holes 12½" and
21½" from the post tops. Cut
1"-dia. dowels to 27" in length
to make the drying rods (N).
Apply glue to the surfaces of
the 1" guide holes, and insert
the rods so the ends are flush
with the outside edges of the
front and back posts. Sand the
dowel ends smooth,
if necessary, after
the glue has dried.
Also give all the wood
surfaces a light finish
sanding before apply-
ing your finish of
choice. We applied
clear polyurethane
directly to the un-
stained, unpainted
wood to create a sur-
face that is easy
to clean.

> **TIP**
>
> *Use special pegboard
> hooks to hang items
> from pegboard. Sold
> at any hardware
> store or building
> center, the hooks can
> be moved from hole
> to hole easily, with-
> out stripping out
> pegboard holes
> (as screws will).*

125

Firewood Caddy

*Make handling firewood easy and clean with our caddy. Jus[
bundle and carry it inside with the leather carrier, and sto
wood in the cedar box.*

CONSTRUCTION MATERIALS

Quantity	Lumber
1	2 × 4" × 4' cedar
1	2 × 2" × 12' cedar
1	1 × 8" × 12' cedar
1	1 × 3" × 6' cedar
3	1 × 2" × 8' cedar
3	1"-dia. × 3' oak dowel

A fireplace becomes a convenient, clean household feature with our firewood caddy. Our caddy is equipped with a leather carrier that slips easily in and out of the frame. Throw the wood onto the carrier, pick it up with the dowel handles, and carry it indoors without a mess. The carrier slides into the frame,

and you don't have [
the wood until the ti
to build a fire. The c
base of the storage b
it easy to clean up ba
wood chips. The fire
caddy is a sturdy, attr
addition to any home

126

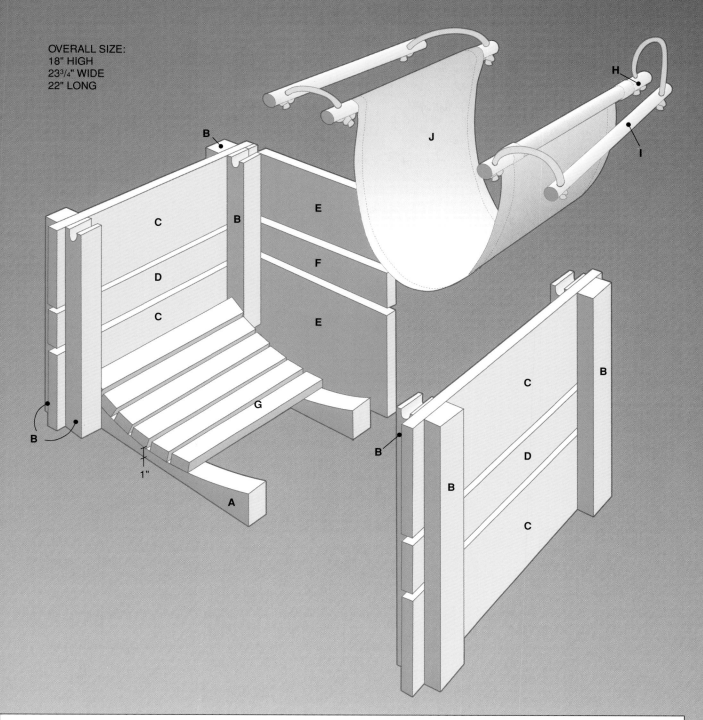

OVERALL SIZE:
18" HIGH
23¾" WIDE
22" LONG

Cutting List

Key	Part	Dimension	Pcs.	Material
A	Base rail	1½ × 3½ × 19¼"	2	Cedar
B	Post	1½ × 1½ × 18"	8	Cedar
C	Wide rail	¾ × 7¼ × 22"	4	Cedar
D	Narrow rail	¾ × 2½ × 22"	2	Cedar
E	Back rail	¾ × 7¼ × 19¼"	2	Cedar

Cutting List

Key	Part	Dimension	Pcs.	Material
F	Middle rail	¾ × 2½ × 19¼"	1	Cedar
G	Slat	¾ × 1½ × 19"	13	Cedar
H	Dowel	1 × 22"	2	Hardwood
I	Handle	1 × 18"	2	Hardwood
J	Carrier	16 × 48"	1	Leather

Materials: Leather (16 × 48"), brass upholstery tacks, moisture-resistant glue, deck screws (1⅝", 2½"), 4d finish nails, ¼"-dia. rope, finishing materials.

Note: Measurements reflect the actual size of dimensional lumber.

Use a flexible tracing guide to draw the arcs.

(above) Drill a 1"-dia. hole centered on the cutting line between two posts.

(left) Cut through the 1"-dia. holes in the 2 × 2's to create four posts with ½"-deep grooves at the ends.

Directions:
Firewood Caddy

MAKE THE BASE RAILS. A base rail is located at the front and rear of the firewood caddy. Each base rail has an arc, which determines the lay of the slats. Start by cutting the base rails (A) to length. Draw the arc by using a thin, flexible piece of metal, plastic or wood as a template, or tracing guide. Tack a casing nail into the center of one base rail, 1" from the top edge. Hook the flexible guide over the nail, then flex each end to the corners. Tack a casing nail at each corner to hold the guide in place as you trace along the strip to draw the arc **(photo A).** Remove the nails, then cut the arc with a jig saw. The arcs should be 1" deep at the center. Sand the arc smooth, then use it as a template for laying out the arc on the second rail.

CONSTRUCT THE FRAME. The frame is made to withstand the inevitable knocks and bumps that will come from loading wood. The posts (B) support the rails on the firewood caddy. They are made from four pieces of 36⅛"-long cedar. Drill a 1"-dia. hole through the center of two of the pieces **(photo B),** and crosscut the four pieces directly through their centers to form eight posts **(photo C).** When you cut the posts to length, you will cut through the centers of the 1"-dia. holes, forming ½"-deep notches on the top edges of the inside posts. Cut the wide rails (C), narrow rails (D), back rails (E) and middle rail (F) to size. Attach the wide and narrow rails to the posts with moisture-resistant glue and 1⅝" deck screws, making sure the inside posts have the notches on the top edges **(photo D).** When the frame is assembled, the wide and narrow rails should extend ¾" beyond the posts' front and back edges. The top and bottom edges of the wide rails should be flush with the top and bottom edges of the posts (see *Diagram*, page 27). There should be a ⅜" gap between

Attach the wide rails flush with the top and bottom post edges.

Place the slats in position to make sure they fit correctly along the arcs on the base rails.

the wide and narrow rails. Finally, attach the back rails and middle rail to the posts with glue and deck screws, forming the U-shaped firewood caddy frame. Use a power drill to continue the notches on the inside posts through the top edge of the back rails. This groove allows the dowels to sit snugly on the frame.

ATTACH THE SLATS. The bottom assembly is made from a series of slats attached to the arcs on the base rails. Begin by attaching the base rails to the inside edges of the posts with deck screws and moisture-resistant glue. Cut the slats (G) to size. Test-fit the slats by laying them across both rails **(photo E).** If their combined width is too wide, plane down the outer slats with a hand plane. Fasten all the slats to the base rails with 4d finish nails.

MAKE THE CARRIER. The carrier section is made from a piece of leather attached to a rope and dowel handle assembly. We chose suede for its pliability and strength. Unlike canvas, suede does not need hemming after it is cut. The

materials in this section can be purchased at most fabric stores. Start by cutting the oak dowels (H) and handles (I) to length. Once the dowels and handles are cut, drill ¼"-dia. holes 3" from the ends of the dowels and 1" from the ends of the handles. These holes are for the ropes and should go all the way through the pieces. Coat the dowel rods with linseed oil before moving on. Cut the carrier material to size, and fasten it to the dowels with brass upholstery tacks **(photo F).** Tape the carrier material in place to make sure it is centered

on the dowels before you drive the upholstery tacks. Because the carrier is expected to carry a fairly heavy load, you should fasten it to the dowel with at least two rows of pins. Finish the handles with linseed oil, and connect them to the dowels with ¼"-dia. × 8"-long ropes, knotted at each end.

APPLY THE FINISHING TOUCHES. Sand out the rough edges with medium-grit sandpaper, and finish the firewood caddy with *twp* clear wood sealer.

Tape the leather to the dowels, and tape the dowels to the worksurface to make attaching the upholstery tacks easy.

End Table

With handy storage pockets for reading materials at each end, this end table makes a perfect companion to your favorite cabin chair.

CONSTRUCTION MATERIALS

Quantity	Lumber
8	1 × 2" × 8' pine
2	1 × 4" × 10' pine
1	1 × 8" × 8' pine
1	¾ × ¾" × 4' pine stop molding

This end table has several benefits that make it ideally suited for a vacation home. It is very functional, with a generous tabletop surface, a spacious shelf and two end pockets for storing magazines or newspapers. It is relatively simple to build, consisting basically of a pair of slat-covered frames, four simple legs and two boxes at the ends. Stylistically, it is highly adaptable, with a slightly contemporary appearance that is tempered by traditional construction methods and a classic shellac finish. And, because it is made entirely from pine, it is very inexpensive to build.

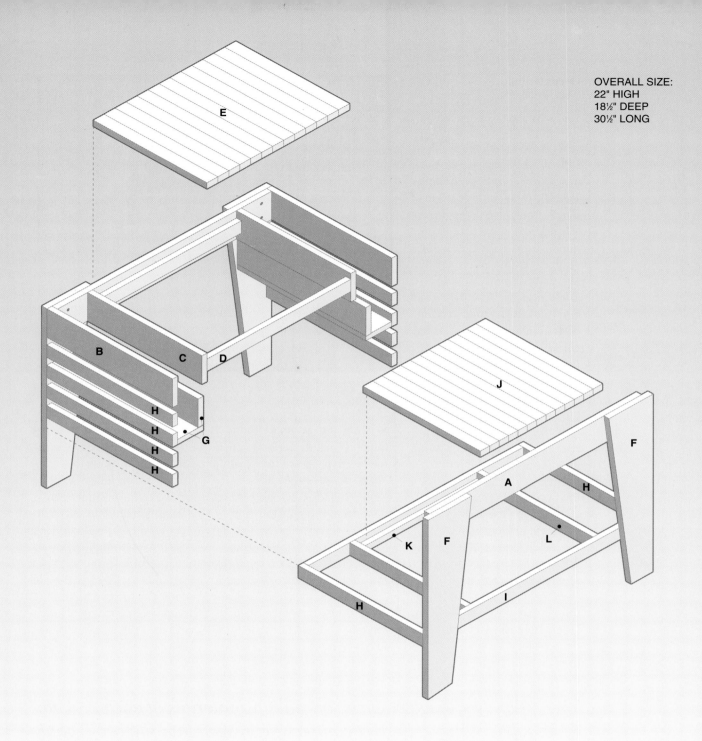

OVERALL SIZE:
22" HIGH
18½" DEEP
30½" LONG

	Cutting List			
Key	**Part**	**Dimension**	**Pcs.**	**Material**
A	Top rail	¾ × 3½ × 29"	2	Pine
B	Top end	¾ × 3½ × 17"	2	Pine
C	Pocket divider	¾ × 3½ × 15½"	2	Pine
D	Top ledger	¾ × 1½ × 19½"	2	Pine
E	Top slat	¾ × 1½ × 15½"	13	Pine
F	Leg	¾ × 6 × 22"	4	Pine

	Cutting List			
Key	**Part**	**Dimension**	**Pcs.**	**Material**
G	Pocket rail	¾ × 3½ × 17"	4	Pine
H	Leg slat	¾ × 1½ × 17"	10	Pine
I	Shelf side	¾ × 1½ × 29"	2	Pine
J	Shelf slat	¾ × 1½ × 15½"	13	Pine
K	Shelf ledger	¾ × ¾ × 19½"	2	Stop molding
L	Shelf cap	¾ × 1½ × 15½"	2	Pine

Materials: Glue, #6 × 1¼" wood screws, 6d finish nails, finishing materials.
Note: Measurements reflect the actual thickness of dimensional lumber.

Directions: End Table

MAKE THE LEGS. The end table legs are tapered on the inside edges to provide greater access to the bottom shelf. Begin by cutting the legs (F) to length from 1 × 8 pine. The legs should be 6" wide at the top and 3" wide at the bottom after cutting. On one end of each leg, mark a point 3" in from one long edge. At the opposite end of each leg, mark a point 6" in from the same long edge. Using a straightedge, draw tapered cutting lines connecting the two points **(photo A).** Use a circular saw with a straightedge cutting guide to cut along the lines, creating the tapers.

MAKE THE TABLETOP FRAME. The frame for the tabletop of the end table is made by fastening two 1 × 4 pocket dividers (C) between the 1 × 4 top rails. Ledgers are then attached to the inside faces of the top rails, between the pocket dividers, to create ledges that support the 1 × 2 top slats. Start by cutting the top rails (A) and pocket dividers (C) to length. Draw a reference line 4" in from each end of each rail to mark positions for the pocket dividers. Apply glue to the ends of the pocket dividers, then position them

Draw tapered cutting lines on the face of each leg board, then cut the tapers with a circular saw and a straightedge cutting guide.

between the top rails, butting the ends of the dividers against the faces of the top rails, just inside the reference lines. Clamp the top rails and pocket dividers in this position, and drive 6d finish nails through the top rails and into the ends of the pocket dividers to reinforce the joints. Cut the top ledgers (D) to length. Position a ledger against the inside face of each top rail, ¾" down from the tops, to create a recess for the tabletop slats. The ends of the ledgers should butt against the insides of the pocket dividers. Attach the ledgers with glue and #6 × 1¼" wood screws, driven through countersunk pilot holes in the ledgers and into the top rails.

INSTALL THE TOP SLATS. Cut the top slats (E) to length from 1 × 2 pine. Sand the ends to remove rough or uneven spots, and also sand the edges of the slats with medium-grit sandpaper to smooth them out. Position the top slats between the top rails so they span across the

frame opening, with the ends resting on the ledgers **(photo B).** Test the spacing to make sure all 13 top slats fit in properly, with no gaps between slats. Attach the top slats to the ledgers with glue and 6d finish nails, driven through pilot holes at each end of each slat. Use a nail set to set all the nail heads. Cut the two top end (B) boards from 1 × 4 pine, and sand the ends smooth. Position the top end boards against the ends of the top rails. Make sure the edges are flush, and attach the end boards with glue and 6d finish nails, driven through the top ends and into the ends of the top rails.

ASSEMBLE THE LEGS & TOP. Position the top upside down on a flat worksurface. Position a leg at each end of the top, making sure the square-cut (untapered) edge of each leg is flush with the outside face of each top end, and the tops of the legs are flush with the top rails. Carefully clamp the legs

TIP

Use a straightedge cutting guide when making tapered cuts. You can buy a straightedge guide designed specifically for use with a circular saw, or you can simply use a straight piece of lumber clamped down to your workpiece. Always make a test cut on scrap lumber first, to make sure you know exactly how far from the cutting line the straightedge needs to be positioned.

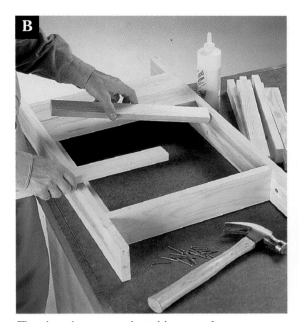

The slats that create the tabletop surface are attached to a ledger inside the top frame.

With the legs clamped in place, drive wood screws through the top rails and into the legs.

in place with bar clamps, and attach them with glue and #6 × 1¼" wood screws, driven through the top rails and into the legs **(photo C).**

BUILD THE STORAGE POCKETS. A storage pocket is located at each end of the end table to create spaces for storing magazines, newspapers and books. The storage pockets are made independently and attached between the legs as individual units. Begin by cutting the pocket rails (G) and leg slats (H) to size. The pocket rails are assembled into right-angle pairs: butt one long edge of a pocket rail against one face of another pocket rail, making sure the ends and edges are flush; attach the pocket rails to each other with glue and 6d finish nails. Use clamps to ensure a solid bond. After the glue on the legs dries, position a leg slat against one long edge of each pocket rail pair, and attach it with glue and 6d finish nails. The pocket edge containing the leg slat will face outward from

the table. Assemble both pockets, then mark a reference line on each leg, 8¼" down from the wider (top) ends. Position the pockets between the legs so one pocket rail face is flush with the reference line. Attach

the pockets with glue and 6d finish nails **(photo D).** The leg slat should be flush with the outside edges of the legs. The remaining leg slats are installed after the major parts of the end table are put together.

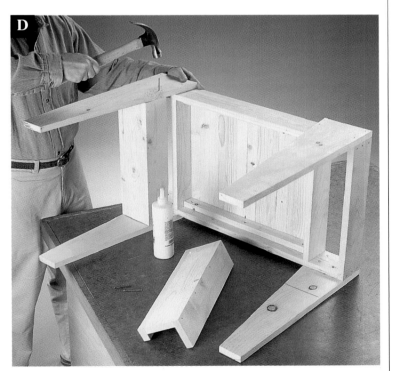

Install the storage pockets between the legs at each end of the end table, using glue and finish nails.

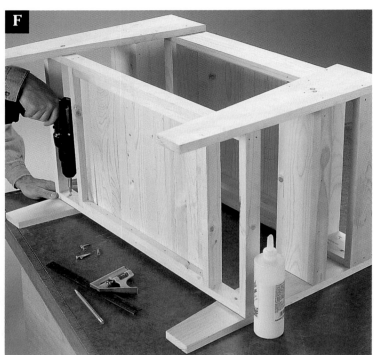

Fasten the shelf caps between the shelf edges to make the shelf frame.

Fasten the shelf with glue and wood screws, driven through the shelf sides and into the inside faces of the legs.

MAKE THE SHELF FRAME. Like the tabletop, the shelf is also built from 1 × 2 slats that are attached to a simple frame. Each shelf side has a piece of stop molding attached on the inside face to support the slats. When the shelf is completed, it is installed between the leg pairs. Begin by cutting the shelf sides (I) and shelf caps (L) to size. Mark reference lines on each shelf edge, 4" in from each end. Set the shelf edges on a flat worksurface, and position the shelf caps between them so their outside faces are flush with the reference lines—all the parts should be on edge. Apply glue to the ends of the shelf caps, and clamp the shelf edges and shelf caps together with bar or pipe clamps. Check to make sure the corners are square. Drive 6d finish nails at each joint **(photo E).** Cut the shelf ledgers (K) to size, and use glue and 6d finish nails to

attach them to the inside faces of the shelf sides, making sure the bottom edges are flush.

ATTACH THE SHELF SLATS. Cut the shelf slats (J) to length from pine 1 × 2, sand the ends and edges, and position them on the shelf ledgers to test the fit. Remove the slats, apply glue to the top of the shelf ledger, and reposition the slats on the ledgers. Drill pilot holes near each end of each slat, then drive 6d nails through the pilot holes to secure the shelf slats.

INSTALL THE SHELF. Use glue and finish nails to fasten a leg slat to each end of the shelf, making sure the edges of the slats are flush with the outside faces of the shelf sides. Position the completed

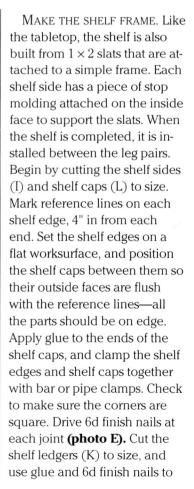

shelf between the leg pairs. The bottom edges of the shelf should be 7" up from the bottoms of the legs. The outside edges of the shelf should be flush with the untapered edges of the legs. Fasten the shelf with glue and #6 × 1¼" wood screws, driven through the shelf sides and into the inside faces of the legs **(photo F).**

ATTACH THE LEG SLATS. Attach the remaining leg slats between the legs, flush with the untapered edges **(photo G).** Unlike the table slats or shelf slats, the leg slats should have ¾"-wide gaps between slats. Use the slats that are already installed as reference points for setting the layout for the rest of the slats. Use glue and 6d finish nails to attach the ends slats.

APPLY FINISHING TOUCHES. Sand all the wood surfaces with a power sander, using medium-grit sandpaper, then finish-sand the entire project with fine (150- or 180-grit) sandpaper. Wipe the wood clean with a rag dipped in mineral spirits. Because pine is a soft wood, it is usually a good idea to apply a coat of sanding sealer before applying your finishing materials. Sanding sealer allows coloring and topcoating products to be absorbed into the wood more evenly. Read the manufacturer's directions before application. For a simple, traditional finish, we used amber shellac to finish the end table. A centuries-old product, shellac provides a protective topcoat, while imparting a warm glow to the wood. And as shellac ages, it tends to darken somewhat, creating an antique appearance. We brushed on three coats of shellac, sanding lightly with very fine sandpaper between coats. Fill all nail holes and screw counterbores with tinted wood putty that matches the color of the finished wood **(photo H).** This may require a little trial and error with putty of different colors. Carefully sand the putty level with the surrounding wood after it dries.

Position the leg slats between the legs, and fasten them so they are spaced evenly and the outer faces are flush with the outside edges of the legs.

After applying your finish, fill all nail holes and screw counterbores with wood putty tinted to match the color of the finished wood.

Deacon's Bench

At home in the family room, library or entry, this traditional bench provides convenient seating and hidden storage.

CONSTRUCTION MATERIALS

Quantity	Lumber
1	¾" × 4 × 8' birch plywood
1	1 × 4" × 8' pine
2	1 × 6" × 8' pine

With a bench seat that flips up to expose a storage compartment, this deacon's bench is a great place for storing phone books, favorite novels or a lap-top computer—best of all, it provides some roomy seating in the process. Perfect for an unused nook of your den or family room, or even in the hallway, the deacon's bench makes the most of a traditional design, combining functional seating with convenient storage. And you can throw a few pillows onto the bench seat to add another level of comfort and style as you take advantage of a quiet moment to relax, call a friend or get a little extra work done at home.

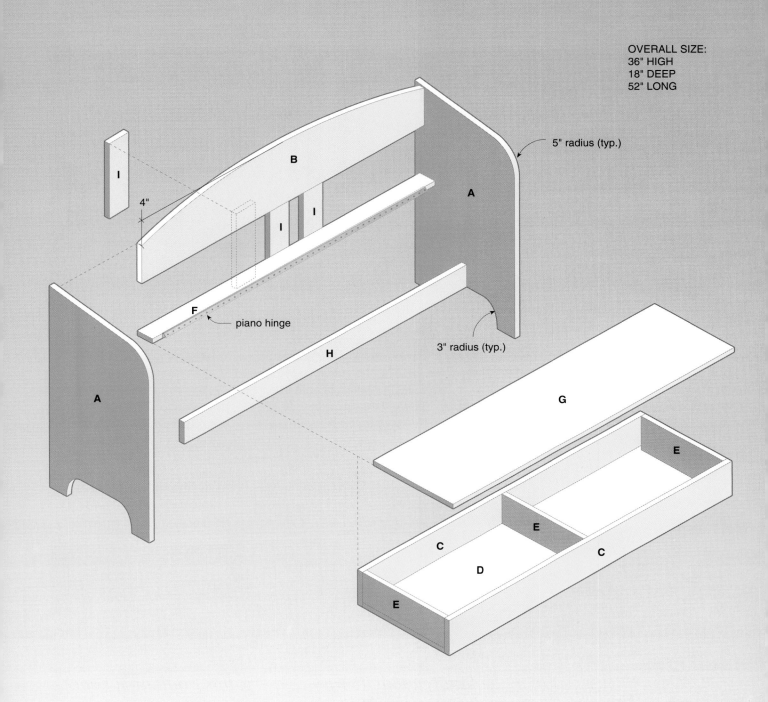

OVERALL SIZE:
36" HIGH
18" DEEP
52" LONG

5" radius (typ.)

4"

B

I

I

I

A

A

F
piano hinge

3" radius (typ.)

H

A

G

E

C

E

D

C

E

Cutting List				
Key	Part	Dimension	Pcs.	Material
A	End panel	¾ × 18 × 32½"	2	Plywood
B	Backrest	¾ × 10 × 50½"	1	Plywood
C	Seat rail	¾ × 5½ × 50½"	2	Pine
D	Bottom	¾ × 14½ × 50½"	1	Plywood
E	Lid support	¾ × 4¾ × 14½"	3	Pine

Cutting List				
Key	Part	Dimension	Pcs.	Material
F	Hinge rail	¾ × 2¾ × 50½"	1	Plywood
G	Lid	¾ × 14¼ × 50¼"	1	Plywood
H	Bottom rail	¾ × 3½ × 50½"	1	Pine
I	Slat	¾ × 3½ × 12"	3	Pine

Materials: Wood screws (#6 × 1¼", #6 × 2"), wood glue, ¾" birch edge tape (50'), 1½ × 48" piano hinge, finishing materials.

Note: Measurements reflect the actual thickness of dimensional lumber.

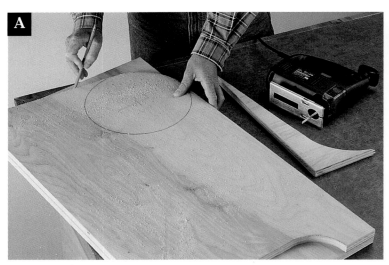

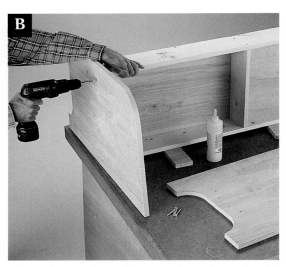

After cutting one end panel to shape, use it as a template for marking cutting lines onto the other end panel.

Fasten the seat frame between the end panels with glue and wood screws.

Directions:
Deacon's Bench

MAKE THE END PANELS. Cut all plywood parts from birch plywood, using fine-tooth blades on your circular saw and jig saw, then apply self-adhesive veneer edge tape to the exposed edges to give them a smooth, finished appearance. Countersink all the screws; you will fill the screw holes with wood putty before you paint the project. Start by cutting the end panels (A) to size. Designate a top, bottom, front and back to each end. The best way to ensure uniform end panel shapes is to make the cuts on one end panel, then trace its shape onto the other end panel. To cut the arches on the bottom edges of the end panels, start by setting a compass to draw a 3"-radius semicircle. Set the point of the compass as close to the bottom edge as possible, 6" in from the front edge, and draw the semicircle. Draw another 3"-radius semicircle on the bottom edge, 6" in from the back edge. Draw a straight cutting line connect-

ing the tops of the two semi-circles, and cut along the cutting line with a jig saw. The tops of the end panels slant downward from front to back and have a rounded top, front corner. Use a compass to draw a 5"-radius circle near the top, front corner; position the point of the compass 7" down from the top edge and 5" in from the

front edge. Draw the circle, then draw a straight line from the top, rear corner to the top of the circle. Cut along the line with a jig saw, and sand the cuts smooth. Position the finished end panel on top of the uncut end panel, and trace the shape **(photo A).** Cut the second end panel to shape with a jig saw, and sand it smooth.

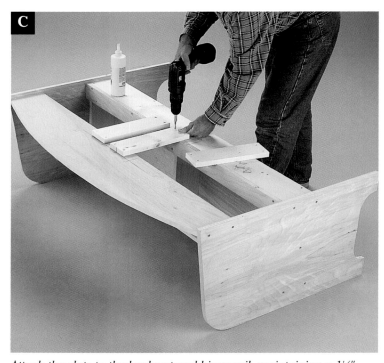

Attach the slats to the backrest and hinge rail, maintaining a 1½"-wide gap between slats.

138

MAKE THE BACKREST. The backrest fits between the end panels and has a sweeping arc cut along the top edge. Cut the backrest (B) to size, and use a thin, flexible straightedge to draw an arc at the top. Drive one finish nail at the center of the top edge and another along each side edge, 4" down from the top edge. Hook the straightedge around the center nail and inside the nails along the sides. Trace the arc with a pencil, then cut it with a jig saw. Sand the edges smooth. Use a household iron to apply self-adhesive veneer edge tape to the front, top, and back edges of the ends, and to the top and bottom edges of the backrest.

MAKE THE SEAT. The seat is a simple rectangular frame with a plywood bottom. The frame is made by attaching three lid supports between two seat rails, flush with their top edges. Cut the lid supports (E) and seat rails (C) to size. Position two lid supports between the seat rails so their outside faces are flush with the ends of the seat rails. Drill pilot holes, and fasten the seat rails with glue and #6 × 2" wood screws, driven through the seat rails and into the lid supports. Center the remaining lid support between the seat rails, and fasten it with glue and wood screws. Cut the seat bottom (D) to size, and fasten it in place in the recess formed between the bottom edges of the lid supports and the bottom edges of the seat rails. Next, mark reference lines on the ends, 11¾" and 17¼" up from the bottom edges. Stand the seat frame on a seat rail, supported by a ¾"-thick scrap

board. Apply glue to the outside face of the outside lid supports. Set the ends on their back edges, and position them against the outside lid supports so the frame is centered between the reference lines. Drive #6 × 1¼" wood screws through the ends and into the lid supports to secure the parts **(photo B).** Set the backrest on a ¾"-thick piece of scrap, and fasten it between the ends so the bottom edge of the backrest is 26" up from the bottoms of the ends. Use glue and 2" wood screws, driven through the ends and into the backrest to attach the backrest between the ends.

ATTACH THE RAILS & SLATS. The rails are attached between the ends. One rail is positioned near the bottoms of the end panels to add strength to the project. Another rail is positioned on the back seat rail—this rail will be attached to a long hinge when you attach the seat lid. Finally, decorative vertical slats are fastened to the bench to span the gap between the backrest and seat. Start by cutting the bottom rail (H) to size. Position the bottom rail between the ends so it is centered and its bottom edge is flush with the top of the arch. Cut the hinge rail (F) to size, and sand it smooth. Stand the

Fasten the lid to the hinge rail with a 1½ × 48"-long piano hinge.

bench upright, and fasten the hinge rail between the end panels; the bottom of the hinge rail should sit squarely on the seat frame, and the back edge of the hinge rail should be ¾" in from the back edges of the end panels. Cut the slats (I) to size, and sand them smooth. Center the first slat between the end panels, and attach it with glue and #6 × 1¼" wood screws. Fasten a slat on each side of the middle slat so there are 1½"-wide gaps between slats **(photo C).**

APPLY FINISHING TOUCHES. Cut the lid (G) to size. Apply veneer edge tape to all the edges, and sand the lid smooth. Use a 1½ × 48"-long piano hinge to fasten the lid to the hinge rail **(photo D).** Remove the hinge, and fill all countersunk holes with wood putty. Finish-sand the project, and finish as desired. We applied a semi-gloss latex paint. Reinstall the piano hinge.

Folding Table

*Sturdy, spacious and portable, this indoor/outdoor
table folds up for storage.*

CONSTRUCTION MATERIALS

Quantity	Lumber
5	2 × 4" × 8' pine
6	1 × 6" × 8' pine
3	1 × 4" × 8' pine

Bigger and better than a card table, this efficient folding table can provide surplus seating at a moment's notice when company arrives. With more than 15 square feet of table surface, it is roomy enough for six adult diners. But when folded up for storage, it shrinks to a diminutive 3 × 3' package that is less than 12" thick—small enough to fit into just about any closet.

If you live in a house or apartment where outdoor security is an issue, this folding table can be stationed on your patio or balcony, then carted inside for times when you are not at home. If you plan to use the table outdoors, be sure to apply exterior-rated paint.

OVERALL SIZE:
29¼" HIGH
36" DEEP
63½" LONG

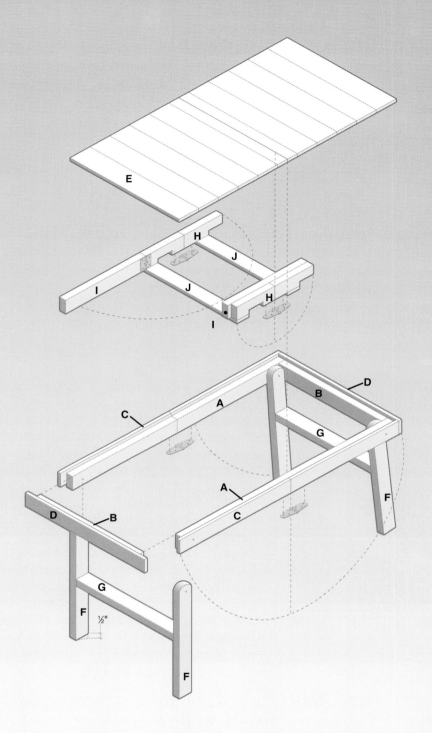

Cutting List

Key	Part	Dimension	Pcs.	Material
A	Side rail	1½ × 3½ × 62"	2	Pine
B	End rail	1½ × 3½ × 31½"	2	Pine
C	Side skirt	¾ × 3½ × 63½"	2	Pine
D	End skirt	¾ × 3½ × 34½"	2	Pine
E	Slats	¾ × 5½ × 34½"	11	Pine

Cutting List

Key	Part	Dimension	Pcs.	Material
F	Legs	1½ × 3½ × 28½"	4	Pine
G	Stretcher	1½ × 3½ × 28⅜"	2	Pine
H	Cleat	1½ × 3½ × 22"	2	Pine
I	Sweep	1½ × 3½ × 23"	2	Pine
J	Guide	¾ × 3½ × 28"	2	Pine

Materials: Wood glue, deck screws (1¼", 2", 2½"), 1½ × 6"-long strap hinges (4), 2 × 2" brass butt hinges (2), ⅜ × 4½" carriage bolts with lock nuts (4), 1"-dia. washers (8), finishing materials.

Note: Measurements reflect the actual size of dimensional lumber.

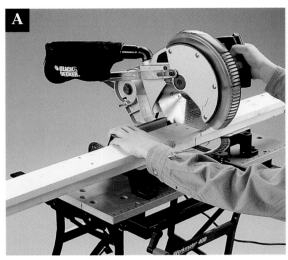

After attaching the side rails and side skirts, cross-cut them in half.

The middle slat is rip-cut in half and attached on each side of the hinged joint between the sides of the tabletop frame.

Attach the guides to the cleats, flush with the edges of the notches.

Directions: Folding Table

MAKE THE SIDE SECTIONS. Before permanently assembling the tabletop frame, the side sections are made. When fastening the parts, countersink all the screw holes. Start by cutting the side rails (A), end rails (B), side skirts (C) and end skirts (D) to size. Position a side skirt against each side rail. Make sure the side skirts overhang the side rails by ¾" on one long edge. This ¾"-wide overhang

will face the top on the completed table, creating a lip for the slats (E) to sit on. Center the side skirts on the side rails so ¾" of the side skirts extends beyond the side rails at each end. Clamp the side skirts to the side rails, and attach the parts with 1¼" deck screws. Leave the middles of the side skirts and side rails free of screws so they can be cut in half. Once the side skirts and side rails are attached, draw reference lines across the center of the side skirts. Cut along the reference lines with a power miter box, cutting the boards into two equal lengths **(photo A).** Connect the halves with 6" brass strap hinges, attached to the bottom edges of the side rail halves. Unscrew the parts and hinges before proceeding.

ATTACH THE END SECTIONS. Like the side sections, the end sections are made with rails and skirts. Position the end rails between the side rails, flush with the side rail ends. Apply glue, and drive 2½" deck screws through the side rail faces and into the end rails.

Position an end skirt against each end rail. Like the relationship between the side rails and side skirts, there should be a ¾"-deep ledge from the tops of the end skirts to the tops of the end rails. This ledge is for the slats to sit on. With the ends of the end skirts flush with the side rails, drive 1¼" deck screws through the end skirts and into the side rails and end rails. Reattach the side skirts with glue and wood screws, and reattach the strap hinges in their former positions.

ATTACH THE SLATS. Begin by cutting the slats (E) to size. Rip-cut one slat in half, using a circular saw and a straightedge guide. This halved slat will fit in the middle of the tabletop. Position one half of the ripped slat on each side of the cut at the center of the side rails. Butt the halved slat pieces together at the center so no gap is apparent. Attach each half to the side rails, using glue and 2" deck screws **(photo B).** Position the other slats across the tabletop frame, spaced evenly, and attach them with 2" deck screws. Drill ⅜"-dia. holes for carriage

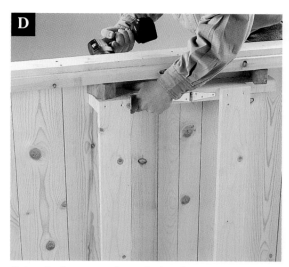

Drive deck screws through the slats and into the cleats below.

Fit the legs into place and attach them with carriage bolts, washers and lock nuts.

bolts through each end of the side skirts and side rails. Center the holes 4¼" in from the ends of the side skirts and 1¾" up from the bottoms of the side rails. The holes will be used to attach the legs.

MAKE THE LEGS. Cut the legs (F) and stretchers (G) to size. At one end of each leg, mark a point along one long edge, ½" in from the end. Draw a reference line from that point to the opposite corner on each leg. Cut along the reference lines with a circular saw. These slanted ends will be the bottoms of the legs. At the other end of each leg, use a compass to draw a centered, 1¾"-radius semicircle. Mark the center of the semicircle where the point of the compass was in contact with the workpiece. Drill a ⅜"-dia. hole for a carriage bolt through the centerpoint. Sand the legs smooth. Use a combination square to draw a reference line across one face of each leg, 14" down from the top. Position the legs in pairs on your worksurface. Slide a stretcher between each leg pair with their top faces on the ref-

erence lines. Drill pilot holes, and attach the stretchers between the legs with glue and 2½" deck screws.

MAKE THE CLEATS. Start by cutting the cleats (H) to size. The cleats are notched on one long edge to allow the table to fold in half. Each notch is 1" deep. To mark the notches, draw reference lines across one edge of each cleat, 3½", 7¼" and 18½" from one end. Use a pencil to shade from the 3½" line to the 7¼" line, and from the 18½" line to the ends of the cleats. These shaded areas mark the notches. Cut the notches with a jig saw, then cut each cleat in half. Attach the cleat halves with strap hinges, positioned across the centerline.

ATTACH THE SWEEPS & GUIDES. The sweeps (I) and guides (J) are attached to the cleats to form a locking mechanism. Cut the sweeps and guides to size. Position the guides on the cleats, flush with the edges of the notches. Attach the guides to the cleats with glue and 2½" deck screws **(photo C).** Turn the tabletop upside down, and position the

cleats and guides inside the tabletop so their hinged centers align. Use 1¾"-thick spacers to center the cleats between the side rails. Trace the cleat outline onto the table slats with a pencil. Remove the cleats, and drill pilot holes through the slats in the tabletop. Insert the cleats and guides. Fasten them to the bottom of the table with glue and 2" deck screws **(photo D).** Make sure the center joints on the tabletop line up with the center joints on the cleats. Attach 3" brass butt hinges to one end of each sweep, then use the hinges to attach a sweep to one end of each cleat. Make sure the sweeps are attached at opposite ends of the cleats.

APPLY FINISHING TOUCHES. Fasten the legs inside the tabletop, using carriage bolts, washers and lock nuts **(photo E).** Check for smooth operation, then remove the hardware and fill all countersunk screw holes with wood putty. Sand the surfaces with medium sandpaper, and apply primer and paint. Reattach the legs.

Corner
TV Center

This sleek TV center fits snugly into a corner, but with its beautiful birch tones and open design you may be tempted to put it on display in the middle of your living room.

PROJECT
POWER TOOLS

If finding a decent spot to house your television set is like trying to put a square peg in a round hole, we've got just the solution for you. This trim TV center tucks neatly into a corner, keeping it out of the traffic flow and conserving pre-cious wall and floor space. And as an added benefit, it automat-ically orients the TV screen so it can be seen from anywhere in the room.

Beyond its admirable effi-ciency, however, this special home furnishing is downright beautiful. Rich wood tones come to life in the all-birch ply-wood construction. The subtle veneer tape along the exposed edges makes even close view-ers believe this TV center is made from expensive hard-wood. And the wide-open design has an unassuming ele-gance that won't overwhelm other furnishings in the room.

Ample storage on adjustable shelves adds another useful component to this versatile pro-ject. The shelves are supported by simple shelf pins so they can be moved up and down in ac-cordance with your storage de-mands. And believe it or not, all the parts for this TV center are cut from a single sheet of plywood.

CONSTRUCTION MATERIALS

Quantity	Lumber
1	¾" × 4 × 8' birch plywood

144

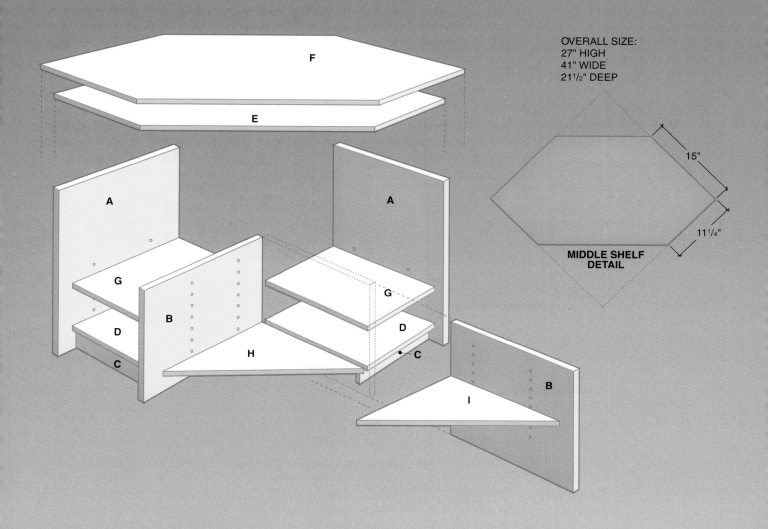

OVERALL SIZE:
27" HIGH
41" WIDE
21½" DEEP

15"

11¼"

**MIDDLE SHELF
DETAIL**

	Cutting List			
Key	**Part**	**Dimension**	**Pcs.**	**Material**
A	Side panel	¾ × 15 × 26¼"	2	Birch plywood
B	Center partition	¾ × 15 × 17¼"	2	Birch plywood
C	Kick plate	¾ × 2½ × 10½"	4	Birch plywood
D	Bottom shelf	¾ × 13½ × 10½"	2	Birch plywood
E	Middle shelf	¾ × 26¼ × 26¼"	1	Birch plywood

	Cutting List			
Key	**Part**	**Dimension**	**Pcs.**	**Material**
F	Top shelf	¾ × 29 × 29"	1	Birch plywood
G	Adjustable shelf	¾ × 13¼ × 10½"	2	Birch plywood
H	Fixed ledge	¾ × 14 × 14"	1	Birch plywood
I	Adjustable ledge	¾ × 14 × 14"	1	Birch plywood

Materials: Wood glue, ¾"-wide self-adhesive veneer tape, 1½" wood screws, finish nails (4d, 6d), ⅜"-dia. birch plugs, shelf pins, tack-on glides, finishing materials.

Note: Measurements reflect the actual size of dimensional lumber.

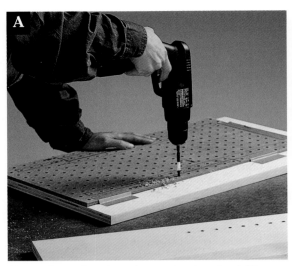

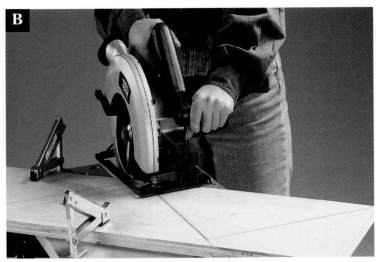

Use a piece of pegboard as a template for drilling shelf-pin holes in the side panels and center partitions.

Lay out the 14 x 14" triangle-shaped fixed ledge on a piece of plywood and cut out the ledge using a circular saw.

Directions: Corner TV Center

MAKE THE SIDE PANELS & CENTER PARTITIONS. Start by cutting the side panels (A) to size from birch plywood using a circular saw and straightedge. Measure up from the bottom of each panel 3¼" and down from the top 12", and draw lines across the panels. Lay the end panels flat on the worksurface, marked sides up, then place a 12 × 24" piece of pegboard onto one panel. This will be used as a drilling template for the shelf pin holes. Line the pegboard up with the bottom edge and a side edge of the panel. Use duct tape to hold the pegboard in place. Drill ¼"-dia × ⅜"-deep holes for the shelf pins along two columns in the pegboard **(photo A).** One column should be approximately 3" in from the flush side of the pegboard and panel and the other column should follow the opposite side of the pegboard. Use a piece of masking

Fasten the kick plates to the center partitions, with the front plate 3" back from the front edge of the partition, and the rear plate flush.

tape wrapped around the drill bit to mark the ⅜" depth. Drill only the template holes that are between the marks on the panel. Repeat the process for the other side panel. Next, cut the center partitions (B) from birch plywood using a circular saw and straightedge. Lay the partitions flat on a worksurface and measure up from the bottom 3¼" and down from the top 3" and draw lines across the partitions. Use the same piece of pegboard as earlier and lay it on top of a partition, flush

with the bottom edge and a side edge. Let the pegboard hang over the top edge of the partition. Use duct tape to hold the pegboard in place. Drill out two columns of holes between the marks on the partitions as you did previously on the side panels. Repeat the process for the other partition, then turn the partitions over and repeat the drilling procedure. Drill only to the ⅜" depth stop (the masking tape on the drill bit) to

Position the center partition corners together snugly, and fasten the partitions to the fixed ledge with glue and screws.

Fasten the bottom shelf to the kick plates, between the side panels, using glue and 4d finish nails.

avoid drilling through the other sides of the partitions. When all side panels and center partitions have been drilled for shelf pins, stand the panels on their back edges, one at a time, and apply adhesive-backed wood veneer tape to the front edges. Use a heat gun or a household iron to heat the tape, activating the adhesive. Apply pressure to the veneer tape with the iron (see *photo F*), a putty knife, or a wood block to bond it to the plywood edge. You may find it helpful to use a small J-roller to press the wood tape onto the panel edge after heating and pressing with the iron. Trim the wood tape edges with a utility knife, then hand-sand with 100-grit sandpaper to smooth out the seams and edges. Don't use a power sander for this, it may be too aggressive for the veneer tape. Apply veneer tape to the back edges of the panels, then to both edges of the remaining panels. Sand the faces of the side panels with medium (100-or 120-grit) sandpaper, then finish-sand with fine (150- or 180-grit) sandpaper. Use care with power sanders so you don't sand through the veneer tape.

BUILD THE FRAME. Lay out the fixed ledge (H) dimensions on a piece of plywood by marking a line 14" along one side and another 14" across, then connecting the end points. Cut along the line with a circular saw **(photo B).** Apply veneer tape to the diagonal edge of the fixed ledge, then sand and smooth as necessary. Cut the kick plates (C) from birch plywood using a circular saw. Sand the fixed ledge and kick plates. Attach the kick plates to the center partitions, positioning the front plate 3" back from the front edge and flush with the bottom of the partition, and positioning the back plate flush with the back edge of the partition **(photo C).** Measure up from the bottom of the partitions on the drilled side 2½" and mark a line, then lay one center partition assembly on its side, resting on the flush-mounted kick plate. Place the fixed ledge on-edge on the worksurface and butt the other edge up to the center partition, positioning the fixed ledge on the layout line. Attach the fixed ledge to the center partition

TIP

There is an easy way to make a pair of matching triangle-shaped pieces with 45° diagonals in one simple cutting procedure. Cut your material into a square with dimensions equal to the length of the 90° sides of the triangle. Then cut the square diagonally to create matching triangular pieces.

with glue and counterbored #6 × 1½" wood screws. Stand the center partition upright on the worksurface and place two 2½" spacer blocks under the fixed ledge to support it at the proper elevation. Position the other center partition assembly against the fixed ledge, with the corner of the partition tight to the corner of the adjacent center partition. Secure the center partition assembly to the fixed ledge with glue and screws **(photo D).** Place a mark on the bottom of the side panels, 3" from the front edge. Position the side panels against the kick plates, lining up the front plates with the marks at the bottoms of the panels, so the rear plates are flush with the back edges of the side panels. Secure the side panels to the kick plates with glue and screws.

BUILD & INSTALL THE SHELVES. Start by cutting the bottom shelves (D) to size from ¾"-thick birch plywood, using a circular saw and straightedge.

Apply birch veneer tape to both ends of the shelves, then trim and sand the tape. Fasten the bottom shelves to the side panels and kick plates with glue and 4d finish nails **(photo E).** Next, lay out the middle shelf (E), following the *Diagram* on page 39, on a 26¼ × 26¼" piece of ¾" plywood. Start in one corner, measure over 15" along the edge and place a mark. Then, from the same corner, measure up 11¼" along the adjacent edge and place a mark. In the opposite corner, measure over 11¼" along the edge. Then, measure up 15" along the adjacent edge. Now, connect the 11¼" marks to each other and connect the 15" marks to each other. Cut along the lines using a circular saw and straightedge.

Apply veneer tape to the cut edges **(photo F),** since these will be the exposed front and back edges after installation. If the edges are not perfectly smooth, sand them smooth using a power sander. Place the

Apply self-adhesive veneer tape to the shelf edges, using a household iron to press the tape in place, while activating the glue.

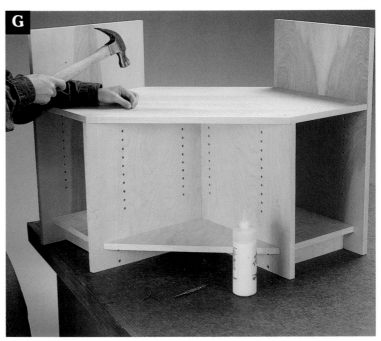

Fasten the middle shelf to the center partitions and side panels, using glue and 6d finish nails.

Secure the top shelf to the side panels with glue and screws.

middle shelf on the center partitions and fasten with glue and 6d finish nails **(photo G).** Drive finish nails through the side panels and into the shelf edge to secure it in place. Next, lay out the top shelf (F), following the *Diagram* on page 39, on a 29 × 29" piece of ¾" plywood. Starting in one corner, measure over 16½" along one edge and place a mark. Then, from the same corner, measure up 14" along the adjacent edge and place a mark. On the opposite corner, measure over 14" along the edge (this should be the same side as the previously marked 14" side). Then, from the same corner, measure up 16½" along the adjacent edge and place a mark. Now, con-

nect the 14" marks to each other and connect the 16½" marks to each other. Cut along the lines using a circular saw and straightedge. Smooth any rough saw cuts with a power sander. Apply veneer tape to the edges of the top shelf (all edges will be exposed, so they all need to be covered with tape). Trim the veneer tape flush with the top and bottom of the plywood, using a utility knife, then sand the edges. Finish-sand the surfaces of the top shelf. Lay the top shelf on the side panels and line it up so there is a 1" overhang at the outside faces and front edges

of the side panels. Drill counterbored pilot holes through the top and into the side panels. Counterbore so there is enough room for wood plugs (⅜"-dia. × ¼"-thick is common). Fasten the shelf to the side panels using glue and screws, then glue wood plugs into the counterbores. Sand the wood plugs until level with the wood surface.

APPLY THE FINISHING TOUCHES. Start by making the adjustable components. Cut the adjustable shelves (G) and adjustable ledge (I) from ¾"-thick plywood. Apply veneer tape to the front edges of the adjustable shelves and the adjustable ledge. Trim the veneer tape with a utility knife, then sand the edges and surfaces. Finish-sand the entire TV center lightly. Fill any open nail holes, defects or voids with a quality wood filler tinted to match the color of the wood stain (if any) you plan to apply. Sand filler or putty level with the wood. Wipe away sanding residue with a rag dipped in mineral spirits or a tack cloth. Apply a sanding sealer product to the TV center and to the adjustable shelves if applying a darker stain (sealer helps the wood accept the stain evenly, minimizing blotches). Apply the stain (if any), then topcoat the wood after the stain has dried. We brushed on two thin layers of satin-gloss polyurethane. When dry, install tack-on glides at the bottoms of the partitions and side panels, then insert the shelf pins for the adjustable shelves and ledge. Rest the shelves and ledge on the pins, adjusting them as needed to fit your TV components.

PROJECT
POWER TOOLS

Poker Table

*A removable top converts this conventional game table
into a custom poker table.*

CONSTRUCTION MATERIALS

Quantity	Lumber
1	¾" × 4 × 8' birch plywood
4	1 × 4" × 8' oak
2	1 × 4" × 8' pine
2	1 × 6" × 6' oak
2	2 × 2" × 6' pine
2	⅜ × 1⅛" × 7' oak stop molding
2	¼ × ¾" × 7' pine shelf nosing

The top of this table is designed especially for poker, with an eight-sided playing surface and trays to hold the chips. But for those times when you just need a simple card or game table, the poker tabletop pulls off to create a small four-sided table.

Each leg pulls out easily for storage, but is held securely in place by carriage bolts and wing nuts. With the oak legs and heavy-duty construction, you can play the game without worrying about an untimely collapse—this is no flimsy, fold-down card table. The exterior components are made from oak, while the interior frame-work and tabletops are made from pine and oak plywood.

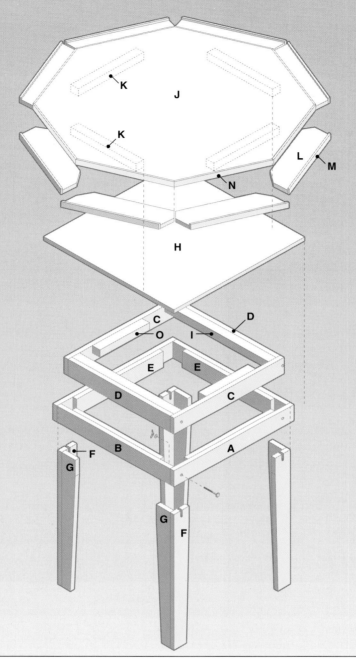

OVERALL SIZE:
31½" HIGH
48" WIDE
48" LONG

Cutting List

Key	Part	Dimension	Pcs.	Material
A	Apron side	¾ × 3½ × 30"	2	Oak
B	Apron end	¾ × 3½ × 28½"	2	Oak
C	Liner side	¾ × 3½ × 27"	2	Pine
D	Liner end	¾ × 3½ × 25½"	2	Pine
E	Filler block	¾ × 3½ × 21½"	4	Pine
F	Leg front	¾ × 3½ × 30"	4	Oak
G	Leg side	¾ × 2¾ × 30"	4	Oak
H	Main top	¾ × 32 × 32"	1	Plywood

Cutting List

Key	Part	Dimension	Pcs.	Material
I	Main cleat	1½ × 1½ × 25½"	2	Pine
J	Poker top	¾ × 48 × 48"	1	Plywood
K	Poker cleat	1½ × 1½ × 16"	4	Pine
L	Tray	¾ × 5½ × 18"	8	Oak
M	Tray trim	¾ × 1¹⁄₁₆ × 18"	8	Stop molding
N	Poker trim	¼ × ¾ × *"	8	Shelf nosing
O	Short cleat	1½ × 1½ × 9"	2	Pine

Materials: Wood screws (#6 × 1¼", #6 × 2", #6 × 2½"), 1¼" brads, wood glue, ¾"-dia. × 3"-long carriage bolts with washers and wing nuts (4), ¾" birch veneer edge tape (15'), finishing materials.
Note: Measurements reflect the actual thickness of dimensional lumber. *Cut to fit.

Use a straightedge guide and scrap-plywood stop blocks when cutting leg tapers with a circular saw.

Position the liner assembly inside the apron assembly so it fits against the filler blocks.

Directions: Poker Table

MAKE THE LEGS. The table legs are designed for heavy-duty support. They are tapered from the top to the bottom. Each leg is made from two 1 × 4 boards butted together. Start by cutting the leg fronts (F) and leg sides (G) to length from 1 × 4" oak. Before cutting the tapers on the leg fronts and leg sides, draw accurate cutting lines. First, designate a top and bottom to each workpiece. Mark a point on the bottoms of the leg fronts, ½" in from one long edge, then draw a mark 3½" down from the tops of the leg fronts on the same long edge. Draw a cutting line connecting the two points on the leg fronts. The leg sides are more narrow than the leg fronts. To draw the cutting lines on the leg sides, mark a point on the bottom of each leg side, 1¼" in from one long edge. Measure and mark a point 3½" down from the top and ¾" in from the same long edge. Draw cutting lines connecting the two points on the leg sides. Use a circular saw with a straight-edge guide to cut along the cutting lines **(photo A).** Support the leg fronts and leg sides with a piece of scrap plywood as you cut them to size. Edge guides made from scrap and stop blocks screwed down at the ends and sides of the workpieces keep the leg parts steady as you cut them. For most ac-curate results, start the taper cuts at the bottom ends. Once the leg sides and leg fronts are cut to shape, butt the unta-pered edges of the leg sides against the leg fronts. With the leg fronts and leg sides flush, drill evenly spaced, counter-bored pilot holes through the leg fronts. Fasten the parts with

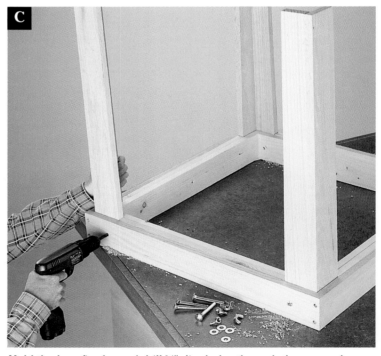

Hold the legs firmly, and drill ⅜"-dia. holes through the apron, legs and liner for carriage bolts at all corners.

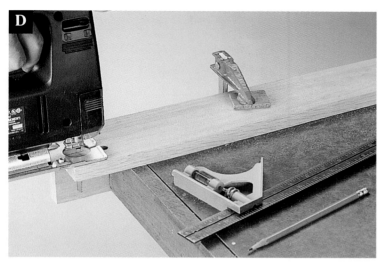

Cut a notch from the top of the leg fronts down to the carriage bolt hole to make it easier to remove and install the legs.

glue and #6 × 2" wood screws, driven through the leg fronts and into the leg sides. Fill all counterbored screw holes with ⅜"-dia. flat wood plugs. Sand the legs smooth.

MAKE THE APRON. The apron is a frame that holds the legs securely at the corners and supports the tabletops. The apron is actually a frame within a frame, made from strong, solid oak on the outside with a less expensive pine liner and filler blocks. L-shaped gaps at the corners of the apron hold the legs, which are secured with carriage bolts and wing nuts. Start by cutting the apron sides (A) and apron ends (B) to size.

Position the apron ends between the apron sides with the the outside faces of the apron ends flush with the ends of the apron sides. Drill counterbored pilot holes, and use glue and #6 × 2" wood screws to fasten the parts. Cut the liner sides (C) and liner ends (D) to size from 1 × 4" pine. Position the liner ends between the liner sides, making sure the edges are flush. Drill pilot holes, and fasten the liner ends between the liner sides with glue and #6 × 2" wood screws, driven through the liner and into the apron. Draw reference lines on the inside faces of the apron sides and apron ends, 3½" in from each corner. Cut the filler blocks (E) to size, and fasten them between the reference lines, using glue and countersunk #6 × 1¼" wood screws. With the apron on a flat surface, set the liner assembly inside the apron **(photo B),** and fasten the liner assembly to the filler blocks with glue and #6 × 2" wood screws.

ATTACH THE LEGS. The legs are inserted into the gaps at the corners of the frame, and secured with carriage bolts. Start by sliding the wide ends of the legs into the gaps at each corner of the apron frame. They should fit snugly, with their tops flush with the apron top. Mark the outside faces of the apron sides for carriage-bolt holes.

Fasten the main top to the liner by driving screws through the main cleats and short cleats and into the liner and filler blocks.

153

Center the holes 3¼" in from the apron side ends. With the legs held firmly in place, drill a ⅜"-dia. hole through the apron, legs and liner at each corner **(photo C).** Remove the legs. At the top of the leg fronts, use a jig saw to extend the holes all the way to the top of the leg fronts **(photo D).** These notches allow you to remove the legs for storage without having to remove the carriage bolts. Insert the legs, and push the carriage bolts through the holes. Slide washers on the bolts, and attach wing nuts to secure the legs in place. If one or two legs do not fit precisely, try switching them around— you may find a better fit.

MAKE THE MAIN TOP. The main top is used as a game table and as a base for the poker tabletop. Begin by cutting the main top (H), main cleats (I) and short cleats (O) to size. Sand the parts smooth, and use a household iron to apply self-adhesive birch veneer edge tape to all four edges of the main top. Trim and sand the excess edge tape. Draw reference lines on one face of the main top, 2¼" in from each edge. Center the main cleats and short cleats on the main top with their outside edges on the reference lines. Fasten the cleats, making sure the main cleats are on opposite sides. Test-fit the main top on the apron. If the main top doesn't fit, realign the cleats. Fasten the main top to

TIP

Although we chose a natural oil finish for the poker table, these projects are traditionally covered with green felt. Green felt can be purchased at any fabric store. If you choose to cover the poker table with felt, use contact cement to fasten it down. Wrap the felt around the top before attaching the poker trim molding.

Carefully draw the cutting lines for the poker top, using a straightedge and a homemade compass.

the liner by driving 2½" countersunk screws through the main cleats and into the liner and filler blocks **(photo E).**

MAKE THE POKER TOP. The poker top is a large octagonal tabletop with ledges to hold poker chips. Cleats are attached on the bottom of the poker top so it can be centered over the main top. To cut the poker top (J) to size, start with a 48" square piece of plywood. Marking the octagonal cutting lines requires a little basic geometry. First, draw reference lines between opposite corners, locating the center of the workpiece. Mark the centers of the edges on each of the four sides. Draw lines across the poker top, connecting opposing-edge centerpoints. Next, construct a homemade bar compass by drilling a centered screw hole at one end of a 1 × 2" piece of scrap. (The scrap piece must be at least 25" in

length.) Drill another centered hole for a pencil, 24" up from the first hole. Drive a screw through the first hole and into the poker top center point. Slip a pencil into the remaining hole, and rotate the bar compass to draw a 48"-dia. circle on the poker top. Using a straightedge, draw cutting lines connecting the points where the reference lines intersect with the circle **(photo F).** Cut along the cutting lines with a circular saw, and sand the poker top to smooth out any rough edges or saw marks. To cut the poker trim (N) to fit against the poker top sides, use a power miter box or a backsaw and miter box to cut a 22½° outside bevel at one end of a poker trim piece. NOTE: 22½° is commonly marked on miter boxes, circular saws and radial-arm saws. After cutting

154

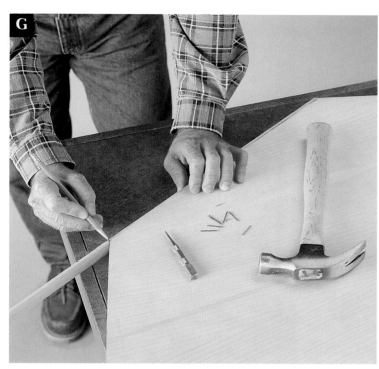

Mark the trim pieces to fit the edges of the poker table, and cut them to length with a 22½° bevel.

down. Use glue and #6 × 1¼" wood screws to fasten the trays to the poker top at each straight edge. The trays should extend 3½" beyond the poker top edges, so use a piece of 1 × 4 as a spacer between the tray trim and the poker top edges as you fit the pieces together. Cut the poker cleats (K) to size, and center them on the poker top centerlines. (The poker cleats hold the poker top in place while it sits on the main top.) Center the poker cleats on the lines, and make sure their inside edges are 16⅛" in from the center of the table. Fasten the poker cleats with glue and #6 × 1¼" wood screws **(photo H).**

APPLY FINISHING TOUCHES. Set all nail heads and fill all nail holes with untinted, stainable wood putty. Glue ⅜"-dia. oak plugs into all screw counterbores, then sand to level. Finish-sand all surfaces, and ap ply your finish of choice. We used three coats of tung oil.

this bevel, position the poker trim against one edge of the poker top. Mark the trim where the next point contacts it **(photo G),** then cut another bevel that slants in the opposite direction from the bevel at the other end. Attach the trim piece to the poker top with glue and 1¼" brads, and continue cutting and measuring the poker trim to fit the table. Fill all the brad holes with wood putty, and sand the edges smooth when dry.

ATTACH THE TRAYS. Trays are attached to each edge of the octagonal poker top to hold poker chips. Cut the trays (L) and tray trim (M) to size. In order for the trays to fit on the underside of the poker top, the inside corners on one long edge on each tray are trimmed off at a 45° angle. Draw cutting lines at each end of one long edge, forming a triangle with 2"-long sides, and use a power

miter box or a circular saw to cut the corners. Use glue and 1¼" brads to fasten the tray trim to the square long edge of each tray so the bottoms are flush. Turn the poker top upside

Fasten the poker cleats to the underside of the poker table, 16⅛" in from the centers.

Futon Frame

A comfortable sofa by day, this futon frame converts easily into a spare bed frame for overnight guests.

If you've put off buying a futon because the frames are expensive and complicated to use, wait no more. Designed to hold a full-size futon mattress, our futon frame is built entirely of inexpensive pine. The result is an incredibly sturdy, reliable frame at a fraction of the cost of commercial frames. Instead of the complicated hardware that adds so much to the cost of most futon frames, we developed a trouble-free system of folding frames that attach to one another with heavy-duty hinges. You won't even need to move the futon mattress to turn your sofa into a bed. By day, the futon is a casual sofa for reading or relaxing. When bedtime rolls around, simply slide the seat frame forward to convert your futon sofa into a sturdy, full-size bed your guests will love.

CONSTRUCTION MATERIALS

Quantity	Lumber
14	2 × 4" × 8' pine
7	1 × 6" × 8' pine

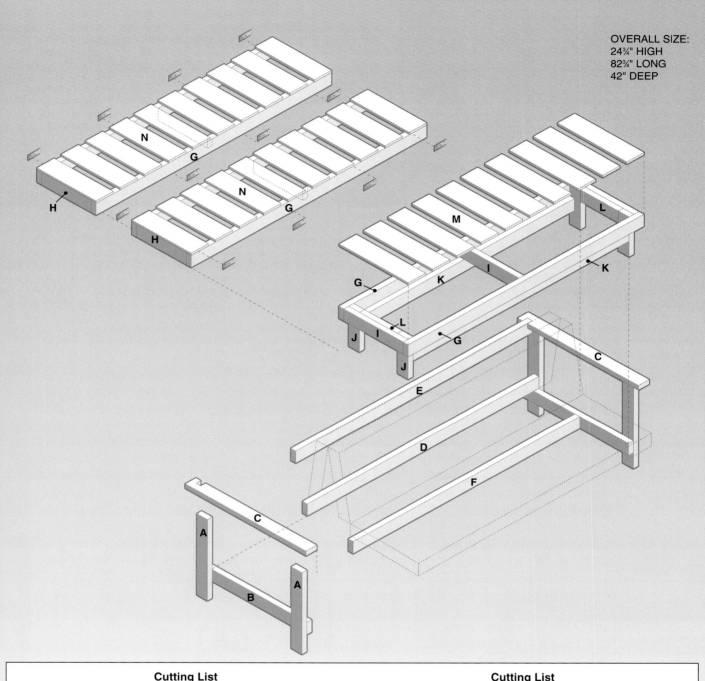

OVERALL SIZE:
24¾" HIGH
82¾" LONG
42" DEEP

Cutting List

Key	Part	Dimension	Pcs.	Material
A	Post	1½ × 3½ × 23¼"	4	Pine
B	Outer rail	1½ × 3½ × 34"	2	Pine
C	Armrest	1½ × 3½ × 38½"	2	Pine
D	Back rail	1½ × 3½ × 75¾"	1	Pine
E	Backrest	1½ × 3½ × 78¾"	1	Pine
F	Cross rail	1½ × 3½ × 72¾"	1	Pine
G	Frame rail	1½ × 3½ × 75"	6	Pine

Cutting List

Key	Part	Dimension	Pcs.	Material
H	Back stretcher	1½ × 3½ × 16"	6	Pine
I	Seat stretcher	1½ × 3½ × 19"	3	Pine
J	Leg	1½ × 3½ × 11½"	4	Pine
K	Leg stretcher	1½ × 3½ × 69"	2	Pine
L	Leg brace	1½ × 3½ × 12"	2	Pine
M	Seat slat	¾ × 5½ × 22"	10	Pine
N	Back slat	¾ × 5½ × 19"	20	Pine

Materials: Wood screws (#6 × 2", #6 × 2½"), wood glue, 3 × 3" butt hinges (12), nylon furniture glides (8), finishing materials.

Note: Measurements reflect the actual thickness of dimensional lumber.

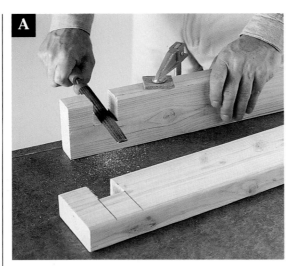

Use a wood file to make clean, straight edges on the notches in the armrest.

Directions: Futon Frame

MAKE THE ARMRESTS. The futon frame is essentially a combination of four 2 × 4 frames that work together. The outer frame supports all the other frames. This frame stays in place while the futon is folded or unfolded. The armrests are notched at the back end to hold the backrest. All the rest of the parts are simply cut to length, drilled and sanded. Counterbore all the visible screw holes for ⅜"-diameter plugs. Cut the armrests (C). The armrests attach to the tops of the posts with glue and screws. They are notched to hold the backrest. To mark the notches, lay the armrests together edge to edge. Draw a 1½" square along the inside edge of each armrest, starting 1½" in from one end. Cut the notches with a jig saw. To get a tight-fitting notch, cut just inside the cutting lines, then use a wood file to remove the last fraction of wood and clean up the cuts **(photo A).**

ASSEMBLE THE ARMREST FRAMES. Cut the posts (A) and outer rails (B) to length. Use a pad sander with medium-grit paper to remove splinters, smooth out rough spots, and sand away any grading stamps. The outer rails fit across the inside faces of the posts to support the back frames when the futon frame is unfolded. To mark reference lines for the outer rails on the posts, lay the posts side by side in pairs with the ends flush. Draw lines across the pairs of posts, 8" from the bottom ends. Position the outer rails against the posts so the top edges of the rails are on the lines and the ends of the rails are flush with the edges of the posts. Apply glue to the joints and secure them with 2½" screws. If glue oozes from the joints, let it dry and scrape it away later with a chisel. While the glue is drying on the rails and posts, prepare the armrests. Attach an armrest atop each pair of posts so the inside edges are flush. The back edge of the rear post should be flush with the front of the notch and the front post should be 1½" from the front of the armrest. Use glue and 2½" screws to secure the armrests to the posts **(photo B).**

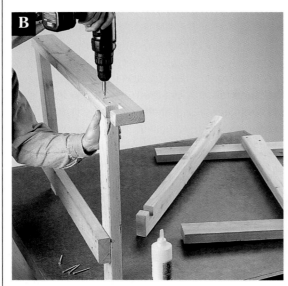

Make sure the armrest notches are on the same side of the posts as the outer rails.

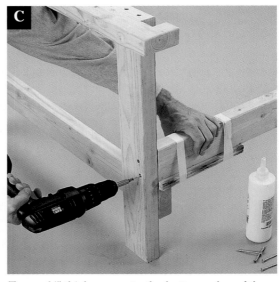

Tape a ¾"-thick spacer to the bottom edge of the back rail to create a gap between the back rail and the outer rail.

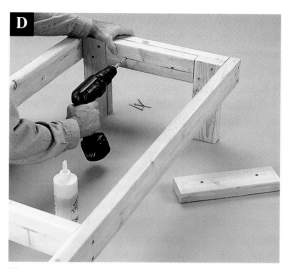

The leg braces hold the the legs firmly against the frame rails to prevent wobble.

Space the slats in the seat frame so the gaps align with the back frame.

COMPLETE THE OUTER FRAME. Cut the back rail (D), backrest (E) and cross rail (F) to length. Tape a ¾"-thick piece of scrap to the bottom edge at each end of the back rail. The scraps are spacers that will hold the back rail at the correct height as it's fastened between the rear posts. Drill counter-bored pilot holes for #6 screws centered along the back edge of the rear post, 9¾" and 11¼" from the bottom. Apply glue to an end of the back rail and rest the spacer on the outer rail. Support the back rail level and flush with the back edge of the post, then drive 2½" screws through the post to secure the back rail **(photo C),** and remove the spacers. Fasten the other end of the rail. Next, fasten the backrest in place. Drill a pilot hole through the face of each end of the backrest, ¾" from the end and ¾" up from the bottom edge. Brush glue sparingly inside the notches, then slide the backrest along the post and up into the notches until the top edges are flush. Drive 2½" screws through the pilot holes in the backrest

into the back edge of the post, then add deeply counterbored screws driven through the sides of the armrests into each end of the backrest. Finally, fasten the cross rail between the outer rails, 17" from the rear posts, using glue and counterbored 2½" screws. Glue wood plugs into all the visible counterbore holes and sand the outer frame to round the corners and edges.

MAKE THE SEAT FRAME. The seat frame carries most of the weight, so it's heavier and has legs. To make the seat frame, cut two frame rails (G), and the seat stretchers (I). Mark the centers of the frame rails. Stand the seat rails on edge, then fasten the seat stretchers between the rails with glue and 2½" screws. Fasten a stretcher at each end of the rails, and one in the middle. Cut the legs (J), leg stretchers (K) and leg braces (L). Lightly round the bottoms of the legs. Rounding the bottom edges helps keep the legs from splintering as the futon frame is pushed and pulled to convert it from bed to sofa. When attaching the legs

and leg braces, simply countersink the pilot holes because the screw heads will not be visible. Fasten a leg to each inside corner of the seat frame, using glue and screws. Butt the legs tightly against the corners with the narrow edge of each leg against the frame rail. Keep the tops of the legs flush with the rails. Drive 2½" screws through the legs and into the rails to secure them. The leg braces fit tightly between the legs and against the outer seat stretchers to lock the legs into their upright position. Apply glue to the faces of the braces before fastening them between the legs, flush with the tops of the seat stretchers **(photo D).** To further support the legs, drill counterbored pilot holes along the outside edges of each leg, 1" and 2½" from the bottom edges of the seat stretchers. Glue, then

TIP

When working with pine, fasten and seal the pieces as quickly as possible to keep individual boards from warping. This is especially important in a piece of furniture like this futon frame, where moving parts interact and there is not a lot of room for error. Pine can dry out or take on moisture quite quickly, and the amount of warping that can occur can be dramatic.